1993 BUYING GUIDE

Special year-end issue
The December 15, 1992, issue
of CONSUMER REPORTS
Volume 57, No. 13

 The body of this book is made with recycled paper.

Contents

6 Major kitchen appliances

Microwave ovens	7	Dishwashers	15
Ranges	10	Ratings	18
Refrigerators	12		

24 Small kitchen appliances

Blenders	24	Coffee appliances	29
Food processors	26	Toasters & toaster ovens	32
Portable food mixers	27	Ratings	34

44 Laundry appliances & detergents

Washing machines	44	Detergents & other laundry products	51
Clothes dryers	47	Ratings	54
Steam irons	49		

61 Home theater

TV sets	65	Stereo headphones	77
VCRs	68	Walkabout stereos	78
Laser-disc players	71	Compact-disc players	80
Camcorders	71	Cassette decks	81
Stereo receivers	73	Compact stereo systems	84
Loudspeakers	76	Ratings	86

108 Photography

Cameras & lenses	109	Film processing	116
Tripods	114	Ratings	118

122 Recreation & exercise

Exercise equipment	123	Bicycles	128
Running shoes	125	Ratings	131
Tennis racquets	127		

139 Home workplace

Home copiers	140	Cordless telephones	146
Typewriters & word processors	141	Telephone answerers	147
Computer printers	143	Ratings	150
Printing calculators	145		

CONSUMER REPORTS (ISSN 0010-7174) is published 13 times a year by Consumers Union of the United States, Inc.,101 Truman Avenue, Yonkers, N.Y. 10703-1057. Second-class postage paid at Yonkers, N.Y., and at additional mailing offices. Canadian postage paid at Mississauga, Ontario, Canada. Canadian publications registration no. 9277. Title CONSUMER REPORTS registered in U.S. Patent Office. Contents of this issue copyright © 1992 by Consumers Union of the United States, Inc. All rights reserved under International and Pan-American copyright con-

165 Personal Health

Blood pressure monitors	165	Oral irrigators	172
Toothpaste	168	Sunscreens	173
Mouthwash	170	Ratings	175
Electric toothbrushes	171		

186 Home Environment

Fans	186	Water treatment	194
Air-conditioners	188	Ratings	200
Air cleaners	192		

208 Cleaning Products

Household cleansers	209	Hand-held vacuums	212
Paper towels	210	Ratings	214

224 Paints

Paints & stains	224	Ratings	232
Paint removers	230		

240 Yard & Garden

Lawn mowers	241	Chippers/shredders	246
String trimmers	243	Gas barbecue grills	247
Tillers & cultivators	245	Ratings	249

268 Auto Products

Tires	268	Child safety seats	273
Batteries	270	Ratings	276
Security systems	271		

281 Autos

Recommended 1992 cars	282	Reliable used cars	312
Ratings of 1992 cars	294	Used cars to avoid	315
How to buy a new car	306	Repair records	317
How to buy a used car	309	Owner satisfaction	357

361 Repair Histories   371 Product Recalls   385 Index

Illustrations by Chris Gall

ventions. Reproduction in whole or in part is forbidden without prior written permission (and is never permitted for commercial purposes). CU is a member of the International Organization of Consumers Unions. Mailing lists: CU occasionally exchanges its subscriber lists with those of selected publications and nonprofit organizations. If you wish your name deleted from such exchanges, send your address label with a request for deletion to CONSUMER REPORTS, P.O. Box 53029, Boulder, Colo. 80322-3029. Postmaster: Send address changes to the same address.

About Consumers Union

Consumers Union, publisher of CONSUMER REPORTS, is a nonprofit organization established in 1936 to provide consumers with information and advice on goods, services, health, and personal finance and to work toward improving the quality of life for consumers.

Consumers Union is a membership organization. Paid subscribers may become members in one of three ways: by written application; by sending in a nomination to the Board of Directors; or by voting in the annual election of CU's Directors (ballots are mailed to all paid subscribers). There is no financial or other obligation.

No advertising. We accept no advertising and buy all the products we test on the open market, so we are not beholden to any commercial interest. Our income is derived solely from the sale of CONSUMER REPORTS and our other publications and from nonrestrictive, noncommercial contributions, grants, and fees.

Our Ratings and reports are for the use of our readers. Neither the Ratings nor the reports may be used in advertising or for any commercial purpose. CU will take all steps to prevent commercial use of its material, its name, or the name of CONSUMER REPORTS.

Contributions. Contributions to Consumers Union are tax-deductible. Contributors of $1000 or more become Lifetime Members, receiving a lifetime subscription to CONSUMER REPORTS and other benefits. Bequests are another way to help ensure CU's programs. For information, write to Consumers Union, Box NR, 101 Truman Ave., Yonkers, N.Y. 10703-1057.

About Consumer Reports

CONSUMER REPORTS is published monthly, except in December when it comes out semi-monthly; the Buying Guide is the thirteenth issue. Reproduction of CONSUMER REPORTS in whole or in part is forbidden without prior written permission (and is never permitted for commercial use).

Subscriptions. U.S. rates: $22 for 1 year, $38 for 2 years, $54 for 3 years, $86 for 5 years. Other countries: add $6 per year. (Canadian rate is $33 if paying in Canadian dollars; Goods & Services Tax included GST #127047702.) For subscription service or to change a mailing address, write to Subscription Director, CONSUMER REPORTS, P.O. Box 53029, Boulder, Colo. 80322-3029. Please attach or copy your address label from the back cover of a monthly issue.

EXECUTIVE DIRECTOR: Rhoda H. Karpatkin.
BOARD OF DIRECTORS: James A. Guest, Chair; Jean Ann Fox, Vice Chair; Betty Furness, Secretary; Teresa M. Schwartz, Treasurer; Robert S. Adler, Carol M. Barger, Christine A. Bjorklund, Jean S. Bowers, Joan Claybrook, John K. Crum, Clarence M. Ditlow, Michael Jacobson, Richard L. D. Morse, Sharon L. Nelson, Joel J. Nobel, Milton M. Pressley, Peter M. Sullivan, Julian A. Waller.

Readers' letters. We welcome comments or questions about our reports. They should be sent to CONSUMER REPORTS, P. O. Box 2015, Yonkers, N.Y. 10703-9015.

Back issues. Back issues of CONSUMER REPORTS up to 11 months old are available as supplies permit from Back Issue Dept., CONSUMER REPORTS, P.O. Box 53016, Boulder, Colo. 80322-3016; single copies are $4; the Buying Guide, $10. Your local library may also have back issues on file.

Other media. CONSUMER REPORTS is available online through CompuServe, Dialog, Nexis, and Prodigy, and on CD-ROM. Reports are also available on microfilm from UMI, 300 N. Zeeb Rd., Ann Arbor, Mich. 48106. Address inquiries to Consumers Union, Electronic Publishing Dept., 101 Truman Ave., Yonkers, N.Y. 10703-1057.

ABOUT THE BUYING GUIDE

The Buying Guide collects, in one handy volume, buying advice and evaluations of hundreds of brand-name products. We report on autos, video and audio gear, kitchen and laundry appliances, tools, yard and garden equipment, cameras, and more.

The Buying Guide also provides information on the reliability of brands, information available only from CONSUMER REPORTS. See the Frequency-of-Repair charts for automobiles and the repair histories for other products. In addition, there's a compilation of all product recalls published in the monthly issues of CONSUMER REPORTS (October 1991 through September 1992).

For further information on a subject, check the most recent report in CONSUMER REPORTS. You'll find a four-year index to the magazine at the back of the book, following the index to the Guide.

About our Ratings. Ratings are based on laboratory tests, panel tests, reader surveys, and expert judgments of products bought in stores. Ratings are usually based on estimated overall quality without regard to price. If a product is judged high in quality and appreciably superior to other products tested, we give it a check rating (✓). If a product offers both high quality and relatively low price, we deem it A Best Buy.

A Rating applies only to the brand and model listed, not to other models sold under the same brand name, unless so noted. We can't conduct special tests or provide information beyond what appears in CONSUMER REPORTS. We choose models to test after considering factors such as reader interest, the extent of a product's availability, current consumer expenditures, and new designs.

Availability. Because of the time required for testing and reporting, some of the models listed here might not be available. Products that we know have been discontinued are marked Ⓓ in the Ratings. They may be available in some stores. For some products, we've been able to identify a "successor model" to what was tested. A successor, according to the manufacturer, is similar in performance to the item tested, but it may have different features. Such products are marked Ⓢ in the Ratings.

Prices. Most prices, especially for big-ticket items, have been updated for the Buying Guide. The prices we give, unless otherwise noted, are manufacturers' approximate or suggested retail. Discounts may be substantial, particularly for electronics and camera equipment.

MAJOR KITCHEN APPLIANCES

Microwave ovens 7	Dishwashers 15
Ranges 10	Ratings..18
Refrigerators 12	

Consumers usually acquire kitchen appliances the same way audio enthusiasts build sound systems: item by item from different manufacturers. Our tests over the years confirm the wisdom of that approach—no single company has ever swept the kitchen-appliance field for sheer excellence.

Past satisfaction with a particular brand is no guarantee of future happiness either. Most of the top 25 appliance brands in the U.S. now come from the "Big Five": General Electric, Whirlpool, Maytag, Raytheon, and Frigidaire. General Electric brands include its namesake, *Hotpoint*, and *RCA*. Whirlpool owns *KitchenAid*; Maytag, the *Jenn-Aire, Magic Chef*, and *Admiral* brands. Raytheon sells *Amana* and *Speed Queen* machines; Frigidaire, *White-Westinghouse, Gibson, Kelvinator, Tappan*, and *Frigidaire* products.

To make the market even more confusing, companies may not manufacture all the brands they sell. Microwave ovens, for instance, are nearly all made by Japanese or Korean manufacturers.

Many stores now want to sell goods that take up less space and move faster than bulky ranges, refrigerators, and the like. So department stores have given up much of the major appliance business, except for microwave ovens. Although discount chains have taken up some of the slack, you'll generally find fewer places selling major appliances than in the past.

The price paid for a given appliance depends largely on where you live. In cities and suburban areas, where competition among mass merchandisers is keen, prices tend to be lower than elsewhere. Appliances are not discounted as sharply as audio and video equipment, but sales are common. Discontinued models, which are sometimes only slightly different from their newer replacements, may be a source of greater savings.

As with most products, the more you pay, the more frills you get. But dishwashers don't lend themselves to the addition of frills as readily as electronic products such as microwave ovens. Though manufacturers do try to give ranges, refrigerators, and dishwashers the kind of electronic controls microwaves have, white goods for the most part work fine without glitz. Some frills, notably ice-makers and water dispensers in refrigerators, can actually make an appliance less reliable, as our Frequency-of-Repair surveys show.

Stylistically, stainless steel and sleek white-on-white or black-on-black "Euro-style" finishes offer quite a contrast with the avocado green and harvest gold of yesteryear. Built-in appliances, designed to be installed flush with surrounding cabinets, have inspired trim kits that give regular appliances the same custom look.

On the whole, new appliances are far stingier with energy than their predecessors. In fact, Federal standards for power-hungry refrigerators mandate that models built in 1993 be 25 percent more efficient than permitted in 1990—and the 1990 standards are typically 4 percent tougher than the 1987 standards. For a ballpark idea of energy costs, take a look at the bright yellow guide labels on big-ticket appliances. The labels provide an estimate of yearly energy costs, based on national average utility rates and, in smaller print, other rates. They also tell how a particular model compares in efficiency with others like it.

While manufacturers often warn against plugging major appliances into extension cords, many people do so anyway. The possibility of a short circuit or fire increases when an appliance is plugged into an extension cord incapable of handling the power load. If you must use an extension, buy a heavy-duty cord.

MICROWAVE OVENS

▶ Repair histories on page 364.

The "zapper" provides a fast, convenient way to defrost frozen foods, warm leftovers, and bake potatoes. It doesn't heat up the kitchen, it's clean, and it saves energy. But it has its limitations. Microwave ovens don't do justice to roasts and other meats, and no self-respecting pastry chef would dream of baking in one. Our surveys show that few readers actually cook from scratch in a microwave oven.

The choices

Size and power. Microwave ovens come in small, medium, and large sizes—and in some lines, sizes in between. When appliance makers talk about "compact" or "large" ovens, they mean the size of the cooking cavity, which ranges from less than half a cubic foot to more than three times that. Inside dimensions, while roughly the same as those outside, reflect how efficiently the manufacturer has designed the cabinet. Some models are low and long; others are on the boxy side. Big ovens typically sit on a countertop; smaller models may allow under-cabinet mounting, and mid-sized ovens, over-range mounting.

Size aside, the main difference between a big and small oven is the amount of power produced by the magnetron, the part that generates the high-energy microwaves that do the cooking. The magnetron in a full-sized oven is usually 650 to 900 watts, in mid-sized models, 600 to 800 watts. In small ovens, it's generally 500 to 700 watts.

Because of the greater power, big ovens can heat food about one-third faster than small ones, a difference especially noticeable when cooking large quantities. In addition, many cookbooks and convenience-food package instructions are written solely for high-wattage ovens. (A less powerful model requires tinkering with the time or power levels specified in recipes.)

Big ovens can accommodate lots of food—several containers of leftovers, many strips of bacon, or a large casserole. But they take up lots of space—they're typically 22 to 24 inches wide and 15 to 19 inches deep. Prices list from $250, but discounts are common.

The smallest ovens, just a bit larger and more expensive than a toaster oven, may be too small to hold a 10-inch dinner plate or a frozen dinner. But for basic chores, like popping corn or warming beverages, you may not need more capacity. Small ovens list for $100 or so.

Mid-sized ovens, a popular compromise, are quickly becoming the preferred size among consumers. Though they save just a few inches of counter space—they're typically 20 to 24 inches wide or less and 13 to 18 inches deep—they are considerably less bulky than a big oven. And there's little sacrifice in the way of capacity, power, or versatility. Mid-sized models list from about $180.

Microwaves plus. Manufacturers have come up with various hybrid appliances, chiefly to remedy the microwave oven's cooking deficiencies. The microwave/convection oven works fast, like an ordinary microwave. Like a traditional range oven, it browns food nicely. In convection cooking, air is heated by a concealed electric element and circulated inside the oven by a fan, crisping the outside before the heat works its way from the outside in. You can cook with convection or without. Most such ovens can be set for a full range of temperatures from 200° to 450°F. Price: typically $350 to $650 list.

An offshoot of the microwave/convection oven, the microwave/thermal oven relies on the natural circulation of heat to brown food. In our tests, the microwave/convection design worked better.

Features to look for

Bare-bones models have a mechanical rotary timer and may not beep to tell you the food is ready. But as often happens, features once found solely on high-end products now grace smaller, cheaper models. Here's a rundown of what to look for when shopping:

Electronic controls. Seconds count in using this appliance, so we recommend electronic controls. (A mechanical timer could miss the mark by 20 or 30 seconds.) Touchpads vary in readability and ease of programming. On better models, numbers and letters are printed clearly, and the control pad is well labeled and laid out so the buttons are near one another when an operation requires a sequence of commands. Good displays are large and well lit.

Ordinary heating commands are usually straightforward. To zap something on full power, you press number keys to select the time, then hit Start. (Some models make you hit a Cook or Time button first. With a few models, you set the power level, too.) Programming the oven's automated features can be more vexing. We like models with prompts that take you through each command step by step.

Power levels. Most larger ovens have 10; some have 100. We find five well-spaced settings are plenty. In a few inexpensive ovens, power remains constant. Models with a high-power default automatically cook at that power unless programmed otherwise.

Temperature probe. Like a meat thermometer, a temperature probe in a microwave oven monitors a food's internal temperature and either turns off the oven or switches to a lower "keep warm" setting when the preset temperature is reached. Few of CU's readers who own a probe said they actually use it, according to our surveys.

Moisture sensor. This keeps track of cooking progress by tracking the moisture level in the oven as the food releases steam. We think this type of sensor is much handier than a probe, but readers say they don't often use it.

Multistage cooking programs. These programs tell the oven to cook at one power level for a while, then switch to another—helpful for recipes that call for 10 minutes at high power and 5 at a reduced setting, or for going directly from Defrost to Cook. Basic models typically allow two programs; fancier models offer several.

Automatic defrosting. Any microwave can adequately thaw out food if you break apart defrosted pieces and turn the food occasionally. An automatic-defrost setting reduces the labor. With some ovens, the feature works by lowering the power level over the thawing period; with others, it works for a programmed time period, based on the item's weight. Highly automated ovens signal when to turn the food or remove defrosted sections. They may also go into a "standing" mode periodically to let the temperature equalize. The models that thaw the best—without burning the edges of food and leaving icy spots elsewhere—may not be the swiftest, since uniform thawing takes time. More than half our readers regularly use their oven's auto-defrost feature.

Programmed cooking. Electronic controls give a microwave oven various programming capabilities. Many models have preset programs that adjust the cooking time and power level for specific tasks, such as reheating a cup of soup. Some models allow you to enter cooking instructions for your own recipes into computer memory or call up programmed instructions for a variety of foods at the touch of a button.

Turntable. A turntable improves heat distribution, but it's not a substitute for turning the food by hand. A turntable that isn't recessed or removable cuts down on an oven's usable capacity.

Conveniences. Inspect any oven, plain or fancy, for basic conveniences. Can you see through the window to check on the progress of a dish? A dim interior light, coarse screen, or dark door pane limits visibility. Does the oven have a shelf? It comes in handy for cooking more than one dish at a time. Other useful touches include: a lip or tray to contain spills; and especially, a clearly written, logically organized instruction book.

The tests

Our evaluation includes a judgment of heating speed, based on the temperature increase when heating measured amounts of water for a fixed time interval, and a battery of cooking tests, most of them designed to gauge evenness of heating, a major concern in microwave cooking. We defrost ground beef, warm leftovers, and bake potatoes, popcorn, and brownies. With the bigger and fancier ovens, we prepare entrées like meat loaf and quiche. We also measure usable capacity and review conveniences.

Buying advice

Consider the space available and how you plan to use the oven. Given the smallest ovens' limited capacity and power, we suggest buying one only if kitchen space is truly at a premium. In our opinion, mid-sized models are the best for the money. Many cost just a little more than small ovens but cook faster and come with more features. And they're still small enough to fit under a cabinet or sit on the kitchen counter without hogging it.

Specifically, we recommend the top-rated *GE JEM31K001*, $209, from our November

1991 report; it is one of the few models from that report that is still available.

A convection oven is free from many of the flaws of microwave cooking. But those flaws appear only when you use the microwave for real cooking—not just heating food. You'll have to learn new cooking methods to take advantage of a microwave/convection model. For broiling and baking, a regular oven is probably best.

GAS & ELECTRIC RANGES

▸ Repair histories on page 365.

No kitchen appliance is showcased more than the range. The lowly stove of yesteryear is today's "cooking center," which may consist of a single basic range or a series of advanced cooking appliances. Your choice depends largely on budget, personal preference, and cooking style. But the layout of your kitchen, the available fuel source, and the conveniences you desire may also influence what you buy.

The choices

The kitchen's cabinetry and floor plan will probably dictate the range's width (21, 24, 30, 36, and 40 inches are the usual sizes) and whether the range fits between counters, is built into the countertop and cabinets, or stands alone.

Configurations. Catalogs and showrooms feature dual-oven ranges and ranges with a microwave oven above the cooktop and a regular oven below. You can also find those combinations as built-ins—the cooktop installed in an island or counter, the oven or ovens in the cabinetry. Despite all those designs, many people still want a simple freestanding range with four elements or burners and a self-cleaning oven.

Gas or electric? This decision often depends on the utility hookup available. If you can choose gas or electric but have no preference, here are a few points to keep in mind:

Gas burners respond quickly and let you see heat levels. Gas cooktops also remain usable in power outages. A gas range is more expensive than a comparable electric model (there's more inside plumbing), but typically costs less to operate, especially now that automatic spark igniters have by and large replaced pilot lights.

The broiler in an electric range generally browns better over a wider area than a gas broiler, we've found. Electric ranges are also less likely to break down and need repair.

Cooktop types. Besides the familiar electric coil element or gas burner, there are solid-disk elements, glass-ceramic cooktops, and modular cooktops that let you substitute a rotisserie, grill, griddle, or deep-fryer for two elements.

New in gas cooking are burners sealed to the top of the range to stop spills from seeping below.

Electric models with solid-disk elements are also easier to clean because food spills can't get under the disks. Ads claim solid disks offer better low-temperature control (for maintaining a simmer), a claim our tests didn't confirm. Further, solid elements take longer to heat and cool than coil elements and require cookware with an extra-flat bottom to cook evenly.

Smooth cooktops, with heating elements under a sheet of ceramic glass, fared poorly in tests done many years ago. They wasted energy, cooked slowly, and demanded elaborate care. A new generation using different technology promises improvement.

The new cooktops work in one of three ways: with radiant elements, halogen elements, or induction elements. Radiant elements cook food much as coils and disks do—with radiant heat and conduction. With a halogen element, light from a halogen-gas "bulb" produces the heat. With an induction element, a magnetic field created under a steel pot heats the pot and its contents.

Features to look for

Self-cleaning oven. A self-cleaning oven is almost standard nowadays. A high-heat cycle (usually two to four hours at temperatures as high as 1000°F) turns any accumulated goop into ash. When the cycle is complete, you wipe away the residue with a damp sponge. This worthwhile option adds $50 to $100 to an oven's price.

A dwindling number of models come with a "continuous-cleaning" oven. Instead of extreme heat, they rely on a special textured surface that absorbs grime during routine cooking. Our tests some years ago didn't show this approach to be particularly effective. Some continuous-cleaning ovens have regular porcelain-enamel oven floors, removable for cleaning at the sink.

No-frills ranges must be cleaned manually, a messy job that can involve the use of acrid, highly toxic oven cleaners.

Cooktop KP. Some designs make cleanup particularly easy. Look for a cooktop you can prop up or remove. A deep well and minimum clutter under the cooktop make it easy to reach spills. Other features to facilitate cleaning: seamless corners and edges (especially where the cooktop joins the backguard, as found on some electric ranges); a glass backguard instead of a painted one (glass won't scratch as easily); and porcelain rather than shiny metal drip bowls.

Capacity. Ovens in models with similar exterior dimensions often differ in capacity because of shelf supports and other protrusions. Some ovens won't let you cook a turkey and a casserole at the same time. A well-designed cooktop can hold a big stockpot on a back burner and still accommodate a saucepan or skillet on the other side, and a pot on the rear burner won't block the controls.

Conveniences. An oven window is a plus if you can see inside clearly. Indicator lights can be a help depending on their number and location. Choosing between a mechanical clock and a digital model isn't as simple as it might seem; we think mechanical clocks are apt to be more troublesome in the long run. Color-coded controls may help you match control to function. Storage drawers are handy for a kitchen short on space. Electronic touchpad controls, instead of knobs and dials, may add more to the price of the range than they're really worth.

Safety considerations

Unlike electric coils, solid-disk elements remain gray even when very hot, so you may forget they're turned on. And they take a long time to cool down. But disks have one safety feature coils and gas burners lack: They automatically reduce their wattage if a pot boils dry.

On any range, when you use oven and cooktop together, the front of the cooktop can get hot enough to burn. That area also gets hot during the self-cleaning cycle.

With any electric range, you must leave the door slightly ajar when you broil, to let the air circulate. Some models have a broil shield, which manufacturers claim makes the job safer. We've found the shields awkward; further, they obstruct your view of the food and interfere when you want to flip a hamburger or steak.

The tests

Two important criteria of cooktop performance: how fast the burners heat and how well they hold a low temperature for slow cooking. We judge speed of heating by the time it takes to warm measured quantities of water. To test simmering prowess, we melt baking chocolate in a heavy saucepan, keep it over low heat for 10 minutes, and check for scorching. We judge evenness of oven and broiler heating by baking cakes and broiling hamburgers. We evaluate each oven's self-cleaning by baking on and removing a special blend of gunk. We also assess cooktop cleanability.

Buying advice

Our reader surveys over the years tell us electric ranges are more reliable than gas models. Electrics are also less expensive. A typical 30-inch freestanding electric range with four coil elements and a self-cleaning oven below lists at around $450 to $600; a comparable gas range sells for $500 to $700. Electric ranges offer more burner options—coils, disks, or smooth tops—and boast superior broiler performance.

But gas ranges have their advantages: It's cheaper to cook with gas than electricity. The heat is easily and directly controlled. And gas ranges remain usable in a blackout.

No matter what type of range you're considering, look for a model with logically placed, understandable controls; a simple, easy-to-clean cooktop; and room for a variety of pots and pans.

REFRIGERATORS

▶ Ratings start on page 18. ▶ Repair histories on page 363.

Refrigerators, one of the biggest energy-consuming appliances in the home, have chalked up impressive gains in efficiency. Today's models work on about one-third less energy than those of a decade ago. Responding to consumer demand and Government prodding, manufacturers continue to devise new ways to reduce energy use, and now, scramble to meet stiff new Federal energy standards for 1993. In the future, refrigerators are likely to be better insulated, boast an energy-thrifty compressor, and run on a refrigerant friendlier to the environment than the chlorofluorocarbons in use at present, which are set to be phased out.

Efficiencies notwithstanding, a refrigerator's use of electricity still adds up over its expected 17-year life span. Your cumulative electricity bills can eventually amount to twice the appliance's purchase price, so choosing an energy-efficient model can mean real savings over time. Energy costs depend largely on the capacity and type of refrigerator you buy. But the design matters, too. Our tests regularly show a spread in the amount of electricity similarly configured models consume.

The choices

These are the main types you'll find:

Top-freezer. The most common format, top-freezer models are generally least expensive to buy and cheapest to run; they also give you the widest choice of capacities, styles, and features. The eye-level freezer, though smallish, generally has a large usable capacity and offers easy access to its contents. Its fairly wide shelves make it easy to reach things at the back, but vegetables and other items stored on bottom shelves are awkwardly out-of-reach. Nominal capacity ranges from about 10 to almost 25 cubic feet; width ranges from 24 to 34 inches. A typical 20-cubic-foot unit sells for $650 to $850.

Side-by-side. These larger models (nominally about 19 to 27 cubic feet, 30 to 36 inches wide) usually appeal to the luxury market, costing more to buy and run than other types. Side-by-side models come in a fairly wide selection of capacities, styles, and features. Advantages that may justify the expenditure: You can store more food at eye level in both compartments. The tall, thin shape of the compartments makes it easy to find stray items (but hard to get at items in the back). Doors are narrower than those of a top-freezer model, requiring less clearance in front for opening. The freezer is larger than in comparable top- or bottom-freezer models. Selling price: $900 to $2000, depending on size.

Bottom-freezer. These models, a tiny part of the market, give you fairly wide, eye-level shelves in the refrigerator and easy access to its contents, and a bigger freezer than that of top-freezer models with the same overall capacity. That advantage is offset by the pull-out basket, which reduces usable space. However, bottom-freezer models are more expensive ($900 to $1100) than top-freezer units and can be more expensive to run than other types. The location of the freezer at the bottom means you have to crouch or bend to get at it. And features such as an in-door water dispenser are unavailable. Nominal capacity: 18 to 22 cubic feet; width, about 32 inches.

Built-in refrigerators. Built-ins are expensive appliances (usually $2000 and more) sized from 10 to 33 cubic feet. Designed to be installed flush with the surrounding cabinets, they can be faced with custom door panels to match the cabinetry. To achieve that look, built-ins are only 24 inches deep, a half-foot shallower than conventional models; they're also taller and wider than typical refrigerators. Installation can be a major expense. Just squeezing the machines through existing doorways can be a problem.

Compact models. At the other end of the scale are refrigerators with a nominal capacity of six cubic feet or less. The best-selling models of this type, popular in dormitories and playrooms, are cubes—scaled-down versions of regular-sized refrigerators. In this segment of the market, you'll find familiar appliance names, such as *General Electric* and *Whirlpool,* and also names known better for electronic products, such as *Sanyo* and *Goldstar.* Prices range from about $100 to $300.

Mechanically, compacts are old-fashioned. Freezers, typically within the refrigerator compartment, get no colder than 15° or 20°F and can keep ice cream for only a few hours before it goes soupy. If you adjust the control to make the freezer colder, items in the refrigerator compartment freeze, too. These models don't automatically defrost. And if our experience is typical, the consumer has nearly a 25 percent chance of buying a sample with a major problem, such as a bum thermostat.

Features and conveniences

When evaluating a regular refrigerator, we use a 70-item checklist to gauge how easy the unit would be to live with (the compact-model list has only 23 items). Minor things—poorly placed shelves, bins that don't glide smoothly—can mount up to major dissatisfactions in daily use.

Temperature controls. These are typically dials in the refrigerator area. With some designs, you may have to move food to make adjustments. Some models have more controls—a simple louver or valve, typically for crispers or meat-keepers. In our experience, the effectiveness of these controls varies.

Electronic touchpad controls, available on high-end models, are usually easy to use. They can show when a door is ajar, when the unit is excessively warm, and when to clean the coils. In addition, such controls can flag problems needing repairs.

Shelves and bins. As a rule, the shelves in the refrigerator compartment can be rearranged; so can some freezer shelves and door shelves. Tempered-glass shelves, increasingly common, are preferable because they confine spills to one level. Sliding shelves help you find stray items. Removable bins can be handy for ice cubes.

On models higher in a manufacturer's line, you may find a utility shelf fitted with storing and serving containers that are microwaveable; adjustable extra-deep door shelves for holding gallon containers; movable retainers on door shelves to hold odd-shaped items; or a built-in beverage container with spigot.

No-frost operation. This is practically a given these days, except on compact models. Most self-defrosting models defrost about once a day, after their compressor has run for a fixed number of hours.

Ice and water. Ice-makers, ice dispensers, and water dispensers jack up a refrigerator's price by $200 to $250. The plumbing connections for ice-makers and dispensers also come in kit form for as little as $70 to $100. Such devices should be used routinely to keep them in working order and to keep their contents tasting fresh.

An ice-maker can be a mixed blessing. It can take up a cubic foot of valuable freezer space and nearly double the chance you'll need repairs. Although the ice-maker is built-in, the refrigerator must still be connected to the kitchen's cold-water line, a job do-it-yourselfers may be able to handle after checking local plumbing codes. Most ice-makers shut off when their bin is full or when you raise and lock a wire arm. Don't expect large quantities of ice: The models we've seen produce about four to six ice-trays' worth a day.

Through-the-door ice dispensers can drop just a few cubes into a glass or fill an ice bucket. We like the push-in cradle arrangement, as is found on some soda fountains. Dispensers using overhead push buttons often send ice to the floor instead of into the glass. Don't expect to get lots of cold water from a dispenser—reservoirs typically hold about 1½ quarts.

The tests

Our tests for compact models are less rigorous than for a regular refrigerator since they are not designed to have very cold freezers. The inside of a regular model ought to hold steady at 37° F; the freezer should stay at 0°. Compacts should hold compartments at 35° and 15°, respectively.

We place each model in a test chamber and challenge the unit to keep that temperature balance at various room temperatures, including extreme heat. We check for temperature uniformity; temperature accuracy of the meat keeper (it should be 30° to 35°, slightly cooler than the temperature in the main compartment); the crisper's ability to retain moisture (to prolong the life of vegetables); and speed of ice-making. We also measure noise.

Energy use

The yellow EnergyGuide sticker the Government requires on refrigerators compares electricity consumption among models of a given capacity range. When comparing those guides, it's important to make sure the models are in the same cubic-foot class and that the labels note the same national electricity rate.

Because of U.S. Department of Energy standards, models manufactured in 1990 or later have to meet more energy-efficient standards than ones made before. Standards will be tightened again on January 1, 1993. An inside faceplate sometimes gives the date of manufacture.

To conserve energy, you should clean a refrigerator's condenser coil a few times a year with a special brush or a vacuum.

When the coil collects dust, it becomes less effective at dissipating heat and may reduce efficiency. Some models put the coil at the rear; it gathers less dust there but is hard to get at. Others have the coil in front, at the bottom. If you have more than one refrigerator in use, you can save a lot of energy by shutting off one.

Small refrigerators such as compacts generally use energy less efficiently than larger models.

Buying advice

Decide on the type; then decide on capacity. Too large a model may be needlessly expensive, besides wasting space and energy. If your old model was big enough, then a similar-sized unit will probably suit your needs.

Kitchen space is another consideration. Check how much clearance the door or doors need in front and at the side. Some doors demand up to an extra foot on the side so you can slide out bins and shelves.

In general, models with features such as an ice-maker and a water dispenser break down far more often than models without them. See repair records for refrigerators on page 363 and weigh the importance of such features carefully.

DISHWASHERS

▶ Repair histories on page 365.

An automatic dishwasher won't necessarily clean better than hand washing, but it could be a cheaper way to wash dishes. Modern dishwashers use relatively little hot water—less than you'd likely use if you're accustomed to washing dishes under a faucet spewing hot water.

The choices

There are two main types, built-in models and freestanding, portable models. Mechanically, the two are similar.

More than 30 years ago, most models sold for $300 to $400. Today, almost half the dishwashers sold still sell for less than $400. You can spend nearly twice as much, but not necessarily for a machine that does the dishes better.

Built-ins. Most people choose a built-in, which is designed to be permanently attached to a hot-water pipe, a drain, and electrical lines. They generally fit into a 24-inch-wide space under the countertop between two kitchen cabinets. A few compacts are made to fit an 18-inch space.

Portables. These have a finished exterior, wheels, a plug-in cord, and a hose assembly you attach to the sink faucet each time you use the machine. Most portables can be converted to an under-cabinet installation.

Features and conveniences

Buying higher in a line typically buys a unit with electronic controls and specialized cycles, promoted to tackle chores beyond everyday dishwashing.

Controls. Manufacturers' flagship models couple electronic touchpads with "systems monitor" displays. The circuitry logs the time for various dishwasher operations, and some monitor the energy that each operation consumes. Some displays flash warnings about clogged drains, blocked wash-arms, open detergent dispensers, and so on. Some models have a hidden touchpad that locks the controls to keep kids from playing with them—a worthwhile feature.

Simpler models let you set everything

with push buttons, or with buttons and a dial. By and large, these basic controls work just fine.

Cycles. A cycle is a combination of washes and rinses. Normal or Regular generally comprises two washes and two or three rinses. A Heavy cycle can entail longer wash cycles, another wash, hotter water, or all of the above. A Light cycle usually includes one wash. Rinse and Hold rinses while you accumulate a full load. Those basic cycles are really all you need.

Extra cycles—with names such as Pot Scrubber, Soak and Scrub, and China and Crystal—help justify a higher price tag. Regardless of what the names imply, a machine cannot scrub the way abrasive cleaners and old-fashioned muscle can. Nor can a dishwasher baby your heirloom crystal or good china. The machine jostles dishes and the harsh detergents could etch them. Gold trim may be especially vulnerable.

Energy-saving features. Some booster heater systems check the water temperature, automatically heating it, if necessary. That allows you to keep your water heater at a lower, more economical setting. A Delay-Start setting lets you program the dishwasher to do its work several hours later, say, when off-peak energy rates are in effect. Most dishwashers let you choose between a heated dry cycle and plain air drying. A few also use a blower to aid drying, though some other machines did just fine without one.

Noise. One big complaint about dishwashers is that they're loud. So quiet operation has become a main selling point. While dishwashers as a whole have become less raucous over the years, few models are truly quiet. In our tests, we've found no particular correlation between price and noise. However, in a given brand line, the more expensive models tend to have better soundproofing.

Racks. Most racks hold the cups and glasses on top, plates on the bottom. (*Maytag* and *Jenn-Aire* machines load the opposite way.) Some models have racks with folding shelves to let you squeeze in extra cups and glasses. Some models have provisions for adjusting the upper rack for tall glasses. Flatware baskets are typically in the main dish rack. *Whirlpool* machines place their baskets on the door.

Energy use

It doesn't take much electricity to run the pump, motor, and heating element—something like one kilowatt-hour, which works out to less than a dime's worth of electricity at average rates. No-heat drying saves a penny or two.

Most of the energy a dishwasher uses is in the form of hot water from your water heater. If you don't rinse dishes before you load—and there's no need to—a dishwasher uses no more water than hand washing in a dishpan. An electric water heater will use about 20 cents of electricity to provide the 11 gallons of 140°F water the typical unit consumes in one load. If you use the dishwasher once a day, the total comes to about $100 a year. Figure about half that cost for a gas-fired water heater, two-thirds for an oil one. Lowering the water heater's thermostat to 120° will reduce the cost by a few dollars.

The tests

We judge performance by how well a dishwasher cleans place settings soiled with some of the most challenging foods we can find: dinner plates smeared with chili, spaghetti, and mashed potatoes; luncheon plates with fried egg yolk, peanut butter, raspberry jam, and cheese spread; sauce dishes with cornflakes and milk, oatmeal, and stewed tomatoes; and cups stained with coffee, glasses with milk and juice. We let the soiled dishes stand in the machines overnight. We run many loads in each machine, half at 140° and half at 120°. Most machines clean a bit better at the hotter setting.

Buying advice

We still find substantial performance differences among various brands of dishwashers—more than what we usually see with other major appliances. Price and performance in a dishwasher don't always go hand in glove. Electronic controls add substantially to the cost but buy no edge in cleaning. Solid performers with dials and push buttons cost less than $500.

When shopping, look at the racks with your dishes in mind. Construction is important, too. A porcelain-coated steel interior resists abrasion better than plastic but can be chipped. Stainless steel can be dented but is most durable.

How to Use the Ratings

- Read the article for general guidance about types and buying advice.
- Read the Recommendations for brand-name advice based on our tests.
- Read the Ratings order to see whether products are listed in order of quality, by price, or alphabetically. Most Ratings are based on estimated quality, without regard to price.
- Look to the Ratings table for specifics on the performance and features of individual models.
- A model marked Ⓓ has been discontinued, according to the manufacturer. A model marked Ⓢ indicates that, according to the manufacturer, it has been replaced by a successor model whose performance should be similar to the tested model but whose features may vary.

18 SIDE-BY-SIDE REFRIGERATORS

RATINGS SIDE-BY-SIDE REFRIGERATORS

Better ◐ ◐ ○ ◑ ● Worse

▶ **See report, page 12.** From Consumer Reports, May 1991.

Recommendations: The top-rated *Amana* and its essentially similar brandmate offer a winning combination of performance, efficiency, and convenience. The plainer model, the *SZD27K*, lacks niceties you may find easy to live without—touchpad controls, an LED monitor, alarms, and a smarter defrost circuitry. The next three models in the Ratings—the *GE*, the *Hotpoint*, and the *Sears* are all made by GE. They offer convenience and efficiency similar to the *Amanas* and performed almost as well in many respects.

Ratings order: Listed in order of estimated quality. Bracketed models had essentially identical overall performance; listed alphabetically. The price is the approximate retail as quoted by the manufacturer; actual retail may be lower. Price does not include plumbing hardware. The annual energy costs are based on the 1990 national average electricity rate of 7.9¢ per kilowatt-hour. ⓢ indicates model has been replaced by successor model; according to the manufacturer, the performance of the new model should be similar to the tested model but features may vary. See right for new model number and approximate retail price. ⒹⒹ indicates model discontinued.

Brand and model	Price	Annual cost	Temp. uniformity	Crisper humidity	Ice & water dispensers	Ice-making	Noise	Overall convenience	Capacity, cu. ft. ⓣ	Advantages	Disadvantages	Comments
Amana SZD27K ② ⓢ	$1490	$116	◐	◐	○	◐	○	◐	16.7	C,D,E,G,H,I,J,O,P,R,S,W,Y,AA	—	C,D,G,I,J,M,O,T
General Electric TFX27VL ⓢ	1475	115	○	◐	◐	◐	○	◐	16.7	C,E,G,H,K,O,U,W	a,h	B,E,F,I,N,P,U
Hotpoint CSX27DL ⓢ	1320	115	○	◐	◐	◐	○	◐	17.2	C,E,G,H,K,U,W	a,h	B,N,P,U
Sears Kenmore 50771 Ⓓ	1385	115	○	◐	◐	◐	○	◐	16.7	A,C,F,G,H,O,U,W	a,h	B,I,J,N,U
Whirlpool ED27DQXW Ⓓ	1520	124	◐	◐	◐	◐	○	◐	15.7	A,B,C,D,F,G,H,I,K,M,W,Z	j	B,E,G,I,J,K,T
KitchenAid KSRS25QW ⓢ	1535	114	○	●	◐	◐	◐	◐	16.0	A,C,F,G,I,L,M,R,W	j	B,D,E,G,I,J,K,O,S,T,X
General Electric TFX27FM	1685	133	○	◐	◐	◐	○	◐	16.4	C,E,G,H,K,O,U,W,X	a,h,p	B,E,F,N,P,U,V
Admiral CDNS24V9	1150	109	◐	●	◐	◐	○	○	16.0	C,H,K	f,i,l,q	B,D,H,I,L,O
Jenn-Aire JRSD246	1355	107	◑	●	◐	◐	◐	◐	15.3	C,E,H,I,L,R	f,i,o	B,C,G,H,I,J,L,O,R
Maytag RSW24A ⓢ	1580	107	◑	●	◐	◐	○	◐	15.1	C,E,H,I,K,L,O,Q,R,V	d,i,n,o,q	A,B,E,G,H,I,J,O,R,W

SIDE-BY-SIDE REFRIGERATORS 19

Brand and model	Price	Annual cost	Temp. uniformity	Crisper humidity	Ice & water dispensers	Ice-making	Noise	Overall convenience	Capacity, cu. ft. [1]	Advantages	Disadvantages	Comments
Frigidaire FPCE24VWL [D]	$1100	$116	◐	◒	◒	○	◐	○	15.4	C,F,H,I,N,O,T	b,e,f,g,m,o	E,G,I,O
Kelvinator FMW240EN [D]	1235	116	◐	○	◒	◒	◐	○	16.0	T	b,c,e,f,k,m,o	E,Q
White-Westinghouse RS249M [S]	1000	116	◐	○	◒	◒	◐	○	15.4	F,K,T	b,c,e,f,m,o	H,I

[1] As measured by CU.
[2] Essentially similar brandmate **SZDE27K**, $1780, also tested.

Successor Models (in Ratings order)
Amana SZD27K is succeeded by SZD27M, $1699; GE TFX27VL by TFX27VM, $1425; Hotpoint CSX27DL by CSX27DM, $1250; KitchenAid KSRS25QW by KSRS25QX, $1549; Maytag RSW24A by RSW2400A, $1580; White-Westinghouse RS249M by RS249MC, $949.

Performance Notes
Except as noted: • Ability to maintain set temperature judged excellent. • Ability to compensate for changes in room temperature judged good. • Performance under severe conditions judged good. • Meat-keeper temperature judged very good or excellent.

Features in Common
All have: • Adjustable glass shelves in refrigerator. • Temperature-controlled meat-keeper. • Anticondensate heating, judged effective in controlling exterior condensation. • At least 1 crisper drawer, at least partly sealed. • Bulk-storage drawer in bottom of freezer. • Door-shelf retainers, bins, or both, that are easily removed for cleaning. • 4 rollers on base, the front pair adjustable for leveling. • Parts and labor warranty for at least 1 yr. on entire unit, 5 yr. on sealed refrigeration system.
Except as noted, all: • Can maintain 37°F in refrigerator, 0° in freezer. • Have adjustable shelves/bins on refrigerator door. • Have textured steel doors. • Have plastic seamless liner. • Have door stops. • Met 1990 U.S. Energy Dept. efficiency requirements.

Key to Advantages
A—Controls are easy to reach.
B—Some refrigerator shelves slide forward for easier access.
C—Refrigerator door has removable bins whose height can be adjusted.
D—Freezer door has removable bins whose height can be adjusted.
E—Some freezer shelves adjustable.
F—Freezer baskets slide for easier access. (On **White-Westinghouse** and **Frigidaire**, baskets can be removed to convert space to shelves.)
G—Refrigerator door has at least 1 shelf that can easily fit 1-gal. milk containers.
H—Bookend-type "snugger(s)" on refrigerator door shelves keep small containers upright (**Frigidaire** uses fingerlike tabs).
I—2 crisper drawers.
J—Sliding freezer shelf for cans.
K—Separate deli/utility drawer.
L—Some drawers are on rollers.
M—Fast-freeze shelf above ice-maker.
N—Juice-dispenser jug on inside of door.
O—Comes with microwaveable containers for storing, heating, and serving.
P—Beverage area on door shelf has separate temperature control.
Q—Separate ice and water dispenser lock-outs.
R—Performance under severe conditions judged very good.
S—Crisper's humidity controls judged very effective.
T—Has rear condenser coils; need cleaning less often than bottom-mounted coils but refrigerator must be moved from wall to clean.
U—Defrost drain-tube opening easily accessible for cleaning.
V—Locks on rollers to curb rolling.
W—Lets user select cubes or crushed ice.
X—Electronic monitor, diagnostic system.
Y—Dispenser area has night light, which can be set to turn on automatically after dark.

Ratings Keys continued

20 SIDE-BY-SIDE REFRIGERATORS

Z–Ability to compensate for changes in room temperature judged very good.
AA–Ability to compensate for changes in room temperature judged excellent.

Key to Disadvantages
a–Upper shelf area of freezer door warmed more than most during defrost.
b–Lacks separate On/Off control arm for ice-maker; ice bin must be physically removed to stop ice-maker.
c–Butter door will not stay open by itself.
d–Ice and water dispensers difficult to operate.
e–Requires at least 3-in. clearance on top and 1 in. on bottom for air circulation.
f–Lacks door stops.
g–Doors are smooth, not textured; may show smudges more readily.
h–Drip pan cannot be removed; hard to clean (but water may evaporate faster).
i–Condenser wrapped in metal "shroud," which curbs dust but makes cleaning hard.
j–Drip pan must be lifted over a wire brace; hard to remove.
k–Freezer on 2 samples could not reach zero in some tests because absence of baskets allows inlet air ducts to be blocked.
l–Crisper drawers lack adequate stops.
m–Ice dispenser can be activated even when freezer door is open resulting in ice falling on floor.
n–Ability to maintain set temperature judged very good, not excellent.
o–Ability to compensate for changes in room temperature judged fair.
p–Performance under severe conditions judged fair.
q–Meat-keeper temperature judged only fair or good.

Key to Comments
A–For models sold in 1991, sealed-refrigeration system warrantied until 12/31/99.
B–Meat-keeper is sealed.
C–Standard door trim accepts optional decorator door panels.
D–Has white handles.
E–Has brown or tan door-seal gasket.
F–Has almond-colored door interior.
G–Crisper(s) have humidity control.
H–Chart in freezer lists food-storage times.
I–Has wine rack.
J–Has 2 lights in refrigerator.
K–Has 2 lights in freezer.
L–Separate leveling legs to prevent rolling.
M–Entire cabinet, not just doors, is textured.
N–Has metal interior liner.
O–5-yr. warranty on liner except door.
P–Limited lifetime warranty on plastic drawer.
Q–1-yr. $100 freezer food-loss protection.
R–Second-yr. parts-only warranty.
S–Sixth-through-tenth-yr. parts-only warranty on sealed-refrigeration system.
T–Unlike other models that circulate hot refrigerants, these models have an anticondensate heater, judged effective in controlling exterior condensation.
U–Company claims meat-keeper control can convert meat-keeper to spare crisper.
V–Door-within-door "Refreshment Center."
W–Repositioning meat-keeper and utility drawer may improve or worsen temperature performance.
X–Glass butter dish, not plastic.

*W*HAT THE RATINGS MEAN

■ The Ratings typically rank products in order of estimated quality, without regard to price.

■ A product's rating applies only to the model tested and should not be considered a rating of other models sold under the same brand name unless so noted.

■ Models are check-rated (✓) when the product proved to be significantly superior to other models tested.

■ Products high in quality and relatively low in price are deemed Best Buys.

TOP-FREEZER REFRIGERATORS

RATINGS: TOP-FREEZER REFRIGERATORS

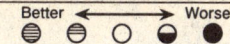

▶ See report, page 12. From Consumer Reports, July 1992.

Recommendations: Among the basic models, the *GE TBH18JP* top-freezer model, $610 on average, performed well and cost the least to operate. The high-scoring *Hotpoint* and *RCA* models may be better suited for households in the South because of their ability to withstand high room temperature. The deluxe top-freezer models, the side-by-sides, and the bottom-freezer model did as well or better but they all cost more to buy or operate.

Ratings order: Listed by types; within types, listed in order of estimated quality. Except where separated by bold rules, closely ranked models differed little in quality. Models judged about equal are bracketed and listed alphabetically. Price is the approximate retail as quoted by the manufacturer; actual retail may be lower. Ⓢ indicates tested model has been replaced by successor model; according to the manufacturer, the performance of new model should be similar to the tested model but features may vary. See page 22 for new model number and suggested retail price, if available. Ⓓ indicates model discontinued.

Brand and model	Price	Annual cost	Temp. uniformity	Reserve capacity	Meat-keeping	Crisper humidity	Ice-making	Noise	Convenience	Width, in.	Capacity, cu.ft.	Advantages	Disadvantages	Comments
BASIC TOP-FREEZER MODELS														
General Electric TBH18JP	$610	$71	⊜	○	○	◖	⊜	⊜	○	29¼	13.8	I,L,P	c,n	A,C,F
Hotpoint CTX18EP	505	81	⊜	⊜	○	◖	⊜	⊜	○	29¼	14.8	I,L,P	c	C,F
RCA MTX18EP	550	81	⊜	⊜	○	◖	⊜	⊜	○	29¼	14.8	I,L,P	c	C,F
Sears Kenmore 60821 Ⓓ	530	79	⊜	⊜	◖	●	◖	⊜	◖	31	14.8	B,M,Q	e,f,j,l	E,M
General Electric TBX18PR	485	81	⊜	⊜	○	◖	⊜	⊜	⊜	29¼	14.3	L,P	c	C,E,F
Montgomery Ward 19514 Ⓢ	530	93	⊜	○	◖	⊜	⊜	○	◖	31½	15.1	B,I,N	o	H,L,T
Whirlpool ET18ZKXX	555	76	⊜	⊜	◖	●	⊜	○	○	29½	14.6	B,F,H,L,N,S	b,i	D,F,R,T
Amana TM18QB	600	81	○	⊜	⊜	●	⊜	○	◖	32	14.0	N	a,l	A,B,E,G,K,L,M
Magic Chef RB19-2A	545	93	⊜	○	◖	⊜	◖	○	◖	31½	14.4	B,E,I,N	k,o	B,D,H,K,L,T
Admiral NT19L6	595	93	○	◖	●	◖	⊜	○	◖	31½	14.4	B,I,N	k,l,o	B,D,H,K,L,T
Gibson RT19F5WX Ⓓ	580	80	○	○	○	○	◖	⊜	◖	31	14.5	Q	b,g,h,k	C,E,K,M,P
Tappan 95-1971 Ⓓ	615	80	○	○	○	◖	⊜	○	◖	31	15.1	Q	b,g,h,j,k,m	F,N,P,R

Ratings continued

22 TOP-FREEZER REFRIGERATORS

Ratings continued

Brand and model	Price	Annual cost	Temp. uniformity	Reserve capacity	Meat-keeping	Crisper humidity	Ice-making	Noise	Convenience	Width, in.	Capacity, cu.ft.[1]	Advantages	Disadvantages	Comments
White-Westinghouse RT193M [D]	$460	$82	⊖	○	—	○	○	⊖	⊖	31	14.9	H,Q	g,h,k	E,F,P,R
Frigidaire FPDA18TP [D]	515	80	●	⊖	—	○	●	⊖	⊖	29¾	14.8	I,Q	e,g,h,l	E,K,P,Q
Kelvinator TSK180JN [D]	500	101	○	○	○	○	⊖	⊖	⊖	31	14.8	Q	d,g,h,l	M,P,R

DELUXE TOP-FREEZER MODELS

Amana TX18Q [D]	665	81	⊖	⊖	⊖	⊖	○	○	⊖	32	13.8	C,G,K,N	a	A,B,G,K,T
KitchenAid KTRC18KX	675	76	⊖	⊖	⊖	⊖	●	○	○	29½	14.6	A,B,D,F,H,K,N	i	B,F,K,T
Maytag RTS19A [D]	700	88	⊖	○	⊖	●	⊖	○	○	31½	13.9	A,B,E,F,I,K,N,O	—	A,H,K,T
Caloric GFS187 [D]	585	79	○	⊖	⊖	●	●	⊖	○	31	14.1	A,B,L,M,Q	c,f	F

BUILT-IN SIDE-BY-SIDE MODEL

| Amana SZI20M [D] | 1200 | 98 | ● | ⊖ | ⊖ | ○ | ⊖ | ⊖ | ⊖ | 36¼ | 14.7 | C,D,F,G,J,N,S | f,n | A,B,F,G,J,K,S,U |

SIDE-BY-SIDE MODEL

| General Electric TFX20D [S] | 800 | 104 | ○ | ○ | ⊖ | ⊖ | ⊖ | ⊖ | ○ | 30¼ | 15.2 | C,D,G,J,L,P,R | n | A,D,H,I,K,O,Q,S,U |

BOTTOM-FREEZER MODEL

| Whirlpool EB22RKXXW | 840 | 103 | ○ | ⊖ | ○ | ⊖ | ⊖ | ⊖ | ⊖ | 32¾ | 15.9 | D,G,H,J,K,L,N,R | f,n | B,F,G,T |

[1] As measured by CU.

Successor models (in Ratings order) Montgomery Ward 19514 is succeeded by Signature 19534, $530; GE TFX20D by TFX20DR, $800.

Performance Notes
Except as noted: • Ability to maintain a set temperature in center of mainspace and freezer judged excellent. • Ability to compensate for changes in room temperature judged excellent or very good. • Accuracy of initial settings of controls for ideal temperature balance judged at least good.

Features in Common
All have: • At least 1 dairy compartment. • 4 rollers on base. • Textured doors. • Warranty of 1 yr. or more covering parts and labor of entire unit; 5-yr. warranty on sealed refrigeration system.

Except as noted, all have: • Energy-saver switch. • Thermostat that can maintain 37°F in refrigerator, 0° in freezer. • Adjustable front rollers for leveling. • \ re shelves. • Plastic bottom shelf. • Fixed-position door shelves. • Seamless plastic liners. • Door stops. • Meat pans or drawers. • 2 crisper drawers. • Doors that can be hinged on left or right. • Provision for installing ice-maker. • Depth with door open of between 56 to 61 in. • No side clearance required for removal of drawers.

Key to Advantages
A–Energy-saver switch has light or red bar to show position.
B–Controls judged easiest to reach.
C–Meat-keeper's temperature control judged more effective than most.

TOP-FREEZER REFRIGERATORS 23

D–Crispers have front and rear seals, which tended to reduce moisture loss.
E–Lighted controls.
F–At least 2 lights inside refrigerator.
G–Light in freezer.
H–At least 1 door shelf for 1-gal. containers.
I–At least 1 extra-deep freezer-door shelf.
J–Freezer basket slides out for easy access.
K–Ice-cube tray and bin compartments.
L–At least 1 utility bin.
M–Sweated less than most with energy-saver switch on.
N–Removable drip pans.
O–Locking rollers to keep unit from rolling.
P–Condenser coils easier to clean than most.
Q–Condenser coils, mounted vertically behind unit, may collect less dust.
R–Light bulbs located behind plastic barriers.
S–Meat-keeper and crispers provide excellent visibility of contents.

Key to Disadvantages
a–Handle has sharp edge that could pinch a small child's hand.
b–Handle could pinch small child's hand.
c–Freezer warmed more than most in defrost.
d–Anticondensate heaters judged somewhat less effective than most.
e–Lacks door stops.
f–At least 1 freezer-door shelf judged narrow.
g–Freezer controls harder to use.
h–Freezer could not reach 0° in some tests.
i–Door shelves judged not as sturdy as most.
j–Dairy-compartment door doesn't stay open.
k–Crisper drawers lack adequate stops.
l–Dairy compartment provides poor view of contents.
m–Confusing markings on energy-saver switch.
n–Door took more force to open than most.
o–Wide, shallow ice tray judged relatively hard to load into freezer.

Key to Comments
A–Sealed meat-keeper.
B–At least 1 crisper has humidity control.
C–1 high-humidity, 1 low-humidity crisper.
D–Glass bottom shelf in refrigerator.
E–Molded side shelf supports.
F–2 dairy compartments or 1 full-width dairy compartment.
G–Entire cabinet has textured finish.
H–Cabinet has semismooth paint.
I–Porcelain-on-steel interior liners.
J–Comes with ice-maker.
K–5-yr. warranty on cabinet liner (**Amanas, Magic Chef, Admiral, Frigidaire, Kitchen-Aid, Maytag**); lifetime warranty on crisper drawers (**GE**); 10-yr. warranty on compressor replacement (**Gibson**); 2-yr. warranty on parts for sealed refrigeration system (**KitchenAid**).
L–Separate leveling legs prevent rolling but make unit hard to move for cleaning.
M–Door area or dispenser in freezer for juice cans.
N–Removable, reversible molded wire shelf in freezer.
O–"Hot loop" (not switchable heater) for condensate control.
P–Ability to maintain balanced temperature judged good.
Q–Ability to compensate for changes in room temperature judged good.
R–Accuracy of initial settings of controls judged fair or poor.
S–Depth with door open of 45 to 46 in.
T–Side clearance of between 16 to 21 in. required for removal of drawers.
U–Side clearance of between 13 to 17 in. on right and 10 in. on left for removal of drawers. No side clearance needed with **Amana** if lower door bins are removed.

How objective is CU?

Consumers Union is not beholden to any commercial interest. It accepts no advertising and buys all the products tested on the open market. CU's income is derived from the sale of CONSUMER REPORTS and other publications, and from nonrestrictive, noncommercial contributions, grants, and fees. Neither the Ratings nor the reports may be used in advertising or for any other commercial purpose. Consumers Union will take all steps open to it to prevent commercial use of its materials, its name, or the name of CONSUMER REPORTS.

Small Kitchen Appliances

Blenders 24	Coffee appliances 29
Food processors 26	Toasters & toaster ovens 32
Portable food mixers 27	Ratings 34

For years, the small appliances section of the hardware store or department store moved sleepily, rousing only for the nonce-appliances that show up at holiday time or for the occasional machine like the food processor that changes kitchens across the land. But of late, new designs have given coffee makers, blenders, mixers, and other previously boring small appliances new interest—and new sales.

The trend began in the early 1970s when Krups, the German appliance maker, redesigned the automatic drip coffee maker pioneered by Mr. Coffee. Krups and another German company, Braun, have since redesigned small motorized kitchen items, founding new subtypes of appliances (such as handheld blenders) along the way.

The European look of sleekly styled plastic and understated controls has spread to products from toasters to teapots. Meanwhile, a retro look developed a following, notably with blenders and toasters styled in the chrome and colors of the 1950s.

One result of the new attention to design is that there's a tremendous range of prices for products that do essentially the same thing. The retro *Waring* blender costs $100, for instance, while less-styled models cost $20 to $40.

BLENDERS

▶ Ratings on page 36.

Blenders became established appliances in the 1930s, when Stephen J. Poplawski developed a machine that excelled at making his favorite drink, the malted milk shake. Standard blenders today are much like the Depression-era prototypes, but innovative designs are reshaping the market. Beyond the basic choices of handheld versus standard model are the handheld hybrids that are very portable.

The choices

Handheld models. In just the past few years, sleek handheld models have emerged to challenge the traditional blender, capturing about a third of blender sales.

The handheld hybrids consist of a cylindrical hand grip with the motor housing inside and, at the other end, a blade shaft. A handheld model weighs around a couple of pounds, which makes it fairly easy to maneuver. It's also convenient to use, since the blended food or drink may be eaten or sipped from the container in which it was prepared. And handheld models are simple to clean; merely hold the blades under hot running water.

Handheld blenders are ideally suited to mixing liquids, such as drinks. With the help of other blades, they can handle more tasks. Prices range from about $20 to $80.

Standard models. The standard blender—a mixing pitcher with a rotating blade driven by a motor in the base—is more powerful than its handheld rivals and hence more versatile. Besides mixing liquids, it can blend or chop some solid foods, such as grinding peanuts into peanut butter, grating cheese, and making gazpacho. The old-fashioned blender also boasts more features than its handheld cousin—generally lots of speeds (the handheld ones usually offer only one or two). Some include a Pulse feature for quick bursts of blending. Prices range from $20 to $100.

Features to look for

Controls. Fewer controls make cleaning the base easier and operation simpler. On standard models, look for a wide range of speeds, not a lot of speed selections. A half-dozen are enough for most chores. Pulse, which keeps the blades whirring only as long as you depress the control, is especially useful when it works with more than one speed. Handheld models are usually limited to one or two speeds, which suffices for mixing liquids. Especially handy is a continuously variable speed.

Containers. Markings that aid measuring are an obvious convenience. Wide-mouth containers make cleaning and loading food easy. Standard blenders come with plastic or glass containers, handheld models with plastic ones. Plastic is lighter than glass but may not hold up as well in the dishwasher. Blend-and-store containers minimize cleanup.

Storage. Short and/or coiled cords simplify storage. While handheld units are small enough to go into a drawer, a design that lets the device stand on its head makes temporary storage easy, and a rack makes long-term storage easy.

Accessories. Interchangeable blades extend the usefulness of handheld models beyond mixing liquids, making it possible to mince, whip, blend, beat, and chop.

The tests

We put all models through a series of trials: blending diet drinks, milk shakes, gazpacho soup, and whipping cream. With the more muscular standard mixers, we judge their prowess at grating Parmesan cheese and grinding peanuts into butter.

We also test for electrical leakage by spilling milk onto the base of each standard blender and subsequently taking current readings in three places on the base.

Buying advice

If your blending tasks include but extend beyond mixing liquids, consider a standard blender. Differences among them tend to be slight, so it's sensible to let convenience, features, and price guide your choice. A handheld model lets you mix and serve in the same container. If you make a lot of foamy drinks, it's your best choice.

FOOD PROCESSORS

▶ Ratings of processors on page 34, choppers on page 41.

Food processors, introduced amid much fanfare by Cuisinarts Co. two decades ago, easily chop vegetables for a soup or stew. They also make quick work of salad fixings like onions, mushrooms, and cucumbers, and they're handy for such baking chores as crumbling graham crackers for a cheesecake crust or mixing a pastry dough.

But for mashing potatoes or whipping cream, an electric mixer remains the tool of choice. And for liquefying foods, puréeing baby food, or concocting exotic drinks, nothing tops a standard countertop blender. See the chart on page 38.

The choices

Compact vs. full-sized. Food processors come in compact and full-sized incarnations. Within those categories, sizes vary greatly. Because one manufacturer's "compact" can have a larger processing bowl than another's "full-size," we created our own definitions. Those we consider full-sized have a bowl that holds between 5¼ and 12¼ cups of food when filled to the rim. Price: around $35 to $300. Compacts, priced from around $30 to $95, hold from 2½ to 4¼ cups. Even by that definition, some compacts are taller than full-sized models.

Full-sized processors are useful if you're an active chef with an ambitious menu or regularly make large meals. Compact models demand a bit less kitchen space, of course, and they're easier to lift and clean. To create copious quantities, you just make another batch.

Minis and shooters. Variations on the basic food-processor theme exist as well. Miniature food choppers, which cost anywhere from $20 to $35, chop, grind, and purée in small quantities, half a cup or so at a time. They cannot, however, slice or shred. Another option, the salad gun, is essentially a feed tube equipped with a motorized cone holding a blade that slices or shreds. Although simple to clean and move around, these relatively inexpensive devices (basic ones for under $30) tend to be less convenient and not nearly as effective or versatile as a food processor.

Features and convenience

Chute. With most machines, sliced or shredded food simply drops into the bowl, which must be emptied when full. Other machines use various means to keep food from filling the bowl: a separate chute you can attach to divert the flow; or a device that can "sling" food out of the bowl, into a container through an opening in lid.

Bowl. All food processors have a transparent plastic work bowl, most with a convenient handle. Bowls can hold more dry food than wet. Once a bowl is filled to capacity with a thin liquid, it will usually leak when you process.

Blades and disks. An S-shaped metal chopping blade and a slicing/shredding disk are standard. Some models have separate slicing and shredding disks. Additional attachments, sometimes standard or sold separately, include thin and thick slicing/shredding disks, a cheese-grating disk, and a disk for cutting french fries. Attachments such as a plastic whipping attachment for cream or a plastic dough-mixing blade, are less worthwhile.

Feed tube and pusher. With most models, you slice or shred food by dropping it through a feed tube on the bowl's lid, using a plastic pusher when necessary. With some models, you have to trim food so it will fit in the tube. With models that lack any tube, you generally have to remove the lid to add food. On a couple of models, the tube is big enough to swallow a medium-sized tomato and incorporates a slender tube, for thin foods.

Controls and safety. No model can be turned on unless its lid and bowl are latched, a safety provision. All full-sized models and most compacts have an On/off switch and a Pulse provision, which keeps the machine running as long as you depress a switch.

Some models have touchpad controls instead of switches or are activated by moving the lid in and out of a latch on the housing. The switching mechanism may be part of the handle. That's inconvenient—it can cause you to turn on the machine continuously when you want pulse and vice versa.

One speed is all you should need for food processing. And that's what you'll find on all compacts and most full-sized models. Multiple speeds or variable speed controls are overkill.

Cleaning and storage. Machines with clean lines and an absence of food-trapping gaps are easiest to clean. Tough to clean: feed tubes that are large and convoluted. Most components can be washed in a dishwasher. Be sure to place them on the top rack, away from the heating element. And don't let blades soak in water overnight, lest they rust.

The tests

To judge the processors, we spend hundreds of hours chopping, slicing, shredding, and mixing more than 30 different foods. Our heavy-duty tasks include chopping, whipping, blending, and puréeing various foods. To judge grinding, we crush peanuts, graham crackers, and beef cubes. For the chopping and slicing tasks, we use carrots and prosciutto, among other foods. We follow manufacturers' suggestions, but we also experiment to get the best results.

Buying advice

Most people who own a food processor probably don't use it very often. But when you need to chop, purée, mix, or slice on a grand scale, you may be glad to have a processor around. A busy cook or baker of bread is probably best off with a full-sized machine. If you're a less enthusiastic cook and aren't making food for a crowd, a compact model should fill the bill nicely.

You needn't pay top dollar. Processors that come with a Cadillac price, such as the *Cuisinarts* and *Waring Professional*, may be big and hefty, powerful, quiet, and well-apportioned, but less expensive models work quite well and may be more convenient.

PORTABLE FOOD MIXERS

▶ Ratings on page 39.

Portable hand mixers have earned a permanent place in the kitchen because of their convenience and versatility. Lightweight and compact, the mixers excel at blending cake batter, mashing potatoes, and whipping cream. Heftier versions, introduced in recent years, can even handle bread dough.

Portable mixers come in plug-in or cordless, battery-powered versions. Beyond that, models differ in the power of the motor, the number of speeds, and the beaters.

The choices

Plug-in models. An unadorned, basic mixer offers three to five speeds, ejectable beaters, and sells for as little as $15 at discount. The new, muscular mixers are a compromise between powerful stand mixers, which are costly and take up a lot of space, and inexpensive, compact portables. The advantage of a strong motor lies in its ability to keep the beaters turning through the stickiest dough, a challenge that could burn out a lesser machine. A special power-boost switch on some models often provides the extra muscle needed. The fancier models have price tags of up to $55.

Cordless models. Cordless mixers free you from the wire but they must be kept on a charging base that's plugged into an electrical outlet when not in use. Package claims suggest that cordless units pack lots of power. They don't. They're also expensive. Prices range from $35 to $70.

Of course, hand mixers aren't the only way to fix food. See the chart on page 38.

Features and convenience

Most portables weigh between 1¾ and 2¼ pounds. With time-consuming tasks, heavier models may begin to feel leaden. Too light a mixer, though, may lack clout as well as heft. A comfortable handle makes weight easier to bear.

Speeds. Although many models offer a generous number of speeds or even continuously variable speed, we've found that three well-spaced settings—slow, intermediate, and fast—are plenty. The slower the slow speed, the better to reduce spattering.

Thumbwheel speed controls are more difficult to set than the typical On/off speed switch. If the control is located toward the front of the handle, you can hold the mixer and adjust the speed singlehandedly. Look for a switch that's clearly labeled, located on top of the handle, and that sequentially moves from Off to Slow, Medium, and High.

Beaters. In addition to the basic beaters, some mixers come with such useful extras as a dough hook and a balloon whisk. For most chores, beater shape doesn't much matter. For whipping cream, however, a wire whisk is best. More important is the number of beaters: Some cordless models have only one; they don't mix food as well as those with two.

Stainless-steel whisks or wire beaters tend to be easier to clean and offer better corrosion resistance than conventional chrome-coated ones.

Storage. A mixer with its beaters in place should stand on a countertop without toppling over. Mixers with a narrow heel rest provide little stability.

A plug-in mixer doesn't require much space in a drawer or cupboard. Many can be mounted on a wall. Some models have clips on their housing to hold the beaters. For a cordless model, you need room near an outlet for the charging base.

The tests

We beat cake batter and cookie dough, whip cream, and mash potatoes. If a mixer comes with a dough hook, we also knead bread. Since cordless mixers aren't designed for heavy work, we add a separate trial for them: We make batches of butter-cream frosting.

Buying advice

Spending $50 on a mixer isn't necessary if you're primarily going to use it to mash potatoes once in a while. For occasional use, a conventional plug-in portable will do nicely. Our tests turned up solid performers, with convenient controls and a stable heel rest, selling for about $15 at discount.

If you bake, consider a powerful plug-in model, perhaps even a stand mixer. Although some mixers can manage dough, it takes quite a firm grip on the mixers to keep the dough hooks from recoiling. Many routine tasks leave cordless mixers wheezing.

COFFEE APPLIANCES

▸ Ratings of espresso makers on page 42.

Americans consume about one-third of all the coffee grown in the world—enough to make some 400 million cups a day. While some devotées boil their brew in a pot or swear by a percolator, the appliance of choice these days is a drip-style maker—usually an electric model. Mr. Coffee pioneered the automatic drip machine in 1973, and it's still one of the leading brands. But European companies such as Krups transformed the coffee maker into a fashionable as well as functional appliance.

Another popular European import is the coffee known as espresso—a thick, dark, liquid with foamy head, or *crema*. The word espresso comes from the Italian for "pressed out," since in making espresso, water is forced by pressure through the coffee grounds. But a good cup of espresso doesn't come cheap. The best esoteric machines can be apparatuses that can cost hundreds of dollars.

Part of the coffee-making mystique holds that you can't make great coffee without grinding your own beans. Coffee-grinding appliances range from slim little choppers to coffee mills nearly as tall as a drip coffee maker.

DRIP COFFEE MAKERS

Among drip-style makers, there are two types: manual and electric. Both types brew the same way.

The choices

Electric. Most automatic-drip machines have four parts: a water tank, basket to hold the filter and coffee, a carafe to catch the flowing liquid, and a hotplate to keep the filled carafe warm. A device in the machine's base heats the water and hot plate. To brew a pot, you pour a measured amount of cold tap water into the tank and flip a switch.

Electric models come in various capacities, from junior-sized four cuppers to full-sized machines that can brew 12 cups at once. List prices start at around $30, but discounts are common.

Manual. The simplest manual-drip brewers consist of nothing more than a cone to hold the paper filter and coffee grounds and a glass carafe. The process consists of pouring boiling water over the grinds. Cost: $15 or less.

Features to look for

Carafe. The carafes that come with most drip coffee makers are glass and can be washed in the dishwasher—important, because to make good-tasting coffee, the carafe must be kept squeaky clean.

Some carafes come with a glass-lined thermal carafe that doubles as a serving pitcher. That frees you from having to leave the carafe in the coffee maker to stay warm. An insulated carafe, however, is tougher to keep clean than a glass one because it's more delicate. Some carafes have "cup" markings to help measure water.

Basket. A basket that's attached to the coffee maker rather than one that sits atop the carafe saves having to fiddle with hot grounds before you can serve the coffee.

'Drip stop.' This prevents the last few drops from splashing on the hot plate when you remove the carafe.

Clock/timer. This feature shuts off the hot plate automatically. One variation of this feature can cycle the brewing on again at the same time next day, but since the coffee in a coffee maker loaded with grounds overnight will lose flavor, we don't think it's such a good idea.

Features not to look for

Of questionable worth are heating systems that say they lessen the need for "descaling"—purging the buildup of minerals in the coffee maker's tank and tubes. A solution of water and vinegar will do. Nor do we see much point in brew-strength control to vary the potency of the brew. It's easy enough to adjust the amount of coffee used.

The tests

To judge drip coffee makers, expert tasters sip hundreds of cups of coffee freshly brewed by the machines. We use the same brand of coffee and the same amount of grounds for each cup.

Buying advice

A coffee maker is only as good as its ability to turn out consistently good-tasting brew. Most units do that. Better models are also a pleasure to use. Manual-drip coffee makers can turn out a decent cup of coffee and list for $15 or less.

ESPRESSO MAKERS

Not surprising, espresso makers require more fussing than drip coffee makers. The basic technique requires you to fill the maker with water and then spoon coffee grounds into the filter holder—a device shaped somewhat like an ice cream scoop. You must fill the holder with precisely the right amount of coffee, tamped to the correct firmness, before twisting the holder in.

The choices

Stovetop models. The simplest type, they work like a percolater to push water up through the grounds. They're easy to use and the parts screw together with a modicum of effort. They're also inexpensive, priced generally under $20. But they don't force the water through the grounds with enough pressure to extract a really good cup of espresso, and they lack the ability to steam milk for cappuccino.

Steam machines. These use water heated under pressure to make both the espresso and the steam needed for brewing or frothing milk. In general, they perform better than the stovetop models but require practice to master. They list from $60 to $150.

Pump and piston-operated models. Better still are pump machines and piston-operated makers. Both, however, are elaborate and expensive. Pump machines, $170 to $375 list, incorporate an electric pump to force water through coffee grounds. They can be tricky to use and require some time to set up. Piston machines, which retail for $700 to $1000, rely on a hand-operated piston to force water through the grounds. While the piston gives you optimal control over extraction of the brew, it is even fussier and more elaborate than pump models.

Features to look for

Instructions. Clear instructions facilitate the use of these complicated devices. We found a big difference in the clarity of instructions from machine to machine.

Steam nozzles. Most espresso makers have a separate steam nozzle to froth milk for cappuccino. Easiest to use is a nozzle that injects air along with the steam in the correct proportion.

Clean-up. A machine's design determines ease of cleaning. Spills are typically most difficult to remove from steamers.

Filter basket. This should be easy to open, fill, mount, and remove.

The tests

An expert taster sips espresso made by each unit. The espresso is made with bottled water and the same brand of freshly gound coffee.

Buying advice

If you wish a small cup of foamy, syrupy, authentic espresso or cappuccino, be prepared to pay for the privilege. Finicky but fashionable piston units work well, but at more than $600, enthusiasm for espresso must border on the fanatic. Steamers are priced considerably lower, but they're not in the same league as the better pump models.

COFFEE GRINDERS

There are two basic types of grinders:

The choices

Choppers. Cylindrical in shape and with a whirling blade that sits inside a small covered cup, this type of grinder dominates the market. Choppers retail for about $15 to $30.

Coffee mills. These larger machines grind the beans between a pair of wheels. Grinders cost about $45 to $150.

In our experience, just about any chopper or grinder is able to mash beans fine enough to make a good drip or espresso coffee.

Mills work slower than choppers because the beans have to travel through the grinding wheels. In general, choppers can process enough beans in 15 seconds or less to make eight cups of drip-grind coffee; the mills take longer, typically needing 30 to 60 seconds.

Anyone who has been around a coffee grinder before will remember the racket it makes. A minute of a mill's noise is reason enough to consider a chopper.

Minor spills of grinds are inevitable. Mills tend to be a bit messier than choppers, in part because you have to remove the ground-coffee holder. With a chopper, you use the lid to pour grounds directly into the coffee maker.

Features to look for

Capacity. Brewing a full pot of coffee (10 five-ounce cups) requires about 2½ ounces, just about a chopper's maximum. Mills hold enough to make four to five pots.

Controls. With a mill, you pour the beans into a hopper, set a dial to adjust the coarseness of the grind, and flip a switch. Usually the controls are easy to operate.

Some mills have a timer and cup-portion control that doubles as an On/off switch; when enough beans have passed between the grinding wheels, the mill shuts off automatically. Once you've found the right setting, the mill will deliver the same grind batch after batch.

A chopper is less precise. Its blade rotates as long as you maintain pressure on a switch or lid.

The tests

Our coffee-grinding tests are modeled on a standard industry trial to determine fineness and uniformity. We grind small and large batches of beans, then pass the grounds through a nest of increasingly finer sieves. We also use dark-roasted espresso beans because they're more brittle than brown-roasted beans.

Buying advice

Grinding coffee doesn't demand extreme precision. Mills are fancy, but choppers work just as well overall. And choppers cost a lot less, too. They don't hold as much as mills, but that's not important unless you regularly make more than 10 cups at a time.

Regardless of the type of grinder, it's important to wipe it clean after each use. Oils left over from the grinding can turn rancid, affecting the taste of the next batch.

TOASTERS & TOASTER OVENS

A toaster's primary job is to make toast, which most do adequately, we found. The toaster oven and toaster-oven broiler offer no improvement on this basic task. Nor do the mini ovens bake or broil as well as a full-sized range oven. Their particular strength lies in the ability to perform a variety of small cooking tasks: heating rolls and leftovers, making grilled sandwiches, baking potatoes. And they brown foods readily, unlike a microwave oven.

The choices

Toasters. The mechanics of the pop-up toaster haven't changed much since Toastmaster pioneered the device in 1926. Until recently, about the biggest difference among models was their capacity: either two- or four-slice versions. Now, however, there are models with a single elongated slot, the better to toast oversized slices, and models with wide slots, for browning bagels, English muffins, and the like. We've found that the opening has to measure at least 1⅛ inches for most thick items to fit. Some models advertised as "wide slot" have an opening no broader than the standard three-quarters of an inch. No four-slice toaster we've tested has done a good job with thick slices.

Other innovations include models designed for mounting beneath a kitchen cabinet (to free up counter space), an all-plastic housing, which remains cooler to the touch than traditional chrome, and electronic controls rather than the customary mechanical timer or electric thermostat. Prices range from around $15 to $60 for typical one- and two-, and four-slice machines and $30 to $60 for typical four-slice models.

For retro toast, Waring sells a four-slice luncheonette-style toaster that's straight out of the 1950s. The price is out of this world: $320.

Toaster ovens and toaster-oven broilers. Toaster ovens have elements that heat food from above and below. Toaster-oven broilers can also switch on their top element alone. Toaster ovens sell for about $40 to $65, toaster-oven broilers for about $45 to $130. More money usually buys sturdier components and conveniences—"continuous clean" coating, fancy controls, slide-out crumb tray.

As toasters, the devices are lethargic and tend to leave bread underdone on the top and striped on the bottom. The most spacious models can accommodate six slices; the least roomy, just two. Bulky items like bagels and English muffins fit into the oven easily enough, but many models have a hard time toasting them.

As ovens, they aren't precise, even though they have control knobs marked in degrees. Inconsistent temperatures are also common, a result of the on/off cycling of the heating element. But imprecision and inconsistency don't matter much if all you want to do is warm up a snack or dinner.

As broilers they often aren't hot enough. It takes high heat to turn out steaks and burgers that are well browned on the outside with a touch of pink on the inside. With some models, you're likely to end up with meat that's well done by the time the exterior is nicely browned. Broiling with any oven demands a watchful eye. Dripping grease can spatter, smoke, and cause a fire.

Features and conveniences

Controls. You can interrupt toasting on most models by raising a lever. Some toasters also have a control knob that raises the toast immediately. Still others have a "keep-warm" setting that lets the toast stay put, basking in the toaster's residual heat instead.

A well-designed four-slice toaster should have separate controls for each pair of slots. Then you needn't heat all four elements just to toast a slice or two, and you can vary doneness. Some toaster ovens and toaster-oven broilers have an On light. Others have elements that turn off when the door opens and stay off until the oven is turned on again. Other worthwhile controls include a timer that shuts off the machine and a mode-selector switch that prevents the oven and broiler from operating at the same time.

Cleanup. Something as elemental as a crumb tray can make cleanup a snap. Better than no crumb tray is a slot on the bottom of the toaster through which crumbs can be shaken.

With toaster ovens and toaster-oven broilers, a removable rack and a detachable door make the cleaning task easier.

Removing baked-on stains is easiest with appliances that boast an unobstructed cooking cavity. Don't be overly impressed by models that tout a "continuous clean" interior. Such an interior is supposed to absorb and disperse food spatters. In reality, it mostly masks the buildup. On some cookers, the finish can interfere with the smooth travel of the toasting rack (a little vegetable oil on the edges keeps the rack moving freely).

A baking pan made of plated or porcelain-coated steel is sturdier and easier to scour than an aluminum one.

The tests

We look for toast that comes out predictably, uniformly browned, the same color on each side, each slice toasted in the same way. We toast one slice of white bread at a time, in full batches, and in consecutive batches. We further test the ovens and broilers by broiling burgers and steak and baking potatoes.

In addition, we measure the air temperature inside the cookers to gauge accuracy of the control settings. We also note conveniences.

Buying advice

If you eat a lot of toast, buy a toaster. In general, we prefer the two-slice models. If your tastes run toward toasted bagels or thick hand-slices from crusty loaves, consider a machine that has a wide slot. A four-slice model is good for cooking large quantities; look for a model that has separate controls for each pair of slots.

If you eat a little toast but a lot of other items, consider a toaster oven or a toaster-oven broiler. It won't make terrific toast, but it can make tuna melts, bake potatoes, warm rolls, broil a steak, and more. Look for features that make cleaning easy and operation safe. And be sure the model is roomy enough. Some can't hold more than two slices of toast or two burgers.

RATINGS FOOD PROCESSORS

Better ← → Worse
● ⊖ ○ ⊝ ●

▶ **See report, page 26.** From Consumer Reports, August 1992.

Recommendations: The top-rated model, the *Braun UK11*, $104, boasts generous capacity (11½ cups); except for noise, it got high marks in most tasks. The *Panasonic*, $84, was nearly as good and much quieter.

Ratings order: Listed by types; within types, listed in order of estimated quality. Closely ranked models generally differed little in quality. Price is the estimated average, based on prices paid nationally in mid-1992. A * denotes the price CU paid (an average wasn't available). Capacity is of dry food, with bowl filled to rim and S-shaped chopping blade in place.

Brand and model	Price	Capacity, cups	Heavy-duty tasks	Convenience	Noise	Whip cream	Blend soup	Grind graham crackers	Chop garlic	Slice Mozzarella	Slice Carrots	Slice Pepperoni	Advantages	Disadvantages	Comments
FULL-SIZED MODELS															
Braun Multipractic UK11	$104	11½	○	⊖	●	⊖	○	○	⊖	○	○	○	C,H,K,N	—	B,I,L,O,R
Panasonic Kitchen Wizard MK-5070	84*	8¼	○	⊖	⊖	○	○	⊖	⊖	⊖	⊖	⊖	A,I	h	I,M
Cuisinart DLC-7 FPC	300	12¼	⊖	⊖	⊖	●	⊖	⊖	⊖	○	⊖	⊖	A,E,M	f	F,J,L,N,O,T,X
Cuisinart Custom 11 DLC-8M	188	10	⊖	⊖	⊖	○	⊖	○	⊖	⊖	○	○	A,E,M	f,i	F,I,J,N,O,T,X
Regal La Machine II K588GY	65	9½	○	⊖	⊖	○	●	○	○	⊖	⊖	⊖	B,K,M,N	—	A,W
Hamilton Beach 714W	63*	8	○	⊖	●	○	⊖	⊖	⊖	⊖	⊖	⊖	F,L,M	i	B,I,S
Waring Professional PFP15	230*	7¾	⊖	⊖	⊖	○	○	○	⊖	⊖	○	⊖	—	e,i	F,H,J,R,X
Moulinex 305	70	6½	⊖	⊖	○	○	○	○	⊖	○	⊖	⊖	A,M,N	h	D,E,M,O,Q
Braun Multipractic MC100	60	6½	⊖	⊖	○	⊖	⊖	⊖	⊖	○	○	○	K,N	h,k	I
Braun Multipractic MC200	80	6½	⊖	○	⊖	⊖	⊖	○	⊖	○	⊖	○	K,N	h,k	D,I,M
Regal La Machine I K813GY	37	6½	⊖	○	○	⊖	○	●	○	○	○	●	K,M	h,i	A,O
Sunbeam Oskar 3000 14201	90	5½	⊖	⊖	●	○	⊖	⊖	⊖	○	⊖	○	D,N	d,i	C,G,M,U

FOOD PROCESSORS 35

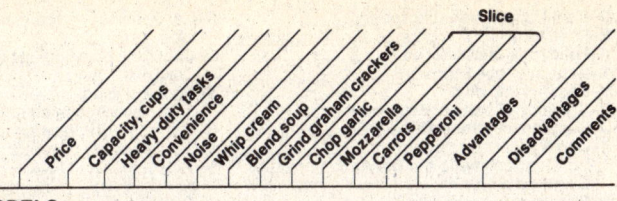

Brand and model	Price	Capacity, cups	Heavy-duty tasks	Convenience	Noise	Whip cream	Blend soup	Grind graham crackers	Chop garlic	Mozzarella	Carrots	Pepperoni	Advantages	Disadvantages	Comments
COMPACT MODELS															
Cuisinart Little Pro Plus	$94	4¼	—	◐	◐	○	○	◐	◐	○	◐	◐	A,B,G,M	—	J,K,O,T
Black & Decker Shortcut CFP10	38	4¼	—	◐	◐	○	◐	◐	◐	○	◐	◐	A,B,J,M	—	P,U
Black & Decker Handy Shortcut HMP30	30	2½	—	◐	○	○	○	◐	◐	○	◐	○	A,M	a,g	U
Sunbeam Oskar 14181	35	2¾	—	●	●	○	◐	◐	○	◐	◐	—		a,b,c,j	V

Performance Notes
All were judged excellent to good at puréeing carrots, grinding peanuts, chopping carrots and prosciutto, slicing mushrooms. • Very good to good at grinding beef cubes. • Excellent to very good at shredding zucchini and cabbage.

Features in Common
All have: • See-through plastic chop/mix bowl and lid. • Effective safety-interlock switch. • Plastic food pusher. • Pads or feet under base.
Except as noted, all have: • Handle on chop/mix bowl. • Lid with feed tube. • Metal S-shaped chopping blade that rusted when soaked in salt water. • 1 metal reversible shredding/slicing disk with finger holes or other provision to aid removal and installation. • Separate On/off switch, Pulse provision, and 1 speed. • Cord between 3 and 4 ft. long. • 1-yr. repair/replacement warranty.

Key to Advantages
A–Controls well marked, easy to use.
B–Slicing/shredding disk easier and safer to mount and remove than most.
C–Has reversible thin/thick disks for slicing or shredding, disk for grating cheese, and disk for french fries. All worked well.
D–Coarse shredding disk worked well.
E–Feed tube handles slender and large-sized foods (but see Disadvantage f).
F–Can slice or shred food into bowl or expel it through lid's built-in chute.
G–Comes with both regular lid and chute for slicing or shredding.
H–Can process nearly 4 cups of liquid without leaks.
I–Can process 3⅓ cups of liquid without leaks.
J–Can process 1½ cups of liquid without leaks.
K–Blade stops instantly when switched off.
L–Chopping blade didn't rust.
M–All blades can be stored in bowl.
N–Has place to store cord.

Key to Disadvantages
a–Chop/mix bowl lacks handle.
b–Chop/mix bowl lacks feed tube; chute option cumbersome.
c–Lacks Pulse switch; for On/off and Pulse, lid must be rotated through latch on housing.
d–On/off/pulse switch on handle; inconvenient.
e–Touchpad On/off and Pulse switches require more effort than others.
f–Feed tube assembly hard to use and to clean.
g–Feed tube inconveniently narrow.
h–Blade inserts pose slightly greater danger of cut fingers than others.
i–Because these models leaked, we blended only a half-recipe of soup. The **Sunbeam, Hamilton Beach,** and **Waring** leaked most.
j–Leaked more than other compacts when processing liquids; held only ¼ cup.
k–Hole on blade hub can admit foods, which can create a mess.

Key to Comments
A–Must lock On switch for continuous action.
B–2 speeds.
C–6 speeds.

Ratings Keys continued

36 BLENDERS

D–Continuously variable speeds.
E–Feed tube has narrow side and wide side.
F–Feed tube at back of lid.
G–Bottom of bowl convex.
H–Has 3-prong plug.
I–Some or all parts not dishwasher safe.
J–Separate slice and shred disks.
K–Citrus juicer attachment.
L–Whisk attachment; the **Braun** has one, the **Cuisinart** a pair.
M–Plastic whip accessory.
N–Plastic dough-mixing blade.
O–Comes with hard plastic spatula.
P–Has insert to guide slim food down feed tube.
Q–Chopping blade comes with cover.
R–Cord 5½ ft. long.
S–Cord 2 ft. long.
T–3-yr. repair/replacement warranty.
U–2-yr. repair/replacement warranty.
V–5-yr. warranty on motor.
W–Tallest model at 17¼ in.; may present storage problem.
X–Among heaviest models: **Waring**, 15½ lb.; **Cuisinart DLC-7 FPC**, 14¾ lb.; **Cuisinart 11 DLC-8M**, 12¼ lb.

RATINGS BLENDERS

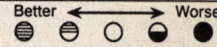

▶ **See report, page 24.** From Consumer Reports, June 1992.

Recommendations: Performance did not vary greatly among standard models. Let price, convenience, and features guide your choice. Among handheld models, the *Singer 795* is our favorite; we rated it A Best Buy.

Ratings order: Listed by types; within types, listed in order of estimated quality. Price is the estimated average, based on prices paid nationally in early 1992. A * indicates the manufacturer's suggested retail (an average price wasn't available).

Brand and model	Price	Container [1]	Speeds	Diet drink	Milk shake	Whipped cream	Gazpacho	Parmesan cheese	Peanut butter	Convenience [2]	Advantages	Disadvantages	Comments
STANDARD													
Osterizer 852-20	$40	G	12	◐	○	◐	⊖	⊖	⊖	⊖	C,M	—	H,W,Y
Osterizer 890-20	42	G	7	◐	○	◐	⊖	⊖	⊖	⊖	D,M	—	H,X
Osterizer 887-20	40	P	5	○	○	○	⊖	⊖	⊖	⊖	D,M	—	H
Hamilton Beach 609W	25	G	6	○	○	●	⊖	⊖	⊖	○	B,D,F,K,N	f	N,Y
Osterizer 5000-08	69	G	1	○	○	◐	○	⊖	⊖	⊖	E,F,I	h,j	H,V,Z
Waring NB5-1	37	P	2	◐	●	●	⊖	⊖	◐	⊖	B,D,I,J,L	—	B,F,U,AA
Black & Decker HB15	25	P	2	○	○	●	⊖	⊖	◐	⊖	E,F,I,J,L,P	a,g	A,E,F,R
Hamilton Beach 722	20	P	6	○	○	●	⊖	⊖	⊖	⊖	B,E,N	—	C,N
Hamilton Beach 5306B	52	G	2	○	○	○	⊖	○	⊖	⊖	B,I,K	f,j	S
Sears 68175	37*	G	14	○	○	●	⊖	○	⊖	○	B,E,K,N	f	G,N,S,Y

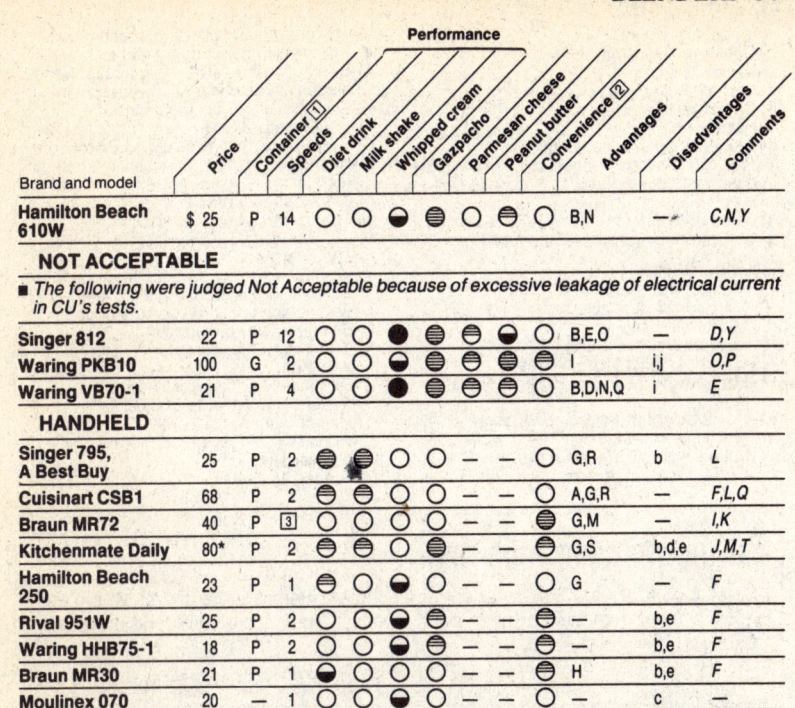

BLENDERS

Performance ratings columns: Price | Container [1] | Speeds | Diet drink | Milk shake | Whipped cream | Gazpacho | Parmesan cheese | Peanut butter | Convenience [2] | Advantages | Disadvantages | Comments

Brand and model	Price	Container	Speeds	Diet drink	Milk shake	Whipped cream	Gazpacho	Parmesan cheese	Peanut butter	Convenience	Advantages	Disadvantages	Comments
Hamilton Beach 610W	$25	P	14	○	○	◐	◉	○	◐	○	B,N	—	C,N,Y

NOT ACCEPTABLE

■ *The following were judged Not Acceptable because of excessive leakage of electrical current in CU's tests.*

Brand and model	Price	Container	Speeds	Diet drink	Milk shake	Whipped cream	Gazpacho	Parmesan cheese	Peanut butter	Convenience	Advantages	Disadvantages	Comments
Singer 812	22	P	12	○	○	●	◉	◉	◐	○	B,E,O	—	D,Y
Waring PKB10	100	G	2	○	○	◐	◉	◉	◉	◉	I	i,j	O,P
Waring VB70-1	21	P	4	○	○	●	◉	◉	◉	○	B,D,N,Q	i	E

HANDHELD

Brand and model	Price	Container	Speeds	Diet drink	Milk shake	Whipped cream	Gazpacho	Parmesan cheese	Peanut butter	Convenience	Advantages	Disadvantages	Comments
Singer 795, A Best Buy	25	P	2	◐	◐	○	○	—	—	○	G,R	b	L
Cuisinart CSB1	68	P	2	◐	◐	○	○	—	—	○	A,G,R	—	F,L,Q
Braun MR72	40	P	[3]	○	○	○	○	—	—	◉	G,M	—	I,K
Kitchenmate Daily	80*	P	2	◐	◐	○	◉	—	—	◉	G,S	b,d,e	J,M,T
Hamilton Beach 250	23	P	1	◐	○	◐	○	—	—	○	G	—	F
Rival 951W	25	P	2	○	○	◐	◉	—	—	◉	—	b,e	F
Waring HHB75-1	18	P	2	○	○	◐	◉	—	—	◉	—	b,e	F
Braun MR30	21	P	1	◐	○	○	○	—	—	◉	H	b,e	F
Moulinex 070	20	—	1	○	○	◐	○	—	—	○	—	c	—

[1] Key to container: G=glass; P=plastic.
[2] Rankings are relative with each category of blender.
[3] Continuously variable speed.

Features in Common

All standard models: • Have removable blade assembly. • Have rubber feet to improve stability. • Are 12½ to 15½ in. tall.
Except as noted, all standard models: • Have 5-cup container, marked in 1-cup intervals, and handle. • Have removable insert in lid. • Have 3- to 3½-ft. cord. • Were relatively noisy. • Come with 1-yr. warranty.
Except as noted, all handheld models: • Come with clear plastic container that holds about 2 cups when full. • Have single 2-prong blade. • Can be rested temporarily on their flat top. • Come with 1-yr. warranty.

Key to Advantages

A–Container marked clearly in quarter-cups.
B–Container marked in half-cups.
C–Pulses on all 12 speeds.
D–Pulses on 2, 3, or 4 speeds.
E–Pulses on single speed.
F–Quieter than other standard blenders.
G–Storage rack for blender, blades, and container.
H–Has storage rack for blender.
I–Single On/off switch; base is easier to clean than most. See Disadvantage h.
J–Cord is coiled; easy to store.
K–Has wide-mouthed container; easy for loading food and cleaning.
L–Can chop ice without water, according to mfr.; our results were very good.
M–Very wide range of speeds.
N–Wide range of speeds.
O–Wide range of speeds at high rpm's.
P–Takes up less counter space than others.
Q–Lid has built-in strainer.
R–Has blending, whipping, and chopping blades.
S–Has beating, whipping, mincing, and chopping blades.

Key to Disadvantages

a–Blades rusted after we "blended" water

Ratings Keys continued

for several hours.
b–Container lacks markings.
c–Lacks container.
d–Container holds only a cup or so.
e–Container is opaque.
f–Hard to pour liquid without dribbling.
g–Processed carrots not smooth.
h–Protruding switch judged more likely than most to be damaged or turned on accidentally.
i–Blade unit hard to unscrew for cleaning.
j–Chrome-finished base highlights dirt.

Key to Comments
A–Marked 4-cup capacity.
B–Marked 4½-cup capacity.
C–Marked 5½-cup capacity.
D–Marked 6-cup capacity.
E–Container twist-locks on base.
F–Mfr. says plastic container dishwasher safe.
G–Has 2 blend-and-store containers.
H–Mfr. says container not dishwasher safe, but we washed it without damage.
I–Optional chopping attachment available.
J–Has grating and grinding attachments.
K–Comes with whisk attachment.
L–Safety guard around interchangeable blades makes it hard to remove them.
M–Available only from the distributor.
N–Has 2-ft. cord.
O–Has 6-ft. cord; may be awkward to store.
P–Has 3-prong plug that can mitigate effects of leakage current when used with a grounded receptacle.
Q–18-mo. warranty.
R–2-yr. warranty.
S–3-yr. warranty.
T–90-day warranty against manufacturing defects. From 90 days to 12 years, mfr. will replace unit at 50 percent of cost.
U–5-yr. warranty on motor.
V–1-yr. warranty came with only 1 of 3 samples.
W–Essentially similar to **852-08**.
X–Essentially similar to **890-08**.
Y–Has speed-shift selector.
Z–Runs on a single speed, but will pulse on a lower speed.
AA–Hinged lid flips up.

BUYING THE RIGHT FOOD FIXER

Not all food-fixers are equally adept at all chores. Here are the chores where the typical blender, handheld blender, portable mixer, stand mixer, and food processor stand out.

	Standard blender	Handheld blender	Portable mixer	Stand mixer	Food processor
Puréeing vegetables	✔				✔
Blending mayonnaise	✔				✔
Mixing frozen drinks	✔				
Making milk shakes	✔	✔			
Whipping cream			✔	✔	
Mashing potatoes			✔		
Mixing cake batter			✔	✔	
Mixing pie crust					✔
Mixing cookie dough				✔	✔
Kneading bread dough				✔	✔
Crumbling crackers					✔
Chopping, shredding, slicing vegetables					✔
Chopping parsley					✔
Grating Parmesan	✔				✔

PORTABLE FOOD MIXERS 39

RATINGS | PORTABLE FOOD MIXERS

Better ◄——————► Worse
⊜ ⊖ ○ ⊘ ●

▶ See report, page 27. From Consumer Reports, July 1991.

Recommendations: For occasional mixing, look for a good price on a plug-in model. If you bake, however, we recommend the top-rated *Krups 725*, if you can still find it, or its successor, *745*.

Ratings order: Listed by types; within types, listed in order of estimated quality, based on performance and convenience. Except where separated by a bold rule, closely ranked models differed little in quality. The price is the manufacturer's suggested retail. ⓢ indicates model has been replaced by successor model; according to the manufacturer, the performance of the new model should be similar to the tested model but features may vary. See page 40 for new model number and suggested retail price, if available. Ⓓ indicates model discontinued.

Brand and model	Price	Speeds	Performance	Ease of setting	Beater-eject ease	Advantages	Disadvantages	Comments
PLUG-IN ELECTRIC MIXERS								
Krups 725 ⓢ	$50	3	⊜	⊜	⊜	A,D,F,G,K,L	f,g	D
KitchenAid KHM3WH	55	3	⊜	⊜	⊜	A,D,G,H	f,g,r	E
Kenwood A177 Ⓓ	36	3	⊜	⊜	⊜	H,K	—	C
Moulinex 748 Ⓓ	45	①	⊜	⊘	○	C,D,F,G,L	g,j,r	D,E
Farberware D2770	30	5	⊜	⊜	⊜	E,J	b	—
Sunbeam 03161	22	4	⊜	⊜	⊖	G,I	b,r	—
Hamilton Beach 103C Ⓓ	41	①	⊜	○	○	A,C,J	b,r,s	I
Black & Decker M175	30	5	⊜	⊜	⊜	B	b,f,r	J
Rival 435 Ⓓ	29	5	○	⊜	⊜	B,C,J	a,e	H
Toastmaster 1743 Ⓓ	15	3	⊜	⊜	⊜	E,J	a	—
Sunbeam 03181	35	6	⊜	⊜	⊘	A,B	r	—
Waring HM5-1	23	5	⊜	⊜	⊜	J	a,m	—
Waring HM20-1	30	12	⊜	⊜	⊜	—	—	G,K
Sunbeam 03921	47	①	○	⊜	⊜	C	e,q	A,E,K,L,N
Rival 433	22	3	○	⊜	⊜	J	e	H
Black & Decker M24S	22	3	○	⊜	⊜	E	a,e	J
Cuisinart CM-4	55	3	○	⊘	⊜	D,H	d,k,p	A,D,H
CORDLESS MIXERS								
Cuisinart CM-3	70	3	○	⊘	⊜	D,H,M,N	d,k,p	D
Waring HM115-1	50	2	⊘	⊘	⊘	M	c,k,l,n,p,r,t	A,F,K,L
Black & Decker Handymixer 9210	43	2	●	⊘	—	H	h,i,k,p	B,F,K,L,M
Proctor Silex M399 Ⓓ	35	3	●	⊜	—	M	h,i,o	B,K,N

① *Speeds continuously variable.* **Hamilton Beach** *has 14 marked settings;* **Moulinex** *and* **Sunbeam**, *8.*

Turn page for Ratings Keys

PORTABLE FOOD MIXERS

Successor Model
Krups 725 is succeeded by 745, $50.

Features in Common
All cordless models have: • Recharging storage base that can stand on countertop or be mounted on wall, and that should be left plugged into an electrical outlet.
Except as noted, all: • Weigh 1¾ to 2¼ lb. • Have 2 metal beaters that fit in either of 2 sockets. • Were judged excellent at mixing cake batter and whipping cream, very good at mashing potatoes, and good at mixing cookie dough. • Have an easy-to-set speed control at front of handle. • Have convenient beater- or whisk-ejection mechanism. • Are stable when resting on heel base with beaters in place.
Except as noted, all: • Plug-in models have 4- to 5½-ft. power cord.

Key to Advantages
A–Better than most at mixing cookie dough.
B–Has burst-of-power feature.
C–Low speed slower than most, reducing spattering.
D–Stainless-steel whisks (wire beaters on **Cuisinart CM-4** and **CM-3**) judged easier to clean and more corrosion-resistant than conventional beaters.
E–Clips on motor housing to store beaters.
F–Heavy batter did not collect in whisks.
G–More stable than most on heel rest.
H–Motor housing easier to clean than most.
I–Has cord wrap at heel rest.
J–Keyhole on housing for wall hanging.
K–Comes with wall bracket for storage.
L–Comes with dough hooks for mixing small quantities of bread dough.
M–Indicator light shows that unit is charging.
N–Has greater battery capacity than others.

Key to Disadvantages
a–Whipped cream more slowly than most.
b–Whipped cream slightly slower than most.
c–Labored heavily when mixing cookie dough; slowed when mashing potatoes.
d–Slowed somewhat when mixing cookie dough.
e–Needed extra time to produce smooth mashed potatoes.
f–Heavier than most, about 2½ lb.
g–Beaters are not interchangeable.
h–Has only 1 beater; poor with heavy mixing tasks; produced coarsely textured cakes.
i–Lacks beater-ejection mechanism.
j–Thumbwheel speed control was more difficult than most to set, and display does not show entire setting spectrum.
k–Pulses at low-speed setting; switch must be held down for continuous operation.
l–Handle may be too wide for small hands.
m–Handle less comfortable than most.
n–Feels somewhat unbalanced in use.
o–Lacks heel rest.
p–Very narrow heel rest on pistol-grip handle provided little stability.
q–Less stable than most on heel rest.
r–Noisier than most at high speed.
s–Chrome-finish shows fingerprints.
t–Has limited battery capacity.

Key to Comments
A–Weighs 1½ lb.
B–Weighs less than 1 lb.
C–Beaters must be inserted before speed control is set.
D–Beaters or whisks have 1 or more plastic parts.
E–Claims to have electronic speed control.
F–Speed control located under handle.
G–Has 12 speed choices; in tests, speeds 7 and 8 proved to be slower than speed 6.
H–Power cord approx. 6 ft. long.
I–Power cord is removable.
J–Has bowl-scraper accessory.
K–Has balloon-whisk accessory.
L–Has plastic stir-paddle accessory.
M–Has spiral-whisk accessory.
N–Has drink-mix rod.

ABOUT PRICES IN THE BUYING GUIDE

Prices for most products, notably big-ticket items such as kitchen appliances, home-electronics gear, and gardening equipment, have been updated for the Buying Guide. The prices we give, unless otherwise noted, are approximate or suggested retail as quoted by the manufacturer. Discounts may therefore be substantial, especially for electronics and camera equipment.

FOOD CHOPPERS 41

RATINGS FOOD CHOPPERS

Better ← → Worse

▶ **See report, page 26.** From Consumer Reports, August 1992.

Recommendations: Our favorite is the *Moulinex*, $25, which holds a generous 3½ cups of dry food. Even though it has been discontinued, it may still be available in some stores. The *Krups*, $31, performed nearly as well but was very noisy.

Ratings order: Listed in order of estimated quality. Closely ranked models generally differed little in quality. Prices are estimated average based on prices paid nationally in mid-1992. A * denotes the price CU paid (an average wasn't available). Capacity is in dry cups; liquid capacity is much less. ⒹD indicates model discontinued.

Brand and model	Price	Capacity, cups	Noise	Puréed carrots	Ground peanuts	Ground beef cubes	Chopped garlic	Chopped citrus peel	Advantages	Disadvantages	Comments
Moulinex Maxi Chopper 094 Ⓓ	$25*	3¼	○	◒	◒	○	○	◒	A,B	b,d	A,H
Krups Mini Pro 708	31	2¼	●	◒	◒	◒	◒	◒	C	d	—
Cuisinart Mini-Prep DLC-1	35*	2½	●	◒	◒	◒	◒	◒	C	a,d	C,D,G
Black & Decker HC20	21	1¼	○	○	◒	○	◒	◒	—	c	F
Sunbeam Oskar Jr. 14131	21	1¼	◒	◒	◒	○	◒	○	—	—	B,F
Kenwood CH100	23*	1¼	○	○	◒	○	○	●	—	d	E

Performance Notes
All: Were either very good or excellent at grinding graham crackers, grating Parmesan cheese, and chopping parsley, carrots, onions, and prosciutto.

Features in Common
All: • Have see-through plastic bowl that lacks handle. • Have 1 metal chopping blade with plastic hub. • Have switch that must be held down to activate machine.
Except as noted, all: • Have 1 speed. • Have 1 or more holes for adding liquid during use. • Have separate On/off switch. • Cords measure 2½ to 3½ ft. long. • Have 1-yr. repair/replacement warranty.

Key to Advantages
A–Bowl marked in cups, ounces, and liters.
B–Makes small milk shake, judged very good.
C–Has place for cord storage.

Key to Disadvantages
a–Vibrated and moved on counter during use.
b–Must disassemble to add ingredients during use.
c–No hole in lid for adding liquids during use.
d–Blades rusted in saline solution.

Key to Comments
A–Top-mounted motor. Turns on when motor housing is pressed onto bowl's cover and push button is activated.
B–Lid latch is On/off switch.
C–Reversible blade has blunt position, for grinding, and sharp position.
D–Has separate levers for high and low speeds.
E–Cord is 5½ ft. long.
F–2-yr. repair/replacement warranty.
G–18-mo. repair/replacement warranty.
H–1-yr. repair warranty.

RATINGS ESPRESSO MAKERS

Better ⬌ Worse

▶ **See report, page 30.** From Consumer Reports, November 1991.

Recommendations: The top-rated *Gaggia 41276*, $420, delivered an authentic espresso or cappuccino. The less expensive *DeLonghi CE-20*, $169, A Best Buy, offers similar performance but is less convenient.

Ratings order: Listed by types; within types, listed in order of estimated quality. Bracketed models were judged equal in quality and are listed alphabetically. Price is the manufacturers' suggested or approximate retail price. ⓈI indicates tested model has been replaced by successor model; according to the manufacturer, the performance of new model should be similar to the tested model but features may vary. See right for new model number and suggested retail price, if available. ⒹI indicates model discontinued.

Brand and model	Price	Coffee quality	Milk frothing	Ease of use	Cleaning ease	Max. cups	Weight, lb.	Advantages	Disadvantages	Comments
PUMP										
Gaggia 41276	$420	◕	◕	◕	◕	2	17½	A,B,D,F,H,I,M	—	B,I
Rotel S240 Espressomat Ⓓ	264	◕	◕	◕	◕	2	9½	A,C,D,F,G,H,K,M	—	A,I
Krups 969 L'Espresso Plus	300	◕	◕	◕	◕	2	10½	A,E,F,H,K	—	E,I,L,M
Rancilio Sienna R400	299	◕	◕	◕	◕	2	12	A,B,D,F,I,K	—	I
DeLonghi CE-20, A Best Buy	169	◕	◕	○	◕	2	6½	A,D,F,G,I,K	i	I,L
Cuisinart EPM7 Ⓓ	300	◕	◕	○	○	2	11½	A,B,D,K,L	b,c,j	D,F,I,L
Gaggia 10553 Gran Gaggia	225	◕	◐	◐	○	2	6½	H,I,K,L	d,f,g	C,I
Bosch TKA 4811 US Espresso Ⓢ	220	○	○	◐	◕	4	6	A,J,K	a,g	B,I
PISTON										
La Pavoni Europiccola	795	◕	◕	◐	◕	2	12	A,G,I	d,e,j,k	H
STEAM										
Krups 972 Il Primo	130	○	◕	◕	○	4	4	J	—	I,L
Braun E200T Espresso Master	150	○	○	◕	○	4	4½	A	h	J
Krups 963 Espresso Mini	100	◐	◕	◕	○	4	4	J	—	I,L
Salton EX-10 Three For All ①	130	○	◕	○	◕	4	8	A	b,d	I,L
Conair CEM-400 Cuisine Ultra Series Ⓓ	90	○	◕	○	○	4	4	J	b,d	K
Maxim EX 152 Expres	60	○	◐	◕	○	4	4	A,E	—	I,L
Gaggia 42029 Fantastico II Ⓓ	100	○	●	○	○	4	4½	L	b,d,h	I
STOVETOP										
Gaggia 42044 Classica Ⓓ	18	◐	②	○	○	6	1	—	d,h	G

① *Combination drip-coffee and espresso maker.*   ② *Lacks provision for frothing milk.*

ESPRESSO MAKERS

Successor Model
Bosch TKA 4811VS is succeeded by 4821US, $220.

Features in Common
All pump and piston machines: • Are electric. • Brew coffee directly into cups. • Have nonskid feet. • Come with coffee-measuring scoop.
All steam machines: • Are electric. • Consume between 470 and 780 watts. • Have nonskid feet, glass carafe, plastic body.
Except as noted, all pump and piston machines: • Lack swiveling steam nozzle. • Consume between 900 and 1250 watts.

Key to Advantages
A–Removable drip tray.
B–Very large drip tray.
C–Adjustable brew temperature.
D–Large water tank; **Gaggia's** very large.
E–Comes with videotape user's manual.
F–Removable, easy-to-empty water tank.
G–Water level easy to see.
H–Designed for continuous coffee making.
I–Comes with tamping tool.
J–Removable parts are dishwasher safe.
K–Steam nozzle swivels.
L–Comes with steam-nozzle cleaning tool.
M–Built-in cup warmer.

Key to Disadvantages
a–Coffee holder very difficult to open when hot.
b–Signal light dimmer than others.
c–Water tank cumbersome to fill.
d–Loose filter basket; tends to drop out while being emptied.
e–Boiler section hot to the touch when in use.
f–Excessive vibration during brewing.
g–Steam nozzle too short for deep containers.
h–Does not come with coffee measuring scoop.
i–Button must be held down while frothing milk.
j–Can spray grounds about if filter holder removed too soon after brew cycle.
k–Tends to dribble water on countertop.

Key to Comments
A–2 samples had defective filter holder.
B–Power draw between 1400 and 1500 watts.
C–Power draw approx. 675 watts.
D–Comes with water filter.
E–Can also use prepacked pods of grounds.
F–Disk attachment to help put head on coffee.
G–3-mo. warranty.
H–3-mo. warranty, excluding heating element.
I–12-mo. warranty.
J–12-mo. warranty, excluding surface finishes.
K–24-mo. warranty.
L–Toll-free phone number for service questions.
M–**Krups 964**, $300, essentially similar; no videotape manual; can't use prepacked pods.

WHAT THE RATINGS MEAN

■ The Ratings typically rank products in order of estimated quality, without regard to price.

■ A product's rating applies only to the model tested and should not be considered a rating of other models sold under the same brand name unless so noted.

■ Models are check-rated (✓) when the product proved to be significantly superior to other models tested.

■ Products high in quality and relatively low in price are deemed Best Buys.

Laundry Appliances & Detergents

Washing machines 44	Detergents & other laundry
Clothes dryers 47	products: 51
Steam irons 49	Ratings 54

Walk down the laundry products' aisle in the supermarket, and you'll hear the secret to whiter, brighter clothes shouted by powders, packets, and liquids. Elbow-to-elbow with detergents on store shelves, old-fashioned soap, fabric softeners, boosters, bleach, and other special-purpose cleaners make their own claims. Meanwhile, appliance manufacturers go to considerable lengths to make washers, dryers, and irons sleeker, smarter, and more convenient.

Do flashy new appliances work any better than plainer, simpler ones? Not necessarily. Just about any modern washer, dryer, or iron does a decent job. Spending more for an appliance generally buys fancier features and perhaps greater capacity but not always better performance.

The same holds true for detergents. All detergents clean clothes. Most also whiten, brighten, and remove at least some stains. Some products work better than others, but you may not be able to tell the difference unless your clothes are badly soiled. Boosters, bleach, spot removers, and softeners can sometimes be useful, but they're not always essential.

Washing Machines

▶ Ratings on page 56. ▶ Repair histories on page 362.

Washing machines are among the least glamorous and most put upon household appliances. In fact, the typical washer takes a pounding for 13 years, on average. With any long-lived appliance, manufacturers have a lot at stake when replacement time rolls around. So they've added niceties such as extra cycles and electronic controls not only to make a washer look jazzier and seem more convenient, but to help endow it with a distinct personality. Uniqueness is increasingly important since just five companies manufacture more than a dozen leading brands. In addition to selling washers under its own marquee, Whirlpool makes the machines that sell under the *Sears Kenmore* and *KitchenAid* names. Maytag, known for its line of premium washers, is the parent company of *Magic Chef*, which makes machines sold under its own label as well as the *Admiral* and *Norge* nameplates. General Electric washers bear the names *GE*, *Hotpoint*, and *RCA*; White Consolidated Industries sells washers under the *Gibson*, *Kelvinator*, *White-Westinghouse*, and *Frigidaire* logos. *Amana* and *Speed Queen* washers are made by the Raytheon Corp.

The choices

Washers come in several designs and sizes and range in price from about $300 to more than $800. Most models in a brand's line are remarkably similar. They often boast the same design and use the basic components—wash tub, agitator, transmission, pump, and so on. What can you expect by spending more? Typically, a larger number of cycle and speed combinations, more capacity, and a wider selection of water temperature and fill options.

Type. The basic choice is between top- and front-loaders. Top-loaders are the biggest sellers in this country. Front-loaders use about half the amount of water, but are costlier, more prone to repair, and don't hold as much. In addition, selection is limited to *White-Westinghouse* and a few imported brands.

Size. Most washers (and their companion dryers) are "full-sized" models 27 inches wide. Tub capacities usually vary between "large" or "extra large." There are oddball models for special installations—ones that piggyback with a dryer or have a built-in dryer on top, and "portable" rolling ones that hook up to a sink.

Multiple speeds. Most washers have more than one wash/spin speed. A second, slower speed allows certain laundry to be handled more gently. Although some washers offer additional speeds, two choices—a normal-speed agitation with normal spin and slow agitation/slow spin—are adequate for most needs.

Features and convenience

Venturing higher in a manufacturer's line buys frills, not performance. Controls that operate with buttons, levers, and dials, for example, may be slightly more difficult to manipulate than the touchpads found on top-of-the-line machines, but they're often less complex and cheaper to service. Here are other options to consider:

Extra cycles. Regular, Permanent Press, and Delicate are all you need for most uses. The cycle you choose may determine the speed and water temperature as well; though on many models, you must choose those two. Costlier machines offer a soak/prewash for badly soiled laundry or an extra rinse cycle at the end. You can accomplish the same result manually by simply resetting the dial.

Temperature settings. You generally need only three wash temperatures: hot, warm, and cold, followed by a cold rinse. High-end washers offer hot and warm wash temperatures, followed by a warm rinse. But warm water doesn't rinse any better than cold. (Although, a warm wash and rinse are recommended for washable woolens.) And it wastes energy. Sears and Frigidaire supply a few of their washers with an electronic temperature sensor that measures incoming water temperature and blends hot and cold to reach preset targets. The feature solves the occasional problem of too-cold water that fails to dissolve detergent. But adjusting your hot and cold spigots for a warmer wash temperature solves the problem as well.

Water levels. The most economical way to wash is to do a full load. When that's not practical, you can save water, detergent, and energy by adjusting the fill level. On most large-tub models, minimum fill requires roughly half as much water as the maximum fill, or 20 to 30 gallons per wash. A choice of three fill levels is sufficient; some machines offer four or are continuously adjustable.

Finishes. More and more machines use plastic-based finishes for the top and lid instead of the traditional porcelain or baked enamel. The newer coatings, with trademarked names like Dura-Finish or Enduraguard, are tougher than enamels, but softer than porcelain.

Tubs. More plastic is used inside, too. Some machines have a plastic tub, which should work as well as the porcelain-coated steel type. The polypropylene tub included with some models, including those made by White Consolidated Industries, comes with a 25-year warranty.

Special features. Some machines have dispensers that release bleach and fabric softener. Some include an alternate agitator that's supposed to be kinder to delicates. Others boast a little basket that fits inside the main tub for very small loads. A few others are equipped with a "suds-saver" feature that pumps the used wash water into an external tub so it can be reused for the next load.

The tests

Given a good detergent and enough space for laundry to swish around freely, any washer should do a decent job. We measure water and energy usage, tub capacity, noise, water extraction, and the ability to cope with unbalanced loads.

Washers vary a lot in the amount of noise they generate. They also vary in the amount of water and electricity they use. Energy consumption hinges on how much hot water is used, since heating water accounts for most of a washer's energy cost. A typical top-loader (with an extra-large tub) doing six hot wash/cold rinse loads a week uses $112 worth of electrically heated water or $37 worth of gas-heated water a year, at average utility rates. By contrast, a front-loader would consume only $42 in electricity, $14 in gas, for the same amount of laundry. If you wash in warm water, you cut those costs by half.

Capacity is determined by tub size and the design of agitator. Our tests show that washers deemed "extra large" can differ in capacity by as much as 50 percent.

Buying advice

Look for a brand with a solid repair history and don't buy more machine than you need. Top-of-the-line washers with fancy electronics and specialized settings don't provide the best value. A three-cycle, two-speed model should be ample for most chores.

A top-loading machine is easier to load and unload than front-loaders and holds more laundry. Installation and servicing are easier, too. But if conserving energy and water is a priority, consider a front-loader. Be aware, though, that pickings are slim and they cost a lot. Indeed, if you heat your water with gas or oil, the payback for the initial investment could exceed the machine's life expectancy. Front-loaders are also more apt to break down.

And keep an eye out for ad specials, especially in newspapers. Manufacturers such as Maytag, Speed Queen, GE, and Whirlpool have beefed up their promotions, including rebates and money-back guarantees.

CLOTHES DRYERS

Ratings on page 54. Repair histories on page 362.

Just about any modern dryer will dry clothes adequately. If it's your habit to throw a mixed load of jeans, shorts, towels, and nightgowns into the dryer and collect it the next morning, chances are you'll never notice the subtle performance differences that separate one machine from the next.

To compensate for that inherent sameness, dryer manufacturers go to great lengths to make their products distinct. Some sophisticated machines do everything for you. Others require plenty of human help. But the highly automated dryer may not be worth the several hundred dollars extra it costs.

The choices

Dryer prices vary from under $200 to more than $700. Spend more, and you'll likely get electronic touchpad controls, greater drum capacity, more automatic settings, and a moisture sensor to control the drying time rather than a thermostat, which is less precise. Here are the basic choices:

Gas or electric. If you have the choice, you're probably better off with a gas model. Gas models tend to cost around $40 to $60 more than comparable electric models, but you'll quickly make that back in lower operating costs. In our cost-comparison tests, based on average utility rates, it cost us 14 cents to dry a 12-pound mixed load in a gas model, versus 44 cents in an electric one. The extra plumbing in a gas dryer, however, often makes it slightly more trouble-prone.

Size. Full-sized models are 27 to 29 inches wide with a drum of 5 to 7 cubic feet. Some brands offer only one size drum across the complete model line; others offer a larger drum in top-line machines. The bigger the drum, the more easily a dryer handles bulky items, such as a comforter. Manufacturers also make compact models, usually electric, and often able to be stacked on a companion washer, with a capacity of about 3½ cubic feet. Compacts can be plugged into a regular outlet instead of a heavy-duty 240-volt line, but drying will take much longer. Compacts generally sell for less than $330.

Features and convenience

Here's what to consider:

Cycles. Dryers typically offer two or three automatic drying cycles—Regular, Permanent Press, Knit/Delicate, for instance—as well as timed and unheated settings. A "More Dry to Less Dry" range on the automatic settings lets you fine-tune the setting based on the size and composition of each load. (That control is useful to retain dampness for easier ironing.) Automatic drying cycles reduce the chances of overdrying, thus saving energy. Low-end dryers may offer just a timer.

Thermostat or moisture sensor. The oldest, simplest approach to automatic drying relies on a thermostat to control the heat and the timer. A thermostat checks the load's dampness indirectly. As the clothes dry, air leaving the drum gets progressively hotter. When it rises enough, the thermostat cycles the heat off and the timer advances until the heat goes on again. The process is repeated until the heating portion of the cycle has ended. Newer designs sense moisture more accurately, using sensors in the drum that touch the clothes to gauge dryness. Models with moisture sensors may be limited to manu-

CLOTHES DRYERS

facturers' flagship upper-end dryers.

Controls. Like other major appliances, top-of-the line dryers are equipped with electronic controls. Electronic touchpads make it simple to choose from many options, but they add a lot to the machine's cost and are pricey to repair as well. And they may not be as informative as regular dial controls, which indicate roughly where you are in the cycle. At the other end of the scale, cheap models sometimes put too many choices on too few controls, which makes them hard to use.

Finish. Most dryers have a baked-enamel finish on the cabinet top and drum that is not as scratch-resistant as porcelain.

Added tumble time. Most dryers allow you to extend the period of cool tumbling after the end of the automatic dry cycle—anywhere from 15 minutes to as much as a couple of hours. This useful feature, sometimes called "Wrinkle Guard" or "Press Guard," helps keep clothes from wrinkling if the cycle is completed and the dryer is not emptied right away.

Less useful is a "Wrinkle Remove" or similarly named feature that promises to save you some ironing. It takes clean, wrinkled clothes and puts them through a short spell of tumbling at low or no heat followed by a cool-down. The feature can be duplicated on any machine with a temperature selector merely by setting the selector to low or no heat and the time to, say, 20 minutes.

Other features. Most models have a buzzer or other warning that sounds the end of the drying cycle; the signal's loudness is adjustable in many models. Some dryers also sound off when the lint filter is full and needs emptying.

A drum light can be useful for hunting down errant socks, even in a well-lit laundry room. A number of fancier dryers also come with a drum rack for drying sneakers and other items without tumbling.

Most doors open to the right so you can position the laundry basket in front of the opening. A door that opens down creates a handy shelf, but can also force you to stretch to reach into the drum.

The tests

We judge a dryer's prowess by seeing how well it handles a number of assignments at the appropriate automatic settings. We dry large loads of towels, jeans, and shirts, and small heaps of underwear, shorts, shirts, and hand towels. We also fill the machines with permanent-press shirts, and do loads of delicates—nylon lingerie, pajamas, nightgowns, and blouses.

A good dryer should dry laundry thoroughly, without heating the fabrics too much. The machine should also turn off promptly when the clothes reach the degree of dryness selected.

Buying advice

If you have a choice between an electric or gas dryer, opt for the gas model. Although gas dryers cost more initially, they're much more efficient than electric models. The energy saving in the first year of ownership should make up for the price difference.

Look for a model that offers automatic drying cycles. Timed cycles are best used just for small loads, which can confound the automatic setting on some machines. Models with a moisture sensor can further help reduce wasteful overdrying. But you'll have to spend an extra $30 to $60 to get that feature.

Electronic controls can add pizzazz to a machine's looks but don't improve performance, we've found.

Whichever dryer you end up choosing, make sure to clean the lint filter regularly. Ideally, that's after every use. Lint that's allowed to build up in the exhaust duct could cause a fire.

Steam Irons

▸ Ratings on page 59.

Ironing is not one of life's great joys. But if you want to look well groomed, it's a necessary part of owning clothes; be they wrinkle-prone cotton and linen or so-called permanent-press. The process for removing wrinkles is simple: Steam makes the material more pliable, the pressure of the iron sets it straight, and the heat dries it out. The more steam an iron produces, the better the effect. Manufacturers, cognizant of that correlation, are bolstering the steam-producing capability of many models in their lines.

The current crop of irons is a diversified lot. Bare-bones models that simply get hot and ooze steam are still available, but fanciful irons in designer colors that shut off automatically, spray, and vary steam output dominate the market. Competition has a lot to do with the evolution of the species. Nowadays familiar brands as *Sunbeam*, *Proctor-Silex*, and market-leader *Black & Decker*, fight for shelf space with dressy—and pricey—foreign-owned brands such as *Rowenta*, *Tefal*, *Krups*, *Sanyo*, and *Panasonic*.

The choices

Irons come in plain and fancy, large and compact packages. In fact, some appliances designed to remove wrinkles aren't irons at all; they're steamers that relax creases with a steady stream of warm mist. Here's the breakdown:

Regular irons. Even bare-bones models these days steam. Their cost: $25 or less. The vast middle of the market is occupied by full-sized irons that spray and steam. Many also beep, light up, work without a cord, and shut themselves off automatically. Prices vary greatly—$30 to $100.

Professional-type products. Heavy, bulky irons with vast steam-making capability can cost $200 or more. Unlike the familiar household iron, these models typically consist of a soleplate tethered by a water tube/power cord to a base with a cavernous water tank. Professional irons are cumbersome to carry, require a lot of storage space, and may lack amenities such as an automatic shutoff, nonstick soleplate, and spray feature.

Steam presses. Costlier still—perhaps more than $500—these measure a couple of feet in length and weigh upward of 30 pounds. A press is best suited for those who sew—it's just the thing for doing the small flat sections of a garment under construction or for fusing interlacings to fabric.

Travel irons and steamers. Scaled-down and sometimes odd-looking versions of regular irons are small and light enough to fit in a bag. The irons generally perform more robustly than the steamers. But steamers, which emit mist either continuously or intermittently, offer an advantage: You don't need a flat surface or ironing know-how. These portable machines cost between $20 and $50.

Features and convenience

Some features offer real advantages. Others are nice but not necessary.

Automatic shutoff. This turns off an upright iron that hasn't been moved for 10 minutes or so. On most shutoff models, the feature also works if the iron is left in the horizontal, ironing position for about 30 seconds. A valuable safety feature, automatic shutoff has become far more common than it was just a few years ago. Nearly half of all irons—including some

STEAM IRONS

inexpensive models are equipped with automatic shutoff.

Spray and steam. A built-in spray squirts warm water from a nozzle on the iron's prow; a burst-of-steam feature blasts steam from the holes in the soleplate. These features help set creases or remove the stubborn wrinkles in clothing made of natural fibers. The newest twist, a variable-steam feature, lets you adjust the steam level to match the temperature setting and so, presumably, improve performance. We don't think it offers much benefit, since irons tend to generate less steam at lower temperatures.

Cordless irons. They allow greater freedom of motion, but they must be constantly returned to a plug-in base for reheating.

Cord handling. Most irons and cords now have some kind of swivel to keep their rear-mounted cord from interfering with your wrist. Some manufacturers market irons with a cord that can be attached to the left side, for left-handers.

Temperature control. A fabric guide emblazoned on the iron helpfully guides you to the setting that's best suited for different fabrics. Adjusting the thermostat is not always easy. On many models, the thermostat is inconveniently positioned under the handle or on the side of the housing.

Water tank. The bigger the tank, the longer the steam lasts. Most irons are filled through an opening near the handle. If that tank has a narrow throat, the water can back up and spill easily. The best models have a removable tank that can be filled on or off the iron. Clear plastic water tanks make it easy to tell how much water is left. Most, however, still rely on the time-honored vertical tube.

Most manufacturers say it's all right to use tap water, except in areas with very hard water. If you use distilled water, they advise switching to tap water occasionally. In any case, empty the iron immediately after each use to prevent clogging and corrosion.

Other features. Most irons have a soleplate coated with a nonstick finish such as Silverstone. That finish is easier to keep clean than an aluminum soleplate but it's no easier to push. Some irons have indicator lights that show if they are plugged in or warming up, or emit a beep before automatically shutting off. Some models have grooved or notched soleplates for ironing around buttons.

The tests

We test the irons much as they're used, on a variety of fabrics. We measure the heat at various settings. Then, we go to the ironing board. We also measure the duration and intensity of each iron's steaming.

Buying advice

Before rushing out to buy a fancy iron, consider the tasks you routinely perform. If you're fond of linen suits, look for an iron that steams and sprays copiously. If you use an iron occasionally to touch up permanent-press items, perhaps all you need is a plain steam iron. Automatic shutoff is a worthwhile feature increasingly available for no great premium.

It's a good idea to handle any iron before buying it. It should feel comfortable in your hand, and its controls should be clear and easy to set.

DETERGENTS & OTHER LAUNDRY PRODUCTS

Few products are marketed as aggressively as laundry detergents. Soap makers spend a quarter-billion dollars a year promising the cleanest, fluffiest laundry and herald even minute changes in formulation with a flurry of advertising and coupons. In turn, consumers spend some $4-billion a year for detergent. Although there are lots of brands, industry giants Procter & Gamble, Colgate-Palmolive, and Lever Brothers dominate. Despite all the promises and products, detergents tend to be more alike than not.

Laundry washed with soap instead of detergent doesn't need softening. But modern detergents clean fabric fibers so thoroughly that they can leave clothes feeling scratchy. While line-dried clothes don't build up static, synthetics, especially, are prone to accumulate an electric charge in a dryer. Hence the need for fabric softeners.

By thinly coating the fibers of fabric with a waxy film, fabric softeners solve both the problem of static and the problem of clothes that are too clean. Humectant chemicals help the fabric retain moisture, neutralizing the static charge that otherwise causes socks to cling. Lubricants in the softener let the fibers glide past each other, reducing wrinkling. They also separate a napped fabric's fibers and stand them on end, which makes a towel feel fluffy.

A third weapon in the cleaning arsenal—boosters-plus-detergents—was created for times when something looks readier for the rag pile than the hamper. Boosters are sometimes useful for stains too stubborn for a regular detergent. Usually, they aren't much more effective than detergent alone.

The choices

Cleaning products come in a hodgepodge of liquids, powders, concentrates, sticks, sheets, pumps, and sprays—each with its own characteristics. Here are the realities the ads don't mention.

Detergents. It's in a manufacturer's financial interest to convince you that a particular task needs a special detergent. Such "niche marketing" is a way to sell two or three products where one might do. Truth is, all detergents clean clothes. Most also brighten, remove stains to some extent, and work in a variety of water temperatures. That's true whether or not a manufacturer decides to make any of those attributes a selling point. There are some differences worth noting, however.

Liquid detergents tend to be pricier than powders, but they allow easier pretreatment of stains. Once considerably less effective than powders, many liquids now clean as well or nearly as well.

Superconcentrated powders are the newest wrinkle in the detergent market. Packaged in easy-to-tote, compact containers, a carton not much larger than a lunchbox can hold enough powder for more than 40 loads.

Fabric softeners. First marketed in the late 1950s, fabric softeners originally came as a creamy liquid, often pink, that was added during the washer's rinse cycle. Rinse liquids are still around, but today they're competing against more convenient products—dryer sheets and detergent-softener combinations.

Made of fiber or foam, dryer sheets are impregnated with softener. You throw a sheet into the dryer along with the laundry. Heat releases the softener.

Combination products. "All-in-one" products—with colorsafe bleach, fabric softener, or stain-fighting enzymes—seem convenient but the results leave something to be desired. Detergent-fabric softener combinations, for instance, haven't done particularly well at cleaning or softening in our tests.

Detergent-softeners contain both products. The softener is present in the wash cycle, and the manufacturer relies on special chemicals to make sure that it sticks around for the rinse cycle. Single-use packets of detergent-plus-softener have detergent inside, which dissolves during the wash; the fibers of the bag, which are laced with softener, go into the dryer with the rest of the laundry.

Laundry boosters. Easiest to use for small stains are booster sticks, which rise from a tube like lipstick does. You rub booster onto the stain, then launder in the usual way. Liquid boosters, like sticks, must be rubbed in, which can be a chore for lots of stains. Aerosols and pump sprays are a bit easier to apply. You douse the stain, then wash the garment. Powders are the handiest for treating a large load. Instead of applying booster to the stained area, you simply pour it into the washer along with the detergent. Powders can also be used for presoaking.

Hand-laundry detergents. Specialty products like *Woolite* are promoted as a gentler alternative to regular detergents. Such products work, our tests have shown, but so do dishwashing liquids, which are very similar in composition to hand-laundry detergents except for whitening agents. The name-brand products charge a premium. Store-brand versions of these detergents cost less. But dishwashing liquids are the best buy.

What makes them work

For centuries, people did their laundry with a fat-and-alkali mixture known as soap. Trouble is, when soap and hard water mix, an ugly scum forms on both the fabric and washer. Today's synthetic laundry detergents eliminate the problem. But their components are a far cry from fat and alkali. Modern laundry products work through the combined action of a number of key ingredients:

Surfactants, or surface active agents, are dirt removers. They act much as soap does, emulsifying oil and grease and the dirt they bind, allowing them all to be washed away. There are hundreds of such chemicals, which can be classed as three types. Anionic surfactants work best in hot, soft water and are very effective on oily stains and removing mud and clay. Nonionic surfactants are less sensitive to water hardness; they excel at ridding oily soils from synthetics at cool wash temperatures. Many liquids contain this type. Cationic surfactants are more common in fabric softeners and detergent-softener combinations.

Builders enhance the cleaning efficiency of the surfactants by softening the water. Phosphates are the quintessential builders. (Phosphates, found only in powdered detergents, have taken the rap for spurring the growth of algae, which can eventually transform a lake into a bog in a process known as eutrophication. So they're banned in about a third of the country.) Nonphosphorus powders may combine old-fashioned washing soda with extra ingredients to make up for the lack of phosphorus. Liquid detergents like *Wisk* and *Surf* contain water-softening chemicals such as sodium citrate.

Whitening agents, also known as optical brighteners, are colorless dyes that give laundry an added glow in sunlight and fluorescent light, making garments appear a bit brighter.

Enzymes help break down complex soils—especially proteins, such as those in blood, egg, or grass stains—so they can be more easily removed. Some people, however, may experience skin irritation upon contact with enzymes. You can generally tell if a detergent contains enzymes

DETERGENTS & OTHER LAUNDRY PRODUCTS

by checking the ingredient list for substances ending in the suffix "-ase."

All-fabric bleach, a popular addition to powders, is not as good as chlorine bleach at whitening, but it's gentler. All-fabric bleaches—sodium perborate tetrahydrate is the most common—are safe on most materials and dyes.

The tests

We judge detergents on their ability to perform three tasks: removing tough stains from white cotton-polyester swatches, keeping loosened soil from settling back on fabric, and brightening fabrics. We run swatches of stained material through matched washers and dryers under identical laundering conditions. Stains include mud, grass, makeup, grape juice, tea, and spaghetti sauce. Detergent is added according to label instructions.

We challenge boosters on swatches treated with the same tenacious stains we give our detergents. We use each according to label instructions and wash under identical conditions with a regular nonphosphorus detergent powder recommended for use with a booster.

To judge fabric softeners, we ask a panel of staffers to compare the softness of freshly laundered cotton terry washcloths treated with the softeners. To see how well each product dissipates static electricity, we use an electrostatic-field meter to measure the charge of each load of washcloths as it emerges from the dryer.

Buying advice

On an ordinary load of laundry, the range of performance among detergents would be clean to cleanest, not dirty to clean. Some products work a bit better, especially on tough stains like tea, grass, and grape juice. On the other hand, we haven't found any detergent that works on black ink or used motor oil.

Some products can now remove used motor oil, a stain previously too tough for any detergent or booster, so it might be worthwhile to have a booster on hand for the spills even the best detergent can't tackle. Products in stick form are the costliest; powders, the least expensive.

Regular detergent can be used as a spot remover, too. Just rub a bit of liquid detergent directly into the stain before laundering in the usual way. Some powdered detergents shouldn't be used as spot removers, according to their labels. For products without such a caveat, try this method: Combine a spoonful or so with a bit of water until it forms a paste, then rub it into the stain with an old toothbrush.

There's little correlation between the price of a detergent and its cleaning ability, we've found. Look for special promotions, and buy what's on sale. You'll pay more for the convenience of liquids or premeasured packets. You'll also pay more for buying green, although there's no evidence to suggest that so-called natural brands are any better for the environment than regular brands.

Almost all fabric softeners reduce static; dryer sheets are particularly good. On the whole, rinse liquids soften better than other types. Detergent-softener combinations are the least effective.

Expect to pay around 10 cents per use for liquids, less than 10 cents for dryer sheets, and as much as 30 cents per use for combination products. Like detergents, softeners are heavily promoted. Buy dryer sheets by price. Some supermarket brands cost half as much as big name brands but soften about as well.

CLOTHES DRYERS

RATINGS CLOTHES DRYERS Better ◄——► Worse

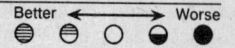

▶ **See report, page 47.** From Consumer Reports, January 1992.

Recommendations: For capacity, convenience, and performance, consider the electric and gas *Maytags* and the electric *Sears 60941*. Less expensive but still generous in capacity are the two high-rated *Whirlpools*. Lower-rated and lower-priced models are likely to be just as satisfactory, although they tended to overdry.

Ratings order: Listed by types; within types, listed in order of estimated quality. The price is the approximate retail as quoted by the manufacturer; actual retail may be lower. Ⓢ indicates model has been replaced by successor model; according to the manufacturer, the performance of new model is similar to the tested model but features may vary. See right for new model number and approximate retail price, if available. Ⓓ indicates model discontinued.

Brand and model	Price	Drum volume	Mixed load (large)	Mixed load (small)	Permanent-press	Delicate fabrics	Convenience	Advantages	Disadvantages	Comments
ELECTRIC DRYERS										
Maytag DE9900	$600	◒	◒	◒	◒	◒	◒	D,F,H	o,p	A,E,O,P,R,S,V
Sears 60941 Ⓢ	630	◒	◒	◒	◒	◒	◒	A,C,D,E,F,G	—	A,E,K,L,Q,V
Whirlpool LE9800XS	450	◒	◒	◒	◒	◒	◒	A,F,G	d,l,p	A,D,E,I,L,M,R,V
Sears 60931 Ⓢ	520	◒	◒	◒	◒	◒	◒	C,E,F,G	a,h	C,D,E,K,L,V
Speed Queen AEE953W	410	◒	○	◒	◒	◒	◒	B,D,F,G	i	A,R,S
RCA DRB2885M	310	◒	◒	◒	◒	◒	◒	I	i,o	O,V
General Electric DDE9500M	400	◒	◒	◒	◒	◒	◒	I	i,o	E,O,V
Magic Chef YE20J-N5	370	◒	○	◒	◒	◒	○	B,G	f,j,o	H
KitchenAid KEYE860W	495	◒	◒	◒	○	◐	◒	F,G,H	c,d,h,p	C,E,I,J,L,M,P,T,U,V
Amana LE3902W	390	◒	○	◒	◒	◒	◒	D,F,G	g,i	A,P,R,S
Montgomery Ward 7640 Ⓢ	375	◒	◒	◒	◒	◒	○	G	f,k,o	H
Whirlpool LE9500XT	380	◒	◒	◒	◒	○	◐	F	d,h,l,n,p	E,I,L,M,V
White Westinghouse DE800K	350	○	◐	◐	○	◒	◒	—	b,i	E
Hotpoint DLB2880D Ⓓ	345	◒	◐	○	◒	◒	○	I	a,i,o	F,O
Gibson DE27A7X	325	○	◐	◐	◒	◒	○	—	b,i,k,n	H,P
Frigidaire DECIF-W-2	380	○	◐	◐	◒	◒	◒	—	a,f,j,k	H

CLOTHES DRYERS

Ratings indicate:
- ○ = lower rating
- ◐ / ◑ = middle ratings
- ● = higher rating

Brand and model	Price	Drum volume	Mixed load (large)	Mixed load (small)	Permanent-press	Delicate fabrics	Convenience	Advantages	Disadvantages	Comments
Kelvinator DEA500	$270	○	●	○	○	◐	○	—	a,e,m,n	B,G
Roper EL6050	330	○	◐	○	○	○	●	—	a,e,h,k,n,p	C,E,I,L,M
GAS DRYERS										
Maytag DG9900	645	◐	◐	◐	◐	◐	◐	D,F,H	o,p	A,E,O,P,R,S,V
Whirlpool LG9801XS	440	◐	◐	◐	◐	◐	◐	A,F,G	l,p	A,D,E,I,L,M,R,V
Sears 70931 [S]	500	◐	◐	◐	◐	◐	◐	C,E,F,G	a,h	C,D,E,K,L,V
Speed Queen AGE959W	450	◐	○	◐	◐	◐	◐	B,D,F,G	i	A,R,S
Magic Chef YG20J-N5	405	◐	◐	◐	◐	◐	○	B,G	f,j,o	H,N
General Electric DDG9580M [S]	420	◐	◐	◐	◐	○	◐	I	i,o,q	E,O,V
White-Westinghouse DG800K	390	○	●	●	○	◐	◐	—	b,i	E,N
Frigidaire DGCIF-W-2	380	○	●	○	◐	◐	◐	—	a,f,j,k	H,N

Successor Models (in Ratings order)
Sears 60941 is succeeded by Sears 61951, $749; Sears 60931 by 62931, $579; GE DDE9500M by DDE9500R, $400; Montgomery Ward 7640 by 7643, $330; Sears 70931 by 72931, $620; GE DDG9580M by DDG9580R, $449.

Features in Common
All have: • At least 1 automatic dryness-control cycle. • No-heat setting. • 4 leveling legs. *Except as noted, all have:* • Thermostat for gauging dryness. • Provision for choosing extended cool-down after automatic cycle. • Automatic controls able to recognize already-dry loads and turn off heat cycle within 20 to 40 min. • Timed cycle with at least 60 min. drying time. • Rotary timer dial. • End-of-cycle signal, from 2 to 5 sec. long, that can be adjusted for loudness or turned off entirely. • Drum light. • Lint filter removable from inside the drum. • Raised edge on top to contain spills. • Baked-enamel finish on cabinet top and drum. • Door that opens to right. • 1-yr. warranty on parts, labor.

Key to Advantages
A–Automatic dryness control recognized already-dry load sooner than most (in 5 min. or less) and turned off heat cycle.
B–Maintained cooler temperatures (under 140°F) than most with delicate loads.
C–Quieter than most when tumbling.
D–Programmable cycle memory.
E–Light makes controls easier to see.
F–Signals when lint filter is full.
G–Rack for drying without tumbling.
H–Porcelain-coated top.
I–Porcelain-coated drum.

Key to Disadvantages
a–Automatic dryness control didn't recognize already-dry mixed and permanent-press loads and turn off heat within 40 min.
b–Automatic dryness control didn't recognize already-dry mixed loads and turn off heat cycle within 40 min.
c–Allowed 200°F temp. with delicates.
d–Noisier than most when tumbling.
e–No extended cool-down at end of cycle.

Ratings Keys continued

56 WASHING MACHINES

f–Cycle selector turns only in one direction.
g–End-of-cycle signal too faint.
h–End-of-cycle signal too short.
i–Overly long end-of-cycle signal.
j–Seemingly endless end-of-cycle signal.
k–End-of-cycle signal cannot be adjusted or turned off.
l–End-of-cycle signal cannot be turned off.
m–No end-of-cycle signal.
n–No drum light.
o–Drum light dimmer than most.
p–No raised edge on top to contain spills.
q–Deeply recessed gas connection made it difficult to check tightness of connection.

Key to Comments
A–Electronic controls with touchpads.
B–Single-control model, with only 1 heat setting in automatic cycle; fabric-cycle selector determines dryer temperature.
C–Continuous range of heat control in all cycles.
D–Extended cool-down after auto cycles.
E–"Wrinkle remove" feature as separate cycle.
F–Maximum timed cycle only 50 min. long.
G–Mixed-load and delicate-fabric performance reflects use of single permanent-press cycle. Maker suggests using timed cycle.
H–Delicate-fabric performance reflects use of automatic permanent-press cycle. Maker suggests using timed cycle.
I–Lint filter can be pulled up from top of cabinet.
J–Has removable fabric-softener dispenser.
K–Has clothes hanger that mounts on dryer.
L–Door opens downward.
M–Vents only from rear.
N–Vents from rear, right, or bottom.
O–Vents from rear, left, or bottom.
P–1-yr. warranty on labor; 2-yr. on parts.
Q–3-yr. warranty on parts and labor.
R–Warranty has 5-yr. coverage on electronic controls.
S–Warranty has 5-yr. coverage against rust on certain parts.
T–Warranty has 5-yr. coverage on electrical element and cabinet assembly.
U–Warranty has 10-yr. parts-only coverage against rust on drum.
V–Moisture sensor gauges dryness.

RATINGS WASHING MACHINES

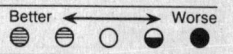

Better ← → Worse

▶ See report, page 44. From Consumer Reports, August 1992.

Recommendations: Between manual and electronic controls, we think the manual controls offer better value. The best models with manual controls were the *Sears 29841*, $500, and the *KitchenAid KAWE860W*, $575. The *Roper AX6245V*, $430, is a bare-bones variant of those two.

Ratings order: Listed by type of controls; within types, listed in order of estimated quality. Except where separated by a bold rule, closely ranked models differed little in quality. Price is the approximate retail as quoted by the manufacturer; actual retail may be lower. Ⓢ indicates tested model has been replaced by successor model; according to the manufacturer, the performance of new model should be similar to the tested model but features may vary. See page 58 for new model number and suggested retail price, if available. Ⓓ indicates model discontinued.

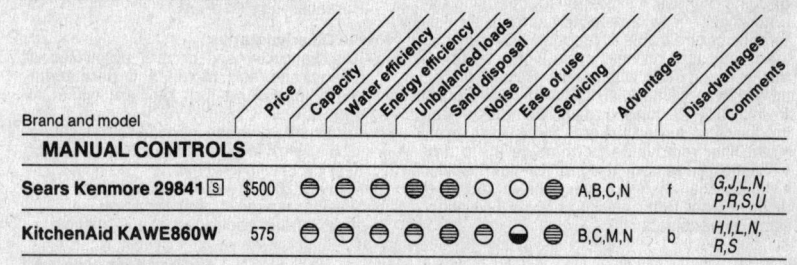

Brand and model	Price	Capacity	Water efficiency	Energy efficiency	Unbalanced loads	Sand disposal	Noise	Ease of use	Servicing	Advantages	Disadvantages	Comments
MANUAL CONTROLS												
Sears Kenmore 29841 Ⓢ	$500	◒	◒	◒	◒	◒	○	○	◒	A,B,C,N	f	G,J,L,N, P,R,S,U
KitchenAid KAWE860W	575	◒	◒	◒	◒	◒	◒	◐	◒	B,C,M,N	b	H,I,L,N, R,S

WASHING MACHINES 57

Brand and model	Price	Capacity	Water efficiency	Energy efficiency	Unbalanced loads	Sand disposal	Noise	Ease of use	Servicing	Advantages	Disadvantages	Comments
Whirlpool LA9500T	$470	◐	◐	◐	◐	○	◐	◐		C,M,N	b	G,I,L,N,R,S
Roper AX6245V ⓢ	430	◐	◐	◐	◐	◐	○	○	◐	C	a,b,d	G,I,L,N,R
Ward Signature 2000 6589	390	◐	◐	◐	◐	◕	○	◐	○	J,K,M,N	h	B,G,I,K,N,P,R,S,T
Ward Signature 2000 LNC6532 Ⓓ	400	◐	◐	◐	◐	○	○	○	●	C	—	A,G,J,R
Maytag A9800	640	○	○	○	①	○	○	◐	◐	B,J,K,M,N	b,c,d	H,I,L,R,S,T
Speed Queen AWM551 Ⓓ	395	○	○	○	①	◐	○	◐	◐	J,K,N	c	C,H,I,S
Amana LW3303W Ⓓ	445	○	○	○	①	◐	○	◐	◐	J,K	c	C,F,H,I,R
White-Westinghouse LA700M Ⓓ	450	○	○	◐	◐	○	◐	◐	○	C,J,K,N	h	B,G,J,K,N,S,T
Frigidaire WCIL	395	○	◐	◐	◐	○	◐	◐	○	J,K,M,N	f	B,G,J,K,N,P,S,T,U
GE WWA8858M Ⓓ	410	○	◐	◐	◐	●	○	●	●	B,C,J,K,M	—	G,I,M,O,R,T
Hotpoint WLW3700B Ⓓ	375	○	◐	◐	○	◐	◐	◐		B,C,K	g	G,I,L,M,T

■ *The following model was downrated because it lacks warm wash—a frequently used, energy-saving choice—on its permanent-press cycle.*

| **Magic Chef W20J-4S** | 480 | ◐ | ◐ | ◐ | ● | ○ | ○ | ◐ | ● | C | e | A,H,J |

ELECTRONIC CONTROLS

Sears Kenmore 21951	815	◐	◐	◐	◐	◐	○	◐	◐	B,C,D,F,G,I,J,K,L,M,N	f	D,G,J,L,N,Q,R,S,U
Whirlpool LA9800XT	580	◐	◐	◐	◐	◐	○	○	◐	C,D,L,M,N	b	E,G,I,L,N,R,S
Maytag A9900	735	○	○	○	①	○	○	◐	◐	B,D,G,H,J,K,L,M,N	b,c,d	E,H,I,L,R,S
Speed Queen AWE951 Ⓓ	455	○	○	○	①	○	○	○	○	D,F,G,J,K,L,M	c	C,E,H,I,R,S
Frigidaire WA8600P	480	◐	●	●	◐	○	◐	○	◐	C,D,E,F,G,H,J,K,L,M,N	d	B,E,G,J,K,N,Q,R,S

SUDS-SAVER MODEL

| **Maytag A9700W** ② | 610 | ○ | ③ | ④ | ① | ◐ | ○ | ◐ | ◐ | B,J,K,N | b,c,d | H,I,L,O,R,T |

① *Performance varied from ◐ to ○.*
② *Manual controls.*
③ *Score when machine is in regular mode and score for suds-saver mode.*
④ *Score in regular mode; scored slightly higher in suds-saver mode.*

Turn page for Ratings Keys

58 WASHING MACHINES

Successor Models (in Ratings order)
Roper AX6245V is succeeded by RA57245A; Sears 29841 by 22481.

Performance Notes
Except as noted, all were judged very good at collecting lint.

Features in Common
All: • Have bleach dispenser. • Provide at least 2 agitation and spin speeds. • Have variable water-level controls. • Did about equally well extracting water from laundry in our tests.
Except as noted, all: • Have only hot, warm, or cold wash, cold rinse. • Have porcelain-coated steel tub, painted top. • Have softener dispensers. • Have instructions on lid. • Agitation and spin speeds chosen automatically when you select cycle or fabric type. • Have self-cleaning lint filter system. • Are limited to max. drain height of 48 or 60 in. • Have lip on top to contain minor spills. • Have 1-yr. parts/labor warranty. • Have lids hinged at back.

Key to Advantages
A–Electronic temperature control to blend hot and cold water worked well.
B–Porcelain top and lid.
C–Self-adjusting legs at rear.
D–Timer shows remaining time for cycle.
E–Digital clock.
F–Delay start.
G–Programmable custom cycle settings.
H–Settings between Cold/Warm and Warm/Hot.
I–Dial light.
J–Softener dispenser easy to use and clean.
K–Large bleach dispenser, judged better than others. **Sears Kenmore** delays dispensing until late in the wash cycle.
L–Has end-of-cycle signal.
M–Has extra rinse setting.
N–Slow agitation available with warm wash/warm rinse; possible advantage for woolens.

Key to Disadvantages
a–No softener dispenser.
b–Top has no lip to help contain spills.
c–Moderately unbalanced load stopped Spin cycle.
d–No instructions on lid.
e–Only hot or cold wash in permanent-press.
f–Lid doesn't open completely to lie flat.
g–Lacks soak/prewash settings.
h–Judged good at collecting lint.

Key to Comments
A–Painted steel tub with extended warranty.
B–Plastic tub with extended warranty.
C–Stainless-steel tub with extended warranty.
D–All parts and labor warrantied for 3 yr.
E–5-yr. parts warranty on electronic controls.
F–5-yr. parts/labor warranty on transmission.
G–5-yr. parts warranty on transmission.
H–10-yr. parts warranty on transmission.
I–Transmission warranty covers all parts.
J–Transmission warranty covers some parts.
K–Lid locks during Spin cycle.
L–Readers complain that slots under agitator snag laundry; that didn't happen in tests.
M–Can be installed to 96-in. drain height.
N–Can be installed to 72-in. drain height.
O–Lacks self-cleaning lint filter.
P–Controls judged better than others for visually impaired people.
Q–Electronic temp. control didn't work.
R–Warm rinse available with hot wash.
S–Warm rinse available with warm wash.
T–Separate control for agitation and spin.
U–Lid hinged from left.

ABOUT CU'S REPAIR HISTORIES

Thousands of readers tell us about their repair experiences with autos, appliances, and electronic items on the Annual Questionnaire. Using that unique information can improve your chances of getting a trouble-free car, washing machine, TV set, or other product. See the Frequency-of-Repair charts starting on page 317 and the brand repair histories starting on page 361.

STEAM IRONS 59

RATINGS STEAM IRONS

Better ← → Worse

▶ **See report, page 49.** From Consumer Reports, January 1991.

Recommendations: Of the top two models, the *Black & Decker* was easiest to use. The *Norelco* was a better steamer.

Ratings order: Listed by types; within types, listed in order of estimated quality. Bracketed models ranked the same (listed alphabetically). Price is the approximate retail as quoted by the mfr. Weight ranges from 2 to 3 lb., excluding water or cordless models' base units. **Key features: A** = automatic shutoff; **B** = burst of steam; **C** = cordless; **C/C** = cord or cordless; **N** = nonstick soleplate; **S** = spray. ⓢ indicates tested model has been replaced by successor model; according to the manufacturer, the performance of new model should be similar to the tested model but features may vary. See page 60 for new model number and suggested retail price, if available. ⓓ indicates model discontinued.

Brand and model	Price	Key features	Water capacity, fl. oz.	Steaming rate	Ease of setting	Ease of filling	Water gauge	Advantages	Disadvantages	Comments
FULL-FEATURED IRONS										
Black & Decker F640S	$71	A,B,N,S	7	○	◒	◒	◒	H,O,P,Q,T	v	B,F,P,T
Norelco 760se ⓢ	60	A,N,S	6½	◒	○	◒	◒	A,G,J,O,P,T,U	g,k,m	C,L,W
Proctor-Silex I2747	56	A,B,N,S	6	○	◒	◒	○	B,K,O,S	q	J,P
Panasonic NI682E	80	A,N,S	7	○	○	◒	◒	C,F,L,N,R	b,k	B,C,L,M,S,V
Black & Decker F610SA	56	A,N,S	7	○	◒	◒	◒	I,O,P,T	v	B,F,T
Rowenta DA-49 ⓓ	65	B,S	6	◒	●	◒	◒	B,D,E,O,P,Q,U	e,f,k,m,u	O,P,U,X
Proctor-Silex I2725 ⓓ	40	B,N,S	6	○	◒	◒	○	B,M,S	h,q	—
Tefal 1648	60	B,N,S	7	◒	●	◒	◒	B,D,E,G,U	e,f,i,m,p,s,u	A,E,K
Rowenta CS-01	110	B,C/C,S	8	○	●	◒	◒	B,C,O,P,Q	b,e,f,k,m,u	C,D,M,O,R,T,U,X
Sunbeam 12631	35	A,N,S	8	◒	○	○	●	B,F,M,O,T	d,f,g,j,k,o,r	I,M,T
Panasonic NI-333E	32	N,S	6	○	◒	◒	◒	N	—	C,M,V
Black & Decker F416WHS	43	A,B,N	6	●	○	◒	○	M,U	r	B,G,N,P,T
PLAIN IRONS										
Sunbeam 11500	20	N	8	◒	○	●	●	B	a,d,f,g,j,k,o,r,t	H,T
Black & Decker F363	22	—	6	○	◒	◒	—	—	g,r,t	G,T
Proctor-Silex I1321	20	—	6	●	○	●	—	S	c,l,n,q,t	G,Q

Turn page for Ratings Keys

60 STEAM IRONS

Successor Model
Norelco 760se is succeeded by 518, $63.

Features in Common
All: • Draw 1000 to 1200 watts.
Except as noted, all: • Have temp. control at front of handle and fabric guide under handle. • Have rear-mounted cord that pivots, wraps around body for storage. • Can iron near buttons. • Have tube water gauge. • Have light to show iron is heating. • Have 1-yr. repair-or-replace warranty.

Key to Advantages
A–Spray more effective than others.
B–Very good temperature range.
C–Tank can be filled on or off iron.
D–Comes with a cup; makes filling easier.
E–Large, clear tank.
F–Covering for tank opening.
G–Self-clean valve removes for cleaning.
H–Lights and audible signals indicate temperature.
I–Push-on control turns on iron, light.
J–3 lights show iron is plugged in, is heating, or has shut off.
K–2 lights show iron is plugged in or has shut off.
L–2 lights show iron is plugged in or heating.
M–Light shows iron is plugged in (**Sears** and **Sunbeam** light flashes when iron shut off).
N–Dry/steam button on handle easy to use.
O–Variable steam feature.
P–Variable steam control on handle very convenient.
Q–Easy to switch between burst-of-steam and spray.
R–Cord stays out of way in use; it's also retractable for storage.
S–Cord mounts left or right.
T–Self-cleaning feature worked well.
U–Convenient cord wrap.

Key to Disadvantages
a–Water can pour out of tank if cap is opened.
b–Housing below tank gets hot enough to burn.
c–Iron must be tilted to fill.
d–Horizontal water gauge; not accurate when iron is standing.
e–Limited number of fabrics in guide.
f–No permanent-press setting.
g–Steam dropped off greatly after 10 min.
h–Dry/steam button interferes with controls.
i–Dry/steam button not well marked; pressing burst-of-steam button can deactivate steam button.
j–Less stable standing than most.
k–Temperature control under handle.
l–Temperature control on side.
m–No Off mark on thermostat.
n–No button notches or grooves.
o–Large buttons stick in groove.
p–Shallow button notches; a problem with large buttons.
q–Side-mounted cord drags on fabric.
r–Back-mounted cord hits wrist.
s–Soleplate has ridges; dirt tends to collect.
t–No indicator light.
u–Lower housing gets hot enough to burn.
v–No provision to store cord.

Key to Comments
A–Reaches higher temperature than others.
B–Light goes out when iron has shut off.
C–Large water tank is dark.
D–Going from corded to cordless use is easy.
E–10-yr. warranty for soleplate damage.
F–Vertical water gauges are dark.
G–Dry/steam button on handle.
H–Rocker switch under handle for dry/steam.
I–Variable steam control under handle.
J–Variable steam control on handle.
K–Fabric guide on temperature control at front of handle.
L–Fabric guide on heel.
M–Indicator light on left side.
N–Automatically shuts off after 10 min. of inactivity, regardless of position.
O–No groove or notches, but ironed adequately around buttons.
P–1 sample defective.
Q–Distilled water is preferred, especially in areas with very hard water. Tap water should be used on occasion.
R–Large hole on housing under removable water tank should *not* be filled with water.
S–Retractable cord should be pulled all the way out during use.
T–2-yr. repair-or-replace warranty.
U–Valve system is designed for tap water, except in extremely hard water areas. Mfr. recommends demineralizer.
V–1-yr. repair warranty.
W–Has 30-day money-back guarantee. Iron must be shipped prepaid to mfr.
X–3-yr. repair-or-replace warranty.

HOME THEATER

TV sets 65	Stereo headphones 77
VCRs 68	Walkabout stereos 78
Laser-disc players.........................71	Compact-disc players 80
Camcorders 71	Cassette decks 81
Stereo receivers 73	Compact stereo systems 84
Loudspeakers 76	Ratings...86

The idea of home theater—watching movies on a big-screen TV set with a good sound system—has changed home-entertainment products in myriad ways:

■ Most all stereo TV sets can now be connected to a sound system, and more and more sets come with beefed up audio amplifiers capable of directly driving external loudspeakers. Sets with a 27-inch screen are now the premier sellers, and sets with a screen of 30 inches or more are becoming commonplace.

■ Most mid-to-high-priced stereo receivers are now "audio/video" receivers, capable of serving as the switching center for a home-theater system. And many not-so-expensive models now come with special sound-effects abilities like Dolby Surround and Dolby Pro Logic. These systems decode a special sound track that adds ambience such as the rumble of airplanes or ricochets. Dolby Surround uses four speakers; Dolby Pro Logic, five.

■ Speakers, once available only in pairs, are now available singly, the better to set up these "ambience" sound systems.

■ Hi-fi sound is now a common feature in VCRs, the machines that started home theater.

■ Laser-disc players, once considered something of a technological dodo, have taken on new life, primarily because they promise superb picture and sound quality.

■ Remote controls have become a product unto themselves, many capable of day-to-day operation of the whole show.

At its fanciest, a home theater can cost more than a car. But setting up a home theater can be as simple as hooking up the TV to a pair of powered speakers (cost: as little as $150) or adding a patch cord to connect the TV set to the stereo (about $5). Or you can update a component or two in your present setup. Even if you're building a system from scratch, you can do it for well under $2000 and still get good performance. Here's what to consider:

Decide which component is the center. Until recently, there was no choice. It had to be the stereo receiver, whether or not you normally watch TV and listen to music in the same room. But many big-screen TV sets can now drive external speakers directly and switch among several video sources. Plan on spending at least $600 for a 27-inch set with those audio and switching capabilities.

If you already have a TV set with an audio output, you can set up a receiver-based system for much less. A receiver, its amplifier more powerful than what's currently built into TV sets, can produce the best sound. And a receiver-based system is more versatile than a TV-based system. A separate receiver costs as little as $150. For an A/V model that decodes Dolby Surround sound, figure at least $250.

Set up the speakers. Some TV sets have built-in "psychoacoustic effects," which enable speakers only a couple of feet apart to simulate the spaciousness of full-blown stereo. Still, these effects can't compare with the sound produced by a set of good loudspeakers placed for maximum effect. Expect to pay $350 to $400 for a main pair. The pair of "rear," adjunct speakers in a Dolby setup can be cheaper, since that channel carries only untaxing mid-range frequencies.

A proprietary system called THX, developed by LucasFilm, maker of "E.T." and the "Star Wars" trilogy, takes Dolby sound a step farther by using specially designed equipment. Originally custom fitted only to movie theaters, a home THX system can be installed by a contractor for around $12,000. A cheaper way to get part of the THX sound: speakers from Cambridge Sound Works that follow the THX standard closely. *The Surround,* as these speakers are dubbed, are priced at $399 a pair. Another alternative is Atlantic Technologies' *Pattern Home Theater* system, priced at $1200, which includes unobtrusive "satellite" speakers, a large powered subwoofer, and a Dolby decoder.

In a two-speaker setup, you'd put the speakers on either side of the TV set. With the four speakers of a Dolby Surround system, the second pair should be pointed away from the listener, since you want the ambience sounds to seem as if they're coming from all around you. The fifth speaker in a Dolby Pro Logic setup goes near the TV screen.

Many high-quality speakers, particularly those of American origin, have an impedance rating of four ohms. (Impedance measures resistance to electric current.) But many receivers, particularly Japanese products, are designed to work with speakers rated at six ohms or more. Using the wrong speakers can overheat and damage receiver circuits, especially when playing steadily at high volumes. Multiple speakers complicate the picture. Two sets of speakers connected in parallel, as some receivers do when driving two sets, is a more difficult load than the same two sets connected in series, as is done by other receivers. Check the speaker and receiver specifications to be sure that components are compatible before you buy.

Choose the playback devices. At a minimum, a home theater needs a hi-fi VCR. Hi-fi models are now fairly inexpensive, available at discount for less than $400. The price of laser-disc players has been plunging, as well, to less than $400.

Consider the remote control. If all the components in a home theater are the same brand, there should be little problem in running the basic functions with just one remote, probably the TV's or the VCR's. In a setup of mixed brands, you may want a universal remote. These "learning" or "code-entry" remotes now come with high-end TV sets and VCRs. They can be bought separately, too, for $40 and up. But don't count on tossing out the remotes you've collected—you'll still need them to perform specialized functions.

The rest of the gear. To round out the home-entertainment possibilities, there are camcorders, tape decks, and CD players.

Connections. Connectors range from phono plugs to multipronged S-connectors; wires, from thin speaker wire to coaxial cable. Avoid thin speaker wire; ordinary lamp cord is better for hooking up speakers. Be sure to trim the ends of the wires carefully to avoid the two wires' shorting together. Audio cables should be kept away from power cords to avoid excess "hum."

CABLE SYSTEMS AND HOME THEATER

Cable reception, theoretically perfect, can founder in three places: The signals transmitted from the cable company can be inferior; the distribution system—the cable and associated equipment—can degrade them, or the cable-converter box can introduce problems.

Cable boxes. Today's cable-ready sets are designed to present channels as if broadcast directly to the set's antenna. Cable boxes—set-top converters and descramblers—act as electronic middlemen, one more link for signals to negotiate before they're fed to your set. Unfortunately, the boxes are sometimes a weak link. Many cable subscribers must use the boxes to get premium channels like HBO; in some systems, subscribers must use them for all channels.

Cable boxes often render a TV set's remote control useless for changing channels. You'll likely need the cable company's remote—at perhaps a dollar or two in monthly charges—merely to change channels. One remedy: "code-entry" remotes, which work some brands of cable boxes.

Hooking up a VCR to a set with a cable box is apt to be cumbersome and to add a layer of complexity to programming the VCR. Further, the box can make it difficult or impossible to view two channels simultaneously on a set with the picture-in-picture (PIP) feature. In the worst cases, you may need *two* boxes to display PIP.

Cable sound. When cable systems were first being wired, no one envisioned that expectations of a TV set would change so. Less than superlative audio might have gone unnoticed before the days of hi-fi TV. Now, poor sound just gets reproduced more faithfully.

Even though you may watch programs that are broadcast in stereo and even though your TV or VCR indicates it's receiving stereo signals, your cable company may not properly process the signal. If your "stereo" sound is practically mono, the problem is likely to be most noticeable with Dolby Surround and other ambience effects, which need clear stereo separation.

More annoying, noise can be introduced into the system—and the fancier the system, the worse it will sound. Buzz can come from the extra information that many cable systems use in scrambling the signal. If that's the problem, your only recourse is to complain to the cable company and hope that it will soon upgrade its equipment or switch to another scrambling method. Hum can result from electrical power leaking into the audio signal. That problem, which can be caused by voltage differences in electrical grounds, may be more easily solved by the cable company.

Some cable systems simulcast the audio track of their pay channels on a separate frequency in the FM band, with potentially far better sound quality; some systems also include the basic channels or at least the music channels, like MTV. Many A/V receivers are set up to receive such simulcasts. (The simulcasts are assigned broadcast frequencies where there are no local radio stations on the dial.) There may be an extra installation or monthly charge to hook up your stereo receiver to the cable.

Our basic shopping advice is easily summed up: Shop around, and don't buy more than you think you need.

Buying electronic gear

Home electronics equipment is often sharply discounted from the list price. The amount of discounting depends to some extent on where you buy. Audio/video salons tend to charge list or close to it; discount houses and mail-order sources usually provide better deals, but you have to know exactly what you want.

Often, the benefits of spending more and moving up the brand line are small but tangible improvements in performance, convenience, or versatility. Sometimes, however, you pay extra for a name and a look. Manufacturers of electronics aim for two different markets, the ordinary consumer and the "prestige" customer. The mass-market brands, such as *RCA* and *Panasonic* in video and *Pioneer*, *Technics*, and *JVC* in audio, are widely available in stores and by mail, usually at a substantial discount. Prestige brands, such as *Proton* and *ProScan* on the video side and *NAD* and *Luxman* on the audio side, are sold primarily through specialty audio and video dealers, with little discounting. Some companies, such as Sony, RCA, and Panasonic, make separate lines of merchandise to reach both markets. Our tests have shown no substantive performance advantage for the prestige brands. Indeed, prestige audio brands tend to give you fewer features and less power for the money than mass-market brands. On the other hand, the control panels on many prestige products are models of simplicity.

Aficionados of hi-fi equipment have always put together a system one piece at a time, shopping carefully for just the right speakers or the cassette tape deck nonpareil. Our tests confirm that a single company rarely excels at making every component. Keep in mind, however, that the differences in performance we find between the best and the rest are often fairly small. Even "rack systems," the everything-provided audio systems snubbed by audiophiles, can, at their best, produce good sound.

What to look for in a remote control

Too few remote controls appear to have been designed for human hands, eyes, and brains. And since many functions of today's TV sets and VCRs can be performed only with the remote, there's ample opportunity to contemplate the device's failings.

You can tell the products whose manufacturers have given humans proper consideration—the buttons are well spaced and differentiated by color and shape, the labels have good-sized lettering and plenty of contrast, and the keypad can be used instinctively because it's logically arranged. Common design flaws include:

■ Row after row of identical minuscule buttons—they're torture on the eyes and hard to manipulate.

■ Often-used buttons, like a TV set's Mute or a VCR's Pause, that are hard to locate.

■ Lack of ergonomic awareness. The least convenient remotes are bulky and cluttered and force you to use two hands: one to hold the device and another to push the buttons. The best are well-balanced and fit comfortably in one hand.

■ Inelegant software design. Some remotes make you press an additional key—"Enter"—to access a channel. On some models, you're forced to wade tediously through screen after screen of menus to locate the setting you want to adjust.

The jargon used to describe the types of remotes can be confusing, but there are three main types:

Dedicated remotes can operate only a single component. They're typically found on the least expensive TV sets, VCRs, and receivers. Remotes for cassette decks, CD players, and laser-disc players are generally product-specific as well.

Unified remotes operate at least one other product of the same brand, but often only in a limited way. Receiver remotes, for instance, tend to have lots of buttons for surround-sound speaker balance, but only On/off, Volume, Mute, and channel selection for a TV set.

Universal remotes, usually furnished with high-end TV sets, VCRs, and receivers, operate devices from different manufacturers. Increasingly, they're sold as a stand-alone product. Universal remotes come either preprogrammed with digital codes for dozens of major brand components ("code-entry" remotes) or are of the "learning" variety. To program a learning remote, you place it head-to-head with the remote whose commands you want to mimic, then press the buttons you want it to learn.

TV SETS

▸ Ratings on pages 86 & 94.   ▸ Repair histories start on page 367.

Television sets are the closest thing to a commodity product in the world of major consumer electronics. They're assembled all over the world to well-worked-out specifications. As a result, we've come to expect good performance in mainstream products. Quality tends to falter at the edges of the market. At the low end, you find extremely cheap or off-brand sets. With new products, innovation sometimes strains the limits of technology, as with miniature TVs, or an idea hasn't been fully realized, as happened with the first generation of TV/VCR hybrids.

The modern mainstream TV set, especially those with a screen size of 20 inches or more, is typically designed to be part of an audio-video system. Such "monitor/receivers" generally have sufficient inputs and outputs for connection to other parts of the audio-video system.

Picture tubes have become better and brighter in recent years. More than 20 years ago, Sony introduced its breakthrough Trinitron system, with a grill-like metal screen inside the tube that allows greater brightness while keeping the image sharp. More recently various manufacturers have introduced the Invar tube. The tube takes its name from invar, the nickel-iron alloy used to make the tube's special "shadow mask," a device that helps aim the electron beams at the phosphors of the tube. Ordinary shadow masks bend when they get hot, allowing the electron beams to go out of line and making the color blotchy and distorted. Invar, however, can stand up to the heat of all the electrons needed to create an exceptionally bright picture.

Companies often extol their sets' high

resolution. The current broadcast and cable-TV format allows at best for 330 lines of this "horizontal resolution," a measure of how sharply the tube can display closely spaced vertical lines. Most of the sets we've tested can resolve 320 lines or so, good enough for most TV-watching. If a set lacks a comb filter, however, it may resolve only about 270 lines. S-VHS videotapes and laserdisc players can produce 400 to 425 lines, a resolution a high-resolution set ought to reproduce when fed this signal directly.

To deliver a more detailed picture—one with more "definition"—the set needs more information. The existing broadcast-signal format limits definition. The images on today's best TV screens are very close to the best that's possible from broadcasts.

The future of the medium lies a quantum leap away: HDTV, for high-definition television. It will use an extra wide screen with more scan lines to deliver images rivaling those seen at the movies. The system's audio will provide CD-quality sound.

If you're in the market for a TV set, don't wait for HDTV. HDTV sets aren't expected to turn up on store shelves until 1995 or later, and such sets will be priced high until enough people want them so that they're produced in quantity. A set bought now won't become unwatchable with the coming of HDTV, the Government has promised.

In the meantime, wide-screen models ready for adaptation to HDTV are beginning to show up. These transitional models use IDTV (improved definition television), a technology that's been around for a few years. IDTV paints the lines of the picture consecutively instead of alternately, effectively removing obtrusive scan lines from the image on the screen. Other signal-processing circuitry makes outlines and edges clearer. What results is an extraordinary picture. When our engineers tested a $4000 27-inch *Sony* model in 1989, its picture was the best they'd ever seen on any TV set available to consumers.

The few IDTV sets on the market are costly, priced hundreds of dollars more than conventional sets of similar size (screens of 32 or 35 inches).

TV sound has also improved over the past decade. As stereo telecasts and hi-fi sound tracks on videotapes have become commonplace, the ability to decode multichannel TV stereo (MTS) has also become commonplace.

Good sound starts with good fidelity—the ability to reproduce the wide tonal range now available. Sound from the best sets now compares quite favorably with that of a decent compact component system.

But good tone quality alone cannot provide the sound effects that some movies beg for. Speakers are not far enough apart to hear stereo in all its glory.

The "side-firing" speakers on some models offer a better illusion of stereo, as long as the TV is not enclosed in household cabinetry. More and more TVs have built-in amplifiers to power extra speakers. Some sets offer electronically enhanced stereo, or "psychoacoustically" altered sound, as an alternative to hooking up external speakers. In those sets, electronics manipulate the audio cues reaching listeners' ears to promote the illusion of a wider sound stage. It's most effective in movies with exotic sound effects, but it can make dialogue sound unnatural. The more expensive *RCA* and *Sony* models tested use SRS (sound retrieval system), developed by Hughes Aircraft. Zenith calls its competing system SEq (for spatial equalization), and JVC calls its system Bi-Phonic.

The choices

In the world of television, screen size defines the subtype. There are other, oddball sizes and designs, but these are the main variations you'll find:

Mini. Color TVs with screens of three

inches or so are still in the fancy-gadget stage of evolution. The pictures, provided by liquid-crystal displays (LCDs) rather than by a regular TV's cathode-ray tube, formerly had to be viewed nearly straight on to be pleasing. Also, bright outdoor lighting made the picture all but vanish. New TFT active-matrix LCD TVs are much improved in these areas. The best ones cost as much as a full-sized TV: $300 to $600 at discount.

13-inch sets. TVs of this size aren't regarded as a household's main set, so manufacturers tend to make them plain (though the cabinets may come in "decorator colors"). As a rule, expect monophonic sound, sparse features, a remote control, and a price tag of $200 to $300 at discount.

20-inch sets. With corners squared off, 19-inch sets grew to 20 inches on the diagonal in most brands. (Some 19-inch sets are still available.) Once the standard living-room set, TVs of this size are increasingly regarded as a second set. Don't expect high-end picture refinements such as comb filter and a high performance picture tube. You can expect a very good to acceptable picture, stereo capability, plus extra inputs to accept direct programming from a VCR and laser-disc player. This size offers a wide array of features and sells for $250 to $500 at discount.

27-inch sets. The squared-off successor to the 25- and 26-inch set, this size is usually a feature-laden heavyweight designed to be the primary TV. Such sets cost $500 to $1000 at discount. Sound systems are fancy, remotes typically complex and versatile.

Bigger still. As the concept of the home theater catches on, direct-view sets with screens of 29 to 35 inches or more and projection sets with screens up to 10 feet on the diagonal are showing up on the market. Those with a regular picture tube typically cost $1000 to $2500, but top-of-the-line models can be priced well over $3000 and weigh hundreds of pounds. Projection sets start at less than $1200 and typically cost $1500 to $3000. Projection TVs are now bright enough to be viewed from the sides and in rooms with normal light.

Features to look for

Comb filter. Circuitry that improves resolution and cleans up image outlines.

Remote control. Just about all TV sets these days come with an infrared remote control. The simplest such device may only switch the set on and off, change channels, and adjust volume. More versatile units can mute sound, shut the set off with a timer, block a channel from view, and control a VCR. For details, see the discussion of remote controls on page 64.

Electronic channel scan. Direct tuning, which lets you hop from one station to another, is standard. "Auto program" automatically inserts your active channels in the scan sequence. Most sets let you delete little-watched channels from the scan.

Cable ready. These sets have a coaxial cable jack on the back and can receive cable TV signals (except for scrambled premium movie channels) without using the cable company's decoder box. This feature is now commonplace. Higher-end models offer two cable (antenna) inputs, for basic and for scrambled channels.

MTS stereo. MTS (multichannel TV sound) means the set has a built-in stereo decoder and amplifier to reproduce stereo broadcasts. Some lower-end 20-inch sets from RCA and GE create a pseudo-stereo sound instead of the standard MTS variety.

Inputs/outputs. Audio and video jacks are found mostly on sets 20 inches and larger. For hooking up a hi-fi VCR, laser-disc player, camcorder, or sound system, the TV set needs at least one video and one stereo audio input, and one stereo audio output.

The tests

Our standard panoply of TV tests includes laboratory measurements and viewer judgments. Experienced staffers evaluate key aspects of picture quality: clarity, color fidelity, and contrast.

In addition, we test for a set's ability to handle such factors as less-than-perfect signals. Audio quality is measured much as we do for sound-system components.

Buying advice

With good picture quality the norm these days, the choice of a TV set is likely to hinge on several other factors—features, reliability, price, or perhaps the design of the remote control. If it's possible, try out the remote functions before buying the set, to see how convenient they are to use

Don't put too much stock in comparisons of the picture you see on TV sets displayed in a store. You can't be sure those TV sets are getting a uniform picture signal or that they have been uniformly adjusted.

VCRs

▶ Ratings on page 91. ▶ Repair histories on page 366.

Sales of VCRs have rebounded to the high levels of the 1980s. Those sales are no doubt fueled by enticements from manufacturers such as hi-fi models priced at as low as $300.

Sound isn't the only thing that has been improving on VCRs. On-screen programming is now standard on virtually all models, with some manufacturers going a step further by incorporating innovations like VCR Plus. Fancy features—such as a jog-shuttle control and flying erase head, which are an aid in editing—keep trickling down from the high-end models. Some features that stubbornly remain on top-of-the-line models: improved formats like S-VHS, sophisticated editing capabilities, and digital special effects.

These days, nearly all VCRs use the VHS format. The Beta format has all but vanished; only Sony, its inventor, still sells Beta equipment, primarily to the TV industry, to Betaphiles, and to consumers outside the U.S.

Newer formats such as 8mm and its cousin, Hi8, have come along to accommodate a new breed of small-sized camcorders, and a small number of VCRs that are sold in those formats. Like Beta-format machines, those formats do not accept VHS cassettes.

The choices

VCRs cost anywhere from less than $200 to more than $1500. Certain key features mark off rough price levels.

The basic VCR. While some very low-priced models exist that are just playback machines, called VCPs for video cassette players, the workhorse product among VCRs has been the low-priced ($250 to $300) two-head player with monophonic sound. Two play/record heads are all you need for everyday recording and playback.

Four-head models. An extra pair of heads offers some advantages. Four-head VCRs offer cleaner freeze-frames in the EP speed and may produce a slightly better picture during regular playback. Four-head models have recently overtaken two-head models in sales and may soon be regarded as the basic VCR. Four-head models start at about $300.

Hi-fi. Hi-fi stereo is resoundingly better than the older "linear" stereo technology, which lays sound tracks along the edges of the tape. Hi-fi VCRs record the audio tracks as diagonal stripes across the tape's width under the video portion. The result is near-CD quality sound, with virtually no flutter or noise and excellent reproduction across a wide range of audio frequencies. Hi-fi VCRs use two extra heads on the drum and so are sometimes called "six-head" machines. Discount prices of $350 to $450 are typical.

Super VHS. You'll pay a premium of about $200 for this technical refinement. S-VHS gives a sharper picture than normal VHS. S-VHS also stands up better if you're making multiple tape-to-tape copies. To get the most from the S-VHS format, you need a source of S-VHS pictures, such as an S-VHS camcorder. The VCR must also be connected to a high-resolution TV set—preferably a model equipped with an S-Video jack.

This format is partially compatible with regular VHS—an S-VHS machine can tape and play in VHS mode, but an S-VHS tape can't be played in a regular VHS machine (although more and more conventional VHS machines offer "Quasi-S-VHS" playback capability to allow this). To record in S-VHS, you need special S-VHS tapes; the player automatically senses which type of tape and which mode to tape in.

S-VHS models generally cost $600 to $1300 at discount.

Features to look for

Year by year, fancy features migrate down from higher-priced models to lower-priced ones.

Remote control. Even low-end models usually come with a remote. For more information, see "What to look for in a remote control" on page 64.

HQ. HQ (for "high quality") refers to small technical refinements that reduce some of the video noise and other picture defects that a VCR can introduce into a recording. Virtually every VHS VCR is designated HQ.

Programming. On-screen programming is almost universal. The VCR shows a menu on the TV screen that walks you through the process of choosing times and dates for programs you want to record, up to several days or weeks in advance.

Even though on-screen programming is a great improvement over previous methods it's still too hard for many people. So manufacturers keep devising new, easier ways to program. VCR Plus, widely sold for $60, now also comes incorporated in many VCRs. It uses the special three- to seven-digit program code that appears in the TV listings of many newspapers and magazines to enter the time and channel information automatically. Matsushita has come up with a separate remote just for programming, available as the Program Director on most *Panasonic* models and, as the Pro-Commander, for *Quasar* models. You enter each piece of basic information—date, start time, stop time, and channel—by turning a set of dials one by one until all the correct numbers appear on the device's LCD display and send the information to the VCR with the Transmit button.

Camcorder jack. All VCRs let a camcorder of any format be plugged in. More and more models have the jack on the front of the VCR, where it's easy to reach.

Picture tricks. They include such features as multiple-speed slow-motion and fast-motion, frame advance, freeze frame, and picture-in-picture capabilities. On the whole, we'd say that they're flashy gimmicks rather than truly useful additions.

Taping features. One-touch recording (OTR) simplifies taping. A tape-time-remaining indicator can save the frustration of running out of tape five minutes before the end of the movie. Index search lets you mark the tape and then move rapidly to the next mark. Real-time search or "go to" lets you enter the length of the program

HOW TO CHOOSE THE RIGHT VIDEOTAPE

It's not difficult look for major brands and buy by price. Our tests show very little difference among major brands. Stock up whenever videotape is on sale. That may be fairly often, since manufacturers have shifted their focus from product innovation to packaging and promotion.

One way the companies are trying to sell more tape is by promoting special tape for special uses ("everyday," "special recording applications," and so forth). Our tests have shown little or no difference between the regular grade and the high-grade tapes. Nor is there any reason to pay extra for special "hi-fi" tape-any tape can record high-quality sound in a VCR that records in the VHS hi-fi format. (Our tests do show some small differences among brands in recording linear stereo tracks.)

Be wary of off-brand tapes. Even those that display legitimate VHS or 8mm logos, supposed assurance that manufacturing standards have been satisfied, can be substandard. It's ironic that at a time when the differences between major brands of videotape have all but disappeared, the assurances of quality implied by the brand name itself have become more important.

---

you want to skip in minutes and then speeds through that length of tape. A Skip button advances the tape in 30-second increments.

Tape-editing functions. Of interest mainly to those who make home videos, these include: flying erase heads, for glitch-free assemble edits; an Edit switch that boosts the signal when dubbing to improve the quality of second-generation tapes; a synchro-edit jack to coordinate a camcorder (of any format) or second VCR used as a source; advanced editing features such as insert editing; a jog-shuttle control, which helps locate a tape segment by running the tape backward or forward at continuously variable speeds; audio and video dubbing abilities; and a character generator for adding written titles or captions.

The tests

Our engineers check performance at both SP (standard play) and EP (extended play) speeds. We make tapes on each machine, then play them back on laboratory monitors. A panel of staffers judges them for blurriness, graininess, streaking, and unnatural-looking edges to images.

In the laboratory, CU engineers measure the same tuner factors we check in TV sets—sensitivity to weak signals and selectivity for blocking out adjacent signals. Our audio tests measure the same factors we check on tape decks—flutter, signal-to-noise ratio, and frequency response. And of course, we evaluate how easy a VCR is to use.

Buying advice

The current VCR market is replete with good performers. A two-head VCR or a basic four-head model is all you need if you're primarily interested in taping TV programs for viewing later.

If you want to take advantage of movies with a stereo sound track or hook the VCR into your stereo system as part of a home theater, consider a hi-fi VHS model.

Unfortunately, there's no standardization of synchro-editing features. If you're interested in editing lots of tapes, check that the VCR and camcorder have compatible synchronization provisions.

Laser-Disc Players

Though they've never sold as well as VCRs, laser-disc players enjoy several potential advantages. As movie-playing machines, they can run rings around conventional VHS decks. Their picture quality from the discs can be much higher, and sound quality is excellent. A player can rapidly skip to any desired portion of a program and, unlike tapes, discs don't wear with repeated use. Alas, disc players lack a VCR's versatility: You can't record on a disc (at least not yet), and the rental-movie market offers only limited disc selections. Mail-order clubs and retailers sell regular movies on disc for $20 to $30 apiece; special editions may cost $100 or more.

The choices

To ease consumers' qualms about the hodgepodge of disc formats that have arisen, manufacturers have made most of the players compatible with all formats (including CAV, CLV, and CD-V). They've also given them the ability to play audio compact discs, hence the term "combi player." List prices start at about $500 and range upward to more than $1000.

Features to look for

CD changer. Available on some upscale models, this lets you play several CDs (but not laser discs) without pause.

Double-sided play. This is a major convenience, but it's a pricey one. It plays both sides of a laser disc without having to flip the disc over by hand. It comes with machines selling for several hundred dollars more than a basic model.

Other features. There are many digital frills, including special video effects, esoteric means for preselecting tracks, and various methods for editing from disc to tape.

Buying advice

Picture quality is apt to be good with any model, so choose features first, then shop for the best price.

Camcorders

▸ Ratings on page 99.

Every year, camcorders offer better and better value, as innovations cascade from top-of-the-line products. List prices begin at about $700 and go up to more than $2500. New top-of-the-line features include a color LCD viewfinder and a "wide-screen" mode.

Manufacturers' claims notwithstanding, picture quality falls off in very dim light. Companies make much ado of "lux" numbers, but there is little agreement on how the specification is measured, making such "ratings" meaningless.

Fewer companies make camcorders than all the brand names might lead you to think. Sony also makes *Ricoh, Nikon,* and *Yashica* models, for instance; Sanyo Fisher makes *Olympus* and *Sunpak*; JVC, some *Minolta* models; and Matsushita, *Panasonic, Quasar,* and *Magnavox.*

The choices

Buying a camcorder means making a commitment to a particular format, either VHS, VHS-C (a compact form of VHS), or

72 CAMCORDERS

8mm, another compact format. Each of those also comes in a "high band" version that provides better horizontal resolution: S-VHS, S-VHS-C, and Hi8. Except for the improved resolution of high-band models, none of the formats is inherently superior in the pictures it takes. The major differences: sound quality, the bulk of the camera, and ease of playback.

Full-sized VHS. This was the old standard, now fading. Models of this type are heavy and bulky. The only advantage to the size: Shoulder mounting makes for slightly steadier shooting. Standard VHS cassettes are widely available; T-120 (two-hour) tapes cost about $3 each. The camcorder can double as a VHS VCR to play rented movies. Full-sized VHS is the bargain format now, with retail prices of $700 or less on discontinued models.

8mm. Small, light, easy to tote, 8mm is the hot format. Cassettes run up to two hours. Sound quality is better than all except hi-fi models in the other formats. Cassettes cost about $5. For playback, it's a simple matter to connect a cable from the camcorder to your TV or VCR. You can also connect the camcorder to your VCR to make copies or edit tapes in your VCR's tape format; 8mm VCRs are available. List prices range from about $700 to $2000 or more.

VHS-C. JVC introduced this compact version of VHS. Its cassettes are playable in a VHS VCR, directly on a few VCR models or with an adapter (supplied with the camcorder) that will work with any VHS VCR. Cassettes hold just 30 minutes at fast speed, 90 minutes at slow speed, and cost $6 apiece; tapes with longer running times are reportedly on the way. List prices start at $900.

Features to look for

Standard features include: a motorized zoom lens that lets you make closeups of subjects within an inch of the lens; automatic exposure and sound-level controls; and a flying erase head that helps deliver clean scene changes even if you rerecord something.

Autofocus. Also standard. It keeps the image sharp as the subject or the camera moves about. In our tests, both types worked well most of the time, but neither was infallible.

Automatic white balance. This circuitry keeps colors normal under different lighting conditions.

Electronic image stabilization. High-end models have this feature, which helps iron the jitters out of hand-held shots by digitally magnifying the center portion of the scene. Too much camera movement, though, soon defeats the EIS. A tripod is still the best tool for steady shots (see the report on tripods on page 114).

Digital gain-up. A fairly new feature, it helps create passable pictures in dim light. It works by slowing the shutter speed. The downside: Moving subjects or fast panning leave a blur.

Sound. The 8mm format has audio capabilities inherently superior to all except hi-fi VHS and VHS-C models. The built-in mike in most camcorders is better suited for capturing speech than music.

Remote control. More and more commonplace, a remote makes it easier to use the camcorder for playback and editing. It also works as an alternative to a self-timer. Many 8mm camcorders come with one, which is especially handy when using the camcorder to play back tapes because tapes made in those models can't be played back directly in a VHS VCR.

Special picture effects. Simple effects, such as fade in and fade out and a range of shutter speeds, are standard. Effects found on some middle-of-the-line models and up include time lapse, freeze frame, and other digital effects.

Title generator. Some models permit superimposing printed titles and captions created with a built-in character generator. Others provide a means to photograph and superimpose titles from art work or signs. Most let you select a color for the title.

Connections. Camcorders usually come with all the cables and connectors needed to play back tapes through a TV set or copy them on a VCR. Most can record from those sources as well.

Date/time labeling. This lets you superimpose the date, the time, or both by pressing a button.

The tests

We shoot a series of test subjects under a variety of lighting conditions and play the tapes for a panel of trained viewers to judge clarity, color accuracy, and low-light performance. Our audio tests, for frequency response and flutter, are done much as we test tape decks.

Buying advice

VHS and VHS-C are slightly more convenient for playback of tapes, but that's about their only advantage. Compared with VHS, 8mm and VHS-C cameras are much easier to lug around and the pictures are about as good. With any type, you'll need a tripod for professional results. For fast panning, a tripod-mounted compact is more manageable than a tripod-mounted VHS model because the compact's viewfinder is at the rear.

RECEIVERS

▸ Ratings on page 89.

The receiver, heart of the audio system, has lately become the heart of the audio/video system as well. For a product that remained essentially unchanged for years, that's a big shift in capability.

In addition to acting as a switching center, a receiver amplifies audio signals from other components and its radio tuner. Receivers, particularly those without mechanical switches and knobs, use few moving parts and tend to last a long time. Our tests have shown that, regardless of price, the amplifier portion almost always performs very well. Where brands differ is in amplifier power output, in FM radio performance, and in such conveniences as input jacks for plugging in ancillary equipment.

The choices

The premium charged for video capability depends on the brand. Some companies, such as Pioneer, Sony, and JVC, have switched virtually their entire lines over to audio/video receivers. Other companies retain audio-only receivers at the low end of their lines. Some prestige brands offer nothing but audio receivers, but even these are starting to recognize video functions as more than a frill.

List prices range from $150 to more than $1500, with many models clustering around $400 to $500. The majority of brands are sharply discounted, however. By spending more, you don't necessarily get better sound. You get:

Power. Low-end receivers may produce only 35 to 45 watts per channel of amplifier power, while higher-end models crank out 100 watts or more and come with a separate amplifier to drive the surround-sound speakers that are an essential part of a home theater.

How much you need depends on your speakers, the size of the room, and the type of music you play. The need for extra power is easily and often exaggerated. In most applications, 50 watts per channel is ample. Receivers in the 100-watt range are necessary only if you're driving multiple pairs of loudspeakers at loud volumes in large spaces or are using speakers that are particularly inefficient.

Audio "ambience." These effects simulate the acoustics of a stadium or concert hall and are now common on middle-of-the-line receivers. Mid-priced models now often come with Dolby Surround (special circuitry that deciphers sound effects encoded on many movie videos).

Models with Dolby Pro Logic (which allows a fifth speaker to carry sound from the direction of the TV screen) are dropping in price. Some of the cheapest Dolby Pro models lack an amplifier to power the fifth speaker. A recent innovation on many Pro Logic receivers is Dolby 3 Stereo, a feature that lets you experience all five channels in the surround mode without the rear ambience loudspeakers. Sounds that would normally emanate from the rear speakers are rerouted to the front three speakers and dispersed at slightly lower volume than the sounds for the other channels. We think rear speakers provide a much more dramatic effect.

Audio/video switching. An A/V receiver is essentially a control center to select the component you want to hear from—either a video source such as a TV set, VCR, or laser-disc player, or an audio source such as a CD, cassette tape, or radio. A remote control to handle most functions comes with all but the cheapest receivers these days.

HOW MUCH POWER DO YOU NEED?

These days, even inexpensive receivers have plenty of power. But if you want a close idea of how much amplifying power your system actually needs, here's now to figure it:

Determine the volume and "liveness" of your listening room. A space with hard floors, scatter rugs, and plain wood furniture will be acoustically live. One with thick wall-to-wall carpet, heavy curtains, and upholstered furniture will be relatively dead. Locate the room size and type on the chart below and note the multiplier. That figure, multiplied by a speaker's minimum power requirement, as noted in our speaker Ratings, will give you the watts-per-channel needed.

Let's say you have a 4000-cubic-foot room with average acoustics and want to use speakers that require 12 watts of power. The multiplier from the chart, 1.5, times 12 equals 18. At a minimum, you would need an amplifier with 18 watts of power per channel to drive those speakers at moderately high volume. To be safe, double that figure and look for a receiver that produces 35 watts or so. To do justice to compact discs or especially demanding music, increase that figure to about 50 watts.

POWER MULTIPLIERS

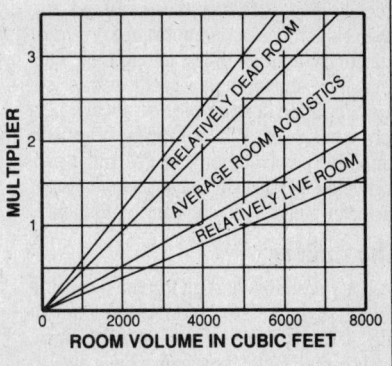

Elaborate controls. Mass-market receivers tend to accrete knobs, dials, levers, and lights as you move up the product line. More controls do more, but they make the product more complicated. Prestige brands, on the other hand, make a virtue of simplicity—no flashy display, often no remote control, limited switching and dubbing capability, even on high-priced models.

Features to look for

Some receiver features—a pulsing bar graph of the sound "profile," say—may do more for a product's image and marketability than for its usefulness. Here are features we find most useful:

Graphic equalizer. You find this fancy tone control for "contouring" the sound starting with middle-of-the-line models. Equalizers with less than seven adjustment levers, or bands, as they are called, don't accomplish much more than regular bass and treble controls. A few high-end models now offer digital signal processing.

Quartz-locked digital tuning. This has replaced the analog dial tuner on all but a few lowest-priced models. Such tuners typically have several rows of station presets, some with fairly powerful programming or classification capabilities. Manual tuning is generally accomplished with an Up/Down Seek button that searches for the next listenable station along the dial. Handiest are tuners that step in 200-kilohertz increments, the distance between FM channels in the U.S., but tuners that step in 100- or even 50-kHz increments are common. When you tune past either end of the band, wraparound tuning jumps automatically to the opposite end.

Switched outlets. They let you plug other components into the receiver so you can shut off the whole system when you turn off the receiver.

Tone-control bypass. It's useful for temporarily defeating tone settings so you can listen to a recording in its pristine form.

Loudness switch. It boosts the bass when the volume is down to compensate for the human ear's insensitivity to bass at low volume.

Mute switch. It reduces volume without changing the volume-control setting.

The tests

Our evaluation includes a judgment of convenience, based largely on the control layout, and a standard battery of laboratory tests, chiefly of the FM tuner. A stellar tuner reproduces sound that's free of residual background noise and distortion. Sensitive enough to pull in weak signals, it also resists interference from electrical sources, aircraft, and other radio signals.

Buying advice

If you want to power only a modest system, a low-end receiver, rated at 50 watts per channel or less, should be fine. Many list at less than $300.

Although some low-priced models can handle a TV/VCR/stereo setup without a problem, you'll probably have to buy higher in the line if you want the receiver to be the heart of a home theater. Receivers in the $350-to-$450 range typically come with Dolby Pro Logic and enough jacks to accommodate a complicated system and enough power to run more than one set of speakers.

Before buying any receiver, make sure it matches your other components. See "How much power do you need," opposite.

LOUDSPEAKERS

▸ Ratings on page 106.

Good sound depends more on the loudspeakers than on any other component, so money invested in speakers can buy more performance than money spent elsewhere. In setting up a system, speakers are the last place to economize.

Speakers in our tests tend to differ most in their ability to handle the bass. But that doesn't mean the models we tested all sound the same—differences elsewhere in the audio spectrum give each model its own distinctive sound. That's where your own taste comes into play. Additionally, what you hear is affected by the size and furnishings of the listening room, by speakers' placement, and even by type of music.

The choices

Classic loudspeaker configuration has not changed much in 30 years: a rigid box containing a large bass speaker, the woofer, and a much smaller treble speaker, the tweeter. There may also be a third speaker, the mid-range, that handles middle tones between the highs and lows. While most speakers direct all the sound out the front, others are designed to radiate some sound upward or to the rear, bouncing sound waves off a nearby wall.

To make a big, loud bass, a speaker needs a big woofer. Speaker manufacturers have long tried to design around that fact of physics, with some success. Some miniature speakers, for instance, can deliver more bass than their size would imply, though at the expense of volume. A newly popular type of speaker, the three-piece "subwoofer/satellite" system, separates the tweeter and mid-range speakers from the bass subwoofer. The tweeter and the mid-range speakers, which supply much of the stereo effect, are small and fit unobtrusively amongst furnishings, while the large bass section can be concealed behind a sofa or in a corner behind the TV set.

List prices for speakers run from $100 or so a pair to $1000 and up, with low-priced models clustered around $300 and mid-priced models around $500 per pair. What more money primarily buys, at every size level, is a deeper reach into the bass range. Here are the main choices:

Miniature speakers. Most are smaller than a shoebox and list for $200 to $400 a pair. Most are seriously deficient in reproducing bass. A subclass of miniature speakers is the "powered" speaker, which has its own built-in amplifier.

"Ambience" speakers. Small and relatively inexpensive (typically less than $200 per pair), these speakers are suitable for use as the adjunct speakers in a Dolby Surround system. Many are sold singly, to serve as the center-channel speaker in a Dolby Pro Logic setup. Note that "ambience" speakers don't need much bass capacity, as that chore is relegated to the main speaker pair.

Bookshelf speakers. They can fit on a normal bookshelf sideways, at the expense of about 1½ feet of books. Bookshelf speakers typically list for $200 to $550 per pair. They're appropriate for undemanding listening in medium-sized rooms or as the second pair of speakers in a surround-sound system.

Medium-sized speakers. Standing about two feet high and a foot wide and deep, they're the speakers of choice for playing at loud volume in a medium-sized room. They can fill even a large room with fairly loud sound. When speakers reach this size, the woofer can be big enough to push the large volumes of air needed to reproduce a full, rich, loud bass sound. Figure on spending $250 or more for a decent pair.

Large speakers. Speakers that occupy three or more cubic feet of space may cost from $700 to thousands of dollars. They're necessary for filling a very large room, but overkill in a smaller setting. In this size one also finds audiophile equipment, such as "electrostatic speakers," in which tall, thin plastic diaphragms replace speaker cones.

The tests

Speaker performance is measured by laboratory instruments in an echo-free chamber and in a 14-by-23-foot carpeted, furnished room. For main speakers, we measure accuracy from a frequency of about 30 Hertz in the bass to about 16,000 Hz in the treble and rate it on a 100-point scale. For ambience speakers we don't test them at frequencies below 100 Hz.

Tweaking a receiver's tone controls can improve a speaker's accuracy and also help compensate for a room's acoustical drawbacks. Most listeners find it difficult to pick the more accurate of two models if the spread in our scores is eight points or less.

We also measure the minimum power the receiver must supply to a speaker to produce fairly loud sound in a medium-sized room.

Buying advice

It's important to audition loudspeakers yourself. In an audio store's listening room, try to duplicate the speaker position you'll use at home. Compare only two pairs of speakers at a time; stay with the pair you prefer and judge it against the next. Take an LP or CD whose music you know well, one that gives both bass sounds and treble a workout.

It's also important to get return privileges in case the speakers don't sound satisfactory at home. Once you have a model in mind, be sure your receiver will be able to supply enough power to the speakers and that speaker impedances are not too low for the amplifier to handle (see "How much power do you need?" on page 74).

STEREO HEADPHONES

Headphones have come a long way in recent years. Some now rival the acoustic accuracy of high-quality loudspeakers. Models of that sort use a magnet-and-coil dynamic driver that functions essentially like a miniature loudspeaker. Headphones suitable for use with home sound systems typically come with price tags in the $50 to $150 range. The plastic and foam-rubber models designed for use with walkabout stereos are priced at $10 and up.

The choices

Headphones can sit on or around the ears. The best design for you may depend on the shape and size of your ears. Headphones also differ in how much of an acoustic cocoon they provide. Here are the types:

Closed-seal. These models cut out much of the surrounding sound, while letting out little of the sound that might disturb others.

Semi-open. Models of this design give you a reasonable chance of hearing the phone ring or the baby cry.

Open-seal. These models keep you in touch with your surroundings, but they leak a fair amount of sound.

Headphones also differ in their cord arrangements. The traditional Y-shaped cord, attached to both earpieces, makes the headphones a trifle hard to put on. Single-cord models are more convenient. Cords may be coiled or straight.

A few models do away with the cord, relying on infrared light to transmit the sound signal. Unfortunately, the infrared system may introduce background noise and interference. You also lose sound anytime something opaque comes between the headphones and the stereo.

The tests

We measure sound accuracy on an acoustic mannequin known as Kemar (for Knowles Electronics Manikin for Acoustic Research). We install precision microphones wired to computer-controlled test equipment in place of Kemar's eardrums. The microphones hear what you would hear, and the computer tells us how close the sound comes to the ideal. The main inaccuracy, we've found, is an exaggerated mid-bass. To assess overall bass capability, we measure mid-bass distortion at moderate and high volume, noting the frequency at which bass volume drops by half.

To assess comfort during headphone use, we ask a panel of staffers to report on what the various headphones are like to wear.

Buying advice

Be sure to check that the headphones are compatible with the impedances of your components. Receivers and CD players are usually no problem, but some cassette decks require high-impedance headphones. Equipment such as walkabout stereos may need high-sensitivity headphones to achieve satisfactory loudness.

With any headphones, users may not realize how loud the music has become. If sounds seem muffled and words are hard to distinguish after you've taken headphones off, you may have suffered temporary hearing loss. When those symptoms progress to a tickling sensation or ringing in your ears, there's a danger that the hearing loss could become permanent.

WALKABOUT STEREO PLAYERS

A bit more than a decade into their existence, walkabout stereos are a familiar part of the American audio landscape. Unlike the boom box, that other teen-age listening device, the walkabout lets the listener enjoy the music without inflicting it on everyone else within earshot.

Instead of speakers, walkabouts—a.k.a. personal portables, pocket-sized tape players or, after the market-leading brand-name, *Walkmans*—come with headphones. The typical walkabout has a cassette player and an AM/FM radio tuner, but you can buy walkabouts that have just one or the other. If you're willing to spend about $300, you can even get a walkabout that plays CDs. There's also a Sony DAT walkabout for the audiophile who must have the ultimate in on-the-go digital sonic purity—and who doesn't mind spending about $850 to get it.

The headphone cable on a walkabout acts as the FM antenna, so when you move, the signal strength reaching the antenna varies considerably. If you use the radio where stations are distant and signals weak, reception may be difficult to get, especially if you use the walkabout while jogging.

Sony invented the walkabout and remains the major brand. Others in the market: Sanyo, Panasonic, Emerson, and Aiwa.

The choices

The name of the game in walkabouts is smallness; manufacturers have managed to cram decent sound and performance into machines little bigger than a couple of tape cassettes.

Radio/tape players. Unless you confine your listening to either tapes or radio, you'll want a walkabout that offers both functions. Those models average $50 or so, though feature-laden models run to $200 and beyond.

Tape players. The average cassette-only model costs about $25, and it's typically smaller and lighter than the units with radio tuners—a consideration if you plan to hook the player on your waist while jogging. (The bounce of jogging causes noticeable flutter in these machines, though the act of running is likely to make critical listening impossible anyway.)

Radios. Most walkabouts with just a radio tuner are even cheaper (typically, less than $20) and lighter (no tape-drive mechanism).

Features to look for

The typical radio/tape player has the basics you need to play a cassette (Play, Stop, Fast Forward, and Rewind) or dial in a station (AM/FM band, Tuning). Features beyond the basics include:

Autoreverse. If you're jogging and don't want to fumble with tape controls, it's handy to have the player automatically switch to the other side of the cassette.

Digital tuning. The precision of Digital tuning does away with the often frustrating attempt to dial in a station with the traditional thumb wheel. The selected radio station is displayed on a small LCD screen.

Preset tuning. Available on models with digital tuning, this lets you program up to 16 of your favorite stations.

Bass booster. Sold under names like "Megabass," this feature puts more oomph in the low range.

Water resistance. "Sports" models offer some protection from rain and sweat. Some models also claim moderate impact resistance.

Recording. Few models can record, but for people who want to tape lectures or interviews, a walkabout with a built-in microphone is a good choice.

Noise suppression. In our tests, units with Dolby B had significantly less tape hiss than those without.

Other features. Models with automatic stop turn themselves off automatically after rewinding, to save the battery. On some models, unplugging the headphone stops the tape. A Hold button keeps you from accidentally turning the unit on or changing a station. Scan and Seek tuning make it easier to find radio stations. And dual headphone jacks let a friend listen in. Some models have remotes.

The tests

A cassette-playing walkabout is, at its heart, a tape deck, so we test for such features as tape noise, flutter, and speed accuracy. We also check frequency response through the supplied headphones and directly at the headphone jack, to see how well the walkabouts would function when hooked up to a stereo system.

For units with a radio, we check sensitivity—the ability to pull in a weak radio signal—for both AM and FM bands; selectivity—how well the tuner rejects interference from stations close on the dial; and tuning ease.

We measure battery life for both tape and radio operation; you get a lot more out of a battery if you listen to the radio than play tapes.

Buying advice

Most walkabouts produce surprisingly good sound, roughly equivalent to what you would hear with a low-priced home audio system. When you pay more than about $50, you get such convenience and performance features as digital tuning with station-presetting capability, Dolby noise suppression, and a bass booster. Higher-priced units also tend to be more compact.

Don't buy more than you need. If radio reception where you live is weak, you may be better off with a unit that only plays tape. Or if you never listen to tapes, a radio-only model can save both money and considerable weight.

"Sports" models are typically bulkier than other walkabouts, but their cases provide some protection against water and occasional bumps and jolts.

COMPACT-DISC PLAYERS

▸ Ratings on page 97.   ▸ Repair histories on page 369.

Virtually every CD player we have tested is capable of reproducing superb hi-fi sound. All the traditional indicators of quality sound—wide dynamic range, accurate ("flat") frequency response, and freedom from noise and distortion—can be taken for granted. The minor differences we've noted in sound-reproduction capabilities just wouldn't be apparent except to a laboratory instrument or an expert listener. Performance differences are confined to how well the players overcome adverse conditions such as being bumped or playing a damaged disc.

The choices

The world of CD players can be divided into three main parts:

Table-model components. These are the biggest-selling type. They come as single-disc models and multiple-disc changers. Prices start at less than $100 for a low-end single-disc player, though most sell for between $100 and $300.

One changer design uses what's called a magazine, a slide-in box the size of a small, fat paperback book. Magazines typically hold six discs, but some models take more.

The alternative changer design is a carousel, holding five or six discs. That design has the advantage of being somewhat easier to load. Some carousels use a slide-out drawer, while others load from the top. Top-loading models cannot be sandwiched into a stack of other stereo components.

Portable players. Some are scarcely bigger than the disc itself, others are part of an overgrown boom box. Portable models list from about $150 for a small, simple unit to more than $800 for a fancy "system." Basic models may have only rudimentary controls. More elaborate versions come with features such as a rechargeable battery pack, a built-in radio tuner, cassette deck, or a panoply of controls similar to what you find on a fancy table model. Many boom-box systems have detachable speakers with a bass-boost feature. Portables can easily be hooked into a sound system.

Features to look for

The CD world is rife with jargon referring to technical specifications, particularly those connected with the conversion of digital information to analog sound waves: "oversampling," "dual digital/analog converters," "bit stream" technology, triple laser beams, and so forth. None of that stuff is apt to make a major difference you can consistently hear, our tests have shown.

The extras on a CD player don't always go hand-in-hand with price. Less expensive models may be just as generously endowed with features as more expensive ones.

Standard on all models are features that

let you play, pause, stop, select a track, or program selected tracks to play in the order you choose. (Changers let you skip from one disc to another.)

Also typical is a display that indicates which track is being played and the elapsed playing time and a remote control. Common options, even on basic models:

Shuffle play. This mixes the playing order into a random sequence. Look for non-repeat shuffle.

Numeric keypad. It lets you program by punching in track numbers directly rather than fussing with Up/down buttons. It's common on remotes, less so on consoles.

Calendar display. It starts off by showing the number of each track on the disc; as the disc plays, the track numbers disappear one by one.

On/off pause. It's handier than having to hit Play to resume playing.

Fade control. This makes the music fade out slowly, then stop.

Programming aids. Programming for a CD player is simply a matter of instructing the unit to play tracks in a particular order. Some players can even remember your programs. This feature, called favorite—track selection or custom file, involves the player's reading a code on each disc and filing your program for that disc under the code for later reference.

Taping aids. Running total adds up track time as you're programming the disc so you can tell how many tracks will fit on the tape you're using. A calendar display on the console is also handy for copying. It reminds you of the tracks you've already programmed. Taping is easiest with such special features as auto-edit. When you punch in the recording time of one side of a tape, the CD player suggests a track order to fit the time. With a player that allows synchronized recording, you don't even have to be present during the taping. You merely connect a cable from the player to a deck of the same brand that has auto-reverse. When the deck is ready to record on the second side, it sends a signal to the CD player, and the taping continues.

The tests

In addition to making the usual sound checks, we see how well the players can cope with adversity: bumps and purposely defective discs. We also measure how fast the players can jump from track to track.

Buying advice

Take good audio performance for granted and let price and features be your guide. Changer models now cost just slightly more than single-play units and offer the convenience of hours of uninterrupted play. We prefer the carousel, since it's easier to load than the magazine type.

If uninterrupted playing isn't crucial, consider a single-play model. It's likely to offer more features than a comparably priced changer.

CASSETTE DECKS

Ratings on page 102.

The familiar cassette tape was originally developed for recording voices rather than as a medium for reproducing high-fidelity music, so it was born with a limited ability to capture the whole audible spectrum and burdened with a high level of background hiss. It has taken considerable technical cleverness to overcome those impediments. Now, the best of the modern cassette decks are able to reproduce music that's pleasing

82 CASSETTE DECKS

to any but the most critical listener.

Tape cassettes still far outsell compact discs, an inherently superior medium, for obvious reasons. Cassettes—cheap, portable, and widely available—allow you to make your own recordings. But conventional tape has to compete against new digital technologies that play back and record:

■ Digital audio tape (DAT) cassettes have had a toehold in the U.S. for a couple of years. DAT delivers virtually the same fine high-fidelity sound as a compact disc. But the tiny DAT cassettes aren't compatible with conventional cassettes, so a DAT owner is faced with the prospect of building a new tape library of digital cassettes. DAT decks also incorporate copy-protection circuits that allow users to make perfect copies of recordings, but prevent copying those copies.

■ Digital compact cassette decks (DCC), a new medium that will begin to appear in stores late this year, go DAT one better in that they can play conventional cassettes. For recording (on digital tape), DCC relies on a data-compression process that leaves out the parts of a musical program that are masked by other sounds. In essence, it records only what you're apt to hear and ignores inaudible sonic information. Like DAT, DCC decks will have copy-protection circuitry.

■ The Mini Disc, or MD, developed by Sony, promises to be the first consumer-priced compact disc-style medium that can record as well as play. Using data-compression technology similar to that used on digital compact cassettes, the Mini Disc is a 2½-inch disc said to play up to 74 minutes.

Promising as these new technologies seem, they won't send cassette tape the way of the LP record overnight. If you already have an extensive collection of tapes, it makes sense to stay with a conventional tape deck. If you choose the right deck, you won't sacrifice much in the way of performance. Some of the decks we've recently tested can deliver sound that approaches the quality of digital tape or CD.

The choices

Component tape decks list from $150 or so to well over $1000. But since discounts are common, an outlay between $200 and $500 should be sufficient to get you a deck that performs well. Spend less, and you'll most likely sacrifice performance. Spend more, and you'll get more features, which may or may not improve performance significantly.

Among component decks, there are two principal types:

Single-deck machines. They're generally regarded as "serious" machines, geared to the audio-buff market. We've found that the single-tape drive is often a cut above the pair of drives in a comparably priced dual-deck machine.

Dual-deck machines. Also called "dubbing" decks, they lend themselves to making copies of tapes and to playing two cassettes in sequence. For that convenience, you usually have to give up something in performance. In past tests, we've found they tended to suffer more from flutter than single-deck models.

Finally, one can hook up some walkabout tape players to a stereo system. Their basic playing performance can be very acceptable, although the small controls may not be very convenient.

Features to look for

Here are the most useful features:

Adjustable bias control. Modern tape coatings have the potential to deliver a wider dynamic range than the standard ferric oxide (Type I) tape. By increasing the "bias" (an ultrasonic signal the deck uses to reduce distortion), many decks can handle chromium dioxide (Type II) and metal

HOW TO CHOOSE THE RIGHT AUDIO TAPE

Blank tapes differ in several ways:

Type. This refers to the type of coating used. Type I tapes, the cheapest, have a ferric-oxide coating. They're suitable for basic recording chores, especially if the material is undemanding, like background music, or playback conditions less than superb, as in a car. Type II tapes, with an improved ferric-oxide coating, are also called "high bias" tapes. They're good for more demanding recordings, such as making high-quality recordings from LPs or copying CDs for an autosound system. Type IV tapes, or "metal" tapes (their iron coating is in metallic form), have the widest dynamic range, our tests have shown. The most costly type, they should be reserved for recording live music and copying compact discs. Note that metal tape may not be recordable on some decks that can play it back.

Grade. Manufacturers additionally split their offerings into various grades—"HD-M," "Ux-Pro," "DX1," and so forth. Coatings, and thus performance, do vary, according to our tests, though perhaps not as much as manufacturers would like consumers to think.

Time. The total play time is indicated by the "C" number—C-60, C-90, and so forth. A C-90 tape plays 45 minutes on a side. Relatively new: 100-minute tapes meant for taping two CDs.

(Type IV) tape. If a deck has automatic tape-type switches, it is able to sense the type of tape loaded and switches bias accordingly. To fine-tune the bias setting, some decks have a manual control you set by ear. Some decks boast the convenience of an auto-bias control that fine tunes the bias for you, which obviates the need for a lot of fiddling.

Noise-suppression circuits. Numerous techniques have been employed to mute tape hiss, including reformulating the tape itself. Most recorders lean heavily on electrical signal processing to reduce noise. Standard are Dolby B and Dolby C; virtually all prerecorded cassettes use Dolby B. Better still, though now available only on mid- to high-priced models, is HX Pro, which expands the treble range just about wide enough to capture the dynamic range of a CD, and the new Dolby S, which records at near-digital quality. Another system, *dbx*, has all but disappeared.

Autoreverse reverses the tape automatically when it reaches the end, so you can hear both sides without having to flip the tape. Dual decks often go that one better. Many models can play both sides of two tapes in sequence, a feature called relay play.

Music search locates a selection by looking for the silent gap between selections.

Tape scan helps locate a desired selection on a tape. It moves from song to song, playing the first few seconds of each.

Remote control. Remote controls for tape decks are probably less useful than for other components, if only because you do have to approach the machine anyway to insert or remove a cassette. The typical tape-deck remote is a small gadget with tiny buttons.

Recording-level meters. These days, meters are lighted bar graphs rather than swinging needles. If you do a lot of recording, look for a deck with 12 or so segments on its recording-level meter. They make it easier to establish the peak level of the music you are recording and to set the appropriate level.

Three heads. A deck with three heads

doesn't necessarily produce better recordings than one with two heads, but is more convenient to use for recording. The third head makes it possible to monitor the recording as it is being made. On machines with a bias adjustment, the third head makes it easier to fine-tune the bias setting.

Record mute. This feature inserts a silence between selections when you record continuously, say from a CD or an LP. The silences act as signposts for the music search and scan features.

Quick reverse. This senses the leader tape at the end of a cassette, and immediately switches the tape's direction.

Dubbing. Dual decks dub (copy) tapes with the press of a button. Many decks have an edit dub feature that allows you to pause the recording deck while you change tapes or fiddle with the playback deck. A high-speed dubbing feature cuts recording time in half, but also degrades the music somewhat.

CD synchro. This feature helps coordinate recording from a CD. It requires using a same-brand CD player. Pushing a Synchro button cues up the deck and starts recording the instant the music begins.

The tests

We check decks for speed accuracy and flutter, which can make music sound wavery or watery. We measure frequency response—how smoothly a deck responds to sounds. We also measure dynamic range—the span between the loudest and the softest sound a unit accurately records.

Buying advice

If you plan to make a lot of tapes, look for a deck with three heads, an adjustable bias control, and Dolby B, Dolby C, and HX Pro noise-suppression circuitry. If you'll be taping CDs, you may want to pay extra for Dolby S circuitry or at least auto edit or synchro edit features. If you're interested in copying tapes, look for a dual-deck unit.

For mostly playing tapes, look for Dolby B circuitry, autoreverse, and music search.

COMPACT STEREO SYSTEMS

Compact stereos are for people who want an inexpensive system in one easy-to-buy and easy-to-use package. Also called "integrated-component systems," they descend directly from the all-in-one stereo radio/phono/tape players available a few years ago. They may take the shape of separate components, usually in a cabinet.

A step up from the compact system is a "mini sound system." These components, sold individually or as a package, make a system that's smaller and generally better finished than the typical compact system.

The choices

Compact systems. They typically include a digitally tuned receiver that delivers 5 to 30 watts per channel, a compact-disc player, a dual-cassette tape deck, a remote control, and sometimes a phono turntable. The better systems have better-quality components: The amplifiers are more powerful. Speakers are two-way (with woofer and tweeter) instead of one-way. Tape decks can handle Type II tape as well as Type I. The CD player has a motorized CD drawer instead of a manual one.

Compact systems sell for $200 to $700 at retail. The better systems give you a lot of hardware for the money. The worse ones give you a lot of mediocre hardware for the money. Most receivers do a reasonably good job of pulling in weak FM radio signals and plucking a station off a crowded di-

COMPACT STEREO SYSTEMS

al. Unfortunately, the loudspeakers are generally poorly made boxes, unable to faithfully reproduce the audio spectrum. On most systems, the speakers can't easily be switched for better ones. The tape decks work adequately and are fairly free of flutter, the wavering sound that results when tape moves at an uneven speed.

Since it's virtually impossible to buy a bad-sounding CD player—even in a compact system—the CD player is likely to be the best part of the package. But with the typical compact system's puny receiver and speakers, you won't fully capture the sound.

A few compact systems have a turntable. Lack of a turntable may be a blessing, though, judging by the performance of the models that have them. The ceramic cartridge provided almost ensures mediocre performance. (A magnetic cartridge is usually better.)

Mini systems. Minis look like downsized component systems, complete with shoe-box-sized loudspeakers and, in some lines, subwoofers as well. Most come with an AM/FM stereo receiver, compact-disc player, and dual-cassette deck, and often no turntable or inputs for one. In some lines, these systems are packaged with sophisticated features, including Dolby Surround and Pro Logic sound. Typical list prices: $600 to $1200.

The tests

We put the compact systems through the same tests we run for standard hi-fi components.

Buying advice

People serious about good stereo sound should pass up compact systems. Compacts are made for undemanding listening. They'd probably be fine for youngsters devoted to the Top 40 and for people who just want some background music in the house. But don't expect sound quality much better than that of a boom box.

If space constraints are severe, a miniature component system can provide decent sound in a small package. Otherwise, you can put together a good, basic component system for less than the cost of a mini system: $150 to $200 for a receiver more powerful than any compact systems'; $150 for a plain, single-play CD player; $200 to $300 for a cassette deck; and $150 to $200 for a pair of speakers. Total: $650 to $850.

HOW TO GET MORE INFORMATION

Check out what we've said in CONSUMER REPORTS. For the date of recent reports, refer to the four-year index in the back of the Buying Guide or the date noted on each Ratings table. Back issues are available at most libraries or can be ordered. You can also get the latest new- and used-car price information. For details, see page 307 (new cars) and page 310 (used cars).

RATINGS LARGE-SCREEN TV SETS

▶ **See report, page 65.** From Consumer Reports, March 1992.

Recommendations: The 27-inch set is a reasonable size for the home theater. Among the 20 tested sets, our first choice is the *RCA F27230ES*. It vied for top honors with the *Sony KV-27EXR20*. Several high-rated models represent good value as well as good quality: the *Quasar SX-2730FE*, the *Toshiba CX-2780A*, the *Zenith SJ2771W*, and the *RCA F27201GG*.

Brand and model	Price	Overall score	Image quality	Color fidelity	Brightness	Geometric distortion	Interlace	Color control	Airplane flutter	Adjacent channel	Fringe VHF	Fringe UHF	Spark rejection
RCA F27230ES	$919	90	◒	◒	◒	◒	◒	●	○	◒	◒	◒	◒
Sony KV-27EXR20	900	88	◒	◒	○	◒	◒	◒	◒	○	◒	◒	○
Quasar SX-2730FE [S]	650	87	◒	◒	●	●	◒	◒	◒	◒	◒	◒	○
Toshiba CX-2780A [D]	690	86	◒	◒	●	◒	◒	◒	◒	◒	●	○	○
Sony KV-27EXR90 [S]	910	85	◒	◒	●	○	◒	◒	◒	◒	◒	◒	○
Zenith SJ2771W	749	85	◒	◒	◒	●	◒	◒	◒	◒	◒	◒	○
Hitachi CT-7893B [D]	735	84	◒	◒	○	◒	○	◒	◒	◒	○	○	○
Mitsubishi CS-2715R [S]	800	84	◒	◒	◒	◒	◒	◒	◒	◒	◒	◒	○
Panasonic Prism CTN-2794S [D]	760	84	◒	◒	●	●	◒	◒	◒	○	○	○	◒
RCA F27201GG [S]	575	84	◒	◒	○	◒	◒	◒	◒	◒	○	○	●
Fisher PC1627	700	83	◒	◒	○	○	◒	◒	◒	◒	○	○	○
JVC AV-2771S [S]	710	82	◒	◒	●	○	○	◒	●	○	○	○	○
Sylvania SPA2751/ Magnavox RP2780A [1][S]	600 520	82	◒	◒	●	◒	◒	◒	◒	○	●	●	◒
Zenith SJ2775BG	879	82	○	◒	●	◒	◒	◒	◒	◒	◒	●	○
Emerson TS2760D [S]	440	80	◒	◒	●	○	◒	◒	◒	○	●	●	●
GE 27GT612	569	80	◒	◒	○	◒	◒	◒	◒	○	◒	●	●
Philips 27S242C [D]	720	80	◒	◒	●	◒	○	◒	◒	○	○	●	●
Samsung TC2750S [S]	480	77	○	◒	◒	◒	◒	◒	◒	◒	◒	○	○
Sharp 27A-S300 [S]	625	74	●	◒	◒	○	◒	◒	◒	◒	◒	○	○
Goldstar CMT-2708A [S]	470	70	●	○	○	○	○	◒	◒	○	○	○	○

[1] *According to mfr., these models are identical.*

LARGE-SCREEN TV SETS 87

Better ← → Worse
◓ ◐ ○ ◑ ●

Ratings order: Listed in order of overall score, based primarily on picture and sound quality. Differences in score of 7 points or less are judged not very significant. Models with identical scores are listed alphabetically. Price is the suggested retail as quoted by the manufacturer; actual retail may be lower. ⓢ indicates tested model has been replaced by successor model; according to the manufacturer, the performance of new model should be similar to the tested model but features may vary. See page 88 for new model number and suggested retail price, if available. ⒹMagnifier indicates model discontinued.

Audio tone	Ease of use	Remote control	Code entry	Video	Audio	Advantages	Disadvantages	Comments	Brand and model
◐	○	○	✔	2/1	2/2	A,B,F,I,O	—	B	RCA F27230ES
○	◓	◑	✔	2/2	2/1	A,B,E,F,G,K,M,S,T	d,f,i,n	A	Sony KV-27EXR20
◓	◓	○	✔	1/0	1/1	L,O	g,i	A	Quasar SX-2730FE ⓢ
○	○	◑	✔	2/0	2/1	B,F,I	m	A,B,E	Toshiba CX-2780A Ⓓ
◓	◓	◑	✔	2/1	2/2	A,B,E,F,G,K,M,N,S,T	d,f,i,n,r	A,B,F	Sony KV-27EXR90 ⓢ
◓	○	◓	✔	1/1	1/1	B,L	q	C	Zenith SJ2771W
○	◓	●	—	3/1	3/2	F,J,K,L,M,N,T,U	d,f,i	A,C	Hitachi CT-7893B Ⓓ
○	◓	◑	—	2/1	2/1	B,K,L,M	d		Mitsubishi CS-2715R ⓢ
◓	◓	○	✔	1/0	1/1	A,I,L,O	g		Panasonic Prism CTN-2794S Ⓓ
○	○	◓	✔	2/1	2/2	A,B,F,O	r		RCA F27201GG ⓢ
○	○	○	✔	2/0	2/1	J,K	f,i,k		Fisher PC1627
○	○	○	✔	1/1	1/2	A,E,F,H,I,L,N,Q,T	g,r	A,B	JVC AV-2771S ⓢ
○	○	○	✔	1/0	1/1	I,R	e		Sylvania SPA2751/ Magnavox RP2780A ⒾⓈ
○	○	◓	—	1/1	1/1	A,B,D,I,L	b	C	Zenith SJ2775BG
◐	◐	◑	—	1/1	1/1	A,C,E	a,d,f,i,k,l,q		Emerson TS2760D ⓢ
●	○	◓	✔	1/0	1/1	E,O	a,o,p	A	GE 27GT612
◓	○	○	✔	1/1	1/2	A,B,F,H,K,N,P	r		Philips 27S242C Ⓓ
○	○	●	—	2/1	2/2	A,E,F,K,S	c,d,k	A,D	Samsung TC2750S ⓢ
◐	◐	◓	✔	1/0	1/1	K,Q,	h,i,j,k,m		Sharp 27A-S300 ⓢ
○	◐	○	—	1/1	1/2	B,N	k,r	A	Goldstar CMT-2708A ⓢ

Turn page for Ratings Keys

88 LARGE-SCREEN TV SETS

Successor Models (in Ratings order)
Quasar SX-2730FE is succeeded by SX-2741HE, $900; Sony KV-27EXR90 by KV-27EXR9S, $1150; Mitsubishi CS-2715R by CS-27EX1, $699; RCA F27201GG by F27202GG, $669; JVC AV-2771S by AV-27BP3, $930; Sylvania SPA2751/Magnavox RP2780A by SPC2754/RP2781C, $749; Emerson TS2760D by TS-2761D, $900; Samsung TC2750S by TC2770S, $670; Sharp 27A-S300 by 27C-S300, $900; Goldstar CMT-2708A by CN29C10, $600.

Performance Notes
All: • Have hi-fi outputs with excellent frequency response and satisfactory freedom from noise and distortion.
Except as noted, all have: • Excellent or very good black-level retention. • Fair or poor color correction. • Adequate stereo separation at audio outputs. • Horizontal resolution of about 320 lines with RF input and at least 400 lines with auxiliary video inputs. • Moderately overscanned picture, losing 10-12 percent at sides. • Picture unaffected by low line voltage.

Features in Common
All have: • Remote for basic functions. • Keypad on remote but none on receiver. • Capacity for at least 99 cable channels. • Audio output level to external amplifier that can be adjusted by the TV's volume control.
Except as noted, all have: • Essential TV controls duplicated on console. • Separate bass, treble, and balance controls. • Stereo and SAP (separate audio program) capability. • Automatic and manual selection of scannable channels. • Remote that can control a VCR of same brand. • Comb filter for better resolution of fine detail. • S-video inputs.

Key to Advantages
A–Can drive external speakers without need for additional amplifier.
B–Can produce enhanced stereo surround effect from normal stereo sources; **RCA F27230ES** and **Sony KV-27EXR90** were particularly effective.
C–Headphone jack.
D–Remote can learn commands.
E–Can be programmed for timed on/off cycles.
F–Channel blockout feature.
G–Each audio/video input retains level and other settings specific to it, to tailor settings for different video sources.
H–At least 2 sets of audio/video settings can be recalled, for different viewers' preferences.
I–Picture-in-picture (PIP) feature allows viewing a second source simultaneously.
J–Jacks on front of set.
K–On-screen help menus guide viewer through features and adjustments.
L–Switchable video noise reduction (VNR) to "smooth" noisy pictures.
M–Switch selects reddish or bluish background whites (other models use mfrs.' preference).
N–Can display stations' call letters.
O–Commercial skip timer lets viewer look at other channels for approx. length of a commercial.
P–Internal clock can retain correct time for at least 10 min. during power interruption.
Q–Can automatically scan active channels.
R–Menus in English or Spanish.
S–Overscans less than most.
T–Notch filter for cleaner outlines.
U–Color correction judged very good.

Key to Disadvantages
a–Cannot receive second audio program (SAP) audio channel.
b–Overscans more than most, so loses more picture at sides of screen.
c–Channel blockout cannot be unlocked easily if access codes are forgotten.
d–Remote control must be used to reinstate a deleted channel.
e–No active-channel autoprogram feature.
f–Picture controls on remote only.
g–Picture size shrinks or expands noticeably at low line voltage.
h–No tone controls.
i–Tone controls on console only.
j–On-screen menu uses colors that may be difficult for colorblind viewers.
k–Instruction book less clear than most.
l–No Stereo/Mono Select switch; selection is automatic but sometimes erroneously triggered by noise.
m–No internal clock.
n–No indicator to show SAP is selected; mutes on non-SAP broadcasts if SAP is selected by mistake.
o–No comb filter, so limited to 270 lines of horizontal resolution at RF input.
p–Tone control alters treble, but not bass.
q–No S-video input.
r–Black-level retention judged average or fair.

Key to Comments
A–Side-firing speakers.
B–Can produce simulated stereo sound.
C–Room-light sensor compensates for varying room brightness.
D–Remote cannot control VCR of same brand.
E–Can produce "theatre, stadium, club," and "hall" sound ambience.
F–ASC circuitry samples picture, compares it with an "ideal," and attempts to adjust.

MID-PRICED RECEIVERS 89

RATINGS MID-PRICED RECEIVERS — Better ◄———► Worse

▶ **See report, page 73.** From Consumer Reports, March 1992.

Recommendations: Overall performance was high and differences between models slight. The models with Dolby Pro Logic Decoder and built-in amplifiers are better equipped for playing sound tracks used in the home theater.

Ratings order: Listed by types; within types, listed in order of overall score. Models with equal scores are listed alphabetically. A difference in accuracy of 8 points or less is not significant. Price is the suggested retail as quoted by the manufacturer; actual retail may be lower. Ⓢ indicates tested model has been replaced by successor model; according to the manufacturer, the performance of new model should be similar to the tested model but features may vary. See page 90 for new model number and suggested retail price, if available. Ⓓ indicates model discontinued.

Brand and model	Overall score	Price	Pro Logic Decoder	Convenience	Control layout	FM tuner performance	AM tuner performance	Measured power (8/6/4 ohm)[1]	Surround power[2]	Pro Logic power[3]	Advantages	Disadvantages	Comments
POWERED PRO LOGIC/DOLBY SURROUND MODELS													
Pioneer VSX-51 Ⓢ	95	$580	✔	◕	◕	◕	◕	115/130/149	18	25	A,B,C,E,F,G,I	b,c	C,E,I
Pioneer VSX-4800 Ⓢ	94	490	✔	◕	◕	◕	○	118/133/148	20	20	A,B,E,F,I	b,c	C,I
Kenwood KR-V7030, A Best Buy Ⓢ	89	380	✔	◕	◕	◕	◕	122/141/107	15	65	A,B,C,E,H,I	a	I
Kenwood KR-V8030 Ⓢ	89	450	✔	◕	◕	◕	◕	138/159/120	15	75	A,C,E,H	a	G,I
Sony STR-AV1070 Ⓢ	89	465	✔	◕	◕	◕	◕	133/156/185	15	15	A,B,C,E,F,I	c	B,C,D,E,I
Technics SA-GX710 Ⓢ	89	570	✔	◕	○	◕	◕	139/159/105	30	60	C,F,G,I	a	D,F,I
Fisher RS-646	85	400	✔	○	◕	◕	◕	145/157/[4]	20	20	A,B,G,J	c,f,h	D
JVC RX-805VTN Ⓢ	84	465	✔	○	◕	◕	◕	116/133/[4]	20	50	C,E,F,G,I	c,d	B,C,G
Technics SA-GX505 Ⓢ	84	375	✔	◕	○	○	◕	126/145/81	10	10	C,F,G	a,e	F,I
Denon AVR 610	82	600	✔	○	◕	◕	○	79/96/119	20	75	B,I,J	a,d,e	C,D,H,I,J
DOLBY SURROUND MODELS													
Onkyo TX-906 Ⓢ	95	425	✔	◕	◕	◕	◕	104/122/145	12	—	A,B,C,D,I,J	a,f,g	A,C,E,H
Kenwood KR-V6030, A Best Buy Ⓢ	89	285	—	◕	◕	◕	◕	122/141/109	15	—	A,B,C	a,h	—
Pioneer VSX-3900S Ⓢ	89	335	—	○	◕	◕	◕	110/123/136	18	—	B,I	b,c	B,C
Fisher RS-636	88	350	—	○	◕	◕	◕	119/134/129	20	—	A,G	f,h	D
JVC RX-705VTN Ⓢ	87	370	✔	○	○	◕	◕	109/127/[4]	20	—	C,E,F,I	c,d,g	B,C
JVC RX-505VTN Ⓢ	86	275	—	○	○	◕	◕	85/97/[4]	20	—	C,E,F,G,I	c,d	B,C

Ratings continued

90 MID-PRICED RECEIVERS

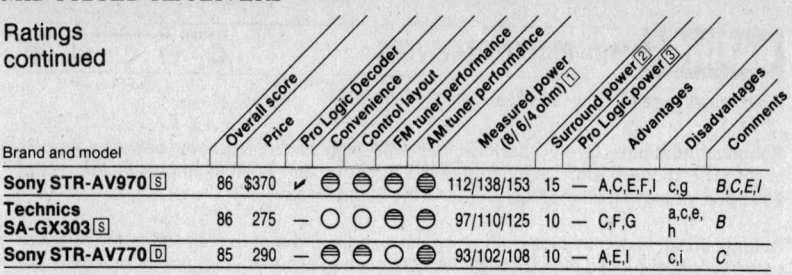

Ratings continued

Brand and model	Overall score	Price	Pro Logic Decoder	Convenience	Control layout	FM tuner performance	AM tuner performance	Measured power (8/6/4 ohm)[1]	Surround power[2]	Pro Logic power[3]	Advantages	Disadvantages	Comments
Sony STR-AV970 Ⓢ	86	$370	✔	⊖	⊖	⊖	⊖	112/138/153	15	—	A,C,E,F,I	c,g	B,C,E,I
Technics SA-GX303 Ⓢ	86	275	—	○	○	⊖	⊖	97/110/125	10	—	C,F,G	a,c,e,h	B
Sony STR-AV770 Ⓓ	85	290	—	⊖	⊖	○	⊖	93/102/108	10	—	A,E,I	c,i	C

[1] The watts-per-channel output of each receiver at impedances typical of loudspeakers.
[2] The watts-per-channel output to the rear, surround-sound speakers, at 8 ohms, per mfr.
[3] The mfr.'s 8-ohm power rating of the center Pro Logic channel.
[4] Mfr. does not recommend receiver for use with 4-ohm speakers.

Successor models (in Ratings order)
Pioneer VSX-51 is succeeded by VSX-52 Elite, $750; Pioneer VSX-4800 by VSX-451, $435; Kenwood KR-V7030 by KR-V7040, $479; Kenwood KR-V8030 by KR-V8040, $599; Sony STR-AV1070 by STR-D1090, $630; Technics SA-GX710 by SA-GX630; JVC RX-805VTN by RX-807VTN, $640; Technics SA-GX505 by SA-GX530; Onkyo TX-906 by TX-SV303 Pro, $460; Kenwood KR-V6030 by KR-V6040, $349; Pioneer VSX-3900S by VSX-401, $395; JVC RX-705VTN by RX-707VTN, $520; JVC RX-505VTN by RX-507VTN, $390; Sony STR-AV970 by STR-D990, $480; Technics SA-GX303 by SA-GX330.

Performance Notes
General: • Excellent frequency response, stereo separation, and AM rejection. • Channel balance and amplifier show typical gain.
Amplifier: • Excellent signal-to-noise ratio and freedom from distortion.
Phono preamplifier: • Excellent signal-to-noise ratio and freedom from distortion. • Resistance to overload within expected range. • Input impedance suitable for typical phono cartridge. • Input capacitance suitable for typical cartridge; 125 to 300 picofarads, except as noted.

Features in Common
All have: • Digitally tuned FM stereo and mono AM tuners. • 1 magnetic phono input. • Up/down Seek tuning. • Backup power source to retain memory of station presets. • Tuner that automatically "wraps" from one end of band to other and that moves in 100-kHz increments. • Headphone jack. • 2 or more CD/Tape/Aux inputs. • Connections for 2 pairs of speakers. • FM and AM indoor antennas plus connection for external AM antenna.
Except as noted, all have: • Bass and treble tone controls instead of graphic equalizer.

• 20 or more station presets. • Capability to accommodate 2 decks. • Clear indication of selected source. • Tuning display readable from at least 30° above horizontal. • Secondary speakers connected in parallel when both pairs switched on. • FM antenna connection for both 300-ohm twin lead and 75-ohm cable.

Key to Advantages
A–Numeric keypad.
B–Controls marked more clearly than most.
C–Can turn off tone controls to listen to CDs.
D–Has signal-strength indicator.
E–Readout can display station call letters.
F–Can "memorize" settings.
G–On/off Loudness-compensation switch.
H–Variable Loudness control.
I–Has variable delay to rear speakers.
J–Control panel simpler than others.

Key to Disadvantages
a–No audio Mute switch on main unit.
b–Display not readable from 30° angle.
c–Speaker pairs connected in series.
d–Audio input jacks not color coded.
e–Only 1 recording output for tape deck.
f–Lacks 75-ohm antenna input.
g–Power amplifier for Pro Logic separate.
h–Remote lacks rear speaker control.

Key to Comments
A–Has low phono-input capacitance.
B–Has graphic equalizer.
C–Simulated surround-sound modes.
D–Audio/video inputs on front panel.
E–Can play 2 sources at once.
F–Tone control and parametric graphic equalizer to fine-tune broad range of frequencies.
G–Flip-up door conceals additional controls.
H–"B" speaker controls inconvenient.
I–Has Dolby 3 stereo.
J–Allows 16 station presets.

RATINGS HI-FI VCRS

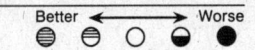

Better ← → Worse

▶ **See report, page 68.** From Consumer Reports, March 1992.

Recommendations: If you play mostly rental tapes, look to the top dozen or so models, all of which had excellent pictures at standard speed. Frequent time-shifters should consider models with good extended-play ratings and easy programming.

Ratings order: Listed in order of overall score. Differences of less than 8 points are judged not very significant. Models with identical scores are listed alphabetically. Price is the suggested retail as quoted by the manufacturer; actual retail may be lower. Ⓢ indicates tested model has been replaced by successor model; according to the manufacturer, the performance of new model should be similar to the tested model but features may vary. See page 92 for new model number and suggested retail price, if available. Ⓓ indicates model discontinued.

Brand and model	Price	Overall score	Picture quality scores (SP/EP)	Programming ease	Adjacent channel rejection	Fringe reception (VHF/UHF)	Linear flutter (SP)	Features	Remote use	Advantages	Disadvantages	Comments
Sony SLV-585HF	$549	90	93/80	◐	○	◐/○	○	◐	○	A,B,C,H,I,L,N,P,S,U,V,BB,CC	j	A,J,K,L,N,P,Q,S,U
Fisher FVH-4903	450	89	98/86	○	◐	◐/○	◐	◐	○	B,J,K,N,O,P,S,BB	h	A,I,J,N,P,Q,R,V,AA
Mitsubishi HS-U54 Ⓢ	475	89	96/81	◐	◐	◐/◐	◐	◐	○	A,B,H,K,M,N,O,V,W,X,Z,CC	b	A,J,K,L,P,W,BB
Sanyo VHR-9406 Ⓢ	370*	89	100/84	○	○	◐/○	○	◐	○	B,J,K,M,N,O,P,S	a,h	A,I,J,Q,R,V,AA
Sony SLV-686HF Ⓢ	530	89	94/76	◐	◐	◐/○	○	◐	◐	A,B,C,H,I,L,N,P,Q,S,U,V,BB,CC	—	A,H,J,K,L,N,P,Q,S,U
Hitachi VT-F351A Ⓓ	415	86	94/80	◕	◐	◐/○	○	◐	○	A,B,J,M,N,P,S,U,Z	b	A,J,P,Q,S,CC
Goldstar GVR-A465 Ⓢ	370	85	96/71	○	◐	◐/○	◐	◐	○	A,B,C,E,J,L,N,O,P,R,V,AA,BB	b,h	A,I,J,O,P,Q,R,T
ProScan PSVR60 Ⓢ	530	84	93/77	◐	○	◐/○	◐	◐	◐	B,E,G,J,P,S,U,V,CC	b	A,G,I,J,P,Q,S,BB
Toshiba M-647 Ⓢ	405	83	94/76	○	◐	◐/○	◐	◐	◐	B,J,L,M,N,P,V,AA	a,b,e	J,O,Q,R
Panasonic PV-4070 Ⓓ	550	82	89/77	○	○	◐/○	◐	◐	◐	B,D,F,H,J,M,N,P,Q,R,S,V	b,d,e,f	D,E,H,I,J,K,L,O,R,S,U,Y,Z
Zenith VRJ420HF Ⓓ	365	81	94/80	◕	○	◐/○	◐	○	◕	B,E,J,N,R,V	a,g	A,I,J,K,Q,R,T

Ratings continued

92 HI-FI VCRS

Ratings continued

Brand and model	Price	Overall score	Picture quality scores (SP/EP)	Programming ease	Adjacent channel rejection	Fringe reception (VHF/UHF)	Linear flutter (SP)	Features	Remote use	Advantages	Disadvantages	Comments
Panasonic PV-4164 [D]	$435	80	89/74	○	○	◐/○	○	◐	◐	B,F,I,J,M,O,P,S,V,Y,Z	a,b	A,C,I,K,L,O,P,Q,R,W,Y,Z
Philips VR6065AT [D]	465	80	92/76	○	○	○/●	◐	○	◐	B,J,M,S,V	b,c,j	A,B,F,J,O,Q,Y,DD
Sharp VC-H75U [D]	500	80	89/78	○	◐	◐/○	◐	○	●	B,J,K,N,S,T,V,Z,BB	b,h	I,J,Q
Quasar VH6415 [D]	380	79	88/74	○	○	◐/○	○	◐	◐	B,F,J,M,O,P,S,V,X,Y,Z	a,b	C,I,J,O,Q,R,W,Y
JVC HR-D910U	550	78	89/75	●	◐	◐/○	◐	◐	○	B,C,J,K,L,N,W,X	a,b	J,K,M,N,P,Q,S
RCA VR680HF [S]	435	78	84/72	◐	◐	◐/○	○	◐	●	B,G,J,L,M,N,Q,S,U,V	a,b	A,I,J,Q,R,S
Magnavox VR9062AT [S]	405	77	89/73	○	○	○/●	◐	○	●	B,J,M,S,V	b,c,j	A,B,J,O,Q,Y
Memorex MD-100 [S]	500	77	90/70	○	◐	◐/○	◐	○	●	B,J,K,N,S,T,V,Z,BB	b,h	I,J,Q,EE
Samsung VR8501 [S]	305	76	84/79	●	○	◐/●	◐	◐	◐	B,J,N,V	a,b	I,R,X
GE VG4216 [S]	375	72	85/71	○	◐	◐/○	◐	○	◐	B,J,N,S,V	a,b,d,h	A,I,O,R
Sears LXi Cat. No. 53483	325	70	86/71	○	◐	◐/○	◐	○	●	J,P,R	b,c,d	A,I,Q,R,T,Z

Successor Models (in Ratings order)
Mitsubishi HS-U54 is succeeded by HS-U56, $499; Sanyo VHR-9406 by VHR-5406, $300; Sony SLV-686HF by SVL-696HF, $649; Goldstar GVR-A465 by GVR-B465, $430; ProScan PSVR60 by PSVR61, $599; Toshiba M-647 by M-648, $405; RCA VR680HF by VR667HF, $549; Magnavox VR9062AT by VR9162, $379; Samsung VR8501 by VR8702, $530; GE VG4216 by VG 4217, $399.

Performance Notes
All had: • Excellent frequency response and adequate stereo separation for MTS. • Average to good signal-to-noise performance in SP and EP audio linear-track recordings. • Good-quality freeze frames in EP and SP mode. • Fair to poor flutter and mediocre audio response in EP linear-track recordings.
Except as noted, all had: • Excellent or very good MTS separation and linear audio response.

Features in Common
All have: • Digital quartz tuners with automatic set and add/delete. • On-screen programming from remote control. • Daily and weekly programming. • Remote control with numeric keypad. • One-button quick record with offset. • Ability to record in SP and EP speeds and play back at SP, LP, and EP speeds. • Tape counter with memory. • Automatic rewind at end of tape. • Ability to eject tape with power off. • Ability to turn on automatically when a cassette is inserted. • 2-way speed search. • Hi-fi stereo. • Stereo and SAP (secondary audio program) reception capability. • Vertical lock controls to minimize freeze-frame jitter.
Except as noted, all have: • Programming capability of 8 events, 365 days in advance. • 125 cable channels. • Warranty of 12/3/12 mo. on parts, labor, and heads.

Key to Advantages
A—10 min. or more power backup.
B—Tape counter can count in hrs./mins.
C—Tape handling judged faster than average.
D—Remote has 7 programmable buttons.
E—Code entry remote control.
F—Optional special programming device easier to use than regular programming methods.
G—Built-in VCR Plus programming device.
H—Jog-shuttle on remote control.
I—Jog-shuttle on console.
J—Tracking control on remote control.
K—Tracking control located on console and remote.
L—Shows recording time remaining on tape.
M—"Go-to" searches by time or number.
N—Index search.
O—Can search for unrecorded tape segment.
P—Front-mounted audio/video jacks.
Q—Good assemble editing capability.
R—Headphone jack with volume control.
S—Input selection on console.
T—Channel add/delete on console.
U—Remote can control more than one VCR.
V—Pause switch toggles on and off.
W—Dual stereo audio output jacks.
X—Automatic picture sharpness control.
Y—Can play, but not record, S-VHS tapes.
Z—Tamper-proof switch.
AA—Automatic tape speed; will record in SP as long as possible, then switch to EP.
BB—Console viewing angle wider than average.
CC—Owner's manual better than average.

Key to Disadvantages
a—No audio level meters.
b—Clock and counter share digits on console.
c—Tape handling slower than most.
d—Console viewing angle narrower than most.
e—No rear input video jacks.
f—Remote control flimsier than others.
g—No tape counter on console.
h—Owner's manual poorer than average.
i—MTS separation judged good.
j—Linear audio response judged good.

Key to Comments
A—Unified remote can control same-brand TV.
B—Can display all active channels at once.
C—Optional bar-code programmer.
D—Includes bar-code scanner.
E—Audio record-level controls.
F—Audio has ambience enhancement.
G—Bass boost.
H—Audio/video dub.
I—Can record in LP speed.
J—Automatic tracking.
K—Slow-motion forward or backward.
L—Reverse playback.
M—Display dimmer.
N—Picture sharpness control.
O—On-screen calendar.
P—Auto head cleaner, not tested.
Q—Can set tape speed on timed recordings.
R—Simulcast recording capability.
S—Can use special control cable with certain camcorders or VCRs to facilitate editing.
T—Rudimentary title generator to add titles.
U—Programming capability: 8 events/30 or 31 days in advance.
V—Programming capability: 6/365.
W—Programming capability: 4/28 or 30.
X—Programming capability: 4/365.
Y—99 cable channels.
Z—Warranty: 12/12/12 mo. on parts, labor, and heads.
AA—Warranty: 12/3/0 mo.
BB—Warranty: 12/6/12 mo.
CC—Warranty: 24/3/24 mo.
DD—Warranty: 24/12/36 mo.
EE—Warranty: 12/3/3 mo.

About CU's Repair Histories

Thousands of readers tell us about their repair experiences with autos, appliances, and electronic items on the Annual Questionnaire. Using that unique information can improve your chances of getting a trouble-free car, washing machine, TV set, or other product. See the Frequency-of-Repair charts starting on page 317 and the brand repair histories starting on page 361.

RATINGS 13- AND 20-INCH TV SETS

▶ See report, page 65. From Consumer Reports, November 1992.

Recommendations: The *Zenith SJ2071W*, $385, is the clear choice among 20-inch sets. Unfortunately, that brand has a relatively poor repair history (see page 367). Any of the models in the upper half of the Ratings would also make a good choice. Among 13-inch sets, the *Sharp 13A-M100*, $220, stands out. Any of the top five is also a good choice.

Rating symbols legend: ratings use filled/partial/open circle glyphs for each attribute (Picture quality: Clarity, Color fidelity, Brightness, Geometric distortion, Interlace, Color control; Reception factors: Airplane flutter, Adjacent channel, Fringe VHF, Fringe UHF, Spark rejection).

Brand and model	Price	Overall score
20-INCH SETS		
Zenith SJ2071W	$385	85
Sanyo AVM2051 [S]	270	76
GE 20GT372	290	75
JVC AV20BM3	365*	74
RCA F20600ET	370	74
Goldstar CMT-2108A	280*	73
Panasonic CTN-2056S [S]	320	73
Sears Cat. No. 43218 [S]	280*	72
Sharp 20A-S300	325*	71
Emerson TS2041D [S]	275	70
Admiral 12692	300*	69
Magnavox RS2080	325	69
Sony KV-20TS27	410	69
Hitachi CT2043B	380	68
Toshiba CF-2055A	330	65
13-INCH SETS		
Sharp 13A-M100	220	85
GE 13GP237	250	82
Sony KV-13TR24	280	82
Magnavox RR1330	195	80
Toshiba CF1313A [S]	220	76
Panasonic CTP-1351R	219*	72
Zenith SJ1325W	240	70
Emerson TC1369	250*	60
Goldstar CMT-4072X	190	60

13- & 20-INCH TV SETS

Better ← → Worse
◐ ◑ ○ ◒ ●

Ratings order: Listed in order of overall score, based primarily on picture and sound quality. Differences in score of 8 points or less are judged not very significant. Models with identical scores are listed alphabetically. Price is the estimated average, based on prices quoted and paid nationally in late 1992. A * indicates the price we paid (an average price wasn't available). ⑤ indicates tested model has been replaced by successor model; according to the manufacturer, the performance of new model should be similar to the tested model but features may vary. See page 96 for new model number and suggested retail price.

Tone quality	Ease of use	Remote control	Video	Audio	Advantages	Disadvantages	Comments	Model
								20-INCH SETS
○	○	◑	1/1	1/2	A,C,D,E,F,Q,R	—	C,D,E,I	Zenith SJ2071W
●	◑	◑	1/0	1/1	D,H	d	A,F,G,I	Sanyo AVM2051 ⑤
●	◑	◑	1/0	1/1	E,G,J,M,Q,R	—	E,G,I,J	GE 20GT372
○	◑	◑	1/0	1/1	C,D,J,K,L,N	b,j	A,I	JVC AV20BM3
●	◑	◑	1/0	1/1	E,G,J,M,P,Q	—	E,G,J	RCA F20600ET
○	○	○	1/0	1/1	C,D,E,J,L,N	—	E,I	Goldstar CMT-2108A
●	◑	○	1/0	1/1	C,J,M	—	I	Panasonic CTN-2056S ⑤
◒	◑	◒	0/0	0/0	D,H	d	A,F,G	Sears Cat. No. 43218 ⑤
●	◑	◑	1/0	1/0	D,N,Q	g	E	Sharp 20A-S300
◒	◑	◒	0/0	0/0	C,J	b,d	F	Emerson TS2041D ⑤
○	○	◑	1/0	1/1	C,D,E,R	—	I	Admiral 12692
◒	○	○	1/0	1/0	Q	c,g	E	Magnavox RS2080
●	◑	◒	1/0	1/1	D,J,K	b,d	H,I	Sony KV-20TS27
●	◒	◒	1/0	1/1	A,H,I	b,d	F,I	Hitachi CT2043B
◒	○	○	1/0	1/1	C,D,N	b,g,j	I	Toshiba CR-2055A
								13-INCH SETS
○	◑	◑	0/0	0/0	E,N	a,g	—	Sharp 13A-M100
◒	◑	◑	0/0	0/0	E,H,J	—	—	GE 13GP237
◒	◑	◑	1/0	1/0	J,K,R	b,d	H	Sony KV-13TR24
○	◒	◑	0/0	0/0	E,H,O	c,f,g,i	B	Magnavox RR1330
◒	◑	◑	0/0	0/0	N	b,g	—	Toshiba CF1313A ⑤
●	◑	○	1/0	1/0	B,J,M	j	—	Panasonic CTP-1351R
●	◒	◑	1/0	1/0	E	e,j	—	Zenith SJ1325W
◒	○	○	0/0	0/0	B	b,d,f,g,h,j	—	Emerson TC1369
●	◑	◒	0/0	0/0	—	b,g,j	—	Goldstar CMT-4072X

Turn page for Ratings Keys

13- & 20-INCH TV SETS

Successor Models (in Ratings order)
Sanyo AVM2051 is succeeded by AVM2052, $329; Panasonic CTN-20565 by CTP-2056S, $389; Sears Cat. No. 43218 by 43248, $280; Emerson TS2041D by TS2042D, $500; Toshiba CF1313A by CF1327B, $300.

Features in Common
All: • Have sleep timer and last channel recall. • 20-inch sets can receive broadcast stereo. • Can receive at least 99 cable channels. • 13-inch sets measure about 15x15x15 (within 2 in. for each dimension).
Except as noted, all have: • Ability to make essential adjustments to picture or sound from remote or console. • Automatic and manual channel bypass to retain only those channels you wish to view. • A clock. • Picture sharpness control. • Numeric keypad on remote.
Except as noted, all lack: • Tone controls. • Comb filter that improves resolution of fine details. • Remote that can control a same-brand VCR. • SAP (separate audio program).

Performance Notes
Except as noted, all have: • Excellent or very good black-level retention. • Fair or poor color correction. • Pictures that shrink or distort badly at low line voltage (100 V). • Moderately overscanned picture, losing up to 12 percent at sides. • Horizontal resolution of about 280 lines at RF input and video inputs.

Key to Advantages
A–Can produce pseudo-stereo surround effect and normal stereo.
B–Has headphone jack; when inserted, internal speakers are disconnected.
C–Has separate bass, treble, and balance controls.
D–Can receive SAP.
E–Picture unaffected by low line voltage (100V).
F–Comb filter allows resolution of about 330 lines at RF and 400 lines at composite video inputs.
G–Has an S-VHS video input.
H–On-screen help menus guide you through features and adjustments.
I–Has switch to select hue of background whites; others use mfrs.' preference.
J–Can be programmed to automatically turn on during the next 24-hour period; Emerson TS2041D can repeat daily.
K–Has channel blockout feature to restrict viewing of selected channel(s).
L–Can display stations' call letters along with channel number.
M–Skip timer lets viewer look at other channels for the approximate duration of a commercial.
N–Can automatically scan channels with programming, pausing at each.
O–Has carrying handles or wells.
P–Has a built-in FM radio.
Q–Can program via code entry.
R–Color correction judged average.

Key to Disadvantages
a–Horizontal overscan a bit worse than others, so loses more picture at sides of screen.
b–Remote control must be used to reinstate a deleted channel.
c–Lacks active channel autoprogram feature.
d–Picture controls not on console; on remote only.
e–Picture controls not on remote; on console only.
f–Instruction book less clear than most.
g–Lacks clock.
h–Lacks sharpness control.
i–Lacks numeric keypad.
j–Black-level retention judged average or fair.

Key to Comments
A–Has side-mounted speakers, which improves stereo imaging, but limits use in some entertainment systems.
B–Can be reset to put picture settings in factory preset positions.
C–Has defeatable room-light sensor which can compensate for varying room brightness.
D–Has defeatable video filter to "smooth" noisy pictures.
E–Controls VCR of same brand.
F–Tone controls not on console; on remote only.
G–Has high frequency boost/cut tone control.
H–When SAP is selected, mutes without indication on non-SAP broadcasts.
I–Output level to amplifier is controlled by set's volume control.
J–Produces pseudo-stereo surround effect when "stereo" selected.

CD PLAYERS

RATINGS CD PLAYERS

Better ⬅ ⊖ ⊖ ○ ◐ ● ➡ Worse

▶ **See report, page 80.** From Consumer Reports, March 1992.

Recommendations: To the average listener, all the tested players deliver superb sound. Choose models for convenience and features.

Ratings order: Listed by types; within types, listed in order of overall score. All were judged excellent in sound quality. Differences in score of less than about 7 points were judged insignificant. Models with identical scores are listed alphabetically. The price is the suggested retail as quoted by the manufacturer; actual retail may be lower. ⓢ indicates tested model has been replaced by successor model; according to the manufacturer, the performance of new model should be similar to the tested model but features may vary. See page 98 for new model number and suggested retail price, if available. ⒹⒹ indicates model discontinued.

Brand and model	Price	Overall score	Disc-error correction	Track-finding speed	Bump immunity	Taping convenience	Features & convenience	Track keypad	Remote volume control	Advantages	Disadvantages	Comments
LOW-PRICED PLAYERS												
Onkyo DX-702 ⓢ	$185	88	⊖	⊖	○	⊖	⊖	✔	—	B,D,E,F,I,M	d	B,O
Kenwood DP-2030 ⓢ	150	85	⊖	⊖	⊖	○	⊖	✔	—	B,F,I	—	—
Philips CD40 Ⓓ	150	85	⊖	⊖	●	●	⊖	—	—	A,C,D,I,M,Q	i	G
Pioneer PD-5700 ⓢ	150	85	⊖	⊖	⊖	○	⊖	✔	✔	A,B,D,E,J,K	f	C
Sony CDP-491 ⓢ	145	83	⊖	⊖	⊖	⊖	⊖	✔	—	A,B,D,E,J,R	—	J
Technics SL-PG300	170	83	○	⊖	⊖	⊖	⊖	✔	✔	B,C,E,I,J,K,M	d	C,K
JVC XL-V241TN ⓢ	135	79	●	⊖	⊖	⊖	⊖	—	—	B,D,E,I,P,Q	d,f	C
Magnavox CDB-502	200	79	○	⊖	⊖	○	○	—	—	A,B,D,I,M	h,i,l	—
Sherwood CD-3010R	180	79	○	⊖	●	○	⊖	✔	—	A,B,C,D,F	—	—
Sears LXI Cat. No. 97525	120	75	⊖	○	○	⊖	●	—	—	—	a,b,c,e,g,i,k,l	N
Optimus CD-1760 ⓢ	120	74	○	●	○	⊖	○	—	—	I,K	e,g,i,k,l	N
Sharp DX-R250 Ⓓ	130	74	●	○	⊖	⊖	○	—	—	—	d,e,g,i,k,l	—
HIGH-PRICED PLAYERS												
Onkyo Integra DX-706	750	90	⊖	⊖	○	○	⊖	✔	✔	B,C,E,F,G,I,J,L,M,P,R	d,l	B,O
Sony ES CDP-X222ES ⓢ	370	89	⊖	⊖	○	⊖	⊖	✔	✔	A,B,C,D,E,F,G,H,I,J,L,O,P,Q,R	—	B,H,J
Denon DCD-970 Ⓓ	335	87	⊖	⊖	●	⊖	⊖	✔	✔	B,E,F,J,L	—	A,E,J,M
Yamaha CDX-750 ⓢ	300	85	⊖	○	⊖	○	⊖	✔	✔	B,D,E,F,G,H,I,L,Q	f	A,B,F

Ratings continued

CD PLAYERS

Ratings continued

Brand and model	Price	Overall score	Disc-error correction	Track-finding speed	Bump immunity	Taping convenience	Features & convenience	Track keypad	Remote volume control	Advantages	Disadvantages	Comments
Technics SL-PS900	$450	84	○	◒	○	◒	◒	✔	✔	B,C,E,F,I,J,L,M,N,P,Q,R	d	A,B,C
Proton AC-422	350	83	◒	◒	●	○	○	—	—	I,M	a,b,i,j,l	L
Luxman DZ-122	400	82	○	◒	◒	○	◒	✔	✔	A,B,E,K,L	—	A,B,I,J,M
Pioneer Elite PD-41 ⑤	560	82	◒	◒	○	○	○	—	—	B,D,Q	f,g,i	A,B,C,F
Harman/Kardon HD7500II ⑤	265	81	○	◒	○	◒	◒	✔	—	A,B,C,F,L,Q	k	—
NAD 5440	430	81	◒	◒	●	●	◒	—	✔	B,C,D,G,I,K,L,P	g,k,l	A,D
Carver SD/A-450	500	78	●	◒	◒	○	○	✔	—	B,C,E,I,Q,R	d,g	A,J
Nakamichi 4 ⑤	330	77	○	◒	◒	●	○	—	—	B,I,P	d,f,k,l	A,F

Successor Models (in Ratings order)
Onkyo DX-702 is succeeded by DX-703, $230; Kenwood DP-2030 by DP-2040, $199; Pioneer PD-5700 by PDS-501, $290; Sony CDP-491 by CDP-497, $220; JVC XL-V241TN by XL-V251TN, $210; Optimus CD-1750 by 15CD-1760, $120; Sony ES CDP-X222ES by CDP-X229ES, $400; Yamaha CDX-750 by CDX-660, $399; Pioneer Elite PD-41 by PD-52, $500; Harman/Kardon HD7500II by HD-7525; Nakamichi 4 by CD-4, $345.

Features in Common
All have: • Play, Pause, Stop, and Program functions. • Audible scan free of pitch distortion, for shuttling rapidly through a track. • 3-inch-CD compatibility without adaptor.
Except as noted, all have: • Remote control. • Headphone jack. • Ability to program 20 or more tracks. • Running total of program time. • Shuffle feature. • Calendar display. • 1-yr. warranty on parts and labor.

Key to Advantages
A–Has music-sampling function.
B–Shows time remaining on disc.
C–Can repeat part of a track or disc.
D–Can repeat a track.
E–Has auto-edit feature for taping.
F–Has auto-space feature.
G–Has delete-track function.
H–Has favorite-track selection.
I–Has multiple-speed scan in play mode.
J–Has music-peak finder.
K–Has index display but not select.
L–Has variable/fixed-level analog outputs.
M–Fast scan is faster than most.
N–Has function switches that can be programmed by user.
O–Can remember volume, index settings, and assigned titles of memorized discs.
P–Has lower excess distortion and better low-level linearity than most.
Q–Has index selection on remote.
R–Has fade control on remote.

Key to Disadvantages
a–Will not display track number and time together.
b–No remote control.
c–Time is shown only in scan mode.
d–No on-off pause control on remote.
e–Measured excess distortion, though minor, slightly higher than others.
f–Low-contrast lettering on remote.
g–No headphone jack.
h–No scan feature on remote.
i–No running total of program time.
j–Low-contrast lettering on console.
k–Lacks shuffle feature.
l–Lacks calendar display.

Key to Comments
A–Has digital output.
B–Has optical-digital output.
C–Has synchronizing jack for a tape deck.
D–Has dynamic-range compressor.
E–Has speed control.
F–2-yr. warranty on parts and labor.
G–3-yr. warranty on parts, 2-yr. on labor.
H–3-yr. warranty on parts and labor.
I–5-yr. warranty on parts and labor.
J–Has variable fade.
K–Fade can be used only in Program.
L–Remote control is optional extra.
M–Variable fade is on console only.
N–Able to program 16 tracks.
O–Remote will also control an **Onkyo** deck.

CAMCORDERS

RATINGS CAMCORDERS

Better ← ⊜ ⊝ ○ ◐ ● → Worse

▶ **See report, page 71.** From Consumer Reports, March 1992.

Recommendations: No camcorder format clearly outshines another. You'll find models representing the major formats at the top of the Ratings. Any of the models in the top half of the Ratings would make a good choice. See the list of similar models on page 100.

Ratings order: Listed in order of overall score, which covers mainly picture quality. Models with identical scores are listed alphabetically. A difference of less than 10 points in score is not significant. Price is the suggested retail as quoted by the manufacturer; actual retail may be lower. ⓢ indicates tested model has been replaced by successor model; according to the manufacturer, the performance of new model should be similar to the tested model but features may vary. See page 100 for new model number and suggested retail price, if available. ⓓ indicates model discontinued.

Brand and model	Price	Format	Overall score	Weight, lb.[1]	Clarity (best/worst)	Low light	Autofocus performance	Freq. response, built-in mike	Freq. response, external mike	Flutter	Indexing[2]	Advantages	Disadvantages	Comments
Sony Handycam CCD-TR81	$1500	Hi8	95	2¼	⊜/⊝	○	⊝	○	⊜	⊜	—	A,B,D,I, P,R,S	e,q	B,F
Sharp Slimcam VL-L30U ⓓ	745	VHS	93	5½	⊜/—	○	⊜	◐	⊝	⊝	A	C,D,J, P,U	c,e,h, q	I,K
Panasonic PV-41 ⓢ	1125	VHS-C	92	2¼	⊜/⊝	○	⊝	○	○	⊝	A	B,C,F, M	c,e,g, l,m, o,p,q	C,G,I, O,Q
Fisher FVC-990 ⓓ	950	8mm	91	2	⊝/—	●	⊝	○	⊜	⊝	—	B,D,I,K, P,R	c,e,p, q	B,D,E, F,K,M, R,S
Sony Handycam CCD-F401	1000	8mm	91	3¼	⊝/—	○	⊝	◐	⊝	⊝	—	B,C,L, N,O,P, R,U	k	B,F,G, M
RCA Pro 8 PRO820A ⓓ	840	8mm	88	2¾	⊝/—	○	⊝	○	⊝	⊝	—	A,G,K, L,R,U, V	f,h,k, p	B,D,E, F,N,R, S
Hitachi VM E25A	1099	8mm	86	2¼	○/—	○	⊝	◐	⊝	⊝	—	E,H,I,K, R,V	c,d,e, i,o,p	B,F,K, O,Q,S
Magnavox Easycam 8 CVM720 ⓓ	896	8mm	86	2	⊝/—	○	⊝	⊝	⊝	⊝	—	M,Q,T	c,d,e, o,p	F,J,K, L,N
Fuji Fujix-8 F60 Wide ⓓ	800	8mm	85	2	⊝/—	●	⊝	○	⊝	⊝	—	B,C,D, E,V	b,c,e, f,o,q	B,D,F, H,O,P, S

[1] Rounded to the nearest quarter-pound, with tape and battery aboard.
[2] Key to indexing: **A** = automatic; **M** = manual.

Ratings continued

CAMCORDERS

Ratings continued

Brand and model	Price	Format	Overall score	Weight, lb. [1]	Clarity (best/worst)	Low light	Autofocus performance	Freq. response, built-in mike	Freq. response, external mike	Flutter	Indexing [2]	Advantages	Disadvantages	Comments
Magnavox CVM620 [D]	$896	VHS-C	85	2¼	◐/○	●	◐	○	○	◐	A	C,J,K, M,T	c,e,g, m,o	C,F,J, N
Canon Canovision 8 E61 [S]	745	8mm	81	2½	○/—	○	◐	◐	◐	◐	—	G,L,U, V	d,e,f, h,j,k, o,p,q	B,D,F, K,N,O, R
Memorex MC-153 [D]	899	8mm	81	2¾	◐/—	◐	○	○	◐	◐	—	B,C,D, L,U	a,f,j, k,p	A,B,H, N,O
Canon UC1	1499	8mm	79	1¾	○/—	●	○	○	◐	◐	—	B,C,T, V	c,e,h, n,o, p	B,F,K, O
JVC GR-AX5	996	VHS-C	75	2½	○/○	○	◐	●	—	◐	M	K,N,P, Q	c,d,e, g,l,o	B,F,I,J, K,S

[1] Rounded to the nearest quarter-pound, with tape and battery aboard.
[2] Key to indexing: **A** = automatic; **M** = manual.

Successor Models (in Ratings order)
Panasonic PV-41 is succeeded by PV-42, $1299; Canon 8 E61 by E210, $1299.

Similar Models
Sony Handycam CCD-TR81: Nikon VN-700, Ricoh R-88H, Yashica KX-H1; Panasonic PV-41: Quasar VM-518; Fisher FVC-990: Olympus VX-82, Sunpak SV-11, Zenith VM8300; Sony Handycam CCD-F401: Ricoh R-861; Magnavox Easycam 8 CVM720: Chinon C8-SC98; Magnavox CVM620: Panasonic PV-19, Quasar VM-515; JVC GR-AX5: Minolta C-618.

Performance Notes
All except **JVC GR-AX5** had excellent color accuracy. It was a notch below the best.

Features in Common
All have: • Automatic focus, exposure, white balance, audio level control. • Fastest shutter speed, 1/1000 sec. or faster. • CCD image sensor. • Tripod socket. • Flying erase head. • "Quick review" that shows last seconds of previous scene. • Ability to show elapsed time or time remaining on tape. • Clock that typically can record time and date. • Automatic shutoff. • Low-battery signal. • AC power pack/battery charger. • Ability to play back through TV or VCR. • Adjustment for moderate near- or far-sightedness. • Macro-focus capability. • Dew indicator.
Except as noted, all have: • Manual and power zoom. • Zoom ratio of 8. • Contrast autofocus. • Manual white balance feature. • Manual focus with button for temporary autofocus. • Headphone jack. • External microphone jack. • "Tally" light to indicate recording. • Fade feature for picture and sound; picture fades to black. • Audio/video inputs. • Provision to operate from car cigarette-lighter socket. • Snap-on lens cap attached with string. • Separate non-rechargeable clock battery. • Warranty of 12 mo. on parts, 3 mo. on labor.

Key to Advantages
A–Exposure can be adjusted manually.
B–Can superimpose titles shot from artwork.
C–Backlight-compensation button.
D–Variable-speed power zoom.
E–Built-in lens cover.
F–Electronic image stabilizer.
G–Built-in character generator for titling.
H–Can superimpose any of 24 graphics.
I–Stereo sound.
J–Audio & video dubbing (**Sharp**, only audio dub).
K–Special control cable to aid in editing.
L–Also has manual zoom.
M–Charger can discharge battery to rejuvenate.
N–Beep confirms start and stop of taping.
O–Single-cord setup for playback on TV set.
P–Switch to restore all automatic settings.
Q–Can automatically date-stamp first scene.
R–Wind-noise suppression setting.
S–Scale in viewfinder for zoom or exposure.
T–Built-in clock battery recharges automati-

cally from main battery.
U–Accessory shoe for video light or microphone.
V–Self-timer.

Key to Disadvantages
a–No warning in viewfinder for manual color-balance setting.
b–No tape counter or elapsed-time display in playback.
c–Motorized manual focus—an inconvenience.
d–No external microphone jack.
e–No momentary autofocus button.
f–Autofocus doesn't work in macro mode.
g–No audio/video input jacks.
h–No separate low-tape warning indicator.
i–Viewfinder can't be tipped up.
j–Viewfinder doesn't collapse for storage.
k–Bulkier than most other 8mm models.
l–Low-contrast lettering on controls.
m–Two dual-function buttons not dual-labeled.
n–Can't change tape when on tripod.
o–No headphone jack.
p–No remote-control jack.
q–Cover on clock battery or jacks easy to lose.

Key to Comments
A–Comes with carrying case.
B–Comes with wireless remote (opt. on **JVC**).
C–Comes with video light.
D–Time-lapse feature.
E–Short-burst animation feature.
F–Heavier, larger-capacity battery available.
G–Lighter, smaller-capacity battery available.
H–No adapter for operating from car battery.
I–No tally light.
J–Fade does not affect sound.
K–Fades to white (**Fisher** to white or black).
L–Additional fade modes.
M–Dynamic range slightly wider than most.
N–Dynamic range slightly narrower than most.
O–Warranty exceptions: **Memorex**, 3 mo. on parts and labor; **Hitachi**, 2 yr. on parts, 3 mo. on labor; **Panasonic** and **Canon**, 6 mo. on image sensor; **Fujix**, 1 yr. on parts and labor.
P–Zoom ratio of 6; also has separate wide-angle setting.
Q–Digital special effect can extend zoom ratio to 12:1 for **Panasonic**, 64:1 for **Hitachi**.
R–Infrared autofocus.
S–Lacks manual white balance feature.

How to Use the Ratings

■ Read the article for general guidance about types and buying advice.

■ Read the Recommendations for brand-name advice based on our tests.

■ Read the Ratings order to see whether products are listed in order of quality, by price, or alphabetically. Most Ratings are based on estimated quality, without regard to price.

■ Look to the Ratings table for specifics on the performance and features of individual models.

■ A model marked Ⓓ has been discontinued, according to the manufacturer. A model marked Ⓢ indicates that, according to the manufacturer, it has been replaced by a successor model whose performance should be similar to the tested model but whose features may vary.

MID-PRICED CASSETTE DECKS

RATINGS MID-PRICED CASSETTE DECKS — Better ◐ ◑ ○ ◐ ● Worse

▶ **See report, page 81.** From Consumer Reports, March 1992.

Recommendations: Buyers must first decide whether to get a single-well or a dual-well deck. Dual decks are handy for copying tapes and for playing two tapes in sequence, but for that convenience you usually have to give up some performance. Among single-well decks, consider the check-rated *Aiwa AD-F810* for its top-notch sound. In fact, any of the next seven single-well decks produced and reproduced very good sound. Let price and features guide your choice. Among dual models, we recommend the *Sony TC-WR875*. See also Features table on page 105.

Ratings order: Listed by types; within types, listed in order of estimated quality, based on overall score. Differences in score of less than 10 points are judged not very significant. Models with identical scores are listed alphabetically. Price is the suggested retail as quoted by the manufacturer; actual retail may be lower. ⓢ indicates tested model has been replaced by successor model; according to the manufacturer, the performance of new model should be similar to the tested model but features may vary. See opposite for new model number and suggested retail price. ⓓ indicates model discontinued.

SINGLE-DECK MODELS

Brand and model	Overall score	Price	Record/play flutter	Mid-frequency, Dolby B	Mid-frequency, Dolby C	High-frequency, Dolby B	High-frequency, Dolby C	Record/play frequency response	Overall convenience	Controls	Advantages	Disadvantages	Comments
✓ Aiwa AD-F810	94	$400	◐	○	◐	○	◐	◐	◐	◐	E,H,I	—	U,V
Sony TC-K670 ⓢ	91	280	◐	○	◐	◑	○	◐	◐	◐	C,E,H	j	L,U,V
JVC TD-V541TN	88	380	◐	○	◐	◑	◐	◐	○	○	—	g,j	K,L
Technics RS-BX606	88	400	◐	○	◐	◑	◐	◐	○	◐	G,H	—	U
Nakamichi Cassette Deck 2 ⓓ	87	360	◐	○	◐	◐	◐	◐	◐	○	C,E	b	N,V
Carver TD-1200 ⓓ	86	360	◐	○	◐	○	◐	●	◐	◐	D	b,f,i,k	D,S
Yamaha KX-530	86	399	◐	○	◐	◐	◐	◐	○	◐	D,G,H,K	—	R,U,V
Sansui D-X211HX-R ⓓ	85	200	◐	○	◐	◐	◐	○	◐	—		g,h	K,T
NAD 6340	83	399	○	○	◐	◐	◐	◐	●	◐	D	b,f,g,i,k,l	D,O,Q
Onkyo TA-R401	82	380	◐	◑	◐	◐	◐	◐	○	○	G	g	K
Pioneer CT-S609R ⓢ	82	240	◐	◑	◐	○	◐	◐	◐	◐	E	g	K,M
Fisher CR-9070	80	350	◐	○	◐	◑	○	◐	◐	○	B,C,E,F,H	j	H,U,V

MID-PRICED CASSETTE DECKS 103

Brand and model	Overall score	Price	Record/play flutter	Mid-frequency, Dolby B	Mid-frequency, Dolby C	High-frequency, Dolby B	High-frequency, Dolby C	Record/play frequency response	Overall convenience	Controls	Advantages	Disadvantages	Comments
Kenwood KX-7030	80	$379	◒	●	◒	◒	●	◒	◒	○	A,C,G,H,I,K	a,j	K,U
Denon DDR-780 [D]	79	400	◒	●	◒	◒	○	◒	◒	◒	—	g,j	U
Harman/Kardon TD-4400	79	419	◒	●	○	●	○	◒	◒	◒	E,K	g,i,k	—
DUAL-DECK MODELS													
Sony TC-WR875	88	500	◒	○	◒	◒	◒	◒	◒	◒	C,F,H,J	d,j,m	M,U,V,W,X
Sony TC-WR775 [S]	83	285	○	○	◒	◒	◒	◒	◒	○	C,F,H,J	g,k	M,Q,W,X
Denon DRW-850	82	500	◒	●	◒	◒	◒	◒	◒	◒	—	g,k	J,W,X
Kenwood KX-W8030 [S]	80	280	◒	●	◒	◒	◒	◒	◒	○	B,C,F,G,H,J,K	a,d,g	K,W,X
Pioneer CT-W850R [S]	80	380	◒	●	◒	◒	◒	◒	◒	◒	E,F	g	E,G,K
Sansui D-X311WR [D]	80	280	◒	●	◒	◒	○	◒	◒	◒	F,J	g,h	J,K
Yamaha KX-W332 [S]	79	375	◒	●	◒	●	○	◒	○	◒	—	e,g,h,k	M
Carver TDR-2400	78	500	◒	●	◒	◒	◒	◒	◒	◒	E,G	e,h,l,m	B,D,S
JVC TD-W505TN [D]	78	210	○	●	◒	◒	◒	◒	◒	◒	E,J	g,h,j,k	B,C,F,I,J,K
Onkyo TA-RW470 [D]	77	370	◒	●	◒	◒	◒	◒	◒	◐	J	e,h,k	B,C,F,M,N
Teac W-580R [D]	77	250	○	●	◒	◒	○	◒	◒	◒	F,J,K	d,e,g,h	B,K,M,W,X
JVC TD-W805TN	76	380	◒	●	◒	◒	◒	◒	◒	○	E,J	d,g,j,l	K,W,X
Technics RS-TR555 [D]	74	270	◒	●	◒	◒	◒	◒	◒	◒	J	c,m	K,M,P,W,X
Pioneer CT-W550R [D]	71	250	◒	●	○	●	◒	◒	◒	◒	E,F	h	K,M
Radio Shack Optimus SCT-89 [D]	71	300	◐	●	◒	◒	○	◒	◒	◒	F	a,e,h	B,M
Pioneer Elite CT-WM77R [S]	70	365	◒	●	○	◒	◒	○	◒	◒	E,H,J	g,j	A,E,J,K,M,W

Successor Models (in Ratings order)
Sony TC-K670 is succeeded by TC-K690, $350; Pioneer CT-S609R by CT-S601R, $320; Sony TC-WR775 by TC-WR790, $380; Kenwood KX-W8030 by KX-W8040, $379; Pioneer CT-W850R by CT-W801R, $390; Yamaha KX-W332 by KX-W362, $429; Pioneer CT-WM77R by CT-WM70R, $510.

Performance Notes
All were judged: • Excellent or very good in frequency response during playback. • Excellent or very good in playback flutter.
Except as noted, all dual-deck models were judged: • Excellent or very good in maintaining frequency response in dubbing.

Ratings Keys continued

MID-PRICED CASSETTE DECKS

Features in Common
All have: • Dolby B and C noise reduction. • Auto-stop at end of play, rewind, or fast forward. • Light-touch controls.
All dual-deck models have: • Autoreverse on both decks. • High-speed dubbing. • Relay (continuous) play from one deck to the other.
Except as noted, all have: • Dolby HX Pro. • Automatic tape-type selection. • Record level control with left-right balance. • Headphone jack. • No input for microphone. • Tape counter for each well. • Record-mute button that inserts blank spot on tape. • FM multiplex filter. • Ability to record using external timer. • Width of 16½ to 17½ in. • Depth of 10¾ to 15 in. • Height of 4½ to 5¾ in. • Ability to rewind a 90-min. tape in 2 to 2½ min. • 1-yr. warranty on parts and labor.

Key to Advantages
A–Can store auto-bias settings for all tape types.
B–Can store bias settings for 1 tape type.
C–Can start playing automatically after rewind.
D–Control to adjust high-frequency response during play.
E–All operating modes clearly indicated on display.
F–Can skip long blank portions of tape during play.
G–Can play 1 selection repeatedly.
H–Record-level meter more finely graduated than most.
I–Rewind time, less than 2 min., faster than most.
J–Allows edit changes in dub mode.
K–Intro scan; samples selections for a few seconds apiece.

Key to Disadvantages
a–Can record with only 1 button; risks accidental erasure.
b–Lacks automatic tape-type recognition.
c–Has separate record-level control for each channel.
d–One deck lacks bias adjustment.
e–One deck lacks tape counter.
f–Lacks record-mute button.
g–Difficult to see tape once it's loaded.
h–Record-level meter more coarsely graduated than most.
i–Lacks headphone jack.
j–Power must be on to eject cassette.
k–Cannot use external timer to record or play.
l–Rewind time slower than most—exceeds 2½ min.
m–Worse than most in maintaining frequency response in dubbing.

Key to Comments
A–Changer model—can hold up to 6 cassettes and play selections from each.
B–Microphone inputs.
C–Separate external-microphone record-level control.
D–Record-level control ganged but can move separately.
E–No channel-balance control.
F–Can mix narration onto existing recording.
G–Can control level of dubbed material.
H–In record mode, has automatic fade-in/fade-out control.
I–Pitch control.
J–Single tape counter for both decks.
K–Record functions can be synchronized with same-brand CD player.
L–Extra audio input connects deck to CD player directly.
M–Lacks FM multiplex filter.
N–Lacks Dolby HX Pro.
O–Switch can compress dynamic range—good for making copies of CDs for walkabout player or autosound system. May be helpful for hearing-impaired listeners.
P–Has DBX noise reduction.
Q–Tape-takeup tension higher than usual.
R–Rewind gets faster if button held down.
S–Simulated "rack handles" add 2 in. to front-panel width.
T–2-yr. warranty on parts and labor.
U–Headphone volume control.
V–Cassette backlight.
W–Has relay record function.
X–Has simultaneous record function.

ABOUT PRICES IN THE BUYING GUIDE

Prices for most products, notably big-ticket items such as kitchen appliances, home-electronics gear, and gardening equipment, have been updated for the Buying Guide. The prices we give, unless otherwise noted, are approximate or suggested retail as quoted by the manufacturer. Discounts may therefore be substantial, especially for electronics and camera equipment.

FEATURES — MID-PRICED CASSETTE DECKS

▶ See report, page 81 and Ratings, page 102. From Consumer Reports, March 1992.

Brand and model	Three heads	Autoreverse	Quick reverse	Auto return	Memory rewind	Meter segments	Tape counter [1]	Cue/review	Music search	Remote	Same-brand remote
SINGLE-DECK MODELS											
Aiwa AD-F810	✔	—	—	—	✔	16	E	✔	✔	✔	—
Sony TC-K670	✔	—	—	—	✔	15	E	✔	✔	—	—
JVC TD-V541TN	✔	—	—	✔	✔	14	D,E,TR	—	✔	—	✔
Technics RS-BX606	✔	—	—	—	✔	15	D,E	—	✔	—	—
Nakamichi 2	—	—	—	—	✔	13	D	—	—	—	✔
Carver TD-1200	—	—	—	—	—	13	M	—	—	—	—
Yamaha KX-530	—	—	—	✔	✔	16	E,TR	—	✔	✔	—
Sansui D-X211HX-R	—	✔	✔	✔	—	6	M	✔	—	—	✔
NAD 6340	—	—	—	—	—	12	M	—	—	—	—
Onkyo TA-R401	—	✔	✔	—	—	10	E,TR	—	✔	✔	✔
Pioneer CT-S609R	—	✔	✔	—	—	10	D,E	—	✔	—	✔
Fisher CR-9070	✔	—	—	—	✔	16	E	✔	✔	—	✔
Kenwood KX-7030	✔	—	—	✔	—	17	E	—	✔	—	✔
Denon DRR-780	—	✔	✔	✔	✔	12	E,TR	✔	✔	✔	—
Harman/Kardon TD-4400	—	—	—	—	—	12	E	✔	✔	—	✔
DUAL-DECK MODELS											
Sony TC-WR875	—	✔	✔	—	✔	16	E	—	✔	—	—
Sony TC-WR775	—	✔	✔	—	✔	16	D	—	—	—	—
Denon DRW-850	—	✔	✔	✔	✔	12	E	✔	✔	✔	—
Kenwood KX-W8030	—	✔	—	✔	✔	17	E	✔	✔	—	✔
Pioneer CT-W850R	—	✔	—	—	—	11	D,E	—	✔	—	✔
Sansui D-X311WR	—	✔	✔	—	✔	8	D	✔	✔	—	✔
Yamaha KX-W332	—	✔	✔	—	—	6	M	—	✔	—	—
Carver TDR-2400	—	✔	—	—	—	6	M	✔	✔	✔	—
JVC TD-W505TN	—	✔	—	—	—	8	D	—	✔	—	✔
Onkyo TA-RW470	—	✔	—	—	—	6	E,TR	—	—	—	✔
Teac W-580R	—	✔	—	—	—	8	M	✔	✔	—	✔
JVC TD-W805TN	—	✔	✔	—	—	14	E	—	✔	—	✔
Technics RS-TR555	—	✔	✔	—	—	12	D	—	✔	—	✔
Pioneer CT-W550R	—	✔	—	—	—	9	D,E	—	✔	—	✔
Radio Shack Optimus SCT-89	—	✔	✔	—	—	6	M	—	—	—	—
Pioneer Elite CT-WM77R	—	✔	—	—	—	17	D,E	—	✔	✔	✔

[1] *M* = mechanical; *D* = electronic digital; *E* = elapsed time; *TR* = time remaining.

RATINGS: LOW-PRICED LOUDSPEAKERS

▶ **See report, page 76.** From Consumer Reports, March 1992.

Recommendations: The most accurate surround-sound speaker in our tests is also one of the cheapest: the *BIC Venturi V52S*, at a list price of $178 per pair. For a fifth, center-channel speaker, consider any of the top five models in that group.

Ratings order: Listed by types; within types, listed in order of accuracy score in surround-sound location. Models with equal scores are listed alphabetically. A difference in accuracy of 8 points or less is not very significant. Price is the manufacturers' suggested retail. Key to finish: **Bl**=black laminate over wood; **Bm**=black metal; **Bp**=black plastic; **Bv**=black vinyl over wood; **Gp**=Gray plastic; **Wp**=white plastic; **Wv**=wood-printed vinyl over wood; **W**=wood veneer over wood. ⑤ indicates tested model has been replaced by successor model; according to the manufacturer, the performance of new model should be similar to the tested model but features may vary. See opposite for new model number and suggested retail price, if available. ⓓ indicates model discontinued.

Brand and model	Price	Accuracy [1]	Bass cutoff, Hz. [2]	Impedance, ohms [3]	Minimum power, watts	Dimensions, HxWxD, in.	Finish	Comments
SURROUND-CHANNEL MODELS								
BIC Venturi V52S	$178 pr.	87/86	51	5/8	16	12x7x7½	Bv	D,J,S
Realistic Minimus 77	160	86/80	70	8/8	14	8½x5½x5	Bm	F,L,S
Bose 101 Music Monitor	219	85/80	63	4/4	18	9¼x6¼x6	Bp	F,I,O
Boston Acoustics HD5V	170	84/82	54	5/8	23	9¾x6½x7½	Bv	D,J,P,S
AR Patio Partners ⓓ	220	83/78	62	4/4	23	9x6x9	Bp	F,O,T,V
Cambridge Model Ten	150	83/78	120	5/4	16	6½x4½x3¼	Bp	C,F,J,L,S
Polk M³	200	83/81	60	5/8	16	11½x6½x10	Bp	F,N,P,T
Cambridge The Surround ⑤	399	82/74	93	7/8	16	8½x6x5¾	Bp	G,L,O,S
NHT Zero	200	82/77	82	8/8	20	9x5½x5¾	Bl	F
Realistic Minimus 26	74	82/79	60	8/8	14	11x6¾x5½	Wv	F
Pinnacle PN5+	185	81/83	46	5/6	25	11¼x6¾x7¼	Bv	W
Advent Mini-Advent	180	80/78	70	5/6	14	11x6¾x5¼	Bv	S
Infinity Reference E-L	179	80/80	54	4/6	25	11½x7½x6¾	Wv	—
Phase Tech 235ES	200	79/78	70	6/8	19	10x6½x6	Bp	M
JBL ProPerformer	199	78/72	100	6/8	13	6¼x6x5½	Wp	I,M,Q
Jensen 2652	130	78/76	53	6/8	9	15x11¼x7	W	
JVC SP-XS6BK ⓓ	180	77/71	80	9/8	9	27x8x8	Bv	F,I,P,U,X
Pioneer CS-X5	60	69/62	110	8/8	9	7¾x5¾x5¼	W	F,H,I,P,Y
Yamaha NS-A102	178	69/65	90	5/6	13	11¾x8¾x3½	Gp	I,L,R

LOW-PRICED LOUDSPEAKERS 107

CENTER-CHANNEL MODELS

Brand and model	Price	Accuracy [1]	Bass cutoff, Hz. [2]	Impedance, ohms [3]	Minimum power, watts	Dimensions, HxWxD, in.	Finish	Comments
Design Acoustics PS-CV	$120 ea.	88/82	57	6/8	15	10¼x7x6¼	Bv	—
NHT 1C	170	87/83	50	6/8	24	12x7½x9¼	Bl	A,B,G
Polk CS-100	170	85/79	58	9/8	13	6x18x6¾	Bv	E,S
Pinnacle PN50	125	83/82	43	4/8	36	14¾x7½x6¾	Bv	D,S,W
JBL Pro III	150	82/77	56	4/4	23	6x9x5½	Bp	C,E,N
Boston Acoustics Shielded Satellite	150	77/69	150	5/8	23	8x5x4¾	Bv	C,F,L,O
Altec Lansing 66	200	70/69	47	4/8	23	8x15¾x7	Wp	B,K,L,P,Q,V
Boston Acoustics 404V	129	64/59	83	8/8	9	5½x17x6½	Bv	I,K,P,S
Yamaha NS-C90	149	63/58	79	5/6	14	6x17½x7½	Bv	F,I,S

[1] We determined **limited-spectrum** accuracy over the 80-16,000 Hz frequency range used for a Dolby Surround system's adjunct speakers, and **full-spectrum** accuracy over the wider, 40-16,000 Hz range we use as the chief criterion for judged accuracy of main speakers.

[2] The frequency in the bass at which the sound becomes only half as loud as the rest of the spectrum.

[3] The speaker's resistance to electric current, which determines compatibility with a receiver or amplifier.

Successor Model
Cambridge The Surround is succeeded by The Surround II, $249 pr.

Features in Common
Except as noted, all have: • Spring-loaded connectors that take dual banana plugs or bare wires. • Tweeter and at least 1 woofer. • Removable black grille. • 5-yr. warranty. Except as noted, no center-channel model had a noticeable effect on the TV picture when placed atop TV set.

Key to Comments
A–Atop TV set, had very slight effect on colors at top of picture.
B–Atop TV set, caused very slight sound-related disturbance in picture.
C–Atop TV set, had slight effect on colors at top of picture.
D–Atop TV set, caused slight sound-related disturbance in picture.
E–Atop TV set, caused moderate sound-related disturbance in picture.
F–Connectors do not take double banana plug.
G–Binding-post connectors.
H–Slotted-screw connectors.
I–Full-range driver, rather than woofer and tweeter.
J–Recommended by mfr. for surround- and center-channel use; available singly.
K–Recommended by mfr. for both surround- and center-channel use.
L–Screw slots for wall-mounting.
M–Brackets for wall-mounting.
N–Brackets for wall- or ceiling-mounting.
O–Brackets available for wall-mounting.
P–Grille not removable.
Q–Grille is white.
R–Grille is gray.
S–Resilient adhesive pads to prevent sliding.
T–Triangular design.
U–Floor-standing design.
V–Water-resistant, according to mfr.
W–7-yr. warranty.
X–3-yr. warranty.
Y–1-yr. warranty.

PHOTOGRAPHY

Cameras & lenses 109	Film processing 116
Tripods 114	Ratings 118

Camcorders, popular though they may be, will never entirely replace the still camera. There'll always be a place for vacation snapshots, for wallet-sized pictures of loved ones, and for photographs that mark life's rites of passage—birthdays, graduations, weddings. And that means there'll always be a market for regular cameras and the paraphernalia that goes with them—accessory lenses, tripods, and the myriad attachments that fill camera cases.

Blunder-proof, highly automated compact 35mm cameras have quickly become the amateur's best friend. Equipped with a moderate zoom lens, such cameras are almost as appealing and versatile as more "professional" single-lens reflex models. Disposable cameras—single-use models preloaded with print film—have also become so popular that roughly one disposable camera is sold for every regular camera. When all the pictures are taken, photofinishers turn your film into prints, sometimes in as little as an hour. A good lab can return crisp photos in glorious colors. A bad laboratory—well, don't ask. Read the accompanying report.

For the really conscientious photographer, a sturdy tripod also allows for careful framing and for using exposure settings that might cause blurring if the camera were hand held. For video work, a decent tripod is a must. A tripod specifically built for camcorder use can keep home videos from looking jumpy and jerky.

Shopping for photographic equipment is unusual in some ways. You'll find that few stores ask full list price for a camera or lens. Discounts depend on a store's competition and the amount of customer service and convenience it provides. For rock-bottom prices, check the mail-order ads in newspapers or camera magazines. Mail-order houses in New York and other large cities sell cameras and photography equipment sometimes for as little as half the list price.

Watch out for vendors who go beyond ordinary sales pressure into sharp, even illegal, sales practices. The classic trick is the familiar bait-and-switch: "We're all out of that one, but we have something better...." Protect yourself by refusing substitutes.

A variation on bait-and-switch is the "tie-in." There, you're told you cannot buy an item at a certain price unless you buy something else—a camera case, for instance. Try to find out beforehand which removable pieces—lens caps, straps, cases, and so forth—are standard equipment on whatever you're buying. That way, you won't fall victim to "stripping," where a store strips off standard equipment and then sells it back to you.

Much of the photo equipment available in this country is called "gray market" merchandise, imported by someone other than the manufacturer's authorized U.S. subsidiary. That doesn't mean there's anything wrong with the goods—except that they may come with an "international" or camera store warranty that may complicate obtaining warranty service. Unless the ad specifically says "U.S. warranty," assume the goods are gray market.

A store may tell you your sales slip is your warranty. That means the store, not the manufacturer, assumes responsibility for the warranty period. Some stores may give you a choice of goods with or without a U.S. warranty. For gear least likely to break—tripods and lenses—you don't risk much to forego the premium-priced U.S. warranty if the price is right. For cameras, we'd think carefully about risking expensive camera repairs.

CAMERAS & LENSES

▶ Ratings of zoom lenses on page 118.

The 35mm format has become the standard for professional photographers, serious amateurs, and snapshooters alike. One reason for its appeal is the negative size—about 1x1½ inches, appreciably larger than negatives from disc and 110 cameras. Bigger negatives yield sharper enlargements. Another reason: the variety of color and black-and-white films available.

There are two basic types of 35mm cameras—the compact and the single-lens reflex, or SLR. In addition, 35mm "bridge" designs combine some characteristics of compacts and SLRs. They're aimed at photographers who want more than a compact but less than an interchangeable-lens SLR.

Compact 35s

These pocket-sized models (a few fit in a shirt pocket, most in a coat pocket) are nice for snapshooters with little or no photographic background. Automated film-loading features have made them almost as easy to use as disc and 110 snapshot cameras. List prices for most compacts range from about $80 to $300.

Disposables—single-use camera preloaded with print film—appeared in the late 1980s and have become very popular. Some disposables can be used underwater; some take panoramic shots, for prints about twice as wide as ordinary snapshots. Some even have flash or a telephoto lens. They list for about $9 to $16, depending on type. You shoot the pictures, then return the entire camera for processing.

Lens. Early compact cameras were limited by their single fixed-focal-length lens. These days many compacts come with a zoom lens that goes from a wide-angle lens (say, 35 mm) to a modest telephoto (say, 105 mm) so you can bring in more distant subjects and frame a scene even more precisely.

Exposure. Nearly all compacts have automatic exposure control to help assure proper exposure of the film; a built-in light meter sizes up the lighting and adjusts the lens and shutter accordingly. The system strikes a balance between fast shutter speed (to prevent moving objects from blurring) and small aperture, or lens opening (to enhance overall sharpness). A few models have a "backlight" switch that lets you adjust the exposure when strong light comes from behind the subject. All but the most rudimentary compact cameras have a built-in flash; most fire their flash automatically when it's needed.

Film handling. Most compact 35s have automatic film handling: You drop in the cartridge, pull out enough film to reach a certain mark in the camera, close the camera back, and a motor automatically threads the film. The motor also advances the film after each shot and rewinds it when done.

All but the cheapest compact models read the film's sensitivity from the checkerboard DX-coding on the cartridge and appropriately set the exposure meter. Some can read only the most popular color-print film speeds, ISO 100 and 400, while some read the range of ISOs from 25 to 1600 or even 3200. If you plan to use a variety of film speeds, look for a camera that covers a wide range.

Focusing. None of the compacts we've seen require you to focus. The simplest models, sometimes called "focus-free," have fixed focus, like those in most 110 cameras and older "box" cameras. Cameras that work that way use very small lens apertures to keep all objects more than a few feet away in reasonably sharp focus. They can't take non-flash pictures in as dim light as can a typical autofocus camera.

Compact cameras that focus automatically typically list for more than $100. Autofocus systems set the lens for one of several distance zones. One zone might cover subjects 8 to 10 feet away; another, 10 to 14 feet away, and so on. Some models use only two distance zones (near and far) while some cameras cover a dozen or more. As a rule, the more zones, the better.

Viewfinder. Some compacts have a clear "bright-frame" viewfinder that's easy to use, even with eyeglasses. Others sharply frame the entire image. Our tests have shown such viewfinders to be fairly accurate: What's visible in the frame is pretty much what is captured on film. Worst are ones with indistinct framing that shifts if you move your eye.

Limitations. Compact cameras can stymie an advanced photographer, who might want to use a variety of lenses or override the camera's automatic settings. Compact cameras usually don't allow such control. They don't even let you know *which* settings they've chosen for a picture. If you crave artistic control, compact cameras aren't for you. But many a snapshooter is happy to trade control for convenience and simplicity in a small package.

SLR cameras

Single-lens-reflex cameras were once strictly for serious hobbyists and professionals—photographers who knew how to take advantage of the many ways possible to manipulate lenses, exposure controls, focus, and film types to create artistic effects. Recent innovations have automated so much of this that some SLRs can be as easy to work as a compact 35mm camera. But the main photographic value of an SLR remains not so much in the camera itself as in the additional lenses and paraphernalia you can add that transform the camera into a "system."

Lenses. The distinctive trapezoidal hump at the top of an SLR camera houses a prism mounted over a mirror, an arrangement that lets you see what the lens sees when you look through the eyepiece behind the hump. A built-in light meter also "sees" and evaluates what the lens sees.

The reflected image—the "reflex" in "single-lens reflex"—makes it practical to use a variety of lenses in addition to the "normal" 50 mm or 55 mm lens. Snap on a super-wide-angle lens and you gain appreciable peripheral vision—excellent for panoramas or photographing groups in tight spaces. Switch to a telephoto lens and you're looking through a telescope—excellent for candid shots and bringing in distant objects without having to move in close. Or you can use a zoom lens for a whole range of views. What you see through the lens is what the film will record when you press the shutter.

Thus, an SLR system gives you immense control over point of view and composition. But you're no longer talking about a $300 camera; an SLR system can easily cost several times the price of the camera alone.

For years, the lens typically sold with an SLR was a "normal" 50 mm lens. Now, that lens is likely to be a moderate-range zoom (35 mm to 105 mm or so). Our tests show that the quality of zoom lenses has improved markedly in recent years. Any lapses in sharpness are usually imperceptible except under high magnification.

Automatic exposure controls. Many SLRs are programmed to select both the aperture and shutter speed automatically. SLRs with aperture-priority exposure let you set the lens opening (f-stop) while they automatically select the shutter speed. Those with shutter-priority exposure do just the opposite. Most can be operated in a manual mode as well: Typically, an indicator in the viewfinder confirms when you've manually set a combination of aperture and shutter speed that works for a shot's lighting.

All the exposure systems rely on readings from a built-in light meter. Some systems (spot meters) check lighting only at the very center of the frame, where the subject is likely to be; others (center-weighted) consider the entire frame but give greater weight to the center; yet others (multipattern metering) average the frame's light reading in a more complex manner. SLRs with more than one metering mode let a photographer select the mode used.

Automated film handling. This helps load, advance, and rewind the film. Most cameras with an autowinder also let you fire off a quick series of shots, as fashion and sports photographers are wont to do. Automatic DX-code readers set film speed.

Automatic focusing. Some people find focusing by hand and eye to be tedious and slow. Typically, the center of the viewfinder shows a split image whose halves you must align by turning the lens. Or you must try to sharpen a shimmering microprism ring surrounding the split-image circle in the center of the viewfinder.

Technology has solved the focusing problem as well. At the press of a button, computer chips and a miniature motor can now focus the lens in a split second, generally with pinpoint accuracy. You pay dearly for such convenience: Autofocus SLRs carry list prices of $500 to $1000, several hundred dollars more than the price of a manual-focus model. An autofocus SLR with a zoom lens can easily list for well over $1000 (but discount prices are typically hundreds lower).

Do you really need to spend the extra money for an autofocus SLR? No. Focusing an SLR is tricky only if you've never done it before. With just a little practice, the technique becomes second nature. The same is true of film loading and automatic-exposure control. If you're willing to spend the time to learn the photographic ropes, you can choose a basic SLR, which is the best SLR buy. Some camera makers no longer support their manual-focus cameras with a full line of lenses, however.

If you want a zoom lens, say, for a manual SLR, you may have to settle for a different company's lens or for a second-hand lens.

'Bridge' cameras

These cameras "bridge" the gap between SLRs and compacts—they offer less control than a typical SLR but more versatility than a typical compact camera. With list prices ranging from $600 to $800, these cameras are almost as expensive as a good SLR.

Bridge cameras are built with a non-interchangeable zoom lens whose focal length generally spans 35 mm to 135 mm, a wider range than the zooms typical of compact cameras. Additional features include: a viewfinder that's sometimes the single-lens reflex type; programmed exposure; autofocus; built-in electronic flash (also found on most compacts and even on some regular SLRs); and an autowinder with automatic film threading. Other features vary. With all their automation, bridge cameras are very easy to use. But so are most autofocus SLRs.

From what we've seen in our tests, the lenses on these cameras are about as good as that of a middling SLR zoom—very good but not exceptional. More important, whether or not they had an SLR viewfinder, the bridge cameras' viewfinders didn't let you frame scenes quite as accurately as interchangeable-lens SLRs typically do. What you see in the camera isn't necessarily what you get. Framing errors of 15 or 20 percent are typical. People with the money and time to invest in learning photography will be less limited with an SLR than a bridge model. People without that level of photographic interest may need no more than a cheaper compact 35mm camera.

Flashes

Electronic flash units range from compact, low-powered models with limited features and list prices around $50 to high-powered, multi-featured models with list prices of more than $300.

A camera owner's choice is limited by problems of compatibility. Most camera manufacturers' flash units are "dedicated"; each is designed for one or more models of the same camera brand and won't work satisfactorily with other brands, if at all. Consumers have to rely on salespeople or product literature to tell which flash does what with which cameras.

In general, the expensive units offer more light output and special features. You can tilt the unit toward the ceiling for "bounce" flash, a more pleasing effect than the flatness of head-on flash. They calculate exposure automatically with your camera's metering system or let you override the setting manually. Other features let you diffuse light or lighten shadows about faces.

Most recently, camera manufacturers are tackling "red-eye," the nemesis of built-in flash photography. Some models allow the photographer to flip the built-in flash farther from the lens, so there's less reflection from a subject's retinas. Others "pre-flash"—they first fire to constrict the subject's pupils (which cuts red-eye). Then, after a short delay, they flash for real to take the picture.

The tests

Key tests are for sharpness, a function of a camera's lens and focusing system. The lens chosen for SLRs was the manufacturer's moderate zoom, covering a 35mm to 105mm (or 135mm) range of focal lengths. Some camera companies no longer make a zoom lens for their manual SLR models; those models were rated as if equipped with an aftermarket lens of average quality.

Tests of exposure accuracy tell how capably a camera gauges lighting to adjust its shutter and aperture for a given scene and

Text continues on page 114

A GUIDE TO CAMERA AUTOMATION

Autofocus. Speeds up picture taking. May not work well in dim light or in scenes with little contrast or with repetitive graphic patterns.

Autofocus illuminator. A red beam shines on the subject to help the autofocus work in dim light.

Autowinder. Typically threads, advances, and rewinds film. Lets you capture rapid-fire sequences. A popular convenience.

Bar-code reader. This optional Canon accessory comes with a booklet of pictures showing different photo situations. After selecting the picture that best fits your scene, you scan a bar code under the sample with the pen-like reader. Then you place the reader against the camera to transfer the code to the camera, which sets the aperture and shutter speed.

A cumbersome gimmick, it's sometimes hard to match sample pictures to actual situations.

'Creative expansion' cards. With this Minolta feature, plug-in chips provide special exposure modes. Cards are useful for customizing camera settings, but they're a nuisance to store and change.

Depth-of-field preview. This feature adjusts lens to show how much background and foreground will be sharp, given the lens aperture. May not work in all exposure modes and often too dim to see results.

Depth-of-field mode. An autofocus option that lets you select the nearest foreground and farthest background objects that you want to keep sharp. The camera then tries to adjust aperture and shutter accordingly. Takes the guesswork out of how the final photo will look.

Diopter adjustment. Adjusts viewfinder for moderate near- or farsightedness, so that eyeglass wearers with no astigmatism can focus and shoot without their glasses on. A nice feature for some.

DX film-speed reader. Reads the checkered code on 35mm cartridge to set film speed for proper exposure. Convenient—keeps you from ruining film if you forget to change meter settings. But some systems don't cover all common speeds.

Film-prewind feature. Shoots film "backwards" by first unwinding the entire roll from cartridge. As you shoot, film winds back into the light-tight film cartridge. If you accidentally open the camera in mid-roll, no more than one shot is ruined. A good idea.

Follow-focus mode. Sometimes called "servo" or "continuous focus," this feature keeps a moving subject sharp as long as you hold shutter release partway down and keep the subject centered. Sometimes, though, the camera will take an unfocused shot.

Programmed exposure. Automatically sets both aperture and shutter speed for proper exposure. Works well under all but trickiest lighting—a boon to novices and pros. Some programs, selectable by the photographer, favor background and foreground sharpness; others favor freezing fast action.

Trap-focus mode. After being focused manually, the camera automatically snaps any subject that moves into the center of the frame at the preset distance. This feature comes in handy for wildlife and candid photography.

film. Accurate exposure is essential for shooting slides, but less so for print film, which is more forgiving of over-exposure. Our speed-of-use tests tap overall convenience: We time a pair of experienced photographers as they load, shoot an assigned sequence of photos under a range of conditions, and unload.

Buying advice

Before you shop for a camera, you should decide how deeply you want to get involved in photography. If your commitment goes no further than recording everyday family events, a compact 35mm may be all the camera you need. For a dash of flexibility in framing your shots, consider a compact with a zoom lens.

If you are or expect to become knowledgeable about photography, consider an SLR without autofocus. Equipped with a 50mm lens, a manual-focus SLR lists for $300 to $600. Equipped with a zoom lens to cover a fairly wide range—say, 35mm to 105mm—it would list for about $500 to $750. If money is no object, buy an autofocus model equipped with a zoom lens. Such camera bodies list for $350 to $850, the lenses for $375 to $650.

Whatever type of camera you decide on, select several models that have the features you want. In the store, hold each camera to your eye and check its view, controls, grip, and balance. That's the only way to tell whether you'll be comfortable taking pictures with it.

VIDEO & PHOTO TRIPODS

▶ Ratings on page 119.

Unless you're blessed with rock-steady hands, one of the simplest ways to hold a camera steady is with a tripod, an accessory long used in still photography. Fortunately, today's fast films and quick shutter speeds allow sharp pictures without "camera shake" even if hands aren't so steady. So tripods have become primarily an artistic device, allowing you to compose a picture carefully and maintain that composition securely until conditions are absolutely right or if the shot demands a long exposure time.

For camcorder owners, however, a good tripod is more a necessity if you want your home videos to have a professional look. To achieve smooth "panning" (turning from side to side) or "tilting" (pointing the lens up or down), you need a video tripod.

A full-sized tripod is the most effective way to steady a camera, but there are other options: minipods, diminutive versions that fit into a camera bag or backpack; monopods, with one leg to rest on the ground or hoist above a crowd; car pods, which clamp to rolled-down car windows; and shoulder pods, which brace a camera against the body the way you'd steady a rifle. Some pros even carry a bean bag, which molds itself to various surfaces and on which a camera can rest steady.

The choices

Video tripods. Camcorders, as a rule, do work better with tripods designed specifically for video use. Such tripods have a "fluid" pan head—viscous friction on the pan and tilt motions to ensure smooth motion. Further, you can adjust the amount of friction until the camera sits still when you release the pan handle and yet moves smoothly when you push on it. (Mount a camcorder on a typical photo tripod and you'll see the difference. You must loosen and retighten tilt and pan locks frequently; it's also harder to follow the action without jerky motions.)

Mid-priced video models generally list for $100 to $150 and weigh in around five pounds; some are a pound or so lighter. More expensive models tend to be taller and heavier; less expensive ones, shorter and lighter.

Photo tripods. Because these tripods are less complex mechanically, they're a bit cheaper than video tripods. Photo tripods list for about $80 to $115. They're also lighter, generally weighing in at three to four pounds.

Features to look for

A tripod has three principal parts: a pan head, which anchors the camera and controls its motion; a center column, which supports the pan head and periscopes up and down; and the legs.

Pan head. Video and still cameras need to pan from side to side and tilt up and down. A still camera should also be able to be tilted on its side, to shoot in a vertical format. Some pan heads can perform all three operations, but some lack a side-tilting axis. You can use those tripods to take vertical shots, but to accomplish it you must tip the pan head 90 degrees, loosen the camera-mounting screw, and rotate the camera.

Center column. A geared column lets you raise or lower the camera with a crank. The alternative, a simple tube that you adjust with one hand and lock with the other, works fine if the camera isn't too heavy.

Legs. A tripod's telescoping legs can make it slower or faster to set up. We think legs in three sections work best. Units with more leg sections are more time consuming to set up; those with only two sections may be steadier but aren't as short when folded for carrying and storage.

Look for legs that lock with levers or knobs instead of collets, small threaded rings that tend to jam when dirty. Lever locks are fastest to operate.

Attaching the camera. Most video tripods and some photo models have a quick-release insert—a small fitted plastic piece with a protruding screw—that's supposed to expedite the union of camera and tripod. Instead of making the connection in the traditional way (by holding the camera over the tripod platform and tightening a screw from below), you screw the insert directly into the camera using a coin or screwdriver, then latch that combination onto a matching socket atop the pan head. In theory, the insert should speed setting up. But most such designs, we've found, make a camera less steady.

One feature that works well for camcorders is the use of a tiny pin on the mounting platform of most video tripods and some photo models. The pin, which fits into a corresponding hole on the bottom of a camcorder, prevents the camera from twisting on the tripod during use. Few, if any, still cameras have a hole for the pin, however. Some pins retract, but some must be removed before you attach the camera, a task that sometimes requires a screwdriver.

The tests

Key tests gauge freedom from vibration. For video models, we simulate up and down torque by releasing a weight suspended from a lever arm we place between the camera and the pan head; we then play back the tape frame by frame to measure the jumping and twitching of the images.

For still photography, the camera shutter itself is usually the source of vibration; we use a system of mirrors and projected crosshairs to capture and analyze the jiggling as a 35mm camera shoots at a relatively slow shutter speed.

We gauge speed and ease of use by having testers run through a drill involving set up and using each model to compose a series of shots in both vertical and horizontal formats.

Buying advice

Videos greatly improve when a tripod is used. Hand-held camcorder shots, particularly telephoto shots, are never really steady and rapidly become tiring to watch. Of prime importance: a tripod that is stable and sturdy and that allows for fluid pans and tilts. The surface on which the camera rests should be fairly large and made of a material like cork or textured rubber to keep the camcorder from twisting even if there is no built-in pin to help anchor the camcorder.

A tripod isn't really a must for still photography except in dim light or with long telephoto lenses, which magnify even the smallest vibration. But a tripod lets you frame and compose your shots precisely and permits sharp pictures at long exposure times.

FILM PROCESSING

▸ Ratings on page 120.

All photofinishing companies—from local one-hour outlets to giant mail-order operations—use highly automated equipment. The machinery is geared to deliver good prints of average subjects captured under normal lighting, but it can be easily foiled by out-of-the-ordinary conditions. And the folks running the machines don't always check the prints that come out. It's cheaper for the lab to redo botched jobs only when customers complain. Many never complain about printing errors, perhaps figuring the mistakes were their own fault.

Poor color balance—evidenced by odd skin tones, for example—often results when a bright, single-color background fools a lab's automatic color analyzer. Other common mistakes: overexposed prints, which look too dark, and underexposed prints, which look pale and washed out. Those errors can usually be corrected by the lab, but first a human being has to notice a problem. On the other hand, flat, muddy-looking prints due to underexposed negatives aren't the labs' fault.

Your photographs can also be prey to human error at the lab: mishandled negatives marred by fingerprints, dirt, or scratches; film inadvertently exposed to light during processing; and negatives chopped in half, for instance. Once in a rare while, you may even get someone else's pictures delivered to you. You can't blame that one on the machine.

The choices

Mail-order labs. These businesses operate nationwide, with mailing envelopes that usually double as order forms. They're fairly low-priced—typically $3.50 to $7 for a set of 3½x5-inch prints from a 24-exposure roll.

Minilab chains. These outfits, often found in malls, can deliver prints within a few hours after you drop off film. Many promise one-hour service. You pay a premium price for quick turnaround, generally $10 to $15 for a 24-exposure roll.

Wholesale companies. These processors operate through supermarkets, discount centers, and drugstores. You may never even know the laboratory's name. Qualex is the dominant wholesaler. One of its branches is Kodalux, descended from Kodak's photofinishing operation. Its service is offered primarily through camera stores and prepaid mailers. Prices for wholesalers are comparable to those of the mail-order companies. Turnaround generally takes two days.

The tests

We take hundreds of photos—mainly landscapes and portrait shots—to challenge photofinishers' equipment—using one kind of film *(Kodacolor Gold 100)*. We shoot in various lighting—flash, incandescent, and fluorescent light indoors and sunny and cloudy skies outside. We deliberately over- and underexpose some shots. A tripod set-up lets us duplicate photos and exposures precisely on multiple rolls of film in multiple cameras.

Then we send the film to the processors, staggering sets of rolls over several months, with some rolls timed to coincide with Christmas and vacation time, two busy seasons. We score print quality for all blunders, whether they're caused by a lab's machinery or its personnel.

Buying advice

Three mail-order labs served us best and have consistently done so in three tests over the past eight years. The better processors committed the fewest errors and returned prints generally within eight days, that for under $7 a roll. The wholesale labs were a notch or so poorer but still pretty good overall. You may find it more convenient to drop off film at the supermarket or drugstore than to use a mailer.

Unless you're in a terrible rush, stay away from the one-hour minilabs. Although the best were decent, as a group their results were mediocre, and they charged considerably more than mail-order and wholesale labs.

How to get more information

Check out what we've said in CONSUMER REPORTS. For the date of recent reports, refer to the four-year index in the back of the Buying Guide or the date noted on each Ratings table. Back issues are available at most libraries or can be ordered. You can also get the latest new- and used-car price information. For details, see page 307 (new cars) and page 310 (used cars).

RATINGS ZOOM LENSES

Better ← ⊖ ⊖ ○ ◐ ● → Worse

▶ **See report, page 109.** From Consumer Reports, November 1990.

Recommendations: The only zoom to disappoint us was the *Canon EF 35-80mm*, which mates with the *Canon EOS 700* camera.

Ratings order: Listed by types; within types, listed in order of overall score. For SLRs that use interchangeable lenses, we tested zooms in the 35-105mm or 35-135mm focal range where available. Differences of 5 or more points in score were not judged significant. Models with identical scores are listed alphabetically. Prices are manufacturer's suggested list price. Substantial discounts are available. Bridge cameras come with a built-in lens, included in the camera price.

Brand and model	Overall score	Price	Maximum aperture	Weight, oz.	Smallest field, in.	Sharpness	Chromatic aberration	Flare	Freedom from Distortion	Comments
SLR LENSES										
Minolta MD 35-135mm	95	$650	f/3.5-4.5	18	12	⊖	⊖	⊖	●	B,E
Yashica AF 35-105mm	89	375	f/3.5-4.5	17	13	⊖	⊖	⊖	◐	A,D
Canon EF 35-135mm	88	460	f/4-5.6	15	7	○	⊖	⊖	◐	A,D
Nikon Nikkor AIS 35-135mm	88	645	f/3.5-4.5	21	12	⊖	○	⊖	●	B
Pentax F SMC 35-135mm	87	577	f/3.5-4.5	17	13	○	⊖	⊖	◐	A,D
Olympus AF 35-105mm	86	470	f/3.5-4.5	16	16	○	⊖	⊖	●	D,E
Chinon AF 28-70mm	84	390	f/3.5-4.5	14	11	◐	⊖	⊖	⊖	A,D
Minolta Maxxum AF 35-105mm	84	376	f/3.5-4.5	11	8	◐	⊖	⊖	◐	A,C,D,E
Canon EF 35-80mm	75	180	f/4-5.6	8	5	●	⊖	◐	○	A,C,D
BRIDGE-CAMERA LENSES										
Chinon Genesis 35-80mm	91	—	f/4.1-6.4	—	11	○	⊖	⊖	⊖	A,D
Olympus Infinity 330 38-105mm	90	—	f/4.5-6	—	14	⊖	⊖	⊖	◐	A,D
Ricoh Mirai 105 38-105mm	90	—	f/4.5-6	—	14	⊖	⊖	⊖	◐	A,D
Olympus AZ4 35-135mm	88	—	f/4.2-5.6	—	9	○	⊖	⊖	◐	A,D
Ricoh Mirai 35-135mm	88	—	f/4.2-5.6	—	9	○	⊖	⊖	◐	A,D

Features in Common
All have: • Automatic diaphragm.
Except as noted, all have: • Separate controls for focusing and zooming. • Depth-of-field scale. • No lens hood.

Key to Comments
A–Autofocus lens.
B–Zoom and focus control are combined.
C–No separate macro focusing range.
D–No depth-of-field scale.
E–Lens hood.

VIDEO & PHOTO TRIPODS

RATINGS VIDEO & PHOTO TRIPODS

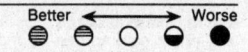

Better ◄——————► Worse
● ◐ ○ ◑ ●

▶ See report, page 114. From Consumer Reports, August 1990.

Recommendations: For camcorder use, any of the top four video tripods would be a good choice. Our first choice is the *Bogen 3170*, $150. The best of the photo tripods is the *Bogen 3000*, $95.

Ratings order: Listed by types; within types, listed in order of overall score, based primarily on tests for steadiness and secondarily on convenience judgments. Differences in score of 7 points or less are not significant. Models with identical scores are listed alphabetically. Prices are manufacturer's suggested retail. Weights are to nearest ¼ lb. Heights are to nearest in.

Brand and model	Overall score	Price	Weight, lb.	Max. height, in.	Min. height, in.	Length, folded, in.	Column travel, in.	Video	Still	Speed of use	Quick-release insert	Advantages	Disadvantages	Comments
VIDEO TRIPODS														
Bogen 3170	95	$150	5½	59	16	25	8	●	●	◑	—	A	f	A,C,E,G,K
Hollywood Titan 2800	92	140	5	63	24	25	12	●	●	◑	●	B	—	A,J
Velbon Stratos 470	92	149	5	63	24	26	11	●	●	●	◑	D	c	E
Vivitar V3000	92	104	5¼	66	24	26	12	●	●	○	○	B	—	I
Slik 503QF	82	140	3¾	59	22	24	13	○	●	●	—	—	c	E
Coast Coastar VTR-80	77	130	4¼	62	24	25	15	○	●	○	◑	—	d	D,E
Cullman T2502	75	145	4	63	24	24	16	○	●	●	◑	A	a	C,F
PHOTO TRIPODS														
Bogen 3000	95	102	4¾	58	16	24	8	●	●	○	—	A	f	B,C,E,G
Tiltall Junior LEO2	93	115	3¾	56	22	23	11	●	●	◑	—	A,C	e	C,G
Star-D D-29 Mini-Pro	88	85	3½	56	22	23	11	●	●	●	—	A	e	C,G
Velbon Victory 450	$83	88	3¾	58	21	22	13	●	●	●	◑	A	b	H
Vivitar 980	83	86	4¾	66	24	25	13	●	●	●	●	B	—	I
Slik U100 Deluxe	77	80	3	57	22	23	13	◑	●	○	—	—	—	E
Coast Coastar VTR-50RA	74	80	2¾	60	21	22	13	◑	●	●	◑	B	—	H

Features in Common
All have: • Adjustable 3-section legs. • 1-piece adjustable column.
Except as noted, all have: • 3-way pan head with pan handle and side-tilt for vertical-format stills. • Geared column with adjustable friction control. • Leg braces and plastic yoke. • Convenient leg clamps that flip sideways to lock. • Rubber leg tips that retract to expose spikes. • Plastic control knobs.

Key to Advantages
A–Pan head can be positioned below center column; helpful for framing low-angle shots.
B–Has handy spring-loaded camcorder pin.
C–Has metal control knobs.
D–Has circular "bubble" level on pan head.

Ratings Keys continued

120 FILM PROCESSING

Key to Disadvantages
a–Center column can be moved even when locked; lacks stop to prevent accidental removal of column.
b–Legs tend to fold when tripod is lifted.
c–Camcorder pin must be reversed to use still camera.
d–No provision for storing camcorder pin when using still camera.
e–Has collet leg locks; requires much more time and finesse to operate than flip locks.
f–Knob-operated leg locks; slower than flip locks.

Key to Comments
A–Pan head lacks side-tilt for vertical-format stills.
B–Has versatile 3-way head with no pan handle.
C–Center column not geared; must be raised or lowered by hand.
D–Geared column has no friction-control adjustment.
E–Has rubber feet without spikes.
F–Feet flip to expose either rubber pads or teeth.
G–Has metal yoke; eliminates need for leg braces.
H–Leg clamps flip up to lock.
I–Leg clamps flip down to lock.
J–Has removable "bubble" level on tilt axis; judged fragile and of little use.
K–Has large cork-covered mounting platform, a good alternative to camcorder pin.

RATINGS FILM PROCESSING

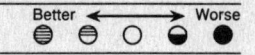

Better ← ⊜ ⊜ ○ ⊖ ● → Worse

▶ See report, page 116. From Consumer Reports, August 1991.

Recommendations: For mail-order service, *Skrudland*, in Texas, and *Mystic Color Lab*, in Connecticut, are your best bet for quality, fast turnaround, and price. Neither the minilabs nor wholesale labs that did best in our tests could match the best mail-order service.

Ratings order: Listed by types; within types, listed in order of picture-quality score. Differences in score of less than 10 points were judged not very significant. The price or price range is for developing and printing one 24-exposure roll of 35mm color-print film, one 3½x5-inch print per negative (or the closest to that size we could obtain). Prices include shipping, handling, and postage, where applicable.

Processor	Price	Picture-quality score	Dirt and scratches	Condition of negatives	Turnaround time, days	Comments
MAIL-ORDER LABS						
Skrudland Photo	$4.77	82	⊜	⊜	8	5311 Fleming Ct., Austin, Tex. 78744. 512-444-0958.
Mystic Color Lab	6.45 [1] [5]	81	⊜	⊜	8	P.O. Box 144, Mystic, Conn. 06355-9987. 800-367-6061. Provides postpaid film mailers.
Seattle FilmWorks [2]	7.50 [5]	81	⊖	○	18	P.O. Box 34065, Seattle 98124-1056. 206-283-9074. New roll of Seattle-brand film returned with order.
Custom Quality Studio [3]	3.84 [1]	78	⊖	⊜	16	P.O. Box 4838, Chicago 60680-4838. Provides postpaid film mailers.
Kodalux [3]	8.00-11.52	76	⊜	⊜	10	Usually found at camera stores; also available via prepaid mailers.

FILM PROCESSING

Processor	Price	Picture-quality score	Dirt and scratches	Condition of negatives	Turnaround time, days	Comments
Clark Color Labs [3]	$3.52	72	○	○	9	P.O. Box 96300, Washington, D.C. 20090.
York Photo Labs	3.51	68	○	●	11	400 Rayon Dr., Parkersburg, W. Va. 26101.
'ONE-HOUR' MINILABS						
Moto Photo	10.17-11.89	75	◐	○	—	Chain of more than 300 outlets in Northeast, Midwest, and South.
CPI Photo Finish	12.09 [4]	74	○	◐	—	Chain of about 300 outlets nationwide, except on West Coast.
Fox Photo 1-Hr. Labs [3]	11.95-16.35 [4]	73	○	◐	—	Chain of about 300 outlets in Southeast, Texas, California, and Hawaii.
Miscellaneous Colorwatch Minilabs	8.58-11.16 [4]	72	○	○	—	Independent labs that advertise Kodak Colorwatch system.
Eckerd Express [3]	10.19 [4]	69	○	○	—	250 minilabs in Eckerd drugstores in Florida, Dallas, Houston, Atlanta, and Charlotte, N.C.
Miscellaneous Non-Colorwatch Minilabs	8.95-10.17	68	○	○	—	Independent labs that don't use Colorwatch.
Fotomat Express	9.99-13.59	66	○	○	—	Minilabs located in Fotomat stores.
Photogo [3]	8.99-9.99 [4]	64	○	○	—	Franchiser of minilabs in Southeast, Midwest, and West.
WHOLESALE PROCESSORS						
Qualex [3]	3.49-5.99	73	◐	◐	—	Processes film anonymously, but Qualex labs (listed in phone book) name retailers using Qualex.
Miscellaneous Non-Colorwatch Wholesalers	4.15-6.39	73	◐	◐	—	Typical of the processors you might be using, if you took film to a drugstore, discount store, or supermarket that didn't advertise use of Colorwatch.
Miscellaneous Colorwatch Wholesalers	3.60-5.99	69	◐	○	—	Labs that process film for stores that display Colorwatch seal.

[1] *Prints are 3½x5¼ in., a size that matches proportions of a 35mm negative better than 3½x5 in.*
[2] *Processes only 35mm film.*
[3] *Uses Kodak Colorwatch system.*
[4] *Price is for 4x6-in. prints.*
[5] *Accepts credit card orders.*

RECREATION & EXERCISE

Exercise equipment 123
Running shoes 125
Tennis racquets 127
Bicycles 128
Ratings 131

Exercise can strengthen the heart, improve circulation, help control weight, reduce cholesterol, ease hypertension, reduce stress, increase muscle tone, and improve sleep. It can also be fun.

Studies have shown that you can perform the exercise of your choice at a moderate pace and still reap rewards. For maximum benefit to the heart and circulatory system, though, you need to move about with an intensity sufficient to raise your heartbeat to an aerobic "target zone." To find the margins of that zone, subtract your age from 220 and multiply that number by 0.70 for the lower limit (0.60 if you're new to exercise) and 0.85 for the upper limit. The greatest cardiovascular benefit comes when you maintain those levels for at least 20 minutes without stopping, and do so at least three times a week.

Almost any exercise will give you some health benefits. Bowling, golf, fishing, tennis, and gardening may not get your pulse pounding, but they're a vast improvement over watching TV. If you want to build muscle tone, no one has improved on resistance training such as weightlifting.

For cardiovascular benefit, you have to find an aerobic exercise you like. Among the best are running, brisk walking, bicycling, rowing, swimming, stair climbing, cross-country skiing, and aerobic dance. Many people "cross-train" among several exercises.

The standard words of caution still apply. If you're out of shape, have a medical problem that could affect your ability to exercise, or are over 40, it's best to consult a doctor before starting out. Don't try to run a marathon the first time you put on your new running shoes. Start with a short workout at moderate effort level and gradually add to duration and intensity. If you feel pain at any point, stop and walk until the pain goes away; if it doesn't, call it a day. Stretch—without bouncing or jerking—before and after each workout.

Finally, don't feel that all your recreation has to have a significant physical effect. There's nothing wrong with relaxing. It's called recharging your batteries.

EXERCISE EQUIPMENT

▸ Ratings of stair climbers on page 131.

You can achieve fitness without buying an expensive machine. At the least, you need a good pair of sneakers and the will to use them regularly. The scenery and fresh air of an outdoor workout can do a lot to keep you from getting bored while exercising.

But Americans love gadgets, and more and more of them have become convinced that exercise devices are key to health and long life. Sales of treadmills, exercise bikes, stair climbers, and other home-gym paraphernalia continue to rise.

Workouts on an exercise machine have advantages. You can use it when bad weather might otherwise encourage sloth. You can exercise in the privacy of your own home, even in the dead of night. There's no risk of injury from potholes, dogs, muggers, or cars. Terrain doesn't determine the effort you must expend. You can stop anytime without being miles from home. And you may be able to get a better workout, since a good machine makes it easy to maintain your target-zone pace.

Some machines work just the lower body. Others can improve the tone of the whole body. But if your reason for exercising is to achieve cardiovascular fitness, the kind of exercise matters less than the amount of effort you put into it as long as you are using the larger muscle groups. Your choice should be governed by personal preference and cost. When weighing cost versus benefits, keep in mind that a machine you don't enjoy is likely to turn into an expensive coat rack.

Before settling on a machine, it's a good idea to ask your doctor if you're making the right choice. Some people with back problems, for example, might be advised to avoid rowing machines. Those with knee problems might be warned away from stair climbers. The obese should probably avoid running on a treadmill (walking is O.K.).

Treadmills

In essence, a treadmill is a belt stretched between two rollers and driven by a motor. Most treadmills let you adjust the incline to simulate hills and increase the strenuousness of the workout. A monitor tells you how fast you're going, how far and long you've gone, and such things as heart rate and an estimate of the calories burned.

Machines vary in the type and size of motor. The type of motor—ac or dc—affects the way the machine works. An ac motor runs at full speed all the time, relying on a transmissionlike pulley system to vary the speed of the belt. Most such models can start up at full speed—a rude surprise if you're standing on the belt at the time. Manufacturers recommend you straddle the belt while starting up. The speed of a dc motor can be regulated, so machines with a dc motor avoid this problem. All models, whether ac or dc, come with a speed control that you gradually turn up as you start to walk.

Motor sizes vary from half a horsepower to one horsepower or more. The more power, the better the ability to handle heavy loads or high speeds. Walking or jogging can be done on any unit, but running requires a treadmill that goes at least 5 mph.

Inexpensive brands include *Proform, Vitamaster, Sears, Tunturi, Voit,* and *DP.* Precor, Trotter, and Quinton make expensive versions.

Cost. The machines most homeowners buy range from about $400 to $1000. The more you spend, the bigger the motor, the wider and longer the belt, and the higher the top speed. More expensive machines have automatic incline adjustments and easy-to-use controls. The typical machine priced under $500 is designed for walking, not running; the top speed is likely to be less than 5 mph. The least expensive machines, we found in our tests, often suffer from various design flaws and develop such ills as faulty controls, worn drive mechanisms, and balky motors over time. You can also spend up to several thousand dollars for the kind of treadmill used in health clubs. They're better built and should last much longer.

Exercise value. Walking at a brisk pace, jogging, and running are excellent aerobic conditioners. Increasing the incline can boost the exertion level of even a 3-mph walk to an aerobic level for a regular runner. Walking and running also improve lower-body muscle tone.

Features to look for. A slow minimum speed makes starting safer. Automatic incline adjustments are helpful; treadmills that use pins to change the slope are a bother. A long and wide belt and full-length handrails make for comfortable, safe use.

Exercise bikes

There are two main types of exercise bikes. As you pedal "single-action" models, you drive a resistance device, such as a flywheel. The main advantage of a flywheel bike is that you can change resistance with the twist of a knob.

"Dual-action" models let you also pump handlebars back and forth with your arms. Some have their handlebars coupled with the pedals; as you move the handlebars the pedals rotate. Others use hydraulic shock absorbers for arm resistance. Most use a fan for resistance, but some use a flywheel instead. To increase resistance on a fan model, you move arms and legs faster. While you're pedaling, the fan can cool you—in theory. But some models, we've found, produce barely a zephyr.

There are a couple of variations as well. Recumbent models let you sit in a chairlike seat rather than perch on a bike seat. That arrangement works the hamstring muscles more than an upright bike and is helpful for people who have back problems or trouble with balance. Training stands hook a resistance device to a regular bicycle to make it an exerciser. If you already own a bike, a stand is a way to use it indoors at a much lower cost than an exercise bike.

Exercise bikes are made by bicycle companies such as Schwinn and Ross, as well as companies like Tunturi and Vitamaster that first made their name in the exercise-equipment field. Lifecycle makes home and health clubs versions that include programmable "courses" of hills and flats.

Cost. The models we tested ranged from about $150 to $700. High-tech, health-club-style bikes can cost upwards of $1500. Bikes that cost less than $150 tend to be flimsy and jerky.

Exercise value. Cycling is an excellent aerobic conditioner. Pedal-only models work the lower body; dual-action bikes add an upper-body workout.

Features to look for. The flywheel should rotate smoothly and the resistance control should be easy to work. The seat should be well padded and comfortably shaped. A monitor keeps track of how far you've "traveled" and the time. Pedal straps let your legs work on the upstroke as well as the downstroke. On dual-action models, "coaster" pedals let your feet momentarily stop while your arms do the work.

Stair climbers

Currently one of the more popular types of exercise machine, stair climbers are essentially levers attached to a resistance device. Your legs pump the levers as if you were climbing stairs. A monitor displays steps-per-minute, time, and calories burned.

Dual-action models work arms as well as legs. Additionally, models vary according to how they apply resistance—with a hydraulic piston, flywheel, drive train, or through air resistance. On many models, the "steps" are linked—as one goes down, the other goes up. Other models have independently moving steps.

Stairmaster is a leading brand of health-club models; *DP, Tunturi, Precor,* and *Sears* are popular brands among the home models.

Cost. Stair climbers range in price from less than $100 to more than $3000, but many models meant for home use sell for less than $500.

Exercise value. Aerobic plus lower-body muscle toning. Since your feet stay on the levers, the stress of going up and down a real flight of stairs is reduced.

Features to look for. Pedals and handles positioned so that a comfortable posture can be maintained. Smooth pedal motion. Stability. Monitors that are clear and not complicated. Easy-to-adjust resistance. Pedals that provide a comfortable and secure stance. Comfortable handles.

The tests

In addition to thoroughly examining the way a piece of equipment works and how it's put together, testers use each piece of equipment, sometimes extensively. When appropriate, we devise machines to supplement the human workouts. We also check convenience factors such as how easy any monitors are to use; comfort factors such as how much a treadmill vibrates; and safety factors such as the security of seat-adjustment pins.

Buying advice

The more expensive machines, we've found in our tests, generally run more smoothly, have a greater range of speeds or motions, and can be expected to stand up to harder use than those at the lower end of the price range. Very inexpensive machines typically suffer from shoddy workmanship, cheap materials, and poor design. But you can find poor design in machines at the high end as well. In particular, watch out for overly complicated monitors.

To get an idea of the type of machine that's best for you, try some out. Health clubs typically have several.

In the store, try the model you're considering if possible. Be alert for things like loose parts, grating noises, and anything that causes discomfort. Inquire about return privileges in case you don't like it once it's home. In the case of a treadmill, which can't be easily transported, make sure in-home service is available.

RUNNING SHOES

▸ Ratings on page 134.

They're not called sneakers anymore. Nowadays, if you're a runner—or want to look the part—you need running shoes. And you'll also need about $50 for a decent pair. Besides helping you look good, a good pair of running shoes can reduce the risk of injury from the sport, a risk that is likely to increase the more you weigh and the more miles you run.

The choices. The major running-shoe manufacturers like Nike and Reebok spend many millions on advertising. Those two companies account for about half of the running shoes sold in this country. Other brands you will encounter in the stores and on the road include: *New*

Balance, Adidas, Asics Tiger, and *Saucony.*

Running shoes are sold by mail as well as in athletic footwear, sporting goods, and department stores; unless you're sure of your size and brand preference, buy at a store with knowledgeable salespeople and where you can try the shoes on.

A running shoe typically consists of an upper made of synthetic suede and breathable nylon; a toe box (the front of the upper) that's big enough so you can wiggle your toes; a heel counter and heel stabilizer to cup the heel and control lateral motion; a thin foam insole (a.k.a. sockliner) for some cushioning; a midsole that provides most of the cushioning and support; and an outsole, the bottom of the shoe, made of durable carbon rubber with lugs, grooves, or a waffle pattern for traction.

Features to look for

Comfort. A comfortable running shoe has good arch support and adequate, but not overly spacious, toe room. It doesn't pinch or cause pain during or after running and is free of protrusions that can chafe the opposite leg. Its heel pad cushions, but doesn't restrict, the Achilles tendon.

Cushioning. The cumulative toll from thousands of footstrikes during a run can cause painful and disabling bone and joint injuries. Cushioning in a running shoe, especially the midsole, absorbs some of the shock. Manufacturers use a variety of midsole materials, including compressed gas, plastic foam, silicone gel, and rubber balls. Advertising hype notwithstanding, none proved clearly superior in our tests.

Flexibility. Proper running form calls for the foot to land on the heel and roll forward, bending at the base of the toes as it pushes off. A running shoe should be flexible enough to allow that bending to take place easily.

Stability. Some people's feet roll to the inside when they run (called pronation); others' roll to the outside (supination). Some shoes are designed to help control either tendency without clamping your foot like a boot.

Ventilation. Porous materials in the shoe's upper let sweat evaporate and reduce the chance of foot or shoe odor.

Other features. Reflective tabs make you more visible to motorists at night. Some shoes have lacing systems that let you adjust shoe tightness more precisely. The weight of running shoes can vary by several ounces; over a long run, the differences add up.

The tests

We ask panelists to run over varied terrain with several pairs. Machines supplement the panel judgments. One machine uses a foot prosthesis and an accelerometer to measure cushioning. We used high-speed video to determine each shoe's stability during running. We test ventilation by stuffing a wet sock into a shoe's forefoot and measuring the amount of water that evaporates during a test period in an environmental chamber.

Buying advice

If you're buying running shoes just to wear to the supermarket, almost any brand will do. But runners should be a little choosy. Find a store that has knowledgeable salespeople and sells a number of brands. (Friends who are runners may be able to recommend a store.) Use these tips to help make your choice:

■ Find out if you're a pronator or supinator by looking for wear on your present shoes—a pronator will have more wear on the inside of the outsole, a supinator on the outside. If the wear is even, you have a neutral running style, and don't need shoes with special motion control. Ask the salesperson for a shoe that's right for your running style.

- Shop at the end of the day (when feet are their largest), and wear the socks you'll wear for running.
- If your feet are different sizes, buy for the larger foot. Use an insert to fill any gaps in the other shoe.
- Look for such defects in workmanship as a shoe that tilts to the side or poorly attached seams and layers of shoe material.
- Run a few steps and stop short to see if your feet slide inside the shoes, a sign the shoes are too big. Check for adequate toe room by pushing down at your longest toe—there should be a thumbnail-sized space. Make sure the heel counter is snug around the back of your foot. Test the flexibility of the shoes by going up and down on your toes; the shoes should bend easily.

TENNIS RACQUETS

▸ Ratings on page 136.

Innovations in racquet materials and design have wrought major changes in tennis over the last 20 years. In the early 1970s, metal racquets of tubular aluminum and steel became widely available and mildly popular. But not everyone was convinced that they conferred real advantages over traditional laminated-wood frames. Much the same held true for several revolutionary models fabricated from fiberglasslike composite materials.

In 1976, Prince startled the tennis world with an aluminum racquet whose head nearly doubled the hitting area. Since 1980, a limit of 178 square inches has been set to govern head size, but that's still much bigger than any racquet made so far.

Another change is the racquet's weight. Through the use of graphite fibers and various concoctions of space-age chemistry, racquet manufacturers have managed to pare two to four ounces off the weight packed by the old wood frames without sacrificing strength.

To make racquets stiff, manufacturers molded graphite and other fibers into them. To make them even stiffer, they fattened the beam—the front-to-back dimension of the frame. "Widebody" racquets, which were introduced by Wilson in 1987, now dominate the market.

The choices

The most visible names in tennis racquets are *Wilson* and *Prince*. Performance-related factors include such things as weight, head and grip size, and stringing tension and material. Your choice depends on your strength and your style of play. As racquets have changed, so have prices. Most premium-quality racquets fall in the $100 to $300 range.

Performance features

Head size. Hitting area—the entire strung area of the head—ranges from 85 to more than 115 square inches. Racquet heads are commonly available in four sizes: midsize, midplus, oversize, and oversize plus. In our tests, larger heads tended to provide more power and stability and less control.

Stringing. Only relatively inexpensive racquets are sold prestrung; with others, you can customize the stringing to suit your game. Gut strings, made from animal intestines, are resilient but they are not as long-lasting as nylon, the alternative. Nylon is typically cheaper. Stringing prices range from as little as $12 or so for basic nylon to more than $50 for a fancy gut. The rule of thumb is that you restring a racquet as many times per year as you play per week.

Grip size. Most racquets come in five grip sizes, from 4⅛ to 4⅝ inches. The actual measurement doesn't always match the label, so make sure to check it for proper fit. Most racquets have eight-sided, beveled handles to help you place your hand properly, but some are more rounded. You can build up a too-small handle with overwrap or reduce a too-large one by replacing the original grip with thinner wrapping.

Weight and balance. By the standards of old-fashioned wooden racquets, today's models are remarkably light—typically two or three ounces less than wood racquets. Many racquets are head-light, meaning the balance point (unstrung) is nearer the handle than the head. That makes a racquet more maneuverable. Others are head-heavy for more stability. You can change a racquet's balance point by adding lead tape to the frame.

The tests

Intermediate and advanced players of varying abilities judged a racquet's power, control, stability, touch (how it transmits the feel of the ball on the strings), and maneuverability.

We use machines to determine balance, swing weight (the ease of starting and stopping the swing), and to gauge the stiffness of the frame. We also determined the size of the racquet's "sweet spot," the area in the center of the head where you get the most power.

Buying advice

The racquet you choose should complement your strokes, style of play, and meet your budget.

In the end, the best way to pick a racquet is to play with it—at least a half hour if possible. Most pro shops are happy to lend racquets.

BICYCLES

Walk into a bicycle store and you'll see a profusion of models across a broad range of types. All these types and variants of types reflect the specialization that has occurred in the past decade. More and more, manufacturers cater to several distinct classes of bike rider: recreational, fitness, commuter, racer, around town, or off-road. Which bike is best for you depends on where and how you ride.

The choices

Bike prices range from about $100 for a discount store clunker up to thousands for an elite model. Expect to pay $200 to $500 for a competent model. The world of bicycles can be divided into three main types:

Mountain bike. This is the most popular type sold in the U.S. With fat, knobby tires, 26-inch-diameter wheels, flat handlebars, and a sturdy frame, the mountain bike moves competently over rough terrain, but can feel a bit ungainly on pavement. A scaled-down variant, the city bike, is designed for the lighter demands of urban streets and dirt roads.

Road bike. This lightweight, thin-tired bike designed for racing or touring comes with "drop" handlebars. Fast and efficient, but not as comfortable as some people like, it doesn't ride as well on rough surfaces as other types. Although road bikes are

DON'T FORGET THE HELMET

Whether you ride your bike 30 miles a day or 30 miles a year, a helmet, adjusted for a snug fit, should be worn on every ride. For our last reeport (May 1991), we tested helmets in a cross-section of styles and sizes. Most of our high-rated helmets were no-shell models. They generally performed best in all our tests except those for penetration resistance.

For maximum protection, a snug fit is critical. Here's how to check:

Buy the smallest size that fits comfortably. Use the sizing pads (included with most helmets) to refine the fit. Put the helmet on, and try to push it to the sides, front, and back. If it moves enough to create a gap between your head and the pads, use thicker pads. If the helmet is still loose, get a smaller one that touches your head at the crown, sides, front, and back.

Adjust the straps. With the helmet level across your forehead just above your eyebrows, the front strap should be close to vertical. The back strap should lie straight, just below the ear, without any slack. Straps should meet just below the hinge of the jaw, in front of the ear.

Test the fit. With the chin strap buckled, the helmet shouldn't move when you shake your head or push from the sides, front, or back. If it does, use thicker pads or select a smaller helmet. The helmet shouldn't roll back or forward on your head when you push up on the front or back. If it does, tighten the straps. The chin strap should feel tight when you open your mouth.

---

the best choice if you ride fast or ride far, primarily on smooth pavement, they've declined in popularity.

Hybrid bike. Introduced about five years ago and making great strides in popularity, this type uses a lightweight frame, flat handlebars, and moderately knobby tires to marry a mountain bike's strength and comfort with a road bike's efficiency. A hybrid is a good choice for commuters or those who travel a dirt road now and then.

Features to look for

Frame. The diamond-shaped chassis—a bicycle's foundation—determines whether the bike will fit you. The frame is a major factor in the bike's weight and handling ability.

Frames are made from various materials: heavy steel on the cheapest bikes; lightweight aluminum or carbon fiber, or exotic metals like titanium on the most expensive. Frames for the typical $300 to $500 model are chromium-molybdenum steel or lightweight aluminum. Chromoly mountain and hybrid bikes weigh about 30 pounds; a carbon-fiber road bike can weigh as little as 18 pounds. A frame's stiffness and geometry also affect a bike's performance.

Handlebars. Their size and shape influence riding efficiency and comfort. The bent-over posture required by road bikes, and to a lesser extent, performance-oriented mountain bikes and hybrids, reduces wind resistance and shocks from bumps. That posture also lets muscles work more efficiently. But such benefits are unimportant for casual rides on pavement, where an upright position may be preferred.

Gears. These let you pedal comfortably despite changes in road slope. With three sprocket wheels in front and six to eight in the rear, most mountain bikes and hybrids have 18 to 24 speeds. Off-road, we consider

18 the minimum needed. On pavement, 12 or 14 speeds are usually enough.

Just as important as the number of gears are a bike's highest and lowest gear numbers. These numbers sum up the interaction between the front and rear gears, and the wheel size. For challenging off-road rides, the lowest should be 28 or less. A road bike for general use should have a low of 40 or less. High gears around 100 help speed you downhill on roads.

Shifters. These cause the derailleurs to move the drive chain from one sprocket wheel to another. Long a deterrent to would-be riders, old-fashioned "friction" shifters can be difficult to master until you develop a feel for them. "Indexed shifters"—a more recent development—make changing gears far easier.

The most convenient indexed shifters are the "push-button" or "wishbone" type found on many mountain bikes and hybrids. One caveat for off-road riding: If these shifters are thrown out of alignment by a fall, they cannot revert to friction shifting. Above-the-bar levers offer indexing with a friction mode as backup. For rough riding, that type may be the wiser choice.

Brakes. Road bikes typically use caliper brakes, poised over the tire. Most mountain and hybrid bikes have cantilever brakes mounted directly on the front wheel fork and the seat or chain stay. According to our tests, these are able to stop a bike quickly and controllably. If you ever ride in wet weather, avoid steel-rimmed wheels. In our wet-brake tests, they required a greater distance to stop than wheels with aluminum rims.

Tires. A major factor in handling ability, they are easily changed to suit the terrain. For rough trails, they should be at least 1.9 inches wide, with very aggressive treads. Such tires produce a "buzzy" ride on pavement, though; there, smoother tires are better.

Saddle. This won't affect performance much, but may limit how often or how long you ride. Look for one that's comfortable. Saddles are easy to change—don't let a poor saddle stop you from buying an otherwise good bike. Some manufacturers claim that seats filled with siliconelike "gel" reduce shock and vibration. But our testers—of both sexes—have found them no more comfortable than other types of bike seats.

The tests

Our engineers test bikes in a variety of terrains and conditions. They navigate mountain bikes and hybrids through mud, sand, and gravel, around rocks, over dirt roads, and on pavement. All bikes' brakes are tested, wet and dry, for control and for stopping ability from 15 mph. We also put bikes through high-speed turns to gauge handling and ride over bumps to assess shock absorption.

Buying advice

Bicycle models and components change every year, but the basic characteristics of a good bike remain the same.

Narrow the field by selecting among bikes with frames that fit the rider. To find the right size, the rider should straddle the crossbar with both feet flat on the floor. Allow 3 inches clearance between crossbar and crotch for mountain bikes, 2 inches for hybrids, and 1 inch for road bikes. We recommend that both men and women buy a bike with a crossbar if they intend to ride more than just casually.

Most of a bike's components can be easily changed by the dealer. Before buying, ride the bike to make sure you like how it handles; that your posture, the saddle, and the pedals feel comfortable; and that the brakes respond evenly, without grabbing, as you increase hand pressure on the brake levers.

STAIR CLIMBERS 131

RATINGS STAIR CLIMBERS

Better ◄——► Worse
⊖ ⊖ ○ ⊝ ●

▶ **See report, page 124.** From Consumer Reports, May 1992.

Recommendations: If a "stepper" climber is your preference, give first consideration to the *CSA E541*. Nearly as good was its brandmate the *CSA E512*, which we judged A Best Buy. To add an upper-body workout, we recommend the *Precor 730e*. If you prefer a "ladder" climber, consider the *BMI/Helix SC8000*.

Ratings order: Listed by types; within types, listed in order of estimated quality based on ergonomics, performance, reliability, and safety. Closely ranked models are similar in quality. Price is the manufacturers' suggested retail. A * denotes approximate retail, according to the manufacturer. [D] indicates model discontinued.

Brand and model	Price	Action [1]	Ergonomics	Rigidity, stability	Smoothness	Resistance adjustment	Monitor's ease of use	Reliability	Safety	Advantages	Disadvantages	Comments
STEPPERS												
CSA E541	$400	S	⊖	⊖	⊖	⊖	⊖	⊖	○	C,D,E,F,J,L,N,O,R	z	N,Q,T,AA,JJ,MM,OO
Precor 730e	650	D	⊖	⊖	⊝	⊖	⊖	⊖	○	F,H	j	B,D,V,X,FF,GG,KK,LL
Precor 725e	625	S	⊖	⊖	○	⊝	○	⊖	○	H,N	—	G,R,FF,GG,JJ,KK,PP
CSA E512, A Best Buy	160	S	○	○	⊖	●	⊖	⊖	⊖	A,F	k,p,r	H,X
Spirit 766UBC	500	S/D	○	⊖	⊖	⊖	⊖	⊖	○	F,H,N	d,l,q,r,bb	A,B,E,G,T,Z,JJ,MM
Precor 718e	399	S	⊖	⊖	⊖	⊝	⊖	○	○	A,G,H	s,w	G,V,X,FF,GG,KK,LL
Spirit 660	575	S	○	⊖	○	⊝	⊖	○	○	A,H,N,O	g,q,r,bb,ee	G,T,Z,JJ,MM,PP
Wynmor Wynstep 17-W690	360	S	○	⊖	○	○	⊖	⊖	○	A,G,M,N,Q	b,cc	F,G,M,Q,JJ,KK,MM,OO
Tunturi C401	219	S	○	⊖	○	○	⊖	○	○	D,H	a,q,x,dd	G,M,X,DD,JJ,KK,MM,NN
Quinton Cross Country Climber	549	D	○	○	○	○	○	⊖	○	D	f,r,z,cc	C,D,M,O,T,CC,EE,JJ,PP
Impex QS900SR	149	S	○	○	⊖	⊝	○	○	○	H	r,w	H,X,FF
Impex SNT600	199	D	○	⊝	⊖	⊝	○	○	⊖	A,G,H	r,w	B,E,T,Z,BB,JJ,MM
Lifestyler (Sears Cat. No. 28552)	180	S	○	○	○	○	⊝	⊖	○	E	b,q,t,w,z	H,M,R,S,U,Y,JJ,KK,MM,NN
BMI 4500	129	S	⊝	○	○	⊝	○	○	○	H	a,w,ee	H,T,Z
Stamina Stepper 975	94*	S	○	○	⊖	⊝	○	●	○	H	b,o,w,y,bb	H,T,Z,GG,KK,MM

[1] **S** = single-action; **D** = dual-action; **S/D** = single or dual action.

Ratings continued

132 STAIR CLIMBERS

Ratings continued

Brand and model	Price	Action [1]	Ergonomics	Rigidity, stability	Smoothness	Resistance adjustment	Monitor's ease of use	Reliability	Safety	Advantages	Disadvantages	Comments
STEPPERS *continued*												
ProForm Airobic Trainer	$299	S	○	○	◐	◉	◒	●	○	A,D,I	b,g,cc	H,J,K,P,W,FF,II,NN,QQ
BMI 8660	199	D	○	◒	○	◐	◒	○	◐	A,H,N	a,e,r,w,z,cc	B,D,T,Z,JJ,MM
DP Airgometer 17-0800 [D]	443	S	◐	◒	◐	—	◒	○	○	A,E,M,Q	b,g,h,m,v,bb,cc	F,H,J,Q,JJ,KK,MM,OO
DP Quantum 17-0629	222	S	◐	●	◐	●	◒	○	○	E,G,M,Q	b,p,w,y,z,bb,cc	G,Q,FF,JJ,KK,MM,OO
Lifestyler 3000p (Sears Cat. No. 28502)	230	S/D	○	●	○	◒	◒	◐	◐	J	j,n,q,t,w,y,z,cc	B,E,H,R,S,U,Y,JJ,KK,MM,NN
LADDERS												
BMI/Helix SC8000	299	S/D	○	◒	○	◉	◐	◉	○	A,B,G,J,N,O	a,c,g,i,n,r,u,aa,cc,ee	B,E,H,I,X,HH,JJ,MM
Tunturi C614	699	S/D	◐	◉	○	◉	◐	◐	◒	A,H,J,K,P	c,h,i,k,n,q,s,u,aa,cc,dd,ee	B,E,G,L,X,JJ,KK,MM,NN
Impex MC1000	225*	D	◐	●	◐	○	○	○	◒	—	a,b,c,h,r,u,x,z,aa,cc	B,E,M,X,BB,HH,JJ,MM

[1] S = *single-action;* D = *dual-action;* S/D = *single or dual action.*

Features in Common

All: • Require assembly. • Can be tipped over backward during careless use. • Ladder-type climbers have movable arm pegs with two positions, for users of different heights.

Except as noted, all: • Have dependent pedal motion (stepping down on one raises the other). • Have up/down timer. • Have counter that tracks steps taken. • Have lever-type pedals that pivot reasonably high on the support column. • Have variable resistance levels. • Use shock absorbers for resistance, adjustable by moving each absorber's mount backward or forward along its pedal lever. • Include electronic monitor. • Can be tipped to side during careless use. • Provide toll-free number for parts and service.

Except as noted, all monitors: • Use AA batteries. • Shut off automatically when not in use. • Scan through functions. • Beep at set tempo.

Key to Advantages
A–Less apt to tip to side than most.
B–Three hand-peg positions.
C–Handrail has forearm rests and adjusts for height and fore-and-aft positions.
D–Easier than most to assemble.
E–Wheels make model easier to move than most.
F–Quieter than most.
G–No room-light reflections on monitor.
H–Manual and/or markings on unit warn of danger to fingers from moving parts.
I–Resistance can be adjusted by preset program or manually without stopping exercise.
J–Resistance adjusted with single knob that controls both pedals; no need to stop exercise.
K–Pedal straps allow pulling as well as pushing.
L–Simulates exercise bicycle with optional seat.
M–Calorie counter more accurate than most.
N–Wide pedals; relatively comfortable.
O–Pedals stay horizontal through entire stroke.
P–Pedals can pivot to stay horizontal.
Q–Displays actual pulse; sounds alarm if pulse rises or sinks below preselected target range.
R–Displays actual pulse; sounds alarm if pulse exceeds preselected target level.

STAIR CLIMBERS

Key to Disadvantages
a–No warnings in manual or on machine to keep children away.
b–Low-pivoting pedals may slant foot uncomfortably and may pinch careless bystander.
c–Open trolley track poses pinching hazard.
d–Moving handles can pinch user's fingers against stationary handlebar.
e–Moving handles can injure bystander at pivot and shock-absorber mount.
f–Beginners can lose balance mounting.
g–Irregular pedal action can cause discomfort to knees.
h–Knees can bang into frame.
i–Single-action handlebar too low.
j–Arm levers can brush chest during deep step.
k–Pedals smaller or narrower than most.
l–Large diameter of single-action handlebar can make it uncomfortable to grasp.
m–Resistance not adjustable; too high for fast-cadence workout.
n–Resistance settings not indexed.
o–Resistance settings tend to slip.
p–Must unscrew knob under pedal and reposition shock absorber to change resistance.
q–Cramped display or small markings make monitor hard to read.
r–Beeps at each step; may be annoying.
s–Actual step-per-minute rate can exceed capacity of display.
t–No auto-off; monitor drains batteries if left on.
u–Monitor too high or low for easy viewing.
v–Routine adjustment of drive chain requires taking much of machine apart.
w–Pedal cable or rope broke in reliability test.
x–Shock absorbers leaked oil in reliability test.
y–Replacing broken cable relatively difficult.
z–Monitor may not count small steps.
aa–Harder to move around than most.
bb–Harder to assemble than most.
cc–Noisier than most.
dd–Room-light reflections can obscure display.
ee–No toll-free number for parts and service.

Key to Comments
A–Available as single-action machine without electronic display (Model **766**).
B–Arms can be used actively or passively.
C–Arms must be used actively.
D–Step down with your right foot and the right arm lever moves away from you.
E–Step down with your right foot and the right arm lever moves toward you.
F–Can use with back against support, facing away from machine, but poor body position or low resistance makes workout ineffective.
G–Has front rail or handlebar.
H–Has side rails.
I–Flywheel resistance.
J–Fan resistance.
K–Fan cools face, but may dry eyes.
L–Drum-brake resistance.
M–Resistance adjusted by dial on each shock absorber; stop workout to make adjustment.
N–Hydraulic oil-transfer resistance.
O–Monitor is optional.
P–Electronic display and resistance adjustments need 120-volt ac; adaptor included.
Q–Monitor measures pulse with ear clip.
R–Monitor gives visible, not audible, cadence.
S–Monitor displays all functions at same time.
T–Pushing pedal turns monitor on.
U–Monitor has graphic display of workout.
V–Monitor cannot be turned off.
W–Monitor shows total distance in miles and step rate in mph.
X–No auto-shutoff on monitor, but LCD display uses little power.
Y–Monitor uses 9-volt battery.
Z–Monitor uses flat-cell batteries.
AA–Folds, but folding mechanism tends to jam.
BB–6-mo. warranty on shock absorbers.
CC–5-yr. warranty on frame.
DD–Sold as **C405** at Herman's sports stores.
EE–Available with electronic monitor for $587.
FF–Timer on monitor only counts up.
GG–Monitor has step odometer.
HH–Monitor counts total distance plus total steps.
II–Monitor tracks total distance only.
JJ–Beeps or flashes at a cadence you try to match.
KK–Displays number of steps per minute.
LL–Displays average and maximum cadence for workout.
MM–Calorie counter indicates calories burned so far.
NN–Calorie counter estimates the number per minute you are burning.
OO–Calorie counter also counts down to zero from a preset total.
PP–Pedals move independently.
QQ–Displays speed in mph.

RATINGS RUNNING SHOES

Better ← → Worse

▶ **See report, page 125.** From Consumer Reports, May 1992.

Recommendations: The first choice of both the men's and women's panels was the *Saucony Jazz 3000*, which we dubbed A Best Buy for its high quality and relatively low price. The shoes our panelists liked best performed well in several important respects and deserve first consideration. Among them, let comfort and fit be your guide.

Ratings order: Listed by types; within types, listed in order of estimated quality, based mainly on panel judgments for overall performance, comfort, and cushioning. Price is the suggested retail price, according to the manufacturer. ⓢ indicates tested model has been replaced by successor model; according to the manufacturer, the performance of the new model is similar to the tested model but features may vary. See right for new model number. Ⓓ indicates model discontinued.

Brand and model	Price	Weight, oz. [1]	Performance	Comfort	Cushioning	Flexibility	Ventilation	Stability [2]	Best use [3]	Advantages	Disadvantages	Comments
MEN'S SHOES												
Saucony Jazz 3000, A Best Buy	$68	11	◐	◐	◐	◐	◐	ES	NP/MH	B,C	e	J,T
Nike Air 180	125	12.7	◐	◐	◐	◐	◐	ES	NP/MH	—	a,e,m	A,D,J,L,U
Avia ARC 2040MZ	70	12.2	◐	◐	◐	◐	◐	ES	NP/MH	—	a	N,U
Asics Gel-Lyte III	85	11.2	◐	◐	○	◐	◐	LS	N/MH	A,C	j	B,C,F,I,U
Adidas Torsion Response	85	13	○	◐	◐	◐	◐	VS	NP/MH	C	—	K,T
Asics Gel-Saga	55	11.3	◐	◐	○	◐	◐	MS	N/BM	D	j	H,U
Saucony Azura II	82	11.1	◐	◐	◐	◐	◐	MS	NP/MH	D	k,r	J,K,T
New Balance M997	120	13	○	○	◐	●	●	ES	NP/MH	C,E	b,e,k,l	M,P,T
New Balance M577	80	14.2	○	○	◐	●	●	ES	NP/MH	C,E	b,e,l	H,K,P,S,U
Brooks GFS-110 Ⓓ	99	9.8	◐	○	○	◐	◐	LS	N/BM	D	i,k	T
Reebok Running Pump Ⓓ	130	11.5	○	◐	○	◐	◐	ES	NP/MH	C	f,e,p,r	E,I,J,T
Nike Air Craft Ⓓ	55	10.7	○	◐	○	◐	◐	MS	N/B	—	a,m	A,G,I,J,W,T
Reebok Blaze Ⓓ	55	11.7	○	◐	○	◐	●	ES	N/B	—	a,e,q	G,J,O,V
Nike Air Pegasus Ⓢ	70	11.1	○	○	◐	◐	◐	ES	N/MH	—	a,e,m	A,J,T
Brooks Chariot HF	70	12.3	○	○	○	●	◐	ES	NP/MH	D	h	U
New Balance M495	63	11.8	●	●	○	●	●	VS	NP/MH	C,E	h,l	D,R,U
Etonic StableAir NR Ⓓ	65	13.6	●	●	●	●	○	LS	N/MH	—	a,h,n,o	D,J,U
WOMEN'S SHOES												
Saucony Jazz 3000, A Best Buy	68	9.3	◐	◐	◐	◐	◐	MS	NP/MH	B,C	e	H,T

RUNNING SHOES

Brand and model	Price	Weight, oz.[1]	Performance	Comfort	Cushioning	Flexibility	Ventilation	Stability[2]	Best use[3]	Advantages	Disadvantages	Comments
New Balance W997	$100	10.1	⊖	⊖	⊖	⊖	○	ES	NP/MH	B,C,E	d,e,k,l	K,M,P,R,T
Reebok Running Pump [D]	130	9.4	⊖	⊖	⊖	⊖	○	VS	NP/MH	B,C	f,p,r	E,T
Saucony Azura II	82	9	⊖	○	⊖	⊖	⊖	VS	NP/MH	D	k	C,H,J,K,T
Avia ARC 2040WZ	70	10.9	⊖	⊖	⊖	⊖	○	LS	NP/MH	—	a	N,U
Reebok Blaze [D]	55	10.1	⊖	⊖	⊖	⊖	●	ES	N/B	—	a,e,q	G,J,O,V
Nike Air 180	125	10.3	⊖	○	⊖	⊖	○	VS	NP/MH	—	a,e,m,q	A,D,L,U
Nike Air Craft [D]	55	8.6	⊖	⊖	⊖	⊖	⊖	VS	N/B	—	a,m	A,G,T
Asics Gel-Lyte III	80	9	○	⊖	○	⊖	⊖	LS	N/MH	C	i,j	C,F,U
Nike Air Pegasus [S]	70	8.9	○	○	⊖	⊖	⊖	ES	N/MH	—	a,e,m	A,I,J,T
New Balance W495	60	10.2	○	○	◐	⊖	○	LS	NP/MH	E	a,l	D,H,U
Asics Gel-Saga	55	8.6	○	○	●	⊖	⊖	ES	N/BM	D	c,j	H,U
Etonic StableAir NR [D]	65	11.1	○	●	○	○	◐	MS	N/MH	—	a,h,n,o	D,J,U
Brooks Chariot HF	70	9.5	●	⊖	⊖	○	◐	LS	NP/MH	D	—	U
Adidas Lady Oregon Classic	45	7	●	●	●	◐	⊖	ES	N/BM	F	a,g,h,i	C,Q,R,V

[1] Of each shoe, to the nearest 1/10 oz., for men's size 9D and women's size 7B.

[2] Key to stability: **ES**=extremely stable; **VS**=very stable; **MS**=moderately stable; **LS**=least stable.

[3] Key to best use: **N**=normal-moving feet; **NP**=normal-moving or slightly pronating; **B**=beginners' workouts; **BM**=beginners' workouts to mid-mileage workouts; **MH**=mid- to high-mileage workouts.

Successor Models
Nike Air Pegasus is succeeded by 104005 (men's); Nike Air Pegasus by 105005 (women's).

Features in Common
All: • Have notch or soft pad at heel top. • Have removable insoles.
Except as noted, all: • Have reflective trim for night running. • Lack separate arch-support inserts. • Were judged light- or medium-weight by panelists. • Accept orthotic inserts. • Are white with colored trim.

Key to Advantages
A–Easier to put on than most, said panelists.
B–Better traction than most, said panelists.
C–Reflective trim at rear and sides.
D–Reflective trim at rear.
E–Insole appeared less flattened than most after panel test.
F–Felt especially light to panelists.

Key to Disadvantages
a–No reflective trim.
b–Felt especially heavy to panelists.
c–Not enough arch support, said panelists.
d–Material bunches up in shoe, said panelists.
e–Midsoles stain easily.
f–Protrusions can chafe opposite leg.
g–Not enough heel and midfoot support, said panelists.
h–Caused more aches and pains than most, said panelists.
i–Less traction than most, said panelists.
j–Pebbles got stuck in outsole tread.
k–More outsole wear than most after panel test.
l–Partial separation of upper from midsole after panel test.
m–Insole more flattened than most after panel test.
n–Arch area of insole caused panelists discomfort and blisters.

Ratings Keys continued

136 TENNIS RACQUETS

o–Insole felt wet after ventilation test.
p–No instructions for proper use of pump.
q–When wet, can stain socks slightly.
r–Lost some shock absorption after repeated pounding.

Key to Comments
A–Comes with arch-support inserts.
B–Sizes marked larger than actual.
C–Lacks notch for Achilles tendon.
D–Instructions for cleaning or care.
E–Pump system for adjusting fit.
F–Unconventional tongue; split up middle.
G–Doesn't accept orthotic inserts.
H–More toe room than most, said panelists.
I–Less toe room than most, said panelists.
J–Comes in several colors.
K–Heel height is greater than most—lift is 7/10 in. from forefoot to heel. Shoes are best suited for women who spend a lot of time in high heels.
L–Tongue and upper material may help dissipate sweat.
M–Comes with extra heel pad.
N–"Dynafit" lacing system; designed for better fit.
O–Insole glued, but can be removed.
P–Recommended for heavyset runners.
Q–Not recommended for heavyset runners.
R–Basic color gray, not white.
S–Basic color blue, not white.
T–Slip-lasted.
U–Combination-lasted.
V–Board-lasted.

RATINGS TENNIS RACQUETS

Better ← → Worse

▶ **See report, page 127.** From Consumer Reports, August 1992.

Recommendations: The oversize *Donnay Ultimate Pro*, $200, is a high-power racquet with excellent control. We judged the less expensive *Pro-Kennex Graphite Infinity* A Best Buy, but it has been discontinued and may be hard to find. Among medium-power models, the *Spalding Professional Extreme 95*, $130, had good control and touch. In the same group is the *Spalding Graphite XL 105* (now *Graphite Epic*), A Best Buy at $100.

Ratings order: Listed in groups, according to power level determined by CU's panels of advanced-beginner and intermediate players. Models in the high-power group were judged to transmit more of the swing's force to the ball and to maintain more of its pace in blocking back shots, though perhaps with some loss of control. Within groups, listed according to our intermediate players' assessment of such court-performance characteristics as control, stability, and touch. Price is the manufacturer's suggested retail for each racquet as sold. A * denotes the price CU paid. Most racquets are sold unstrung; exceptions are noted in the Comments. Discounts may be available. ⑤ indicates tested model has been replaced by successor model; according to the manufacturer, the performance of new model should be similar to the tested model but features may vary. See page 138 for new model number and suggested retail price. ⒹD indicates model discontinued.

On-court judgments

Brand and model	Price	Head size [1]	String tension, lb.	Weight, oz. [2]	Control, strokes	Control, serves	Stability	Touch	Maneuverability [3]	Advantages	Disadvantages	Comments
HIGH POWER												
Donnay Ultimate Pro	$200	O	58-67	12.0	◐	◐	◐	◐	V	A,C	e	B,H,O
Pro-Kennex Graphite Infinity, A Best Buy Ⓓ	100	M+	57-67	12.0	◐	◐	○	○	L	A,C	b,d,e	A,J,M,T,X
Wilson T5652 Profile Hammer 2.7si	280	O	53-63	9.6	◐	◐	◐	○	V	A,C	b	B,O,S,Z

TENNIS RACQUETS 137

On-court judgments

Brand and model	Price	Head size [1]	String tension, lb.	Weight, oz. [2]	Control, strokes	Control, serves	Stability	Touch	Maneuverability [3]	Advantages	Disadvantages	Comments
Wilson T5926 Pro Staff 4.5si	$170	O	53-63	12.0	○	◒	◒	○	M	A,C	b	B,O,S
Wilson T5506 Profile 2.7si	200	O	55-65	12.0	◒	○	○	○	M	A	b	B,O,Q,S
Prince Vortex	325	O	45-60	12.0	○	○	○	●	L	A,B,C	—	A,O
Head Discovery SG 720	325	O	65-77	10.4	○	○	○	○	M	C	b	E,I,K,N,O
Prince CTS Blast [D]	169	O	55-70	12.0	○	○	○	○	L	A,B	—	A,O
MEDIUM POWER												
Prince CTS Precision [D]	129	O	50-65	12.0	◒	◒	○	◒	V	B	—	A,O
Spalding Professional Extreme 95	130	M+	58-66	11.2	◒	◒	◒	◒	V	B,C	a,c	F,I,M,S,V,W
Spalding Graphite XL 105, A Best Buy [S]	100	O	55-65	11.2	◒	◒	○	◒	H	C	a	B,C,I,R,W
Head Ventoris 660 [D]	149	M+	63-74	11.2	◒	◒	○	◒	V	C	a	E,K,N,P
Spalding Paradox	250	M+	50-64	10.4	◒	◒	○	◒	V	B,C	c	B,L,P,S,U,V,Y
Donnay WST Cobalt [S]	125*	M+	55-65	11.2	◒	◒	○	◒	V	B,C	a,c	D,H,P
Wilson T5504 Profile 2.7si [D]	200	M+	50-60	12.0	◒	◒	●	○	M	C	a,b	B,P,Q,S
Yonex RQ420	175	O	55-60	12.0	◒	◒	◒	◒	M	A,C	—	C,H
Pro-Kennex Ceramic Infinity [D]	120	M+	57-67	12.0	◒	◒	○	◒	H	B	a,b,d	A,J,T,X
Prince Pro II	60	O	55-70	11.2	◒	◒	○	◒	H	B	—	D,G,M,R
Dunlop Revelation 115 [D]	210	O+	58-70	12.0	◒	◒	○	○	H	A,C	b	C,O
Wilson Graphite Aggressor T5422	60	M+	50-60	12.0	◒	◒	●	◒	M	—	a	D,I,M,R
Dunlop Pulsar 95 [S]	150	M+	55-65	8.8	◒	◒	●	◒	V	—	a,b	A,Q,BB
Prince CTS Precision [D]	129	M+	50-65	12.0	◒	○	●	○	M	B	—	A,P
Wilson T5924 Pro Staff 4.5si	170	M+	48-58	12.0	◒	○	●	○	H	—	a,b	B,P,S
Prince CTS Blast [D]	169	M+	50-65	12.0	◒	○	●	○	H	B	a	A,P
Head Dominion 720	50	O	65-77	12.0	○	◒	●	○	H	—	a,f	D,G,K,M,O,R,AA

[1] Key to head sizes (as specified by mfrs.): midplus (**M+**), with a hitting area ranging from 95 to 104 square inches; oversize (**O**), 105 to 114 square inches; and oversize plus (**O+**), 115 square inches and up. Ratings judgments of models apply only to head sizes tested.

[2] Weight is that of the unstrung frame with a grip size of 4⅝ inches. Stringing with 16-gauge nylon increased weight by six-tenths of an ounce or so.

[3] Key to maneuverability: **V** = very high; **H** = high; **M** = medium; **L** = low medium.

Turn page for Ratings Keys

TENNIS RACQUETS

Successor Models (in Ratings order)
Spalding Graphite XL 105 is succeeded by Epic, $100; Donnay WST Cobalt by Cobalt Pro, $145; Dunlap Pulsar 95 by Pulsar Pro, $150.

Features in Common
All: • Are widebody racquets but with various beam contours, as noted in Comments.
Except as noted, all: • Have graphite or graphite composite frames. • Come in grip sizes 4 1/8, 4 1/4, 4 3/8, 4 1/2, and 4 5/8 in. • Are sold unstrung. • Come with full-length racquet cover. • Carry 1-yr. warranty.

Key to Advantages
A–More forgiving of mis-hits than most, said panelists.
B–Grip more comfortable than most.
C–Better than others at damping vibration, said panelists.

Key to Disadvantages
a–Less forgiving of mis-hits than most, said panelists.
b–Frame unwieldy to some panelists.
c–Actual grip size smaller than marked.
d–Actual grip size larger than marked.
e–Grip more slippery than most.
f–Worse than most at damping vibration, said panelists.

Key to Comments
A–Beam thickest at tip of head, tapering to shaft.
B–Beam thickest at bottom of head, tapering to tip of head and to shaft.
C–Beam thickest at middle of head, tapering to tip of head and to shaft.
D–Beam is straight, with no taper.
E–Beam thickest at tip of head and at throat, and narrowest at middle of head.
F–Beam thickest at throat, tapering to tip of head.
G–Aluminum frame.
H–Frame is made slightly lighter in smaller grip sizes.
I–Not available in 4 1/8-in. grip size.
J–Oddly shaped grip; bulged in middle.
K–Bevels on grip more pronounced than on most.
L–Rounded grip; six-sided grip also available.
M–Cover is only half-length.
N–Model also sold with midsize head (85-94 sq. in.).
O–Model also sold with midplus head.
P–Model also sold with oversize head.
Q–Model also sold with oversize plus head.
R–Sold prestrung.
S–Comes with string damper that can be attached to lower ends of vertical strings.
T–Comes with spare set of string dampers for re-stringer to install.
U–Comes with packet of 17-gauge nylon string.
V–Comes with 3-part bumper/grommet system for customizing balance when racquet is strung.
W–1-yr. warranty includes free string, grip overwrap, and a new bumper/grommet balance system sent 6 mo. after buyer returns warranty registration card.
X–2-yr. warranty.
Y–2-yr warranty; with return of registration card, includes free string, grip overwrap, and a new bumper/grommet balance system sent every 6 mo. during warranty period.
Z–Very high power.
AA–Less power than most.
BB–Name changed to **Pulsar Pro**; identical racquet.

HOME WORKPLACE

Home copiers 140	Cordless telephones 146
Typewriters & word processors..141	Telephone answerers 147
Computer printers......................143	Ratings......................................150
Printing calculators 145	

In the days before office equipment became fully domesticated, the home workplace was the part of the house where do-it-yourselfers used power tools to craft furniture or tune car engines. Today the term could just as easily apply to the room where you balance your checkbook, answer correspondence and return calls, or produce family income.

Increasingly, the new equipment is electronic, so equipping the home workplace now entails familiarizing yourself with new technology and figuring out what you need to get the job done.

For example, you can type a perfectly good letter on a secondhand typewriter, a $300 dedicated word-processing machine, or a $1500 personal computer and printer. The word processor and computer let you make wholesale changes without retyping, and the computer can run software other than a word processor. But for a letter to your Aunt Millie, a typewriter may be just fine—and an old-fashioned pen might be even better.

The range of choices is not as dramatic for telephones, for answering machines, and for home copiers. But improved technology and lower costs are making these products more attractive. Until a few years ago, for instance, photocopiers fell strictly within the realm of professional office equipment. Now perfectly serviceable home copiers can be bought for $400 to $900. Cordless phones now have fewer shortcomings and more conveniences than ever before. Still, money spent for capabilities you'll probably never use is still money wasted.

Shopping for any of this equipment is a lot like buying a TV set or stereo. Quality tends to be good but product lines are in a constant state of flux, and pricing is highly competitive. Because products like printers, calculators, and answering machines are marketed to businesses as well as consumers, you may find the latest models and best prices on the business pages of your local newspaper or in office equipment stores.

HOME COPIERS

▸ Ratings on page 150.

Until 1983, photocopiers were regarded as strictly business and professional office equipment that required a lot of expensive servicing. That's when Canon Corporation devised a way to make the copier components that had needed regular servicing—the toner cartridge and photoconductor drum—disposable and easily replaceable.

Canon's innovation paved the way for a new generation of small, reliable, and fairly economical copiers suitable for home offices. It also made Canon the dominant force in home copiers. A decade later, it still controls nearly two-thirds of the U.S. home copier market. The next biggest brand, *Sharp,* has 20 percent.

The choices

Most home copiers are small, stripped-down machines with a minimum of controls and fancy features. Major features that raise a copier's price: an automatic paper feed and the ability to enlarge and reduce. Home copiers bear list prices ranging from $600 to $1800—$400 to $900 with discounts. In addition, toner cartridges must be replaced periodically. Typical price: about $100. Some models make you put in a new photoconductor drum after every few thousand copies. Typical price: about $140. Others require professional service to replace the drum every 20,000 copies or so. Typical price: about $120 to $200. Supplies (paper, toner, photoconductor) cost about a nickel a copy. But if you figure in the price of the machine, the cost of making a copy can easily run as high as 25 cents.

Features to look for

Paper feed. With automatic feed, you stack 40 to 100 sheets of blank paper (the limit depends on the copier) in a tray; with manual feed, you put it into the machine one sheet at a time.

Exposure control. This lets you adjust to characteristics of originals by making copies lighter or darker. Look for a continuous light-to-dark adjustment scale. A control with only three settings may be too limited for some jobs. Some models have an automatic exposure setting that adjusts itself, but our tests show such controls don't always work effectively.

Enlargement and reduction. This can be useful for making small type more legible or copying a legal-sized or up to a 10x14-inch document onto letter-sized paper. It typically adds a couple of hundred dollars to the cost of the copier.

Bypass tray. This lets you switch easily between plain paper and letterhead.

User-replaceable drum. A copier with an all-in-one cartridge that you replace yourself has a decided edge over one that requires professional service to replace the drum.

The tests

We test cartridge longevity two ways: We run off a variety of originals—text, magazine illustrations, test patterns, and photo prints—until the toner runs out. Then we do the same thing with a plain double-spaced typed page, for which we list cartridge capacity in the Ratings. We also copy onto transparencies, as well as paper of various weights, cotton content, and finish.

Buying advice

A lower-priced copier with manual feed is fine for modest copying chores—the occasional bill or magazine article. But for more than the occasional small copy job, say, a couple of hundred résumés or making multiple copies, feeding in copy paper sheet by sheet doesn't make sense. For such use, it's worth paying extra for the automatic-feed feature. Other special features also add to the cost of a copier, so pick and choose only those you'll really use.

When buying, be sure you know what kind of servicing the machine requires, as well as the the copier's paper capacity and cost of cartridges. Some machines' cartridges inherently produce more copies than others', but the kind of originals you use has a big effect on cartridge life. According to our tests, if you copy only double-spaced typewritten pages, you stand a good chance of exceeding the manufacturer's estimate. Copy enough illustrations heavy in gray and black and you'll get less copies than the manufacturer says.

TYPEWRITERS & WORD PROCESSORS

▸ Ratings on page 154.

The simple typewriter may be all but extinct, but its successor isn't necessarily a multipurpose computer. People who produce mainly typewritten documents of limited length and complexity may be happier with one of two other modern species of writing machine: the word-processing typewriter or the somewhat more ambitious personal word processor.

A step up from the electric typewriter, these machines feature an LCD screen, where you can view and edit your words before committing them to paper. They print with the same sort of daisy wheel—a spinning typewheel whose petals stamp the characters onto paper—that was popular on early computer printers. These high-tech typewriters can store documents for later retrieval and printing. They also check spelling and, in some cases, do rudimentary proofreading.

Less expensive models look a lot like an electric typewriter. Pricier ones resemble a personal computer, complete with detachable keyboard, full-screen display, and diskette slot. Most won't run anything but a word-processing application, but they do it for less money and hassle than a computer.

If you've never typed on anything but a traditional typewriter, you may find the keyboard on these hybrids intimidating at first—some keys perform more than one function and there are others you never saw on your trusty old Royal, keys with names like "Code" and "Alt." But you need not enter the brave new world of word processing all at once: The machines usually have a typewriter mode, in which they work pretty much like a traditional typewriter.

Electronics make functions like moving from place to place on the page and fixing errors quite easy. Usually you can easily fix mistakes on the LCD screen. If the typo prints out, the typical correction method is a sticky tape that lifts the incorrect letters off the paper. Settings like margins and tabs show on the display and can be easily changed. No need to hit a carriage return at the end of every line—these machines return to the next line automatically, a feature known as "word wrap."

Such powers still fall short of what a full-fledged personal computer can do. Someone accustomed to using a PC for word processing would probably find these machines frustrating. Many of the displays are small, with little room for the "help" screens typically available on computers. The printing takes much longer than most computer printers. In our tests, a 170-word, one-page business letter took close to two minutes. The built-in thesauruses tended to be skimpy. And the ability to format a document, such as changing line spacing, may be limited.

The choices

Word-processing typewriter. Of the two types, this is more like the old-fashioned typewriter. It types directly on paper, but does a few things a paper-pounder could never do. It lets you see and change words on the screen before printing, stores a few pages of text you can print later, and checks spelling. These high-tech typewriters suffer from two major handicaps. Their small display—usually no more than a couple of lines of 40 characters each—limits the ability of the machine to instruct the typist on how to use the keyboard. And the lack of a diskette drive limits the permanent storage capacity to about 5 to 10 typewritten pages. Discount prices start at about $100.

Personal word processor. This machine is closer yet to a personal computer but usually unable to run programs other than a word processor. Cheaper models sell at discount for $200 to $300 and look like word-processing typewriters except for a larger pop-up LCD screen and a slot to hold a diskette. More expensive models, priced at more than $300, may look more like desktop computers. The large display makes this type easier to learn and use than a word-processing typewriter. And diskettes provide a nearly unlimited capacity for document storage.

Closer still to a genuine computer are designs like Panasonic's battery-powered "laptop" word processor with a 14-line display or Canon's deluxe word processor with built-in ink-jet printer. Those models are priced in the $500 to $600 range.

Features to look for

Display. The bigger the better. Look for a tiltable screen that's at least seven or eight lines high and 80 characters wide, with pull-down menus that eliminate the need for complicated sequences of keys.

Keyboard. Look for a keyboard that groups keys logically or a machine that comes with color-coded key labels. A detachable keyboard offers more flexibility on your desktop than one that's attached. The most useful key is an undo key. It lets you undo a mistake, such as accidentally deleting a block of text.

Storage. Word-processing typewriters will store about 10 pages as long as the battery holds out. Machines that use a standard 3½-inch diskette, similar to the type used in PCs, can store 120 to 175 pages per diskette. Some machines use special plug-in memory cards, which hold 8 to 16 pages.

Paper handling/typing. This is a weak point with a number of machines. But some models give you an unobstructed view of the line you're typing and some handle index cards and envelopes flawlessly. All make you feed paper one page at a time.

Other features are geared to specific needs. For instance, some typists will appreciate a feature that simplifies form letters. The best word processors print form letters by combining mailing lists with a generic template document. A grammar checker scans a document for simple punctuation errors. Some machines print two columns of text per page, which is helpful for preparing simple newsletters. Word counts come in handy if what you're writing must fit a certain space. Decimal tabs are useful if you need to align columns of figures by their decimal points or their rightmost digit. Special symbols let you type and print non-English accents, currency symbols, and the like.

The tests

We test the machines the way any good typist would—by inserting lots of paper and pressing lots of keys. We judge the feel and layout of keyboards, readability of displays, and the ability to correct typos. We time how quickly they move paper up or down as well as how long they take to print a business letter.

We also pit their spell-checkers against a list of demon misspelled words, and their thesauruses against a list of 40 common words.

Buying advice

Personal computers are now so cheap that a simple PC setup—computer, monitor, printer—makes sense for many people. Such a system can be purchased at discount for much less than $1000. Packaged systems, from computer specialists such as Apple, IBM, or Dell make these systems relatively simple to set up.

Still, a genuine computer may be more technology than you want or need. If your typing workload is light, a word-processing typewriter may do just fine. If you spend a fair amount of time behind the keyboard, it's well worth the extra $100 or so for a personal word processor, with its larger, more readable screen, and diskette drive. Stay away from machines that use plug-in memory cards, which are more expensive than diskettes and store a lot less.

If you buy a machine with a disk drive, be sure it can read and write diskettes compatible with MS-DOS (i.e., IBM-compatible) computers. That capability will come in handy if you need to exchange files with others or if you move on to a PC yourself someday. Note that if you do send documents to a computer, certain formatting elements of your documents, such as underlining or centering, may be lost.

COMPUTER PRINTERS

▸ Ratings on page 162.

Technical innovation and competition are making computer printers better and cheaper than ever. The venerable daisy-wheel printer, an early standard bearer of print quality, has become virtually a relic. Even dot-matrix printers, the dominant breed for the past decade, may be on the brink of obsolescence. Their rapid decline appears assured if the prices of the newest, most technologically advanced printers—ink-jet and laser models—drop much lower.

The choices

Dot-matrix. These printers' tiny metal pins form characters by hitting the paper hundreds of times a second in a shrill whine. The more dots in a printhead's matrix, the smoother and crisper its print. Early dot-matrix models had only nine pins, which formed coarse, sometimes stunted, characters. Later models used more pins, or passed the printhead two or three times over a line, to create a smoother effect.

Today, most printer-makers offer a line of low-cost nine-pin models—typically priced below $200—and a line of 24-pin models priced in the $200- to $650-range. In our tests, 24-pin models turned out decent copy in near-letter-quality (NLQ) mode, their slowest. Nine-pin models are fine for graphics and if text quality isn't important.

Ink-jet. These use an ink cartridge that

feeds an array of nearly microscopic tubes, each with a heating element; when the element is energized, a small ink droplet in the corresponding tube squirts quietly onto the paper. Since the technology doesn't demand much electrical energy, it's often used in small, portable, battery-operated models. In our tests, most ink-jets' output quality was nearly as good as a laser printer's, with very little noise. Ink-jet cartridges are expensive, raising operating costs to about 6 cents a page (excluding paper), about double the operating costs of laser or dot-matrix printers. Ink-jet printers typically cost $350 to $700.

Laser. Using xerographic technology like that in photocopiers, these can reproduce an almost limitless variety of type forms and sizes, as well as complex graphics. Images are electronically created on a light-sensitive drum, usually with a scanning laser. Powdered toner adheres to areas where light touches the drum and then transfers to a sheet of paper, which is briefly heated to fuse the toner permanently. The output is clean and crisp. In our tests, laser printers produced—quietly—nearly perfect renditions of test pages. And they printed each page in 11 to 15 seconds—about half the time of a dot-matrix printer in NLQ mode or an ink-jet. Until recently, laser printers typically cost several thousand dollars. Now prices have dropped below a thousand for most.

Features to look for

Typefaces. Most models can print in at least a couple of distinct typefaces—such as Times Roman, Helvetica, and Courier.

Paper feed. All printers can handle single sheets of letter-sized paper. Laser printers use an automatic feeder tray stacked with blank paper. That's an extra-cost option with most dot-matrix and some ink-jet models. Paper-tray capacity ranges from 30 sheets up to a ream of 20-pound paper.

Dot-matrix models typically use a tractor feed, a sprocketed, treadlike device that pushes or pulls perforated fanfold paper. Some designs put the sprockets on the roller itself. Those pin-feed printers work fine with standard-width continuous paper, but they can't adjust to narrow-width paper or standard one-across mailing labels. Least convenient with continuous paper are printers that have no tractor at all but rely instead on the friction of the roller to advance the paper. That may be O.K. for the first few sheets, but not long after that, the paper is likely to become misaligned.

The tests

We test printers by producing the same two pages, one of text and the other of pie charts. A panel of staff members grades the samples. We also measure the time each machine takes to print a 170-word business letter. Because laser printers need several seconds to warm up, we have them print our letter five times and average the results.

Buying advice

If your needs are limited to routine tasks like correspondence and résumés, a 24-pin dot matrix printer should do the job for relatively little expense. For a few dollars more, an ink-jet printer can provide near-laser quality without taking a toll on your ears, though you will pay a premium for ink—about $20 to $35 for each replacement cartridge.

Consider a laser model only if print quality and speed are extremely important. Fancier laser models—for example, those that feature a printer language like PostScript and cost well over $1000—are only needed for sophisticated desktop publishing. Prices and models change rapidly. Before buying, check prices in computer magazines and the business section of your newspaper.

PRINTING CALCULATORS

▸ Ratings on page 151.

Pocket calculators are fine for speeding up the mathematics of problem solving, but there are important advantages in having a calculator that leaves a paper trail. You can check your entries for errors without keying in the numbers all over again. And you have a permanent record.

Printing calculators today are competent mathematical tools with easy-to-read displays. They include keys not only for the basic arithmetic functions, but also for memory storage, percentage computations, and constant, reciprocal, and power functions. You select decimal placement, floating or fixed. Most have a print buffer, a memory that stores entries as fast as they are keyed in until the printer catches up. You can also turn the print mechanism off. Models mainly differ in convenience and how well they stand up to heavy use.

The choices

Plug-in desktop models. They have large keys that stand well above the keyboard surface and respond with a click to confirm an entry. They sell for $50 to $65.

Desktop portables. These are similar to plug-ins but can also be powered by batteries. As with plug-ins, most have well-designed keyboards. They sell for $25 to $55.

Handheld models. These tend to be smaller, lighter, and a little cheaper than desktop models. The keyboards are small, making them less convenient to use. Their important function keys are grouped above and to the right of the number keys. The print mechanisms tend to be less durable.

Features to look for

Display. Fluorescent displays are easier to see in dim light than liquid-crystal displays, but LCDs draw less power and are easier to see in very bright light. Under normal lighting conditions, both types of display are more than adequate.

Paper and printing. Most models use paper rolls 2¼-inches wide (a standard size) and up to 3¾ inches in diameter. A few models take smaller rolls, which may be hard to find. Printing is typically done with black or purple ink.

5/4 switch. When used with a decimal switch, this performs automatic rounding by increasing the last visible decimal if the next unseen decimal is five or greater.

Special keys. A 00 key inserts two zeros with a single keystroke, speeding up data entry. An average/IT key calls up the number of items in a list being added and can compute an average of their values. A markup/margin key, useful for business calculations, calculates mark-up, mark-down, and gross profit margin. A +/- key changes a positive number to negative and vice versa, helpful when adding negative numbers.

The tests

We gauge keyboard layout and the feel of the keys. We clock printing speed and check noise. Using pneumatic "fingers" to press keys, we assess the durability of keyboard and printer and the limits of the print-buffer capacity. We measure battery life.

Buying advice

Choose a desktop calculator if you want a durable machine with a keyboard designed for rapid data entry. Among the desktops, the plug-in type excelled in our tests. A handheld model is more appropriate for occasional use or situations that demand unusual portability.

CORDLESS TELEPHONES

▶ Ratings on page 159.

At heart, a cordless phone is a walkie-talkie, with a tiny radio transmitter and receiver in both base and handset beaming the conversation between the two. To accomplish that, phone-makers bring together in the handset a transmitter and receiver capable of operating over ranges of up to 1000 feet, a speaker and microphone, a maze of circuits under a push-button dial, and a rechargeable battery, among other things.

The resulting device is not without its shortcomings. Cordless phones can deliver irritating static, distort voices, or quit when carried too far afield. They may connect with signals from a neighbor's cordless phone. Their batteries tend to lose power inopportunely if the handset isn't returned often enough to the charger.

Even so, the millions who buy cordless phones in the U.S. each year have obviously been willing to put up with the shortcomings to gain the conveniences. And happily, the product is improving. Recently tested models had better sound quality and less background noise than cordless models of earlier years. Our tests did show, though, that you will probably sound clearer to the people you call than they sound to you (if they are using a corded phone).

Cordless phones now have enough range to be used anywhere in any size house short of a mansion. Most employ a digital "combination code" between handset and base to discourage others from listening in and to reduce interference from nearby cordless phones. Some let you change codes manually; others do it automatically.

The choices

Basic phones. These usually cost no more than about $100. Their main drawback is that they operate on only one or two radio channels, which makes them more prone than full-featured phones to interference from neighbors' phones.

Full-featured phones. For a bit more money, these phones offer 10-channels, a speakerphone, or both. If you have a lot of neighbors, the extra channels help ensure that their cordless phones don't interfere with yours. Should such a conflict occur, most 10-channel phones let you change channels while continuing to talk. Some go a step further—they select a clear channel when you first turn on the phone.

A speakerphone on a phone's base provides hands-free operation, useful for conversing while doing something else or when your hands tire from holding a handset that could weigh nearly three-quarters of a pound. You can use the base and handset as two ends of an intercom. (Some models have a speaker that is intended for intercom use only, not for calls.) Models that have a dialing keyboard on the base are, in effect, two phones in one.

Features to look for

Here are some features that add to a phone's convenience:

Two-way paging. With this feature, pushing a button on the base or handset causes the other component to sound a paging signal, useful for signaling someone or finding a missing handset.

Ringer in base. This lets you know there's a call, even if the handset is somewhere else.

Out-of-range tone. This feature warns you that you've moved the handset too far from the base.

Speed-call memory. This stores frequently called numbers and lets you dial them using one or two buttons. Many phones can store more than 10 numbers of up to 16 digits each.

Volume control. This boosts the loudness of the handset's speaker or lowers it for those sensitive to loud speech.

Mute or hold. This feature lets you speak with someone nearby without letting the person on the other end of the line hear you.

The tests

We test cordless phones in a variety of ways that simulate actual use. We make calls to and from regular corded phones, checking both sides of the conversation for loudness and quality. We determine the phones' maximum operating range in an open parking lot. And we subject them to a variety of insults, including 8000-volt electrical jolts, 800-volt surges, and falls from a height of several feet onto a hard floor.

Buying advice

If you live in a densely populated area, a 10-channel phone will give you reasonable protection against interference. You may even be able to find one for about the same price as a basic cordless phone. Consider a one- or two-channel model if you live in a rural area and you don't need any frills. Given the heavy discounting of phones, you should be able to get a good basic cordless phone for considerably less than $100.

Don't rely on a cordless phone as the only phone in your house. Most models are rendered inoperative by a power failure or a dead battery.

TELEPHONE ANSWERERS

▸ Ratings on page 156.

Telephone answerers are more popular than ever. Their increased appeal is due to several factors. Improved technology has automated basic functions and shrunk the machine's size. The remote beeper has been replaced by the keypad of the Touch-Tone telephone. And voice-actuated circuits and automatic "timeouts"—the ability to hang up if there's no voice after a few seconds—have made the machines adroit at handling both long and short messages.

The choices

Single microcassette. This type records both the greeting and incoming messages on a single microcassette. Messages are often limited to a minute or two each and, because there's only one tape in the machine, callers must wait for the tape to shuttle forward before they can leave a message. Prices range from $40 to $60.

Dual cassette. The most flexible machines use two tapes—either full-sized cassettes or microcassettes. Callers can leave their message without delay and the greeting can be longer than on a single-cassette machine. A machine that uses an endless-loop tape for greetings is unable to answer calls for about 15 seconds after a call while the tape cycles back to the beginning. Prices range from $70 to $260.

Memory chips. Memory chips similar to those found in computers store the greeting and, on a few machines, the messages. By replacing moving parts with circuits, these machines are less likely to break down. Compared with tape, memory chips are expensive; as a result, the machines that record messages on them restrict recording times. A one-minute limit per call is typical. In our tests, voice quality on these machines was clear, but sounded less natural than messages on tape. These models tend to be small but pricey—ranging from about $100 to $400.

Built-in phone. Some machines combine answerer and phone—cord or cordless—in a single device. That saves space and can cost less than buying a separate phone and answerer, but if either one fails, both go to the repair shop. These "integrated telephone answering devices" typically are priced at $100 or more.

Voice mail. Many local phone companies across the U.S. now offer this alternative to the answering machine. Messages are received and stored by the phone company when you're out or even if your line is busy. You use a Touch-Tone phone to check for or listen to messages. The advantages are obvious—no machine to break down and an increased capability for receiving messages. But you can't screen incoming calls, there's no light to tell you if you've got messages, and charges can run $5 to $10 per month or more, depending on your type of phone service.

Features to look for

Certain basic features have become standard on many machines. These include:

Call screening. This lets you listen to an incoming message as it comes in, helpful in avoiding nuisance calls without missing important ones. If you decide to take a call, many machines automatically stop recording as soon as you pick up any phone in the house.

Number of rings. This lets you adjust the number of rings the machine will wait before it answers, so you don't have to race to the phone to beat the machine's pickup. If you're away, you can set the machine to fewer rings as a courtesy to callers.

Pause and Skip. These let you control playback of recorded messages. Pause temporarily stops a message so you can jot down a name or number. Skip speeds things up by moving the tape back or forward exactly one message.

Call counters. Some machines use a blinking light to signal that messages are waiting. Better are ones that blink the light to tell you how many messages there are. The best displays provide a digital readout of the number of calls. Most counters ignore hang-ups that occur before the beep.

Power backup. Most machines retain their memory at least for a short time in the event of power failure, but some reset the call counter to zero. The best designs use a battery backup (with an indicator that tells you when to replace it) that holds the settings for hours.

Remote control. All machines let you use a Touch-Tone phone to retrieve messages while on the road. Some let you set your own codes; others are preprogrammed. Those with two- or three-digit codes offer the most security.

Toll-saver. This feature lets you avoid a long-distance call when you call to check messages. When there aren't any messages waiting, you set the machine to answer the first call after four or five rings and subsequent messages after only one or two. You save the charge by hanging up after three rings—if the machine hasn't picked up by then, there are no messages.

Higher-priced machines offer features that may someday trickle down to basic models. These include:

Greeting bypass. Callers who don't want to listen to your greeting bypass it by pressing the right Touch-Tone key, usually the asterisk.

Time and date. With this, the machine notes the time and date of each message and announces them in a pleasant voice when you play the message back.

Announce only. This lets you post a greeting—for example, a meeting announcement—without recording incoming calls.

The tests

Our tests of answering machines concentrate on versatility and convenience. We place calls to the machines and play back messages, gauging tone quality of the voice on the message. We note the presence of mechanical and background noise. We try out all the features and assess how easy each answerer is to use.

Buying advice

If your needs are simple and you don't want a new telephone, look for a plain answerer with dual cassettes or with a memory chip for the greeting and a cassette for messages. A number are available for about $60 to $90. If you can live with just short messages, a machine that uses memory chips for greeting and messages is less likely to need repairs.

Among the answering machines with a built-in telephone, there are lots of choices—most of them expensive, unless you need a phone anyway. They range from cordless models with lots of features to plain models.

If you have special needs, shop around—there may be a model with features particularly suited to your circumstances.

---

*W*HAT THE RATINGS MEAN

- The Ratings typically rank products in order of estimated quality, without regard to price.

- A product's rating applies only to the model tested and should not be considered a rating of other models sold under the same brand name unless so noted.

- Models are check-rated (✓) when the product proved to be significantly superior to other models tested.

- Products high in quality and relatively low in price are deemed Best Buys.

RATINGS: HOME COPIERS

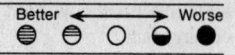

Better ◄——► Worse
◉ ⊖ ○ ◐ ●

▶ See report, page 140. From Consumer Reports, January 1992.

Recommendations: The *Canon PC-6RE* delivered excellent copies with minimal fuss. Consider the *Canon PC-2* for undemanding use and the *Canon PC-1* for occasional use. Both models have been discontinued, but they may still be in some stores.

Ratings order: Listed in order of estimated quality, based on overall score. Differences in score of less than 10 points are not significant. The price, without cartridge, is the approximate retail as quoted by the manufacturer; actual retail may be lower. The price in parentheses is the list price for the cartridge as recommended by the manufacturer. Ⓓ indicates model discontinued. Key to paper feed: **A** = automatic; **M** = manual.

Brand and model (cartridge)	Overall score	Price	Cartridge life	Cost per copy	Exposure consistency	Autoexposure	First copy/subsequent copy, sec.	Paper feed	Paper capacity	Advantages	Disadvantages	Comments
Canon PC-6RE (A30)	95	$800 (145)	6200	4¢	◉	◉	12/7	A,M	100	A,B,E,F,H	g,j	D
Mita CC-20 (CC Proc Unit)	90	600 (197)	6000	4	◉	—	9/7	A,M	100	A,C,D,H	j	D,E
Canon PC-2 (A15) Ⓓ	87	500 (95)	2900	5	⊖	⊖	17/9	A	50	A,G	j,k	B,C,G
Canon PC-1 (A15), A Best Buy Ⓓ	82	390 (95)	2600	6	○	—	17/10	M	—	A,G	j	B,C,D
Sharp Z-76 (ZT-50TDI)	81	1299 (130)	3300	6	○	◐	11/7	A,M	100	D,F,H	a,b,g,i	A,C,D
Sharp Z-50 (ZT-50TDI) Ⓓ	81	495 (130)	4700	5	⊖	◐	10/7	A,M	100	D,E	a,b,g,i	A,C,D
Tandy PPC-750 (63-688)	76	600 (100)	3400	7	○	—	14/10	A	50	—	c,e,f,h,i,j	B,C,D,F
Sanyo SFT-50 (CK50K)	75	795 (149)	5000	5	○	—	15/10	A	50	—	c,d,e,f,h,i,j	B,C,D,F
Xerox 5220 (6R333)	75	500 (135)	3600	5	○	◐	17/12	A	40	D	a,b,c,i	B,C,G

Features in Common

All: • Take letter-size paper. • Can copy from books. • Can make double-sided copies. • Lack provision for leveling. • Operate on ordinary 120-volt power.
Except as noted, all have: • Continuously adjustable exposure control. • Opt. single-color cartridges in blue, brown, green, red.

Key to Advantages

A–Uses all-in-one toner/photoconductor cartridge with enclosed magnetic brush.
B–Stationary platen; convenient when copying from books.
C–Has 20-sheet bypass feed tray.
D–Exposure control clearly labeled.
E–Counter setting can be decreased and increased.
F–Has ability to reduce and enlarge.
G–Ready to copy in 1 sec.
H–Can also take legal-size paper.

Key to Disadvantages

a–Exposure control has only 3 positions.
b–Quarter-inch-wide strip along long edge of platen cannot be copied.
c–Service person required to replace photoconductor drum (every 20,000 copies):

PRINTING CALCULATORS

Tandy, $200; **Xerox,** $195; **Sanyo,** $124.
d–Copy contrast slightly low.
e–Lacks interlock to shut off power when opened (but no shock hazard found).
f–Hot toner fuser more accessible to fingers than most (but has warning label).
g–Paper in feed tray hard to see.
h–Copier can stop with internal fault indication; user must reset by turning copier off.
i–Cartridge is potentially messy to change.
j–Requires centering original along one edge of platen.
k–Copy counter must be manually reset after making multiple copies.

Key to Comments
A–User-replaceable photoconductor drum (required every 9000 copies, $140).
B–Portable model; can be stored on edge (but no provision for storing power cord).
C–Photoconductor drum replaced separately from toner cartridge.
D–Could not reliably make overhead projector transparencies.
E–Dust cover included.
F–Colored toner cartridges available in blue and red only.
G–"Continuous" setting makes copies as long as paper supply lasts.

RATINGS PRINTING CALCULATORS

Better ◀——▶ Worse

▶ See report, page 145. From Consumer Reports, August 1991.

Recommendations: For light use, we suggest a handheld model such as the *Radio Shack EC-3016*. Better suited for hard use and fast entry are desktop calculators, especially plug-in models like the *Casio FR-3200* (now discontinued) or the *Texas Instruments TI-5045 II*. Our first choice among desktop portables is the *Casio HR-100T*.

Ratings order: Listed by types; within types, listed in order of estimated quality. Models judged equal in quality are bracketed and listed in alphabetical order. Price is the approximate retail as quoted by the manufacturer; actual retail may be lower. Ⓢ indicates tested model has been replaced by successor model; according to the manufacturer, the performance of new model should be similar to the tested model but features may vary. See page 152 for new model number and suggested retail price, if available. Ⓓ indicates model discontinued.

Brand and model	Price	Key feel	Ergonomics	Digit size	Printing speed	Printing noise	Keyboard durability	Printer durability	Advantages	Disadvantages	Comments
PLUG-IN DESKTOP MODELS											
Casio FR-3200 Ⓓ	$50	◐	◐	◐	◐	◕	◐	◐	A,D,E,F,G	—	B,K,O,P
Texas Inst. TI-5045 II	60	◐	◐	○	◐	◐	◐	◐	A,B,D,E,F,H,I	p,s	B,I,O
Canon MP15D	49	◐	◐	◐	◐	○	◐	◐	A,E,F,I	—	B,I,S
Sharp EL-1197IV Ⓓ	49	◐	◐	◐	◐	◕	◐	◐	C,D,E,F	—	B,H,N,U
DESKTOP PORTABLES											
Casio HR-100T	30	◐	◐	○	○	○	◐	○	D,F,G,M	u	E,H,N,P
Sanyo CX5523 Ⓓ	55	◕	◐	○	○	○	◐	◐	B,D,F,J,M,N	q,t	A,D,F,L,O,T
Sears 5874 Ⓓ	30	○	◐	○	○	◐	◐	○	B,F	l,q,u	E,I,O,Q

Ratings continued

152 PRINTING CALCULATORS

Ratings continued

Brand and model	Price	Key feel	Ergonomics	Digit size	Printing speed	Printing noise	Keyboard durability	Printer durability	Advantages	Disadvantages	Comments
Canon P41-D	$34	○	⊖	○	○	○	⊖	⊖	L	m	F,G
Sharp EL-1601T [S]	33	⊖	⊖	○	○	○	⊖	⊖	—	m,r	E,J,N,U,V
Radio Shack EC-3017 [S]	50	○	⊖	○	●	●	⊖	⊖	D,L	h,n,q	I,Q
Texas Inst. TI-5029	35	⊖	○	○	○	○	⊖	⊖	—	g,m,o,u	E,L,N
Royal 6600 HD [D]	40	⊖	⊖	⊖	○	⊖	⊖	⊖	A,D,E,K	c,d,j,k,r,u	F,H,S
HANDHELD MODELS											
Radio Shack EC-3016 [S]	35	○	○	⊖	◐	⊖	⊖	⊖	L,M,N	h,m	I,Q
Sharp EL-1611A [S]	25	○	○	○	○	⊖	⊖	⊖	L,M	e,h,m	A,C,E,J,N,Q,U
Casio HR-8A [S]	20	○	○	⊖	○	◐	⊖	⊖	L,M,N	f,h,m,r	A,E,M,P,Q
AEG Olympia PD700	40	○	○	⊖	○	○	⊖	●	L,M	h,m	E,I,Q,T
Canon MP1D	22	○	⊖	⊖	○	⊖	⊖	●	L,M	h,m	E,I,Q,S
Texas Inst. TI-5005 II [S]	29	○	○	⊖	○	⊖	⊖	●	L,M,N	h,m	E,I,Q
Sanyo CX-3554 [D]	25	◐	○	○	⊖	⊖	⊖	●	L	a,b,h,i,m,p	A,C,E,I,R,T

Successor Models (in Ratings order)
Sharp EL-1601T is succeeded by EL1601H, $33; Radio Shack EC-3017 by EC-3018, $50; Radio Shack EC-3016 by EC-3024, $30; Sharp EL-1611A by EL-1611H, $25; Casio HR-8A by HR-8B, $20; Texas Inst. TI-5005 II by 5006, $30.

Performance Notes
Except as noted: • Buffer overrun and resistance to reflection judged above average. • View angle judged good.

Features in Common
All have: • Keys for arithmetic functions, "memory +" and "memory −", percent, paper feed, plus constant, reciprocal, and power functions, floating decimal or fixed decimal-place accuracy selection (see story). • Error/overflow, memory store, negative number display indicators. • Very legible black or purple print. • Paper roll included.
All handheld models have: • LCD display. • Algebraic data entry. • Memory recall/clear key or keys. • Internal paper compartment. • Print/no print key. • Weight 3/4 lb. or less.
Except as noted, all have: • Keys that click when pressed. • 10-digit display. • Selectable add-mode data entry. • 5/4 round-off selector switch. • Non-add print key. • Item counter.
• Provision for power from 4 AA batteries or house current with optional adapter. • Holder for 2 1/4-in.-wide paper roll. • Replaceable ink roller. • Nonslip feet. • 12-mo. parts/labor warranty.
Except as noted, all desktop models have: • Fluorescent display. • "Mixed logic" data entry with separate addition/subtraction and multiplication/division register. • Memory total and subtotal keys. • Replaceable plastic external paper holder. • Weight from 1 to 3 lb.

Key to Advantages
A–Round-up selector switch (see story).
B–2-color print; negative numbers are red.
C–Tax-rate key lets you store local sales-tax rate in memory, add tax to grand total.
D–Key to calculate mark-up/mark-down/gross profit margin.
E–Backspace (entry erase) key.
F–Change-entry (+/−) key.
G–Averaging key.
H–Percent-change key; automatically calculates percent difference between 2 numbers.
I–Sigma switch to automatically add results of multiplication/division calculations to addition/subtraction register.
J–Internal compartment for 2 1/4-in.-wide paper roll.

PRINTING CALCULATORS

K–Very bright display characters.
L–Has auto-off.
M–View angle judged above average.
N–Battery life for printer above average or better.

Key to Disadvantages
a–Lacks nonslip feet; slides on table.
b–Ink roller can't be replaced or refilled, but has reasonably long life according to the manufacturer.
c–Fragile battery terminals.
d–Wires in print-head compartment exposed to potential damage.
e–Memory information lost when unit automatically switches off.
f–No option for add-mode entry, which automatically places decimal point in front of last 2 digits entered.
g–No non-add print key, useful for printing display information without affecting a calculation.
h–No item counter.
i–No external paper holder.
j–Battery cover very hard to remove.
k–Batteries hard to install and remove.
l–Instructions not comprehensive or clear.
m–No "00" digit key.
n–Printer makes annoying noise.
o–Hard-to-read markings for power/printer control and decimal-selector switches.
p–Last printed number on paper tape not in view until next printing cycle.
q–Keys don't click when pressed.
r–Buffer overrun judged worse or much worse than average.
s–Display's resistance to reflection judged average.
t–Display's resistance to reflection judged fair.
u–Battery life for display judged below average.

Key to Comments
A–Has internal paper compartment with see-through cover.
B–Operates on house current only. Has power cord at least 6 ft. long.
C–Uses 3 AA batteries.
D–Uses 4 C batteries.
E–Batteries included.
F–Comes with ac adapter; cord at least 6 ft. long.
G–Fixed-decimal accuracy can be set to 0, 1, 2, or 3 places.
H–Fixed-decimal accuracy can be set to 0, 2, or 3 places.
I–Fixed-decimal accuracy can be set to 0, 2, 3, or 4 places.
J–Fixed-decimal accuracy can be set to 0 or 2 places.
K–Fixed-decimal accuracy can be set to 0, 1, 2, 3, 4, or 6 places.
L–Fixed-decimal accuracy can be set to 0, 2, or 4 places.
M–Fixed-decimal accuracy can be set to 2 places.
N–No 5/4 switch. Automatically rounds off numbers, depending on decimal-switch setting.
O–12-digit display.
P–Has constant function display indicator.
Q–Nonreplaceable folding external paper holder. (Plastic holder on **Sears 5874, Radio Shack EC-3017**; metal on others.)
R–Uses 1½-in.-wide paper roll.
S–Warranty: 12 mo., parts; 3 mo., labor.
T–3-mo. parts/labor warranty.
U–6-mo. parts/labor warranty.
V–Uses algebraic data entry.

What the Ratings Mean

■ The Ratings typically rank products in order of estimated quality, without regard to price.

■ A product's rating applies only to the model tested and should not be considered a rating of other models sold under the same brand name unless so noted.

■ Models are check-rated (✓) when the product proved to be significantly superior to other models tested.

■ Products high in quality and relatively low in price are deemed Best Buys.

154 TYPEWRITERS & WORD PROCESSORS

RATINGS: TYPEWRITERS & WORD PROCESSORS

Better ◖ ◐ ○ ◑ ● Worse

▶ See report, page 141. From Consumer Reports, November 1991.

Recommendations: For short reports and routine correspondence, stick with a typewriter such as the *Sears 53514*. For longer reports and extensive correspondence, it's worth paying $100 or so extra for a word processor equipped with external storage on diskettes. Give first consideration to the top performer: the *Brother WP-760D*.

Ratings order: Listed by types; within types, listed in order of overall score based on performance as word processors. Differences of less than 4 points were judged not very significant. Price is the suggested retail as quoted by the manufacturer; actual retail may be lower. ⓢ indicates model has been replaced by successor model; according to the manufacturer, the performance of new model is similar to the tested model but features may vary. See opposite for new model number and suggested retail price. ⓓ indicates model discontinued.

Brand and model	Price	Score	Working memory, pages	Ease of use	Keyboard layout	Speed	Visibility	Return	Envelopes, cards	Advantages	Disadvantages	Comments
WORD PROCESSORS												
Brother WP-760D	$280	86	16	◖	◖	◐	○	◖	◖	A,C,D,E,I,K,M,R	d,j	*A,H*
Panasonic KX-W900 ⓢ	360	82	18	◖	◐	○	●	○	○	C,E,J,M	c,m	*I*
Panasonic KX-W905 ⓓ	330	82	22	◖	◐	◖	●	○	○	C,E,J,M	c,m	*I*
Brother WP-720 ⓓ	285	80	15½	◖	◖	◐	○	◐	◖	A,D,E,I,K,M,O,R	d	*A,B,J*
AEG Olympia EW410 ⓓ	351	80	12	○	◖	◖	◖	◖	◖	F,G,H	c,p,q	*C,D,G,K*
Smith Corona PWP-90 ⓢ	280	76	16	○	◖	◖	◖	○	○	B,F,G,H,M,N,O,P,Q	c,d,f,n,o,p,q,r	*B,L*
WORD-PROCESSING TYPEWRITERS ①												
Brother AX-550 ⓢ	200	68	11½	◐	○	◖	◖	◐	◖	I,M,O,R	a,c,d,e	*C,F*
Smith Corona SD-860 ⓢ	200	67	8	◐	◖	◖	◖	○	○	E,F,M,N,O,P,Q,R	c,d,f,q,r	—
Sears 53514	200	59	5	●	◐	◖	◖	○	◖	N,O	b,c,d,e,g,h,k,l	*C,E*
Sharp PA-3140II ⓓ	215	56	7½	●	◐	◖	◖	○	○	F,I,J,L,O,P	b,c,d,f,h,i,l	—

① *If judged strictly as typewriters, the* **Smith Corona** *and the* **Sears** *would tie for first place, followed by the* **Sharp** *and the* **Brother**.

TYPEWRITERS & WORD PROCESSORS 155

Successor Models (in Ratings order)
Panasonic KX-W900 is succeeded by KX-955, $590; Smith Corona PWP-90 by PWP 2400, $599; Brother AX-550 by AX-600, $200; Smith Corona SD-860 by XD-5900, $329.

Performance Notes
Except as noted, all were judged to have:
• Above average keyboard touch. • Average spell checkers. • Above average typewriter spacing.

Features in Common
All have: • Single-, double-, and 1½-line spacing. • Automatic centering. • Ability to justify text and to print with a ragged-right and flush-left margin. • Move, Copy, and Delete functions for blocks of text. • Automatic lift-off correction of mistakes on current line. • Paragraph indent. • Spell checker with provision for personal dictionary of at least 100 words. • Comfortable handle.
Except as noted, all have: • Automatic search and replace for word or phrase within the document. • Auto-reformat, to format new text added to an existing document. • Key to delete an entire line. • Four directional cursor keys in diamond or inverted-T pattern. • Ability to use cheaper fabric ribbon instead of carbon-film. • Some international characters. • Fractional spacing or backspacing for corrections. • 90-day labor, 1-yr. parts warranty.
All typewriters have: Nontiltable LCD screen that displays two 40-character lines.
Except as noted, all word processors have: • Tiltable LCD screen that displays seven 80-character lines. • Page-preview to view document layout. • Ability to mix different line spacing and character pitch within a document. • Ability to change right and left margins within a document to set off a subparagraph. • Cursor movement back and forth by word or page.

Key to Advantages
A–Screen contrast better than most.
B–Numbering can start with second page.
C–Has mail-merge for form letters.
D–Hyphen-scan helps break long words.
E–Can store block of boilerplate text for use in different documents.
F–For word (or line) delete, cursor may be positioned anywhere on the word (or line).
G–Undo key to recover text deleted.
H–Screen displays 8 lines.
I–Has punctuation checker (see story).
J–Has built-in thesaurus (see story).
K–Printing is less noisy than most.
L–Gives document's word count.
M–In Typewriter mode, during Spell Check, can automatically correct misspellings.
N–In Typewriter mode, beeps to acknowledge new margin settings.
O–In Typewriter mode, remembers margin and tab settings from last time.
P–Automatic correction: on last 3 lines typed (**Smith Coronas**); on last two lines typed (**Sharp**).
Q–Spell checker judged above average.
R–Typewriter spacing judged much better than average.

Key to Disadvantages
a–Cursor keys in row; less convenient than traditional diamond or inverted-T arrangements.
b–Cannot delete an entire line at one time.
c–No headers and footers for automatically titling each page.
d–Cursor cannot move one word at a time (**Smith Corona** cannot move one page at a time, either).
e–Cannot delete boldface or underlined words automatically; must be retyped to delete.
f–Printing is noisier than most.
g–Search function; no automatic Replace.
h–No Up and Down cursor keys to move conveniently through a stored document.
i–Cannot use more economical fabric ribbon.
j–Much slower in Search and Replace.
k–In Typewriter mode, correction very slow.
l–No fractional- or half-spacing.
m–In Typewriter mode, speed of indexing (moving sheet up or down automatically) much slower than most.
n–No Page-preview feature.
o–Only 1 character pitch and 1 line spacing allowed in a document.
p–Left and right margins can't be changed in document to set off subparagraph.
q–No Auto-reformat feature; extra keystrokes needed to properly format added text.
r–Keyboard touch was judged average.

Key to Comments
A–Has optional thesaurus disk (**Brother WP-760D**, $60) or card (**Brother WP-720**, $100).
B–Optional plug-in memory card (**Brother**, $30; **Smith Corona**, $26).
C–No international characters.
D–Has line-printing function in memory mode.
E–1-yr. parts/labor warranty.
F–90-day labor/5-yr. parts warranty.
G–90-day labor/parts warranty.
H–External memory, 237K.
I–External memory, 353K.
J–External memory, 16K card.
K–External memory, 100K.
L–External memory, 32K card.

RATINGS TELEPHONE ANSWERERS

▶ See report, page 147. From Consumer Reports, November 1991.

Recommendations: The top-rated *Sony TAM-50* ($100) and the *Code-A-Phone 2770* ($89) earned the highest scores—both were good performers offering convenience and helpful extras. If you don't need the extras, consider other high-rated models such as the *AT&T 1306* ($60) and the *Sanyo TAS346* ($79). Seven of the nine models with a built-in phone performed about as well; the *GE 2-9821A* ($70) was a bargain if you can do without frills and don't mind messages limited to two minutes total.

Ratings order: Listed by types; within types, listed in order of overall score, based on performance, convenience, and operation of basic functions. Models with identical scores are listed alphabetically. Differences of less than 10 points in score were judged insignificant. Price is the approximate retail as quoted by the manufacturer; actual retail may be lower. Key to recording mechanism: **D** = digitized recording on memory chips; **M** = microcassette; **SM** = single microcassette for greeting and messages; **C** = conventional-sized cassette; **L** = leaderless conventional-sized cassette; **E** = endless-loop conventional-sized cassette. ⓢ indicates model has been replaced by successor model; according to the manufacturer, the performance of new model is similar to the tested model but features may vary. See right for new model number and suggested retail price. ⓓ indicates model discontinued.

Brand and model	Price	Overall score	Recording mechanism: greeting/message	Time limit, min.: greeting/message	Tone quality of greeting	Tone quality of message	Control layout	Convenience and features	Advantages	Disadvantages	Comments
MODELS WITHOUT PHONES											
Sony TAM-50	$100	90	D/M	1/4 /4	◉	◉	◉	◉	A,F,H,J,K	i,q,v	G,I,Q,S,CC,FF
Code-A-Phone 2770	89	89	D/M	1/4 /—	◉	◉	◉	◉	A,C,D,F,G,J,K	p	G,Q,CC,FF
AT&T 1337	110	88	D	1/1	◐	○	○	◉	C,F,G,H,I,J,K	x	A,L,Q,CC,HH
GE 2-9882A ⓢ	88	88	M	—	◉	◉	◉	◉	C,F,G,I,J,K,L	i,p,s	E,G,Q,CC,FF
AT&T 1323	110	86	M	—/4	○	◉	◉	◉	B,C,E,F,G,H,J,K,L	p,q	I,P,Q,R,CC
AT&T 1332	149	84	M	-1/4	○	◉	○	◉	B,C,E,F,G,H,J,K,L	p	H,I,P,Q,R,CC
Cobra AN-8540 ⓘⓓ	150	84	D/M	1/2 /2	○	◉	○	○	A,G,I	e,h,s,t,u,v,x,y	J,O,T,CC,GG
AT&T 1306	60	83	SM	2/4	○	◉	◉	○	C,G,K	c	M,Q,FF,GG
Sanyo TAS346	79	83	C	—/3	◉	○	◉	◉	A,C,G,I,J	j,r,w	G,Q,S,HH
GE 2-9860F ⓢ	60	80	C	—/4	◉	○	◉	○	G,I,K	j,p,x,y	F,Q,S,FF,GG

TELEPHONE ANSWERERS 157

Brand and model	Price	Overall score	Recording mechanism: greeting/message	Time limit, min.: greeting/message	Tone quality of greeting	Tone quality of message	Control layout	Convenience and features	Advantages	Disadvantages	Comments
Panasonic KX-T1470 [D]	$100	80	C	—	◒	○	○	◒	B,C,D,F,G,I,J,K,L	j,n	G,Q,S,FF
PhoneMate 7210 [D]	70	78	D/M	½/5	●	○	◒	◒	A,D,I,L	d,f,u,y	M,O,Q,T,CC,FF
Radio Shack TAD-412	80	77	L	½/3	○	●	◒	○	F,I,J	m,r,x	D,G,O,FF,HH
Panasonic KX-T1000	69	76	SM	½/1	○	○	◒	○	G,K	c,j,o,u,x	G,M,GG,HH
Unisonic 8742	58	74	SM	1½/1½	◒	◒	◒	◒	A,E,G,J	a,c,j,y	M,Q,S,EE,GG
Record-A-Call 800 [S]	40	70	SM	1/1	◒	◐	◒	●	K	a,c,h,j,s,u,v,x,y	M,DD,GG,HH

MODELS WITH PHONES

Brand and model	Price	Overall score	Recording mechanism	Time limit	Tone greeting	Tone message	Control	Convenience	Advantages	Disadvantages	Comments
PhoneMate 4650 [D]	145	85	E/C	½/5	○	◒	◒	◒	A,C,D,I,J,K,L	d,g,i	G,K,N,Q,S,T,U,CC,FF
AT&T 5600 [2]	260	83	M	—/4	○	○	○	◒	C,D,F,G,H,J,K,L	—	Q,X,Y,BB,CC
Cobra AN-8526 [2]	150	83	D/M	½/2	◒	◒	○	◒	A,G,K	f,j	Q,S,W,Y,AA,GG,HH
GE 2-9821A	70	83	D	⅓/2	◒	◒	◒	○	—	b,h,i,l,o,s,u,x	C,M,Z,CC,GG,HH
PhoneMate ADAM	195	83	D	¼/4½	○	◒	◒	◒	A,C,D,G,H,I,J,K,L	d,y	B,F,G,K,L,M,N,Q,S,CC,FF,HH
Panasonic KX-T4200 [2][D]	150	82	D/M	¼/—	○	○	○	◒	A,C,G,I,J,K	j,n,q,x	G,Q,S,T,X,Y,Z,FF,GG
Panasonic KX-T2634 [D]	168	80	D/M	¼/—	◒	◒	◒	◒	A,C,D,E,F,G,I,J,K,L	j,k,n	G,N,Q,S,T,U,V,Z,FF
Code-A-Phone 7210 [2][D]	100	75	SM	—/2	○	◒	◒	●	A,G	c,k,s,u,x,y	M,O,Y,AA,GG,HH
Radio Shack TAD-252 [D]	180	75	M/M	4½/3	◒	○	◒	◒	F,G,I,J	h,m,n,q,r,x,y	D,G,O,Q,S,U,CC,FF

[1] *Portable.* [2] *Cordless phone.*

Successor models (in Ratings order)
GE 2-9882A is succeeded by 2-9883, $99; GE 2-9860F by 2-9861, $79; Record-A-Call 800 by 700, $40.

Features in Common
All: • Have voice-sensitive (VOX) message recording. • Record and replay messages intelligibly. • Can be switched on from remote phone. • Allow remote retrieval of messages with a touch-tone phone. • Have a built-in microphone for recording greeting. • Have a variable-length greeting time. • Stop playback at end of messages. • Allow pause in playback. • Have a built-in jack for telephone hookup (except models with phones). • May be used on line 1 of 2-line phone jacks. • Do not lose greeting or message during short power outages.
Except as noted, all: Have toll-saver. • Note time and date of call. • Turn off if call picked up at another extension. • Lack remote prompt by voice. • Do not limit message length. • Can announce only. • Can record conversations. • Can record memos, directly or remotely. • Automatically return to the answer setting

Ratings Keys continued

after use of other functions. • Allow fast-forward during playback. • Allow message-repeat during playback. • Automatically save messages after playback. • Do not count hang-ups as calls. • Have preprogrammed remote code. • Detect full Touch Tones in remote code, for better security. • Allow access to remote functions before end of greeting. • Have 1-yr. limited warranty on parts and labor.

Key to Advantages
A–Plays newly recorded greeting automatically for review.
B–Can record a second, optional greeting.
C–Caller can skip greeting by pushing a Touch-Tone button.
D–Machine indicates to callers when tape is full.
E–Code you can give to specific callers makes machine beep to alert you to an important call.
F–New messages can be replayed separately from old, saved ones.
G–Automatically reduces blank space on tape between messages to shorten playback time.
H–Can skip forward or back one full message during playback.
I–Old messages can be erased completely.
J–User-programmed remote access code.
K–Can record memo after remote playback.
L–Has remote prompt by voice.

Key to Disadvantages
a–Toll-saver can't be turned off.
b–No toll-saver or remote message-save.
c–Message recording may be delayed in starting after greeting, due to single-tape design.
d–5-sec. pause by caller may halt recording.
e–Machine may stop recording without any warning to callers who speak too softly.
f–Noisy phone lines may cause continued recording after caller hangs up.
g–Requires a relatively long time to reset between messages.
h–Does not allow recording of memos.
i–Backup batteries lack condition indicator.
j–Call counter resets to zero after power failure.
k–Some functions require a look at instructions.
l–No speaker; not usable for call screening.
m–Playback, reset more complex than most.
n–Rewind and Fast-Forward buttons do not cancel when released.
o–Message playback lacks fast-forward feature.
p–If unit is set on Pause when a call comes in, new message will record over old.
q–Call counter resets to zero even if old messages are saved.
r–Must be manually reset to answer mode after playback.
s–User must wait for entire greeting to play before entering remote retrieval code.
t–Entering remote code at the wrong time may erase greeting.
u–Remote code circuits detect partial Touch Tones; less secure than most.
v–Complex sequence required for remote retrieval of messages.
w–Announce-only mode can't be bypassed by remote user to access other functions.
x–Does not note time and date of call.
y–Does not turn off if call picked up at another extension.

Key to Comments
A–7 min. total time for greeting and messages.
B–5 min. total time for messages.
C–2 min. total time for messages.
D–Hang-ups included in message count.
E–Counter displays number of real messages only; press a button to get number of messages plus hang-ups.
F–To halt answering machine from an extension phone, push a key on the phone.
G–Can use phone company's calling party control (CPC) signal for faster disconnect after message is recorded.
H–Can answer 2 phone lines with separate greetings and message playback.
I–Can beep when messages are waiting.
J–Display notes only time of message.
K–Messages may be played back through built-in telephone receiver for privacy.
L–Allows selective erasure of messages.
M–Machine automatically discards old messages unless Save button is pushed.
N–Messages can be forwarded.
O–Remote use requires Touch-Tone phone with long tones.
P–Voice response will let you retrieve messages from rotary phone.
Q–Allows remote change of greeting.
R–Allows a personalized memo retrievable by special remote code.
S–Has room-monitor feature.
T–Can be used for lengthy dictation.
U–Has speakerphone.
V–Speakerphone can automatically pick up calls.
W–Slightly noisy phone; limited in range.
X–Phone has intercom, remote operation.
Y–Phone has call-screen feature.
Z–Can be mounted on wall.
AA–Can go on wall with optional bracket.

CORDLESS TELEPHONES 159

BB–Extra receiver cradle can go on wall.
CC–Battery for memory backup must be replaced periodically.
DD–6-mo. warranty.

EE–3-mo. warranty.
FF–Can be set to limit message length.
GG–Lacks announcement-only feature.
HH–Cannot record conversations.

RATINGS CORDLESS TELEPHONES

Better ← → Worse

▶ See report, page 146. From Consumer Reports, November 1991.

Recommendations: We recommend a model with a minimum of 10 channels if you live where cordless phones are common. Our first choice is the *AT&T 5500* (now the *5510*), a 10-channel model with a useful array of features.

Ratings order: Listed by types; within types, listed in order of overall score. Overall score is based on performance and convenience. Differences in overall score of less than 8 points were judged insignificant. Models with identical scores are listed alphabetically. Price is the approximate retail as quoted by the manufacturer; actual retail may be lower. ⑤ indicates model has been replaced by successor model; according to the manufacturer, the performance of new model is similar to the tested model but features may vary. See page 160 for new model number and suggested retail price, if available. ⑩ indicates model discontinued.

Brand and model	Price	Overall score	Channels	Listening speech quality	Background noise	Range	Programmable call: numbers/digits	REN ①	Advantages	Disadvantages	Comments
FULL-FEATURED MODELS											
AT&T 5500 ⑤	$180	97	10	◐	◐	○	9/16	1.1	B,I,J,K,L	b,e,f,g,o,t,v	A,F,G,L,N
Radio Shack DuoFone ET-435 ⑩	150	91	10	◐	○	○	30/16	0.8	I,K,L,M	b,v,z	A,L
Panasonic KX-T3910	189	90	10	◐	◐	○	16/16	0.2	D,G,L,M	o,v	A,L,N
Uniden CT-785S	130	89	2	◐	◐	○	10/16	0.2	L,M	c,f,o,v	A,L
Panasonic KX-T3710, A Best Buy ⑩	99	84	10	○	◐	○	10/16	0.2	G	l,n	K,N
Sony SPP-115	139	84	10	○	○	◐	10/16	0.3	A,B,E,G	b,d,l,o,r,w	B,F,J,K,N
Sony SPP-90 ⑤	140	82	2	○	○	◐	13/16	0.2	C,G,M	b,n,o,r,u	A,B,L
Cobra Intenna CP-489 ⑩	119	80	2	◐	●	○	9/17	0.1	F,L	e,j,k,n,q	A,L,N
NW Bell ClearTech II 5520 ⑩	149	73	10	◐	●	◐	10/22	0.9	B,J,K	b,f,h,i,l,w	A,C,I,M
BASIC MODELS											
Toshiba FT-6200	100	88	2	◐	○	◐	10/16	0.2	G,J	—	A,B,H
AT&T 4300 ⑤	80	87	2	○	◐	○	—	0.0	K	b,f,g,l,x	H,K,N

Ratings continued

160 CORDLESS TELEPHONES

Ratings continued

Brand and model	Price	Overall score	Channels	Listening speech quality	Background noise	Range	Programmable call numbers/digits	REN [1]	Advantages	Disadvantages	Comments
SW Bell Freedom Phone FF 1150 [D]	$110	86	1	◒	◒	◒	9/18	2.2	—	a,p,v,aa	A,E
Uniden XC-365	89	86	2	◒	◒	○	10/16	0.2	G,J	f,m,x	B,F
PhoneMate 650 [D]	80	80	1	◒	○	◒	6/16	0.3	I,K	b,e,j,l,w	D,E,K,N
Radio Shack DuoFone ET-414 [D]	110	80	1	○	○	◒	10/16	0.4	H	c,e,j,l,x,z,aa	H,K,N
ITT/Cortelco 3310	89	79	1	◒	○	◒	—	0.4	J	e,l,n,w,z	K,M,N
Cobra Intenna CP-482 [D]	89	78	1	◒	●	◒	9/22	0.1	F,I	e,j,k,v,z,aa	A,F
NW Bell Excursion 3200 [D]	58	74	1	◒	●	○	10/16	0.5	—	k,l,n,s,y	K

[1] *A measure of the power a phone's ringer draws.*

Successor Models (in Ratings order)
AT&T 5500 is succeeded by 5510, $180; Sony SPP-90 by SPP-95, $149; AT&T 4300 by 4305.

Performance Notes
All were judged to have: • Excellent or very good talking quality.
Except as noted, all were judged to have:
• Excellent or very good listening loudness.
• Very good ring loudness. • Good or very good security. • Good or very good hearing-aid compatibility.

Features in Common
All: • Require 120-volt power. • Have switch that lets you choose pulse or tone dialing. • Have last-number redial. • Have battery-charge light. • Can switch to second call if you have call-waiting service.
Except as noted, all have: • Two-way paging. • Talk light on handset. • Switch on handset to turn off power and save battery. • Long tones, rather than short beeps, that sound when numbers are pressed. • Digital security. • Battery and base cord that are easy to replace. • Battery-low light. • Base that can be mounted on wall. • Voltage adaptor at end of power cord. • Autostandby so phone is "on" automatically when you pick it up. • Mute or Hold button. • Handset listening volume switch. • In-use light on base. • Metal antenna on handset. • Ringer in base. • Handset that rests flat in base.

Key to Advantages
A–Selects a clear channel automatically.
B–Displays channel clearly.
C–3 one-touch dialing keys.
D–16 one-touch dialing keys
E–Can be used during power outage.
F–No external antenna on handset; user's hand and arm act as antenna.
G–Short, flexible antenna.
H–No large voltage adaptor at end of cord.
I–Handset can be paged even when in use.
J–Lighted keyboard.
K–Tone for out-of-range.
L–Dialing keyboard on base.
M–Ringer-volume switch on base.

Key to Disadvantages
a–No handset talk light.
b–Dialing tones too short for certain functions.
c–Single light for battery-low and talk.
d–Battery must be changed weekly.
e–No handset volume-control switch.
f–No handset power-off switch.
g–Handset transmitter can't be turned off in power outage and may then drain battery.
h–Handset beeps annoyingly if ac power is off.
i–Loses memory in short power outage.
j–Base phone cord not replaceable by user.
k–Battery hard to replace.
l–No ringer in base.
m–Base ringer can't be turned off.
n–No Mute or Hold button.
o–Large power adaptor; may block both outlets.
p–Cannot always answer while ringer is sounding.
q–No paging.
r–No autostandby.

CORDLESS TELEPHONES

s–Model uses low security "guard-tone."
t–Handset has sharp edges.
u–Speakerphone and handset don't operate at the same time.
v–Didn't work after drop test.
w–Didn't work after electrostatic spark test.
x–No in-use light on base.
y–Security judged poor.
z–Security judged fair.
aa–Hearing-aid compatibility judged poor.

Key to Comments
A–Has intercom.
B–Handset rests on end in base; unstable.
C–Uses standard AA rechargeable batteries.
D–Low battery causes earpiece in handset to turn on.
E–Phone jack on base for connecting answering machine.
F–Charging base cannot be mounted on wall.
G–Noncharging base accessory can be mounted on wall.
H–No in-use light on base.
I–Keypad is on back of handset; you can push buttons by mistake.
J–Channel number doesn't show after dialing.
K–One-way paging.
L–Has speakerphone.
M–Listening loudness judged good.
N–Ring loudness judged louder than others.

How to Use the Ratings

- Read the article for general guidance about types and buying advice.
- Read the Recommendations for brand-name advice based on our tests.
- Read the Ratings order to see whether products are listed in order of quality, by price, or alphabetically. Most Ratings are based on estimated quality, without regard to price.
- Look to the Ratings table for specifics on the performance and features of individual models.
- A model marked Ⓓ has been discontinued, according to the manufacturer. A model marked Ⓢ indicates that, according to the manufacturer, it has been replaced by a successor model whose performance should be similar to the tested model but whose features may vary.

RATINGS: COMPUTER PRINTERS

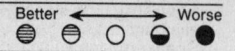

Better ⬅ ⬤ ◐ ○ ◑ ● ➡ Worse

▶ **See report, page 143.** From Consumer Reports, September 1991.

Recommendations: If price is no object, any of the three laser printers we tested would be an excellent choice. You can get almost the same quality for hundreds less from an ink-jet printer like the *Hewlett Packard Deskjet 500*. For routine tasks like letters and résumés, any of the top 18 dot-matrix printers should do the job, at less expense.

Ratings order: Listed by types; within types, listed in order of estimated quality based primarily on quality of text printing. Models judged equal in quality are bracketed and listed alphabetically. Price is the approximate retail as quoted by the manufacturer; actual retail may be lower. ⓈI indicates tested model has been replaced by successor model; according to the manufacturer, the performance of new model should be similar to the tested model but features may vary. See right for new model number and suggested retail price, if available. Ⓓ indicates model discontinued.

Brand and model	Price	Printing quality: text	Printing quality: graphics	NLQ speed [1]	Draft speed	Noise in NLQ mode	Features	Maximum paper width, in.	Ribbon/cartridge price	Advantages	Disadvantages	Comments
LASER												
Hewlett Packard LaserJet IIP Ⓢ	$810	99	99	⬤	⬤	⬤	⬤	8½	$95	B,D,F,G,M	f	F,K
Okidata OL400	700	97	99	⬤	⬤	⬤	⬤	8½	33	B,D,F,G,J,M	—	A
IBM LaserPrinter E	1000	98	99	⬤	⬤	⬤	⬤	8½	259	B,F,G,J,M	—	A,F,K
INK-JET												
Hewlett Packard Deskjet 500	490	92	97	⬤	○	⬤	⬤	8½	20	B,G,H,I,J,L	—	F
Canon BJ-10e Ⓢ	330	95	97	⬤	○	⬤	○	8½	25	L	c,e,f	E,I,K
Diconix 150 Plus Ⓢ	355	50	62	○	○	⬤	○	8½	14	—	d	E,I,K,M
DOT-MATRIX												
Star NX-2420 Rainbow	300	77	81	⬤	⬤	○	⬤	11¾	10	A,B,D,E,F,I,J,L	—	A,B,D,H
Citizen GSX-140 Ⓓ	300	76	77	⬤	⬤	○	⬤	10	8	A,C,D,E,F,I,J	—	A,D
IBM Proprinter 24P Ⓓ	475	83	89	⬤	◐	⬤	11	11	A,H,I,J,L	b	C
NEC P3200	230	82	60	⬤	⬤	○	⬤	11	12	A,C,F,I	b,f	A,B
Tandy DMP240	400	77	72	⬤	⬤	○	⬤	10	10	A,C,D,E,F,I	—	D,J
Epson LQ-510 Ⓢ	265	78	78	⬤	○	○	⬤	10	12	A,C,I,J	—	A,C,G

COMPUTER PRINTERS

Brand and model	Price	Printing quality: text	Printing quality: graphics [1]	NLQ speed	Draft speed	Noise in NLQ mode	Features	Maximum paper width, in.	Ribbon/cartridge price	Advantages	Disadvantages	Comments
Panasonic KX-P1124i	$300	75	76	◉	◉	◐	◉	11¾	$13	A,C,D,E,F,I,K	b	A,B
Star NX-2420 Multifont [D]	310	73	82	◉	◉	◐	◉	11¾	10	A,B,C,D,E,F,I,J	—	A,B
Okidata Microline 380	250	72	82	◉	◉	○	◉	10	11	A,C,F,I,J	—	A,C
Panasonic KX-P1123	200	79	72	◉	◉	◐	◉	11¾	13	A,C,E,F,I,K	b	A,B
Brother XL-1500	300	71	77	◉	◉	◐	◉	10	13	A,C,E,F,I	—	L
Epson LQ-200 [D]	250	77	83	◉	◉	◐	◉	10	8	I,J	—	G
Brother XL-500 (9-pin)	190	71	77	○	◉	○	◉	10	13	A,C,E,F,I	—	K
Panasonic KX-P1124	290	71	84	◉	◉	◐	◉	11¾	13	A,C,E,F,I	b	A,B,I
Citizen 200GX (9-pin)	180	71	81	○	◉	○	◉	10	7	A,C,E,I,J	—	A,B,D
Panasonic KX-P1180 (9-pin) [D]	170	72	80	○	◉	○	◉	11¾	13	A,C,E,I	b	A,B
Laser 190E (9-pin) [D]	200	67	81	○	◉	◉	○	10	6	I	b,c	A,K,J
Epson LX-810 (9-pin) [D]	175	61	78	○	◉	○	◉	10	8	A,C,I	a	A,C,K
Okidata Microline 182 Turbo (9-pin)	340	64	64	◉	◉	○	○	8½	9	—	a,b,c,d	A,C,K,L
Star NX-1001 Multifont (9-pin)	139	57	76	○	◉	○	◉	8½	4	A,I	f	A,B
Tandy DMP 134 (9-pin) [D]	260	54	76	○	○	○	○	10	11	A	c,e	K,J

[1] *Near-letter quality.*

Successor Models (in Ratings order)
Hewlett Packard LaserJet IIP is succeeded by LaserJet II Plus, $1249; Canon BJ-10e by BJ-10ex, $330; Diconix 150 Plus by 180si, $399; Epson LQ-510 by LQ-570, $499.

Features in Common
All: • Can emulate Epson or IBM printers, although some printers do not emulate all features. • Print superscript, subscript, bold, underlined, expanded, and condensed text. • Have a parallel interface. • Have pitch, font, form-feed, line-feed, and printer-select controls on the front or top panel. • Can print non-English characters. • Have a self-test mode to print text samples. • Will fit in a space 11 in. high by 19 in. wide by 24 in. deep. • Require separate cable to connect to computer. *Except as noted, all have:* • Tightest spacing of 17 characters per inch. • Italic text. • Proportional spacing. • LED display on top or front. • Ability to print on business envelopes. • 4 or more typefaces. • Tractor feed, approx. 4-10 in. • 12-mo. or longer warranty.

Key to Advantages
A–Can handle single sheet without removing fanfold paper.
B–Can accept font cartridges.
C–Quick sheet tear-off to save paper.
D–LCD display.
E–Tractor can either push or pull paper.

Ratings Keys continued

164 COMPUTER PRINTERS

F–Menu-type settings to set print modes.
G–"Landscape" setting to print sideways.
H–Can print 24 characters per inch.
I–Can print 20 characters per inch.
J–Cut-sheet feeder holds 100 sheets.
K–Has 8K to 12K buffer size.
L–Has 16K to 37K buffer size.
M–Has 500K or more buffer size.

Key to Disadvantages
a–No proportional spacing.
b–Cable connector intrudes in paper path.
c–Manual not as complete as others.
d–Can't print on business envelopes.
e–No italic text.
f–Cut-sheet feeder holds 50 sheets or less.

Key to Comments
A–Opt. serial interface for long cables.
B–"Quiet" printing mode.
C–Optional pull tractor feed.
D–Can print in color.
E–Can operate on optional ni-cad batteries for 40 to 50 min. per charge.
F–Parallel and serial interface.
G–Single-strike mylar ribbon improves print quality.
H–Color version of **Star NX-2420 Multifont**.
I–Portable.
J–3-mo. warranty.
K–2 or fewer typefaces.
L–Tractor feed, 10-11 in.
M–Tractor feed, 8¾-9 in.

How objective is CU?

Consumers Union is not beholden to any commercial interest. It accepts no advertising and buys all the products tested on the open market. CU's income is derived from the sale of CONSUMER REPORTS and other publications, and from nonrestrictive, noncommercial contributions, grants, and fees. Neither the Ratings nor the reports may be used in advertising or for any other commercial purpose. Consumers Union will take all steps open to it to prevent commercial use of its materials, its name, or the name of CONSUMER REPORTS.

Personal Health

Blood pressure monitors 165	Electric toothbrushes 171
Dental products:	Oral irrigators 172
Toothpaste 168	Sunscreens 173
Mouthwash 170	Ratings 175

An ounce of prevention is worth a pound of cure. Public-health experts reckon that a dollar spent avoiding illness pays off many times over compared with the costs of being sick. While not all illnesses can be prevented, many can; others can be mitigated or kept in check.

For instance, buying a blood-pressure monitor is a wise investment for people who have been diagnosed with hypertension. Taking regular readings at home can help you learn how well your efforts—drugs, diet, exercise—are working.

Prevention is also key to good oral health. Routine and conscientious brushing and flossing remain the best weapons against tooth decay and gum disease. Some toothpastes are better to use than others, we found. And an electric toothbrush is more effective than an old-fashioned brush because, in the same amount of time, it does a more complete cleaning. Dental irrigators are worthwhile for people with braces or extensive bridgework. Many also benefit from special mouthwashes formulated to cut cavities or curb plaque.

Certain cancers are largely preventable. Some 90 percent of skin cancers, for example, are linked directly to sun exposure. It makes sense to apply sunscreen freely.

Blood-Pressure Monitors

▶ Ratings on page 175.

For people diagnosed with hypertension, a home blood-pressure monitor can be a valuable aid in finding the best course of treatment. It can show whether alternatives to drug therapy are working, and how well. For those who do need drug treatment, home monitoring can help the doctor determine the lowest dose that will be effective yet minimize any side effects of a larger dose.

A home monitor also allows patients to chart their progress in controlling pressure, which can be a powerful motivator for staying with a treatment regimen. Home monitoring can be especially useful for people whose blood pressure is driven up by the stress of having a doctor measure it. More typical readings are likely to be obtained at home.

For all those reasons, the National High Blood Pressure Education Program, a Government-sponsored effort, endorses home blood-pressure monitoring for people with documented hypertension, provided monitoring is done in collaboration with a physician and is not used as a means of self-diagnosis.

Blood pressure, the force exerted by the blood against the walls of the arteries, has traditionally been described as height: the number of millimeters that your arterial pressure can push a column of mercury up a vertical tube, abbreviated as "mmHg."

Traditionally, a nurse or doctor wraps an inflatable cuff around the upper arm and inflates it by pumping a rubber bulb. The cuff soon becomes a tourniquet, cutting off blood flow below the elbow. While gradually deflating the cuff, the nurse listens with a stethoscope to the arm's main artery (in the elbow's crook). As blood returns to the lower arm, the onset and cessation of sounds from the artery mark two crucial points: "systolic" pressure, the arterial force as the heart pumps; and "diastolic," the pressure between heartbeats, which is lower than the systolic. Blood pressure is given as the systolic figure over the diastolic, as in 120/80 mmHg, a more or less "normal" value.

The choices

To take your own blood pressure at home, some monitors make you do all the things the doctor or nurse does. Other monitors use electronic circuitry to simplify matters considerably.

Mechanical aneroid models. These are simple, mechanical monitors that use a round dial-type pressure gauge. (Home devices no longer use a mercury column—"aneroid" means "without liquid.") They're relatively cheap at $20 to $30 and can be quite accurate if used properly. Proper use is the big drawback—you must don the cuff, pump it, and listen carefully to the artery as you slowly turn a valve to deflate the cuff, all the while keeping an eye on the gauge's needle. The procedure takes practice but isn't impossible to master. It demands, however, good eyesight and hearing and the dexterity to do things one-handed.

Electronic models. These models sense the pressure changes in the cuff—no stethoscope is needed—and pass data to a microchip in their console, which in turn calculates the systolic and diastolic pressure readings automatically. In no time, your blood pressure and pulse rate flash on a digital display. The machine takes care of determining pressure—no human judgment is required. The circuitry can sometimes err—if you move your arm, say—but an error code is displayed or the reading is so outlandish that it's obviously a mistake.

The cheapest electronic models, at about $40 to $60, have you pump their cuff with a rubber bulb; they handle deflation automatically. More expensive models—ranging from $60 to as high as $200—inflate their cuffs automatically. You put on the cuff and select a starting pressure, typically 30 mmHg higher than your expected systolic reading. You then push a button, and the monitor does the rest.

Recently, electronic models have appeared that take readings from the index finger, so you needn't even roll up your sleeve. You slip the finger into a loop, and the machine does its thing. Electronic finger monitors range in price from $140 to $160.

Features to look for

All arm models have a D-ring to make it easier to don the cuff one-handed—you form a loop and pull the cuff snugly around your arm, then fasten it with the plastic-loop closure. The ends of some cuffs, however, can easily slip out of the metal bar if they don't have a retaining device. Some cuffs are made of limp material, were difficult, or were otherwise cumbersome to handle in our tests.

Features that make mechanical gauges easier to use include the stethoscope's sensor being sewn in place on the cuff (so you needn't hold it down). Also, a sturdy metal deflation valve that works smoothly is easier to control than the plastic valves on some mechanical models.

Some electronic models feature highly readable displays—big, clear numbers that are three-quarters of an inch high.

The tests

An inaccurate monitor can give a false sense of security, alarm unnecessarily, or adversely affect your treatment. So we first checked each unit's gauge, disconnected from the cuff, to see how accurately it registered known pressures. Most were highly accurate.

For mechanical models, the gauge's accuracy determines the best that a unit can work—the rest is up to the user's skill. For electronic models, the circuitry also affects readings, no matter how accurate the gauge. As a result, we did an extensive use test on the electronic models using a cross-section of staffers. We modified the monitors' tubing so that a nurse could take a simultaneous reading with a mercury gauge and stethoscope. By taking multiple readings at each sitting and comparing the nurse's figures with each monitor's, we assessed the average discrepancy of each model (we assumed the nurse was correct) and the model's variability from one reading to another.

Buying advice

Mechanical models offer the best value if you're comfortable with them. They cost as little as $20 and generally proved more accurate in our tests than electronic arm models, provided they're used correctly. With practice most people should have little trouble perfecting the technique. To use them correctly, you'll need good eyesight, hearing, dexterity, and the patience to learn.

The best electronic arm models can be as accurate as the better mechanical units, or nearly so. Those that inflate automatically are easiest to use but most costly. If you don't trust your ability to master a mechanical model, but don't want to pay top dollar, a good compromise is an electronic arm model whose cuff you inflate manually—no big chore—and it could save you about half the price.

With any arm model, it's crucial to use the right size cuff, or you may get erroneous readings. People with large upper arms—more than 13 inches around—may have trouble with the cuffs supplied. It's easy to obtain a larger cuff for mechanical models; medical supply houses sell them. Relatively few electronic monitors offer oversize cuffs as an option; when they do, the cost is $30 or $35.

Stay away from electronic finger models. Because the finger is smaller than the arm and farther from the heart than the elbow is, more factors can interfere with pressure measurement to give false readings. Our tests found the finger monitors' readings grossly variable. As a result, we judged them Not Acceptable.

DENTAL PRODUCTS

▶ Ratings start on page 177.

The U.S. population grew some 10 percent during the 1980s, yet dentists over that span found themselves filling about 30 percent fewer cavities. There's less decay, less gum disease, and fewer teeth being lost in all age groups. Several factors can take credit for the nation's better oral health. Americans now see the dentist more often than they used to and get better care. Fluoride has become widespread in drinking water, helping to build stronger, more decay-resistant teeth in children. And there's been a flood of dental products whose advertising incessantly reminds consumers about the dividends of good hygiene.

Some products are truly new; others, age-old or new twists on old concepts. There's dental "hardware"—special toothbrushes, for instance—and "software"—novel toothpastes and mouthwashes.

You certainly don't need every new product that comes along to keep teeth and gums in good shape. CU's dental consultants believe that routine brushing and flossing still remain the best weapons to fight plaque. But some of the new products may help.

Electric toothbrushes have been transformed into fast-whirring, high-tech "plaque removers" that can clean teeth quite efficiently. Toothpaste formulas have also undergone changes—to offer better cleaning or additional benefits like tartar control or help with sensitive teeth. Other claims, such as pledges of whiter teeth, are less substantial.

Mouthwashes have proliferated, and no longer is "fresh breath" the raison d'être for many brands. Some rinses now play up their medicinal benefits, promising to help teeth and gums over and above ordinary brushing and flossing.

An appliance that makes similar claims, the oral irrigator, delivers a pressurized, pulsating stream through a thin nozzle that you direct against teeth and gums. Irrigators, however, are specialized tools that are not for everyone. *Water Pik* is the major brand.

TOOTHPASTE

Several newer dentifrices rely on old-fashioned baking soda, a mild abrasive and cleaner that earned an undeserved reputation for treating gum disease. Plans for futuristic formulas include antibacterial agents to control plaque germs. The two toothpaste giants, Colgate-Palmolive (maker of *Colgate*) and Procter & Gamble *(Crest)* are now awaiting approval of just such a formula from the U.S. Food and Drug Administration. The controversial germ-fighter, triclosan, is currently used in deodorants in the U.S. and in toothpastes abroad. Another brand, *Viadent,* already includes a plaque-fighting agent extracted from the bloodroot plant.

The choices

We counted 10 basic toothpaste types on store shelves. Some types offer unique benefits:

Regular paste. A basic and effective fluoride formula to help prevent tooth decay.

Extra-strength paste. One brand, *Extra Strength Aim,* packs about 50 percent more fluoride than most other toothpastes, which could help cavity-prone individuals such as older people with receding gums, who often get cavities on the exposed roots of teeth.

Antiplaque paste. All toothpastes fight plaque with brushing action, so most antiplaque claims are throw-aways. *Viadent,* as we've said, does contain a plaque-fighting chemical. The antiplaque agents in some mouthwashes are stronger, however, and can cut plaque and mild gum disease better than toothpaste.

Antitartar paste. These products contain chemicals to slow the buildup of tartar, the rock-hard deposit formed when plaque unites with minerals in saliva. But unlike plaque, tartar above the gumline is generally harmless. And these pastes cannot remove tartar that's already on teeth—that demands professional cleaning.

Desensitizing paste. Receding gums expose softer dental tissue that can make teeth sensitive to heat, cold, or pressure. Special ingredients can block the pain, by disrupting nerve impulses or sealing tubules in teeth. Receding gums also call for a dentifrice of moderate or low abrasiveness; harsher pastes—or overly vigorous brushing—can abrade the exposed dentin.

Smokers' paste. These products are often more abrasive than regular toothpaste, to fight tobacco, coffee, tea, and other stubborn stains.

Children's paste. In flashy colors and unusual flavors, like tutti-frutti, these products are sweet from sorbitol and saccharin, non-nutritive sweeteners. But encouraging the habit through sweetness isn't a good idea. Children should be taught not to swallow any toothpaste to avoid ingesting fluoride.

'Natural' paste. *Tom's of Maine* brand boasts only natural ingredients and flavors and eschews saccharin, but it contains a synthetic detergent, sodium lauryl sulfate, common to many toothpastes.

Soda paste. Baking soda, riding its reputation for treating gum disease, has been added as a mild abrasive and cleaner.

Whitening paste. Special ingredients are supposed to make teeth "whiter." They cannot—the best toothpaste can do is to leave teeth the shade they look after a dental cleaning. Natural tooth color ranges from white to yellow, tan, or even brown. (Cosmetic bleaching by a dentist can actually whiten tooth enamel, but its safety has been questioned by the FDA.)

The tests

Our tests focused on cleaning, using brushing tests on heavily stained animal teeth. Brushing tests also gauged the toothpastes' abrasiveness to dentin, the soft dental tissue exposed when gums recede. And we checked each product's fluoride when purchased and after we'd aged tubes, pumps, and bottles in an oven to simulate two years on a store shelf.

Buying advice

If possible, brush at least twice daily with a fluoride toothpaste and use floss. If your teeth and gums are in good shape, you can brush with just about any fluoride dentifrice. People with receding gums, however, should choose a toothpaste of moderate or low abrasiveness to avoid abrading the exposed roots.

Cleaning stain from teeth is a purely cosmetic concern. But toothpastes do vary appreciably in terms of their cleaning prowess. Abrasiveness sometimes goes hand-in-glove with cleaning, but not always. Steer clear of pricey whitening toothpastes with offbeat ingredients, which might irritate some mouths in the long run, say CU's dental consultants.

Mouthwash

When we surveyed readers, most said that freshening bad breath is the key benefit they look for in a mouthwash. It's a tough job for any rinse, given the myriad causes of bad breath. There's "morning breath," a syndrome identified in *Scope's* ads: Certain bacteria turn protein—from food, shed tissue, and oral debris—into smelly, sulfur compounds. They work especially hard at night, when the flow of saliva all but stops.

Other causes of bad breath include: smoking and drinking; eating foods like onion and garlic; advanced gum disease; and local respiratory-tract infections.

To combat odors from so many sources, mouthwashes rely on their ability to mask offensive odors with pleasant-smelling ingredients such as mint and cinnamon. Those ingredients determine what taste each product leaves in the mouth. Rinses may taste sweet, minty, or bitter and feel cooling or burning.

Unfortunately, the fix is only temporary. Our attempts at masking garlic odor succeeded but briefly, with the bad breath typically returning within an hour of rinsing.

The choices

Breath-freshening isn't the only reason to use mouthwash. Some deliver other benefits as well:

Plaque fighters. Proven plaque-fighting chemicals can help finish the job you start with toothbrush and floss by curbing the oral bacteria that produce plaque. Such rinses can help reverse gingivitis, too. Twice-a-day rinsing is the typical regimen.

The American Dental Association has so far certified two basic plaque-fighting formulas: *Peridex*, a prescription rinse with chlorhexidine, a powerful antibacterial; and that in *Listerine Antiseptic* and a private-label lookalike, *K Mart Antiseptic,* both of which rely on certain essential oils or substances from them.

Other over-the-counter mouthwashes also pack plaque-fighting chemicals but may work somewhat less effectively. *Viadent* toothpaste and rinse both contain a plant extract that curbs plaque significantly when both products are used twice daily. *Cepacol, Scope,* and similar formulas pack cetylpyridinium chloride, another bonafide antimicrobial agent. (Neither brand promotes itself as a plaque-fighter, however.)

Anticavity rinses. Fluoride rinses can protect teeth beyond the fluoride in toothpaste, when used once or twice daily. Brands like *Act, Fluorigard,* or *Listermint* can benefit people especially prone to cavities, six years and older. They include people whose receding gums make the roots of teeth vulnerable and people with reduced salivary flow.

Antitartar rinses. These include the same chemicals as in antitartar toothpaste, which slow the buildup of new tartar above the gumline. They can help people who accumulate tartar most rapidly between dental cleanings and who don't normally use tartar-control dentifrice.

The tests

Volunteers ate garlicky pizza, then rinsed with various products. A sensory expert evaluated their breath at intervals over the next two hours to see how long the rinses could protect.

Buying advice

Don't count on mouthwash to freshen breath very long. Most mouthwashes deliver only in the short term. Choose a product by flavor and price. If you need extra help curbing plaque, gingivitis, tartar, or cavities, choose a special-purpose rinse.

ELECTRIC TOOTHBRUSHES

The American Dental Association—and many dentists—used to hold that any toothbrush can potentially clean teeth well—it depended solely on an individual's diligence. Now, the ADA has been convinced that, for most people, an electric brush takes off more plaque than a regular brush.

CU's dental consultants believe most people can be trained to use a manual brush with excellent results, but most don't brush well enough or long enough. Electric brushes help by covering more area faster, making it easier to brush effectively.

The choices

The first modern electric toothbrushes, introduced some 30 years ago, were scarcely more than regular toothbrush heads rigged with a motor. The brush wiggled up and down in short arcs.

Today's basic electric toothbrush hasn't changed all that much. It's apt to move in small circles or ellipses, which simulate good hand-brushing techniques.

You can also buy fancier "plaque removers" whose whirring, geared business ends bear only slight resemblance to a conventional toothbrush. Nor do these high-tech designs bear much resemblance to each other. One features two rows of five spinning tufts that whirl in one direction and then reverse. Another offers a cup-shaped head that moves back and forth. A third sports a sandwichlike head of bristle disks into which a user bites.

Cost. The simplest electric brushes—with conventionally shaped heads—can be had for around $30. Complex designs generally sell for $80 to $100.

Features to look for

Ease of use. A brush should be easy to set up and maintain—or you won't use it. Some models have finicky internal gearing that must be rinsed and kept clean, lest they clog with toothpaste residue.

Handle. Look for one whose weight and design are comfortable to grip for two minutes, the amount of time brushing should take.

Controls. Make sure they're easy to work. A soft-touch button or slider switch is easier to manage than a small button. Some brushes offer two or three speed settings, to adjust brushing vigor.

Charging time. The longer the time between charging, the more practical a model is for traveling. We found a wide range of "run-down" times, from nearly an hour to about six minutes. If counter space is at a premium, be sure to consider the size of the charging stand.

Extra heads. Brush heads wear out—some in as little as two or three months. The price of replacements can be considerable—$10 or more for some designs. Some models include extra heads, often color-coded, for different family members to use.

The tests

A panel of staffers took the devices home, lived with each for a week, then judged key aspects of "user friendliness." We were particularly interested in how easy models were to set up and maintain. Three dental professionals—two dentists and a hygienist—gave us a professional opinion. We also checked for electrical hazards and found two that failed.

Buying advice

Using an electric toothbrush can improve oral health because most people will brush with one more effectively than they do with a manual brush. People with hand or arm disabilities will find electric brushes a godsend.

Choose a model that's easy to maneuver in the mouth, easy to set up, and easy to maintain. A little bleeding from gums should be expected at first. People especially prone to infection—those given antibiotics routinely before dental work—should check with their dentist before using an electric toothbrush.

ORAL IRRIGATORS

People with extensive dental work—fixed bridges, braces, implants, crowns—often find it difficult to clean their mouths with just brush and floss. An irrigator can flush debris away. For those with advanced gum disease, the dentist may order irrigation twice a day as an adjunct to treatment.

One study found that once-a-day irrigation with plain water was as effective in controlling gingivitis as was twice-a-day rinsing with a powerful antibacterial mouthwash. That's impressive proof that irrigation works to improve gums. Irrigation with an antimicrobial solution or mouthwash works even better than with plain water.

The choices

Most models sold are *Water Piks,* which are more alike than different. Other brands tend to be similar, too. Irrigators cost about $40 to $70, depending on features.

Features to look for

Flow control. A graduated flow control adjusts the stream's force. The best arrangement is a button-dial on the handset that alters pressure when turned and that temporarily stops the flow when depressed, so you can do everything one-handed. Less convenient arrangements have the dial on the base or a valve on the handpiece that must be twisted to stop the flow.

Reservoirs. Capacity varies from 12 to 35 ounces. To do a really thorough job you may need a reservoir on the larger side. Some models also include a spare, smaller reservoir to hold medicated solutions.

Tips. Deluxe models offer two kinds of snap-on tips: blunt tips for regular irrigation above the gumline; and more pointy tips to irrigate periodontal pockets or below the gumline. (Even with blunt tips some solution works its way under the gumline.) Some pointy tips can scratch gums, however, if not used properly.

Wall mounting. Because of the vibration of its motor, an irrigator can "walk" across a bathroom counter. Mounting the unit on a wall eliminates that hazard and makes sure things stay put. Some models include the mounting hardware.

The tests

We tested irrigators much as we tested electric toothbrushes, using a panel of staffers and three professionals. We also checked units for electrical leakage: Two failed.

Buying advice

Most people don't need an irrigator. One is useful, however, for people with extensive bridgework and braces and people with gum disease, as a supplement to brushing and flossing. Some people simply like the gum massage irrigation provides.

Most irrigators are more alike than different. You can narrow the choice by features and price.

Anyone considering an irrigator should first consult with a dentist, since there is potential to harm gums, cheeks, or tongue, or to drive debris deeper into a periodontal pocket, which might cause an abscess.

Sunscreens

Despite decades of warning against it, sunbathing remains one of summer's popular diversions. But where sunbathers see a gorgeous tan, dermatologists see damaged skin—and a mounting number of skin cancers, especially as the protective ozone layer thins over North America.

Unquestionably, using a good sunscreen is the best strategy to let you enjoy the outdoors without becoming a statistic. Until recently, most product claims focused on the sunscreens' blocking ultraviolet B radiation (UVB), which actually burns skin and poses long-term cancer risks. But now many sunscreens also promise protection against ultraviolet A (UVA), a more deeply penetrating ray that doesn't burn immediately yet could be responsible for long-term effects, some dangerous: a loss of skin elasticity that accelerates wrinkling and aging; interference with the immune system; and an increased risk of skin cancer.

The choices

SPFs. Sunscreens vary in how much sun protection they offer. How much you need depends on your complexion, the sun's strength, and the particular formula.

People with fair skin, of course, burn far sooner than those with darker skin; light skin contains less melanin, a protective pigment. Exposure to the sun sparks melanin production as the skin tries to protect itself, producing a tan and some extra protection. The sun's potential to burn also becomes stronger as you move toward the equator, climb higher in altitude, or venture into a reflective background—water, sand, a snowy ski slope, perhaps.

Many sunscreens sold nowadays have an SPF (sun-protection factor) of 15; some are even SPF 30 or more. It takes about 22 minutes for an untanned Caucasian with average skin to get a slight reddish glow in the noonday sun at the height of summer in Miami. Wearing an SPF 15 sunscreen allows that same person to remain outdoors 15 times as long—more than five hours—before reddening occurs.

UVA or UVB blocking. Older formulations concentrated on UVB rays, some blocking the rays physically with opaque chemicals like zinc oxide, others chemically with a mix of ingredients like benzophenone-3 and padimate-O, a PABA relative.

Both approaches also offer some protection against damaging UVA rays. But no one can say how much protection. The U.S. Food and Drug Administration lacks a standard system for evaluating UVA protection.

Only one potent UVA-blocking ingredient, Parsol 1789, has so far been approved by the FDA for use in sunscreens. The chemical offers substantial UVA protection but hasn't yet found its way into many products. Those tend to be among the priciest, though.

Water resistance. Since people both perspire and go swimming when it's hot and sunny, sunscreens need to be waterproof or water resistant. The difference in terms is one of degree. Water-resistant products tend to wash off more easily than do waterproof ones. Some waterproof sunscreens claim extraordinary performance in the water—they say they'll last six hours or even all day. After a long swim, however, you may lose some SPF protection—less hardy products may drop from SPF 15 to, say, 12. In our tests, sunscreens generally lived up to their labeling claims for SPF and for not washing off prematurely.

In any case, it's a good idea to apply more sunscreen to renew a product's protection. But keep in mind that multiple applications do not extend the overall period the sun allows you to remain in the sun without reddening.

'Baby' formulas. "Baby" sunscreens are supposed to be especially gentle, often formulated with a more emollient-lotion base than adult products. That should appeal to people of all ages who have sensitive skin. Most baby products also omit from their formula PABA—related compounds, which can irritate skin and have fallen out of favor in many sunscreen formulas generally.

The tests

We focused on the accuracy of SPF numbers for products not certified by the Skin Cancer Foundation. (That nonprofit foundation certifies that a sunscreen has met FDA guidelines for protection and, as well, does not cause acute skin irritation.) We exposed the arms of volunteers with and without sunscreen to known UVB light, and thus gauged SPFs. To check performance in water, volunteers applied sunscreen, swished their arms for 20 minutes to simulate swimming, then let their arms dry 20 minutes. We expected waterproof products to withstand four such cycles; water-resistant ones, two cycles. The extended-waterproof products got six hours of dunking and drying.

Buying advice

Choose a sunscreen that offers adequate protection along with a fragrance and feel that you can live with. Some lotions are greasy or unpleasantly sticky, for example, and others smell medicinal. Since prices range sevenfold, you can wind up spending a little or a lot—to $4.50 or more per ounce.

Consider a "baby" formula if you have sensitive skin. If you enjoy swimming or plan to be in unusually strong sun for very long periods, choose an appropriate waterproof or high-SPF product. If you have a special reason to be concerned about UVA radiation—very fair skin, perhaps, or a history of skin cancer—consider spending extra money for a Parsol-containing sunscreen, which offers comprehensive protection against both UVB and UVA.

And don't forget to cover the kids: By one estimate, regular use of an SPF 15 sunscreen between ages one and 18 cuts an individual's lifetime risk of nonmelanoma skin cancer by about four-fifths.

HOW OBJECTIVE IS CU?

Consumers Union is not beholden to any commercial interest. It accepts no advertising and buys all the products tested on the open market. CU's income is derived from the sale of CONSUMER REPORTS and other publications, and from nonrestrictive, noncommercial contributions, grants, and fees. Neither the Ratings nor the reports may be used in advertising or for any other commercial purpose. Consumers Union will take all steps open to it to prevent commercial use of its materials, its name, or the name of CONSUMER REPORTS.

BLOOD-PRESSURE MONITORS

RATINGS: BLOOD-PRESSURE MONITORS

Better ← → Worse

▶ **See report, page 165.** From Consumer Reports, May 1992.

Recommendations: Look first to the mechanical monitors for the best value. They are the least expensive type and, if used correctly, are generally more accurate than electronic models. Anyone with poor eyesight, hearing, or dexterity, however, should consider the easier-to-use electronic models.

Ratings order: Listed by types; within types, listed in order of estimated quality, based mainly on consistency in use. (Models judged Not Acceptable are listed alphabetically.) Except where separated by a bold rule, closely ranked models differed little in quality. Price is the manufacturer's suggested retail price.

Brand and model	Price	Self-inflating	Consistency; systolic/diastolic	Ease of use	Instructions	Advantages	Disadvantages	Comments
MECHANICAL MODELS								
Marshall 104	$29	—	◐/◐	◐	◐	B	k,q,r,s,u	—
Omron HEM-18	30	—	◐/◐	◐	○	B	c,k,q,r,s,u	—
Walgreens 2001	20	—	◐/◐	◐	◐	J	c,k,r,s	—
Lumiscope 100-021	30	—	◐/◐	●	◐	—	h,j,k,l,s,u	—
Sunmark 100	22	—	◐/◐	◐	○	—	h,j,k,q,r,s,u	—
Sunbeam 7627-10	31	—	○/◐	●	○	J	h,i,j,k,l	—
ELECTRONIC ARM MODELS								
Omron HEM-704C	130	✓	◐/◐	◐	◐	A,C,E,F,I,J	—	—
Sunbeam 7621	62	—	◐/◐	○	◐	D	g,t	D
Sunbeam 7650	115	✓	◐/◐	◐	◐	C,D,E	b,d,e,t	C
Lumiscope 1081	100	✓	◐/◐	◐	◐	C,D,E,H	b,e,o,t	—
Marshall 91	118	✓	◐/◐	◐	◐	H	m,p	—
AND UA-701	45	—	◐/◐	○	◐	D,H	b,c,e,g,t	B
Omron HEM-713C	90	✓	◐/○	◐	◐	J	m,p	—
Sunmark 144	48	—	◐/◐	○	◐	—	m,p,r	A,B
Omron HEM-413C	52	—	◐/○	○	◐	—	m,p,r	—
Walgreens 80WA	40	—	◐/○	○	◐	J	m,p,r	—
Marshall 80	60	—	◐/○	○	◐	H,J	m,p,r	B
Lumiscope 1065	60	—	◐/○	○	●	D,G,H	d,k,o,p,t	—
AND UA-731	79	✓	◐/◐	◐	◐	C,D,E,H	e,o,t	B
Radio Shack Micronta 63-663	50	—	◐/◐	○	◐	—	m	B
Lumiscope 1060	60	—	◐/●	○	●	D,G,H	k,o,p,t	—

Ratings continued

176 BLOOD-PRESSURE MONITORS

Ratings continued

Brand and model — Price / Self-inflating / Consistency; systolic/diastolic / Ease of use / Instructions / Advantages / Disadvantages / Comments

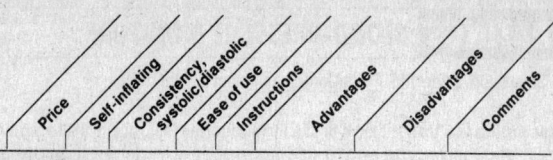

ELECTRONIC FINGER MODELS

NOT ACCEPTABLE

■ *The following models were judged Not Acceptable because of the great variability in the readings they gave. Listed alphabetically.*

Brand and model	Price	Self-inflating	Consistency	Ease of use	Instructions	Advantages	Disadvantages	Comments
Lumiscope 1083	$150	✔	●/●	⊖	⊖	—	f,n,p	—
Marshall F-89	138	✔	●/●	⊖	⊖	—	a,p	A
Omron HEM-815F	130	✔	●/●	⊖	◐	—	a,p	A
Sunbeam 7655-10	156	✔	●/●	⊖	⊖	—	f,n,p	A

Features in Common

Except as noted, all: • Come with storage case or pouch. • Have cuff fitted with metal D-ring to facilitate donning 1-handed. • Measured pressure accurately to within 2 mmHg or less in lab tests. • Allow for rapid cuff deflation in emergency. • Come with 1-yr. warranty.
All mechanical models: • Have dial-type gauge about 2 in. in diameter. • Include stethoscope, usually with sensor attached to cuff to aid in correct placement.
Except as noted, all mechanical models: • Have loop on cuff from which to hang gauge (used in 2-person operation).
All electronic models: • Have liquid-crystal digital readout. • Measure pulse rate (accurate to within 2 beats per minute in tests, except where noted). • Have low-battery indicator.
All self-inflating models: • Automatically deflate cuff when measurement is completed.
Except as noted, all electronic models: • Have push-button On/Off switches (could be turned on inadvertently when packing for storage). • Do not include batteries.

Key to Advantages

A–Cuff somewhat easier to don than most.
B–Stethoscope sounds somewhat easier to hear than most.
C–User can preset any of 4 inflation pressures.
D–Deflation rate can be adjusted, unusual in electronic models.
E–Very large, clear digital readout.
F–Self-contained in hard case, with storage area for cuff, tubing; also protects On/Off switch from accidentally turning on.
G–On/Off slider switch; less likely to be turned on inadvertently when packing unit for storage.
H–Oversize cuff available ($30 to $35).
I–Instruction summary in cover of case.
J–Cuff has prominent mark to aid in correct placement on arm.

Key to Disadvantages

a–Average error substantially greater than most in use tests.
b–Average error slightly greater than most in use tests.
c–Gauge slightly less accurate than most when checked in lab against known pressures.
d–Pulse-rate measurement slightly less accurate than most.
e–End of cuff sometimes slipped out of D-ring.
f–Adjusting finger cuff somewhat difficult.
g–Some testers found cuff harder than others to inflate.
h–Plastic deflation valve flimsy and hard to adjust, which can affect readings.
i–Stethoscope not attached to cuff; makes 1-person operation relatively inconvenient.
j–Plastic stethoscope yoke: May be uncomfortable for some users.
k–Deflation valve must be closed manually each time cuff is inflated.
l–No assembly instructions.
m–Digital readout a bit harder to read than most; user must lean forward.
n–Systolic and diastolic readings not separated on display; numbers can run together.
o–Instructions lack advice that unit should be used in consultation with a physician.
p–No carrying case or pouch.
q–Pouch too small to hold monitor and stethoscope easily.
r–Instructions in relatively small print.
s–Cuff more cumbersome to apply than most

because of attached tubing; **Lumiscope's** cuff is made of floppy material and was hard to keep spread out on the arm.
t–Cuff lacks mark or other indication to aid in correct placement on arm.
u–Cuff lacks loop on outside from which to hang gauge in 2-person operation.

Key to Comments
A–Batteries included.
B–Warranty is only for 90 days.
C–According to manufacturer, model number is now **7650-10**.
D–According to manufacturer, model number is now **7621-10**.

RATINGS TOOTHPASTES

▶ See report, page 168. From Consumer Reports, September 1992.

Recommendations: *Ultra brite Original* proved superior in our cleaning tests, contains adequate fluoride, and isn't overly abrasive. At $1.56 for a six-ounce tube, it's also a bargain. We check-rated it. Other top cleaners to consider: *Close-Up Paste, Gleem, Sensodyne Original*, and *Topol Spearmint Gel*.

Ratings order: Listed in groups based on laboratory tests of fluoride and abrasiveness. Within groups, listed in order of cleaning ability. Toothpastes with the same cleaning ability are listed alphabetically. Price is the estimated average, based on prices paid nationally in mid-1992. A * indicates the price we paid; an average national price wasn't available.

FLUORIDE TOOTHPASTES — MODERATE IN ABRASIVENESS

Product	Package [1]	Size, oz.	Price	Cost per month [2]	Cleaning	Flavor	Comments
✔ **Ultra brite Original**	T	6.0	$ 1.56	$ .58	86	Peppermint	—
Gleem	T	7.0	2.23	.66	79	Spearmint/peppermint	B
Caffree Regular	T	5.0	2.96	1.02	77	Mint	—
Crest Tartar Control Original	P	6.4	2.53	.73	77	Peppermint/anise	B,D,E,H
Crest Tartar Control Fresh Mint Gel	T	6.4	1.99	.53	75	Mint	D,E
Colgate Tartar Control Gel	T	6.4	2.04	.57	74	Peppermint	B,D,E
Pearl Drops Spearmint	B	3.0	3.18	.49	74	Spearmint/peppermint	—
Crest Tartar Control Original	T	6.4	2.00	.53	72	Peppermint/anise	D,E
Ultra brite Gel Cool Mint	T	6.0	1.53	.52	72	Peppermint	B
Colgate Clear Blue Gel	T	6.4	2.06	.71	71	Spearmint	B,D
Crest Cool Mint Gel	T	6.4	1.99	.55	70	Wintergreen	D,G
Crest Regular	T	6.4	2.01	.59	69	Wintergreen	D,G

[1] Key to package: T = tube; P = pump; B = squeeze-bottle.
[2] Based on brushing with one-half in. of paste twice daily.

Ratings continued

178 TOOTHPASTES

Ratings continued

Product	Package [1]	Size, oz.	Price	Cost per month [2]	Cleaning	Flavor	Comments
Crest Sparkle	T	6.4	$ 2.03	$ .51	64	Tutti-frutti	D,G,J
Aquafresh Tartar Control	P	6.0	2.55	.68	63	Peppermint	D,H
Close-Up Tartar Control Gel	T	6.4	1.94	.67	63	Cinnamon	—
Close-Up Anti-Plaque	T	6.4	1.97	.62	62	Spearmint	—
Colgate Tartar Control Paste	T	6.4	2.04	.66	62	Peppermint	B,D,E
Tom's of Maine Cinnamint	T	6.0	3.29	1.07	62	Cinnamon	—
Aquafresh Tartar Control	T	6.0	1.97	.80	60	Peppermint	D
Aim Anti-Tartar Gel	T	6.4	2.24*	.79	58	Spearmint	B,G
Colgate Tartar Control Paste	P	6.4	2.53	.89	58	Peppermint	B,D,E,H
Aim Extra-Strength Gel	T	6.4	1.70	.44	57	Spearmint/peppermint	B,D,G
Mentadent Fresh Mint	P	4.5	2.65*	1.09	57	Peppermint	I,K,L
Slimer Gel	T	3.0	1.79*	1.04	57	Tutti-frutti	B,J
Arm & Hammer Baking Soda Fresh Mint Gel	T	6.3	3.26	1.12	55	Peppermint	B,L
Oral-B Muppets Gel	P	4.6	2.09	.63	52	Tutti-frutti	H,J

■ *The following two products were downrated because they failed fluoride tests.*

Aquafresh	T	6.4	1.98	.79	56	Peppermint	A,D,G
Aquafresh Extra Fresh	T	6.4	1.92	.81	53	Peppermint	A,D,G

FLUORIDE TOOTHPASTES — HIGH IN ABRASIVENESS

Close-Up Paste	T	6.4	1.92	.64	85	Peppermint	—
Topol Spearmint Gel	T	2.7	3.28	1.77	82	Spearmint	B,D,G
Topol Spearmint	T	6.4	5.12	1.32	76	Spearmint	B,D,G
Close-Up Mint Gel	T	6.4	1.92	.64	72	Peppermint	—
Aim Regular-Strength Gel	T	6.4	1.68	.55	70	Spearmint	G
Pepsodent	T	6.4	1.41	.39	58	Wintergreen	—

FLUORIDE TOOTHPASTES — LOW IN ABRASIVENESS

Colgate Baking Soda	T	6.3	3.54*	1.22	51	Peppermint	B,G,L
Colgate Regular	T	7.0	2.08	.74	50	Peppermint	D
Colgate Junior Gel	T	7.7	2.05	.44	39	Tutti-frutti	B,D,J
Colgate Peak	T	6.3	2.78	.97	29	Peppermint	B,G,L
Arm & Hammer Baking Soda Fresh Mint	T	7.0	3.24	1.26	28	Peppermint/baking soda	B,L

■ *The following three products were downrated because they failed fluoride tests.*

Rembrandt	T	3.0	10.16*	4.73	53	Wintergreen	A

TOOTHPASTES

Product	Package[1]	Size, oz.	Price	Cost per month[2]	Cleaning	Flavor	
EpiSmile	P	4.0	$11.00*	$3.90	51	Soapy	A,H,I,L
Aquafresh for Kids	P	4.4	2.05	.89	39	Tutti-frutti	B,D,J
NON-FLUORIDE TOOTHPASTES — MODERATE IN ABRASIVENESS							
Sensodyne Original	T	4.0	3.87	1.29	80	Peppermint	A,C,F
Sensodyne Gel	T	4.0	3.88	1.34	48	Spearmint	A,C,G
NON-FLUORIDE TOOTHPASTES — LOW IN ABRASIVENESS							
Viadent Original Anti-Plaque	T	7.0	4.68	1.40	53	Wintergreen	A
Denquel	T	3.0	3.02	1.77	37	Peppermint	A,B,C,F,G
Butler Protect Gel	T	3.0	2.88*	1.11	20	Wintergreen	A,B,C,F

[1] Key to package: T = tube; P = pump; B = squeeze-bottle.
[2] Based on brushing with one-half in. of paste twice daily.

Key to Comments

A–CU's dental consultants recommend using a fluoride mouth rinse with this dentifrice, which contained insufficient or no fluoride.
B–Unlike most toothpastes, carries an expiration date.
C–Labeled for use on "sensitive" teeth.
D–Carries American Dental Association seal as an effective decay preventive.
E–Carries ADA seal for tartar reduction above the gumline.
F–Carries ADA seal as an effective desensitizer for teeth sensitive to heat, cold, and pressure.
G–Because of product's consistency and packaging, easier to use than most toothpastes by people with hand or arm limitations.
H–Because of product's consistency and packaging, harder to use than most toothpastes by people with hand or arm limitations.
I–Contains bleach, which might irritate the mouth with regular use.
J–Marketed as a children's toothpaste.
K–More packaging material than other products.
L–Contains baking soda, a mild abrasive.

How to Get More Information

Check out what we've said in CONSUMER REPORTS. For the date of recent reports, refer to the four-year index in the back of the Buying Guide or the date noted on each Ratings table. Back issues are available at most libraries or can be ordered. You can also get the latest new- and used-car price information. For details, see page 307 (new cars) and page 310 (used cars).

LISTINGS: MOUTHWASHES

Better ← → Worse
◉ ◒ ○ ◐ ●

▶ See report, page 170. From Consumer Reports, September 1992.

Recommendations: Don't count on mouthwash to freshen your breath very long. However, several products did well in the short term: *Listerine* and similar antiseptic formulas from *Rite Aid* and *K Mart*, *Act Fluoride*, *Colgate Fluorigard*, *Listermint with Fluoride*, *Plax Anti-Plaque Soft Mint*, *Close-up Anti-Plaque*, and *Viadent Anti-Plaque*.

Ratings order: Listed by types; within types, listed alphabetically. Price is the estimated average, based on prices paid nationally in mid-1992. A * denotes the price we paid; an average wasn't available.

RINSES

Product	Price	Size, fl. oz. or oz.	Cost per oz.	Alcohol	Short-term freshening	Flavor	Aftertaste/afterfeel	Color [1]	Comments
Act Fluoride	$3.81	18	21¢	6%	◒ [2]	Sweet, spearmint	Sweet/cool	G	A,B,C,E
Cepacol Mint	4.54	32	14	15	◒	Spearmint, peppermint	Bitter/cool	G	—
Close-Up Anti-Plaque	2.29	12	19	15	◒ [2]	Cinnamon, peppermint	Sweet/cool	R	—
Colgate Fluorigard	3.59	18	20	6	◒	Sweet, spearmint	Sweet/cool	G	A,C
K Mart Antiseptic	1.84	32	6	27	◒ [2]	Eucalyptus	Bitter/hot	A	D,F,I
K Mart Mint	1.82	32	6	19	◒	Spearmint, peppermint	Mint/cool	G	J
Lavoris Mint	3.17	32	10	6	◒	Spearmint, peppermint	Mint/cool	G	—
Listerine Antiseptic	4.19	32	13	27	◒	Eucalyptus	Bitter/hot	A	D,F,I
Listermint with Fluoride	4.36	32	14	7	◒	Sweet, spearmint	Sweet/cool	G	A,E
Plax Anti-Plaque Soft Mint	4.01	24	17	7	◒ [2]	Sweet, spearmint	Sweet/cool	G	—
Rite Aid Antiseptic	1.81	32	6	27	◒ [2]	Eucalyptus	Bitter/hot	A	F,I
Rite Aid Mint	1.99*	40	5	19	○ [2]	Spearmint, peppermint	Mint/cool	G	J
Scope Original Mint	4.47	32	14	19	◒	Spearmint, peppermint	Mint/cool	G	J,K
Signal	3.65	32	11	15	◒	Sweet, spearmint	Sweet/cool	G	E
Viadent Anti-Plaque	4.94	30	16	10	◒	Eucalyptus, mint, spice	Metallic/cool	A	—

[1] Key to color: G = green; R = red; A = amber; W = white.
[2] Product labeling makes no explicit claim about freshening bad breath.
[3] Cost for candy mints is for 1 mint; for **Binaca** aerosol, for 3 sprays per use.
[4] 50% by weight, according to mfr.; roughly equivalent to 58% by volume.

MOUTHWASHES

OTHER PRODUCTS

Product	Price	Size, fl. oz. or oz.	Cost per oz.	Alcohol	Short-term freshening	Flavor	Aftertaste/aftertaste	Color [1]	Comments
Binaca Frosty Peppermint	$2.18*	0.2	5¢ [3]	58% [4]	○	Peppermint	Bitter/cool	—	G,H
Certs Peppermint	.49	0.6	4 [3]	—	○ [2]	Peppermint, chalky	Sweet/cool	W	—
Pep-O-Mint Lifesavers	.48	0.7	4 [3]	—	◐ [2]	Peppermint, chalky	Sweet/cool	W	—
Tic Tac Fresh Mints	.48	0.5	1 [3]	—	○	Vanilla, anise, mint	Anise/cool	W	—

Features in Common
Except as noted, all: • Rinses recommend a dose of 3 tsp. or less. • Are promoted to freshen breath.

Key to Comments
- *A*–Contains fluoride to help prevent tooth decay.
- *B*–Bottle has convenient dose-dispensing pump.
- *C*–Has ADA seal as an effective decay preventive.
- *D*–Has ADA seal for prevention or reduction of plaque and gingivitis.
- *E*–Panelists liked flavor more than most.
- *F*–Panelists disliked flavor more than most—burned more than most and was too medicinal tasting.
- *G*–Spray can ignite if exposed to open flame; no warning on label.
- *H*–Harder than most to use for people with hand or arm limitations.
- *I*–Dose is 4 tsp.
- *J*–Dose is 6 tsp.
- *K*–Panelists complained that the recommended dose was too much.

HOW OBJECTIVE IS CU?

Consumers Union is not beholden to any commercial interest. It accepts no advertising and buys all the products tested on the open market. CU's income is derived from the sale of CONSUMER REPORTS and other publications, and from nonrestrictive, noncommercial contributions, grants, and fees. Neither the Ratings nor the reports may be used in advertising or for any other commercial purpose. Consumers Union will take all steps open to it to prevent commercial use of its materials, its name, or the name of CONSUMER REPORTS.

ELECTRIC TOOTHBRUSHES

RATINGS ELECTRIC TOOTHBRUSHES

Better ◀——▶ Worse
● ◐ ○ ◑ ●

▶ See report, page 171. From Consumer Reports, September 1992.

Recommendations: Our test panel and consultants gave highest marks to the *Braun Oral-B Plaque Remover*, which we check-rated.

Ratings order: Listed in order of overall performance, based on judgments of CU's user panel. Price is the manufacturer's suggested retail for the basic unit and for extra brushes (number of extra brushes shown in parentheses). Discounts are often available. ⒹⒾ indicates model discontinued.

Panel judgments

Brand and model	Price	Price, extra brushes	Handset weight, oz.	Speeds	Brushes, supplied/stored on base	Overall performance	Ease of use	Changing brushes	Cleaning brushes	Charge capacity [1]	Advantages	Disadvantages	Comments
✔ Braun Oral-B Plaque Remover D5545	$99	$10(1)	6	1	4/4	●	●	●	●	●	A	—	A,B,D,G,H
Interplak Family PB-2 Ⓓ	99	13(1)	9	3	2/0	●	●	○	●	●	—	—	C,D,J,K
Water Pik Automatic Toothbrush AT-10W	45	5(4)	6	1	4/4	○	●	●	●	◐	—	—	—
Teledyne Water Pik Plaque Control PC-2000W	50	5(4)	6	1	4/4	○	●	●	●	◐	—	a	—
Interplak Voyager TK-2	99	13(1)	5	3	1/2	○	●	○	○	[2]	B	b	C,D,E,F,L
EpiDent C2500 [3]	79	17(2)	7	2	2/2	●	●	●	○	●	D	c,d	F,M
DentiBrush BT-691-10	35	7(4)	3	1	2/—	●	●	●	●	●[4]	D	a,e	B,I,N,Q
Interplak Plus PB-6	119	13(1)	7	3	4/4	●	●	○	●	●	C	—	D,J,K

① An estimate of how long each brush will run after its batteries have been fully charged. The longest-running should give at least 45 min. of tooth-brushing; the shortest, less than 10 min. The **Dentibrush** should run about 1½ hrs. on a rechargeable "C" cell and about 4 hrs. with an alkaline battery.

② Plug-in model, powered on house current—no batteries.

③ Product has been sold to another company and renamed **OralGiene** but otherwise unchanged, according to company.

④ Based on tests with a typical rechargeable nickel-cadmium "C" cell; a regular alkaline cell would perform even better.

⑤ Brush head holds 2 multitufted disks ("pods"), which may be replaced independently of the head; 1 head and 4 pods list for $6; a set of 8 pods lists for $5.

ELECTRIC TOOTHBRUSHES

Panel judgments

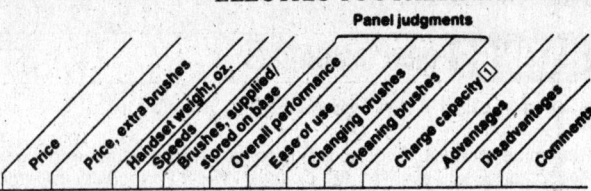

Brand and model: Price | Price, extra brushes | Handset weight, oz. | Speeds | Brushes, supplied/stored on base | Overall performance | Ease of use | Changing brushes | Cleaning brushes | Charge capacity [1] | Advantages | Disadvantages | Comments

CONDITIONALLY ACCEPTABLE

■ *The following model was judged Conditionally Acceptable due to excessive electrical leakage in immersion test; it should be used only with its wall mount.*

Brand and model	Price	Price, extra	Wt	Spd	Br	Perf	Ease	Chg	Cln	Cap	Adv	Dis	Com
Sunbeam Automatic Angle Toothbrush 4205	$66	$5(2)	5	2	4/4	○	◐	○	◐	◐	B	—	A,O,P,Q

NOT ACCEPTABLE

■ *The following model was judged Not Acceptable due to excessive electrical leakage in immersion test; a wall mount is not available.*

| Plak Trac PT-100 | 30 | [5] | 3 | 1 | 2/4 | ○ | ◐ | ○ | ◐ | ○ | — | — | — |

Performance Notes
All: • Clarity of instructions was judged excellent or very good. • Ease of set-up was judged excellent or very good.

Features in Common
Except as noted, all: • Carry American Dental Association seal as effective cleansing devices. • Have 1-yr. warranty on all parts except brushes and brush heads. • Run on built-in rechargeable batteries, not replaceable by user, and include charging stand (base unit), which is connected to house current. • Use 120-volt AC only. • Have adequately long power cord. • Do not include wall mount.

Key to Advantages
A–Timer light flashes after about 2 min. to signal adequate brushing time.
B–Built-in voltage converter for foreign travel.
C–Automatically shuts off if excess pressure is exerted on teeth or gums.
D–Battery can be replaced by user.

Key to Disadvantages
a–Panelists noted excessive vibration when brushing.
b–Coiled power cord judged inconveniently short—only 4 feet.
c–Brush head is bulky, judged hard to maneuver inside mouth.
d–Push-button switch must be held down to operate—judged inconvenient.
e–Some samples had defective battery contacts and didn't work.

Key to Comments
A–Wall mount included.
B–Judged easier to use for people with limited dexterity or ability to grip.
C–Oversized control button available at no cost from manufacturer; makes it easier to change speeds.
D–The American Dental Association has allowed brush to claim significant dental plaque and gingivitis reduction.
E–Foreign plug adapters not available from mfr.; must be obtained elsewhere.
F–Judged harder to use for people with limited dexterity or ability to grip.
G–Buyer has 30-day return/refund privilege.
H–Warranty terms not stated on or inside package.
I–90-day warranty limited to defective material or workmanship; $5 service charge.
J–Wall mount not supplied but available from mfr. at no charge.
K–Storage clips for additional brush heads available from mfr. at no charge.
L–Travel case can store 2 brush heads.
M–Battery charger is separate unit, not a charging stand; the design eliminates the possibility that the charger will be accidentally immersed when plugged in.
N–Has no charger; runs on 1 "C" flashlight battery.
O–Wall mount holds 4 brush heads as well as charger.
P–Travel kit with foreign plug adapters available from mfr.
Q–Lacks American Dental Association seal.

RATINGS ORAL IRRIGATORS

Better ◄──────► Worse

▶ See report, page 172. From Consumer Reports, September 1992.

Recommendations: If you're willing to mount your irrigator on the wall, our condition of Acceptability, you might try the *Colgate Via-Jet Periodontal Irrigator 7500*; our panelists judged it best overall. Otherwise, we recommend one of the three *Water Pik* irrigators; they were roughly equivalent in performance.

Ratings order: Listed in order of overall performance, based on judgments of CU's user panel. Price is the manufacturer's suggested retail.

Brand and model	Price	Reservoir, fl. oz.	Dimensions (WxDxH), in. [1]	Overall performance	Cleaning	Instructions	Ease of use	Advantages	Disadvantages	Comments
Water Pik Professional Dental System WP-32W	$60	35	7x4x7½	◐	◐	◉	◐	A,B,F	—	A,B,F,I
Water Pik Family Dental System WP-30W	70	35	7x4x7½	◐	◐	◉	◐	F	—	F,I
Water Pik Personal Dental System WP-20W	55	25	5½x4x7½	◐	◐	◉	◐	F	a,b	C,F,I

CONDITIONALLY ACCEPTABLE

■ *The following models were judged Conditionally Acceptable due to excessive electrical leakage in our tests. They should only be used with their wall mount.*

| Colgate Via-Jet Periodontal Irrigator 7500 | 60 | 25 | 8½x4½x7 | ◐ | ◐ | ◉ | ◐ | C,D | c | A,B,D,G,I |
| Sunbeam Dental Water Jet 6282-100 | 61 | 12½ | 8½x4¼x5½ | ○ | ○ | ◉ | ◐ | E | d,e | E,G,H,I |

[1] The width and depth, plus the height in use, to the nearest quarter-inch. The tank on the Water Pik WP-32W and WP-30W detach and serve, inverted, as a dust cover. That reduces overall height 3 in.

Features in Common
Except as noted, all: • Have 1-yr. warranty on all parts except irrigator tips. • Supply 4 regular tips, which can be stored in or on base. • Have American Dental Association's seal as acceptable when used as an adjunct to brushing, flossing, and regular professional care. • Run on 120-volt AC. • Have continuous pressure-adjustment control. • Have control on handpiece to stop water flow temporarily without changing pressure setting. • Do not include wall mount. • Have adequately long power cord and water hose.

Key to Advantages
A–Includes secondary 10-oz. reservoir for periodontal rinses.
B–Sulcus (pointy) tips supplied have soft points, judged safer to use.
C–Large, clearly marked pressure-control knob.
D–Judged somewhat less noisy than most.
E–Tips are a bit easier to change than those on other models.
F–Reservoir has permanent volume markings in ounces and milliliters.

Key to Disadvantages
a–Provision for storing only 2 tips on base unit; 1 stores in handpiece, thus increasing overall height.
b–Hose connecting handpiece to base

ORAL IRRIGATORS **185**

judged short, making unit less convenient to use than most.
c–Sulcus (pointy) tips supplied have hard points, judged more likely to scratch gums.
d–Stopping water flow temporarily at handpiece—to switch hands, say—requires user to change pressure setting.
e–Lacks markings on pressure-control knob to help reset pressure to accustomed level.

Key to Comments
A–3-yr. warranty.
B–Includes 2 regular (blunt) and 2 sulcus (pointy) tips, the latter for irrigation below the gumline or into periodontal pockets.
C–Includes 2 regular (blunt) tips only.
D–Includes wall-mounting hardware.
E–Wall mount must be ordered from the distributor for $3.25.
F–Wall mount must be ordered from mfr. for $2.75.
G–Lacks the American Dental Association seal.
H–Judged easier to use for people with limited use of fingers and wrist or difficulty grasping.
I–Replacement tip prices. **Water Piks:** Pik Pocket Tip PP-3, 2 for $10; Jet Tip JT-4, 4 for $4. **Colgate Via-Jet:** 4 for $5. **Sunbeam:** 2 for $5.

How to Use the Ratings

■ Read the article for general guidance about types and buying advice.

■ Read the Recommendations for brand-name advice based on our tests.

■ Read the Ratings order to see whether products are listed in order of quality, by price, or alphabetically. Most Ratings are based on estimated quality, without regard to price.

■ Look to the Ratings table for specifics on the performance and features of individual models.

■ A model marked Ⓓ has been discontinued, according to the manufacturer. A model marked Ⓢ indicates that, according to the manufacturer, it has been replaced by a successor model whose performance should be similar to the tested model but whose features may vary.

HOME ENVIRONMENT

Fans	186	Water treatment	194
Air-conditioners	188	Ratings	200
Air cleaners	192		

Modern technology offers a variety of ways to keep the home healthy and comfortable. Fans and air-conditioners make life bearable in summertime. Using an air-conditioner with a high Energy Efficiency Rating, or better yet, a fan, not only keeps you comfortable and saves money, but helps conserve energy. Room air cleaners aren't the solution to allergies, odors, or dangerous gases, but they can be helpful with dust and the smoke from cigarettes and fireplaces. Water-quality tests can alert you to a hazard like lead, or keep you from wasting money on water-treatment equipment you may not need.

Understanding which problems are present and which treatment methods are practical is the first step to making sure your home environment is safe and comfortable.

FANS

▶ Ratings on page 202.

When it's hot and humid out, most people look to an air-conditioner for comfort. But in some parts of the country—especially where hot days are followed by cool nights—a fan may be all the cooling you need. And it costs much less than an air-conditioner to buy and run. Even those who use an air-conditioner can be helped by a fan. It lets you turn up the thermostat a few degrees and still feel cool.

Today's fans aren't very different than the ones we first reported on 55 years ago—just a motor, propeller, switch, and some housing. Manufacturers arrange those components into a few basic shapes for use in a window, or on the floor or table.

Since fans are so simple, fan-makers rely on small variations in function to stand out from the crowd. Hence, the wide assortment of stands, clamps, and pedestals. Some manufacturers add conveniences like a variable-speed control or thermostat; others resort to pure fashion: making fans in fun colors like neon pink. One company, Vornado, calls its sculptural products not fans, but "air-comfort systems."

As a result of such straining for distinction, you can pay anywhere from less than $20 to more than $100 for fans that do essentially the same thing.

The choices

The major consideration in choosing a fan is whether you want to ventilate a room by pulling air in or out through a window or simply circulate the air within a room. Fans of various shapes and sizes are sold for each of these purposes, but not all fans can be used for both.

Ventilating fans. Traditional window fans are made for ventilation, but most box fans are suitable too. Check the manufacturer's instructions first. Some window models are particularly versatile—you can convert them to floor fans by rotating their legs or stands. Other things being equal, a 16-inch fan will move more air than a 12-inch model and a 20-inch fan will move lots more than either. But our tests showed that bigger isn't always better—design differences helped some smaller fans move more air than larger models. The strongest fans tended to make more noise at high speed and generate more turbulence than other models. Prices range from less than $20 to $150.

Since ventilating fans are most effective when placed in or near a window, they run the risk of getting wet during a rainstorm. All but one of the tested models passed our wet electrical shock hazard test. Even so, it's wise to move a fan away from a window when it's wet out.

Circulating fans. These include floor, table, pedestal, and some box fans—any model that isn't used in or near a window. As with window fans, the better air movers tended to be noisier and create more turbulence. This type tends to be smaller and cheaper than ventilating fans. Prices range from $25 to $120.

Features to look for

Variable-speed control. This lets you set the speed more precisely than a control with only a few distinct settings. With a fixed-speed control, you adjust airflow by moving the fan closer or further away.

Thermostat. As on an air-conditioner, this turns the unit off when the room temperature drops to the set level and back on if it warms up. Some models with a thermostat have a light to indicate that the fan remains on even when the blades are still.

Child safeguards. Safe design is important if children are likely to be about. Look for grilles and housings whose openings are small enough or rigid enough to keep fingers from passing through. Some models have a child-resistant switch that, like a pill bottle top, must be pushed and turned at the same time. Still, it's wise to keep any fan out of reach.

The tests

We rigged an open frame to a scale and mounted each fan horizontally to the top of the frame. Then, with the fan blowing straight up, we recorded the force it exerted. We also measured the velocity of the air each ventilating fan moved and how well all fans distributed that airflow within a room. Other tests included a "rain test" for electrical shock hazard and a stability test.

Buying advice

First decide whether you want a fan that will sit in or near the window and ventilate the room or one that just circulates the air within the room. If you're cooling one room, consider a box fan or larger table and pedestal model. For ventilating more than one room, look to large fans or even an attic fan, whose 24- to 42-inch blades can vent an entire house in minutes.

Most circulating fans will do the job fine. If you don't mind the turbulence, a high-velocity unit will stir quite a breeze. If you're sensitive to noise, consider a larger fan.

On low speed, it may move as much air as a small fan on high, and do it more quietly.

To make the most of a ventilating fan's cooling ability, open windows in the rooms you want to cool as soon as the temperature outside drops in the evening. With the fan in a window, exhaust the air at high speed. In general, if you use a box fan near but not in a window, place it 18 to 24 inches from the window for maximum effectiveness.

AIR-CONDITIONERS

▸ Ratings on page 200.

Central air-conditioning cools and dehumidifies the entire house and can be relatively quiet. But a central system can be very expensive if ducts have to be installed. If your budget is tight, one or two room air-conditioners may be a good alternative.

Where utility rates and usage are high, the electricity consumed by a room air-conditioner each year may come close to the initial cost of the machine itself, so you should make operating cost part of your calculation. Every room air-conditioner carries a Government-required yellow Energy Guide label. The big numbers on that label are the model's Energy Efficiency Rating. The higher the EER, the lower the operating cost required to produce a given amount of cooling. We consider a model with a rating of 9.0 or more to be a high-EER device.

The choices

Window. The two main types are the traditional window-installed model and a relatively new design that requires no window. Most room air-conditioners are designed for installation in double-hung windows. Some are specially designed to fit in a casement window or be mounted through the wall. An innovative design by Matsushita shapes the air-conditioner like an upside-down L. Sold under the *Panasonic* and *Quasar* names, this design puts the bulk of the working parts—the compressor and the fan for the condenser—in an outside section below the window. That cuts the noise in the room and reduces the vertical window space occupied to about seven inches—compared with 12 to 15 inches in the typical design. The Frigidaire Company sells a saddle-shaped design that also takes less window space.

Window models seem to have improved in recent years. In our latest tests, they lived up to their claimed ability to remove moisture, spread cool air evenly through a room and, in most cases, started up on their first try under brownout conditions.

Windowless. A few models even advertise that they don't need windows at all—so-called portable windowless air-conditioners. These expensive machines, sold by DeLonghi, Koldwave, and Bionaire, among others, proved disappointing in our tests. What you gain in portability and ease of installation, you lose in cooling ability. The *Bionaire* and *Koldwave* units, indeed, performed so poorly we rated them Not Acceptable as room air-conditioners in our May 1991 report.

Capacity. Air-conditioner cooling capacity is measured in terms of British thermal units, or Btu, per hour. Models are sold in sizes ranging from 4000 to as much as 30,000 Btu/hr. For a small room, a model rated between 5000 and 6000 Btu/hr. should be about right. For a larger room, you might need a model rated at more than 7500 Btu/hr. Use the worksheet on pages 190 and 191 to calculate the right size.

Small room air-conditioners typically cost $300 to $500; mid-sized units, $400 and up.

Features to look for

Energy-saving options. Some models have a built in 24-hour timer that lets you turn an air-conditioner on a short time before you get home rather than leave it running all day. But you can also buy a separate timer that is specially designed to work with most room air-conditioners. An Energy Saver setting, included on many models, cycles the fan on and off with the compressor instead of allowing the fan to run continuously. In this mode, the temperature control typically suffers. It can provide better humidity control but lack of moving air can make the room feel stuffy.

You can also save energy by using a portable fan to improve circulation of the cooled air. With a fan you should be able to raise the air-conditioner's thermostat.

Louvers. Many models lack a good way to direct the cooled air. Directional control is especially important if the air-conditioner will be mounted in a corner or if you want spot-cooling. Models that let you close some of the louvers can throw cool air with more force through the open ones. A vent setting blows some air outdoors and should only be used when the unit isn't cooling. Some models can also draw fresh air in.

Slide-out chassis. This lets you secure the lightweight cabinet in the window, then slide in the works. That simplifies repairs and makes installation safer but time consuming.

The tests

CU tests air-conditioners by mounting them in an environmental chamber—a heavily insulated room partitioned down the middle, between "outside" and "inside." We create an "outdoor" temperature of 95° F, then adjust each air-conditioner's thermostat to the point at which it cools a central portion of the room to about 80°. We also compare each model's dehumidification ability against the manufacturer's claims and take readings from sensors within the inside room to determine how uniformly each unit distributes cool air. To simulate a heat-wave brownout, we boost the outside temperature to 115° and drop the line voltage to as low as 100 volts. At the lower voltage, we run a unit for an hour, turn it off for three minutes, then try to start it again.

Buying advice

If you live where hot weather lingers from mid-spring through mid-fall, consider central air-conditioning. If summers are fairly temperate and dry, a window or whole-house fan may be sufficient. Otherwise, consider a room air-conditioner.

Use the worksheet on pages 190 and 191 to figure out what size unit you need for the room you're going to cool. In the midst of a heat wave, you might be ready to buy the biggest air-conditioner you can afford—without realizing that a high-capacity unit in a small space will not adequately control humidity. If an air-conditioner is too small, of course, it just won't cool enough.

Where two air-conditioners seem evenly matched, choose the one with the higher EER, even if it costs more. The higher price will be offset by lower operating costs.

How powerful an air-conditioner do you need?

This worksheet, adapted from one published by the Association of Home Appliance Manufacturers, can help you estimate how much cooling capacity you need. You'll need a tape measure, scratch paper, and a pocket calculator. The worksheet guides you through the measurements needed to determine the size of the room; the various calculations determine how much heat builds up in the room each hour. Make the measurements listed. For each dimension or area, round it to the nearest whole number before entering it in the appropriate box, and multiply by the factor in bold. (Use the factors in parentheses if the air-conditioner will be used only at night.) If the room is connected to another by an archway or a permanently open door more than 5 feet wide, consider the two rooms as one area and make all the necessary measurements in both rooms.

1. HEAT THROUGH WINDOWS. Calculate the area (height X width) of each window. Take the measurements in inches, then divide by 144 to determine the square footage. Jot down the area of each window for use in step 6. Add the areas, then enter that figure in the appropriate box below and multiply by the factor given.

For single glass.. _____ x **14**= _____
total window area, sq. ft.

For double glass or glass block .... _____ x **7**= _____
total window area, sq. ft.

2. WALLS. Measure the length of all walls, in feet. Consider walls shaded by adjacent buildings as facing north. Write the lengths in the appropriate boxes below and multiply by the factors given.

Uninsulated frame construction; masonry up to 8 inches thick

Outside, facing north +shaded +interior walls .... _____ x **30**= _____
total wall length, ft.

Outside, facing other directions............................. _____ x **60(30)**= _____
total wall length, ft.

Insulated frame construction; masonry more than 8 inches thick

Outside, facing north +shaded +interior walls .... _____ x **20**= _____
total wall length, ft.

Outside, facing other directions............................. _____ x **30(20)**= _____
total wall length, ft.

3. CEILING. Determine the ceiling area (length X width), in square feet. Enter that figure in the box that's appropriate for your house. Multiply by the factor given.

Uninsulated, no space above .... _____ x **19(5)**= _____
ceiling area, sq. ft.

Uninsulated, attic above .... _____ x **12(7)**= _____
ceiling area, sq. ft.

Insulated, no space above .... _____ x **8(3)**= _____
ceiling area, sq. ft.

Insulated, attic above.. _____ x **5(4)**= _____
ceiling area, sq. ft.

Occupied space above... _____ x **3**= _____
ceiling area, sq. ft.

4. DOORS AND ARCHES. Note: If the room has a permanently open door or archway more than 5 feet wide, skip this step and go on to step 5. Otherwise, enter the width of the door or archway and multiply by the factor shown.

_____ x **300(200)**= _____
total width, ft.

5. FLOOR. Note: If the floor is on ground or over a basement, skip this step and move on to step 6. Otherwise, determine the floor area (length X width) in feet and multiply by the factor shown. The floor area is usually the same as the ceiling area.

_____ x **3** = _____
floor area, sq. ft.

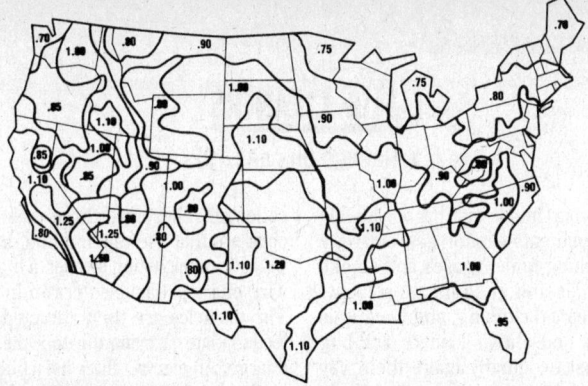

6. SUN THROUGH WINDOWS. Note: If the air-conditioner will be used only at night, or if all windows in the room face north, skip this step and go on to step 7. Using the measurements you made for step 1, enter the total window area for each wall in the appropriate box and multiply by the factor that best describes how the windows are shaded.

		No shades	Inside shades	Awnings	If any windows are glass block, multiply again by 0.5; multiply by 0.8 for storm windows or double glass.	
Northeast	_____ area, sq. ft.	x 60	or x 25	or x 20=	x _____	= _____
East	_____ area, sq. ft.	x 80	or x 40	or x 25=	x _____	= _____
Southeast	_____ area, sq. ft.	x 75	or x 30	or x 20=	x _____	= _____
South	_____ area, sq. ft.	x 75	or x 35	or x 20 =	x _____	= _____
Southwest	_____ area, sq. ft.	x 110	or x 45	or x 30=	x _____	= _____
West	_____ area, sq. ft.	x 150	or x 65	or x 45=	x _____	= _____
Northwest	_____ area, sq. ft.	x 120	or x 50	or x 35=	x _____	= _____

Use only the largest number you calculate

7. SUBTOTAL. Add the figures from steps 1 through 5 and the largest figure calculated in step 6. Enter the sum here and in the box for step 8, below. .... _____

SUBTOTAL

8. CLIMATE CORRECTION. Enter the subtotal from step 7 in the box. Check the map above to find the climate-correction factor for your area. Enter the factor on the line below. Multiply the two numbers.

_____ x = _____
Subtotal from step 7

9. HEAT FROM PEOPLE. Calculate the heat contributed by people in the room. In the box below, enter the number of people who normally use the room (use a minimum of 2). Multiply the figure by the factor given.

_____ x 600 = _____
People in room (min. 2)

10. HEAT FROM APPLIANCES. Add up the wattage of all lights and appliances in the room, not including the air-conditioner itself. Multiply the figure by the factor given.

_____ x 3 = _____
Total wattage

11. TOTAL COOLING LOAD. Add the figures on lines 8, 9, and 10.
Enter the sum on the line at the right. _____

TOTAL

The number you derive tells how much heat builds up in the room each hour. The air-conditioner's cooling capacity (Btu per hour) should nearly match the number you calculated. A difference of about 5 percent between the number you calculated and the air-conditioner's capacity shouldn't be significant.

Air Cleaners

▸ Ratings on page 192.

The air in your house can harbor a wide variety of pollutants—radon gas, cigarette smoke, cooking fumes, gases and smoke from furnaces and gas ranges, solvents from dry-cleaned clothing, and chemicals from paints, household cleaners, and bug sprays. Most eventually make their way outdoors through spaces around windows and doors, but in a tight house, the air-exchange rate can be so low that pollution levels may actually exceed government limits for outdoor air.

Opening windows and eliminating pollution sources are the most effective ways to control indoor pollution. Using an appliance to clear the air can be expensive and—our tests show—at best brings relief from only dust and smoke.

The choices

Many air contaminants are too small to see with the naked eye. To remove objects that small, air cleaners use filtration, electrical attraction, or ozone.

High-efficiency-particulate-arresting filters (HEPA, for short) are the most efficient and expensive filters. These filters snare up to 99.97 percent of particles as small as 0.3 microns. A variant, the pleated filter, traps up to 95 percent of the same particles. By comparison, a room air-conditioner's foam filter traps particles only 10 microns or larger, and no more than 30 percent of the particles at that. But even the best HEPA filter can't catch something as small as a gas molecule. Activated carbon or charcoal filters in HEPA or pleated-filter air cleaners are meant to handle that task but are usually inadequate.

With electrical attraction, airborne particles are given an electrical charge, then collected. There are three main types of cleaners that use this method. In an electrostatic-precipitating cleaner, a high-voltage wire charges particles drawn in by a fan. The particles are then attracted to a collection plate carrying the opposite electrical charge. An electret filter uses fibers with a static charge to trap particles. A negative-ionizer uses fine, electrically charged needles or wire to charge particles, which collect in a filter or, more typically, on walls and furnishings. None of the electrical-attraction cleaners removes gas molecules because the molecules tend to diffuse back into the air rather than stick to a collection plate.

A third approach to air-cleaning uses a high-voltage electrical charge to convert oxygen to ozone, a powerful but toxic gas commonly used to disinfect mildewy boats and deodorize fire-ravaged buildings. At sufficiently high concentrations, ozone attacks and destroys gas molecules and microorganisms. Ozone has no effect on dust and other particulates, however. Further, the ozone generators sold for home use can actually foul the air. The two ozone generators we tested generated unhealthy levels of ozone. Neither cleaned very well. We rated both Not Acceptable.

Cleaners that use these technologies come in various configurations. The type to buy depends on how big an area you need to clean:

Tabletop. These models are usually ionizers or use electret filters. Their fans are quiet but move little air. They're suited to small rooms or the area around a smoker's chair. Typical cost: less than $200.

Room cleaner. If you're cleaning any but the smallest room, you'll need this type with its stronger fan. Most room cleaners are either an electrostatic precipitator or use a HEPA filter. In our tests, most removed dust and smoke far better than even the best tabletop model. Cost: about $200 to over $600.

In-duct cleaners. These go in the ductwork of a central heating or air-conditioning system, where they clean the air for an entire house. There are several types, ranging from sophisticated to simple. The more effective in our tests included a simple filter (about $15) that replaces the existing one in your system. Better yet are complex electrostatic precipitators, which cost about $500 and must be installed by a contractor (about $300). Two potential drawbacks to in-duct cleaners: They work only when the system's fan is blowing, and they can slow air flow through the ducts, raising energy costs.

The tests

We measure air flow and determine clean-air delivery rate (CADR), an industry yardstick, inside a sealed chamber, using very fine laboratory dust and tobacco smoke. Contaminant concentrations are monitored by a laser spectrometer that counts the microscopic particles. To measure odor removal, we use human noses and an extremely sensitive monitor.

Buying advice

First, try to eliminate the source of the pollution or ventilate the room. If the trouble is pollen, an air-conditioner set to recirculate indoor air should do the job. An air cleaner should be tried as a last resort when those measures fail. And if the problem is cigarette smoke, odors, or gases, most cleaners still won't help.

There is no universally accepted performance standard for comparing air cleaners. The closest thing to it is the clean air delivery rate (CADR), a measure that expresses the number of cubic feet of clean air a unit delivers each minute. The CADR, developed by the Association of Home Appliance Manufacturers, is used by some air-cleaner manufacturers on their products.

The CADR is based on both the percentage of particles removed and how quickly they are removed. Tests performed to the appliance association's specifications provide separate CADR numbers for dust, smoke, and pollen.

We believe the CADR numbers alone don't provide a complete picture of an air-cleaner's effectiveness. It's also necessary to know the unit's total airflow rate to properly assess efficiency. For instance, two cleaners may have the same CADR, but the one with the lower total airflow will be the more efficient.

The most effective room models in our tests were electrostatic precipitators and HEPA filters. In general, tabletop models weren't nearly as good; the best of that type were ionizers with electret filters.

We tested four in-duct models. We found the contractor-installed electrostatic precipitators, the *Trion Max 5 1400* ($480) and the *Honeywell F-50E* ($500), nearly as effective as the best room models. Among the two do-it-yourself in-duct filters, the *Newtron 1-1620* ($289) and the *3M Filtrete* ($14), the *3M Filtrete* was only slightly less effective. The *Newtron* was only as effective as a small tabletop air cleaner, at best.

Stay away from ozone generators; the two we tested can generate unhealthy levels of ozone.

Keep in mind that operating costs and maintenance are major considerations when choosing a cleaner. Energy and maintenance costs vary widely among models and, in some cases, can exceed the purchase price within just a year or two. Expect energy costs to range from about $20 to $60. The cost of replacement filters can be quite high, particularly for units using a

HEPA filter. You can expect to spend $30 to $120 for HEPA filters a year; other types will use $20 to $80 a year.

Most air cleaners require little maintenance beyond filter changes and cleanings.

If you choose an electrostatic precipitator you'll need to wash its electronic cell every few months. When the air cleaner makes a crackling sound, you'll know it's time to clean it.

WATER TREATMENT

Despite all the scary news reports, most people's drinking water in the U.S. is not seriously polluted. Public supplies are either comparatively clean to start with or are purified to bring them up to par. Some people who sell water filters and other treatment devices, though, hope you don't know that. The less you know, the more easily they can sell you equipment you may not need.

What gives high-pressure or deceitful tactics an air of credibility is that there are some very real drinking water problems. More than 70,000 water contaminants—industrial and agricultural wastes, heavy metals, radon, and microbes—have been identified. While such contaminants may affect only a fraction of the population, those people have justified concerns.

If you're wondering about your water quality, the first step is to find out what's in the water. If you use a community water system, ask for your utility's latest laboratory test results. If you use a well, try to get information on local water problems from your public works department or the local agricultural extension service.

Testing your water

The surest way to know what's in your water is to test it. The *Nordic Ware Water Test Kit*, about $8 at a hardware store, lets you run a few basic water-quality tests at home. It's easy to use and accurate enough for home use. For an extra $6, the *Nordic Ware* kit offers a mail-in test for lead, a useful option. Unfortunately the kit cannot detect most toxic pollutants. If you suspect you have a problem with, say, organic solvents or pesticides, you need to have your water tested by a professional.

If you have your water tested by someone else, use a reputable, state-certified, independent laboratory, not a company that sells water-treatment equipment. Tests cost from $20 to $200, depending on their complexity. (For more information about selecting a lab, see page 199.) If a test report says your water has a high level of a contaminant, seek confirmation by having the water retested or sent to a second lab before taking costly action.

Pollutants to worry about

Of the thousands of water pollutants, three of the most widespread are lead, radon, and nitrate. Most organic pollutants present only localized problems. Treatment methods are listed in the chart on page 198.

Lead. Significant levels of this toxic metal are more widespread in drinking water than was once assumed, and levels once considered safe are now considered health concerns, particularly for infants and children. Even low-level lead exposure may affect learning ability in children and is associated with elevated blood pressure in adults.

Lead gets in water primarily from corrosion of plumbing. Very soft water, which is more corrosive than hard water, is especially likely to leach lead from soldered pipes and brass fixtures. To help minimize your exposure, use only cold water for cooking and drinking (hot water will dissolve more lead). More important, before drinking, run water for a minute or so to flush the pipes.

If a test reveals that water from flushed pipes contains more than 15 ppb of lead, you may want to install a treatment device. See below for a discussion of devices.

Radon. A naturally occurring radioactive gas, radon probably poses a greater health risk than all other environmental pollutants combined. According to the EPA, radon may cause between 10,000 and 40,000 lung-cancer deaths each year. Most of the risk comes from radon that seeps into homes from the ground. But some well water contains dissolved radon, which escapes into the air in the home from sources like showers and washing machines. Exposure to radon from water may cause between 100 and 1800 deaths a year.

Water-borne radon is usually confined to wells in private or small community water systems. Larger systems generally remove any radon before it reaches the tap. Before you test your water for radon, test the air inside your house. If the level is high and you use ground (well) water, have the water tested. If the air level is low, don't worry about the water.

The level that should prompt remedial action is a matter of dispute. According to an EPA official, you should take action if the water's radon level is 10,000 picocuries per liter or higher (that corresponds to about 1 picocurie per cubic meter of airborne radon). Radon is easily dispersed in outdoor air, so aerating the water before it enters the house is often the simplest solution. Ventilating the bathroom, laundry, or kitchen may also help dissipate the radon. Other solutions include carbon filters (see next column).

Nitrate. High nitrate levels in water pose a risk mainly to infants. Bacteria in their digestive tracts convert it into nitrite, which in turn combines with hemoglobin in the blood to form methemoglobin, which cannot transport oxygen. The resulting ailment, called methemoglobinemia, is rare, but can result in brain damage or death. Some adults, including pregnant women, may also be susceptible to developing methemoglobinemia.

Nitrate in water comes mainly from agricultural activities. Rural families with private wells—especially those with infants or pregnant women—should have their water tested regularly. Some state health departments test wells for free. High nitrate levels may signal that other contaminants are also present.

Treatment choices

If tests show your water supply is contaminated, you can buy bottled water; CU's tests have shown that it's generally pretty clean. If you have a well, you might also try digging deeper to an uncontaminated aquifer. Or you can treat your existing water supply with one of several types of a water treatment device:

Carbon filters. These treat a variety of problems, so they're the most popular water-treatment device. They remove residual chlorine, which improves the water's taste, and can also remove organic compounds—chemicals such as pesticides, solvents, or chloroform. But they won't remove hardness minerals, most heavy metals, or microbes (under certain conditions, they actually breed them).

Carbon filters come in many forms. High-volume filters—in-line filters for about $100—serve a single cold-water faucet. Tiny, faucet-mounted filters with a couple of ounces of carbon cost $20 to $30. Pour-through or pitcher devices cost a few dollars. Whole-house carbon filters ($1500 and up), which have five-foot-high tanks and can be backwashed, are especially useful for removing radon from the whole house's water.

The most practical are in-line filters that treat water at a single location, such as at the kitchen sink. The two main designs are under-sink models and countertop models, which attach with flexible tubes.

Filters and cartridges have to be periodically replaced, at costs ranging from $5 to $100 each time. Manufacturers typically recommend replacing a filter after a certain time or after a given quantity of water has passed through. Some filters have a water meter built in. For a high-volume in-line filter, expect to change cartridges every six months or 1000 gallons.

Reverse-osmosis devices. Reverse-osmosis devices are best at removing inorganic contaminants, such as dissolved salts, ferrous iron, chloride, fluoride, nitrate, and heavy metals such as lead. A carbon filter is incorporated in most reverse-osmosis systems to remove organic chemicals.

But reverse-osmosis devices can be clogged by high levels of hardness minerals. They work slowly, producing only a few gallons of fresh water per day, and they waste several gallons of water for every purified gallon they produce.

At the heart of these devices lies a fine sieve of rolled-up cellophanelike material—a semipermeable membrane that screens out all but the smallest molecules. Under pressure, only water and other small molecules are able to pass through.

Some versions attach to the cold-water line under the sink; others sit on the counter. Under-sink models run $500 to $850, countertop models about $350 to $500.

Filters and membranes need replacement about once every few years. Replacement membranes cost $45 to $234, filters another $25 or so.

Distillers. Distillers boil water, then cool the steam until it condenses. Some models include a tiny carbon filter. Countertop units hold from one-half to 2½ gallons. Prices range from $150 to $429.

Distillers are best for brackish water or water polluted with heavy metals; they demineralize it. Anything that won't boil or evaporate stays behind in the boiling pot. Boiling water can also kill microorganisms, but distillers shouldn't be relied on for that purpose. Distillers aren't effective against volatile organics like chloroform and benzene, which vaporize in the distiller and can wind up in the condensed water. A carbon filter might help remove such chemicals, but the filters incorporated into distillers are too small to do it reliably. Distillers are slow, taking a couple of hours to produce the first quart of water.

Since distillers collect and concentrate minerals, scale can build up quickly and must be cleaned out. And since they heat up, they use a lot of electricity—something like three kilowatt-hours per gallon of water they purify.

Water softeners. Water softeners remove minerals that cause soap deposits, and also remove iron and lead. They don't remove hazardous contaminants like radon, nitrate, or pesticides. They also take a lot of space. A water softener consists of a tank of tiny resin beads loosely coated with sodium ions. When hard water flows in, minerals—principally calcium and magnesium—take sodium's place on the resin. Periodically the softener reverses its flow, taking salt out of a reservoir tank to regenerate the resin beads. The minerals are flushed down the drain.

Some models regenerate at preset intervals, using a timer. More sophisticated models ("demand-control" models) regenerate according to water use. Softeners also differ in size. "Cabinet" units are the most compact.

The average price for a softener is about $1000, but the price varies depending on installation, local water conditions, and dealers that are competitive.

A water softener doesn't require very much care, except for the salt you add now and then. You can adjust the level of salt consumption. A high setting ensures softer water but means more frequent refills. A lower setting saves salt and money, but the resin may regenerate less completely.

Iron removers. Dissolved iron in water can leave rusty brown stains in the bathtub and sink. You can use a water softener to remove the iron, but special-purpose treatments are available for water where hardness is not a problem. An iron remover uses an oxidizing agent to precipitate the iron out. One common design is a canister similar to a water softener. Iron removers cost anywhere from $400 to $650, and are best for removing clear ferrous iron. They can be noisy at times.

Activated alumina lead-removal cartridges. These install on cold-water lines in a standard water-filter housing. If lead is your only problem, this is an effective solution. The cartridges cost about $100, the housing $50.

The tests

Tests were geared to the type of device being tested.

We tested the carbon filters using water spiked with chloroform, one of the most common organic compounds found in drinking water. Chloroform, a possible carcinogen, can often be traced to chemical reactions between dissolved organic matter and the chlorine used to disinfect public water supplies. The water we used contained 1 part per million chloroform, 10 times the maximum permitted by the U.S. Environmental Protection Agency.

We tested the reverse-osmosis devices using water laden with 600 parts per million of sodium chloride (a representative dissolved solid), and 2 to 10 times the Government's allowable limits for lead, cadmium, copper, and barium. We also measured the removal of calcium, a hardness mineral present in moderate amounts in our local supply.

To challenge the filters further, we pumped our test water at an average of 45 pounds per square inch (psi), close to the minimum operating pressure needed for a reverse-osmosis system.

For our primary tests of distillers, we used water spiked with phenol, a chemical related to benzene and typical of a large class of volatile organics. We spiked the water with 0.5 parts per million phenol, a dangerously high level of contamination for related organic compounds.

We also used each unit to distill 50 batches of mineral-laden water. That test showed, in effect, how well the distillers would work with hard water. It also functioned as an endurance test of sorts. We cleaned the units only occasionally, then let them sit uncleaned for a few weeks to see what would happen to their innards.

For the water softeners, we concocted very hard water. We measured the time needed to flush brine through the resin to restore a unit's softening capability and the amount of water used in regeneration for each 1000 gallons of water softened.

For all the devices, we evaluated ease of installation and use.

Buying advice

The chart on page 198 sums up treatment methods recommended for the most common water problems. Before doing business with an unfamiliar water-treatment company, call the Better Business Bureau or a local consumer-protection agency to find out if there are unresolved complaints against it.

If you're looking at carbon filters, the more carbon the better. Based on our tests, small pour-through filters and fist-sized units that thread onto the faucet can im-

198 WATER TREATMENT

prove the taste of water, but are simply too small to remove hazardous chemicals. High-volume under-the-sink or countertop filters do a much better job. Look for those with replaceable filter cartridges.

Cartridges made either with a "carbon block" or granulated carbon are better than those with powdered carbon.

If your carbon filter has a built-in sediment filter and your water contains a lot

Water problems and solutions

Recommended if drinking water contains more than "action level" amounts.

	Action level	Carbon filter	Reverse osmosis	Distiller	Water softener	Iron remover	Activated alumina cartridge	Sediment filter	Aerator
AESTHETIC PROBLEMS									
Dissolved iron	—				✔	✔			
Rust stains	—			✔		✔		✔	
Calcium	—				✔				
Magnesium	—				✔				
Chlorine	—	✔							✔
Salty taste	—		✔	✔					
'Skunky' taste	—	✔							
Total dissolved solids (TDS)	500 ppm		✔	✔					
HEALTH HAZARDS - Organic									
Benzene	5 ppb	✔							✔
Carbon tetrachloride	5 ppb	✔							✔
Lindane	4 ppb	✔		✔					
Methoxychlor	100 ppb	✔		✔					
Trichloroethylene	5 ppb	✔							✔
Trihalomethanes (THM)	100 ppb	✔							
HEALTH HAZARDS - Inorganic									
Arsenic	50 ppb		✔	✔					
Barium	1 ppm		✔	✔	✔				
Cadmium	10 ppb		✔	✔	✔				
Chromium	5 ppb		✔	✔	✔				
Fluoride	4 ppm		✔	✔			✔		
Lead	15 ppb		✔	✔			✔		
Mercury	2 ppb	✔	✔	✔					
Nitrate	10 ppm		✔	✔					
Selenium	10 ppb		✔	✔			✔		
HEALTH HAZARDS - Radiological									
Dissolved radon	10,000 pc/l	✔							✔

of undissolved solids, the sediment part may clog before the carbon is used up. To extend the filter's life, install a separate sediment prefilter upstream of the carbon. A 5- to 10-micron mesh is fine enough. A clear plastic sump on the filter housing will let you see when the cartridge needs changing.

If you're considering a distiller, look at how easy it is to fill or clean. We found little variation in how well distillers removed inorganic compounds.

Any water softener will do an acceptable job of removing minerals, according to our tests. For greatest efficiency and minimum salt consumption where water use varies from week to week, a demand-control model is best.

For iron removal, costlier models have the advantage of removing more iron and regenerating automatically rather than manually. They're designed for high iron levels. Aeration devices can also precipitate and remove iron and also radon.

For removing lead, the least troublesome device is an activated alumina lead-removal cartridge installed on a cold-water line. You could also use a distiller or reverse-osmosis device, but they're needlessly slow if lead is your only water problem.

MAIL-ORDER WATER-TESTING LABS

Companies that sell water-treatment equipment often offer a free or low-cost water analysis as part of the sales effort. Don't depend on that kind of test. It's like asking a barber if you need a haircut. Consult an independent, state-certified lab instead. You can often find one in the Yellow Pages under "Laboratories—Testing."

Or use a mail-order lab. We've identified three reliable ones to date: National Testing Laboratories (6555 Wilson Mills Rd., Cleveland, Ohio 44143; telephone 800-458-3330); Suburban Water Testing Laboratories (4600 Kutztown Rd., Temple, Pa. 19560; telephone 800-433-6595); and Clean Water Fund (29½ Page Ave., Asheville, N.C. 28801; telephone 704-251-0518).

The labs send you a kit containing collection bottles and detailed instructions. You collect water samples and ship them back by overnight package delivery. The labs provide test results and an explanation of the numbers two to three weeks later.

National charges $29 for a lead test. A 73-item scan for minerals, bacteria, and volatile organics costs $89; and a 93-item test that includes pesticides costs $129. A radon test costs $29. Suburban charges $25 for lead, $50 for radon, and $135 to test for 40 items, including bacteria and volatile organics. Clean Water Fund is a nonprofit organization and research project; its tests are for lead in water, paint, soil, dust, and ceramics. Each test costs $12.

RATINGS: MID-SIZED AIR-CONDITIONERS

Key: E ⊖ VG ⊖ G ○ F ◐ P ●

▶ See report, page 188. From Consumer Reports, July 1992.

Recommendations: The top-rated *Friedrich SQ06H10A* stood out as the best performer, but the models in the top half of the Ratings were nearly as good. See also the list of similar models opposite. Let price and energy-efficiency rating narrow the selection.

Ratings order: Listed in order of estimated quality. Price is the approximate retail price, as quoted by the manufacturer. Energy-efficiency ratings (EER) are as certified by the manufacturer. Similar models are models judged comparable in capacity and performance; see listing opposite. Ⓢ indicates tested model has been replaced by successor model; according to the manufacturer, the performance of new model should be similar to the tested model but features may vary. See right for new model number and suggested retail price, if available. Ⓓ indicates model discontinued.

Brand and model	Price	Capacity, Btu/hr.[1]	EER[2]	Moisture removal, pt./hr.	Regular	Energy saver	Uniformity[3]	Directional control	Thermostat Indoors, high	Thermostat Indoors, low	Advantages	Disadvantages	Comments
Friedrich SQ06H10A	$445	6700	10.3	2.1	⊖	○	⊖	○	○	⊖	A,B,K,N	g,l	E,F,J,N,S
Panasonic CW-601JU Ⓓ	405	6000	9.5	1.6	⊖	○	⊖	◐	⊖	⊖	A,D,H,J,L	g,l,m	I,N,O,V
General Electric AME06LA	400	6000	9.5	1.5	⊖	○	⊖	◐	⊖	⊖	A,D,F,H,L	g,l,m	I,N,O
Emerson Quiet Kool 6DC53-A	365	6500	10.0	1.8	⊖	⊖	○	○	○	⊖	C,E,J,L	c	A,C,J,V
Quasar HQ5061DW	435	6000	9.1	1.8	⊖	—	○	⊖	⊖	⊖	C,E,G,H,L	d,g,k,l,o	D,W
Frigidaire FAC067P7B	400	6100	10.0	2.0	⊖	—	○	⊖	⊖	⊖	C,F,G,I,L,M	b,i	H,R,V
Carrier ZMB7061	350	6200	9.4	2.0	⊖	◐	⊖	⊖	⊖	⊖	A,D,H,L,N	f,g,p	B,E,I,K,M,S,V
Sharp AF-602M6	375	6500	9.5	2.1	⊖	⊖	○	○	⊖	⊖	G,L	a,e,g,i,n	A
White-Westinghouse WAC062P7A Ⓓ	320	6000	9.2	2.0	⊖	—	⊖	⊖	⊖	⊖	F,G	h,i,j,k,o	R,V
Sears Kenmore 76069	370	6000	9.0	2.0	⊖	⊖	⊖	○	⊖	◐	E,F,G,H	c,h,i,j,p	F,J,P,Q
Amana 7P2MB	380	6550	10.0	1.8	⊖	—	⊖	⊖	○	⊖	E,F,G,I,L	c,e,i,j	G
White-Westinghouse WAB067P7B	370	6000	9.2	1.7	⊖	—	⊖	○	○	⊖	C,F,I,L	n	J,L,Q,R,S,X
Micro Sonic 2S062A	365	6000	9.2	1.9	⊖	—	⊖	◐	○	◐	C,L	a,f,o	A,C,J,S,T,U,V
Whirlpool ACQ062XW Ⓢ	410	6000	9.0	2.1	⊖	—	⊖	○	⊖	◐	F,G,H	c,h,i,j,p	F,J,Q
Montgomery Ward Signature KMJ-5816	325	6000	8.5	1.4	○	◐	○	◐	⊖	⊖	A,H,L	g,l,m,o	I,O

[1] Cooling capacity as measured in British thermal units per hr.
[2] The higher the energy-efficiency rating (EER), the lower the cost of operation.
[3] Performance of coldest setting with outside temperature at 95°.

MID-SIZED AIR-CONDITIONERS

Similar Models
Panasonic CW-601 JU is similar to GE AME06LA, $400; Quasar HQ5061DW to Panasonic CW-601HU, $450; Frigidaire FAC067P7B to White-Westinghouse WAC067-P7A, $400; Sears 76069 to Whirlpool ACQ062XW, $410; White-Westinghouse WAB06-7P7B to Frigidaire FAB067P7B, $380; Gibson GAB067P7B, $380; Montgomery Ward Signature 2000 5134003, $415; Sears Kenmore 72060, $395; Montgomery Ward Signature KMJ-5816 to Panasonic CW-600JU, $365, Quasar HQ2061DW, $380.

Successor Models
Whirlpool ACQ062XW is succeeded by ACQ062X.

Features in Common
All: • Are rated at 115 volts and 5.6 to 6.5 amp, but can draw more current under adverse conditions. • Should be run on 15-amp circuit protected by time-delay fuse or circuit breaker and grounded outlet. • Are designed for installation in double-hung window, a task we think best handled by two. • Keep window from being opened when properly installed. • Have removable air filter. • Use R-22 HCFC refrigerant. • Have expandable side panels. • Have power cord at least 65 in. long.
Except as noted, all: • Have 3 cooling speeds. • Have adjustable vertical and horizontal louvers. • Have vent control for exhausting some room air. • Started immediately when we restored power in our test of performance at low voltage and in extreme heat. • Have 1-yr. parts/labor warranty; additional warranty covers parts/labor on sealed refrigeration system through 5th yr.

Key to Advantages
A–Slide-out chassis can ease installation and servicing.
B–Low-voltage protection circuitry.
C–At least 1 built-in handle to steady unit during installation.
D–Built-in timer. 12-hr. delay On/Off timer for **Panasonic, GE**; 24-hr. multiple On/Off clock for **Carrier**.
E–Mfr. provides exterior support bracket. (Bracket for **Sears** available as separate parts totaling approx. $15; order as model no. 106.8760693.)
F–Mfr. provides hardware to lock upper window sash.
G–Control markings easy to read.
H–Expandable side panels have metal frames; judged stronger than typical plastic frames.
I–Ventilated room air better than most.
J–Thermostat calibrated in degrees Fahrenheit.
K–Signal light shows when power is on; especially useful in "energy-saver" mode, when fan and compressor shut off together.
L–Filter readily accessible for cleaning.
M–Louvers can be partially closed to increase air thrust or ventilation.
N–Power cord can extend from either side of unit, according to mfr.'s instructions.

Key to Disadvantages
a–Unit had minor difficulty restarting in our test at low voltage and in extreme heat.
b–Bottom of side-panel rail can come out of frame; may be dangerous if unit is picked up by side panels.
c–Sharp corners on grille inside room.
d–Assembly screws provided did not fit into brackets.
e–In high-humidity tests, unit showed either slight drip indoors or spraying and/or dripping outdoors.
f–Controls judged more confusing than most.
g–Side curtains require assembly.
h–Filter judged harder than others to remove and replace.
i–Lacks guard over outdoor cooling fins.
j–Has fixed horizontal (up/down) louvers.
k–Lacks vent feature; can't exhaust room air.
l–Requires more installation time than most.
m–Slide-out chassis exposes unprotected rigid-foam plastic duct to damage when unit is installed or removed.
n–Vent-control markings lack contrast and are hard to read.
o–Only 2 cooling speeds, a minor disadvantage.
p–Outdoor noise on high judged poor.

Key to Comments
A–2nd- through 5th-yr. warranty covers sealed refrigeration-system components only.
B–2nd- through 5th-yr. warranty covers parts for entire unit, with fixed allowance for labor.
C–2-yr. parts warranty on fan motor; 2nd through 5th-yr. labor warranty for sealed refrigeration system at additional cost.
D–2nd- through 7th-yr. warranty covers parts/labor on sealed refrigeration system.
E–Instructions for wall installation.
F–Mfr. recommends periodic oiling of fan motor.
G–Fiberglass insulation in air-discharge duct.
H–Tall top frame/handle may interfere with some window handles; central window handle protruding to 3/8-in. will fit.
I–Requires removal of shipping block or screw.

Ratings Keys continued

202 PORTABLE FANS

J – Cabinetry: Textured steel cabinet (**Sears, Whirlpool**); molded plastic cabinet and base (**White-Westinghouse, Micro Sonic**); textured aluminum cabinet, steel base pan (**Emerson**); plastic base pan (**Friedrich**).
K – 1st sample performed poorly in moisture-removal test; 2nd sample met mfr.'s advertised rating.
L – Thermostat on 2 samples controlled to colder temperature range than did other models.
M – Fresh-air intake and room-air exhaust features.
N – 3-min. time delay may occur when unit turned on.
O – Mfr. provides drain pan for routing away condensate.
P – Mfr. provides air-freshener dispenser and clean-filter indicator.
Q – Has single lever for left-to-right air control.
R – Incorporates at least 1 integral leveling support on exterior.
S – Thermostat lacks specific identification of colder settings.
T – Directs air from 45 to 85 degrees up only.
U – Windowsill angle-bracket helps position and secure unit.
V – Installation instructions explain how to install unit if window has storm sash.
W – Unit's unique "L" shaped design consumes little window space but causes installation difficulties.
X – Unit's saddle shape consumes little window space. Groove in top holds upper window sash.

RATINGS PORTABLE FANS

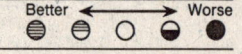

Better ← → Worse

▶ **See report, page 186.** From Consumer Reports, July 1992.

Recommendations: The top-rated *Patton, Lakewood,* and *Galaxy* ventilating fans are high-speed models suited for large rooms or more than one room. Models adequate for single-room use include the *Duracraft DW-612* window model, $45, or the *Lakewood P-223* box fan, $17. For simple air circulation, we favor the *Duracraft DT-16* or the *Windmere KD-16WB*, very quiet models priced at $30 or less.

Ratings order: Listed by type of use; within use groups, listed in order of estimated quality. A model designed for or typically used in windows was considered a ventilating model, regardless of fan type. All others were considered circulating fans. Circulating fans listed below the bold rule on page 204 were significantly lower in quality than those above. Price is the manufacturer's suggested retail; a * indicates price is approximate. Key to type: **W** = window; **B** = box; **F** = floor; **P** = pedestal; **T** = table; **H** = high-velocity. D indicates model discontinued.

Brand and model	Type	Price	Performance	Safeguards	Convenience	Noise (low/high)	Blade diameter, in.	Weight, lb. [1]	Advantages	Disadvantages	Comments
VENTILATING FANS											
Patton WF-1890	W/F/H	$75	◐	◐	●	○/●	18	16	C,E,G,O	f,h,i,l,t	A,C
Lakewood HV-18-WR	W/H	70	◐	○	◐	◐/◐	18	20	D,F,L,O	m	A,C,D
Galaxy 2121 D	W	80*	◐	○	○	◐/◐	20	21	D,F,L,O	f,k	D
Duracraft DW-612	W/F	45*	○	◐	●	○/○	12	7	H	i,p,w	A,C,D

PORTABLE FANS

Brand and model	Type	Price	Performance	Safeguards	Convenience	Noise (low/high)	Blade diameter, in.	Weight, lb. [1]	Advantages	Disadvantages	Comments
Vornado 280AE	W/H	$149	○	○	⊖	⊖/●	11	13	D,G,N	p	A,E
Lakewood P-223	B	17	○	●	⊖	⊖/●	20	10	—	j,m	D
Holmes Air HAWF-1012ER	W/F	60	○	⊖	○	○/○	12	9	D,H,I	h,i,p,w	A,B,C,D
Toastmaster 4437	B	33	○	●	⊖	○/●	20	10	—	b,m,r	A,C,D,F
Galaxy 3746	B	30*	○	○	⊖	⊖/●	20	12	L	b,d	C,D
Lakewood HV-12-WR	W	50	○	○	○	⊖/●	12	12	D,F	f,m,p	A,C,D
Robeson BF20-2393GW	B	20	●	●	⊖	⊖/●	20	9	—	j,m,o	A,D

NOT ACCEPTABLE

■ *The following fan, whose instructions say it can be used in a window, had excessive current leakage in our rain tests.*

Brand and model	Type	Price	Performance	Safeguards	Convenience	Noise (low/high)	Blade diameter, in.	Weight, lb. [1]	Advantages	Disadvantages	Comments
Lakewood P-47/M	B	40	⊖	●	⊖	○/●	20	15	L	m	C,D

CIRCULATING FANS

Brand and model	Type	Price	Performance	Safeguards	Convenience	Noise (low/high)	Blade diameter, in.	Weight, lb. [1]	Advantages	Disadvantages	Comments
Duracraft DT-16	T	27*	○	⊖	⊖	⊖/○	16	7	A,B,G	n	A
Windmere KD-16WB	T	30	○	○	⊖	⊖/○	16	8	B,G,N	—	A
Windmere KS-16WB	P	35	○	○	⊖	⊖/○	16	11	B,G,J,N	c	A
Galaxy 2151S	T	30*	⊖	○	⊖	○/○	16	8	B,G	d,e,n	—
Patton U2-1887	F/H	60	⊖	⊖	○	○/●	18	14	E,G,K,O	f,t	A,C
Holmes Air HAHV-18C [D]	F/H	70	⊖	○	⊖	⊖/●	18	13	G,N,O	—	A,D
Duracraft DS-1600	P	35*	○	○	⊖	⊖/●	16	9	A,B,J	n	A
Holmes Air HAPF-1150	P/F	60	●	⊖	⊖	⊖/○	11	10	M	h,w	A,D,E
Lakewood HV-18-RA	P/H	70	⊖	⊖	○	●/⊖	18	21	E,G,J,K,O	c,d,g,l,t,v	A
Lakewood HV-18	F/H	45	⊖	⊖	○	●/⊖	18	15	E,G,K,O	d,l,s,t	A,C
Galaxy 2157RS	P/H	30*	○	○	⊖	⊖/⊖	16	12	B,G,J	c,e,n	—
Galaxy 2150S	T	24*	●	●	⊖	⊖/⊖	12	7	B,G	d,e,n,w	—
Holmes Air HAOF-1600	T	35	○	⊖	⊖	○/⊖	16	7	B,N	e,r,v	A
Vornado 280 SS	F/H	119	○	○	⊖	⊖/●	11	10	G,N	—	A,E
Lakewood 1645 DX	P	30	●	○	⊖	⊖/○	16	8	B,G,J	c,e,r,u,w	D

[1] *Rounded to the next higher pound.*

Ratings continued

Ratings continued

Brand and model	Type	Price	Performance	Safeguards	Convenience	Noise (low/high)	Blade diameter, in.	Weight, lb. [1]	Advantages	Disadvantages	Comments
Lakewood 1600DX	T	$27	◐	○	◐	◐/○	16	6	B,G	d,e,r,u,w	D
Galaxy 3723N	B	25*	○	◐	◐	◐/◐	20	10	—	a,d,j,m	—
Galaxy 3521	F	25*	◐	○	◐	○/◐	20	9	G	f,o,q,v,w	—

Features in Common
All: • Operate on normal house current. • Use less than 300 watts on high speed.
Except as noted, all: • Have 3 speeds. • Provide 1-yr. warranty on parts and labor. • Require some assembly.

Key to Advantages
A–Child-resistant switch.
B–Horizontal oscillating range of 90 degrees.
C–Adapter for sliding windows is free.
D–Adjustable side panel.
E–3-prong grounded plug.
F–Installation template easy to use.
G–Airflow can angle at least 20 degrees up, at least 10 degrees down.
H–Grille rotates to disperse air.
I–Angles left/right in window, up/down on floor.
J–Adjustable stand height.
K–Can be used as ventilation fan (mfr. recommends using fan near, but not in, window).
L–Has thermostat control. On **Lakewood HV-18-WR**, On/off indicator light shows when thermostat has shut off fan.
M–Backlighted control switch.
N–Grille is easy to remove.
O–Thrust greater than most.

Key to Disadvantages
a–Box fan whose instructions recommend against use in window.
b–Box fan whose instructions don't say whether fan is suitable for use in window.
c–Extensive or difficult assembly.
d–Limited cautions and instructions (though some samples of **Galaxy 2151S** and **Lakewood 1600DX** had adequate instructions).
e–Grille ribs separate easily, can allow contact with blades.
f–Extensive or difficult disassembly needed to clean blades.
g–Stand design makes adjusting height difficult.
h–On some samples, small plastic parts broke in testing (but fan still operable).
i–Window can't close when fan is installed.
j–Rear support legs can break easily.
k–Side panel is hard to alter for small windows.
l–On High, fan may "walk" on smooth surfaces.
m–Large openings in motor housing can permit contact with electrical parts.
n–Plastic grille clips hard to use, broke in testing.
o–Less energy-efficient than most.
p–Ventilated worse than most.
q–Stability worse than others.
r–Controls poorly marked.
s–Vibrated more than most.
t–Has a lot of sharp edges or pointed corners.
u–Hard to adjust angle of fan up or down.
v–Wobbly stand.
w–Thrust performance worse than most.

Key to Comments
A–Warranty exceptions: **Vornado**, lifetime; **Patton**, 25 yr. on parts, 1 yr. on labor; **Lakewood**, 5 yr. on parts and labor; **Toastmaster**, 3 yr. on parts and labor; **Windmere**, 2 yr. on parts and labor; **Holmes Air**, 1 yr. extension for $1; **Duracraft, Holmes Air, Vornado, Windmere,** and **Robeson** charge fee for warranty service.
B–Grille bug screen available for $3.99.
C–Comes fully assembled.
D–Has polarized electrical plug.
E–Variable-speed motor.
F–May be sold as **4433** in some parts of country.

AIR CLEANERS 205

RATINGS AIR CLEANERS

Legend: E ⊜ VG ⊖ G ○ F ◐ P ●

▶ See report, page 192. From Consumer Reports, October 1992.

Recommendations: Give first consideration to the check-rated *Friedrich C90*. It was by far the most effective in our tests and its maintenance costs are among the lowest. The best tabletop unit was the *Pollenex 1850*; however, its $80 annual operating cost is a drawback.

Ratings order: Listed by size; within sizes, listed in order of estimated quality, based primarily on effectiveness in removing dust and smoke. Bracketed models, judged approximately equal in quality, are listed alphabetically. Price is the manufacturer's suggested retail. A + indicates that shipping is extra. ⓢ indicates tested model has been replaced by successor model; according to the manufacturer, the performance of new model should be similar to the tested model but features may vary. See page 206 for new model number and suggested retail price, if available.

Brand and model	Price	Type[1]	Energy[2]	Filter[2]	Smoke removal	Dust removal	Noise High	Noise Low	Weight, lb.[3]	Advantages	Disadvantages	Comments
ROOM MODELS												
✓ Friedrich C90	$399	EP	$25	$34	⊜	⊜	◐	⊜	27	A,D	i	G
Honeywell F59A	600	EP	21	80	⊜	⊜	◐	⊜	38	D,F	—	Q,R
Smokemaster P-600	649+	EP	27	40	⊜	⊜	◐	⊜	39	D,E	i,d	O,Q
Enviracaire EV-35A ⓢ	300	HEPA	57	73	⊜	⊜	●	◐	15	A	e,j	A,G
Austin Air Sierra HEPA PFA-80-AC ⓢ	395+	HEPA	30	52	⊜	⊜	◐	⊜	39	B	a,g,k	A,G,I
Trion Console 250	279	EP	47	60	○	⊜	◐	⊜	35	D	—	A,G,M
Vitaire H200	299	HEPA	24	69	○	○	◐	○	30	A	a,d,g,k	A,F,H,I,J,Q,R
Hepanaire HP50	495	HEPA	26	145	○	○	◐	○	39	—	e,g,k	A,J,R
Cloud 9 Sterilaire 150	325+	HEPA	32	139	○	○	◐	○	27	A	e,g,k	J,L,R
Micronaire P-500	495	EP	34	98	◐	○	●	○	23	D	f,l	A,J,M,R
NSA 7100A	489	HEPA	19	138	◐	◐	○	○	33	A,B,C,F,K	i	A,C,G
Space-Gard 2275	180	PF	12	26	●	◐	◐	⊜	12	—	a	F,G,H

[1] Key to type: *EP = electrostatic precipitator; HEPA = high-efficiency particulate arresting filter; PF = pleated filter; I = ionizer; EF = electret filter; OZ = ozone generator.*

[2] *Our estimate of the cost to run each unit 8 hrs. each day on High, at the national average electricity rate. Filter cost is based on the suggested retail price and the shortest replacement interval recommended by the mfr.*

[3] *Weight is to the nearest pound.*

Ratings continued

AIR CLEANERS

Ratings continued

Brand and model	Price	Type[1]	Energy[2]	Filter[2]	Smoke removal	Dust removal	Noise High	Noise Low	Weight, lb.[3]	Advantages	Disadvantages	Comments
TABLETOP MODELS												
Pollenex 1850	$60	I,EF	$20	$60	○	○	○	◓	8	H,I	a,b,i	A,E,G
Bionaire F-150	180	I,EF	20	68	○	○	◐	◓	7	C,F,H	a,b,j	D,K,P
Trion Super Clean II	129	I,EP	12	40	◐	◐	◐	◓	9	D,J	i	A,G,M,O
Norelco CAM880	147	I,EF	16	120	◐	○	◐	◓	8	F,H,I,J	—	E,G,I
Amcor Air Processor 2135 NI	119	I,EP	4	—	◐	●	○	◓	4	H	a,b	B,G,H,I,N,P
Ecologizer Series 8000	140	HEPA	19	108	●	●	●	◓	9	—	a	C,P
NSA 1200A	179	EF	8	78	●	●	○	○	6	—	—	A,C,G,L
NOT ACCEPTABLE												

■ *The following tabletop models can produce harmful levels of ozone and do not have an automatic control to limit ozone output. Listed alphabetically.*

Alpine 150	449	OZ	5	—	◐	●	●	◓	15	—	h,l	G,H,I
Quantum Panda Plus Q11	499+	OZ	3	—	◐	●	○	◓	9	A,G	c,h	B,G,H

[1] Key to type: EP = electrostatic precipitator; HEPA = high-efficiency particulate arresting filter; PF = pleated filter; I = ionizer; EF = electret filter; OZ = ozone generator.

[2] Our estimate of the cost to run each unit 8 hrs. each day on High, at the national average electricity rate. Filter cost is based on the suggested retail price and the shortest replacement interval recommended by the mfr.

[3] Weight is to the nearest pound.

Successor Models (in Ratings order) Enviracaire EV-35A is succeeded by EV-35B; Austin PFA-80-AC by Healthmate.

Features in Common
Except as noted, all have: • 2 or more fan speeds. • Conveniently located controls. • Rubber or cork pads or legs. • Grounded or polarized plug. • Washable prefilter and/or postfilter. • Activated-carbon or charcoal filter to remove gaseous odors. • On/off light. • Easily accessible cell or filter. • 1-yr. limited warranty. *Except as noted, all lack:* • Handle, wheels, or casters. • Adjustable louvers. • Filter-replacement indicator.

Key to Advantages
A–Has handle.
B–Has wheels.
C–Adjustable louvers direct air flow.
D–Can't be operated if cover is removed.
E–Malfunction indicator light and test button.
F–Filter-replacement indicator or schedule.
G–Self-clean switch cleans ozone power plate.
H–Separate On/off ionizer switch.
I–Separate indicator light for ionizer.
J–Can't run ionizer without fan on.
K–Has indicator light for both speeds.

Key to Disadvantages
a–No indicator light for normal operation.
b–Ionizer runs without fan on.
c–Has only 1 speed.
d–Inconveniently placed control knob.
e–No pads or legs.
f–Made annoying crackling sound.
g–Slight humming sound on Low.
h–High-pitched buzz at high ozone setting.
i–Made humming, vibrating sound on High.
j–High-pitched whine on High.
k–Tools needed to replace filter; a difficult task.
l–Internal electrical and moving parts can be easily reached from outside by a small finger.

AIR CLEANERS

Key to Comments
- A–Warranty exceptions: **Pollenex**, 90 day; **Trion**, 1 yr. on parts; **Hepanaire**, **Vitaire**, and **Micronaire**, 90 day for parts and labor, remainder for parts only; **Enviracaire**, 2 yr. on parts and labor; **Austin Air Sierra** and **NSA**, 3 yr. on parts and labor.
- B–Has spare prefilter.
- C–Chemically treated filter system.
- D–Has 4-stage filter cartridge.
- E–Electret and charcoal filters in 1 cartridge.
- F–No prefilter.
- G–No postfilter.
- H–No activated carbon or charcoal filter.
- I–No grounded or polarized plug.
- J–Front grille acts as a postfilter.
- K–Fragrance cartridge.
- L–Optional fragrance feature.
- M–Has switch position that lets user dry precipitating cell after washing.
- N–Comes with separate tester that indicates when ions are being produced.
- O–Optional wall-mount kit.
- P–Can be wall mounted.
- Q–Optional casters.
- R–Fan motor must be periodically lubricated.

HOW TO USE THE RATINGS

- Read the article for general guidance about types and buying advice.
- Read the Recommendations for brand-name advice based on our tests.
- Read the Ratings order to see whether products are listed in order of quality, by price, or alphabetically. Most Ratings are based on estimated quality, without regard to price.
- Look to the Ratings table for specifics on the performance and features of individual models.
- A model marked Ⓓ has been discontinued, according to the manufacturer. A model marked Ⓢ indicates that, according to the manufacturer, it has been replaced by a successor model whose performance should be similar to the tested model but whose features may vary.

Cleaning products

Household cleansers 209
Paper towels 210
Handheld vacuums.....................212
Ratings..214

Every cleaning job reduces itself to certain basics: a dirty surface, a kind of grime, a cleanser, and a cleaning implement—sponge, rag, mop, steel wool. For years, marketers have played with those variables to concoct "new and improved" potions and to design innovative implements or, at least, improve tried-and-true ones.

One tack in the never-ending battle for your cleaning dollar is specialization. Specialty cleansers have been formulated for just about every site dirt might infiltrate: bathroom cleaners, glass cleaners, appliance cleaners, floor cleaners, metal cleaners, and so on. Other products have taken precisely the opposite approach. All-purpose cleaners present themselves as broad remedies for whatever soils your home, wherever the soil might be.

Convenience makes a sure-fire appeal for products in this category. Some companies have married cleaner and implement. You can now buy wipes premoistened with window cleaner, to use and toss.

Appliance makers likewise add value to their cleaning machines, hoping to persuade people who already own a machine that they need a new and better one. Case in point: the hand-held vacuum. The little vacs are now into their second decade, and companies are outfitting them with brushes, attachments, and additional cleaning capabilities in hopes you'll trade in the old model for one that cleans floors, carpets, and curtains, and even picks up wet debris.

Nor has the environmental angle been forgotten as a selling technique. Companies have rushed out products that play—or prey—on ecological concerns: paper towels from recycled paper, biodegradable cleansers, cleansers in squeeze-bottles and trigger pumps instead of aerosol cans.

Some environmental products offer real benefits to the planet; for many, though, the case is less clear, overstated, or outright misleading. In any event, the environmental aspects of cleaners are often difficult to weigh. The bottom line for most people remains performance.

HOUSEHOLD CLEANSERS

▶ Ratings start on page 218.

You might think that a strong cleanser is crucial for getting dirt out. The fact is, with enough elbow grease, you can at times get away with using just plain water—on lightly soiled windows, say. Likewise, if you're willing to apply some muscle you can often get by with second-string cleaners, which might be cheaper or otherwise more appealing than the stronger ones.

The choices

All-purpose cleaners. A good all-purpose formula can handle an ambitious roster of cleaning chores—appliances, countertops, stovetops, floors, screens and blinds, vinyl and aluminum siding, whitewall tires—even boats and the family pooch, going by some labels.

The all-purpose products' common denominator: their ability to work full-strength on small areas of concentrated, often greasy dirt, spots, and smudges. All-purpose liquids can be diluted for larger areas, like floors. Many attack grease with pine oil, a liquid chemically similar to turpentine. Others pack ammonia, bleach, or other compounds. Some claim special germicidal protection. At best, they can only reduce populations of some germs in a very limited area for a limited time. (If you need stronger germicidal protection, ask your doctor.)

Bathroom cleaners. Manufacturers would have you believe it takes a special cleaner to combat soils unique to the bath—grungy toilets, mildewed showers, smudged faucets. Not so. Vinegar can cut tough soap scum, one of the most demanding bathroom chores. Against mildew, chlorine laundry bleach works just fine, though some bathroom cleaners do pack antimildew agents. (A few such formulas also work to curb fungi that could form new mildew.) Of course, special packaging—premoistened wipes, aerosols, and pump sprays—can make a bathroom cleaner more convenient to use.

Glass cleaners. Anything that sticks to window panes—garden-variety grime, kitchen grease, dirty handprints, tobacco smoke—must be fair game for a glass cleaner. The cleaner should cut through such soils with little effort to leave windows sparkling and free of streaks. Most commercial products rely on ammonia, a powerhouse of a cleaner. A few use lemon juice or vinegar in their formula, the latter a relatively feeble ingredient.

Dishwashing liquids. While water can remove many soils, it's helpless against fats and oils. That's why dishwashing liquids must pack detergent—to suds up and thereby draw grease into the wash water as

---

CU'S RECIPES FOR WINDOW CLEANING

Our home-brew recipes have proven quite effective. For lightly soiled windows, try our lemon cleaner—4 tablespoons of lemon juice in a gallon of water. It's best for cleaning our greasy hand prints and costs only 0.1 cent a fluid ounce. For heavier soil, try our ammonia recipe—one-half cup sudsy ammonia, one pint rubbing alcohol, and one teaspoon dishwashing liquid with enough water to make one gallon. It cleans up our baked-on soil quite well, and it costs only about a penny a fluid ounce.

a foamy emulsion. The more detergent a dishwashing product contains, the more grease it can neutralize. Some brands have much more detergent than others. Since they tend to be the priciest, it may be cheaper to squeeze out more of a less expensive product into the dishpan.

Dishwasher detergents. Powders and liquid "gels" abound to help your dishwasher do its thing. The gel's principal advantage is that it can be applied directly to tough food soils as pre-treatment prior to going into the machine. Gel also slides easily out of the bottle, yet is thick enough to stay in the machine's dispenser until it's needed.

All dishwasher detergents should help remove gummy food debris from plates and flatware and should leave glasses free of film and spots—even in hard water. Dishwasher detergents generally contain phosphorus, which helps to soften water, disperse dirt, and break up grease. (Even areas that have banned phosphorus in laundry detergents allow it in dishwasher detergent.) There are few phosphate-free products on the market, sometimes sold in health-food stores.

The tests

We craft chores to match soils and surfaces to the cleansers being tested. We try the all-purpose cleaners against a painted surface bearing a black-grease concoction and red crayon and pencil marks, for instance. For bathroom cleaners, we use hardened soap scum and mildew-laden tile and tile grout. Our test for glass cleaners is the toughest we could think up: a brown extract of tobacco smoke and tars baked onto glass panes. To gauge the strength of dishwashing liquids, we whip them into hot water and drop in pellets of fat and flour until the suds finally give out. To determine the best dishwasher detergents we run loads of glassware and plates caked with dried, tenacious hominy grits and other foods.

Buying advice

Don't be swayed by special-purpose cleaners, the prima donnas of the cleaning world. A good all-purpose product can make short work of most household cleaning tasks. Indeed, the best bathroom cleansers we found were not specialty products designed for the bath but all-purpose cleaners. You should consider convenience, however. Sometimes a product's dispenser may be worth the extra cost.

Two cautions: Some cleaning products can mar surfaces if spilled or left on for too long. The Ratings give details from our tests. Further, some cleaners should be used only in well-ventilated areas because their bleach fumes are noxious. Others contain chemicals that are sufficiently strong for us to recommend your wearing rubber gloves while working.

PAPER TOWELS

▸ Ratings on page 217.

Paper towels must be up to tackling lots of different tasks—from scouring an oven to sopping up a spill to cleaning a window without leaving lint. Whatever the chore, the towel should stand up to the job, tear off evenly, leave behind as little lint as possible, and not cost a mint. You might also want to consider environmental impact.

The choices

There are dozens of brands: national products, regional labels, supermarket brands. Some are single-ply sheets; others double. Some, made of recycled paper, claim environmental credentials.

Some brands sell themselves for special purposes, as heavy-duty wipes for the garage or workshop or especially for use in the microwave. One brand, *Scottowels Junior,* comes in rolls three inches narrower than normal. The company will provide a free adapter to fit a standard dispenser.

Some specialization is clearly more marketing fancy than performance-based fact. For instance, we could not find any meaningful difference in the appearance or taste of foods microwaved in those special, costlier "microwave" towels and food cooked in cheaper, plain paper towels.

Heavy-duty shop towels live up to their reputation. In our tests tapping brawn, the shop towels beat the strongest regular towels by a good margin.

Environmentally friendly brands didn't do particularly well in our tests. Most brands these days contain some recycled paper, but the exact amount is often "proprietary information." Some paper towels, mostly small and private-label brands, mention their recycled content on the label, but most major manufacturers don't consider that a strong selling point. It's also hard to know what kind of recycled paper or how much of it a particular towel contains.

The tests

We test strength by stretching towels over an embroidery hoop, wetting them, and pouring on lead shot until the paper gives way. The number of plies didn't consistently predict a towel's strength. We also gauge scrubbing strength with an automatic scrubbing machine, a device that methodically rubs a moist towel back and forth over a textured tile until the towel shreds.

We measure how much water and cooking oil each towel can absorb, and how quickly a towel sops up measured amounts of these liquids.

Paper towels with short, weakly anchored fibers tend to shed lint, a particular problem when you clean a mirror or windowpane. To test for linting, we repeatedly rinsed a glass pane with water and wiped the glass dry with a towel.

Buying advice

Paper towels don't always perform uniformly well across the disparate tasks they're asked to do. A fast-absorbing towel, for instance, may turn out to be a weakling when it comes to scrubbing. Much depends on the quality and composition of fiber used, and compromises abound. Still, we've found two brands—*Bounty* and *Viva*—that perform consistently well in our tests over the years.

But paper towels are cheap enough—most brands still cost less than a penny a sheet—so most people can afford to have two brands on hand, perhaps a cheap store brand for everyday uses and a stronger name brand for the more demanding jobs.

Some brands differ in packaging, price, and even performance from one region to another. Further, some brands offer one- and two-ply versions that performed so differently that we consider them essentially different products. We also discovered that most brands have downsized their roll, giving consumers fewer sheets in the last few years. Some are cutting sheets and raising prices.

Buying paper towels that contain recycled paper can't solve the growing problem of solid waste. Paper towels, no matter how "green," cannot themselves be recycled; eventually, most wind up in the landfills and incinerators. Thus the "greenest" paper towel is no paper towel. Most things a paper towel can do, a cloth or sponge can do as well, with less waste of resources.

Handheld Vacuums

▸ Ratings on page 214.

When it first appeared more than a decade ago, Black & Decker's *Dustbuster* filled a unique need: a minisized vacuum for mini messes. The cordless, rechargeable design let users roam, untethered, wherever grime might lead—from an overturned ashtray in the living room to a fallen flowerpot in the kitchen.

The little appliance caught on. Hand-held vacs now account for one of every three vacuum cleaners sold. The major manufacturers—Black & Decker, Royal, and Hoover—have expanded their lines with a host of attachments and with variations on the hand-vac theme, including car vacs, which run off the power for the cigarette lighter, and cordless wet/dry models.

The choices

The main decision is whether to go cordless or buy a plug-in model. Plug-in units would seem to violate the appliance's free-roaming spirit, but they have some advantages. They run until switched off; most cordless models go only about 10 minutes between overnight stays in their charging stand. That may be enough time for most pickup jobs, but it's frustrating when the vacuum poops out before all the soil has been taken up. A long power cord—some models have a 25-foot cord—makes a plug-in vac almost as convenient as a cordless. Plug-in models also tend to have broader nozzles, for faster and wider coverage. Prices of both kinds overlap, ranging from about $30 to $90.

Plug-in models. Most look like a belt sander and come with a six-inch revolving brush built into their business end. The brush turns like a carpet sweeper to beat grime out of carpeting as the vacuum inhales. It works well on hard flooring, too. But some of the more energetic brushes can add to a mess by flinging coarser soils about.

Cordless models. Their business end typically tapers to a three-inch-wide slot that relies solely on suction for pickup; best for hard, smooth floors, countertops, and the like. Some models can handle wet debris and liquids. At about two pounds, cordless models are a pound or so lighter than the plug-ins.

Car vacs. These resemble smaller cordless models, with plain-suction nozzles—except they include a 15- or 20-foot cord to the cigarette lighter. They run off a car's 12-volt electrical system and can be used for extended periods of time without draining the car battery very much.

Features to look for

The right features can add versatility—or unneeded frills. Here's a rundown:

Conversion attachments. A few cordless models include a power brush to transform their suction-only nozzle into a carpet sweeper, like that standard on most plug-ins. The attachment works well but can drain batteries in no time. Some plug-in models with a built-in revolving brush go the other way—they can convert into suction-only units. Sometimes, making the change is a snap; on other models, a hassle.

Brushes, wands. The brushes with some machines clip over the nozzle for doing rugs and upholstery. A wandlike crevice tool focuses suction into small areas. A broad floor nozzle lets you cover more territory.

Dual speeds. Some vacuums offer a two-speed motor; others have an air valve to cut suction. Less suction can be useful for curtains, blinds, or loose-fitting upholstery.

Dirt compartments. Most cordless units come with an internal dust cup, which holds only a cup or two of debris. Some plug-ins have a similar cup; others use a more capacious cloth bag that takes six or more cups. But bags, often held by elastic bands, can be messy to remove, shake out, and reattach.

Upright handle. To save you from stooping, one model includes a long handle, which converts it into an upright vacuum.

Wet pickup. Wet/dry models are cordless, so there's no shock hazard. You must clean the dirt cup scrupulously, lest its soggy contents turn stagnant. A mop might be easier for spills.

The tests

We spread a variety of soils on hard, wood flooring and on low-pile carpeting. Then we count the number of passes each machine takes to remove the debris. Some soils are granular: sugar, sand, lentil-sized gravel. Others are more tenacious: dog hair and potting soil. We also check edge cleaning—how close to a wall each machine can vacuum.

We measure noise levels, too. Some plug-in models are as noisy as full-sized vacuums.

Buying advice

If you'll use a hand vac strictly for spills and small messes, most machines should work well. With some, you may need many extra passes to pick up soils from carpeting.

If your main use will be on carpeting, the plug-in vacs with revolving brushes were strong performers. They typically bested the cordless suction-only models by two notches or more in carpet cleaning and proved at least as effective on hard flooring. Some plug-ins with a revolving brush can be easily converted to suction-only machines, for doing drapery, say.

The car vacs were mediocre workers. If an electrical outlet is close enough to your auto, a lightweight plug-in model may be a better choice.

How OBJECTIVE IS CU?

Consumers Union is not beholden to any commercial interest. It accepts no advertising and buys all the products tested on the open market. CU's income is derived from the sale of CONSUMER REPORTS and other publications, and from nonrestrictive, noncommercial contributions, grants, and fees. Neither the Ratings nor the reports may be used in advertising or for any other commercial purpose. Consumers Union will take all steps open to it to prevent commercial use of its materials, its name, or the name of CONSUMER REPORTS.

214 HANDHELD VACUUMS

RATINGS HANDHELD VACUUMS

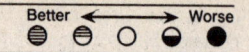

Better ← → Worse
◐ ◑ ○ ◒ ●

▶ **See report, page 212.** From Consumer Reports, July 1992.

Recommendations: The top-rated plug-in—the *Panasonic Jet Flo MC-1060*—combines strong suction with quiet operation and easy emptying. The top-rated cordless, the *Black & Decker DB5400*, delivers decent performance with easy emptying. Among car vacs, the *Black & Decker 9511* stands out.

Ratings order: Listed by types; within types, listed in order of estimated overall quality. Except where separated by bold rules, closely ranked models differed little in overall quality. Models judged about equal in performance are bracketed and listed alphabetically. Price is the manufacturer's suggested retail price or range; + indicates that shipping is extra. Ⓢ indicates tested model has been replaced by successor model; according to the manufacturer, the performance of new model should be substantially similar to the tested model but features may vary. See right for new model number and suggested retail price, if available.

Brand and model	Price	Cleaning carpet	Cleaning smooth surfaces	Blowby	Noise	Emptying dirt	Running time	Dry capacity, cup	Advantages	Disadvantages	Comments
PLUG-IN MODELS											
Panasonic Jet Flo MC-1060	$65	○	◐	◐	◐	◐	—	1¼	A,B,C	—	M,O
Hoover Brush Vac II S1133	60	◐	◐	◐	○	◐	—	1½	A,L	—	M,O
Panasonic Jet Flo MC-1040	38	◐	◐	◐	◐	◐	—	1¼	—	n	M
Eureka Step Saver 53A	35	●	◐	◐	○	◐	—	2	B,E,F	h,n	M
Royal Dirt Devil 513	44-64	○	◐	◐	○	◑	—	6	A,B	a,d,o	A,B,H,J,M,N,O
Sears Klean'n Vac 60071	50+	◐	◐	◐	◑	●	—	11	B,C,D	b,d,h,o	M,O
Sanyo Dustie SC-181	40	○	○	◐	○	◐	—	2	K	k	D,K,N,O
Bissell Featherweight Vac 3103-1	30	○	○	◐	○	◑	—	4	—	a	I,K,N
Hoover Help-Mate S1059-6	45	○	◐	◐	○	◐	—	1¾	—	i,k	L,N,O
Oreck PowerBrush PB-250	89	◐	◐	◐	◑	●	—	11	B,D	b,d,h,o	J,M,O
Douglas ReadiVac R6744	55	◐	◐	◐	◑	◑	—	11	—	b,d,h,o	J,M
Royal Dirt Devil Appliance 103	34-50	◐	◐	◐	○	◑	—	6	—	a,d,o	J,M

HANDHELD VACUUMS 215

Brand and model	Price	Cleaning carpet	Cleaning smooth surfaces	Blowby	Noise	Emptying dirt	Running time	Dry capacity, cup	Advantages	Disadvantages	Comments
Black & Decker DirtVac AC7050 [S]	$58	◐	◉	○	◐	◐	—	11½	B	a,c,f,o	A,B,E,r, H,J,M,N,O
Regina Dirt Magnet DM1800	49	◉	○	●	●	◐	—	8	K	a,c,d,e, g,i,j,o	A,H,M,N,O
CORDLESS MODELS											
Black & Decker Dustbuster Plus DB5400	78	◐	○	◐	◐	◉	11 [1]	2¼	A,G	e	C,E,H,J, L,M,N
Black & Decker Dustbuster Plus 9338A	70	●	○	○	○	◉	15 [1]	1½	G	e,k,m	H,J,M,N
Hoover Dubl Duty S1103 (wet/dry)	50	◐	○	◐	○	◉	6½	2¾	E,J	k,m	—
Black & Decker PowerPro DB6000	72	◐	○	○	○	◉	13½	2¼	A	e,i,k	J,L
Sears Craftsman 17834 (wet/dry)	32+	●	○	●	○	◉	10	4¼	E,I	e,k	G
Black & Decker PowerPro DB2000 (wet/dry)	57	●	○	◐	○	◉	7½	1½	E,I	k	G,J
Black & Decker PowerPro DB3000	57	◐	○	○	○	◉	11½	2¼	A	e,i,k	J
Sanyo Porta Buttler PC-5 [S]	35	●	○	◐	○	◉	7	2¼	H	i,k,m	N
Douglas ReadiVac Pow'r Pac R4030	35	●	○	◐	◐	○	9	1¾	L	k,l,m	J
Black & Decker Dustbuster 9330A	39	●	○	○	○	◉	7½	1¼	—	k,m	J
12-VOLT CAR MODELS											
Black & Decker CarVac Plus 9511	35	◐	○	◐	○	◉	—	1¼	K,L	k	E,J,N,O
Black & Decker CarVac 9509	26	●	○	◐	◐	◉	—	1¼	K,L	k	J
Douglas ReadiVac Autovac R4012	30	◐	○	◐	○	○	—	2	L	k,m	J,N,O

[1] *Power brush cuts battery running time to a minute or two.*

Successor Models (in Ratings order)
Black & Decker DirtVac AC7050 is succeeded by AC7000, $51; Sanyo Porta Buttler PC-5 by PC-5L.

Features in Common
All have: • A plastic housing and washable filter/bag. *All plug-in models:* • Weigh from 1¾ to 4 lb.

All cordless and car vacs: • Have suction-only nozzle about 3 in. wide (exclusive of attachments). • Weigh from 1 to 2½ lb.
Except as noted, all have: • A single-speed motor. • A 1-yr. warranty.
Except as noted, all plug-in models: • Have revolving brushes 5 to 7 in. wide. • Cannot be used as suction-only vacuums.

Ratings Keys continued

HANDHELD VACUUMS

Except as noted, all plug-in and car models have: • A power cord 15 to 20 ft. long.

Key to Advantages
A–Has two motor speeds; gentler setting may be useful for curtains and such.
B–24- or 25-foot power cord, longer than most.
C–Has headlight.
D–Has air-control valve for reducing suction.
E–Has transparent dirt compartment so you can see when it's full. (The **Black & Decker's** tinted compartment is hard to see into.)
F–Opening for rotating brush can swivel upward for stair risers and other vertical surfaces.
G–Accessory power brush (included) was fairly effective and easy to attach.
H–Has charging-indicator light.
I–Wet capacity about 1½ cups.
J–Wet capacity about one cup.
K–Motor housing shaped so power cord winds neatly around it for storage.
L–Cleaned carpeting closer to wall than most.

Key to Disadvantages
a–External dirt bag, somewhat messy to clean.
b–External dirt bag, very messy to clean and difficult to reattach.
c–Test with gravel damaged internal plastic fan.
d–Test with gravel abraded internal parts.
e–May eject grit; wear eye protection.
f–Expelled fine dust through cloth dirt bag.
g–Two of three samples expelled dust through switch recess.
h–Power brush scattered coarse litter more than most.
i–Retaining catch for access to dirt compartment was difficult to release.
j–Handle felt uncomfortable.
k–Nozzle clogged easily in tests with cornflakes.
l–Connector plug disconnects from charging stand every time vacuum is removed, a nuisance.
m–Spring-loaded power switch must be held down to operate vac, a nuisance.
n–Replacing belt for revolving brush more difficult than most.
o–With granular soils, some debris fell out when vacuum was turned off.

Key to Comments
A–Has short (3½-foot) hose.
B–Comes with wand.
C–Comes with ceiling extension for crevice tool.
D–Comes with two wands.
E–Has upholstery brush.
F–Has extra filter cup.
G–Has squeegee for wet pickup.
H–Cleaner attachments can be stored on separate wall bracket (included) or charger cradle.
I–Converts to lightweight upright vacuum with extension handle and broad floor nozzle.
J–Has 2-yr. warranty.
K–Regular nozzle about 3 in. wide, appreciably narrower than on most plug-in models.
L–Wet pick-up kit available for $13.
M–Has revolving brush.
N–Has crevice tool.
O–Has dust brush.

WHAT THE RATINGS MEAN

■ The Ratings typically rank products in order of estimated quality, without regard to price.

■ A product's rating applies only to the model tested and should not be considered a rating of other models sold under the same brand name unless so noted.

■ Models are check-rated (✓) when the product proved to be significantly superior to other models tested.

■ Products high in quality and relatively low in price are deemed Best Buys.

PAPER TOWELS 217

RATINGS | PAPER TOWELS

Better ⊖ ⊖ ○ ⊖ ● Worse

▶ **See report, page 210.** From Consumer Reports, January 1992.

Recommendations: The top-performer—*Job Squad*—may be overkill for any but the toughest jobs. For everyday household spills, look first to any of the top four products but buy by price.

Ratings order: Listed in order of estimated quality. Closely ranked models below *Job Squad* were judged similar in quality. Price is the average price, based on prices paid nationally in late 1991 for a single roll. A * indicates the average price paid by CU.

Product	Plies	Price per roll	Sheets per roll	Cost per 100 sheets	Wet strength	Absorbency	Water absorption	Oil absorption	Tearing ease	Linting	Comments
Job Squad	1	$ .96	45	$2.13	⊖	⊖	⊖	⊖	⊖	⊖	A
Bounty Microwave	2	1.24	80	1.55	⊖	⊖	⊖	⊖	⊖	○	A,H,O
Viva (1-ply)	1	.94	75	1.25	⊖	⊖	⊖	⊖	⊖	○	A
Bounty	2	.92	72	1.28	⊖	⊖	⊖	⊖	⊖	○	A,H,N
Spill Mate	2	.89	100	.89	⊖	●	⊖	⊖	○	○	—
Brawny	2	.82	66	1.24	○	⊖	⊖	⊖	⊖	●	—
Zee	2	.82	90	.91	○	⊖	⊖	⊖	○	○	B,J
Viva (2-ply)	2	.86	77	1.12	○	⊖	⊖	⊖	⊖	⊖	—
Scottowels	1	.83	120	.69	⊖	⊖	⊖	⊖	○	○	B
Safeway	2	.70	100	.70	⊖	⊖	⊖	⊖	○	⊖	—
Start	2	.93	81	1.15	⊖	⊖	⊖	⊖	○	⊖	B,C,D
Scottowels Junior	1	.61	95	.64	○	⊖	○	⊖	⊖	○	B,F
Gala	2	.77	90	.86	⊖	⊖	⊖	⊖	○	○	—
Sparkle	2	.75	90	.83	⊖	⊖	○	⊖	○	○	—
Truly Fine (Safeway)	2	.99*	105	.94	●	⊖	⊖	⊖	⊖	○	—
Mardi Gras	2	.78	100	.78	●	⊖	⊖	⊖	⊖	○	C,H
Marcal	2	.67	100	.67	⊖	⊖	⊖	⊖	○	⊖	C,D,P
Hi-Dri	2	.67	96	.70	⊖	⊖	⊖	⊖	○	⊖	B,C
Green Forest	2	.77	100	.77	●	⊖	⊖	⊖	○	○	C
Pathmark (2-ply)	2	.69	100	.69	●	⊖	⊖	⊖	○	⊖	—
Kroger	2	.57	100	.57	●	⊖	⊖	⊖	○	○	C
Big'N'Thirsty	1	.65	100	.65	⊖	⊖	⊖	⊖	⊖	○	B,K
Seventh Generation	2	1.00*	90	1.11	●	⊖	⊖	⊖	○	⊖	C,E,G,I
So-Dri	2	.58	100	.58	●	⊖	⊖	⊖	○	○	C,H,I
A&P	2	.67	100	.67	●	⊖	⊖	⊖	○	⊖	C,I
Delta	1	.61	100	.61	⊖	●	⊖	●	⊖	○	B
C.A.R.E.	2	.89*	88	1.01	●	⊖	○	⊖	⊖	⊖	D
Pathmark (1-ply)	1	.69	140	.49	●	⊖	●	⊖	⊖	⊖	B

Ratings continued

218 GLASS CLEANERS

Ratings continued

Product	Plies	Price per roll	Sheets per roll	Cost per 100 sheets	Wet strength	Absorbency	Water absorption	Oil absorption	Tearing ease	Linting	Comments
Marigold (Safeway)	1	$.56	90	$.62	◐	◐	●	●	●	○	B
Page	1	.44	75	.59	●	◐	●	●	○	○	B,C,L,M
Cost Cutter (Kroger)	1	.53	75	.71	●	◐	●	●	○	○	B,C

Features in Common
Except as noted, all: • Fit standard dispenser.

Key to Comments
A–Judged softer than most.
B–Judged rougher than most.
C–Made of 100-percent recycled paper.
D–No chlorine bleach used in manufacturing, according to mfr.
E–Unbleached, according to mfr.
F–About 3 in. narrower than most; requires adapter for standard dispenser.
G–Sold by mail order, 30 rolls to a box. For ordering information, call 1-800-456-1177.
H–Wrapper perforated for easier opening.
I–First sheet forms easy-to-grasp pull tab.
J–Samples bought in Washington State judged much slower to absorb oil.
K–Samples bought in Texas judged much slower to absorb water.
L–Samples bought in Maryland judged much more difficult to tear cleanly.
M–Samples bought in Texas produced much more lint.
N–All current single-roll packs will now have 72 sheets, according to mfr.
O–All current single-roll packs will now have 108 sheets, according to mfr.
P–Samples bought in Maryland averaged 67¢ per roll in 3-roll package.

RATINGS GLASS CLEANERS

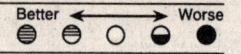

Better ←———→ Worse
● ◐ ○ ◑ ●

▶ See report, page 209. From Consumer Reports, January 1992.

Recommendations: CU's home brews, and even plain water, bested or equalled many store-bought brands. Among commercial products, *K Mart With Ammonia* stood out as the best performer with the best price.

Ratings order: Listed by types. Commercial products are listed in groups in order of ability to clean heavily soiled glass; within groups, listed in order of increasing cost per ounce. For home brews, the price is what we paid for ingredients. For commercial products, the price is the estimated average price for the size we tested, based on prices paid nationally in late 1991. A * indicates the price we paid (a national average price wasn't available). A + indicates an additional shipping charge.

Product	Package [1]	Size, oz. or fl. oz.	Price	Cost per oz. or fl. oz.	Cleaning	Advantages	Disadvantages	Comments
HOME BREWS								
Plain tap water	—	—	—	—	◐	—	—	D
CU's lemon formula	—	128	$ .16	0.1¢	◐	A	b	C
CU's ammonia formula	—	128	1.01	0.8	◐	—	—	—

GLASS CLEANERS

Product	Package [1]	Size, oz. or fl. oz.	Price	Cost per oz. or fl. oz.	Cleaning	Advantages	Disadvantages	Comments
COMMERCIAL PRODUCTS								
K Mart With Ammonia	P	22	$1.56	7¢	◓	—	b	A,L
SOS Extra Strength Ammonia Plus	P	22	2.05	9	◓	—	b	A
Savogran Dirtex	A	18	2.13*	12	◓	—	b	B
Walgreens With Ammonia	P	32	1.69*	5	◓	—	—	—
A&P With Ammonia	P	22	1.62	7	◓	—	b	A
Albertsons With Ammonia	P	22	1.61	7	◓	—	—	A
Lady Lee With Ammonia (Lucky Stores)	P	22	1.49	7	◓	—	—	A
Glass Plus	P	22	2.05	9	◓	—	b	A
K Mart With Ammonia	A	19	1.67	9	◓	—	b	B,F
Windex With Ammonia-D	P	22	2.16	10	◓	—	—	A
Windex With Ammonia-D King Size	A	20	2.27	11	◓	—	—	B
Gold Seal Glass Wax	C	16	1.84	12	◓	—	a,b	G
Scott's Liquid Gold	A	14	1.73	12	◓	—	—	E
Easy Off "Lemonized" With Ammonia	P	22	2.96	13	◓	—	b	A
A&P With Vinegar	P	22	1.19	5	○	—	—	B,H
Kroger Bright With Ammonia+	P	22	1.58	7	○	—	—	A
ClearVue Professional	P	20	1.94	10	○	—	—	B,I,M
Spiffits One Step Towels	T	[2]	2.77	12	○	—	b	A,I
Windex Lemon Fresh with Ammonia-D	P	22	2.19	10	◐	—	—	A,C
Seventh Generation	P	22	4.50+*	20	◐	—	a,b	B,I,M
Sparkle	P	25	2.00	8	●	—	b	A,K
SOS Extra Strength Vinegar	P	22	1.96	9	●	—	—	A,J
Windex Fresh Scent With Vinegar-D	P	22	2.17	10	●	—	b	A,J
Glass Mates Wipes	T	[1]	2.75	14	●	—	b	B,I

[1] P = pump bottle; A = aerosol can; C = pour-can; T = premoistened towel-wipe.

[2] **Spiffits** box holds 24 moist towels; **Glass Mates** canister holds 20 towels. Cost is per towel.

Features in Common
Except as noted, all: • Smell of ammonia.

Key to Advantages
A—Somewhat better than most in cleaning greasy, sooty handprints.

Key to Disadvantages
a—Somewhat worse than most in cleaning greasy, sooty handprints.
b—May stain painted surfaces slightly if spills aren't wiped up quickly.

Key to Comments
A—Easier to use than most, especially for people with hand or arm limitations.
B—Harder to use than most, especially for people with hand or arm limitations.
C—Lemon scent.
D—Odorless.
E—Orange scent.
F—Floral scent.
G—Petroleum odor.
H—Vinegar odor.
I—Alcohol odor.
J—Fruity scent.
K—Solvent odor.
L—Only finger-pump bottle tested; other bottled products sold with trigger pump.
M—**ClearVue** sold mainly in East. **Seventh Generation** sold by mail (1-800-456-1177).
M—**ClearVue** sold mainly in East. **Seventh Generation** sold by mail (1-800-456-1177).

220 DISHWASHER DETERGENTS

RATINGS DISHWASHER DETERGENTS

Better ◀——▶ Worse
⊖ ⊖ ○ ◓ ●

▶ **See report, page 209.** From Consumer Reports, February 1992.

Recommendations: We check-rated *Cascade* powder (the regular-scent version) for admirable cleaning performance at an economical price. *Palmolive Liquid Gel Lemon* was the best of the new gels; its regular-scent version was nearly as good.

Ratings order: Listed by type; within types, listed in order of overall cleaning ability. Price is the estimated average, usually for a 50-ounce container, based on prices paid nationally in late 1991. A * denotes the price we paid (a national average price wasn't available).

Product	Price	Cost per use	Percentage, per label	Grams per use [1]	Phosphorus / Dishes	Cleaning / Glasses, film	Glasses, spots	Comments
POWDERED AND LIQUID DETERGENTS								
✓Cascade	$2.79	12¢	8.1	5	⊖	⊖	⊖	—
Lemon Cascade	2.81	14	8.1	6	⊖	⊖	○	—
Electrasol	2.20	11	7.1	5	⊖	⊖	⊖	—
Kroger Bright	1.91	8	8.7	5	⊖	⊖	⊖	—
Shaklee Basic-D	9.00*	38	8.7	5	⊖	⊖	⊖	B,C,F
A&P Liquid	2.20	14	5.9	5	⊖	⊖	○	A
All	2.16	9	6.1	4	⊖	⊖	⊖	—
Sunlight Lemon	2.82	11	6.1	3	⊖	⊖	⊖	—
White Magic Lemon	2.47	11	8.7	5	⊖	○	○	—
Albertson's Lemon	1.99	8	8.3	5	⊖	⊖	⊖	—
Top Crest	2.15	10	8.7	6	⊖	⊖	⊖	—
Amway Crystal Bright	9.20*	52	8.7	7	⊖	⊖	●	D,F
White Magic	2.42	11	8.7	5	⊖	○	⊖	—
A&P	1.93	9	8.7	6	○	○	⊖	—
A&P Liquid Lemon	2.32	15	5.9	5	○	⊖	◓	A
A&P Lemon	1.89	9	8.7	6	○	◓	○	—
GEL DETERGENTS								
Palmolive Liquid Gel Lemon	2.70*	17	5.8	5	⊖	⊖	⊖	A,F
Palmolive Liquid Gel	2.70*	17	5.8	5	⊖	⊖	⊖	A,F
Cascade LiquiGel	2.80*	18	4.2	4	⊖	⊖	○	E
Cascade LiquiGel Lemon	2.80*	18	4.2	4	⊖	⊖	○	E

[1] *CU's calculation, based on 4 tablespoons of detergent.*

RATINGS: BATHROOM CLEANERS

Better ← ⊖ ⊖ ○ ⊜

▶ See report, page 209. From Consumer Reports, September 1991.

Recommendations: Bathroom cleaners are convenient, and some are very effective on soap scum and mildew. But a good all-purpose cleaner can cost less, clean soap scum as well, and do a better job of inhibiting mildew. Bleach did the best job of removing mildew.

Ratings order: Listed in order of estimated quality, based on cleaning ability and effectiveness at retarding mildew growth. The price is the national average for the size (ounces or fluid ounces) most commonly available. * indicates average price paid by CU shoppers. For towelettes, the size is the number of sheets per box. Dispenser key: **A** = aerosol cans; **P** = pump; **F** = flip-top cap; **S** = screw-cap; **T** = towelettes.

Product	Dispenser	Price/size	Cost per use	Soap scum cleaning	Mildew cleaning	Inhibiting mildew	Surface damage	Comments
Spic and Span Pine [1]	S	$2.82/28	10¢	⊖	⊖	⊖	brass, paint	—
Top Job With Ammonia 2000 [1]	S	2.58/28	9	⊖	⊖	○	brass, paint	—
Woolworth Bathroom	A	1.54*/17	9	⊖	⊖	○	paint	D,G
Easy-Off Instant Mildew Stain Remover	P	2.48/16	16	⊖	⊖	●	brass, paint	B,C,F,G
Clorox Regular Bleach	S	1.25/128	1	⊖	⊖	●	brass, paint	C,G
Earth Rite Tub & Tile	P	2.52/16	16	⊖	○	●	paint	H
Tilex Instant Mildew Stain Remover	P	2.70/16	17	⊖	○	●	brass, paint, steel	B,C,F,G
Descale-It Bathroom Tile and Fixture	P	2.95/16	18	⊖	○	●	brass, paint	G
X-14 Instant Mildew Stain Remover	P	2.76/16	17	⊖	⊖	●	brass, paint, steel	C,F
Eliminate Shower Clean Tub and Tile	P	2.99/16	19	⊖	○	●	brass, paint	G
Dow Bathroom II	P	2.15/17	13	⊖	⊖	●	paint	G
Tough Act Bathroom	P	2.30/17	14	⊖	⊖	●	paint, steel, vinyl	G
Pine Power [1]	S	2.63/28	9	○	⊖	○	paint	—
Ecover Cream [1]	F	3.19/34	9	⊖	⊖	●	brass, paint	—
Fantastik Swipes [1]	T	2.90/24	12	⊖	⊖	●	paint	H
Lime A-Way Bathroom	P	3.34/22	15	⊖	⊖	●	paint	A
Dow Bathroom	A	2.18/17	13	○	⊖	○	paint	—
Lysol Bathroom Touch-Ups	T	2.06/36	6	⊖	●	●	—	H
Lysol Basin Tub & Tile	P	2.13/17	13	⊖	⊖	●	paint, steel	H
Spiffits Bathroom	T	2.85/24	12	○	⊖	○	paint	H,I
Scrub Free Bathroom Lemon Scent	P	2.20/16	14	○	○	●	brass, paint	A,E,H

DISHWASHING LIQUIDS

Features in Common

Except as noted, all: • Powders come in cardboard container. • Liquids and gels come in plastic jug with childproof cap.

Key to Comments

- A–Container has flip-top cap; judged not childproof.
- B–Much less effective when used at lower dose, as suggested on label.
- C–Damaged metallic decoration on china more than most.
- D–Comes in wide-mouth plastic container with screw cap.
- E–Childproof cap fairly hard to open.
- F–**Shaklee** purchased in 47-oz. container; **Amway**, in 48-oz.; **Palmolive** gels, in 65-oz. size.

RATINGS: DISHWASHING LIQUIDS

▶ See report, page 209. From Consumer Reports, September 1991.

Recommendations: The three top-rated products—*Kroger, Sunlight,* and *Ajax*—are good, cheap suds to wash dishes with. Their low usage factor translates into a real cost of less than $2 per quart. Low usage factors indicate the most effective products—those that clean the most dishes per quart.

Ratings order: Listed in order of increasing real cost, as calculated by CU. Price is the average our shoppers paid for 32-ounce bottles (or the closest to that size we could find). The usage factor is the number we derived by testing and statistical analysis to determine how much grease and flour could be added to sudsy water before the suds went away. The lower the factor, the less detergent needed to wash a load of dishes. The real cost is the average price per quart multiplied by the usage factor.

Product	Price	Usage factor	Real cost
Kroger	$1.35	1.0	$1.35
Sunlight	1.82	1.0	1.82
Ajax	1.86	1.0	1.86
A&P	1.42	1.4	1.99
Pathmark	1.49	1.4	2.09
White Magic	2.29	1.0	2.29
Dove	1.69	1.4	2.37
Sweetheart	1.16	2.1	2.44
Crystal White Octagon	1.22 [1]	2.1	2.55

Product	Price	Usage factor	Real cost
Palmolive	$2.56	1.0	$2.56
Dawn	2.70	1.0	2.70
Dermassage	1.49	2.1	3.13
Joy	2.26	1.4	3.16
Ivory	2.46	1.4	3.44
Lux	1.73 [2]	2.1	3.63
Cost Cutter (Kroger)	.78	4.7	3.67
No-Frills (Pathmark)	.79	4.7	3.71
Amway Dish Drops	6.80	0.8	5.44

[1] *Price calculated from 40-oz. size.*

[2] *Price calculated from 22-oz. size.*

BATHROOM CLEANERS

Product	Dispenser	Price/size	Cost per use	Soap scum cleaning	Mildew cleaning	Inhibiting mildew	Surface damage	Comments
K Mart Bathroom	A	$1.66*/17	10¢	○	◐	●	paint	G
Lysol Basin Tub & Tile	A	2.19/17	13	○	◐	●	paint	—
A&P No-Scrub Bathroom	P	1.87/22	9	◐	○	●	brass, paint, steel	A,E,H
Pine Sol Spruce-Ups Lemon Scent [1]	T	2.46/22	11	◐	◐	●	—	H

NOT ACCEPTABLE

■ *The following product was judged Not Acceptable because some containers bought for testing leaked or became swollen within a few months.*

| Tile Plus Instant Mildew Stain Remover | P | 2.11/20 | 11 | ⊜ | ○ | ● | brass, paint | B,C,F,H |

[1] *All-purpose cleaner.*

Key to Comments
A–Strongly acidic; avoid contact with skin. Gloves advised.
B–Strongly alkaline; avoid contact with skin. Gloves advised.
C–Contains bleach; avoid contact with bath mats, rugs, and fabrics.
D–Label warns of extreme flammability and several other hazards.
E–Severe eye irritant, label warns.
F–Not recommended for people with heart or respiratory problems, label warns.
G–Tested container harder to use than some for people with limited hand/arm function.
H–Tested container much easier to use than most for people with limited hand or arm function.
I–Left streaks after cleaning.

How to Use the Ratings

■ Read the article for general guidance about types and buying advice.

■ Read the Recommendations for brand-name advice based on our tests.

■ Read the Ratings order to see whether products are listed in order of quality, by price, or alphabetically. Most Ratings are based on estimated quality, without regard to price.

■ Look to the Ratings table for specifics on the performance and features of individual models.

■ A model marked Ⓓ has been discontinued, according to the manufacturer. A model marked Ⓢ indicates that, according to the manufacturer, it has been replaced by a successor model whose performance should be similar to the tested model but whose features may vary.

PAINTS

Paints & stains 224
Paint removers 230
Ratings 232

Homeowners who balk at repairing a leaky faucet or electrical switch may not think twice about taking a paint brush in hand. But it takes more than enthusiasm to do a good job. You need to choose the right paint, stain, or other finish appropriate for the task. Increasingly, those finishes are water-based formulations rather than messier and environmentally harsher oil-based products.

Surface preparation is critical. To ensure that the new finish will adhere properly, the surface should be clean and smooth. Sometimes that requires stripping caked-on layers of old paint or varnish. Such work is laborious, especially when it requires more than scraping off bits of loose paint. The job can also be hazardous: Paint-stripping techniques commonly involve extreme heat, toxic chemicals, or abrasive tools; and old paint itself often contains lead. But if you spend the extra effort in preparation—scraping, sanding, and washing—you'll improve your chances for long-lasting results.

PAINTS & STAINS

▸ Ratings on page 232.

Paint is the most common way to spiff up a surface. All paints contain pigments (the color), resins (to hold the pigment), and solvents (liquids in which the other components are suspended or dissolved).

Stain, which soaks into wood rather than lying on top of it, is more subtle than paint. When used outdoors, it tends to peel less than paint because it forms less of a film.

Clear finishes such as varnishes protect wood without hiding it at all. Varnish, however, doesn't stand up all that well to sunlight. For more information on what covering suits which surfaces, indoors and

PAINTS & STAINS

out, see pages 226 and 227. Here are the main types:

Latex paint. The resin in latex paint consists of tiny plastic particles suspended in a solvent that's mostly water. Latex paint dries as the water evaporates, leaving a mesh of particles somewhat permeable to air and water.

The water-based chemistry that makes latex paint so easy to brush on and clean up can affect its durability. Latex paint is somewhat more vulnerable to damage from water than oil-based paint and can mar more easily. Latex paints, especially glossier ones, also tend to remain tacky long after they're dry, a problem known as "blocking." That's what causes books to stick to shelving and a window to bond to a window sill.

Alkyd paint. A compound of alcohol and organic acid, usually mixed with vegetable oil and dissolved in petroleum solvents, alkyds are a bit more difficult to handle than latexes. The brush often drags and leaves drips and sags, and paint thinner is required for cleanup.

Alkyd paint dries by oxidation, combining with oxygen from the air to form a watertight skin of hardened resin. The initial hardening process happens over several days but the process may go on for years. Unlike latex paints, alkyds must be applied to a water-free surface to adhere well.

While latex paints are easier to use, alkyds remain unsurpassed when you want smoothness, toughness, a high shine, and water resistance. Alkyds make sense for kitchens and bathrooms and working surfaces such as bookshelves. Alkyd paints also adhere better to weathered exterior surfaces, especially heavily "chalked" ones.

Exterior stain. Stain comes in latex, combination oil-acrylic, or oil-alkyd formulations. Stain contains the same components as paint—solvent, resin, and usually pigment—but in differing amounts. Transparent stain contains only small amounts of pigment; semitransparent stain contains more; and opaque stain, which is close to paint in formulation, more still. As a result, opaque stain can behave more like paint, including, under the right conditions, peeling. Transparent and semitransparent stain provide less surface film and less pigment, so color fades more quickly than it would with paint.

Latex stains go on as easily as latex paints, and they weather well. Oil-based stains weather poorly, and because they're so thin, they tend to spatter and drip when applied.

Interior stain. Oil stain represents the most common type. Most contain "drying oils," such as linseed oil, which seal wood surfaces to an extent. Gel stains are thicker than liquid stains and they won't run on vertical surfaces. Water stains, formulated by mixing powder with water, are highly transparent soluble dyes. They're cheaper than other types of stains, but take considerably longer to dry and don't seal wood. "Spirit" stains are solutions of dyes in strong organic solvents. Like water stains, they're transparent enough to let the wood grain show through in detail, and they won't raise wood grain (water tends to penetrate the wood, raising the tiny fibers in the process).

Clear wood finishes. Finishes such as varnish, lacquer, and penetrating oil seal and protect without hiding the natural beauty of wood grain.

Varnish is essentially paint without pigment, a blend of oils and resins that coats the surface of the wood. The polyurethane so widely used on floors is merely one type of oil-based varnish. Water-based varnishes, which clean up with soap and water, are also available. Either type comes in several gloss levels.

Lacquer is a cellulose derived resin that's dissolved in strong solvents. As the solvents evaporate, the lacquer dries to form a thin, tough film. Another clear finish, penetrating oil, protects wood by soaking into the pores. It doesn't leave a surface coating, as varnish and lacquer do. As a result, penetrating oil doesn't shield wood from abrasion. It's not the optimal choice for floors or furniture subject to heavy use. But it leaves wood with a low luster.

Environmental aspects

The solvents used in paints and other finishes include hydrocarbons and other volatile organic compounds. As the finish dries, those solvents evaporate. Some react with other gases in the presence of sunlight to produce ozone, a component of smog. Both oil- and water-based finishes contain such solvents, but water-based products contain a lot less. As a result, latex products pollute less.

The sale of oil-based paint has been severely restricted in some states, notably California. In response to widening restrictions, manufacturers are reformulating or, in some instances, eliminating oil-based paint from their product lines.

Until recently, most latex paints contained mercury compounds as bacteria-fighting agents. In poorly ventilated rooms, mercury vapor escaping from drying paint could build up to high levels, posing a health hazard. The Government banned

MATCHING EXTERIOR SURFACE TO FINISH

	Latex house	Alkyd house	Wood stain	Trim paint	Porch/deck paint	Cement powder paint	Polyurethane	Aluminum paint	Water-repellant preservative
WOOD									
Clapboard	✔	✔						✔	
Natural siding/trim			✔	✔			✔		
Shutters/trim	✔	✔		✔					
Window frames	✔	✔						✔	
Porch floor/deck					✔				✔
Shingle roof			✔						✔
MASONRY									
Brick	✔	✔				✔		✔	✔
Cement/cinder block	✔	✔				✔		✔	
Porches and floors	✔				✔				
Stucco	✔	✔				✔		✔	
METAL									
Aluminum windows	✔	✔		✔				✔	
Steel windows	✔	✔		✔				✔	
Metal siding	✔	✔		✔				✔	
Copper surfaces							✔		
Galvanized surfaces	✔	✔		✔				✔	
Iron surfaces	✔	✔		✔				✔	

Source: U.S. General Services Administration

mercury from use in interior latex paint in mid-1990; outdoor paint containing mercury must be labeled that it is exclusively for exterior use.

Lead, once widely used in paint pigments and to help oil-based paint dry, was severely restricted in paint made after 1971. But old paint on walls and woodwork may contain lead, and great care must be taken to avoid exposure to lead dust.

Choosing a finish

Here's what to look for:

Interior paint. The range of colors stretches the imagination of copywriters as well as the talents of paint formulators. Gold can be "Warm Sand," blue "Desert Sky," and pink "Heathermist." Even white has its variations: "Cameo," "Navajo," or "Bone." Gloss levels are also variously described, since no standard definitions exist. One brand's "satin" may gleam like another brand's "flat." For a reliable guide to gloss, see our assessment in the Ratings.

Because of their sheen, interior semi-glosses are popular for woodwork—moldings, baseboards, doors, and window frames. And because glossier paint tends to resist dirt and endure scrubbing, it's often the choice for surfaces that need to be cleaned a lot. Flat paint is primarily applied to ceilings and walls.

MATCHING INTERIOR SURFACE TO FINISH

	Latex, flat	Latex, gloss	Alkyd	Varnish	Shellac	Polyurethane	Stain	Floor varnish	Floor paint	Aluminum paint
WOOD										
Floors					✔	✔	✔	✔	✔	
Paneling	✔	✔	✔	✔	✔	✔	✔			
Stair risers		✔	✔	✔	✔	✔	✔			
Stair treads					✔	✔	✔	✔	✔	
Trim/furniture	✔	✔	✔	✔	✔	✔	✔			
MASONRY										
Concrete floors	✔								✔	
Kitchen/bath walls		✔	✔							
New masonry	✔	✔	✔							
Old masonry	✔	✔	✔							✔
Plaster	✔	✔	✔							
Wall board	✔	✔	✔							
METAL										
Aluminum windows	✔	✔								✔
Steel windows	✔	✔	✔							✔
Radiators/pipes	✔		✔							✔

Note: Unless surface has been previously finished, primer or sealer may be required. Consult manufacturer's instructions.

Exterior paints. What to choose for already painted exterior surfaces usually depends on the paint that's already there on the exterior surface. We recommend the same type you used last time—oil over oil, latex over latex. That way, mechanical stresses in the combined film that can lead to blistering and peeling are reduced. For bare wood, we recommend latex over an oil-based primer.

Siding colors tend to be conservative white or subdued pastels, while trim hues are rich and bold. Exterior latex and alkyd paints are formulated to withstand strong sunlight and the weather; most also combat mildew, though latexes usually do better. (Mildew, a fungal deposit that can accumulate on surfaces, particularly in hot, humid conditions, is primarily found on the north, shady side of a structure. It washes off with a solution of bleach and water.)

A white paint that "chalks" continually sloughs off dirt along with the chalky powder, so it appears fresh and clean longer. A dark hue, on the other hand, masks the buildup of dirt. Drying speed, surface stickiness, and smoothness of the dried coating also affect how a paint resists dirt.

Rust-protecting paint. Oil-based products are best because they're tougher and more water resistant than latex paints. Most rust-protecting paint contains rust-inhibiting compounds, but if the surface is prepped correctly, you don't need special products. Grind or sand off all existing rust down to bright metal, prime it, and you can use almost any paint for the top coat. Resist the temptation to try a can of spray enamel. Brushed-on coats are thicker, sturdier, and cover better.

Basement-waterproofing paint. If your basement suffers dampness or mild seepage, a paint might help. Don't count on any paint to halt outright leakage. Even the best basement-waterproofing paints we've tested allow a small amount of water to seep through. The type most resistant to water are oil-based epoxies—expensive, strong-smelling coatings that harden through a chemical reaction between a resin and a catalyst. The epoxy must be mixed in precise proportions and applied promptly to a dry surface.

Next best is oil-based paint specially formulated for use on masonry. Like epoxy, it must be applied to dry walls or it won't adhere. Cement-based powder and water-based paint are also available, but they're not as effective, we've found.

Exterior stain. Color selection is less varied with stains than with paints. Grays, browns, and redwood are the popular colors. Stains rely on absorption into the wood. And if a stain can't soak in, it may not cover well, wear prematurely, and not even stick. Many manufacturers advise against using stain on a painted or otherwise sealed surface. On weathered wood, any stain—latex or oil-based—should have the advantage over paint, which may adhere poorly.

Interior stain. There are limitations to what you can reasonably expect from an interior wood stain. You can't take a raw piece of pine or fir, apply a stain labeled "mahogany" or "walnut," and expect the wood to look like real mahogany or walnut. It may come close, but that's about the best you can hope for.

The most common way to apply stain is to brush it on, let it penetrate the wood, then wipe off the excess—a process open to much individual judgment and error. Wipe too soon, and you may remove more color than you intended. Wait too long, and you may not be able to wipe off the dried excess stain evenly.

Oil stains and oil-based gels are particularly suited for inexperienced hands. They're relatively simple to use, and their colors are easier to control than those of water-based and spirit stain.

Clear wood finishes. With any clear

finish, it's best to apply several thin coats. Trying to do the job with only one or even two heavier coats may result in sagging, wrinkling, or missed spots. Lacquer is the trickiest type of clear finish to apply because it dries quickly and because the second coat dissolves the previous one.

The tests

We judge paint and stain after exposing them to typical conditions. Samples of outdoor paint, for example, are applied to test panels and left outside for many months. We apply rust-protecting paint to metal, then expose it to conditions that promote rusting, such as water and salt fog. We test basement paint by applying it to concrete blocks, then forcing water through the blocks' cavities to gauge how much seeps through the coating.

We evaluate each product for its workability—factors such as brushing ease, leveling (smoothness of the dried coating), and resistance to sagging (dripping) and blocking (residual tackiness). Such properties tend to remain consistent for every color in the brand.

For interior paint, we check how well it resists staining, water, and spattering. We measure gloss levels with an instrument called a glossmeter.

We also test stain and paint for properties dependent on color, such as hiding ability, using a standard chart with stripes of varying intensities of gray. (The chart, invented by CU, is now increasingly used in the industry.) The darker the stripe covered by one coat, the greater its hiding power.

Buying advice

Choose a finish that's compatible with the surface and make sure that surface is clean and smooth. In general, you're better off selecting products from the high end of the brand lines. Over the years, we've learned that bargain paints almost always

STEPS TO A PERFECT PAINT JOB

■ Prime new wood or metal.

■ Clean all surfaces. Use detergent such as trisodium phosphate to remove grease, dirt, grime, or chalk. A solution of chlorine bleach will kill mildew. (Be careful about using bleach with other cleaners—many mixtures can cause hazardous fumes.) Outdoors, a power washer will dislodge flaking or blistered paint along with dirt and chalk.

■ Remove loose paint. Use a paint scraper, wire brush, rasp, or sandpaper. For larger areas, consider a power sander, but only if you're sure the paint is lead-free. If you scrape down to wood, apply a primer.

■ Patch holes in plaster or wallboard with plaster or spackling compound. Sand lightly until smooth.

■ Block rust and water. Remove rust down to bare shiny metal. Cover nail heads that could rust with wood filler and primer. Apply sealer over knots so they don't bleed. Caulk cracks and other sources of moisture penetration.

■ Rough up glossy paint. Use sandpaper or a liquid deglosser.

■ Dress appropriately. Wear goggles and a dust mask when removing paint. Wear rubber gloves for protection against chemical detergents and solvents. Clean up thoroughly. Dust is especially a hazard to children.

■ Use the right tools. Brushes are best for exterior painting, especially on textured surfaces or shingles. Use a natural-bristle brush with alkyd paints, synthetic bristles with latexes. Natural bristles absorb the water in latex paints and become limp and heavy. Use rollers on interior walls and ceilings.

fall down in important qualities such as hiding power and washability.

Prices for indoor and outdoor paints range from $10 to $30 a gallon. Latexes tend to be cheaper than alkyd paints and flat-finish paints cheaper than glossy ones. Stains are priced similarly.

The color you choose affects how much you'll have to buy. Blacks, browns, blues, and greens generally hide quite well in one coat. It's likely to take more applications of a fire-engine red or lemon yellow to cover completely because paint-makers often skimp on costly bright red and yellow pigments. With those and other colors, plan on at least two coats if you're making a substantial color change.

Claims of one-coat hiding assume that you'll spread the paint or stain thickly, typically around 450 square feet per gallon. That's easier to do with a brush than a roller. We've found that with normal rolling, a gallon typically covers 650 square feet, which may offer a film too thin for adequate hiding.

Any finish exposed to bright sunlight is apt to fade somewhat. Among exterior paint, alkyds tend to whiten (and white alkyds to yellow when shaded from the sun). Reds and yellows typically fade the most for the same reason that they don't hide as well as other colors—lightfast red and yellow pigments are quite expensive and are not generally found in house paints. Among exterior stain, oil-based colors tend to fade more than latex.

Paint Removers

▸ Ratings on page 238.

When a finish is severely cracked or peeling, the only way to prevent further deterioration is to take it down to the bare surface. Though the task can be taxing, time-consuming, and sometimes hazardous, it's the basis for a lasting and professional-looking paint job.

The choices

A trip down the aisles of any home center will reveal plenty of gadgets and chemical concoctions to make the job easier. All work in one of three ways: with heat, chemicals, or mechanical force.

Heat guns cause paint to blister and bubble, making it easy to scrape. (Some folks use a propane torch, but we don't advise it because of the fire hazard.)

Chemical strippers, sold as liquids, pastes, or gels, soften and dissolve the old finish so you can scrape or peel it off. The gels and pastes are more effective on vertical surfaces, where liquids tend to run. The products also vary in toxicity. Some are far safer than others.

Abrasive tools, such as shave hooks, power sanders, and gadgets that attach to a drill, rub old paint away. Because they can scratch, these tools are not appropriate for smooth or delicate surfaces. For that reason, chemicals and heat guns are more popular for interior woodwork such as furniture, doors, and moldings.

The hazards

Some chemical paint removers are made with volatile solvents—methanol (wood alcohol), toluene, and acetone. Most are highly flammable, and their vapors can cause headaches, and after prolonged exposure, nerve damage. The solvents contribute to smog as well.

Products made with methylene chloride pose even more insidious risks. A mainstay of paint-removal products for years, methylene chloride can dissolve a variety of tough finishes, including polyurethane and epoxy. However, exposure to its fumes can lead to kidney disease, an irregular heartbeat, and even heart attack. In addition, Federal regulatory agencies have branded it a possible human carcinogen.

Any solvent-based stripper, whether it relies on methylene chloride or other volatile compounds, can be dangerous to use indoors, even with a window open. You'll need to wear neoprene gloves, protective goggles, and a respirator. If you can't work outdoors, use an exhaust fan to ensure good ventilation. Because of such hazards, less onerous chemical strippers have emerged in recent years. The products are safer to breathe, almost odor-free, and less likely to irritate skin. But they take longer to work.

Heat guns pose risks, too. The temperature of the air spewed out of the devices typically ranges from 640° to 875°F, hot enough to sear skin or start a fire. You can also get a nasty burn from the metal nozzle.

Those dangers are especially worrisome if you're working near a child or curious pet. To cut the risk when you've stopped work, some models expedite cooling with a setting that runs the blower with little or no heat. It's an essential feature, in our view.

If you're stripping lead paint, there's another hazard. Any paint dust whipped into the air can be inhaled. When the dust settles, it can still be hazardous to children. Lead paints were used in the U.S. as recently as 1970. If you're removing lead paint, use a safe chemical stripper rather than a heat gun or a method that creates dust.

Performance

Solvent strippers work fast, but leave a sticky film that you may need to remove with mineral spirits. They can remove several coats of paint in two or three hours. The nonvolatile types have to sit several hours or overnight to do as well. Some tend to dry out after several hours. *Peel-Away* products come with a patented cover sheet that keeps the remover moist while it works. You can boost the potency of the other nonvolatile strippers the same way, by covering the stripper with plastic food wrap. After light scraping, gentle scrubbing with a wet sponge or rag removes any residue.

A heat gun is the fastest method. And unlike chemicals, heat guns rarely have to go over the same area twice. Once the hot paint separates from the underlying surface, you can peel it off easily. But a gun can be frustrating when the paint film is very

LEAD-TESTING KITS

We examined two kits that address the need for quick reliable home lead testing, especially in paint. While the readings they give aren't very precise, they reveal whether the paint you're testing contains some lead. (The kits aren't suitable for testing dishware as neither one can tell you how much lead is present. Nor are they sensitive to low levels of lead, so an item that tests negative may not be completely safe.)

Leadcheck Swabs (800-262-LEAD), $17 for 8 tests. It's the easier of the two to use, and it gives results within a minute.

The *Frandon Lead Alert Kit* (800-359-9000), $19.95 for 40 tests. It's somewhat more difficult to use and requires as long as 30 minutes to give results.

If any paint is 20 years old, assume lead is present, and proceed with cautions (see story).

Both kits have been revamped since our tests. Even without retesting, we think the kits are worthwhile and should produce results comparable to the tested ones.

PAINT REMOVERS

thin. Nor will it remove clear finishes. It's also ineffective on painted metal.

The tests

We judge paint-removal methods first on safety, then performance, stripping caked-on layers of paint and varnish from old wooden doors. For chemical-removal methods, we evaluate toxicity, alkalinity, flammability, and tendency to mar wood and metals. For heat guns, we note how close to the painted surface our technicians have to hold the nozzle. We consider handle comfort, overall balance, and length of cool-down.

Buying advice

In general, method makes little difference in the appearance of the results. That makes safety paramount.

Solvent-based strippers, particularly those containing methylene chloride, pose serious health hazards when used indoors. Even with windows open and an exhaust fan, you should still protect your eyes and hands and wear a respirator. Better yet, use solvent products outside.

For immovable items, try one of the less toxic chemicals or a heat gun. Heat guns are faster than chemicals but require careful handling and they shouldn't be used on lead paint. Look for a gun that has a rapid cool-down setting.

Nonsolvent removers typically cost from $20 to $43 a gallon; solvent types, $20 to $27 a gallon. Solvent strippers go farther because a thinner coat goes on and reapplication may not be necessary. Heat guns are inexpensive to use after the initial expense.

RATINGS — INTERIOR LATEX PAINTS: BRAND-RELATED PROPERTIES

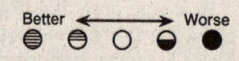

Better ← → Worse

▶ See report, page 224; Ratings of color-related properties, 234. From Consumer Reports, May 1991.

Recommendations: *Pratt & Lambert Accolade* ($31 a gallon) came closest to excellence; we check-rated it for its high quality. Had we judged each color individually, *Accolade* would have been top-rated for all colors except green. Next best overall were *Benjamin Moore Regal Aquapearl* and *Regal Aquavelvet, Pittsburgh Manor Hall Eggshell,* and *Sears Best Easy Living Flat 9500.* The *Sears 9500* had the best green. At $19 a gallon, we rated it A Best Buy.

Ratings order: Listed by groups in order of estimated quality, based on brand- and color-related properties. Within groups, listed alphabetically. Price is the manufacturer's suggested retail, per gallon, rounded to the nearest dollar. Prices marked with * are the average CU paid. Prices marked with ** indicate price for white only; price of colors varies. Substantial discounts are often available. Gloss: **F** = flat; **LL** = low luster; **S** = satin.

Brand and model	Price	Gloss	Stain removal	Scrubbing	Spatter	Blocking	Water resistance
✔ Pratt & Lambert Accolade	$31	LL	◕	◕	◕	◕	○
Benjamin Moore Regal Aquapearl	23**	S	◕	◕	○	◕	○
Benjamin Moore Regal Aquavelvet	23**	LL	◕	◕	◕	◕	●

INTERIOR LATEX PAINTS

Rating symbols: ● = filled, ◐ = half-filled top, ◑ = half-filled bottom, ○ = empty, ⊜ = striped

Brand and model	Price	Gloss	Stain removal	Scrubbing	Spatter	Blocking	Water resistance
Pittsburgh Manor Hall Eggshell	$29	LL	⊜	⊜	○	⊜	⊜
Sears Best Easy Living Flat 9500, A Best Buy	19	F	⊜	⊜	⊜	⊜	●
Devoe Regency 25XX	27*	F	⊜	⊜	⊜	●	◐
Devoe Wonder-Tones Eggshell 34XX	23*	LL	⊜	⊜	⊜	●	⊜
Dutch Boy Super Satin	22	F	⊜	⊜	●	⊜	⊜
Enterprise One & Only Low Lustre	22	F	⊜	⊜	⊜	◐	⊜
Fuller O'Brien Liquid Lustre Eggshell 604	27	F	⊜	⊜	⊜	⊜	◐
Glidden Spred Lo-Lustre 3100	17	S	⊜	⊜	⊜	⊜	⊜
Glidden Spred Ultra Eggshell 4100	22	LL	⊜	⊜	⊜	●	○
Glidden Spred Ultra Flat 4000	20	F	⊜	⊜	⊜	⊜	○
Kelly Moore Acry-Plex Flat 555	23	F	⊜	⊜	○	⊜	○
Kelly Moore Sat-N-Sheen Flat 1610	21	LL	⊜	⊜	○	●	⊜
Pittsburgh Wallhide Flat	22	F	⊜	⊜	⊜	⊜	○
Pratt & Lambert Aqua Satin	30	S	⊜	⊜	⊜	⊜	◐
Pratt & Lambert Vapex Flat	30	F	◐	○	⊜	⊜	●
Sears Best Easy Living Satin 9300	20	LL	⊜	◑	⊜	⊜	●
Sears Easy Living Flat 9700	12	F	⊜	○	⊜	⊜	●
Sherwin-Williams Superpaint Flat	18*	F	◐	○	⊜	⊜	○
Sherwin-Williams Superpaint Satin	19*	F	◐	○	⊜	⊜	○
Tru-Test Supreme E-Z Kare Flat EZ	21	LL	⊜	⊜	⊜	⊜	○
Tru-Test Supreme E-Z Kare Flat EZF	16	F	⊜	○	⊜	⊜	○
Tru-Test Ultra Satin [1]	27	S	⊜	⊜	⊜	●	○
Devoe Wonder-Tones Flat 36XX	22*	F	◐	◐	⊜	⊜	◐
Dutch Boy Dirt Fighter Flat	20	F	◐	[2]	⊜	⊜	◐
Fuller O'Brien Liquid Velvet Flat 602	22	F	◐	⊜	◐	⊜	●
Glidden Spred Satin 3400	17	F	⊜	⊜	◐	⊜	○
Sears Easy Living Satin 9600	16	LL	⊜	⊜	⊜	●	◐
Sherwin-Williams Classic 99	13*	F	◐	⊜	◐	⊜	○
Standard Brands Decade Flat	13	F	◐	◐	⊜	⊜	○
Standard Brands Premium Flat	17	LL	⊜	◐	⊜	⊜	●
Standard Brands Satin	13	S	●	⊜	⊜	●	⊜
Valspar Our Best Quality Acrylic Flat 914	20	F	◐	○	⊜	⊜	●
Wards Great Coat 15 Flat	14	F	◐	⊜	◐	⊜	○
Colony Flat	13	F	●	◐	●	⊜	◐
Dutch Boy Super Kem-Tone Flat	13	F	◑	●	⊜	⊜	◐
Glidden Spred Wall Flat 3200	12	F	●	●	○	⊜	●
Wards Great Coat Satin 10	13	LL	⊜	⊜	●	⊜	◐

[1] New formulation now in stores.
[2] Too variable to rate.

Turn page for Ratings of color-related properties

RATINGS | INTERIOR LATEX PAINTS: COLOR-RELATED PROPERTIES

▶ See report, page 224; Ratings of brand-related properties, 232. From Consumer Reports, May 1991.

Ratings order: Listed by groups in order of estimated quality, based on brand- and color-related properties. Within groups, listed alphabetically. The colors given in the column headings are CU's generic labels; they may be designated on the paint cans by different (and more exotic) names. A ⊖ in hiding means the paint should cover almost any previous

Brand and model	White Hiding, 1 coat	White Hiding, 2 coats	White Fading	Gold Hiding, 1 coat	Gold Hiding, 2 coats	Gold Fading	Pink Hiding, 1 coat	Pink Hiding, 2 coats	Pink Fading
✔Pratt & Lambert Accolade	●	⊖	⊖	⊖	⊖	⊖	●	⊖	⊖
Benjamin Moore Regal Aquapearl [1]	●	⊖	⊖	●	⊖	⊖	⊖	⊖	⊖
Benjamin Moore Regal Aquavelvet [1][2]	●	○	⊖	●	⊖	⊖	⊖	⊖	⊖
Pittsburgh Manor Hall Eggshell	⊖	⊖	⊖	●	⊖	⊖	○	⊖	⊖
Sears Best Easy Living Flat 9500, A Best Buy [2]	⊖	⊖	⊖	○	⊖	⊖	⊖	⊖	⊖
Devoe Regency 25XX [3]	●	⊖	⊖	○	⊖	⊖	●	⊖	⊖
Devoe Wonder-Tones Eggshell 34XX	●	○	⊖	●	⊖	⊖	●	○	⊖
Dutch Boy Super Satin [2][4]	●	○	⊖	●	⊖	⊖	⊖	⊖	⊖
Enterprise One & Only Low Lustre	⊖	⊖	⊖	○	⊖	⊖	●	⊖	⊖
Fuller O'Brien Liquid Lustre Eggshell 604 [1]	●	⊖	⊖	●	⊖	⊖	⊖	⊖	⊖
Glidden Spred Lo-Lustre 3100	●	●	⊖	●	⊖	⊖	●	●	⊖
Glidden Spred Ultra Eggshell 4100 [3][5]	●	○	⊖	●	⊖	○	⊖	⊖	⊖
Glidden Spred Ultra Flat 4000 [3][5]	●	⊖	⊖	●	⊖	○	⊖	⊖	⊖
Kelly Moore Acry-Plex Flat 555 [1][3]	●	⊖	⊖	●	⊖	⊖	⊖	⊖	⊖
Kelly Moore Sat-N-Sheen Flat 1610 [1][3][6]	●	⊖	⊖	○	⊖	⊖	⊖	⊖	⊖
Pittsburgh Wallhide Flat	●	○	⊖	⊖	⊖	⊖	●	○	⊖

[1] Yellow tended to change color when scrubbed with scouring powder.
[2] White grayer than most.
[3] White whiter than most.

INTERIOR LATEX PAINTS

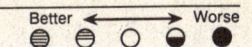

Better ← → Worse

color in one coat. A ⊖ means the paint should cover in one coat if the old color doesn't contrast sharply with the next. Paints judged ○ should cover a similar color in one coat and a darker color in two. Paints judged ◐ and ● will require at least two coats to cover a similar color. Dashes mean a suitable color wasn't available.

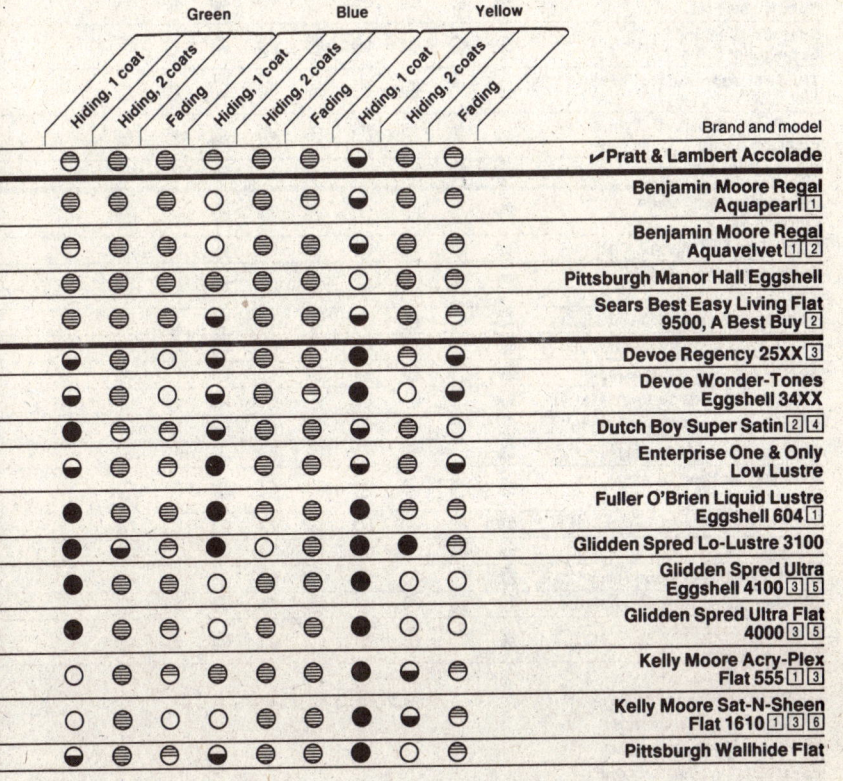

Green: Hiding 1 coat	Green: Hiding 2 coats	Green: Fading	Blue: Hiding 1 coat	Blue: Hiding 2 coats	Blue: Fading	Yellow: Hiding 1 coat	Yellow: Hiding 2 coats	Yellow: Fading	Brand and model
⊖	⊖	⊖	⊖	⊖	⊖	◐	⊖	⊖	✔ **Pratt & Lambert Accolade**
⊖	⊖	⊖	○	⊖	⊖	⊖	⊖	⊖	**Benjamin Moore Regal Aquapearl** [1]
⊖	⊖	⊖	○	⊖	⊖	◐	⊖	⊖	**Benjamin Moore Regal Aquavelvet** [1][2]
⊖	⊖	⊖	⊖	⊖	○	⊖	⊖	⊖	**Pittsburgh Manor Hall Eggshell**
⊖	⊖	⊖	◐	⊖	⊖	⊖	⊖	⊖	**Sears Best Easy Living Flat 9500, A Best Buy** [2]
◐	⊖	○	⊖	⊖	⊖	⊖	⊖	◐	**Devoe Regency 25XX** [3]
◐	⊖	○	◐	⊖	⊖	●	○	⊖	**Devoe Wonder-Tones Eggshell 34XX**
●	⊖	⊖	⊖	⊖	⊖	⊖	⊖	○	**Dutch Boy Super Satin** [2][4]
◐	⊖	⊖	●	⊖	⊖	⊖	⊖	◐	**Enterprise One & Only Low Lustre**
◐	⊖	⊖	●	⊖	⊖	⊖	⊖	⊖	**Fuller O'Brien Liquid Lustre Eggshell 604** [1]
●	◐	⊖	○	⊖	⊖	●	⊖	⊖	**Glidden Spred Lo-Lustre 3100**
⊖	⊖	⊖	○	⊖	⊖	⊖	○	○	**Glidden Spred Ultra Eggshell 4100** [3][5]
●	⊖	⊖	○	⊖	⊖	⊖	○	○	**Glidden Spred Ultra Flat 4000** [3][5]
○	⊖	⊖	⊖	⊖	⊖	●	◐	⊖	**Kelly Moore Acry-Plex Flat 555** [1][3]
○	⊖	○	○	⊖	⊖	●	◐	⊖	**Kelly Moore Sat-N-Sheen Flat 1610** [1][3][6]
◐	⊖	⊖	◐	⊖	⊖	●	○	⊖	**Pittsburgh Wallhide Flat**

[4] Green not a current color.
[5] Gold tended to change color when scrubbed with scouring powder.
[6] Green tended to change color when scrubbed with scouring powder.

Ratings continued

INTERIOR LATEX PAINTS

Ratings continued

Brand and model	White Hiding, 1 coat	White Hiding, 2 coats	White Fading	Gold Hiding, 1 coat	Gold Hiding, 2 coats	Gold Fading	Pink Hiding, 1 coat	Pink Hiding, 2 coats	Pink Fading
Pratt & Lambert Aqua Satin [1][2]	◐	⊖	⊖	⊖	⊖	⊖	◐	⊖	⊖
Pratt & Lambert Vapex Flat [1][2]	◐	⊖	⊖	⊖	⊖	⊖	◐	⊖	⊖
Sears Best Easy Living Satin 9300 [2]	◐	⊖	⊖	⊖	⊖	⊖	●	○	○
Sears Easy Living Flat 9700 [2]	◐	⊖	⊖	◐	⊖	⊖	●	⊖	○
Sherwin-Williams Superpaint Flat	◐	⊖	⊖	⊖	⊖	⊖	◐	⊖	⊖
Sherwin-Williams Superpaint Satin	◐	⊖	⊖	⊖	⊖	⊖	⊖	⊖	⊖
Tru-Test Supreme E-Z Kare Flat EZ [1]	◐	⊖	⊖	⊖	⊖	⊖	◐	⊖	⊖
Tru-Test Supreme E-Z Kare Flat EZF [1]	◐	⊖	⊖	○	⊖	⊖	◐	⊖	⊖
Tru-Test Ultra Satin	◐	⊖	⊖	—	—	—	◐	⊖	⊖
Devoe Wonder-Tones Flat 36XX	●	○	⊖	○	⊖	⊖	●	⊖	⊖
Dutch Boy Dirt Fighter Flat	◐	⊖	⊖	◐	⊖	⊖	◐	⊖	⊖
Fuller O'Brien Liquid Velvet Flat 602 [5]	●	⊖	⊖	⊖	⊖	⊖	●	○	⊖
Glidden Spred Satin 3400 [1][3]	●	◐	⊖	○	⊖	⊖	●	○	⊖
Sears Easy Living Satin 9600 [2]	●	○	⊖	⊖	⊖	⊖	●	◐	⊖
Sherwin-Williams Classic 99	●	○	⊖	⊖	⊖	⊖	●	○	⊖
Standard Brands Decade Flat [3]	◐	⊖	⊖	⊖	⊖	⊖	◐	◐	⊖
Standard Brands Premium Flat [3]	○	⊖	⊖	⊖	⊖	⊖	⊖	⊖	⊖
Standard Brands Satin [3]	●	○	⊖	○	⊖	⊖	●	○	⊖
Valspar Our Best Quality Acrylic Flat 914	●	⊖	⊖	⊖	⊖	⊖	●	⊖	◐
Wards Great Coat 15 Flat [1][2][5]	●	⊖	⊖	○	⊖	⊖	●	○	⊖
Colony Flat	◐	⊖	⊖	●	⊖	⊖	●	○	⊖
Dutch Boy Super Kem-Tone Flat	●	⊖	⊖	◐	⊖	⊖	—	—	—
Glidden Spred Wall Flat 3200 [3]	●	◐	⊖	○	⊖	⊖	◐	⊖	⊖
Wards Great Coat Satin 10 [1][2][5]	●	⊖	⊖	●	○	⊖	●	◐	⊖

[1] Yellow tended to change color when scrubbed with scouring powder.
[2] White grayer than most.
[3] White whiter than most.
[4] Green not a current color.
[5] Gold tended to change color when scrubbed with scouring powder.
[6] Green tended to change color when scrubbed with scouring powder.

INTERIOR LATEX PAINTS

Hiding, 1 coat (Green)	Hiding, 2 coats (Green)	Fading (Green)	Hiding, 1 coat (Blue)	Hiding, 2 coats (Blue)	Fading (Blue)	Hiding, 1 coat (Yellow)	Hiding, 2 coats (Yellow)	Fading (Yellow)	Brand and model
◐	⊖	⊖	○	⊖	⊖	◐	⊖	⊖	Pratt & Lambert Aqua Satin [1][2]
⊖	⊖	⊖	○	⊖	⊖	◐	⊖	⊖	Pratt & Lambert Vapex Flat [1][2]
⊖	⊖	⊖	◐	⊖	⊖	⊖	⊖	◐	Sears Best Easy Living Satin 9300 [2]
⊖	⊖	⊖	◐	⊖	⊖	●	⊖	⊖	Sears Easy Living Flat 9700 [2]
◐	⊖	⊖	○	⊖	⊖	◐	⊖	○	Sherwin-Williams Superpaint Flat
◐	⊖	⊖	○	⊖	⊖	◐	⊖	○	Sherwin-Williams Superpaint Satin
◐	⊖	⊖	○	⊖	⊖	◐	⊖	⊖	Tru-Test Supreme E-Z Kare Flat EZ [1]
◐	⊖	⊖	◐	⊖	⊖	◐	⊖	⊖	Tru-Test Supreme E-Z Kare Flat EZF [1]
○	⊖	⊖	◐	⊖	⊖	◐	⊖	⊖	Tru-Test Ultra Satin
◐	⊖	○	◐	⊖	⊖	●	○	◐	Devoe Wonder-Tones Flat 36XX
●	⊖	○	◐	⊖	⊖	◐	⊖	○	Dutch Boy Dirt Fighter Flat
●	⊖	⊖	●	⊖	⊖	◐	⊖	⊖	Fuller O'Brien Liquid Velvet Flat 602 [5]
●	○	○	◐	⊖	⊖	○	⊖	●	Glidden Spred Satin 3400 [1][3]
◐	⊖	⊖	●	○	⊖	◐	⊖	⊖	Sears Easy Living Satin 9600 [2]
●	⊖	⊖	◐	⊖	⊖	⊖	⊖	○	Sherwin-Williams Classic 99
⊖	⊖	⊖	◐	⊖	○	◐	⊖	⊖	Standard Brands Decade Flat [3]
⊖	⊖	⊖	⊖	⊖	⊖	◐	⊖	⊖	Standard Brands Premium Flat [3]
●	○	⊖	○	⊖	⊖	●	○	⊖	Standard Brands Satin [3]
◐	⊖	⊖	○	⊖	⊖	●	○	◐	Valspar Our Best Quality Acrylic Flat 914
◐	⊖	⊖	◐	⊖	⊖	○	⊖	⊖	Wards Great Coat 15 Flat [1][2][5]
◐	⊖	⊖	◐	⊖	⊖	○	⊖	⊖	Colony Flat
—	—	—	○	⊖	⊖	◐	⊖	●	Dutch Boy Super Kem-Tone Flat
◐	⊖	○	○	⊖	⊖	●	⊖	⊖	Glidden Spred Wall Flat 3200 [3]
●	◐	⊖	●	⊖	⊖	●	◐	○	Wards Great Coat Satin 10 [1][2][5]

RATINGS: CHEMICAL PAINT STRIPPERS

Better ← → Worse

▶ **See report, page 230.** From Consumer Reports, May 1991.

Recommendations: The best was *Peel Away I*, but *Woodfinisher's Pride* performed nearly as well.

Ratings order: Listed in order of overall quality, based on safety, speed, results, and effort needed. Products judged approximately equal are bracketed and listed alphabetically. Price is the manufacturer's average or suggested retail to nearest dollar, per gallon. Ingredients: **A** = alkaline paste; **E** = non-volatile organic esters; **MTA** = methanol, toluene, and acetone solvents; **MC** = methylene chloride solvent.

Brand and model	Price	Cost/sq. ft.	Ingredients	Safety	Speed [1]	Effort	Advantages	Disadvantages	Comments
Peel Away I	$20	$ .60	A	⊖	○	⊖	B	c,f	A,C
Woodfinisher's Pride	32	.40	E	⊖	⊖	⊖	A,B	d,h	B,D
Peel Away 6	43	1.50	E	⊖	⊖	○	A,B	g	A
3M Safest Stripper	20	.50	E	⊖	⊖	⊖	A,B	g,i	B
Easy Off Paint Stripper	25	.80	E	⊖	⊖	⊖	A,B	g	B
Savogran StrypSafer	33	.90	E	⊖	●	●	A,B	d,g	B
Parks No Drip Strip	20	.20	MTA	⊖	●	⊖	—	a,b	—
Savogran FinishOff	20	.30	MTA	⊖	○	●	—	a,b	—
Bix Stripper	20	.30	MTA	●	⊖	●	—	a,b,c,e,f	—
Rock Miracle Paint and Varnish Remover	24	.60	MC	●	⊖	⊖	—	a	—

[1] The time it took to strip five coats of paint from a wood door.

Features in Common
All: • Can be applied with brush. • Are sufficiently viscous for use on vertical surfaces. • May require more than 1 application. • Have adequate instructions, warning labels.
All solvent-based strippers: • Come in metal container with childproof closure.
Except as noted, all: • Did not rust steel or discolor aluminum or wood.

Key to Advantages
A–Less irritating than solvent types.
B–Nonflammable.

Key to Disadvantages
a–Solvent vapors pose health hazards.
b–Flammable.
c–Highly alkaline; skin contact hazardous.
d–Rusted steel.
e–Stained aluminum.
f–Stained or darkened wood.
g–Takes overnight to soften several coats.
h–Dripped more than others when used on vertical surface.
i–Lacks childproof closure.

Key to Comments
A–Comes with plastic-coated paper to be applied over chemical.
B–Performance improved when covered overnight with plastic food wrap.
C–Best applied with spatula, not brush.
D–Mfr. will send $1 in exchange for empty container.

RATINGS: HEAT GUNS

Better ◐ ◐ ○ ◓ ● Worse

▶ See report, page 230. From Consumer Reports, May 1991.

Recommendations: The three top-rated models boast a fan that allows rapid cool-down, an essential feature, in our view.

Ratings order: Listed in order of estimated quality, based on safety, comfort, and number of heat settings. Products judged approximately equal are bracketed and listed alphabetically. Price is the manufacturer's suggested retail. Ⓓ indicates model discontinued.

Brand and model	Price	Weight, oz.	Watts, low/high [1]	Heat settings	Maximum air temp.	Safety	Speed	Handling	Results	Advantages	Disadvantages	Comments
Black & Decker 9754 Ⓓ	$65	23	120/1550	Cont.	730°F	○	◐	◐	◐	B,E,F	—	A
Milwaukee 2000D	50	23	230/1135	Cont.	700	○	◐	◐	◐	B,F	b	C
Milwaukee 750	70	39	60/1700	1	640	○	◐	◐	◐	A,C,D,G	b	B,C
Black & Decker 9756	30	22	630/1240	2	650	◓	◐	◐	◐	—	a	A
Wagner Power Stripper	29	24	715/1440	2	875	◓	◐	◐	◐	E	a	A

[1] As drawn in tests at the lowest and highest heat settings.

Features in Common
All: • Reach dangerously high temperature at nozzle tip. • Can be rested without tipping over. • Can be hung on a hook when not in use. • Have 6-ft., heat-resistant cord. • Have convenient, lockable On/off switch in "trigger" position on handle.
Except as noted, all: • Have plastic body.

Key to Advantages
A–Has fan-only setting for rapid cool-down.
B–Has very low setting for cool-down.
C–Fan air volume adjustable.
D–Switch guard prevents accidental start.
E–Comes with shaped auxiliary nozzle tips.
F–Has continuous rotary heat adjustment.
G–Holding bracket for when not in use.

Key to Disadvantages
a–Lacks setting for accelerated cool-down.
b–Slightly noisier than others.

Key to Comments
A–Double-insulated housing, 2-pronged plug.
B–Has metal housing.
C–Has 3-pronged grounded plug.

YARD & GARDEN

Lawn mowers............................241
String trimmers..........................243
Tillers & cultivators....................245
Chippers/shredders....................246
Gas barbecue grills.....................247
Ratings...249

For many, buying a house with a lawn begins an endless accumulation of tools and power equipment. Storage shed and garage fill up with the paraphernalia necessary to keep up lawn and garden: wheelbarrow, hoses, an assortment of trowels, rakes, shovels, and power equipment such as a lawn mower, a string trimmer, a chipper/shredder, and—for those with a horticultural bent—a garden cultivator.

Of all that power equipment, only the lawn mower might be considered essential. Many people, particularly those with less than a half-acre of yard, probably won't use most other power tools more than once or twice a year. For them, renting makes more sense than buying. Besides freeing up precious storage space, renting equipment eliminates the hassles of servicing that are part of ownership—changing the oil, replacing spark plugs, cleaning or replacing the oil filter, sharpening blades.

Whether you rent or buy, an important consideration is using power tools safely. Follow the safety rules printed at the front of the owner's manual. Gasoline-powered tools deserve special caution—they're capable of killing or severely injuring their operators or people in the vicinity. Fill the fuel tank carefully, after the engine has cooled. Don't handle the blade of a machine unless the engine is stopped and the ignition disabled. For electric tools, don't operate if conditions are wet. Always disconnect the power if you need to handle the blade. In general, don't operate any power lawn tool with children or pets close by. Wear sturdy shoes, long pants and, when it's appropriate, ear and eye protection.

After you've mowed, trimmed, cultivated, and produced mulch for your yard, you might be ready to fire up the barbecue. Today's gas grills take a lot of the hassle out of barbecuing. The grills we've tested are, for the most part, capable of turning out a perfect steak, a nicely charred burger, or a tender salmon filet.

Lawn mowers

▸ Ratings start on page 249. ▸ Repair records on page 370.

Some people with postage-stamp lawns use powerful lawn tractors to cut the grass. And a few hardy souls with vast expanses of green still doggedly perform the weekly mowing chore with a manual reel mower. But it makes more sense to buy a machine that matches the lawn.

The terrain and the landscape also influence the decision. A very hilly half-acre may need a different machine from one that's flat. If your lawn is dotted with trees and flower beds, you'll likely need a walk-behind mower of some type, no matter how large the property is. And even the simplest lawn will need trimming with a walk-behind mower or string trimmer.

Lawn-mowing machines range from $100 you-push-it reel mowers to versatile 20-horsepower tractors costing upward of $5000. Sears and Murray sell about half the lower-priced mowers. Other big names in the mower business—Toro, Lawn-Boy, Snapper, Ariens, Honda, John Deere—stick pretty much to the high end.

Mower manufacturers are betting that consumers' desire to be environmentally sensitive and the urgent problem of overburdened landfills will spur sales of a new lawn-mowing option—the mulching mower or mulching attachment. A mulcher chops clippings into small pieces and blows them down into the turf, hastening the return of nutrients to the soil and reducing the likelihood that the clippings will smother the grass. With no bags of clippings to empty, the mowing job becomes easier, but you may have to mow more frequently to avoid clipping too much grass. Some mulching models can convert to bag-using or chute-using mowers.

Where rainfall is scarce, there is reason to decide against a lawn. You can use half as much water by choosing among less thirsty grasses and plants. For more information, contact your local Cooperative Extension or write to the National Wildflower Research Center at 2600 F.M. 973 North, Austin, TX 78725, Attention: Clearinghouse (enclose $2 for postage and copying).

Safety

The Consumer Product Safety Commission requires manufacturers to equip walk-behind mowers with a deadman control that stops the blade when you let go of a handle. That requirement seems to have helped make mowers safer. Mower-related injuries have dropped to about half what they were just eight years ago. Still, thousands of people receive treatment in hospital emergency rooms every year because of an injury caused by a lawn mower. When you mow, follow these rules:

■ Mow only when and where it's safe. Don't mow when the grass is wet; your foot can slip under the mower. Push a mower across a slope, not up and down; if you have a riding mower or tractor, travel up and down, not across. If the slope is more than about 15 degrees, don't mow at all; the mower can get away from you. Consider planting a different groundcover.

■ Dress for the job. Wear sturdy shoes and close-fitting clothes.

■ Prepare the area. Pick up toys, hoses, rocks, and twigs. Banish anyone nearby, including pets—flying objects can be hurled from the mower.

■ Use gasoline carefully. Fill the mower's fuel tank before you start, while the engine is cold. Before you refill, wait for the engine to cool.

- Keep hands and feet away from moving parts.
- Don't defeat safety devices.
- Don't let young children use a mower.

The choices

Choose a type of mower according to the size of your yard.

Manual reel mower. The original lawn mower has been brought up-to-date with lightweight alloys and plastic parts. A series of blades linked to the wheels slice the grass. For small lawns, up to about 5000 square feet, this is a quiet, no-pollution solution. But it's impractical for all but a small, level lawn. Cost: $100 or less.

Electric mower. The electric versions of the power mower use an electric motor to power a spinning blade. You supply the pushing power. For lawns up to about one-quarter acre, a quiet, fairly low-cost solution. Look for a rear grass-catcher—it works better than a side-mounted bag. A device to let the cord slide across the handle when you change mowing direction keeps the cord from tangling.

The cord does get in the way, and it limits the range. The relatively low engine power makes electrics slower and less effective in tall grass than gasoline-powered mowers. Price: $120 to $300.

Push-type power mower. The typical basic gasoline-powered mower, useful for mowing flat lawns up to about one-half acre and trimming larger lawns, has a one-cylinder, four-stroke, 3½-hp engine that spins a 20- to 22-inch blade. A few models use a two-stroke engine, which requires a gasoline/oil fuel mixture. Some come with oversized rear wheels for smoother rolling on rough terrain.

Look for a deadman control that stops the blade but not the engine when you release the handle (called a blade-brake/clutch), rather than a control that stops both. A blade-brake/clutch is generally found on higher-priced models, but it's worth the cost. Many mulching models are available. On convertible or regular models, a rear grass-catcher bag is easier to maneuver around trees than a side bag. A mower with a deck that extends outboard of its wheels has a better chance of trimming close to a wall or fence than one whose wheels stick out. Metal wheels should hold up better than plastic ones. A folding handle allows compact storage. Electric start eliminates tugging on a rope starter. Price: $100 to $600.

Self-propelled mower. These mowers use the same general design as push-type mowers, but the engine also powers the front or rear wheels. For lawns about one-half acre.

This type is much easier to use, especially on hilly lawns, than push-type and easier to maneuver than sit-down mowers.

Look for the same features mentioned for push-type mowers, plus variable drive speeds and a clutch that lets you "feather" the mower into gear rather than abruptly starting it. Price: $250 to $800.

Riding mower. For lawns about one-half to one acre, these junior tractors typically use an 8- to 10-horsepower engine to power the wheels and a 30-inch blade. They can hold a large grass-catcher, and most have an electric starter. Some take a mulching deck.

Look for one deadman control to stop the engine and/or blade if you dismount, another to stop the engine if you dismount with the mower in gear. Price: $1000 to $2000.

Tractor. For lawns one acre or larger, this is the homeowner's version of the farmer's workhorse. Small versions—called lawn tractors—typically use a 12- to 14-hp engine, mounted in the front, to power the wheels and a 38- to 45-inch cutting deck with two or three blades. Large versions—garden tractors—use a 16- to 20-hp engine.

Mulching decks are sometimes available, as are many other attachments, including such accessories as snow plow and thrower, cultivator, and cart.

Look for hydrostatic transmission, available on fancier models, which permits continuously variable speed. Separate deadman controls are also worthwhile. Price: $1500 to $3500 for lawn tractors, $2000 to $5000 for garden tractors.

The tests

CU tests mowers early each year, as soon as the new models become available. With grass at our New York headquarters brown and dormant in winter, we haul our crop of mowers to a college campus in Florida. We assess each model's adeptness at several tasks: cutting evenly, dispersing clippings without clumping, cutting tall grass, and getting the clippings into the grass-catcher bag. For mowers that mulch the clippings, we see how well they chop and disperse the grass.

We also look for designs that make mowing easier or more of a chore and for anything that increases the risk of injury.

Buying advice

Don't buy more mower than you need. Lawn mowers are heavily promoted in the spring, but the best prices are found after the Fourth of July. No matter when you buy, expect to pay more at a hardware store or specialty mower shop than at a home center, discount store, or catalog retail outlet. But smaller stores typically offer better service, more knowledgeable assistance, and a higher-quality line of mowers.

Mower ads make a big point of easy-starting engines. But almost all mower engines, CU has found, start with a couple of pulls, though 3.5-hp Tecumseh engines have proved a bit quicker than similarly sized Briggs & Stratton engines.

The more complex the mower, the higher the probability that it will need repair. Our readers report that self-propelled mowers need repairs almost twice as often as push-type models of the same brand.

STRING TRIMMERS

▶ Ratings on page 255.

The snipping of grass shears that used to be a part of the suburban weekend serenade has largely given way to the whine of power string trimmers. These machines, either electric- or gasoline-powered, trim areas out of reach of a mower, effortlessly cleaning up even tough weeds and tall grass.

A trimmer works by spinning a plastic line fast enough to slice through stocky vegetation—but with too little inertia to hurt seriously a wayward foot. Still, a lashing from the whirling line can draw blood from bare skin, and the line can fling dirt and debris with considerable force. And gasoline trimmers typically generate around 100 decibels of noise, enough to warrant use of hearing protection. Wear long pants, sturdy shoes, and goggles.

The choices

Gasoline-powered. The heaviest, most powerful type cuts a swath 15 to 18 inches wide. They weigh 9 to 15 pounds, enough to require two-handed operation. Price: $90 to $300.

Two-handled electric. Some cut as well as gasoline-powered models, although the need for an extension cord limits range and convenience. They cut a swath 10 to 17

STRING TRIMMERS

inches wide and weigh less than 10 pounds. Price: $40 to $80.

One-handled electric. For light trimming, it cuts a swath 8 to 10 inches wide and weighs three pounds. Price: $35 or less.

Wheeled string trimmer. These gasoline-powered machines tackle large areas of wood or plantings that are too rough for a power mower or that would require prolonged use of an ordinary trimmer. They cut a swath 17 to 18 inches. Price: $400 and up.

Battery-powered. These trimmers run for about 20 minutes on a charge; they're typically lower in power than electric plug-in types but offer freedom from both an extension cord and gasoline. They cut a swath 6 to 9 inches and weigh 3 to 5 pounds. Price: $35 to more than $100.

Features to look for

Bump-feed string advancement. You tap or bump the trimmer head on the ground, and the line advances. A metal cutter on the head shears off any excess line. Not as common but even more convenient is automatic line-advance.

Brush-cutter blade. A metal blade that can be substituted for the string to cut woody vines up to an inch thick.

Engine/motor location. With a model weighing nine pounds or more, good balance is critical to ease of use. One of the best indicators: an engine or motor mounted high on the shaft, above the main handle.

Shoulder strap. For heavier models, this is another way to improve balance. It also takes some load off arms.

Pivoting trimmer head. For edging with most models, you have to orient the unit so the line spins vertically. A pivoting head makes this easier by letting you grip both handles in their regular position.

Translucent fuel tank. On gasoline-powered models, this makes fuel level easy to check.

The tests

We allowed tough grass, goldenrod, ragweed, timothy, and clover to take over our test lawn and then attacked with all the trimmers. Larger models also got a chance on mature weeds with stiff, seed-encrusted stalks and wild-grape and morning-glory vines.

To simulate trimming by a wall, we lined up rows of 4x4s and let the grass grow tall. For trimmers that seemed capable of the chore, we tried edging around one of our parking lots.

Throughout the testing, our engineers assessed the trimmers' balance, handling, vibration, noise, and ease of feeding out plastic line and changing line spools. For gasoline-powered models, they also assessed ease of starting and servicing.

Buying advice

If your property is large, or if you must tackle heavy growth, consider a gasoline-powered model. But if the tether of an extension cord isn't a problem, the stronger two-handled electrics may make more sense. For trimming a small, well-tended plot, a small one-handled electric is fine.

How to get more information

Check out what we've said in CONSUMER REPORTS. For the date of recent reports, refer to the four-year index in the back of the Buying Guide or the date noted on each Ratings table. Back issues are available at most libraries or can be ordered. You can also get the latest new- and used-car price information. For details, see page 307 (new cars) and page 310 (used cars).

Tillers & Cultivators

▶ Ratings on page 259.

Gardeners who are ready to cast aside their spade might consider a rototiller, a motorized machine that uses revolving blades or tines to till the soil and root out weeds. Although operating a rototiller is a lot easier than using a spade, it is far from effortless. For tilling ground, you'll need plenty of muscle power to keep the machine digging at an effective pace and going where you want it to go. Even the most tractable unit may have to be held back at times or levered up and down to coax the tines to dig in.

Machines with the blades or tines mounted on an axle under the engine or in front of it use the tines not only to dig into the dirt ahead but also to help propel the machine. Rear-tine models, typically larger than front-tine models, use drive wheels to drive the machine forward.

Major brands include mower manufacturers such as Ariens, Honda, Lawn Chief, and Kubota; mass merchandisers such as Sears and J.C. Penney; and lawn-care companies such as Mantis, Lazy Boy, and Troy-Bilt.

The choices

These are the options for churning ground and chopping weeds:

Power weeders. Electric or gas-powered, weeders are essentially power hoes. One type has reciprocating tines; the other has two sets of revolving tines. We found the reciprocating models noisy and fatiguing to use; the others required no effort but were slow-moving compared with lightweight gasoline cultivators. Price: $110 to $400.

Lightweight gasoline-powered machines. They till an 8- to 10-inch swath and weigh less than about 25 pounds. The engine, typically 1.5 hp or smaller, is often hard to start. This type can be hard to keep balanced upright while starting. We found them best suited for clearing weeds between garden rows. Price: $150 to $500.

Compact gasoline-powered machines. These till a swath 14 to 20 inches wide and up to 6 inches deep and weigh 50 to 80 pounds. Compacts are powered by a 2- to 3-hp engine. Price: $280 to $530.

Full-sized machines. They till a swath up to 28 inches wide and weigh well over 100 pounds. This type may be front- or rear-tine. The engine may be up to 8-hp. Price: $500 and up.

Features to look for

Depth stake. This metal bar sticks into the ground to slow the machine and aid in controlling the depth of tilling. The wheels on models with a depth stake serve merely to steady the unit and roll it to and from the work area.

Deadman control. Most models have this vital safety mechanism, which stops the tines and the machine's progress when a lever is released. On lightweights, the throttle lever is the deadman; other machines use a control that deactivates a drive belt or disengages an internal clutch.

Removable tines. If tines are removable, you can adjust them for weeding.

Adjustable handle. A handle that adjusts to different heights is a back saver. It also facilitates storage.

The tests

On small rectangular sodded plots, we ran the machines through two perpendicular passes to find out how deep they could till and how long the job took. We judged penetration ease—whether the tines melt

246 CHIPPERS/SHREDDERS

into the ground or just peck at the surface. We assessed each tiller's ability to break the sod into fine soil. We tested the tillers' ability to cut through tough roots, and to dredge up and cast off rocks.

Buying advice

If you need a rototiller only to establish a new area of lawn, say, you'd do better to rent than to buy. There's no need to buy a rototiller unless you have a vegetable garden or plants that require regular care and weeding.

If your garden is small, or if you'll do mainly weeding, a lightweight model may be the best choice. For weeding alone, consider a power weeder. For a garden of 200 to 500 square feet, consider a compact tiller. For a larger garden, you may need a full-sized machine.

CHIPPERS/SHREDDERS

▶ Ratings on page 262.

As more and more municipalities decline to pick up yard waste, homeowners are forced to find other ways to dispose of leaves, garden litter, and fallen tree limbs. A growing number of people now use a chipper/shredder to reduce the volume of the waste—in some cases, to a tenth its original—and to convert it to useful forms. Shredded leaves make welcome additions to a compost heap, and chipped branches make excellent mulch.

Lawn-care professionals have long used machines to grind up yard waste, but chippers/shredders scaled and priced for homeowners are relatively new. The machines, powered by an electric motor or gasoline-powered engine, typically direct leaves or wood through a hopper or chute to a set of cutters, free-spinning hammers, or flails for shredding or a rotary knife for chipping. The processed chips and shreds issue forth from a discharge port into a plastic can or a bag, or in many cases, on the ground.

Most machines are designed to make it difficult for a careless operator to reach into the workings, but the cutters on some models CU has tested were easily accessible. Some machines gobble up the tamper, the device for pushing material into the hopper. Most blow some of the chips and shreds toward your face, and all are noisy, especially when chipping. Goggles and ear protection are a must.

Garden stores, home centers, and mower shops offer a variety of types and brands. The major brands include: *Sears, MTD, Troy-Bilt, Baker, AL-KO*, and *Flowtron*.

The choices

The choice depends largely on how often you'll use the machine and the size and type of material (leaves, twigs, branches, or all three) you'll stuff into the hopper. Starting with the most modest, these are the possibilities:

Electric chippers. Adequate for twigs and small branches. They're not as powerful as gasoline-powered models so they're much slower. Extension cord required. Price: about $400.

Electric chippers/shredders. For leaves, twigs, and branches up to about an inch in diameter, this type is quieter—and slower than gasoline-powered models. Price: $300 to $400.

Gasoline-powered chippers/shredders. For leaves, twigs, and branches up to three inches in diameter, this type is noisy, but much more powerful and faster than electrics. Some weigh nearly 300 pounds, making transport difficult. Price: $400 to $1300 for 3- to 5-hp models; higher for more powerful models.

Features to look for

Easy transport. Wheels and weight are the critical factors here.

Easy startup. Electric models are easiest, of course. Among gasoline-powered engines, four-stroke engines have proved easier to start than two-stroke engines in our tests.

Variable shred size. On some models, you move a lever to change between fine and coarse. On larger chippers/shredders, you vary the size by changing a discharge screen.

Tamper. The best type is designed specifically for the machine, with a built-in flange to keep it away from the cutter.

Goggles. Most machines blow some material back to your face, making goggles required. Some models provide them.

Cutter safeguard. Look for a model that has long hoppers or chutes that make it difficult or impossible for hands to reach the cutter.

The tests

To test chipping, we fed each chipper or chipper/shredder a series of inch-thick hardwood dowels, along with tree branches of various sizes. We assessed speed, ease of feeding, and amount of vibration and noise.

For our shredding test, we dumped loads of loosely packed leaves into the hopper of each machine and measured the time it took to produce 10 gallons of shreds. We also measured reduction ratio, and judged the ease of feeding leaves.

Buying advice

First, decide whether you can keep a chipper/shredder busy enough to make it worthwhile to buy one rather than rent it. Choose a machine based on the tasks facing it. If your lawn has a lot of large trees given to dropping large dead branches, you may need the power of a gasoline-powered machine capable of handling chipping and shredding.

GAS BARBECUE GRILLS

▶ Ratings on page 265.

Americans hold backyard barbecues twice as often as they did a decade ago. That's due largely to the growing popularity of gas barbecue grills. Gas grills ignite with the push of a button and burn much more cleanly than do charcoal grills, without leaving a heap of ashes to be discarded.

The choices

Plain or fancy, all gas grills work in much the same way. Over the main gas burner of each grill lies a grid covered with volcanic pumice (lava rock) or other material meant to distribute heat evenly. Above that material sits a cooking grate and lid. The whole assembly fits on a wheeled cart that also carries a refillable fuel tank. Most models use propane, but some run on natural gas. On most grills, you have independent control of the right and left sides of the cooking area.

Features to look for

Grate. Look for wide bars. They seal in juices better than thin rods and are less apt to let fish slip through the cracks. Porcelain coating on grates stops rust and speeds cleaning. Cast-iron grates are especially good for searing.

248 GAS BARBECUE GRILLS

Rocks, briquettes, plates. Various materials can be used in grills, but lava rock soaks up dripping grease and has to be replaced periodically. Triangles serve to channel fat and grease to a drip pan, minimizing grease flare-ups.

Igniter. Over the long-term, exposure to grease can make an igniter less effective. Look for an igniter with a protective shield to insulate it from grease.

Timer. Most helpful is the kind that shuts off the gas automatically when the set time has elapsed.

Shelves. Grills with shelves that fold down or come off are easier to store than those with fixed shelves.

Handles. A handle at each side prevents having to reach over the fire when opening the lid.

Window. It's nice to see the food cooking, but unless the window is cleaned often, it won't be very effective.

Transport. Casters or wheels on all four legs make transport easier than if there are only two wheels.

Rotisserie. This feature is handy for slow-turning a roast or chicken. It's an extra-cost option on some models.

Smoker. To give food a smoky taste as wood chips smolder, some models have built-in compartments for holding chips.

Side burner. This resembles a burner on a gas range. It lets you cook something in a pot while you grill the main course.

The tests

Most grills require some assembly, sometimes a daunting project. We evaluate the time and difficulty of putting the grills together.

Following manufacturers' preheating instructions, we clock the time it takes each grate to reach 600°F, the temperature hot enough to sear meat and keep juices in.

Then we grill steaks, hamburgers, chicken breasts, and salmon. The steaks and hamburgers challenge each grill's ability to sear and brown meat while leaving it rare inside. We include chicken and fish because they demand more delicate cooking at lower temperatures.

We also check for temperature uniformity across the entire grate and for such convenience factors as how easy the grill is to clean and how easy the fuel tank is to install.

Buying advice

If you confine your outdoor cooking to charbroiled burgers now and then, you probably won't go wrong with whatever the local discount store has on sale. But if you expect to rely on a grill the way most people do their kitchen range, you'll appreciate the durability and versatility of a well-designed, well-made barbecue grill. In general, we found that the more expensive grills exhibited the best construction.

Considering the time and effort that must be spent in assembling some grills, it might pay to ask the dealer to do the work. Some will do it free; others may charge.

Some grills come in large cartons and weigh as much as 100 pounds, so carrying them home is no small task.

MULCHING MOWERS 249

RATINGS | MULCHING MOWERS

Better ← → Worse
◉ ⊖ ○ ⊕ ●

▶ See report, page 241. From Consumer Reports, June 1991.

Recommendations: Choose among the models rated at least ○ in mulching dispersal. That ensures a competent mulcher. If your mowing habits aren't regular or if once in a while you want a bag of clippings for the compost pile, consider a convertible model like the *John Deere Tricycler 14PB* or the *Honda HR215PXA*.

Ratings order: Listed by types; within types, listed in order of estimated quality. Closely ranked models differed little in quality. Models judged essentially similar in quality are bracketed and listed alphabetically. The price is the suggested retail as quoted by the manufacturer of the mower and, for convertibles, attachments necessary for mulching; actual retail may be lower. + indicates an extra shipping charge. ⓢ indicates model has been replaced by successor model; according to manufacturer, the performance of new model should be similar to the tested model but features may vary. See page 250 for new model number and suggested retail price, if available. ⓓ indicates model discontinued.

Brand and model	Price	Mulching dispersal, reg.[1]	Mulching evenness, reg.[1]	Evenness	Bag capacity	Dispersal	Handling	Operating ease	Catcher use	Advantages	Disadvantages	Comments
MULCHING-ONLY MODELS												
Bolens 8628 ⓢ	$425	◉	○	–	–	–	○	○	–	A,B,C,I,V,X	p	A,C,H,P
Troy-Bilt 8628R	370	◉	○	–	–	–	○	○	–	A,B,C,I,V,X	p	C,H,P
Husqvarna 51M	300	◉	◉	–	–	–	○	○	–	N	e,r,bb	H
Toro Recycler 20217	369	○	○	–	–	–	○	◉	–	I,T,X	ii	H,L,O
White 098R ⓓ	270	○	◉	–	–	–	○	○	–	I,U	o,r,aa,bb,ee	C
MTD 111098R ⓢ	259	○	◉	–	–	–	○	○	–	I	c,o,r,aa,bb,ee	H
Sears Craftsman 38426	230+	○	◉	–	–	–	○	○	–	I,W	d,o,t,aa,ee	A,B,C,H,N
Homelite HM20	330	◉	○	–	–	–	○	○	–	I,X	q	—
Poulan Pro PP800M	370	◉	○	–	–	–	○	○	–	N	e,p,r,bb	H
Rally MR500A	209	◉	○	–	–	–	○	○	–	—	e,p,r,bb	H
Cub Cadet 098R111 ⓓ	285	○	◉	–	–	–	○	○	–	I,U	o,r,aa,bb,ee,gg	C,M
Murray 20800	189	○	◉	–	–	–	○	⊕	–	H,U	e,m,s,aa,ff	A,B,C,H,K,O
Honda HRM21PVA ⓓ	490	◉	○	–	–	–	○	○	–	I,O,U,W	p,aa,bb,dd,ii	A,L,O

[1] *Regular cut was set at about 2¾ in.*

Ratings continued

250 MULCHING MOWERS

Ratings continued

Column headers: Price | Mulching dispersal, reg.[1] | Mulching evenness, reg.[1] | Evenness | Bag capacity | Dispersal | Handling | Operating ease | Catcher use (Non-mulching) | Advantages | Disadvantages | Comments

Brand and model	Price	Mulch. disp.	Mulch. even.	Even.	Bag cap.	Disp.	Hand.	Op. ease	Catcher use	Advantages	Disadvantages	Comments
Atlas AE 2400	$230	◐	○	—	—	—	◐	○	—	B,O,V	e,l,r,y,aa,cc	C,K,M
Wheeler WM-5	219	◐	○	—	—	—	◐	○	—	B,O	e,l,r,y,aa,bb,cc	C,K,M
Yard-Man 11098R [D]	250	○	○	—	—	—	◐	○	—	U	e,m,o,r,aa,bb,ee	C,K
Lawn Chief 91M [S]	230	◐	○	—	—	—	◐	○	—	B,N,O	e,l,r,y,aa,cc,gg	C,K

CONVERTIBLE MODELS

Brand and model	Price	Mulch. disp.	Mulch. even.	Even.	Bag cap.	Disp.	Hand.	Op. ease	Catcher use	Advantages	Disadvantages	Comments
John Deere Tricycler 14PB	625	○	◐	◐	○	○	○	◐	◐	D,F,K,L,P,Q,R,U,W,X	g	A,E,J,O
Honda HR215PXA	610	◐	◐	◐	◐	◐	◐	◐	◐	D,F,K,L,M,U,X	c,g,k,m,t,dd	A,E,J,O
Toro 26562	459	●	◐	◐	◐	○	◐	◐	◐	F,K,L,X	a,k,m,dd,gg	E,O
Lawn-Boy S21ZPM [D]	450	○	◐	◐	◐	◐	◐	○	○	H,I,P,W	e,g,q,t,w,z	A,F,I
Ariens LM21 911041	449	◐	○	◐	◐	◐	◐	◐	○	J,K,X	c,k,m,u	C,F,H,R
Homelite HSD20 [S]	350	●	◐	◐	○	◐	◐	◐	◐	H,I,S,W	a,d,q,s,t,u,w,x,hh	A,B,F,H,I,O
Lawn-Boy M21ZPR [D]	550	○	◐	◐	◐	◐	○	○	◐	G,K,L,M,P,Q,X	h,t	A,D,E,Q
Rally MC500A	189	◐	○	◐	●	●	○	○	◐	B,D,N	e,l,p,v,bb	C,G,H
Lawn Chief 131-J [D]	330	●	◐	◐	◐	○	◐	○	◐	E,L	b,k,r,w,y,bb	C,F,H
Snapper R21507B [S]	420	●	○	◐	◐	◐	◐	○	◐	A,G,L	a,j,p,t,w,x	C,F,H
Wheeler WP31 [D]	360	●	○	◐	◐	◐	●	○	◐	L,N,P	b,i,k,r,w,y,bb,cc,hh	C,F,M
Atlas A131 [D]	360	●	○	◐	●	●	◐	○	◐	L,N,P	b,c,f,i,k,n,r,w,y,bb,cc,hh	A,C,F,N

[1] *Regular cut was set at about 2¾ in.*

Successor Models (in Ratings order) Bolens 8628 is succeeded by 8628B, $370; MTD 111098R by 113-098A, $199; Lawn Chief 91M by 94M, $250; Homelite HSD20 by UT30142, $360; Snapper R21507B by R21500, $390.

Performance Notes
Except as noted: • Dispersal performance in mulching-mode in deep cut was equal to or poorer than performance in regular cut. • Evenness of cut in mulching-mode in deep cut was equal to or better than in regular cut. • Tall-grass cutting was excellent or very good. • Convertible models' score for vacuuming was at least good.

Features in Common
Except as noted, all have: • Deadman control on handle that stops engine and blade when

MULCHING MOWERS 251

released. • 4-stroke, 4- to 5-hp Briggs & Stratton Quantum engine. • Cast-aluminum deck. • 20- to 22-in. swath. • Convenient folding of handle and adjustment for handle height. • Throttle/choke control mounted on handle. • Plastic wheels without bearings. • Paper-element air filter. • 2-yr. warranty on mower and 2-yr./5-yr. warranty on engine/ignition system. • Fuel shut-off valve.
Except as noted, all mulching-only mowers have: • Doughnut-shaped deck chamber.

Key to Advantages
A–Fewer clippings left under mower in mulching.
B–Clippings penetrated below top of grass and to ground better than with most.
C–Made smaller clippings than most.
D–Cut tall grass in mulching mode without stalling, unlike most convertible models tested.
E–Extra blade improved non-mulching mowing.
F–Blade-brake/clutch deadman control stops blade but leaves engine running.
G–Interlock prevents use without grass bag, discharge chute, or mulching plug cover.
H–Easier to push than most.
I–Easier to maneuver than most.
J–Large starter-cord handle, easy to use.
K–Balanced catcher easy to remove/install.
L–Catcher easy to empty.
M–Handle vibrated less than most.
N–Handle more comfortable than most.
O–Less noisy than most.
P–No tools needed for converting.
Q–Sight-glass fuel gauge.
R–Draining oil more convenient than most.
S–Measuring cup for oil-fuel mixing.
T–Dispersal performance in mulching-mode in deep cut judged better than in regular cut.
U–Wheels have ball bearings.
V–Metal wheels.
W–No tools needed to service air filter.
X–No tools needed to adjust handle height.

Key to Disadvantages
a–When mulching, left clippings in clumps.
b–When mulching, left clippings on top of grass.
c–Clippings accumulated under deck in mulching tests.
d–Throttle control mounted on engine. (**Homelite** lacks throttle control.)
e–Hard to jockey from side to side.
f–Clogged in tall grass.
g–Without a catcher, cut a bit less evenly.
h–Clippings may blow in user's face when optional chute is attached.
i–Vacuuming of convertible models in non-mulching mode was judged fair.
j–Engine shut-off control judged unsafe.
k–Harder to push than most.
l–Harder to pull than most.
m–Harder to maneuver than most.
n–Starter rope harder to pull than most.
o–Handle may be too low for some people.
p–Pulling starter rope requires stooping.
q–Deadman control relatively hard to squeeze.
r–Throttle/choke control not precise.
s–Handle vibrated more than most.
t–Noisier than most.
u–Catcher hard to empty.
v–Catcher inconvenient to remove and install.
w–Separate chute needed when using grass catcher; points at user when catcher is not attached.
x–Inconvenient to convert.
y–Flimsy wheel-height adjustment lever covers.
z–Fueling less convenient than most.
aa–Handle height not adjustable.
bb–Adjusting or folding handle inconvenient.
cc–Handle more prone to rust than most.
dd–Mower must be tipped to drain oil. On **Honda**, oil spills onto deck, then drains through hole.
ee–Left-hand wheels stick out; prevent trimming close to walls.
ff–Uncomfortable handle.
gg–Evenness of cut in mulching mode in deep cut judged worse than in regular cut.
hh–Tall-grass cutting judged poor.
ii–Tall-grass cutting judged only average.

Key to Comments
A–Engine variations: 3½-hp Briggs & Stratton Quantum (**Bolens**); 3½-hp Briggs & Stratton Max (**Atlas A131-H**); Honda (**Honda HR215PXA**); 3½-hp Honda (**Honda HRM21PVA**); Lawn-Boy 2-stroke (**Lawn-Boy**); Craftsman Eager-1 (**Sears**); Tecumseh (**Ariens, Murray**); Tecumseh 2-stroke (**Homelite**); Kawasaki (**John Deere**).
B–Fuel-primer bulb instead of choke.
C–Stamped-steel deck.
D–Cast-magnesium deck.
E–Rear-discharge, rear-bagging deck.
F–Side-discharge, rear-bagging deck.
G–Side-discharge, side-bagging deck.
H–No fuel-shutoff valve.
I–Oil-impregnated foam air filter.
J–Combination foam and paper air filter.
K–Starter cord can be mounted on left or right.
L–Irregularly shaped deck.
M–1-yr. warranty on mower.
N–1-yr. warranty on mower and engine.
O–2-yr. warranty on mower and engine.
P–3-yr. warranty on mower.
Q–3-yr. warranty on mower and engine, 5 yrs. on ignition, lifetime on deck.
R–Additional 3-yr. warranty on parts.

RATINGS: SELF-PROPELLED MOWERS

E ⊖ VG ⊖ G ○ F ⊖ P ●

▶ **See report, page 241.** From Consumer Reports, June 1992.

Recommendations: If your lawn is big enough or hilly enough to warrant buying a self-propelled mower, we recommend a model with a blade-brake/clutch safety system. You can't go wrong with any of the 11 such models tested. Our first choice is the *Lawn-Boy M21BMR*, a rear-bagger.

Ratings order: Listed by types; within types, listed in order of estimated quality. Bracketed models, judged about equal, are listed alphabetically. Unless separated by a bold rule, closely ranked models differed little in quality. The price is the manufacturer's suggested retail price for the mower equipped with the attachments to bag, disperse, or mulch clippings. A + indicates an extra shipping charge. ☐ indicates discontinued model.

Brand and model	Price	Evenness	Vacuuming	Bag capacity	Evenness (catcher)	Dispersal (chute)	Mulch dispersal	Handling	Mower convenience	Speeds	Advantages	Disadvantages	Comments
REAR-BAGGING MODELS WITH BLADE-BRAKE/CLUTCH
Lawn-Boy M21BMR	$800	⊖	⊖	⊖	⊖	⊖	⊖	⊖	⊖	3	B,D,E,F,I,K,N,O,Q,U,V	n,q	A,F,G,M
Honda HR215HXA	816	⊖	⊖	⊖	⊖	○	○	⊖	⊖	9	A,D,I,K,L,N,O,U,V	ee	C,F,G,K,M,O
John Deere 14SB	733	⊖	⊖	⊖	⊖	○	○	⊖	○	5	A,E,F,I,L,N,O,R,S,T,U,V	e,s	F,G,K,M,O
Ariens LM21SB 911047	719	⊖	⊖	⊖	⊖	⊖	○	○	⊖	Inf	D,I,K,L,N,U,V	a,f,dd,ii	D,E,H,M
Honda HR215SXA	756	⊖	⊖	⊖	⊖	○	○	○	⊖	3	A,I,K,L,N,O,U,V	e,q,ee	F,G,K,M,O
Kubota W5021SC	755	⊖	⊖	⊖	⊖	○	⊖	⊖	⊖	2	A,F,I,J,L,M,N,O,T,V	e,t,dd,gg	F,G,K,M,O
Lawn-Boy S21BST	699	⊖	⊖	○	⊖	⊖	⊖	⊖	○	1	D,E,F,I,T	h,m	A,F,H,I,P
Toro GTS Recycler 20107	677	⊖	⊖	○	⊖	●	⊖	⊖	⊖	3	E,I,L,M,O,T,U	d,t,dd,ii	E,F,G,I,M
Snapper P21508B	595	○	⊖	○	○	○	●	⊖	○	6	A,B,D,F,J,K,L,O,U,V	r,dd	E,H,O
Yard-Man 122898	538	○	○	⊖	⊖	○	—	⊖	○	6	D,F,I,L,N	m,v,x,aa,bb,dd,ii	H
Homelite HSB21P5C/UT-30149	532	⊖	⊖	⊖	⊖	●	—	○	○	2	F,I,O	q,s,t,bb,dd,gg	E,F,G,M
REAR-BAGGING MODELS WITH ENGINE-KILL
Husqvarna R53S2	690	⊖	⊖	⊖	—	—	—	○	○	Inf	D,E,J,K,N,P,T,U,V	j,m,n,u	A,F,G,M

SELF-PROPELLED MOWERS

Brand and model	Price	Evenness	Vacuuming	Bag capacity	Evenness (With catcher)	Dispersal (With catcher)	Dispersal (With chute)	Mulch dispersal	Handling	Mower convenience	Speeds	Advantages	Disadvantages	Comments
Toro 20216	$558	◐	◐	○	◐	◕	—	○	○	3	E,L,M,O,U,V	d,t	E,F,G,M
Cub Cadet 848E	599	◐	○	◉	◐	◐	◕	◐	◐	6	C,D,F,N,P,V	j,m,r,aa,bb,ii	E,H,M,O,P
Snapper P21509B	574	○	○	◐	○	◐	◕	○	○	6	A,B,D,F,J,K,L,O,U,V	r,y	E,H,O
White 848R Lawncycler	459	○	◐	◉	◐	◐	◕	◐	◐	6	D,F,N,P	j,m,aa,bb,ii	E,H,O,P
Dynamark C2105-500	375	◐	◐	◕	—	—	◐	○	○	5	E,M,N,O,P	a,k,l,u,v,aa,gg	E,G,L,O
Homelite HSD20P/UT-30152	467	◐	◐	◐	◐	○	○	◐	◕	1	A,E,F,H,V	o,p,y,ff	E,F,H,M,N,O,P
J.C. Penney Grasshandler R870C1013	400+	○	◐	◐	◐	◐	○	—	◐	◕	1	C,D,F,N,P	j,m,r,v,aa,bb,ii	H
Lawn Chief 151 ⒹÂ	570	◐	◐	◐	◐	◐	○	◐	◐	2	C,M,O	g,m,t,u,y,gg	H,O
Noma Signature Series C2105-520	439	◐	◐	◕	—	—	◐	○	○	5	E,M,N,O,P,T	a,k,l,u,v,aa,gg	E,G,K,L,O
Murray 21711	288	◐	○	◐	◐	◕	—	○	◕	1	E,N,O,P,V	i,m,n,bb	D,E,G,L
Wheeler WRRBQSP-21	386	○	◐	◐	◐	◕	◐	○	◕	1	A,D,O	l,u,w,aa,hh	G,L,M,P
Rally BP410	309	◐	◐	○	—	—	—	●	◕	1	N,O,P	f,g,h,k,l,p,u,bb	D,E,G,N
Garden Pride 101-9221	299	◐	●	◕	—	—	—	●	◕	1	—	c,d,h,i,j,k,r,u,w,aa	B,E,G,M

SIDE-BAGGING MODELS WITH ENGINE-KILL

Brand and model	Price										Advantages	Disadvantages	Comments
Honda HRS21SA Ⓓ	585	◐	◐	○	◐	○	◐	◐	◕	1	A,E,F,G,H,L,T	e,r,aa,bb,cc,dd,ff,ii	F,I,M,O
Lawn-Boy L21ZSM	535	◐	○	◐	◐	◐	○	◐	◕	1	A,D,E,F,G,T	h,m,y,ff	A,I,P
Toro 16401	438	○	○	◐	◐	◕	—	○	◕	1	F,L,V	e,i,k,bb,ff	B,E,F,I,M
Murray 22751	209	○	○	●	◐	◕	—	○	◕	1	E,H,M,O	g,h,i,aa,cc	D,E,I,J,L,N
Lawn Chief 35	312	○	○	◐	◐	◕	—	○	◕	1	E,F,H,N,O,V	i,k,o,aa,cc	B,D,E,I,J,L
Dynamark C2204-500	330	◐	○	○	◐	◕	—	●	◕	1	—	g,h,i,k,u	B,E,I,L,M,N
Garden Pride 78-9222	308	◐	◐	○	◐	◐	◐	●	◕	1	A,H,M,O	d,i,k,r,aa	B,D,E,I,M,P
J.C. Penney Grasshandler R850C4870	275+	○	●	●	○	◐	—	●	◕	1	E,J,N,O,V	d,g,h,i,k,l,r,u,bb	B,E,I,N

Ratings continued

254 SELF-PROPELLED MOWERS

Ratings continued

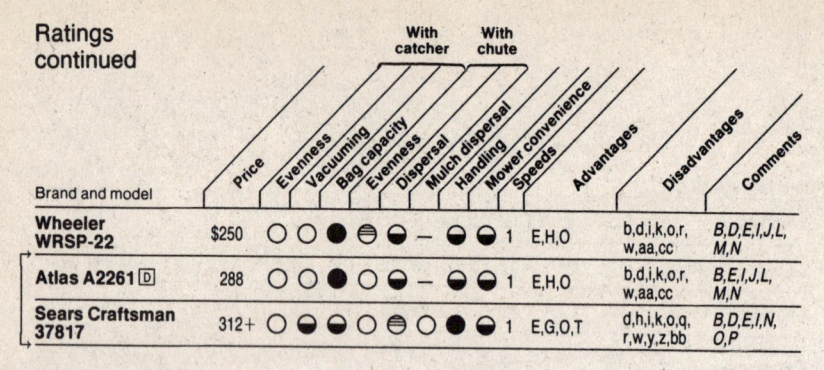

Brand and model	Price	Evenness	Vacuuming	Bag capacity	Evenness (With catcher)	Dispersal (With chute)	Mulch dispersal	Handling	Mower convenience	Speeds	Advantages	Disadvantages	Comments
Wheeler WRSP-22	$250	○	○	●	⊖	⊖	—	⊖	⊖	1	E,H,O	b,d,i,k,o,r, w,aa,cc	B,D,E,I,J,L, M,N
Atlas A2261 D	288	○	○	●	○	⊖	—	⊖	⊖	1	E,H,O	b,d,i,k,o,r, w,aa,cc	B,E,I,J,L, M,N
Sears Craftsman 37817	312+	○	⊖	●	○	⊖	○	●	⊖	1	E,G,O,T	d,h,i,k,o,q, r,w,y,z,bb	B,D,E,I,N, O,P

Performance Notes
Except as noted: • Catcher convenience was good to excellent. • Changing modes was good to excellent. • Mulching evenness very good. • Tall-grass performance was fair or poor.

Features in Common
Except as noted, all have: • Belt- or chain-driven transmission with differential or ratchet mechanism for easier turning. • 4-stroke, 3½- to 5½-hp. engine. • Rear-wheel drive. • Pull starter. • 21-in. cutting swath. • Steel deck. • Convenient way to fold handle and adjust its height. • Fuel- and oil-filler ports at or near top of engine. • Paper-element air filter that requires tools to change. • Fuel shutoff valve. • 2-yr. warranty on mower, 2-yr./5-yr. warranty on engine/ignition system.
Except as noted, all side-bagging models: • Are at least 40 in. wide with bag.

Key to Advantages
A–Relatively few clippings collected under deck in mulching test.
B–Interlock prevents use without catcher, chute, or mulching plug or cover.
C–Electric start, with pull starter as backup.
D–Clutch easy to operate and could be engaged gradually.
E–U turns easier than most.
F–Easier to maneuver than most.
G–Narrower than most side-baggers; mower with bag only 24 to 30 in. wide.
H–Easier to push and pull than most.
I–Easier or more convenient than most to start.
J–Comfortable handle.
K–Relatively easy to shift.
L–Easy to change cutting height.
M–Not as noisy as most.
N–Catcher easy to remove and install.
O–Catcher easy to empty.

P–Single control adjusts height of all 4 wheels.
Q–Mixes oil and gasoline automatically; has oil and fuel sight-gauges at rear of engine housing; engine shuts off if oil too low.
R–Fuel sight-gauge on side of engine housing.
S–Very easy to drain engine oil.
T–No tools needed to service air filter.
U–Speed range relatively wide.
V–Tall-grass performance judged excellent or very good.

Key to Disadvantages
a–Clippings accumulated under deck in mulching test.
b–Clogged discharge chute in regular cutting.
c–Left clippings in clumps in regular cutting.
d–Drive engagement coupled with safety bail; inconvenient to operate; can't engage gradually except on **Toro 20107** and **20216**.
e–Drive engagement was abrupt.
f–U turns more difficult than with most.
g–Difficult to maneuver.
h–Hard to jockey from side to side.
i–Weak traction.
j–Catcher difficult to empty.
k–Did not track precisely in straight line.
l–Harder than most to push and pull.
m–Much harder to pull than most.
n–Front end felt light when catcher was full.
o–Uncomfortable handle.
p–Handle vibrated more than most.
q–Slightly noisier than most.
r–Starter cord hard to pull or requires stooping.
s–Deadman control hard to actuate.
t–Inconvenient to change speeds.
u–Detent in throttle/choke control not precise.
v–Throttle lever judged flimsy.

STRING TRIMMERS 255

w–Catcher difficult to remove and install.
y–Chute points at user when catcher is off.
z–Exhaust blows up at user.
aa–Handle height not adjustable.
bb–Inconvenient to adjust or fold handle.
cc–Fueling and adding oil not convenient.
dd–Mower must be tipped to drain oil.
ee–Changing oil relatively messy.
ff–Catcher has inconvenient zipper closure.
gg–Speed range relatively narrow.
hh–Catcher convenience judged fair.
ii–Changing modes judged fair or poor.

Key to Comments
A–2-stroke engine.
B–Front-wheel drive.
C–Hydrostatic drive.
D–Fuel-primer bulb instead of choke.
E–No fuel shutoff valve.
F–Cast-aluminum deck. (Cast magnesium for **Lawn-Boy M21**; plastic, **Husqvarna**.)
G–Rear-discharge, rear-bagging deck.
H–Side-discharge, rear-bagging deck.
I–Side-discharge, side-bagging deck.
J–Oil-impregnated foam air filter.
K–Combination foam and paper air filter.
L–Starter cord mounts on left or right.
M–Warranty variations: 1-yr. on mower and engine (**Husqvarna, Sears**); 1-yr. on mower (**Wheelers, Atlas**); 1-yr. on mower, 2-yr. on drive mechanism (**Cub Cadet**); 1-yr. on all except blade housing (**Garden Prides**); 2-yr. on mower and engine (**John Deere, Hondas, Kubota, Toros, Dynamark**); 3-yr. on mower and engine, 5-yr. on ignition, lifetime on deck (**Lawn-Boys**); 3-yr. on drive mechanism (**Homelites**); additional 3-yr. on parts (**Ariens**); 5-yr. on deck (**Husqvarna**).
N–22-in. swath (20 in. for **Homelites**).
O–Blade change required for mulching.
P–Mulching evenness was judged good.

RATINGS — STRING TRIMMERS

Better ◀———▶ Worse

▶ See report, page 243. From Consumer Reports, June 1992.

Recommendations: Choose any of the top six gasoline-powered models to tackle large property or heavy growth. If an extension cord is practical to reach your cutting tasks, consider the top two-handled electric models, the *IDC 120* and the *Homelite ST-70*. For very modest tasks, consider a one-handled electric like the *Black & Decker 82300*.

Ratings order: Listed by types; within types, listed in order of estimated quality. Closely ranked models differed little in quality. The price is the manufacturer's suggested retail price for the trimmer and for a replacement spool of string; there may be an additional shipping charge. ▫ indicates model discontinued.

Brand and model	Price (trimmer/string)	Cutting ability	Trimming next to wall	Edging	Balance	Handling	Vibration	Noise	Operating convenience	Spool changing	Advantages	Disadvantages	Comments
GASOLINE-POWERED MODELS													
Stihl FS-36	$130/$5	◐	◐	◐	○	◐	◐	●	◐	○	E,H,I	g,j,p,s	H
Echo GT-1100	165/8	◐	◐	◐	◐	◐	○	◐	◐	◐	A,E,R,T	j,p	B,F,H,J
Sears Craftsman Weedwacker 79715	170/6	◐	◐	◐	◐	◐	●	◐	◐	○	G,H,I,J,N,S	—	D
Husqvarna 26LC	150/7	◐	◐	◐	◐	◐	◐	○	◐	○	G,H,I,N	r	D,H
Ryan 274	89/4	◐	◐	◐	◐	○	◐	◐	◐	◐	A,F,I	p,t,w	—
Weed Eater XT 50	149/8	◐	◐	◐	◐	◐	●	●	◐	○	G,H,I,J,N	—	—

Ratings continued

256 STRING TRIMMERS

Ratings continued

Column headers: Price (trimmer/string) | Cutting ability | Trimming next to wall | Edging | Balance | Handling | Vibration | Noise | Operating convenience | Spool changing | Advantages | Disadvantages | Comments

Brand and model	Price	Cut	Trim	Edge	Bal	Hand	Vib	Noise	OpCon	Spool	Advantages	Disadvantages	Comments
Sears Craftsman Weedwacker 79712	$130/$6	⊖	⊖	⊖	⊖	⊖	●	⊖	○	○	G,H,I,N,S	e	—
IDC 540	109/4	⊖	⊖	—	⊖	○	⊖	⊖	⊖	⊖	B,H,V	h,j,p,t	G
Ryan 284	99/4	⊖	⊖	—	⊖	○	⊖	⊖	⊖	⊖	B,H,V	h,j,p,t,w	G
Homelite ST-185	160/7	⊖	◐	⊖	⊖	◐	⊖	⊖	⊖	⊖	B,C,H,M,O,P,Q,R	d,j,u	G,J
McCulloch MAC 85-SL	160/7	⊖	○	⊖	○	◐	○	●	○	○	B,H,I,N,O,P,Q,R,U	j	G,K
Poulan Pro 114	150/7	⊖	⊖	⊖	⊖	⊖	●	●	○	○	G,H,I,N	—	—
RedMax BT17	160/6	○	⊖	⊖	⊖	⊖	⊖	●	○	○	I,O,P,Q	g,j,k,s,x	H,J
Weed Eater GTI 18 w/Blade	149/8	⊖	⊖	—	○	⊖	⊖	⊖	○	⊖	B,H,J,N,O	c,h,j,q,y	C,G
IDC 500	85/4	○	⊖	○	⊖	○	○	○	⊖	⊖	—	a,p,t	—
Sears Craftsman Weedwacker 79710	100/6	○	⊖	○	⊖	○	⊖	○	○	⊖	E,I,N,S	a,i	—
Homelite ST-155	100/8	○	○	○	⊖	⊖	○	○	⊖	○	M,P,Q,R	a,k,u	J
Poulan Pro 111	119/7	○	○	⊖	⊖	⊖	○	○	○	○	E,I,N	a,i	—
McCulloch MAC 65-SL	100/8	○	⊖	⊖	⊖	⊖	●	⊖	○	○	N,P,Q,R,S	a,i,j,n	H,K
McCulloch Eager Beaver Super	100/7	○	⊖	○	⊖	⊖	●	⊖	○	○	N,P,Q,R	a,i,j,n	H,K
Weed Eater GTI 15T	99/7	○	○	—	○	⊖	⊖	○	⊖	○	N,O	a,c,h,l,m,o,q	C

TWO-HANDLED ELECTRIC MODELS

Brand and model	Price	Cut	Trim	Edge	Bal	Hand	Vib	Noise	OpCon	Spool	Advantages	Disadvantages	Comments
IDC 120	55/4	⊖	⊖	⊖	⊖	⊖	⊖	⊖	○	⊖	⊖	D,E,F	—	—
Homelite ST-70	60/7	○	⊖	⊖	⊖	⊖	⊖	●	○	○	D,E,J	k,u	A,I,J
Sears Craftsman Weedwacker 79805	80/6	⊖	⊖	⊖	○	⊖	○	⊖	⊖	⊖	D,G,K	e	—
Toro 51440	65/7	○	⊖	○	⊖	⊖	⊖	○	⊖	⊖	G,H	b,x	J
Toro 51325	45/6	●	○	⊖	⊖	⊖	⊖	○	⊖	⊖	G,H	b,x	J
Weed Eater 1216	59/7	○	○	⊖	⊖	⊖	⊖	○	○	○	E,F	d,k,m	—
John Deere 72E	84/6	○	⊖	⊖	⊖	⊖	⊖	○	○	○	E,F	d,k	—
Black & Decker 82332	70/6	●	○	○	○	○	⊖	⊖	⊖	⊖	L	b,j	—
The Green Machine 1500/II	80/7	⊖	⊖	—	◐	⊖	●	○	○	○	—	d,e,h,k,v	—
Weed Eater 1212	39/5	●	○	⊖	⊖	⊖	○	○	○	○	—	b,k	—
Sears Craftsman Weedwacker 79902	40/—	●	○	◐	○	⊖	⊖	○	○	○	—	b,k	—

STRING TRIMMERS

Brand and model	Price (trimmer/string)	Cutting ability	Trimming next to wall	Edging	Balance	Handling	Vibration	Noise	Operating convenience	Spool changing	Advantages	Disadvantages	Comments
Black & Decker 82314 [D]	$65/$6	○	○	◐	○	○	◐	○	○	○	—	b,f,j	—
Paramount PT 1400 [D]	59/—	○	○	—	○	◐	○	○	◐	●	—	d,h,l,m,n, u,v,x,z	—
ONE-HANDLED ELECTRIC MODELS													
Black & Decker 82300	30/7	◐	◐	—	○	○	◐	○	○	○	—	b,h,	—
Toro 51230	25/5	●	◐	—	○	◐	◐	◐	◐	○	—	b,h,x	E,I,J
Paramount PT 90 [D]	27/—	●	◐	—	○	◐	◐	◐	◐	○	K	b,h	—
Weed Eater 1208	29/5	●	◐	—	○	○	◐	◐	◐	○	—	b,h	—
Sears Craftsman Weedwacker 79901	25/4	●	◐	—	◐	○	◐	◐	◐	●	—	b,h,x	—
Homelite ST-10	26/6	●	●	—	◐	◐	◐	○	◐	○	J	b,h	I,J

Performance Notes
Except as noted: • User comfort was good to excellent.

Features in Common
Except as noted, all have: • Single string. • "Bump-feed" string advancement. • Curved shaft. • Assist handle that can be adjusted without tools. • Replaceable string. • 1-yr. warranty.

All gasoline models: • Have 2-stroke engine. • Weigh from 9 to 15 lb.

Except as noted, all gasoline-powered models have: • Engine mounted on upper end of shaft behind main handle. • Centrifugal clutch that lets the string coast to stop when throttle is released. • Air filter that requires tools to be removed. • Opaque fuel tank mounted on top or side of engine. • Shoulder strap available.

All electric models weigh from 3 to 9 lb.

Except as noted, all electric models have: • Motor mounted low on shaft, just above cutting head. • Extension-cord retainer.

Key to Advantages
A–Compared with others, cut through heavy growth better than regular growth.
B–Comes with brush-cutter blades, judged effective (but least so with **Weed Eater GTI 18**).
C–Available with optional brush-cutting saw blade, $13, judged exceptionally effective.
D–Motor at top of shaft behind main handle; position enhances maneuverability.
E–Head shifted less than most in edging.
F–Trimmer head can be rotated to facilitate edging with handles in normal position.
G–Assist handle easier to adjust than most.
H–Assist handle more comfortable than most.
I–Main handle more comfortable than most.
J–Fully automatic string-feeding.
K–Automatically feeds string when machine is turned on.
L–Convenient lever advances string from spool on assist handle.
M–Starter-cord handle larger and more comfortable than most.
N–Choke lever especially easy to operate.
O–Ignition-kill switch especially easy to reach.
P–Screws that adjust fuel mixture well exposed for easy access.
Q–Translucent fuel tank; easy to fill and check.
R–Fuel-tank filler opening located below engine, so fuel less likely to spill on engine than with others having top or side filler openings.
S–Retainer on fuel-tank cap.
T–Air filter can be removed without tools.
U–Better balance for above-ground maneuvering than any other model with shoulder strap.
V–Shoulder strap more comfortable and easier to adjust than on most others requiring one.

Key to Disadvantages
a–No clutch. String spins continuously;

Ratings Keys continued

258 STRING TRIMMERS

judged an inconvenience and a possible safety shortcoming.

b–Judged too weak or otherwise unsuitable for trimming heavy growth. (Strings of **Toro 51440** and **Black & Decker 82314** electrics kept breaking as soon as they encountered heavy growth.)

c–Maneuverability and balance worsened when unit was raised or tilted.

d–Balance worsened considerably when unit was raised or tilted.

e–String broke fairly often in heavy growth.

f–String wore faster than others in normal use.

g–Judged awkward for short people to use.

h–Not suitable for edging. No edging instructions provided. Mfr. of **The Green Machine 1500** specifically recommends against edging.

i–Edging required more stooping than with most.

j–Adjusting assist handle more difficult than with most.

k–Adjusting assist handle more irritating than with most; sharp-edged sheet-metal wing nuts tended to dig into fingers.

l–Assist handle can't be fully tightened.

m–Assist handle less comfortable than most.

n–Main handle less comfortable than most.

o–Weaker than other gasoline-powered models when cutting heavy growth.

p–Starter-cord handle uncomfortable.

q–Starter cord awkward to pull with right hand.

r–Ignition switch confusing to use.

s–Choke control less convenient than most.

t–Cover must be removed in order to reach screws that adjust fuel mixture.

u–Throttle trigger (or On/off switch on **Homelite ST-70**) tended to pinch user's finger.

v–On/off switch inconvenient.

w–Ignition-kill switch less convenient than most.

x–Tools required to change spool. On **RedMax BT17**, additional line must be purchased in bulk ($13 for 400 ft.) and wound on spool by hand.

y–User comfort judged fair.

z–User comfort judged poor.

Key to Comments

A–Straight shaft; may help when trimming under shrubs and the like.

B–Optional cutting head with plastic blades ($14) judged ineffective in brush.

C–Vibration-isolation mounting for engine.

D–Vibration-isolation mounting for assist handle.

E–Assist handle molded with main handle, but unit is most comfortably used with one hand.

F–No carburetor-mixture adjustment.

G–Comes with shoulder strap.

H–No shoulder strap available.

I–No extension-cord retainer.

J–2-yr. warranty.

K–2-yr. warranty on engine, 1-yr. on lower drive.

How to Use the Ratings

■ Read the article for general guidance about types and buying advice.

■ Read the Recommendations for brand-name advice based on our tests.

■ Read the Ratings order to see whether products are listed in order of quality, by price, or alphabetically. Most Ratings are based on estimated quality, without regard to price.

■ Look to the Ratings table for specifics on the performance and features of individual models.

■ A model marked Ⓓ has been discontinued, according to the manufacturer. A model marked Ⓢ indicates that, according to the manufacturer, it has been replaced by a successor model whose performance should be similar to the tested model but whose features may vary.

TILLERS & CULTIVATORS

RATINGS: TILLERS & CULTIVATORS

Better ⬤ ◐ ○ ◐ ⬤ Worse

▶ **See report, page 245.** From Consumer Reports, May 1991.

Recommendations: For areas of 200 to 500 square feet, we recommend two compact models, the *J.C. Penney A870C1070A* (now *8500027*) and the *Sears 29823* (discontinued but may be in some stores); both are priced at about $300. Working small gardens or light weeding are tasks best suited to a lightweight model; any of the top five models is fine.

Ratings order: Listed by types; within types, listed in order of estimated quality. Closely ranked models differed little in quality. Price is the manufacturer's suggested or approximate retail. A + indicates an additional shipping charge. [S] indicates tested model has been replaced by successor model; according to the manufacturer, the performance of new model should be substantially similar to the tested model but features may vary. See page 260 for new model number and suggested retail price, if available. [D] indicates model discontinued.

Brand and model	Price	Tilling width, in.	Control[1]	Depth[2]	Speed	Penetration	Sod breakup	Cultivating	Convenience	Advantages	Disadvantages	Comments
COMPACT ROTOTILLERS												
J.C. Penney A870C1070A [S]	$279+	17	○	◐	◐	◐	○	○	◐	H,J,K,R	a,k	R,S
Sears Craftsman 29823 [D]	300+	17	○	◐	◐	◐	⬤	○	◐	A,H,I	i,p,q,y	R,W,Y
Ariens RT-214	489	14	◐	○	◐	◐	◐	◐	○	J,K,N,Q	a,t,v	A,P,V
Sears Craftsman 29852 [D]	280+	14	○	○	○	◐	◐	○	○	A,H,M	h,j,k,l,n,p,r,s,y	B,R,W
Honda F210 K1A	560	20	⬤	◐	◐	◐	⬤	◐	◐	B,C,E,F,J,K,M,P,Q	a,b,k,p	C,J,O,P
Lazy Boy 3LBCT [D]	349	18	◐	◐	◐	◐	○	◐	○	I,R	c,f,i,t,x,y	S
Kubota AT25	589	20	⬤	◐	◐	◐	⬤	◐	◐	C,E,J,K,M,P	a,b,j,k,p,v	D,L,O,P
CONDITIONALLY ACCEPTABLE												

■ *The following compact model has a clutch lever/deadman control that can be locked in the engaged position. Model would be Acceptable if the locking device were removed.*

Lawn Chief 31LC	329	18	◐	◐	◐	◐	○	◐	○	I,R	e,i	S
LIGHTWEIGHT TILLER/CULTIVATORS												
Hoffco Li'l Hoe	270	9	◐	○	◐	◐	◐	◐	◐	A,J,K,L,Q	g,i,l,m,n	M,O
Sears Craftsman 29702	220+	10	◐	○	◐	○	◐	◐	◐	A,J,K,L	g,l,m,n,s	O,R,W
Garden Way Speedy Hoe [S]	349	9	○	◐	◐	○	◐	◐	◐	A,J,K,L,Q	g,m,n	M,O,T,U
Lazy Boy T-5500 [S]	249	9	○	◐	◐	○	◐	◐	◐	A,J,K,L	g,m,n	O

Ratings continued

260 TILLERS & CULTIVATORS

Ratings continued

Brand and model	Price	Tilling width, in.	Control[1]	Depth[2]	Speed	Penetration	Sod breakup	Cultivating	Convenience	Advantages	Disadvantages	Comments
Ariens RC210E	$489	9	○	◐	●	◐	◐	○	◐	B,D,E,F,K,L,O	I,o,r,x	E,M,O,V
Lawn Chief 161LC	220	9	○	○	●	◐	◐	◐	◐	A,J,K,L	l,g,m,n	K
Mantis 20 (Item 7801)	359	8	◐	◐	○	◐	◐	○	○	G,L,O,P,Q,R	l,g,m,n,o,x,y	F,I,Q,U,X
Mantis Electric	359	8	◐	◐	◐	○	◐	○	◐	G,P,R	o,u,v,x,y	H,I,N,Q,U
IDC 400 [S]	150	9	◐	●	●	◐	◐	◐	◐	B,I,K,L,O,Q	a,d,k,i,l,n,o,p,r,s,w,x	G,O,R

[1] *The amount of concentrated physical effort required.*
[2] *After two passes, the second at right angles to the first.*

Successor Models (in Ratings order)
J.C. Penney A870C1070A is succeeded by 8500027, $279+; Garden Way Speedy Hoe by Troy Bilt Mini Tiller, $349; Lazy Boy T-5500 by T1010, $249; IDC 400 by Ryobi 410r, $150.

Features in Common
All: • Compact rototillers have clutch lever to engage tines. • Lightweights have centrifugal clutch and gear drive to engage tines.
Except as noted, all have: • Deadman safety control that, when released, stops movement of tines. • Depth stake to help control forward progress. • Pull-type recoil starter. • Handles that can be adjusted for height and disassembled for storage or transport. • Tines that can be adjusted for cultivation. • Paper-element air filter. • Warranty of 2 yr. on tiller and 1 yr. on engine.
Except as noted, all compact models have: • 4-stroke, 3-hp Briggs & Stratton engine with 2-qt. fuel tank. • Combination of belt drive and chain transmission drive to power tines. • 2 wheels.
Except as noted, all lightweight models: • Have 2-stroke, 1.6-hp Tecumseh engine. • Have 1-pt. fuel tank. • Lack wheels.

Key to Advantages
A–Very comfortable handle grips.
B–Comfortable handle grip.
C–Starting judged convenient.
D–Electric starting; judged very convenient.
E–Engine started more readily than most.
F–Deadman controls more comfortable than most.
G–Soil breakup more thorough than most.
H–Depth stake pivots up conveniently into retaining clip for ground transport.
I–Height adjustment for wheels.
J–Handle height adjusts without tools.
K–Handle can be folded without tools.
L–Easy to fuel. Filler opening is easy to reach; translucent tank shows fuel level.
M–Easier to fuel than most compacts. Filler opening is on top of engine housing or other prominent location. **Kubota** has spill guard with tubing leading to ground.
N–Drive belt easier to replace than most.
O–Convenient carrying handle, placed to make unit well balanced.
P–Servicing judged easier or much easier than average.
Q–Transporting judged much easier than average.
R–Root-cutting judged much better than average.

Key to Disadvantages
a–Wheels that serve as depth stake (on **Ariens RT-214, IDC**) or inadequate restraint of depth stake (on **Honda** and **Kubota**). Designs obliged operator to resort to "leapfrogging."
b–Unit tended to swerve into adjacent, previously tilled swath.
c–Exhaust is directed at operator; a deflector should be installed (see story).
d–Exhaust is directed at operator's right leg.
e–Clutch control judged very uncomfortable; requires too open a grip on handle and, consequently, excessive pressure on palm.
f–Clutch control judged uncomfortable.
g–Unstable standing by itself (**Mantis** can't stand by itself); requires support when refueling.
h–Handle judged too low, even for short operators.
i–Servicing problems: Drive belt harder to replace than most (**Sears**); access to air

TILLERS & CULTIVATORS 261

filter requires tools (**Sears, J.C. Penney, Lazy Boy, IDC, Lawn Chief**); transmission lubricant harder to add than most (**Hoffco**).
j–Clutch-lever sleeves tended to slip off.
k–Changing tine width judged more difficult than with most. **Honda** and **Kubota** lack instructions for changing tine width.
l–Noise judged worse or much worse than average.
m–Hard to start because operator must stand alongside unit.
n–Engine often needed many pulls to start.
o–Tended to bounce while tilling.
p–Tended to leave large lumps of sod or sections of untilled centerline.
q–Handles vibrated more than most.
r–Handles vibrated much more than most.
s–Hard-to-find shutoff switch located on or near engine.
t–Throttle and shutoff located inconveniently on engine.
u–Inconvenient electrical on/off switch.
v–Tines tended to tangle with roots more than most.
w–Relatively ineffective at uprooting weeds when cultivating.
x–Handle height not adjustable.
y–Handle cannot be folded or, for practical purposes, be disassembled.

Key to Comments
A–2-hp Briggs & Stratton engine.
B–2-hp, 2-stroke Tecumseh engine.
C–3-hp Honda engine.
D–3-hp Kubota engine.
E–1.1-hp Tanaka engine.
F–0.9-hp Echo engine.
G–IDC engine; horsepower unspecified.
H–0.5-hp Briggs & Stratton electric motor.
I–No depth stake.
J–Transport wheel retracts when tilling.
K–Combination depth stake/transport wheels; can be reversed.
L–Transport-wheel assembly clamps onto depth stake when needed.
M–Transport judgment given for use with optional wheel kit ($20 for **Hoffco**, $30 for **Garden Way**); without that option, unit must be carried. **Ariens** has optional wheel kit (not tested).
N–Range limited by length of power cord.
O–Oil-impregnated air filter. (**Honda** and **Kubota** have foam cover for air filter.)
P–Transmission to tines is gear drive only.
Q–1-mo. "no risk" warranty; buyers can return unit to dealer for full refund if unhappy.
R–1-yr. warranty on tiller and engine.
S–2-yr. warranty on engine, 5-yr. on ignition.
T–3-yr. warranty on tiller.
U–Tines warranted for life against breakage.
V–Reduced warranty for parts, including tines, subject to normal wear.
W–Tines excluded from warranty.
X–Lightest in weight at 19 lb.
Y–Heaviest in weight at 81 lb.

What the Ratings Mean

- The Ratings typically rank products in order of estimated quality, without regard to price.

- A product's rating applies only to the model tested and should not be considered a rating of other models sold under the same brand name unless so noted.

- Models are check-rated (✓) when the product proved to be significantly superior to other models tested.

- Products high in quality and relatively low in price are deemed Best Buys.

CHIPPERS/SHREDDERS

RATINGS: CHIPPERS/SHREDDERS

Better ⊖ ⊖ ○ ⊖ ● Worse

▶ **See report, page 246.** From Consumer Reports, June 1991.

Recommendations: Give first consideration to one of the four Best Buys in the Ratings. The *Sears 79785* and the *MTD 240-645* (now *243-645*) gasoline models are powerful enough to handle large limbs and bushels of leaves quickly. The electric *Flowtron Leaf Eater* and *Sears Leafwacker* were expert shredders.

Ratings order: Listed by types; within types, listed in order of estimated quality. Closely ranked models differed little in quality. Models judged essentially equal in quality are bracketed and listed alphabetically. Price is the manufacturer's suggested retail price. ⓢ indicates tested model has been replaced by successor model; according to the manufacturer, the performance of new model should be substantially similar to the tested model but features may vary. See right for new model number and suggested retail price, if available. ⓓ indicates model discontinued.

Brand and model	Price	Power[1]	Safety	Chipping speed	Feeding branches	Shredding Speed, leaves	Shredding Speed, twigs	Feeding leaves	Advantages	Disadvantages	Comments
GASOLINE-POWERED CHIPPERS/SHREDDERS											
Sears Craftsman 79785, A Best Buy	$550	5 hp	○	⊖	○	⊖	⊖	⊖	A,C,G	h,j,k,r,t,v,w,z,bb	I,T
MTD 240-645 ⓢ A Best Buy	579	5	○	⊖	○	⊖	⊖	⊖	A,C,G	h,j,r,t,v,w,z,bb	I,O,T
Troy-Bilt Super Tomahawk	1300	5	○	⊖	○	⊖	⊖	○	B,G,L	h,j,n,q,t,aa	H,I,P,R,T
Kemp Master Gardener K6	1088	5	⊖	⊖	○	⊖	⊖	⊖	B,E,N	a,h,l,o,t,aa	I,P,T,V
Baker 612-3.5	879	3.5	●	○	○	○	⊖	⊖	J	d,j,q	E,I,R
Troy-Bilt Junior Tomahawk ⓓ	729	3	○	○	⊖	⊖	⊖	⊖	B,F,N	a,b,h,j,s,y,aa	G,H,P,S
AL-KO B3000	289	3.5	●	⊖	○	●	○	●	E,F	b,c,h,k,r	D,O,T,W
Mighty Mac Mini Mac SC603 ⓓ	569	3	⊖	⊖	⊖	○	●	[2]	●	A,F,J,K,M	b,c,j,l,o	O,R,T
ELECTRIC CHIPPERS/SHREDDERS											
Sears Craftsman 79688 ⓓ	297	10	⊖	●	⊖	⊖	○	○	A,B,E,F,J,K	b,e,p	A,B,I,S,U,W
Flowtron CS-3000 ⓢ	399	12	⊖	○	⊖	○	⊖	○	B,D,E,F	b,f,h,i,k,n,p	A,I,S,T,U,W
AL-KO H1600 ⓓ	299	14	○	⊖	⊖	●	○	●	D,E,F,J,K	b,c,i,k	F,O,W
ELECTRIC LEAF SHREDDERS											
Flowtron Leaf Eater LE800, A Best Buy	99	5.9	○	—	—	⊖	—	⊖	H,I,K	g,j,u,x	K,Q

CHIPPERS/SHREDDERS 263

Brand and model	Price	Power[1]	Safety	Chipping speed	Feeding branches	Speed, leaves (Shredding)	Speed, twigs	Feeding leaves	Advantages	Disadvantages	Comments
Sears Craftsman Leafwacker 79685, A Best Buy	$100	5.9	○	—	—	◉	—	◉	H,I,K	g,j,k,u,x	J,Q
Atlas ALS	130	6	○	—	—	○	—	○	D,H,I	g,j,u,x	B,I,L,Q
Wheeler AWLS	130	6	○	—	—	○	—	○	D,H,I	g,j,u,x	B,I,L,Q
Brave LM-150	273	12	◉	—	—	◉	●	○	G	f,h,j,k	B,F,I,T,W
ELECTRIC CHIPPERS											
Lescha Zak 1800	400	11	◉	◉	◉	—	◉	—	A,F,G,J	f,k,m	B,F,M,T
Mantis Deluxe ChipMate [S]	369	12	○	◉	○	—	◉	—	B,F,G	a,f,h,k,t,aa	C,E,I,N,O

[1] *Power is horsepower for gasoline engines; motor amperage for electrics.*
[2] *Long twigs are chipped, not shredded, says mfr.*

Successor Models (in Ratings order)
MTD 240-645 is succeeded by 243-645, $579; Flowtron CS-3000 by CS-3500, $399; Mantis Deluxe ChipMate by Mantis ChipMate, $299.

Performance Notes
All: • Noise level during chipping was fair or poor.
Except as noted: • Noise level during shredding was average or better.

Features in Common
Except as noted, all: • Come with safety goggles. • Have reversible and replaceable shredding and chipping blades. • Have 1-yr. warranty (all gasoline-powered models have 1-yr. engine warranty). • Models that chip have 1 chipping blade. • Have 2 wheels. • Are fairly difficult to disassemble for servicing. • Can shred twigs up to ½-in. dia. • Lack means to adjust fineness of chips or shreds. • Can discharge into bag or other container.
Except as noted, all gasoline-powered models: • Are approx. 28 in. long, 30 in. wide, 42 in. high. • Have steel hopper and base. • Have engine throttle control. • Require tools to service air cleaner. • Have four-stroke engine. • Weigh approx. 120 lb.
Except as noted, all electric models: • Are approx. 26 in. long, 26 in. wide, 40 in. high. • Have plastic hopper and base. • Weigh approx. 40 lb.

Key to Advantages
A–Control of last piece easier than with most.
B–Comes with shredding tamper.
C–Hopper or ramp swings down to allow leaves to be raked in effectively.
D–Interlock prevents use if housing or hopper is dismantled.
E–Shredder blades can't be reached.
F–Chipper blades can't be reached.
G–Discharges into reusable bag ($25 option for **Troy-Bilt**; $24 for **Lescha Zak**; $19 for **Brave**).
H–Discharges more neatly onto ground than most others.
I–Adjusting fineness of discharge easier than with most.
J–Easier than most to wheel over soft ground.
K–Access for servicing better than most.
L–Has oil-level gauge.
M–Air cleaner can be removed without tools.
N–Vibrated less than most while shredding twigs.

Key to Disadvantages
a–Control of last bit of branch more difficult than most. (**Kemp** recommends against chipping last pieces.)
b–Straight-sided chipping chute; accepts only straight branches.
c–Lacks tamper; simple stick tamper judged unsuitable.
d–Comes with cardboard tamper, which cutters may chew up.
e–Cannot shred twigs larger than ¼-in. dia.
f–Harder than most to feed twigs for shredding.
g–Shredded leaves blew out of hopper.
h–Pieces of twig blew out of hopper.

Ratings Keys continued

CHIPPERS/SHREDDERS

i–Some chips blew out of shredding hopper.
j–Hand could reach cutting blades, though judged unlikely. Nylon-line cutter on **Sears 79685** and **Flowtron LE800** judged very easy to reach.
k–Goggles not included.
l–Discharge messier than most.
m–Discharging chips can bounce at user.
n–Harder than most to adjust fineness of discharge.
o–Couldn't discharge into container.
p–Discharged material clings to bag.
q–Has clutch that must be engaged carefully or engine will stall.
r–Engine harder to start than most.
s–Engine shutoff relatively inconvenient.
t–Harder to move than most.
u–Air cleaner requires frequent cleaning.
v–Dealer must reverse or replace shredding cutters
w–Adding oil requires long funnel.
x–Makes annoying high-pitched noise.
y–Shredded fewer twigs at a time than most.
z–Vibration increased when unit chipped largest branches it's designed to handle.
aa–Vibrated more than most while shredding twigs.
bb–Noisier than most when shredding.

Key to Comments

A–Can be laid on its back to make ramp for raking leaves into hopper; judged ineffective.
B–No tamper provided, but tamping with a stick judged effective.
C–Brake must be used to quickly stop chipping blades.
D–Has two-stroke engine.
E–Has 2 chipper blades.
F–Has steel hopper and base (aluminum hopper on **Brave**).
G–Has plastic hopper.
H–Engine lacks throttle control.
I–Size variations: **Troy-Bilt Super,** 40 in. long; **Kemp,** 53 in. long; **Baker,** 34 in. long; **Sears 79785, MTD,** 49 in. long, 27½ in. high; **Mantis,** 18 in. long; **Flowtron CS-3000,** 36½ in. long; **Wheeler, Atlas,** 34½ in. wide, 52 in. high; **Sears 79688,** 35 in. high, 18 in. wide; **Brave,** 19 in. wide.
J–Comes with 6 sets of replacement cutters.
K–Comes with 18 sets of replacement cutters and 10 collection bags.
L–Comes with 1 set of replacement blades.
M–Comes with replacement chipper blade and necessary tools.
N–Comes with 2 sets of replacement chipper blades, hand pruner, and necessary tools.
O–Has 2-yr. warranty.
P–Unlimited warranty on everything but engine.
Q–Has legs instead of wheels, but light enough to move easily.
R–Fineness of discharge can be adjusted with optional screens ($36 to $50 each).
S–Comes with screen to adjust fineness of discharge.
T–Weight variations: **Flowtron CS-3000, Brave, Lescha Zak,** approx. 60 lb.; **AL-KO B3000,** 51 lb.; **Mighty Mac,** 100 lb.; **Sears 79785, MTD,** 138 lb.; **Troy-Bilt Super,** 234 lb.; **Kemp,** 284 lb.
U–Processed material leaks through gaps in housing.
V–Optional leaf hopper, $46. Kit that includes tamper, safety goggles, tarpaulin for discharge, $39.
W–Shredding cutters aren't reversible.

*A*BOUT PRICES IN THE BUYING GUIDE

Prices for most products, notably big-ticket items such as kitchen appliances, home-electronics gear, and gardening equipment, have been updated for the Buying Guide. The prices we give, unless otherwise noted, are approximate or suggested retail as quoted by the manufacturer. Discounts may therefore be substantial, especially for electronics and camera equipment.

GAS BARBECUE GRILLS 265

RATINGS: GAS BARBECUE GRILLS

Better ◉ ◐ ○ ◑ ● Worse

▶ See report, page 247. From Consumer Reports, July 1991.

Recommendations: The top grills—the *Weber Genesis 4* ($649) and its less elaborate sibling, the *Genesis 2* ($499)—combine fine cooking performance with useful features and conveniences. They've both been replaced, but we expect similar performance from their successors.

Ratings order: Listed in order of estimated quality. Price is the manufacturer's suggested or approximate retail price, excluding propane; actual retail may be lower. ⓈⓈ indicates tested model has been replaced by successor model; according to the manufacturer, the performance of new model should be substantially similar to the tested model but features may vary. See page 266 for new model number and suggested retail price, if available. ⒹⒹ indicates model discontinued.

Brand and model	Price	Max. heat, 1000 Btu/hr. [1]	Warm-up time, min.	Temperature uniformity	Roasting, warming	Overall convenience	Advantages	Disadvantages	Comments
Weber Genesis 4 Ⓢ	$649	35	14	◐	◉	◉	A,C,E,G,H,K,L,N,Q,R,U	—	C,I,K,L,O,U
Weber Genesis 2 Ⓢ	499	35	10	◐	◉	◉	A,E,G,I,K,L,N,Q,R	—	A,C,I,K,L,O,R,U
Ducane 2002SHLPE	666	25	23	◐	○[2]	○	B,D,E,F,H,L,N,P,R,U,W,X	d,f	F,K,M,O,P,Q,R,U
Nordic 73240 Ⓓ	549	40	5	◐	●	◉	A,J,L,S	—	A,B,H,J,L,N,U
Broilmaster D4GCP Ⓢ	659	40	9	◐	◉	◐	B,L,M,N,O,V,X	b	A,D,K,L,P,Q,R,T,U
Thermos 42018401 Ⓢ	219	44	5	◐	○	○	I,L,T	i	H,J,L,O,S
Thermos 44018404 Ⓢ	315	46	8	◐	○	○	I,L	—	H,J,N
Sunbeam 69508 Ⓓ	580	44	9	◐	○	◐	B,H,I,J,M,T	c,e,i	H,J,N,W
Charmglow Classic 0903 Ⓢ	325	42	7	◐	○	○	J	g,h,i	A,G,J,L,N,T,U
Arklamatic 42600 RPB Ⓓ	199	44	7	◐	◐	◐	L,M	b,i	D
Sears Kenmore 15601 Ⓓ	289	44	11	◐	○	◐	J,L,M,T	b	F,O,Q,V,X
Char-Broil 9048 Ⓓ	239	46	5	●	○	◐	B,N	a,b,c,g	E,J,L,N,W
Sunbeam 36201 Ⓢ	396	42	11	○	●	◐	I,M	b,c,h,i	F,J,L,W
Char-Broil 8056 Ⓓ	199	44	5	●	◐	◐	B,N	a,b,c,g	A,E,J,L,O,W

Ratings continued

266 GAS BARBECUE GRILLS

Ratings continued

Brand and model	Price	Max. heat, 1000 Btu/hr.[1]	Warm-up time, min.	Temperature uniformity	Roasting, warming	Overall convenience	Advantages	Disadvantages	Comments
Sears Kenmore 15401	190	42	10	◐	●	◐	L,X	b,i	D,Q,R,V,X
Thermos 30016019 [S]	$149	30	6	○	●	◐	—	b,h	D,J,R
Sunbeam Deluxe 35608 [S]	362	40	20	○	○	◐	I,M	a,b,c,h,i	A,F,J,L,W
Char-Broil 7032 [D]	159	42	4	◐	●	◐	—	a,b,c,g,j	A,E,J,L,W

[1] *As claimed by manufacturer.*
[2] *Has rotisserie system powered by separate burner. Judged ◐ for roasting.*

Successor Models (in Ratings order)
Weber Genesis 4 succeeded by 4000, $649; Weber Genesis 2 by 2000, $499; Broilmaster D4GCP by D47AGP, $674; Thermos 42018401 by 44118005, $219; Thermos 44018404 by 44118401, $315; Charmglow Classic 0903 by 30912, $500; Char-Broil 9048 by 9273, $299; Thermos 30016019 by 32116001, $149; Sunbeam Deluxe 35608 by 35413, $362.

Performance Notes
All: • Performed excellent or very good at grilling steaks and burgers.
Except as noted, all: • Performed excellent or very good at grilling chicken and fish.

Features in Common
All have: • Chrome steel warming grates. • Carts made of tubular steel. • Piezoelectric igniter. • Provision for lighting with match. • Lighting instructions on control panel.
Except as noted, all have: • 20-lb. refillable fuel tank. • Glass window. • Rectangular, cast-aluminum firebox and lid. • Porcelain-coated steel cooking grates. • Burner with 2 independent controls. • Metal casing around igniter to shield it from grease and dirt. • Thermometer. • Fuel gauge. • 2 wheels and 2 casters. • Front lid handle. • Wooden side shelves. • 5-yr. warranty on castings. • 3-yr. warranty on burners.

Key to Advantages
A–Materials and construction judged of much higher quality than others.
B–Materials and construction judged of higher quality than others.
C–Heat sensor shuts off gas if flames go out.
D–Stainless-steel grates designed to catch and vaporize drippings.
E–Valve, burner, and igniter are factory assembled.
F–Glow wire indicates when flame is lit.
G–Has 3 separate burners and controls, and removable bottom panel for easy cleanup.
H–Comes with wood-chip smoker.
I–Screen on burner keeps out insects.
J–Has rotary igniter.
K–More shelf space than others.
L–Fuel tank easier to install than others.
M–1 adjustable grate (3 on **Broilmaster**).
N–Wide grates, good for searing.
O–Has porcelain-coated cast-iron grates, which seared better than others.
P–Galvanized-steel cart and stainless-steel hardware.
Q–Nylon washers on hardware.
R–Instructions better than most.
S–Has timer that can shut off burner.
T–Comes with side burner.
U–Fuel tank attaches to fuel line with quick-connect fitting.
V–Fuel tank attaches with handwheel.
W–Detachable side shelf/cutting board.
X–Handles on sides of lid.

Key to Disadvantages
a–Fuel gauge inaccurate.
b–Grate under lava rock bare steel; may rust.
c–Inconvenient to light with match.
d–Much less shelf space than others.
e–Heavy lid is difficult to handle.
f–Igniter button not readily visible.
g–Igniter unprotected from grease/dirt.
h–Fuel tank is inconvenient to attach.
i–Knobs got much hotter than others.
j–Grilling of chicken and fish judged not as good as others.

Key to Comments
A–At least one burner section blew out in lid-drop test.
B–Nickel-plated steel and aluminum lid.
C–Porcelain-coated steel and aluminum lid.
D–Uses lava rock to radiate heat.
E–Uses charcoal-type briquettes.
F–Uses ceramic briquettes.
G–Uses cast-iron plates.
H–Uses porcelain-coated steel plates.
I–Uses porcelain-coated steel triangles.
J–Mfr. has toll-free customer-service line.
K–Lacks window.
L–Has fold-down front shelf.
M–Lacks temperature gauge.
N–Comes with mechanical timer and alarm.
O–Side shelves disconnect or fold down.
P–Fuel tank must be purchased separately.
Q–Lacks fuel gauge.
R–Has only 2 wheels.
S–Has glass side and front shelves.
T–10-yr. warranty on castings.
U–5-yr. warranty on burners.
V–1-yr. warranty on burners.
W–Life-time warranty on castings.
X–1-yr. warranty on castings.

How to get more information

Check out what we've said in CONSUMER REPORTS. For the date of recent reports, refer to the four-year index in the back of the Buying Guide or the date noted on each Ratings table. Back issues are available at most libraries or can be ordered. You can also get the latest new- and used-car price information. For details, see page 307 (new cars) and page 310 (used cars).

Auto products

Tires 268
Batteries 270
Security systems 271
Child safety seats 273
Ratings 276

The cost of owning a car doesn't end when you drive out of the showroom, of course. If you own a car for any length of time, you'll have to replace its tires and battery. Anyone wary of car thieves might want a security system. And if you've got an infant or toddler, a child-safety seat is a must as well.

With tires, choosing the right size is important. The key to shopping for a battery is freshness. But first you have to crack the codes. We tell you how.

Auto-security devices come in simple and complex packages, some little more than a siren; others, sophisticated systems that disable the engine and set the headlights flashing.

We also provide a guide to infant carriers, "convertible" car seats, and booster seats. Infant seats provide the best fit for a newborn. A convertible seat can be used facing rearward for babies then, reversed for toddlers and larger children. A booster seat works when a child is too big for a convertible seat and not tall enough for the car's own seat and shoulder restraints.

Tires

Tires determine in large part how smoothly and safely the car rides, steers, accelerates, and brakes. Yet even the best tires are products of compromise; enhancing one characteristic often entails some sacrifice of another. A chunky tread pattern, for instance, may give better winter traction but poorer performance on dry roads. Stiff sidewalls may give sharper steering response and a harsher ride.

Of the many dozens of tire brands crowding the market, most are owned or controlled by half a dozen corporate giants—Bridgestone, Continental, Goodyear,

Michelin, Pirelli, and Sumitomo. But that doesn't mean all the brands are more similar now than in the past. Fact is, most tire makers produce a wide range of models that differ considerably in price and performance. Even within a given tire model, one size may perform differently from another.

The choices

While there are tires designed for dry roads or for mud and snow, all-weather, or all-season, tires make sense for most people. Other factors being equal, all-season tires grip as well as conventional tires on dry and wet roads—and better than conventional tires on ice and snow, although not as well as snow tires in deep snow. Radials have all but replaced bias-ply and bias-based tires. So-called performance models tend to be biased in favor of superior road grip and cool running at high speeds, advantages that may come at the expense of a smoother ride, cold-weather traction, and tread life.

You can tell a lot about a tire by the coding molded into the sidewall. The U.S. Department of Transportation requires tire manufacturers to state the following on all passenger-car tires:

Size. A typical tire-size designation is P185/70R14 87S. The "P" stands for a P-metric-size tire.

The "185" is the nominal width of the tire's cross section in millimeters. And the "70" indicates the height of the sidewall—or, more precisely, the ratio of sidewall height to cross-section width. Thus on a 185/70R14 tire, the height of the sidewall is about 70 percent of 185mm, or 130mm. (The tire industry refers to that ratio as the "aspect ratio.")

The "R" stands for radial construction. The "14" is the diameter, in inches, of the metal wheel that the tires are designed to fit.

The "87S" is a service designation consisting of a load index and speed symbol. The speed symbols are as follows: S stands for 112 mph; T for 118; U for 124; H for 130; V for 130+.

Load and pressure. Say the designation is "Max load 590 kg (1301 lbs) @ 240 kPa (35 psi) max press." If the tire is inflated to 35 pounds per square inch, the maximum recommended pressure, it can safely support 1301 pounds. Four such tires should support 5204 pounds (total weight of car, passengers, and luggage).

Tread wear. An index based on how quickly the tread wears under conditions specified by the Government, relative to a "standard" tire. The index won't tell you exactly how long the tire will last on your car; driving conditions vary too much. But a tire with a tread-wear index of 200 should wear about twice as long as one with an index of 100 under like conditions.

Traction. A measure of the tire's ability to stop on wet pavement under specified conditions. Grades range from A (highest) to C (lowest). All but one of the tire models we tested are labeled A.

Temperature. A measure of the tire's resistance to heat buildup under simulated high-speed driving. Again, grades range from A (highest) to C (lowest). All the tires we tested are graded B.

Note that the tire manufacturer, not the DOT, performs the tests for tread wear, traction, and temperature. Snow tires are not required to list those three indices.

Date of manufacture. Every passenger car carries a DOT identification number—for example, DOT B9PA B55X 101. The last three digits identify the week and year of manufacture. For example, "101" means the tenth week of 1991. That date is important for two reasons: Tire compounds harden with age, so you should look for a tire made no more than a year ago. Also, when tires are recalled, the date of manufacture can help determine whether the tire is affected by the recall.

The test

Before testing starts, we break in the tires by driving them for more than 500 miles. Then we subject them to various road conditions on our asphalt test track: braking on wet and dry pavement, cornering at progressively faster speeds, and coasting 2100 feet from 40 mph, to judge rolling resistance, which affects fuel economy. In addition, our test drivers evaluate how quickly, accurately, and quietly a tire responds to the steering wheel.

We don't test for tread wear. The Government requires tire makers themselves to run such tests and to imprint an estimate of tread wear on the sidewall of all passenger-car tires. We include those tread-wear estimates in the Ratings.

Buying advice

The perfect tire—one ideally suited to all road conditions and driving styles—has yet to be invented. As a result, you have to accept tradeoffs. In our judgment, all-season tires provide the best combination of characteristics for most drivers.

A tire's list price means little. Many dealers offer sizable discounts, and special promotions may further reduce the price.

BATTERIES

▶ Ratings on page 279.

The typical auto battery contains six cells, which are small compartments filled with metal plates immersed in sulfuric acid and water. This electrolyte fosters a reaction between the plates, generating current that the battery can deliver on demand. Batteries used to require regular refilling with distilled water, because the lead alloy in the plates led to "gassing" during the charging cycle, breaking down the water's component molecules into hydrogen and oxygen gas that escaped through cell vents. Modern-day auto batteries use different alloys to slow that reaction and reduce the water loss.

The choices

There are three principal types of batteries on the market today: low-maintenance, maintenance-free, and "dual." Low-maintenance batteries have caps or covers over their cells to permit periodic checking and refilling. Maintenance-free batteries are designed to reduce water loss further; indeed, some have no refill caps. On the downside, maintenance-free batteries may not fare as well as low-maintenance batteries after deep discharges. The dual type is a new design. It typically combines a low-maintenance battery with separate backup cells that can be activated to supply extra emergency power.

Size. Manufacturers further categorize batteries by group size—24, 26, 34, and so forth—which denotes the size of the case (but has no direct bearing on the power output). You probably won't find the group-size number in your car's owner's manual, so you may have to check the label on the old battery or refer to the battery dealer's handbook.

Cold-cranking amps. In addition, manufacturers rate the cold-cranking amperage (CCA) of their models. The CCA is the amount of current a battery should be able to deliver at 0°F without dropping below a certain cutoff voltage for 30 seconds—which translates into the battery's ability to supply power long enough to start your car in below-freezing weather. For our last report, we tested two popular power ranges: batteries with a claimed CCA of 455 to 550 and those with a claimed CCA of 600 to 650.

The tests

We judge performance using standard industry tests. First, we make sure each battery is fully charged. Then we check each model's cold-cranking amperage and reserve capacity. The number for reserve capacity, given in minutes, describes a battery's ability to continue supplying power to the engine and accessories if the car's charging system fails. We've found that many models fail to match their claimed cold-cranking ability. Conversely, experience has shown that most batteries meet or exceed their claimed reserve capacity.

The shipping code, which usually appears on a sticker affixed to the battery or a stamp on the battery case, reveals the approximate age of a battery. It may be a string of letters and numbers, but all the information a consumer needs is in the first two characters. Usually, the code starts with a letter that corresponds with the month—"A" for January through "L" for December (some codes omit "I"; for them, "M" indicates December). The second character of the code is a numeral that stands for the year. Thus, a code starting "A2" indicates that the battery was shipped in January 1992; "B2" indicates February 1992, and so on. (Delco reverses the letter and the number; a Delco code starting with "2C" indicates the battery was shipped in March 1992.)

Buying advice

If your old battery has served you well, replace it with a fresh one that has comparable cold-cranking amperage. There's usually no reason to buy a more powerful battery: You'll pay for power your car may never need.

SECURITY SYSTEMS

In 1991, more than 1.5 million cars were stolen in the U.S. Many more were broken into by thieves in search of audio equipment and other booty. Car thieves like to work quickly. A professional thief can unlatch a car door in less than a minute, and even an amateur with crude tools doesn't need much longer. But car thieves want to work furtively, too. So auto security devices are designed to scare a thief off with an alarm or to make the theft such a time-consuming job that the thief gives up.

The choices

Most alarm systems contain the same types of components: a dashboard-mounted display to warn away thieves, one or more sensors to detect a break-in, a siren to attract attention, a remote control to arm and disarm the system, and a control module to run the works. In the more sophisticated "two-piece" systems, siren and control module are separate components. The simpler "one-piece" systems put those parts in a single housing. Alarm systems may be armed actively or passively. With active arming, a system won't work unless you press a remote control after leaving the car. A passive system arms itself after the last protected opening on the car is closed, a feature known as "last-door arming." With some systems, you can elect active or passive arming, but you usually have to make that choice at installation time. A panel of CU staffers enlisted to try out the systems tested preferred passive systems. Professionally installed systems typically cost $200 to $1500. Systems designed for self-installation typically range in price from $60 to $350.

Features to look for

The more forms of resistance an alarm system presents, the more likely it is to foil a break-in.

Siren. It should sound long enough to attract attention, but not so long that a false alarm disturbs the peace. Several cycles of a minute or two each should be adequate. Two-piece systems are more likely to work that way than one-piece systems. In addition to sheer volume, a siren can call attention to itself by cycling through several unique sounds. Having the parking lights or headlights flash at the same time the siren sounds is another attention-getter.

Engine disabler. This important feature prevents the thief from starting the car. Most manufacturers recommend you set up the system to disable the starter. But a disabled starter is an indication to a thief of the presence of a security system, increasing the chances of it being found and bypassed. Whereas, disabling the fuel pump or the ignition system is more effective, because both disable the car without advertising the presence of the security system or its location. But doing so leaves a small risk that the disabler could malfunction while you're driving and cause the engine to stall.

Intrusion sensors. The more types of sensors the better. A sensor should protect all parts of the car equally. It should be designed so you can easily vary its sensitivity by tightening a screw or adjusting a stem. Types of sensors include: shock sensors, which detect a sharp blow to the vehicle's body; motion detectors, which react to jacking, swaying, or bouncing motions; and glass-breakage sensors, which respond if someone tampers with or breaks any of the car's glass.

Hood and trunk protection. Models that monitor electrical usage help protect doors, hood, and trunk. For instance, the alarm sounds if someone opens the door and the courtesy light goes on. If the car lacks courtesy lights under the hood or in the trunk, the alarm system should come with a set of switches to protect hood and trunk.

Remote panic alarm. Standard on most systems, this allows you to trigger the alarm with the remote control if you see someone trying to break into the car or if you see someone suspicious approaching while you're in the car.

Remote door lock. This is a useful feature for cars with power locks. When you arm the system, it automatically locks the doors and unlocks them when disarmed.

Conveniences. These are important to the ultimate success of any alarm system. For instance, a remote control that operated from a long distance might let you control the system from your living room or set off the panic alarm at a safe distance from the car. Other handy features include an emergency override to disarm the alarm if the remote is missing or out of order; a valet switch (on passively armed models) to turn the system off when you hand the car over to a parking attendant; a dashboard display that tells you if the alarm was triggered while you were away; and well-written operating instructions.

The tests

After installing a system in a car, we judge its effectiveness based on the performance of its key components: siren, engine disabler, intrusion sensors, and door, hood, and trunk protectors. For instance, we measured each siren's output with a sound-level meter six feet in front of the car in an outdoor lot. We also evaluate ease-of-use and convenience factors, based on our engineers' expert judgment, and the experiences of a panel of staffers who let us install the systems in their cars.

Buying advice

Look for a model that's easy to use. Next, look for important features such as a disabler, dashboard display, and hood and trunk protection.

Many auto security systems on the market are sold by specialized auto security shops or car-alarm dealers and are professionally installed. Choose an installer with care. In our experience, skill levels and fees vary considerably from one shop to another. People who prefer to install their own systems may have a hard time installing a sophisticated system; they generally take a high level of skill. First you must figure out where to mount all the alarm-system components—the siren in the engine compartment, control box in the passenger compartment, sensors in the firewall, pin switches at the hood and trunk, the LED display on the dashboard—and run the wiring between them. Then there's a good deal of mechanical skill needed in actually putting the parts in place so that they'll work.

If you've installed electronic car equipment before, you have some inkling of what you're in for. But if you've never drilled through sheet metal or poked around under the dashboard, installing an alarm is likely to be frustrating and perhaps damaging to your car.

CHILD SAFETY SEATS

▶ Ratings on page 276.

A crash at 30 mph will propel an unrestrained 15-pound baby with some 300 pounds of force, the equivalent of a fall from three stories. It won't help that baby to be cradled in the arms of an adult. An adult wearing a safety belt lacks the strength and reactive skills to hold onto the child. And the body of an unbelted adult propelled forward by the same crash will likely crush the child with one to two tons of force.

According to the National Highway Traffic Safety Administration (NHTSA), child safety seats can cut the risk of death or serious injury by about 70 percent. State laws reflect that reality. Every state requires children, usually those under the age of four or weighing 40 pounds or less, to travel by car in an approved child safety seat. Unfortunately, many parents ignore those laws and others use the seats incorrectly. A U.S. Department of Transportation survey found that 16 percent of parents didn't use a car safety seat for their children. And of the parents who did use a seat, 36 percent used it incorrectly.

The choices

Safety seats range in price from around $20 to $120 and come in three types: infant-only, for birth up to 20 pounds or 27-inches tall; convertible, for children from birth up to 40 pounds or 40 inches; and booster, generally for children weighing 30 to 50 pounds.

Infant seats. This type provides the snuggest fit for a newborn. It's shaped like a shallow shell that keeps a baby semi-reclined, and it's installed in the car so that the baby rides backward. The back of the shell, in combination with a simple harness, provides restraint in a head-on crash by spreading the forces across the infant's back. Infant seats can also double as infant carriers, feeding chairs, or rockers.

Convertible seats. They are so called because they can be used for infants and faced rearward—the safest way for infants to travel—and later be converted to face forward to hold a larger child, weighing 20 to 40 pounds. Many convertible seats combine shoulder and crotch straps with a padded shield, shaped either like a T or a bar. They're convenient to use and provide good protection for toddlers but they're not the best choice for very small infants. On the models we examined, the shields would be head-high on a small infant; not only could they obscure the infant's face, but they could prevent the restraining harness from fitting snugly against shoulders and chest. In our judgment, the only convertible seats suitable for very small infants (10 to 12 pounds or less) are those with a five-point harness, one that has straps over the shoulders and thighs, and a crotch strap, all fastening to a single buckle at the child's lap. A five-point harness can be adjusted to conform to the size and shape of any child's body and thus hold it securely.

Booster seats. Most booster seats simply elevate the child; the car's safety belts provide all the restraint. A few booster models can be strapped in with the car's belts and have a shield that restrains the child.

Features to look for

Seat attachments. Safety seats are typically held in place by the car's safety belts. Look for models that allow plenty of room to weave those belts through the seat frame or slots in the shell. Installation is more difficult on models that have long, narrow tunnels or slots for the belts. Make sure that the padding doesn't interfere with the belts and that the buckles are easy to fasten and unfasten.

Shields and straps. Buckling a child into the safety seat itself depends largely on how easily you can position the harness, adjust the straps, and fasten the latch. Securing a baby in an infant-only seat isn't much of a problem. Most have a V-shaped three-point harness that slips over the head and then buckles at the foot end. Booster seats are relatively easy to use, too. Most simply involve tightening the vehicle's own safety belts around the seat. For those with a shield, you lift or remove the shield to let the child in, reposition it, and tighten the car's safety belt around the front of the shield; the shoulder belt then goes behind the child.

Among convertible models, seats with a T-shaped shield and shoulder straps take the least amount of work. You can pull out a length of webbing, slip the strap and shield over the child's head, and latch the T-shield to the seat in a single motion. Manipulating a five-point harness takes a bit more doing. You need both hands to gather the belts together and insert two separate latch plates into a single buckle. Bar-shield models require more overhead clearance when the bar is in the overhead, open position than the other types, and with most of them, you have to lengthen the straps to raise the bar-shield every time the child gets out.

Seats with an automatic belt-retracting mechanism for the harness tend to be the easiest to adjust.

The tests

Since 1981, NHTSA has required manufacturers of child safety seats to certify that their seats would pass rigorous crash tests. In one key test, a safety seat holding a 33-pound child-sized dummy is mounted on an impact sled that simulates a head-on crash into a rigid barrier at 30 mph; the seat must remain intact and keep the dummy's head from pitching too far forward. The NHTSA standard includes a similar test using a 17½ pound dummy. The standard doesn't include tests for rear or side collisions. Nor does it specifically address the problem of finding the right kind and size of seat for a child.

Because the Federal Government routinely monitors compliance with its safety standards, we don't try to duplicate its safety tests. Instead, we evaluate the seats mainly in terms of ease of installation and use.

Buying advice

Parents of newborn infants may choose among infant-only and convertible models. But for the first few months, at least, an infant-only seat makes more sense. It fits snugly and protects with a harness system designed expressly for infants. It's also light enough to carry easily.

If you want a safety seat that will follow the growth of your child, choose a convertible model, but choose carefully. If your infant is small, restrict your choice to models with a five-point harness; they may be less convenient, but they provide better protection for infants whose heads can't clear the shields of other convertible models.

Convertible seats with T-shields and bar-shields are adequate for large infants and toddlers, children grown tall enough for their necks to clear the top of the shield. Among the booster seats for still older children, consider a model that can be strapped in place.

DEFECTIVE SAFETY SEATS

Child safety seats are among the most commonly recalled consumer products. Last year alone, our Recalls column alerted readers to problems affecting some 8½-million seats.

The problems are often minor, but they also include serious defects like faulty buckles, broken shields, or unsecured harness straps. In most instances, the entire seat need not be replaced. Instead, the manufacturer will supply substitute parts and replacement instructions free—if you ask.

Trouble is, safety-seat recalls rarely make headlines. Few publications other than CONSUMER REPORTS routinely publicize them. The National Highway Traffic Safety Administration has established a toll-free hotline so consumers can find out the recall status of specific models. The number is 800-424-9393. Before calling, you'll need to know the brand, model, and date of manufacture. That information appears on every seat.

Late in 1992, the NHTSA will require manufacturers to provide a registration card with each seat. Once completed and returned, the card will allow a company to notify seat owners automatically if a problem exists. For now, only two companies—Century and Fisher-Price—provide registration cards.

RATINGS: CHILD SAFETY SEATS

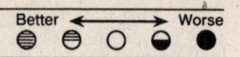

Better ⬅ ⇨ Worse

▶ **See report, page 273.** From Consumer Reports, January 1992.

Recommendations: For infants, the best of the tested seats are the *Century 590* and the *Evenflo Travel Tandem*. They combine comfort, convenience, and portability. The similar *Century 565* and *Evenflo Joyride* lack a stationary base. Convertible models allow for a child's growth. Any of four tested models are worthy of consideration. All four sport the 5-point harness, ideal for small infants. For children tall enough for their neck to clear the top of the shield, we recommend a T-shield or bar shield, found on the *Century 2000* and *3000* and the *Fisher-Price 9101*. For older children, consider the *Gerry Double Guard* booster seat.

Ratings order: Listed by types; within types, listed except as noted in order of estimated quality, based mainly on convenience. Models judged equal in quality are bracketed and listed alphabetically. Price is the manufacturers' suggested or approximate retail price. ⓢ indicates tested model has been replaced by successor model; according to the manufacturer, the performance of new model should be similar to the tested model but features may vary. See opposite for new model number and suggested retail price, if available. ⓓ indicates model discontinued.

Brand and model	Price	Harness [1]	Space needed	Ease of use [3]	Installation [3]	Cleanability	Advantages	Disadvantages	Comments
INFANT SEATS									
Century 590 series	$65	TP	15 in.	⊖	⊖	⊖	A,B,C,D,F	—	B,N
Evenflo Travel Tandem series	65	TP	14	⊖	⊖	●	C,D,F	—	B,N,O
Century 565 series, A Best Buy	67	TP	14	⊖	⊖	○	A,B,C	—	B,N
Evenflo Joyride Convertible series	45	TP	14	⊖	⊖	●	C,D	—	B,O
Century 560 series ⓓ	30	TP	14	⊖	⊖	○	A,B,C	k	B,N
Cosco Dream Ride 709 ⓢ	76	TP	14	⊖	⊖	●	D,G	—	D
Cosco 487 TLC series	30	TP	15	⊖	⊖	○	—	i,k	B
Fisher-Price 9149	50	TS	14	○	⊖	○	A,B,C,D	a,k	D
Kolcraft Rock'n Ride series	39	TP	14	⊖	⊖	●	—	i,l,m	D
Gerry Baby Guard with Glide series	55	TP	17	⊖	○	●	C,H	i	B
CONVERTIBLE SEATS									
■ *The following models are judged suitable for toddlers and infants who can be placed in a semi-upright position.*									
Century 1000 STE series	65	FP	17/15	○/○	⊖/⊖	⊖	A,I,K	—	C,G
Evenflo Ultara V 230186	99	FP	17/17	○/○	○/⊖	⊖	E,J	—	C,E,G,K,O

CHILD SAFETY SEATS

Brand and model	Price	Harness [1]	Space needed	Ease of use [3]	Installation [3]	Cleanability	Advantages	Disadvantages	Comments
Cosco 690-BTO	$55	FP	7/18	○/○	◉/◉	◉	—	q,i	B,E
Renolux Standard GT 2000 series	55	FP	16/16	○/●	◉/◉	◉	—	e,g	B

■ *The following models are judged more suitable for large infants and toddlers than for small infants.*

Brand and model	Price	Harness	Space	Ease	Install	Clean	Adv	Dis	Comments
Century 2000 STE series	75	TS	17/15	○/◉	◉/◉	◉	A,I	i	C,G,N
Century 3000 STE series	85	BS	17/15	●/◉	◉/◉	◉	A,I	i	C,G,H,N
Fisher-Price 9101	80	TS	17/16	○/◉	◉/◉	○	A	b	B,F,J
Cosco 790 Luxury Auto Trac series [D]	109	TS	7/18	○/◉	◉/◉	◉	E	j	B,E,F,J
Century 5000 STE series	103	BS	17/15	●/◉	○/◉	◉	A,I	i	C,E,G,L,N
Evenflo One Step Deluxe 223145 [D]	83	BS	15/16	●/○	◉/◉	○	—	g	B
Kolcraft Playskool 77002	79	BS	16/15	●/○	◉/◉	◉	—	—	A,C,I
Cosco Comfort Ride series	65	BS	7/18	◉/○	◉/○	◉	—	j	B,E,G
Gerry Guard SecureLock series	90	BS	15/13	◉/○	○/◉	○	—	c	C,J
Kolcraft Dial-A-Fit II Auto-Mate series	59	TS	16/15	◉/○	◉/◉	◉	—	f	C,I,N
Kolcraft Traveler 700 series	69	BS	16/15	●/○	◉/◉	◉	—	l	C,I
Evenflo Seven Year series	110	BS	18/18	●/●	○/◉	○	—	g,h	C,K,M,O

BOOSTER SEATS

Brand and model	Price	Harness	Space	Ease	Install	Clean	Adv	Dis	Comments
Gerry Double Guard series	55	SS	16 [2]	◉	◉	◉	L	—	N
Kolcraft Tot Rider Quik Step series [S]	30	SF	16	◉	◉	◉	—	e	—
Century CR-3 series	34	R	15	◉	◉	◉	A,M	e	—
Cosco Explorer series	30	SS	17	◉	◉	◉	—	—	—
Century Commander 4813	28	SS	15	◉	◉	◉	A	e	—
Evenflo Sight-Seer 241145	32	SS	16	◉	◉	◉	—	d	O

[1] Harness key: **TP**=3-point; **FP**=5-point; **TS**=T-shaped shield; **BS**=padded barshield with shield that swings forward (**SF**), sideways (**SS**), or can be removed (**R**).

[2] 11 in. when used with shield.

[3] For pairs of judgments: The first is for rear-facing, the second, forward-facing.

Successor Models (in Ratings order)
Cosco Dream Ride 709 is succeeded by Proam Ride 719, $55; Kolcraft Tot Rider Quik Step by Tot Rider II, $34.

Features in Common
All are: • Certified to meet Federal safety standard.
Except as noted, all: • Come fully assembled.

Ratings Keys continued

CHILD SAFETY SEATS

- Have upholstery that can be removed for cleaning. • Have instructions and provision for securing instructions to unit. • Lack warranty information. • Lack registration card. • Lack visual guide for proper backrest angle. • Infant seats have handle. • Convertible seats have 1 or 2 reclining positions, 2 or 3 harness positions. • Booster seats cannot be belt-attached to vehicle.

Key to Advantages
A–Mail-in registration card provided.
B–Guide for proper backrest angle.
C–Fits in shopping cart.
D–Foldable canopy shields infant from sun.
E–2 headrests.
F–Can be easily detached from stationary base.
G–Converts to car bed.
H–"Rocks" infant if used as free-standing seat.
I–Harness has 2 crotch positions.
J–Reclining-mechanism control on front of seat.
K–Crotch-strap makes buckle fairly easy to operate.
L–Can be belt-attached or used without shield.
M–Can be used with or without shield.

Key to Disadvantages
a–Tested samples required assembly. Newer samples may come fully assembled.
b–Some older units may require assembly.
c–Upholstery not adequately secured to seat on several samples.
d–Instructions appear only on label on seat.
e–Lacks provision to secure instructions to unit.
f–Crotch-strap buckle fairly hard to latch.
g–Harness length judged harder to adjust than most.
h–Shield could pinch child's fingers.
i–Metal parts may burn child in hot weather.
j–Tools needed to remove upholstery.
k–Lacks handle.
l–Mfr. says not to remove upholstery.
m–Error in instructions may cause seat to be installed improperly. Newer samples may have corrected instructions.

Key to Comments
A–Inflatable headrest and lumbar "pillows."
B–2 positions for harness at shoulders.
C–3 positions for harness at shoulders.
D–1 position for harness at shoulders.
E–Extra lumbar padding.
F–Mfr. advises owners to inspect latch/buckle frequently to assure proper operation.
G–Front pull strap convenient in front-facing position but not in rear-facing position.
H–Mfr. says this model shouldn't be used with small infants.
I–Strap length adjusted by turning knob.
J–Strap length adjusted automatically.
K–Soft strap webbing.
L–Adjustable bar-shield pad.
M–Converts to booster seat, but not easily.
N–Buckle requires strong hand to release.
O–1-yr. warranty.

WHAT THE RATINGS MEAN

■ The Ratings typically rank products in order of estimated quality, without regard to price.

■ A product's rating applies only to the model tested and should not be considered a rating of other models sold under the same brand name unless so noted.

■ Models are check-rated (✓) when the product proved to be significantly superior to other models tested.

■ Products high in quality and relatively low in price are deemed Best Buys.

AUTO BATTERIES 279

RATINGS AUTO BATTERIES

Better ◄———► Worse
◉ ⊖ ○ ◐ ●

▶ See report, page 270. From Consumer Reports, October 1991.

Recommendations: Consider first the *Delco Freedom 24-60*, the *Interstate 24-42*, and the *Energizer*. Those three, with a cold-cranking capacity ranging from 455 to 525 amps, were the only ones to consistently deliver the power they claimed to have.

Ratings order: Listed by types. Standard batteries listed in groups by manufacturers' cold-cranking amperage range; within groups, listed in order of performance in CU's cold-cranking test. The price is the manufacturer's suggested retail price. Discounts may be available.

Brand and model	Price	Group size	Mfr. rated [1]	Performance	Mfr. rated [2]	Measured [2]	Full	Prorated	Comments
STANDARD BATTERIES									
Delco Freedom 24-60	$68	24	525 amp ⊖	95 min.	114 min.	3 mo.	60 mo.	A,B
Interstate 24-42	56	24	455 ⊖	90	91	6	42	—
Energizer	40	26	525 ⊖	80	85	—	60	—
Douglas 24-6000	56	24	535 ⊖	100	106	12 [3]	60	E
Motorcraft BX-24	62	24	550 ⊖	105	108	3	60	F
Deka 524MF	75	24	525 ⊖	80	93	3	60	A,E
GNB High Energy 26HE60	50	26	530 ⊖	85	92	—	60	A
Exide Motorvator	40	26	530 ◐	—	79	3	65	G
Napa Power 9460	73	24	515 [4] ◐	80	85	3	60	—
Exide Driver's Edge 24-60	62	24	515 [4] ●	80	81	3	60	—
Deka 624MF	85	24	650 ⊖	110	115	3	65	A,E
Sears DieHard 43224	60	24	600 ⊖	115	118	12	60	—
Exide Driver's Edge 24-72	72	24	600 [4] ○	85	100	3	72	—
Napa The Legend 7524	83	24	600 [4] ○	115	112	3	75	—
Douglas 24-7000	67	24	650 ○	115	124	12 [3]	70	E
DUAL BATTERIES									
DieHard DualStart 43501	120	34	525 (800) ◐	70 (105)	77 (128)	12	60	D,H,I
Interstate X2 Booster	132	34	525 (800) ◐	70 (105)	81 (132)	6	60	D,I
GNB Champion Switch	70	24	[5] (640) ◐	[5] (108)	70 (107)	12	12 [6]	C

[1] *Numbers in parentheses are the rated cold-cranking amps for both portions of battery.*
[2] *Numbers in parentheses are the reserve capacities for the main battery plus backup.*
[3] *Without warranty card and proof of purchase, 90 days.*
[4] *Ratings taken from code on battery case.*
[5] *No CCA or reserve-capacity claim for main battery; tested at 480 CCA.*
[6] *Dealer may add 60 mo. prorated warranty period.*

Turn page for Ratings Keys

AUTO BATTERIES

Features in Common
Except as noted, all are: • "Low-maintenance" batteries, with removable covers for access to cells.

Key to Comments
- *A*–"Maintenance-free" battery. The **Delco Freedom 24-60** is fully sealed.
- *B*–Has built-in hydrometer that gives approximate charge status of 1 cell only.
- *C*–Sealed "Pulsar" technology battery.
- *D*–Vent caps awkward to remove for servicing.
- *E*–**Deka** available east of the Mississippi; **Douglas** available east of the Rockies.
- *F*–Distributed by Ford Motor Co.
- *G*–Available at K Mart.
- *H*–Available only at Sears.
- *I*–Comes with side-terminal adapters for group size 78 use.

How objective is CU?

Consumers Union is not beholden to any commercial interest. It accepts no advertising and buys all the products tested on the open market. CU's income is derived from the sale of CONSUMER REPORTS and other publications, and from nonrestrictive, noncommercial contributions, grants, and fees. Neither the Ratings nor the reports may be used in advertising or for any other commercial purpose. Consumers Union will take all steps open to it to prevent commercial use of its materials, its name, or the name of CONSUMER REPORTS.

Autos

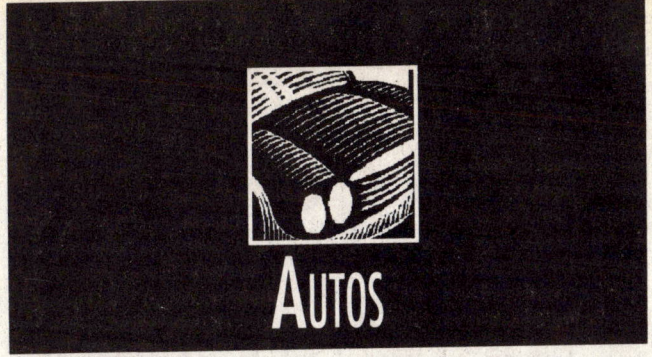

Recommended 1992 cars 282	Reliable used cars........................312
Ratings of 1992 cars 294	Used cars to avoid......................315
How to buy a new car 306	Repair records............................317
How to buy a used car................309	Owner satisfaction 357

Given the average $16,000 selling price of a new car, car shoppers must be more careful than ever when considering this most expensive of regular purchases. To guide you in the right direction, we provide information about performance, price, and reliability.

Performance. We summarize the results of our most recent road tests of widely sold passenger cars, vans, and utility vehicles. We present that information in specific Recommendations as well as hierarchical Ratings. For those who want more information on recently tested models, the Ratings tell you the issue date of the last full report in CONSUMER REPORTS.

Price. The same new car could cost you $1000 more than it does the next buyer because the price on the sticker bears little relationship to selling price. A car typically costs the dealer about 85 percent of sticker, and if you know how to negotiate, the dealer may let you have it for close to cost. The report on page 306 takes you step by step through the process of buying a new car, making sure you get the best deal.

The selling price for a used car depends on conditions and accessories, the region of the country, and whether the sale is private or through a dealer. Although any used car is a risk, it also offers the best value. Compared with a new car, a used car costs less, depreciates more slowly, and is cheaper to insure. The report on page 309 tells you how to lessen the risk and arrive at the best value.

Reliability. You can better your odds of getting sound transportation by narrowing your choices to models with a demonstrated record of reliability. A list of those that fared best in our Frequency-of-Repair records, based on readers' experiences with more than 635,000 cars, begins on page 312. Those records also pinpoint a number of models you would be wise to avoid (page 315). The Frequency-of-Repair charts begin on page 317.

We'll also tell you how thousands of subscribers answered the question "Would you buy that car again?" See page 357.

The recommended 1992 cars

The summary descriptions of the models we recommend in the following pages are listed in overall Ratings order. In general, recommended models are those that performed competently in recent tests and have proved at least reasonably reliable. (In a few cases, we've recommended models not recently reported on—because they've been reliable and because we've had favorable experience with them either in the past or presently. Those are listed at the end of each group.)

We divide the car models into categories. Small cars provide basic, general transportation. Sporty cars include performance-oriented coupes, sports cars, and convertibles. Compact cars provide practical transportation for small families. Mid-sized cars are the classic "family car." We've divided them into two groups—those that cost less than $25,000 and those that cost more. Large cars are big and bulky, with comfortable seating for up to six. Minivans are the successors to the station wagon. Sport/utility vehicles are increasingly popular as runabouts and family wagons.

Small cars

Acura Integra

The sportiest sedan designed by Honda. Superb handling and braking. The 1.8-liter Four provides brisk acceleration. Overdrive automatic transmission usually shifted smoothly. Heating is somewhat spotty, but the climate-control system is otherwise excellent. Logical controls and displays for the most part, and a surprisingly large trunk for such a small car. The front seats and driving position are virtually ideal for most people, but the rear seat is uncomfortable. Due for redesign in 1993.

Mazda 323/Mazda Protegé

Good value in its class. The 323 is the two-door version; the Protegé, the four-door. The 1.8-liter Four in the Protegé runs flawlessly and gives peppy acceleration. Overdrive automatic transmission shifts smoothly except during brisk acceleration. Crisp, responsive handling in normal driving, but controlling tail wag sometimes took skillful steering when the car was cornering near its limits. Braking is excellent, as are controls and displays. A mediocre heater lets down the otherwise competent climate-control system. For added performance, consider the LX version, with a more powerful engine and other sports-oriented equipment.

Honda Civic

Completely redesigned for 1992, the Civic now has a driver's-side air bag as standard equipment, a big plus. It is a peppy, tight-handling car. Good ride for a small car. Routine handling was good; emergency handling was smooth. Excellent braking. Antilock brakes work very well but available only in the top-of-the-line model. Excellent driving position. Comfortable front seats; tight rear seating. Excellent controls/displays, except for horn location. Excellent climate-control system. Exceptionally reliable.

GEO PRIZM/TOYOTA COROLLA

An impressive all-around performer, with a smooth, peppy 1.6-liter Four. Smooth-shifting automatic transmission. Handling is steady and safe, but not quick or crisp. Relatively good ride. Excellent brakes. Very good driving position and front seating, but uncomfortable rear seat. Very good heating, excellent ventilation and air-conditioning. Faultless displays; controls present minor irritations. The GSi version offers a more powerful engine and other sporty equipment. The Prizm's twin, the Toyota Corolla, provided mediocre driver protection in Government crash tests. Due for redesign in 1993.

SATURN

Exceptional first-year reliability, a breakthrough for a car designed and built in the U.S. The 1.9-liter Four in the base version provides impressive fuel economy, but it's rough and noisy and its acceleration is pokey. Much nicer are the higher-line versions, with their peppier engine, more closely spaced gears, and sportier suspension. The automatic transmission shifts too often, especially in the base version. The rear seat is especially uncomfortable. Unique bolt-on plastic front fenders, door skins, and quarter panels are dent-resistant and easy to replace when damaged. Good controls—another breakthrough for GM, which had been paying too little attention to ergonomics. Note: Late-production Saturns offer an air bag. Station wagon version due in 1993.

MERCURY TRACER/FORD ESCORT

A pleasant design, based in part on powertrain and chassis parts from the Mazda Protegé. Performed competently in most of our tests, though the brakes were a bit disappointing. The Escort LX-E handled well; nimble in routine handling. The 1.9-liter Four ran smoothly, but acceleration wasn't especially peppy. (The 1.8-liter, 16-valve Four is more powerful.) Smooth-shifting overdrive automatic transmission. Comfortable front seats, relatively comfortable rear seat. Excellent climate-control system, controls, and displays. Roomy trunk for such a small sedan. Note that the Tracer, assembled in Mexico, performed slightly better in our tests than the essentially similar Escort, and has been more reliable.

NISSAN SENTRA

The sports-sedan appearance and relatively high level of performance could make you forget that this is an economy car. The 1.6-liter Four starts and runs well and accelerates amply. Very good normal handling; not as good in emergency maneuvers. Excellent brakes, but rather long stopping distances. Comfortable front seats, despite the low driving position. Very uncomfortable rear seat. Spotty heating, excellent ventilation. Excellent controls/displays.

DODGE/PLYMOUTH COLT, EAGLE SUMMIT, MITSUBISHI MIRAGE

Though not tested recently, these cars, all built by Mitsubishi, have performed well in the past and have proved reliable. New for 1992 are wagon versions of the Plymouth Colt Vista and Eagle

RECOMMENDED CARS

Summit. The sedan and hatchback are due for redesign in 1993.

Ford Festiva

This tiny model, designed by Mazda of Japan and manufactured by Kia in Korea, has a somewhat better seating package than do most other small commuter cars. Its tiny, 1.3-liter Four delivers very impressive fuel economy—37 mpg overall, in our last tests—and surprisingly peppy performance. Excellent handling and braking.

SPORTY CARS

Nissan 300ZX

A true sports car rather than a sporty car, the 300ZX combines excellent overall performance with enough creature comforts to make it a useful vehicle. Rear-wheel-drive chassis delivers excellent balance for crisp handling. A driver's-side air bag is standard, as are antilock brakes. The clutch pedal is too far forward in relationship to accelerator and steering wheel. Seats are very comfortable. Reliability should be average.

Dodge Stealth/Mitsubishi 3000GT

Mitsubishi's answer to the Chevrolet Corvette. Exotic-car performance (especially with the 3.0-liter twin-turbo V6 and all-wheel drive in highest-trim-line version). Precise five-speed manual transmission, but clutch pedal is too far forward. Front seats are comfortable for all but very tall or very portly people. Consider the car a two-seater; the rear seat can handle only small children or luggage. Superlative sports-car handling and braking. The adjustable suspension is an affectation, as is the adjustment for exhaust sound. Awkward controls, clear displays. Excellent climate-control system. Early data showed average reliability.

Mazda RX-7

All-new in late 1992 as a 1993 model, the RX-7 is billed as a pure sports car and the compromises made in its design are all oriented toward performance. Acceleration, braking, and handling from the rear-wheel-drive chassis are all superb. Driving position is low, with no adjustments, and headroom is very tight in the small, two-seat cabin. Ride is very stiff, even for a sports car. Reliability is expected to be average.

Subaru SVX

Although billed as a sports car, the four-seater is a remarkably good passenger car, as long as you don't expect to use the rear seat often. All-wheel-drive, a driver's side air bag, and antilock brakes provide both active and passive safety. Ride is smoother and quieter than other sports cars. Although an all-new design, previous Subaru models have had good repair records so the SVX can be expected to follow suit.

Mazda MX-6

A good combination of driving fun and practical family transport. The GT version's 2.2-liter turbocharged Four starts and runs flawlessly and provides exceptional acceleration. (The nonturbo engine in the cheaper trim lines should satisfy all but hot-rodders.) The five-speed manual transmission shifts crisply. Excellent handling and braking. Very comfortable driving position and front seating. Skimpy knee room and toe space in rear seat. Fairly quiet. Unpleasant ride on back roads. Competent climate-control system. Awkward controls, excellent displays. 1993 model is already available.

TOYOTA CELICA

All the usual Toyota virtues—and sporty-car drawbacks. The 2.2-liter Four provides smooth, snappy performance. Crisp-shifting five-speed manual transmission with well-chosen gear ratios. Excellent handling; quick and precise response and lots of road feel. The brakes provide short, straight stops. Comfortable though firm ride. Very comfortable driving position, though with serious blind spots at the rear corners. Comfortable, deeply contoured front seats; very uncomfortable, claustrophobic rear seating—barely more than a package shelf with safety belts. Excellent climate-control system, controls, and displays.

MAZDA MX-5 MIATA

A two-seat convertible that feels much like the Lotuses, Austin-Healeys, and MGs of yesteryear—including the noisy, harsh ride. But the cockpit is weathertight, and the reliability record is typical Mazda; in other words, little pieces aren't likely to fall off as you drive. The 1.6-liter Four gives sprightly performance. Crisp-shifting five-speed manual transmission. Nimble handling, precise steering, and excellent brakes. Rear-wheel drive. Tall riders felt cramped even with the top down and claustrophobic with the top up. Excellent climate-control system. Very good controls, excellent displays. The 1991 model scored much better than average in owner satisfaction.

TOYOTA MR2

Fun on the road—but only for two. No rear seat. Mid-engine design and rear-wheel drive combine to provide superlative normal and emergency handling. The 2.2-liter Four runs smoothly and accelerates strongly. Precise five-speed manual transmission. Excellent braking. Very comfortable driving position and seats. Moderate noise level on most roads, worse at speed. Two trunks, front and rear; both are skimpy. Nervous ride. Excellent climate-control system, controls, and displays. Difficult to service some engine components.

NISSAN NX2000

A new model for 1992. The NX series has as its base model the NX1600; the top-of-the-line model is the NX2000, which we tested. It has a smooth and powerful powertrain, quick and steady handling, and a quiet ride for a small sporty car. As expected, the rear seat is essentially unusable for adults. A driver's-side air bag is a plus feature. Antilock brakes are available only on the NX2000 model. We expect this new model to be reliable.

SATURN SC

A sport coupe version of the Saturn SL2 sedan with its own unique front-end styling. The twin-cam version of Saturn's engine is standard. Acceleration in the manual transmission version that we tested was very strong, better than in many more-expensive models. The SC has a driver's-seat height adjustment, a plus for these sporty cars. A driver's-side air bag and antilock brakes are optional. The Saturn SC is quieter than most sporty cars at steady speeds. The engine is noisy when revved. Saturns have developed an excellent repair record in their first year.

Mitsubishi Eclipse/ Eagle Talon/Plymouth Laser

A refined design—comfortable and remarkably quiet. Handles nicely, and even its base 1.8-liter Four gives good acceleration. But it lacks the special nimbleness and pickup that thrill-seekers might want. Larger engines, available in more expensive versions, would provide more snap at the cost of fuel economy. Stops were sure and steady, if a bit long. Firm, supportive front seats; reserve the rear seat for short, nimble, and uncomplaining folks. Very good heater, excellent ventilation and air-conditioning. Excellent controls/displays.

Honda Prelude

Completely redesigned for 1992. Very well equipped even in base version, but considerably more expensive than last year's model. Now has a driver's-side air bag, an important safety plus; a passenger air bag is available as an option in certain models. Only higher trim lines have antilock brakes and four-wheel steering.

Nissan 240 SX

A rear-wheel-drive model. Relatively large, 2.4-liter Four provides quick acceleration but mediocre fuel economy. Very precise shifter. Firm and busy ride. Quick and responsive handling, but somewhat tricky at the limit. Exceptionally reliable.

Compact Cars

Mitsubishi Galant

A desirable model that combines crisp, sporty handling with comfortable seating front and rear. The 2.0-liter Four accelerates responsively. Electronically controlled automatic transmission shifts smoothly except during light acceleration at low speeds. Electronic steering in the GS version lets you adjust steering effort. Excellent brakes. Firm, nervous ride. Excellent climate-control system, controls, and displays. Provided mediocre driver protection in Government crash tests. The 1990 model scored much better than average in owner satisfaction. Due for replacement in 1993.

Honda Accord

One of the best-selling models in the U.S. Acceleration with the 2.2-liter Four is as strong as that of many compacts' V6s. Electronically controlled automatic transmission shifts a bit abruptly and whines. Smooth, nimble handling. Short, straight stops, but the antilock brakes pulse obtrusively. Stiff, nervous ride; somewhat better with a full load.

Rather noisy inside. Low but comfortable front seats, with excellent driver visibility. Three adults can fit in the rear without feeling pinched. Excellent climate-control system and displays.

INFINITI G20

A sporty sedan, with focus on handling. Powerful 2.0-liter Four is both responsive and economical. Overdrive automatic transmission shifts smoothly in normal driving, more aggressively during hard acceleration. Relatively light weight makes for nimble steering response, but the handling can be a bit tricky at the limit, when the rear end tries to swing out. Excellent brakes. Stiff but not punishing ride. Supportive front seats; driver's seat allows lots of adjustment. Comfortable rear seat. Excellent climate-control system, controls, and displays. Large trunk. Hard-to-service engine compartment.

BMW 325i

Everything a sports sedan ought to be, except for weak bumpers. Its 2.5-liter inline Six accelerates powerfully, and the overdrive automatic transmission shifts smoothly. A manual setting lets you hold any gear—useful when starting out on slippery roads. Rear-wheel drive. Precise, nimble routine handling; carves through winding country roads with the best of sports cars. Crisp and responsive emergency handling. Brakes superbly. Stiff but well-controlled ride. Comfortable front seats, but the steering wheel isn't centered directly in front of the driver, an annoyance, and it doesn't tilt. Rear seat isn't comfortable for three. Excellent climate-control system. Controls need some minor improvements; excellent displays. Small trunk.

SUBARU LEGACY

Despite its name, the Legacy has inherited little from its Subaru ancestors—a good thing. The 2.2-liter Four doesn't growl and throb like other Subaru engines. Electronically controlled automatic transmission shifts smoothly except for an occasional driveline shudder when accelerating moderately in overdrive. Steady normal handling. Tail-happy tendency at the track required quick and skillful steering correction. Excellent brakes. Smooth, quiet ride. Excellent front seats; somewhat cramped rear seat. Excellent climate-control system, controls, and displays.

MAZDA 626

One of our recommended models for years. Scored well in critical areas. The 2.2-liter Four runs well but rasps during hard acceleration. Electronically controlled overdrive automatic transmission shifts smoothly except during acceleration from low speeds. Competent though not sporty handling. Excellent brakes. Firm but satisfactory ride on all but the worst roads. Comfortable front seats. Roomy but unsupportive rear seat. Marginal heater, excellent ventilation and air-conditioning. We disliked the horn buttons on the steering-wheel spokes. Excellent displays. Large, expandable trunk. 1993 replacement is now available.

NISSAN STANZA

Quite a nice car, but emphasizes performance over comfort. The 2.4-liter Four provides impressive acceleration at the cost of fuel economy. Smooth-shifting electronic overdrive automatic transmission. Crisp, responsive handling and sure, steady braking. Comfortable seating both front and rear. Harsh, relatively noisy ride. Excellent controls and displays. Deep, roomy trunk. Replaced by Nissan Altima.

Volvo 240

This model is long in the tooth. Climb in, and it's 1968—the year this tall, boxy rear-wheel-drive design made its debut. But its performance remains competent if not exciting. We've tested this model several times over the years, monitoring the design changes that Volvo has made. Excellent crash-test results. The most important recent improvement is the addition of antilock brakes. The station wagon version boasts cavernous cargo room.

Mid-sized Cars
Under $25,000

Toyota Camry

Those looking for an excellent sedan need look no further. The Camry may lack the panache of the similar Lexus ES300, but it provides far more overall value. We tested the Deluxe version, with a four-cylinder engine, and the XLE, with a V6. The higher-line 3.0-liter V6 is more spirited than the basic 2.2-liter Four, but the Four is thriftier and handles more nimbly. Electronically controlled overdrive automatic transmission shifts smoothly. Excellent brakes. The XLE V6 had the edge in ride and interior quietness. Very good front seating; excellent with power adjustment. Adequate rear seating. Versatile climate-control system, excellent controls and displays. Roomy trunk.

Nissan Maxima

Performance, practicality, and reliability, all in one package. We tested the sports-oriented SE. The 3.0-liter V6 runs flawlessly and delivers spirited acceleration. Smooth-shifting overdrive automatic transmission. Very good emergency handling. Short, straight stops with no brake fade. Taut, well-controlled ride; very quiet inside. Excellent driving position and front-seat comfort; rear seat is wide enough for three adults. Excellent climate-control system and controls, very good displays. Scored higher than average in owner satisfaction.

Ford Taurus / Mercury Sable

Our favorite domestic sedans. The 3.8-liter V6 in our latest test car performs superlatively, as does the standard 3.0-liter V6. Electronic overdrive automatic transmission shifts very smoothly. Safe but not sporty handling. Powerful but touchy brakes. Comfortable, quiet ride. Excellent driving position and front-seat comfort; available with bench front seat that holds three. Remarkably comfortable rear seat, even for six-footers. Excellent climate-control system and displays. We disliked the horn buttons on the steering-wheel spokes. Roomy trunk. We recommend the middle-of-the-line GL version for best value. Reliability should be average.

Toyota Cressida

A well-equipped car nicely combining sportiness and luxury. But the Cressida is beginning to show its age. It has irritating motorized front shoulder belts instead of air bags. A 3.0-liter Six and overdrive automatic transmission power this rear-wheel-drive model. Antilock brakes are optional. Seating is a bit tight front and rear. Excellent climate-control system and controls and displays. This model to be discontinued in 1993.

Mid-Sized Cars
Over $25,000

Lexus LS400

Combines advanced engineering with almost every conceivable comfort, safety, and convenience feature, making this the highest-scoring car we've tested to date. The 4.0-liter V8 provides effortless acceleration. Exceptionally smooth-shifting overdrive automatic transmission. Rear-wheel drive. First-rate handling (except on snow, where the car felt twitchy). The brakes inspire confidence, and the Lexus's ride is the best we've experienced. Comfortable accommodations front and rear. Excellent climate-control system; first-rate controls. Scored much better than average in owner satisfaction during the first year of production.

Infiniti Q45

Awesome acceleration from the 4.5-liter V8 and exceptional handling in both normal and emergency driving make the Infiniti the sportiest of the luxury sedans. But the rear-wheel drive, performance tires, and impressive power made the car skittish on slippery roads, despite the limited-slip differential. Exceptionally smooth-shifting overdrive automatic transmission. Despite the car's sporty feel, one couldn't ask for more amenities. Tall drivers should check head and leg room. The rear seat could be better for three. Very good climate-control system. Controls emphasize form over function.

Lincoln Continental

All the comforts and conveniences the domestic auto industry could muster, plus two air bags. Standard air suspension gives superb, quiet ride (at least on good roads), but sluggish and sloppy handling. The 3.8-liter V8 runs without a hitch and provides adequate acceleration. Smooth-shifting overdrive automatic transmission. The spacious cabin accommodates six; limousine-like leg room in the rear. Huge trunk. Complex but logical controls.

Lexus ES300

A fine balance of luxury and sportiness in a smaller package than the Lexus LS400. The ES300 does just about everything well, scoring higher than the Lexus ES250, which it replaced. Sophisticated and lavish, much like the bigger Lexus LS400, but nimbler and sportier. The 3.0-liter V6 provides powerful acceleration. Exceptionally smooth-shifting overdrive automatic transmission. Firm and composed ride, even with a full load. Supportive, fully adjustable front seats; roomy rear seat. Excellent controls and displays.

BMW 535i

A sporty package. Responsive acceleration from the 3.5-liter inline Six and superb handling make this rear-wheel-drive sedan a pleasure to drive. Exceptionally smooth-shifting overdrive automatic transmission. Antilock brakes provided one of the shortest stopping distances we've recorded. Road-hugging ability on winding back roads comes at the expense of a rather stiff ride. Skittery on slick roads. Tall drivers may need more head room. Scant rear-seat knee room. Especially well-designed safety belts. Versatile climate-control system; complex controls. Frail bumpers are costly to repair.

VOLVO 740/940/960

These roomy rear-wheel-drive models share sedan and station wagon bodies. The 740 and 940 are powered by a 2.3-liter Four; some models come with a turbocharger. The 960, new in 1992, has a 3.0-liter Six. A driver's-side air bag and antilock brakes are standard equipment. Provided excellent driver-front-passenger protection in NHTSA crash test.

ACURA LEGEND

Redesigned last year, the Legend continues to set standards in its class. The car now has a more powerful 3.2-liter V6 and antilock brakes. The L and LS versions have air bags for driver and passenger. Well-designed controls, comfortable front seats, and a fairly spacious rear seat make this a worthwhile luxury sedan.

MAZDA 929

The competent but bland 929 has been replaced by a totally new design for 1993. Air bags for the driver and passenger are standard, as are antilock brakes. The sleek Jaguar-like exterior covers a higher performance 3.0-liter V6. Rear-wheel drive. The interior is a mixture of modern control layouts and older-style details. A solar-cell sun roof can charge the battery in winter or ventilate the interior in summer.

MITSUBISHI DIAMANTE

A gadget-lover's delight (and most of the gadgets work quite well). Computers control the variable-assist power steering, suspension, starting traction on slippery surfaces, interior temperature, door locks, and interior lighting. The 3.0-liter V6's performance didn't measure up to that of the sportiest models in this class; its strong acceleration was most apparent at speeds well above the legal limit. The overdrive automatic transmission usually shifted smoothly. The car is relatively heavy, and the poundage takes its toll on nimbleness and acceleration. Wagon version is due in 1993.

MERCEDES-BENZ 300

The solid, expensive 300 series hasn't been redesigned in any major way since it was introduced in 1986. A driver's-side air bag is standard; the optional passenger air bag takes the place of the glove compartment. Antilock

RECOMMENDED CARS

brakes are standard. A 2.6-liter Six, a 3.0-liter Six, and a 2.5-liter turbo Five diesel are available in the 300 series; the 400E comes with a 4.2-liter V8, the better to compete against the likes of such cars as the Lexus and Infiniti. Most models have rear-wheel drive—but both the sedan and wagon are available with a sophisticated all-wheel-drive system.

LARGE CARS

PONTIAC BONNEVILLE

Fun to drive if equipped with sport suspension. The 3.8-liter V6 provided excellent acceleration. Responsive, smooth-shifting overdrive automatic transmission. Exceptionally short stops on dry pavement. Front-wheel drive adds to the roominess. The optional sport suspension delivers ride and handling reminiscent of a European sports sedan—that is, firm ride and precise, fast handling. Seating is better suited to four passengers than five or six. Noisier than most large cars, but not objectionably so. Slow defrosting. Uncomplicated controls. Reliability has waxed and waned; the best we expect is average.

FORD CROWN VICTORIA/ MERCURY GRAND MARQUIS

A 1992 redesign (introduced in the spring of 1991) that retains a traditional full frame and rear-wheel drive. New, the 4.6-liter V8 is smaller than its predecessor but more powerful and more fuel-efficient. Quick steering response in normal driving; safe but sloppy handling in abrupt maneuvers. Rides well when fully loaded. Roomy accommodations and very good climate-control system. Huge trunk. Suitably equipped, this sedan can tow a 5000-pound trailer. A Touring Sedan version with a more powerful V8 and special handling suspension is available. Big Fords tend to be troubleprone in their first year of ownership; after that, reliability generally improves to better than average.

OLDSMOBILE 88 ROYALE/ BUICK LE SABRE

Overall personality depends on equipment. With the standard suspension, it's a typical big car, in the worst sense of the term. Quiet, floating ride on most roads; bumpy on rough roads. The optional touring suspension makes for more responsive handling, much like that of the Pontiac Bonneville, cousin to the 88 Royale and Le Sabre. Very comfortable seating for five adults. Overdone, inefficient controls in the Oldsmobile; the Buick's layout is somewhat better.

Minivans

Toyota Previa

Contemporary styling and innovative design. Unique mid-engine layout and rear-wheel drive. With light load, drives like a good sedan. With full load, the 2.4-liter Four struggles, and handling and ride suffer. The overdrive automatic transmission doesn't shift smoothly. Adequate seating accommodations, spotty heating, gimmicky controls. Converting from people carrier to cargo hauler is time consuming, but placement of the 2.4-liter Four under the driver's seat increases usable cargo space. All-wheel drive is available and recommended.

Dodge Grand Caravan / Plymouth Grand Voyager

These stretched versions of the Caravan/Voyager offer really useful room behind the third seat. The troublesome automatic transmission appears to be improving and since these minivans offer among the best packaging and overall performance, they are back on our recommended list. The standard driver's-side air bag is a plus, and the built-in child seat option is a nice feature for those who need it. The all-wheel-drive version offers excellent traction and control in bad conditions, but the regular front-wheel-drive model is still superior to the rear-drive Toyota Previa or Mazda MPV. Overall reliability has not been as good as that on the short-chassis models.

Pontiac Trans Sport

An innovative, versatile package with modular seating and plastic body panels. You may not like the view from behind the wheel; driving position needs improvement. Seats are comfortable, however. The 3.1-liter V6 gives adequate acceleration. Smooth-shifting three-speed automatic transmission. (A 3.8-liter V6 and overdrive automatic transmission are now optional.) Nimbler than most vans in normal driving. Brakes feel numb but stop well. Steady ride on highways; a full load smooths out the ride on back roads. Competent climate-control system. Cluttered controls.

Mazda MPV

A good people carrier, but rear-wheel drive and nonremovable rear seat limit cargo room. Second seat can be removed, but not easily. Commanding driving position and comfortable front and second seats. Reasonably responsive acceleration from the 3.0-liter V6. Smooth-shifting overdrive automatic transmission. Pleasant normal handling, sloppy in emergency maneuvers. Adequate heating and ventilation; marginal air-conditioning. Logical controls. Provided mediocre driver protection in Government crash tests. All-wheel drive is available.

Sport/Utility Vehicles

Nissan Pathfinder

Feels the most like a passenger car; competent ride and handling. But the cargo compartment is small and awkward to expand. Quick acceleration from the 3.0-liter V6. The overdrive automatic transmission occasionally lurched into gear. Sure and straight braking. Inhospitable rear seat, with awkward access. Slow-warming heater, but excellent ventilation and powerful air-conditioning. Tiny, annoying controls. Rear head restraints and optional door-mounted spare tire interfere with view to the rear.

Jeep Grand Cherokee

A brand new model for 1993. This Cherokee is larger and more expensive than the previous Cherokee models. It has a driver's-side air bag and 4-wheel antilock brakes, both plus features. A full or part-time four-wheel-drive is available. Interior space is not as large or useful as that in the Ford Explorer, the Mitsubishi Montero, or Isuzu Trooper. Overall ride and handling is quite good for the type. Previous models have had a poor reliability record; this model is designed for better quality. We hope the reliability improves.

Ford Explorer/Mazda Navajo

A better-handling and generally more competent replacement for the Ford Bronco II. Large cargo area, especially in four-door Explorer model, and very comfortable seating. (The Navajo, built by Ford, comes only in two-door form.) With suitable equipment, this vehicle can tow a 5700-pound trailer. The 4.0-liter V6 provides better acceleration and fuel economy with manual transmission than with automatic, but both transmissions shifted smoothly. Easily shifts to part-time four-wheel drive with convenient push button. Clumsy but safe handling. Bumpy ride on all but the smoothest roads; a full load makes matters even worse. Quiet inside. Uneven heating, generous ventilation and cooling. Well-designed controls.

Isuzu Trooper

A brand new model for 1992, with a more powerful V6 engine. The new Trooper is very large inside and luxuriously equipped. Only part-time four-wheel drive is offered. Four-wheel antilock brakes are optional on the top-line model. Ride is typical of the type; handling is clumsy. Reliability of this model has not yet been established; that of previous models has generally been worse than average.

Mitsubishi Montero

A new model for 1992, larger and more luxurious than previous Monteros. Four-wheel antilock brakes are standard on the top-line model, optional on the mid-line model. Selectable full-time four-wheel drive is standard. Interior package is much the same as the Trooper, as is the ride. Handling is quite clumsy, improved in four-wheel drive. Acceleration is slower than the Grand Cherokee or Isuzu Trooper, but still adequate. Previous versions of the Montero have had an average reliability record.

RATINGS 1992 CARS

Ratings order: Models are listed in order of estimated quality, based on road and track tests and on judgments of comfort and convenience. The mpg data refer to the car equipped as tested; see the last full report for details.

Major options [1]

Make and model	Predicted reliability	Bumper damage, front/rear	Overall mpg	Air bag, driver/passenger	Antilock brakes	Auto transmission	Air-conditioning
SMALL CARS							
Acura Integra	◓	$0/$0	25	NA	S[2]	O	O
Mazda Protegé	◓	0/0	26	NA	NA	O	O
Mazda 323	◓	—	—	NA	NA	O	O
Honda Civic	◓	0/0	29	S/NA	S[2]	O	O
Toyota Corolla	◓	0/0	25	NA	NA	O	O
Geo Prizm	◓		26	NA	NA	O	O
Saturn SL2	◓	379/0	27	O/NA	O	O	O
Mercury Tracer	○	0/0	29	NA	NA	O	O
Ford Escort	◐	0/0	27	NA	NA	O	O
Nissan Sentra	◓	0/0	28	NA	O[2]	O	O
Toyota Tercel	◓	0/0	35	NA	NA	O	O
Subaru Loyale	○	0/0	26	NA	NA	O	S
Hyundai Excel	●	175/121	29	NA	NA	O	O
Mitsubishi Precis	—	—	—	NA	NA	O	O
Hyundai Elantra	●	0/666	25	NA	NA	O	O
Plymouth Sundance	○	369/0	28	S/NA	NA	O	O
Dodge Shadow	○	—	—	S/NA	NA	O	O

[1] *Key to major options:* **S** = standard; **NA** = not available; **O** = option.
[2] *Available in top-of-the-line version only.*

RATINGS OF 1992 CARS

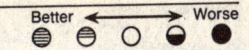

Better ⬅ ➡ Worse

Body styles (Coupe / Hatchback / Sedan / Wagon)	Comments	Last full report	Make and model
— ✓ ✓ —	The sportiest sedan designed by Honda. A mediocre rear seat is the only drawback. Redesigned for 1993.	May '90	**Acura Integra**
— — ✓ — / — ✓ — —	Good value in its class. Somewhat twitchy emergency handling.	May '90	**Mazda Protegé / Mazda 323**
— ✓ ✓ —	New for 1992. Still performs well.	May '92	**Honda Civic**
— — ✓ ✓ / — — ✓ —	Good all-around transportation for a small family, but an uninviting rear seat. Redesigned for 1993.	July '90 / May '90	**Toyota Corolla / Geo Prizm**
✓ — ✓ —	GM's newest, plastic-paneled import fighter. Exceptional first-year reliability. New wagon for 1993.	May '92	**Saturn**
— — ✓ ✓ / — ✓ ✓ ✓	A pleasant design, much improved over earlier small Ford sedans.	May '91 / May '92	**Mercury Tracer / Ford Escort**
✓ — ✓ —	Good value. An inexpensive sedan with sporty styling and performance.	May '92	**Nissan Sentra**
✓ — ✓ —	An "entry level" model. Base version is cheap to buy and run but feels cheap.	March '91	**Toyota Tercel**
— — ✓ ✓	Reliable but crude. Torpid, growly engine and sloppy handling.	July '90	**Subaru Loyale**
— ✓ ✓ — / — ✓ — —	If you drove it without knowing how inexpensive it is, you'd still think it was cheap.	May '90	**Hyundai Excel / Mitsubishi Precis**
— — ✓ —	New for 1992. Needs improvement.	May '92	**Hyundai Elantra**
— ✓ ✓ — / — ✓ ✓ —	Competes with Japanese imports in price, but not in comfort, performance, or economy. New V6 and convertible for 1993.	March '91	**Plymouth Sundance / Dodge Shadow**

Ratings continued

RATINGS 1992 CARS continued

Make and model	Predicted reliability	Bumper damage, front/rear	Overall mpg	Air bag, driver/passenger	Antilock brakes	Auto transmission	Air-conditioning
SPORTY CARS							
Nissan 300ZX	○	$125/$0	21	S/NA	S	O	S
Dodge Stealth	○	0/788	20	S/NA	O	O	O
Mitsubishi 3000GT	—	—	—	—	O	O	O
Chevrolet Corvette	●	0/379	17	S/NA	S	S	S
Mazda RX7	○	0/0	19	S/NA	S	O	S
Subaru SVX	—	0/0	19	S/NA	S	S	S
Mazda MX-6	⊖	0/0	25	NA	O	O	O
Toyota Celica	⊖	0/0	27	S/NA	O	O	O
Mazda MX-5 Miata	⊖	0/0	30	S/NA	O	O	O
Toyota MR2	⊖	0/0	28	S/NA	O	O	O
Nissan NX2000	⊖	0/0	28	S/NA	O	O	O
Saturn SC	⊖	0/0	30	O/NA	O	O	O
Mitsubishi Eclipse	⊖	517/0	29	NA	O	O	O
Eagle Talon	○	—	—	NA	O	O	O
Plymouth Laser	⊖	—	—	NA	O	O	O
Mazda MX-3	⊖	266/0	28	NA	O	O	O
Toyota Paseo	⊖	0/0	33	NA	NA	O	O
Hyundai Scoupe	●	319/582	32	NA	NA	O	O
Volkswagen Corrado	—	1042/1207	25	NA	O	O	S
Geo Storm	○	0/146	29	S/NA	NA	O	O
Mercury Capri	●	0/0	28	S/NA	NA	O	O

[1] Key to major options: **S** = standard; **NA** = not available; **O** = option.

RATINGS OF 1992 CARS

Better ←——→ Worse

Coupe	Hatchback	Convertible	Comments	Last full report	Make and model
					SPORTY CARS
—	✓	✓	Does everything a sports car should do. Convertible new for '93.	Sept '92	**Nissan 300ZX**
—	✓	—	Mitsubishi's answer to the Corvette. In twin-turbo version, blazingly fast.	April '92	**Dodge Stealth / Mitsubishi 3000GT**
✓	—	✓	Fast and brutal. A performance champ, but a reliability dud.	Sept '92	**Chevrolet Corvette**
—	✓	—	A pure sports car. A 1993 model.	Sept '92	**Mazda RX7**
✓	—	—	This is a Subaru? A refined GT more than a true sports car.	Sept '92	**Subaru SVX**
✓	—	—	Even the nonturbo versions should be quick enough. Usable rear seat. Redesigned for 1993.	Oct '90	**Mazda MX-6**
✓	✓	✓	All the usual Toyota virtues, and several of the usual sporty-car drawbacks.	Oct '90	**Toyota Celica**
—	—	✓	The vintage British sports car resurrected in Japan, minus many of the frustrations.	April '90	**Mazda MX-5 Miata**
✓	—	—	Outstanding performance. But only two seats and scant luggage room.	Oct '90	**Toyota MR2**
—	✓	—	NX2000 is the real NX. Smooth powertrain, nice handling.	July '92	**Nissan NX2000**
✓	—	—	Good performance and handling. Excellent reliability so far.	July '92	**Saturn SC**
—	✓	—	Civilized and relatively inexpensive joint effort by Chrysler and Mitsubishi.	Oct '91	**Mitsubishi Eclipse / Eagle Talon / Plymouth Laser**
—	✓	—	Nippy handling. New for '92, smallest V6 available.	July '92	**Mazda MX-3**
✓	—	—	A sheep in wolf's clothing.	July '92	**Toyota Paseo**
✓	—	—	Sleek, macho styling let down by a bargain-basement heart.	Oct '91	**Hyundai Scoupe**
—	✓	—	A supercharged engine—but the promise of performance unfulfilled. New V6 for '92 addresses performance deficiency.	Oct '90	**Volkswagen Corrado**
✓	✓	—	Lives up to its sporty image, not only in performance but in discomfort as well.	Oct '91	**Geo Storm**
—	—	✓	A sporty car should be fun to drive—and the Capri isn't.	April '91	**Mercury Capri**

Ratings continued

RATINGS OF 1992 CARS

RATINGS 1992 CARS continued

Major options [1]

Make and model	Predicted reliability	Bumper damage, front/rear	Overall mpg	Air bag, driver/passenger	Antilock brakes	Auto transmission	Air-conditioning
COMPACT CARS							
Mitsubishi Galant	⊖	$0/$0	24	NA	O	O	O
Honda Accord	⊖	0/333	24	S/NA	S	O	S
Infiniti G20	⊖	0/0	24	NA	S	O	S
BMW 325i	○	1325/0	21	S/NA	S	O	S
Subaru Legacy	⊖	0/0	23	O/NA	O	O	S
Chrysler Le Baron	◐	0/0	23	S/NA	O	O	O
Plymouth Acclaim	◐	0/0	24	S/NA	O	O	O
Dodge Spirit	◐	—	—	S/NA	O	O	O
Mazda 626	⊖	0/0	24	NA	O	O	O
Ford Tempo	●	0/0	24	O/NA	NA	O	O
Mercury Topaz	●	—	—	O/NA	NA	O	O
Nissan Stanza	⊖	0/388	21	NA	O	O	O
Audi 80	—	0/0	22	S/NA	S	O	S
Volkswagen Passat	●	698/51	24	NA	O	O	O
Buick Skylark	—	91/0	21	NA	S	S	O
Oldsmobile Achieva	—	0/0	24	NA	S	O	O
Pontiac Grand Am	—	0/705	25	NA	S	O	O
Chevrolet Corsica, Beretta	◐	0/0	25	S/NA	S	O	O
Pontiac Sunbird	○	0/0	24	NA	S	O	O
Chevrolet Cavalier	◐	—	—	NA	S	O	O

[1] Key to major options: **S** = standard; **NA** = not available; **O** = option.

RATINGS OF 1992 CARS

Better ← → Worse

Coupe	Sedan	Wagon	Comments	Last full report	Make and model
					COMPACT CARS
—	✔	—	A desirable model that offers superior performance and superior reliability. Redesign due in 1993.	July '91	Mitsubishi Galant
✔	✔	✔	One of our perennial favorites. But only the pricey EX comes with antilock brakes.	March '92	Honda Accord
—	✔	—	Accent on handling and performance, though luxury amenities are in abundant supply.	August '91	Infiniti G20
✔	✔	—	Pure driving fun—everything a sports sedan should be, except for the weak bumpers.	Feb '92	BMW 325i
—	✔	✔	This automaker's top sedan model. It scored well in critical areas.	March '90	Subaru Legacy
—	✔	—	In performance, personality, and reliability, it's no match for the best compacts.	March '92	Chrysler Le Baron
—	✔	—	A competent though unexceptional car. Reliability needs improvement.	June '91	Plymouth Acclaim / Dodge Spirit
—	✔	—	One of our recommended models for years. The LX version is the best value. Redesigned for 1993.	July '91	Mazda 626
✔	✔	—	Improves a bit each year, but it's still no more than a journeyman performer. Reliability needs improvement.	May '91	Ford Tempo / Mercury Topaz
—	✔	—	Emphasis on handling rather than comfort, acceleration rather than fuel economy.	March '90	Nissan Stanza
—	✔	—	A competent performer overall, but blighted by a lack of refinement.	August '91	Audi 80
—	✔	✔	A disappointing car; some high spots, but riddled with annoyances.	July '91	Volkswagen Passat
✔	✔	—	An adequate performer, no more.	June '92	Buick Skylark
✔	✔	—	An underachiever in basic version.	June '92	Oldsmobile Achieva
✔	✔	—	Highly styled, but not much more.	June '92	Pontiac Grand Am
✔	✔	—	No better than average in most respects. Corsica is 4-door version; Beretta, 2-door.	June '92	Chevrolet Corsica, Beretta
✔ ✔	✔ ✔	— ✔	Despite some improvements, this decade-old design can no longer compete.	May '91	Pontiac Sunbird / Chevrolet Cavalier

Ratings continued

RATINGS 1992 CARS continued

MID-SIZED CARS

Make and model	Predicted reliability	Bumper damage, front/rear	Overall mpg	Air bag, driver/passenger	Antilock brakes	Auto transmission	Air-conditioning
Lexus LS400	◒	$0/$0	19	S/NA	S	S	S
Infiniti Q45	◒	0/0	17	S/NA	S	S	S
Lincoln Continental	○	0/0	18	S/S	S	S	S
Lexus ES300	◒	415/0	21	S/NA	S	O	S
Toyota Camry	◒	0/0	21	S/NA	O	O	O
BMW 535i	◒	994/328	17	S/NA	S	S	S
Volvo 960	○	0/0	20	S/NA	S	S	S
Acura Legend	◒	0/0	20	S/S [2]	S	O	S
Nissan Maxima	◒	461/0	21	O/NA	O	O	S
Ford Taurus	○	0/0	21	S/O	O	S	O
Mercury Sable	○	—	—	S/O	O	S	S
Mazda 929	◒	0/0	20	S/S	S	S	S
Mitsubishi Diamante	◒	0/0	20	S/NA	O	S	S
Chrysler New Yorker Salon/Dodge Dynasty	●	320/0	21	S/NA	O	S	S
	●	—	—	S/NA	O	S	O
Acura Vigor	◒	0/360	23	S/NA	S	O	S
Audi 100	—	0/0	21	S/NA	S	O	S
Oldsmobile Cutlass Supreme	●	0/0	21	NA	O	S	S
Buick Regal	●	0/0	20	NA	O	S	S
Chevrolet Lumina	●	0/0	22	NA	O	S	O

[1] Key to major options: **S** = standard; **NA** = not available; **O** = option.
[2] Not available on base model.

RATINGS OF 1992 CARS

Better ◀———▶ Worse

Coupe	Sedan	Wagon	Comments	Last full report	Make and model
					MID-SIZED CARS
—	✔	—	Competes successfully with the world's top luxury cars.	June '90	**Lexus LS400**
—	✔	—	Performance and handling that shame most sports cars.	June '90	**Infiniti Q45**
—	✔	—	Big and roomy, with all the amenities that Detroit can muster.	June '90	**Lincoln Continental**
—	✔	—	Luxurious, but scored only slightly better overall than its cheaper cousin, the Toyota Camry.	Feb '92	**Lexus ES300**
—	✔	✔	One of our all-time favorites.	March '92	**Toyota Camry**
—	✔	—	The best sports sedans surpass it in several ways, but not in sheer driving fun.	June '90	**BMW 535i**
—	✔	✔	Very comfortable. Lots of safety features. A fine family sedan.	August '92	**Volvo 960**
✔	✔	—	Smooth and refined. A large and comfortable sedan.	August '92	**Acura Legend**
—	✔	—	Performance, practicality, and reliability in one package.	August '91	**Nissan Maxima**
—	✔	✔	Redesign for 1992 makes this fine model even finer.	March '92	**Ford Taurus**
—	✔	✔		March '92	**Mercury Sable**
—	✔	—	A Japanese Jaguar, smooth ride. Competent rear-wheel-drive handling.	August '92	**Mazda 929**
—	✔	—	Technological tour de force; electronically enhanced performance and luxury.	Feb '92	**Mitsubishi Diamante**
—	✔	—	Comfortable seating. Smooth, quiet ride. Troublesome automatic transmission.	Jan '91	**Chrysler New Yorker Salon/Dodge Dynasty**
—	✔	—	As its name implies, it accelerates vigorously. Comfort takes a back seat.	Feb '92	**Acura Vigor**
—	✔	—	Needs considerable improvement. Fussy and idiosyncratic. High depreciation.	August '92	**Audi 100**
✔	✔	—	Many minor annoyances add up to disappointment.	Jan '90	**Oldsmobile Cutlass Supreme**
✔	✔	—	Competent though unexceptional. Large and heavy.	July '91	**Buick Regal**
✔	✔	—	Smooth, quiet on good roads; sloppy in the boonies.	June '91	**Chevrolet Lumina**

Ratings continued

RATINGS 1992 CARS continued

Major options [1]

Make and model	Predicted reliability	Bumper damage, front/rear	Overall mpg	Air bag, driver/passenger	Antilock brakes	Auto transmission	Air-conditioning
LARGE CARS							
Pontiac Bonneville SE	○	$0/$0	20	S/NA	O	S	S
Ford Crown Victoria LX	○	0/0	20	S/O	O	S	S
Mercury Grand Marquis	○	—	—	S/O	O	S	S
Oldsmobile 88 Royale	○	0/0	19	S/NA	S[2]	S	S
Buick Le Sabre	○	—	—	S/NA	S	S	S
Chevrolet Caprice Classic	◐	0/0	18	S/NA	S	S	S
Buick Roadmaster	◐	688/0	17	S/NA	S	S	S

Major options [1]

Make and model	Predicted reliability	Bumper damage, front/rear	Overall mpg	Air bag, driver/passenger	Antilock brakes	Auto transmission	Air-conditioning
MINIVANS							
Toyota Previa	◐	$537/$460	18	S/NA	O	O	S
Dodge Caravan	○	110/555	20	S/NA	O	O	O
Plymouth Voyager	○			S/NA	O	O	O
Chrysler Town and Country	—			S/NA	S	S	S
Dodge Grand Caravan	◐	—/—	17	S/NA	O	S	O
Plymouth Grand Voyager	●			S/NA	O	S	O
Pontiac Trans Sport	○	0/0	17	NA	S	S	O
Chevrolet Lumina APV	●	0/455	18	NA	S	S	O
Oldsmobile Silhouette	◐			NA	S	S	S
Ford Aerostar	◐	796/649	16	S/NA	S[2]	O	O
Mazda MPV	○	1218/1589	16	NA	S[2]	S	O
Chevrolet Astro	●	497/532	15	NA	S	S	O
GMC Safari	—			NA	S	S	O

[1] Key to major options: **S** = standard; **NA** = not available; **O** = option.

RATINGS OF 1992 CARS

Better ⬅ ➡ Worse

LARGE CARS

Coupe	Sedan	Wagon	Comments	Last full report	Make and model
—	✓	—	The sportiest model in GM's big-car stable with sport suspension.	Jan '92	**Pontiac Bonneville SE**
—	✓	—	Rear-wheel drive, easy towing, and a serene ride with six aboard.	Jan '92	**Ford Crown Victoria LX**
—	✓	—			**Mercury Grand Marquis**
—	✓	—	Unless you opt for the sporty suspension, this is your father's Oldsmobile.	Jan '92	**Oldsmobile 88 Royale**
—	✓	—			**Buick Le Sabre**
—	✓	✓	Comfortable, but with sloppy road manners. Awkward to maneuver in tight traffic.	Jan '91	**Chevrolet Caprice Classic**
—	✓	✓	Soft to the point of decadence. A big, heavy throwback to the Chrome Age.	Jan '92	**Buick Roadmaster**

MINIVANS

Regular	Extended	Comments	Last full report	Make and model
✓	—	Our top choice in minivans. All-Trac version a good bet for slippery conditions.	Oct '92	**Toyota Previa**
✓	—	A competent van with fine crash protection.	Feb '91	**Dodge Caravan**
✓	—			**Plymouth Voyager**
—	✓	Two-wheel drive or all-wheel drive. Versatile and efficient people and cargo carrier. AWD improves already good traction.	Oct '92	**Chrysler Town & Country**
—	✓			**Dodge Grand Caravan**
—	✓			**Plymouth Grand Voyager**
✓	—	New 3.8L V6 + 4 speed automatic. A versatile cargo hauler; modular seats are easy to fold, reposition, remove.	Feb '91	**Pontiac Trans Sport**
✓	—		Feb '90	**Chevrolet Lumina APV**
✓	—			**Oldsmobile Silhouette**
✓	✓	Chassis tweaks have made it less truck-like. 4WD provides impressive action.	Oct '92	**Ford Aerostar**
✓	—	A good people carrier, limited cargo room. 4WD version needed for slippery roads.	Oct '92	**Mazda MPV**
✓	✓	Excellent for carrying people, cargo, or towing but drives like a truck. Two-wheel drive or all-wheel drive.	Oct '92	**Chevrolet Astro**
✓	✓			**GMC Safari**

[2] *Rear wheels only.*

Ratings continued

RATINGS 1992 CARS continued

Make and model	Predicted reliability	Bumper damage, front/rear	Overall mpg	Air bag, driver/passenger	Antilock brakes	Auto transmission	Air-conditioning
SPORT/UTILITY VEHICLES							
Nissan Pathfinder	○	—	18	NA	S [2]	O	S
Jeep Grand Cherokee	—	—	16	S/NA	S	O	O
Ford Explorer	◖	—	15	NA	S [2]	O	O
Mazda Navajo	○	—	—	NA	S [2]	O	O
Isuzu Trooper	◖	—	15	NA	S [2]	O	O
Mitsubishi Montero	○	—	15	NA	O	O	O
Toyota 4Runner	◒	—	16	NA	S [2]	O	O
Jeep Cherokee	●	—	17	NA	O	O	O
Chevrolet S10 Blazer	●	—	17	NA	S	O	O
GMC Jimmy	●	—		NA	S	O	O
Oldsmobile Bravada	—	—	18	NA	S	S	S
Isuzu Rodeo	○	—	15	NA	S [2]	O	O

[1] Key to major options: **S** = standard; **NA** = not available; **O** = option.
[2] Rear wheels only.

RATINGS OF 1992 CARS

Better ⬅ ➡ Worse

2-door wagon	4-door wagon	Comments	Last full report	Make and model
				SPORT/UTILITY VEHICLES
—	✔	Feels much like a passenger car.	Sept '90	Nissan Pathfinder
—	✔	Much improved over the Cherokee; still not as roomy as Explorer.	Nov '92	Jeep Grand Cherokee
✔ ✔	✔ —	Much-improved replacement for Bronco II; better handling, more cargo room.	Nov '92	Ford Explorer Mazda Navajo
—	✔	Roomy and refined SUV. Part-time 4WD only.	Nov '92	Isuzu Trooper
—	✔	Offers full-time 4WD. Redesigned with loads of creature comforts. Very sloppy handling.	Nov '92	Mitsubishi Montero
✔	✔	Its jacked-up body hinders access without markedly improving ground clearance.	Sept '90	Toyota 4Runner
✔	✔	A practical though unsophisticated model.	Sept '91	Jeep Cherokee
✔ ✔	✔ ✔	Crude and poorly finished, with body shakes, rattles, and a punishing ride.	Sept '90	Chevrolet S10 Blazer GMC Jimmy
—	✔	It's marketed as a cushier Chevy Blazer. Has full-time 4WD too.	Sept '91	Oldsmobile Bravada
—	✔	Sleek, sporty looks betrayed by sluggish performance and a ravenous thirst for fuel.	Sept '91	Isuzu Rodeo

How to Buy a New Car

Given depressed new car and truck sales, consumers have an edge when it comes to buying a new car. Dealerships whose normal eagerness has turned to anxiety are often willing to let some models go for surprisingly low markups. And rebates, once dangled as a carrot to clear the lot of leftovers, are more substantial than ever and common throughout the model year.

Still, it takes a savvy shopper to buy the most car for the fewest dollars. You should know what the car cost the dealer and whether there are any current factory-to-dealer incentives, which aren't always publicized. Armed with that kind of information, you can negotiate up from cost rather than down from the sticker price—and save hundreds, even thousands of dollars.

Do your homework

First decide on the type and style of car that best suits your needs. Then narrow the field to specific makes and models in your price range. (The Ratings of the 1992 cars and the Frequency-of-Repair records can help you select the best models.) Don't fall in love with any one car even if we've top-rated it (recommended cars include many good models in all sizes and price categories). You'll probably end up paying too much for it. Unless the salesperson knows you are willing to walk out of the showroom and shop elsewhere, he or she has little incentive to offer you the lowest possible price.

Next, decide on the equipment you want in your new car. Most models are sold in two or more trim lines (basic, deluxe, etc.). Each trim line has a different base price and a different selection of standard equipment.

In some cases, a more expensive trim line may be cheaper than a basic model dressed up with options. Sometimes the options you want aren't available in a lower trim line. But you may pay for extras you don't want with the higher line.

Often, option packages include some useful and some frivolous equipment. It's usually cheaper to buy a package than to pick and choose options, but only if you want all or most of the extras that it includes.

You can visit dealerships to determine what equipment is included in the various trim lines and what options are offered. The automakers' colorful brochures provide that information, but you won't see a word about prices. For that, you're left to the fanciful figures on the sticker or to better sources outside the showroom.

Learn the dealer's costs

Dealer cost typically runs 80 to 90 percent of sticker price. Precise information is available from the Consumer Reports Auto Price Service, which provides printouts for any make, model, and trim line. Each printout notes the standard equipment, list price, and dealer cost of the basic car. It itemizes, by invoice number, all available factory-installed options and options packages with list prices and dealer cost.

The service has been broadened this year to include all current cash rebate offers, including the unadvertised rebates to dealers. Since the dealer has the option of pocketing that rebate or passing all or part of it on to the consumer, knowledge of such offers can provide useful leverage when you bargain.

Using the printout, you can prepare a worksheet that describes the car you want, its dealer cost, and its list price. The worksheet can save lots of time, and probably spare you from a well-rehearsed sales pitch. Most important, it can save you lots of money.

Include on the worksheet the complete name of the car—make, model, and trim line—and next to it, the dealer cost and list price from the printout. Under that, in columns, list the invoice number and name of each option you want, its dealer cost, and its list price. At the bottom of each column, write in the destination charge from the printout. Finally, total both columns. The difference between the two totals is the room for negotiation.

If there's a factory-to-dealer rebate on the car, subtract its value from the dealer cost tally. (In effect, such a rebate reduces the dealer cost.) If there's a factory-to-customer rebate, the check will be mailed directly from the manufacturer to you. Or if you prefer, you can sign it over to the dealer as part of the down payment.

How much over dealer cost should you expect to pay? It depends on the car. Vehicles in great demand command a higher markup. Some luxury cars and sporty models may command a premium. But on a mid-priced domestic car in good supply, you may have to pay as little as $150 to $300. But $500 over invoice is still a reasonable deal. (The dealer may also receive an additional payment, called a holdback, from the manufacturer at year's end. That typically amounts to 2½ to 3 percent of the base sticker price.)

Afterthoughts

The price you're quoted during these initial negotiations, however, may not be the bottom line. Dealers have come up with an amazing array of add-ons that are designed to improve their profits.

The most common are "packs"—extras added by the dealer or regional distributor to pad the price of the car. One of the most common is a "protection package" that includes a fabric finish, a paint sealant, rustproofing, and undercoating. These are of little or no value to the car buyer, but very profitable for dealers.

Some packs on popular cars are nothing but a dealer's demand for profit over and above that built into the manufacturer's price structure. If a sticker lists ADP, ADM, or AMV, be aware that those are abbreviations for "additional dealer profit," "additional dealer markup," and "additional market value." Don't pay them.

Another costly extra is an extended warranty, also commonly referred to as a service contract or mechanical breakdown insurance. Given the three-to-seven-year protection plan common with today's new cars, an extended warranty is not worthwhile unless it's an unreliable car.

Some dealers charge a "conveyance" fee, a charge for the paperwork involved in selling and registering the car. We've come across a charge of $10 to $20 for filling the gas tank. Many dealers add an advertising surcharge —of as much as $400 per car—

AUTO PRICE SERVICE

Consumer Reports Auto Price Service gives you the facts you need to help negotiate a better deal. Here's what you get: a computer printout showing the current list price and dealer's cost for the car you want and for every factory-installed option; current information on factory-to-dealer rebates and factory-to-customer incentives; a listing of the optional equipment (if any) recommended for your car by the Consumer Reports Auto Test Division. To order, write: Consumers Reports Auto Price Service, Box 8005, Novi, Michigan 48050. Prices: $11 for one car; $20 for two; $27 for three; each additional, $5.

to cover regional advertising by the area's dealer association. (National advertising is included in the car's price.) If the dealer insists on charging such a fee, ask to see proof on the invoice. The fee won't appear on the window sticker.

Occasionally, a salesperson may point out that the figures on your worksheet don't include dealer preparation. In most cases, they shouldn't. Dealer preparation is almost always included in the base price of the car.

All too often, dealers will call attention to packs and fees as an afterthought—when it's time to sign the sales contract—not when the offer you've made has been accepted. They may use them as a negotiating point: That way when they cut the price of a pack or waive a fee, buyers feel they're getting a break. They're not.

Keep the deal simple

Don't discuss trade-ins or financing until you have a firm price quote.

Trade-ins. Salespeople usually ask whether you have a trade-in early in the negotiations. Your answer should be "no." (You'll have plenty of time to reconsider later.) If you talk trade-in too soon, the dealer can sour a good deal on the new car with a bad deal on the old one—or vice versa. The numbers become so garbled you don't know how much you paid for the new car or got for the old one.

Whether you decide to trade your old car or sell it privately, you should have a good idea of its market value. You can learn what your car is worth by calling Consumer Reports Used-Car Price Service (see page 310), which provides up-to-the-minute price information.

Financing. When sales are sluggish, dealers often try to boost business by offering below-market loans from the manufacturer. Compared with typical bank rates, promotional rates can save hundreds of dollars over the life of a loan. In many cases, however, low-rate financing applies only to certain models or to short-term loans. If low-interest financing isn't available on the car you want, don't accept the dealer's financing until you've shopped around. A credit union, a bank, or even some auto-insurance companies may offer more favorable terms.

The contract

Take time to read the sales contract—including the small print—before signing. If you see something you don't like—or if you don't see something that should be included—ask to have changes made.

If you'll be turning in your old car on delivery of the new one several weeks later, the contract might allow the dealer to reappraise your car at that time. That's fair. Anything can happen to your car in the intervening weeks that might affect its value.

Make sure the sales contract states that you have the option to void the agreement and get your down payment back if something goes wrong (failure to deliver by the specified date, for example). And make sure an officer of the dealership signs the agreement. The salesperson's signature alone may not be binding.

How to Buy a Used Car

The average new car costs more than $16,000 these days, and it will depreciate by nearly 30 percent the first year. A used car not only costs less to buy, it also costs less to insure, and loses its value more slowly.

The used-car marketplace, however, can be an unsavory bazaar. Prices are highly elastic and subject to haggling. Paint and polish can be liberally applied to mask evidence of wear and tear, and odometers are frequently rolled back to hide the car's true mileage. In addition, only Connecticut, Massachusetts, Minnesota, New York, and Rhode Island have effective lemon laws to protect buyers from dealers who sell faulty merchandise. Protection extends to all but the oldest and cheapest used cars.

Although you can't eliminate the risk when buying a used car, you can better your odds of getting sound transportation by learning how to shop.

Eyeing the field

First, figure out what kind of car suits your life-style and budget. Four-door sedans and station wagons usually provide the best used-car value. Chances are they've led a kinder, gentler life than high-performance models. Convertibles, sporty coupes, and luxury models remain pricey even when used and often come with expensive-to-fix electronic extras like cruise control and power windows.

Next, consider cars that have held up well in the past. Our Frequency-of-Repair records, based on readers' experiences with more than 635,000 cars, describe the repair histories of 1986 to 1991 models. The better the car scored in the past, the less likely it is to have problems in the future. From those data, we have derived a list of reliable used cars. (Prices quoted in that list may vary depending on the region in which you buy, the options, and the condition of the car you're buying.) We used the same data to identify models to avoid. However, the older the car, the less important our records and the more important an inspection.

To find out how much a model sells for in your area, you can use the Consumer Reports Used-Car Price Service described in the box on page 310. Price information also appears in various printed guides, which are available in public libraries.

Where to buy

There are ample sources of used cars, some less risky than others. It's best to buy a used car from someone you know. Tread cautiously with other private sellers. When responding to an advertisement, ask about the car's condition and mileage, if it's been in a wreck, and why it's being sold. Also, ask if the seller is a dealer. If so, and the ad omitted that fact, watch out—you could be dealing with an unethical operator.

Private sellers should charge less than a dealer because they don't have to worry about overhead and markup. The downside of buying privately is that the vehicle usually comes without a guarantee.

New-car dealers who sell used cars generally charge top dollar. But that's where you're likely to find the cream of the crop: late model trade-ins with low mileage. Other advantages are that such dealerships have repair facilities and they often provide a warranty. Independent used-car dealers usually charge less, but their stock may not be as desirable.

Avoid "gypsy" used-car lots commonly found in poorer neighborhoods. These come-and-go operations sell cars at rock-bottom prices, but the quality of the merchandise is suspect. Your safest bet is to find a dealership that's been around for some time and then ask the Better Business Bureau whether any complaints have been lodged against it.

Cars repossessed by lenders are periodically auctioned off. Check newspapers for advertisements. Such cars may be risky because they may not have had the best care. Auto-rental agencies such as Hertz, Avis, and National offer some cars to the public. While these cars may have been driven long and hard, most have had the advantage of regular servicing. And some companies provide a limited warranty. You can call the agencys' toll-free numbers to learn the location of their nearest used-car lot.

Looking for trouble

Never buy on looks alone. After you've found a car that catches your fancy, give it a thorough inspection—on the lot, on the road, and at the service station. Bring along a friend to help troubleshoot.

Here's what to look for:

Fluids. When the engine is cold, open the radiator cap and inspect the coolant; it shouldn't be rusty. Greenish-white stains on the radiator cap denote pinholes. To check the transmission, warm up the engine and remove the dipstick. The fluid should be pinkish; it shouldn't smell burned or contain metal shavings.

Leaks. Puddles or stains beneath the car are a bad sign. So is excessive residue of lubricants on the engine, transmission, hoses, or other underhood components.

Body. Rust is ruinous. Check the wheel wells and rocker panels, the door edges, and the trunk floor. Rust can also hide beneath peeling paint. Fresh welds in the underbody point to an accident. So does ripply body work, a part whose color or fit doesn't seem to match, and new paint on a late-model car. Fresh undercoating on older cars also is a giveaway.

Tires and suspension. A car with 24,000 miles or less should have its original tires. Uneven tread wear indicates an accident or poor wheel alignment. In front tires, uneven tread wear may spell serious suspension damage. Grab the top of each tire and shake it. If there's play or a clunking

USED-CAR PRICE SERVICE

Consumer Reports Used-Car Price Service quotes purchase and trade-in prices over the telephone for 1984 to 1992 cars and light trucks. (Prices for '92 models will be available beginning in January 1993.) The service provides up-to-date price information that takes into account the caller's region of the country, the vehicle's mileage, major options, and general condition. It also offers the vehicle's Trouble Index, based on CU's Frequency-of-Repair data for hundreds of recent-model vehicles.

The telephone number for the price service is 1-900-446-1120. The call costs $1.75 a minute and must be made from a touch-tone phone. Expect the call to take five minutes or more. You'll be charged on your phone bill. Have the following facts about the car on hand when you call: model name or number, model year, mileage, number of cylinders, the car's general condition, and major options, such as air-conditioning or sun roof.

This service is not available for Alaska and Hawaii residents. In certain other areas, 900 service is also unavailable.

sound, suspect loose or worn wheel bearings or suspension joints. Bounce the car a few times by pushing down each corner. When you let go, the car should rise and then settle. If it keeps bouncing, the struts or shock absorbers need replacing.

Interior. A saggy driver's seat means heavy use. On a low-mileage auto, the pedals shouldn't be too worn or brand new. Musty odors suggest a water leak, a costly fix that may be hard to find.

The road test

Plan to spend at least half an hour driving the car at various speeds on a variety of roads. But before you turn on the ignition, unlock the steering and turn the wheel. It shouldn't have much free play. Start the car to check its gauges and play with its gadgets. Switch on the lights and signals.

Engine. The car should start easily and pick up smoothly. Pings or knocks may be corrected with higher-octane fuel or a tune-up. Or they could signal costly problems. Ask a mechanic.

Transmission. A manual transmission shouldn't grab suddenly and make the car buck. An automatic shouldn't slam into gear or slip as you drive.

Brakes. Speed up to 45 mph on a flat stretch of road. Apply the brakes firmly. The car should stop quickly, evenly, and in a straight line. Repeat the exercise. To check for leaks in the brake system, press firmly on the pedal for 30 seconds. It shouldn't sink to the floor.

Alignment. Have someone stand behind the car while you drive straight ahead. The front and rear wheels should line up. Forget about the car if it scuttles sideways; it probably has a bent frame. Veering to one side may be less serious; the wheels may simply need alignment.

Smoke. Blue exhaust smoke from the tailpipe means the car is burning oil—a costly fix. Billowy white smoke is serious as well. It means water is entering the combustion chamber. White vapor emerging briefly from the tail pipe on a cold morning is harmless. Black smoke generally means that the fuel system needs adjustment.

Comfort, noise. Suspension work might be in order if the car bounces or rattles over rough road at local speeds. Sputtering sounds from beneath the chassis indicate exhaust-system leaks.

A car that's passed muster to this point is ready to be examined by a reliable mechanic. If you don't have one, call your local American Automobile Dealers Association, which offers diagnostic services around the country. The National Highway Traffic Safety Administration (800-424-9393) can tell you if the model has ever been recalled. Also, check the Product Recalls chapter on page 371 for recalls of cars published in CONSUMER REPORTS from October 1991 through October 1992. If the car has been recalled, ask the seller for proof the problem was corrected.

How objective is CU?

Consumers Union is not beholden to any commercial interest. It accepts no advertising and buys all the products tested on the open market. CU's income is derived from the sale of CONSUMER REPORTS and other publications, and from nonrestrictive, noncommercial contributions, grants, and fees. Neither the Ratings nor the reports may be used in advertising or for any other commercial purpose. Consumers Union will take all steps open to it to prevent commercial use of its materials, its name, or the name of CONSUMER REPORTS.

GOOD & BAD BETS IN USED CARS

The list of reliable used cars includes 1986 to 1990 models whose overall repair records were considerably better than average for their model year, according to our Frequency-of-Repair records.

The list of used cars to avoid includes '86 to '90 models whose overall repair records are considerably worse than the average for cars at their model year. Problems with the engine, transmission, clutch, and body rust—troubles likely to be serious and costly to repair—weighed more heavily than other problems in forming these lists.

The reliable cars are grouped by price as reported in the April 1992 issue of CONSUMER REPORTS. Most are likely to have dropped to a lower price by 1993. Prices are Midwestern averages for cars with average mileage, air-conditioning, AM/FM cassette stereo, and automatic transmission. (Prices for sporty cars, pickups, and sports/utility vehicles are for manual transmission.) Cars to avoid are listed alphabetically by nameplate.

RWD = rear-wheel drive; **FWD** = front-wheel drive; **2WD** = two-wheel drive; **4WD** = four-wheel drive.

Reliable used cars

$2500-$3000
86 Chevrolet Nova
87 Chevrolet Sprint [1]
88 Ford Festiva
86 Isuzu Pickup (2WD)
86, 87 Mitsubishi Pickup 4 (2WD)
86 Toyota Tercel (2WD)

$3000-$3500
86 Mazda 323
86 Mazda Pickup
86 Nissan Pickup 4 (2WD)
86 Nissan Stanza [1]
86 Toyota Pickup 4 (2WD)

$3500-$4000
86 Chevrolet S10 Pickup 4, V6 (2WD)
88 Chevrolet Spectrum [2]
86 Honda Civic
87 Isuzu Pickup (2WD)
88 Mitsubishi Pickup 4 (2WD)
87 Nissan Sentra [1]
86 Nissan Stanza Wagon (2WD)
86 Toyota Corolla (FWD)

$4000-$4500
87 Chevrolet Nova
87 Chevrolet S10 Pickup V6 (2WD)
87 Dodge Ram 50 Pickup 4
89 Ford Festiva
86 Ford Thunderbird V8
86 Honda Civic CRX
87 Mazda 323
86 Mazda 626
87 Mazda Pickup
87 Nissan Pickup 4 (2WD)
88 Nissan Sentra (2WD)
86 Toyota Corolla SR5 (RWD)
87 Toyota Pickup 4 (2WD)
86 Toyota Tercel Wagon (4WD)

$4500-$5000
88 Chevrolet Nova
87 Chevrolet S10 4 [2], V6 (2WD)
89 Dodge Colt, Plymouth Colt (2WD)
89 Geo Spectrum
87 Honda Civic

88 Mazda 323
86 Mazda 626 Turbo
88 Mazda Pickup
86 Mercury Cougar V8
86 Nissan 200SX 4 [2]
86 Nissan Pickup V6 (2WD)
86 Nissan Stanza Wagon (4WD)
87, 88 Pontiac Fiero 4 [2]
87 Toyota Corolla, Corolla FX-16 [2]
86 Toyota MR2
88 Toyota Pickup 4 (2WD)
87, 88 Toyota Tercel (2WD)

$5000-$6000
86 Acura Integra
87 Chevrolet Caprice V6
88 Chevrolet S10 Pickup 4, V6 (2WD) [2]
88 Chrysler Le Baron GTS
88 Dodge Ram 50 Pickup 4
89 Eagle Summit
90 Ford Festiva
86 Honda Accord

RELIABLE USED CARS

88 Honda Civic
87 Honda CRX
87 Honda Civic Wagon (4WD)
88 Isuzu Pickup (2WD)
87 Mazda 626 [1]
89 Mazda Pickup
86 Mercury Grand Marquis
89 Mercury Tracer
86 Nissan Maxima [2]
88, 89 Nissan Pickup 4 (2WD)
87 Nissan Pickup V6 (2WD)
87 Nissan Stanza, Stanza Wagon (2WD)
87 Pontiac Fiero V6 [2]
88, 89 Subaru Coupe (2WD) [2]
88 Subaru Sedan & Wagon (2WD) [2]
86 Toyota Camry 4
88 Toyota Corolla FX-16
87 Toyota Corolla SR5 (RWD)
87 Toyota Tercel Wagon (4WD)
86 Toyota Van (2WD)

$6000-$7000
87 Acura Integra
87 Chevrolet S10 Pickup V6 (4WD) [1]
90 Dodge Colt, Plymouth Colt (2WD)
89 Dodge Ram 50 Pickup 4
90 Geo Metro
87 Honda Accord
89, 90 Isuzu Pickup (2WD)
89 Mazda 323
87 Mercury Grand Marquis
90 Mitsubishi Pickup 4 (2WD)
87 Nissan 200SX V6
88 Nissan Pickup V6 (2WD)
88 Nissan Pulsar NX
89 Nissan Sentra (2WD)
88 Nissan Stanza
88 Pontiac Fiero V6 [2]
86 Saab 900
89 Subaru Sedan (4WD), Sedan & Wagon (2WD)
89 Suzuki Sidekick (4WD)
87 Toyota Celica (2WD)
88 Toyota Corolla (FWD)
86 Toyota Cressida
87 Toyota MR2
87 Toyota Pickup 4 (4WD) [2]
89 Toyota Pickup 4, V6 (2WD)
89, 90 Toyota Tercel (2WD)
87 Toyota Van (2WD)

$7000-$8000
90 Eagle Summit
87 Ford LTD Crown Victoria
89 Ford Probe 4 [1]
87 Ford Thunderbird V6
90 Geo Prizm
89 Honda Civic
88 Honda CRX
88 Honda Civic Wagon (4WD)
86 Honda Prelude
90 Mazda 323
88 Mazda 626 [1]
88 Mazda MX-6 [1]
90 Mazda Pickup
86 Mazda RX-7 [2]
90 Mitsubishi Mirage
86 Nissan 300ZX
87 Nissan Maxima [2]
90 Nissan Pickup 4 (2WD)
89 Nissan Pickup V6 (2WD)
89 Nissan Pulsar NX
88 Nissan Stanza Wagon (2WD)
89 Oldsmobile Cutlass Ciera 4
89 Subaru Coupe (4WD)
90 Subaru Loyale Sedan & Wagon (2WD)
89 Subaru Wagon (4WD)
86 Toyota 4Runner 4 (4WD)
87 Toyota Camry 4
88 Toyota Celica (2WD)
89 Toyota Corolla (FWD, 4WD)
90 Toyota Pickup 4 (2WD)
88 Toyota Pickup 4, V6 (4WD)

$8000-$9000
88 Acura Integra
86 BMW 325 Series (2WD) [1]
88 Buick Electra V6
88 Chevrolet S10 Blazer V6 (2WD) [1]
88 Dodge Caravan 4
89 Dodge Spirit Turbo 4 [2]
88 Ford LTD Crown Victoria
90 Ford Probe 4
89 Geo Tracker (4WD) [1]
88 Honda Accord
89 Honda CRX
87 Honda Prelude
86 Lincoln Town Car
89 Mazda 626 [1]
90 Mazda Protege
87 Mazda RX-7
88 Mercury Grand Marquis
88 Mitsubishi Galant Sigma V6
89 Nissan Stanza
88 Oldsmobile 88 V6
90 Plymouth Acclaim 4 [2]
90 Subaru Loyale (4WD)
88 Toyota Camry 4 (2WD), (4WD) [1], V6
89 Toyota Celica (2WD)
90 Toyota Corolla (FWD)
87 Toyota Cressida
88 Toyota MR2
89 Toyota Pickup 4 (4WD)
90 Toyota Pickup V6 (2WD)
86 Toyota Supra
87 Volvo 240 Sedan
86 Volvo 740 Sedan & Wagon [1]

$9000-$10,000
89 Acura Integra
86 Acura Legend [2]
87 Audi 5000 Quattro Turbo
87 BMW 325 Series (2WD)
86 BMW 528e
90 Buick Century V6
88 Dodge Grand Caravan 4

[1] *Manual transmission only.*
[2] *Automatic transmission only.*

Listings continued

314 RELIABLE USED CARS

89 Ford F150 Pickup 6 (2WD)
89 Ford Probe GT 4
90 Ford Taurus V6
90 Honda Civic, Civic Wagon (4WD)
87 Lincoln Town Car
89 Mazda MX-6 [1]
89 Mitsubishi Galant 4 (2WD)
89 Nissan 240SX
87 Nissan 300ZX [1]
88 Nissan Maxima [2]
88 Oldsmobile 98 V6
90 Oldsmobile Cutlass Ciera 4
90 Plymouth Laser
87 Toyota 4Runner 4 (4WD)
89 Toyota Camry 4 (2WD)
90 Toyota Corolla (4WD)
89 Toyota MR2
87 Toyota Supra
87 Volvo 240 Wagon
87 Volvo 740 Sedan

$10,000-$12,000
90 Acura Integra
87 Acura Legend [2]
88 Audi 5000
89 Buick Electra V6
89 Buick Le Sabre V6
88 Cadillac De Ville
89 Dodge Caravan Turbo 4 [1]
90 Eagle Talon (2WD)
89 Ford LTD Crown Victoria
89 Honda Accord
90 Honda CRX
89 Honda Prelude
87 Lincoln Mark VII
88 Lincoln Town Car
90 Mazda 626 [1]
88 Mazda 929
89 Mazda MPV 4
90 Mazda MX-6 [1]
88 Mazda RX-7 [2]
90 Mercury Sable
90 Mitsubishi Eclipse (2WD)
90 Mitsubishi Galant 4 (2WD)
90 Nissan 240SX

88 Nissan 300ZX
87 Nissan Pathfinder (4WD)
90 Nissan Pickup V6 (4WD)
90 Nissan Stanza
90 Plymouth Laser Turbo
90 Pontiac Bonneville (FWD)
90 Subaru Legacy (2WD) [1]
88 Toyota 4Runner 4 (4WD)
89 Toyota Camry V6
90 Toyota Celica (2WD)
90 Toyota Corolla Wagon (4WD)
88 Toyota Cressida
89, 90 Toyota Pickup V6 (4WD)
87 Toyota Supra Turbo
88 Volvo 240 Sedan
87 Volvo Sedan & Wagon, Turbo
87 Volvo 760 Sedan Turbo

$12,000-$15,000
88 Acura Legend [2]
88 Audi 5000 Turbo
88 BMW 325 Series (2WD)
87 BMW 528e
86 BMW 535i
90 Buick Le Sabre V6
88 Cadillac Fleetwood
88 Cadillac Seville
90 Honda Accord
89 Mazda 929
90 Mazda MPV 4, V6
90 Mazda MX-5 Miata
89 Mazda RX-7
89 Mitsubishi Montero V6
90 Mitsubishi Montero V6 [2]
89 Nissan Maxima [2]
88, 89 Nissan Pathfinder (4WD)
90 Oldsmobile 88 V6
90 Subaru Legacy (4WD)
90 Toyota 4Runner 4 (4WD)
89 Toyota 4Runner V6 (4WD)
90 Toyota Camry 4 (2WD)
89, 90 Toyota Camry 4 (4WD)

90 Toyota Camry V6
89 Toyota Cressida
88 Toyota Land Cruiser Wagon
88 Toyota Supra
88 Volvo 740 Sedan & Wagon, Turbo [2]
89 Volvo 240 Sedan & Wagon
90 Volvo 240 Sedan
88 Volvo 240 Wagon
87 Volvo 760 Turbo Wagon

$15,000-$20,000
89 Acura Legend [2]
89 Audi 100
90 Audi 100 [2]
89 Audio 200 Turbo
89 BMW 325i Series (2WD)
88 BMW 528e [1]
87, 88 BMW 535i
89, 90 Cadillac De Ville
89 Cadillac Eldorado
89, 90 Cadillac Fleetwood
89 Cadillac Seville
90 Honda Prelude
90 Infiniti M30
90 Lexus ES250 [2]
90 Mazda 929
90 Nissan Maxima [2]
90 Nissan Pathfinder (4WD)
90 Saab 900
90 Toyota 4Runner V6 (4WD)
90 Toyota Cressida
89 Toyota Supra
90 Volvo 240 Wagon
90 Volvo 740 Sedan & Wagon [1], Turbo Sedan [2]

$20,000-$25,000
90 Acura Legend [2]
90 Audi 200 Turbo [2]
89 BMW 525i
90 Cadillac Seville
89 Mercedes-Benz 190E 2.6
87 Mercedes-Benz 300E
86 Mercedes-Benz 420 SEL

USED CARS TO AVOID

90 Nissan 300ZX [2]
90 Volvo 740 Turbo Wagon [2]

$25,000-$30,000
89 BMW 535i
89 Mercedes-Benz 300E
87 Mercedes-Benz 420 SEL

86 Mercedes-Benz 560 SEL

$30,000 AND UP
90 BMW 735i
90 Infiniti Q45
90 Lexus LS400
89 Mercedes-Benz 300CE, 300TE

90 Mercedes-Benz 300SL, 300CE, 300E (2WD), 300TE (2WD)
86 Mercedes-Benz 560 SEC, 560 SL

[1] *Manual transmission only.*
[2] *Automatic transmission only.*

Used cars to avoid

BMW
7 Series, 88

Buick
Century 4, V6, 86
Estate Wagon, 87
Le Sabre V6, 87
Regal V6, V6 Turbo (RWD), 87; V6 (FWD), 89
Skyhawk 86-89
Somerset, Skylark 4, 86-89; V6, 86

Cadillac
Brougham, Fleetwood Brougham (RWD), 90
Eldorado, 86

Chevrolet
Astro Van V6 (2WD), 89-90; (4WD), 90
Blazer, 86-90
Camaro V6, V8, 86-90
Caprice V8, 90
Cavalier 4, 86-88, 90; V6, 86-90
Celebrity 4, 86; V6, 88
Corsica, Beretta 4, 88-89; V6, 88-89
Corvette, 86-90
Lumina 4, V6, 90
Monte Carlo V6, V8, 86-87
Pickup C10/1500-20/2500 V8 (2WD), 86-90
Pickup K10/1500-20/2500 V8 (4WD), 86-90
S-10 Blazer V6 (2WD), 89; (4WD), 86-90
S-10 Pickup 4 (2WD), 89; V6, 90
S-10 Pickup V6 (4WD), 88-90
Spectrum, 86
Sportvan V8, 86-90
Suburban, 86-90

Chrysler
Imperial, 90
Le Baron Sedan, Wagon (including Turbo), 88
Le Baron Coupe 4, Turbo 4, 88-89; V6, 90
New Yorker V6 (FWD), 89

Dodge
Aries, 87, 89
Caravan V6 (2WD) [1], 89-90
Colt Vista Wagon (2WD) [2], 86; (2WD) [1], 87; (4WD) [2], 86
D/W 100-250 Ram Pickup V8, 86-90
Dakota Pickup V6 (2WD), 88-90; (4WD), 88-89
Daytona 4 (including Turbo), 86-90; V6, 90
Dynasty 4, 89
Grand Caravan (2WD), 89-90
Monaco, 90
Omni, Charger, America, 86, 87, 89
Ramcharger, 87, 89
Ram B150-250 Van V8, 86-90
Shadow (including Turbo), 87, 89

Eagle
Medallion, 88
Premier V6, 88-90

Ford
Aerostar Van V6 (2WD), 86-88, 90; (4WD), 90
Bronco V8, 86-90
Bronco II (2WD), 87; (4WD), 86
Club Wagon V8, 86-90
Escort, 86-88
F150-250 Pickup 6, V8 (2WD) [2], 87; 6 (4WD), 86, 88; V8 (4WD), 86-90
Mustang 4, 86-90; V8 [2], 90
Probe Turbo 4, 90
Ranger Pickup V6 (4WD), 86-87
Taurus 4, 86-90; SHO V6, 89
Tempo (2WD), 86-89
Thunderbird Turbo 4, 86, 88; V6, 89-90; SC V6, 90

[1] *Avoid automatic transmission.*
[2] *Avoid manual transmission.*

Listings continued

USED CARS TO AVOID

GMC
S15 Jimmy V6 (4WD) [2], 88; V6 (4WD), 89-90

Hyundai
Excel, 86-90
Sonata 4, 89-90

Isuzu
Trooper II V6, 89

Jaguar
XJ 6, 86-90

Jeep
Cherokee 6 (2WD), 90
Cherokee/Wagoneer 6 (4WD), 86-90
Comanche Pickup 6 [2], 89
Grand Wagoneer, 86-89
Wrangler 6, 87-90

Lincoln
Continental V6 (FWD), 88-89

Mazda
626 [1], 87-90; 626 Turbo [1], 88
MX-6 [1], 88-90

Mercury
Cougar V6, 89-90
Lynx [1], 86
Topaz (2WD), 86-89

Mitsubishi
Montero V6 [2], 90

Oldsmobile
Eighty-Eight V6, 86-87
Ninety-Eight V6, 86-87
Custom Cruiser Wagon, 86
Cutlass Calais 4, 86-88
Cutlass Ciera 4, V6, 86
Cutlass Supreme V6 (FWD), 88-90

Plymouth
Grand Voyager V6, 87-90
Horizon, Turismo, America, 86-87
Reliant, 86, 89
Sundance, 87
Voyager V6 (2WD) [1], 90

Pontiac
6000 4, 86-87; V6 (2WD), 87, 89
Bonneville (FWD), 87

Fiero GT V6 [2], 88
Firebird V6, V8, 86-89
Grand Am 4, 86-87, 89; V6, 86-87
Grand Prix V6 (FWD), 88-90
Le Mans, 88-89
Sunbird 4, 86-87

Saab
900, 900 Turbo, 89
9000, 9000 Turbo, 89; 9000 Turbo [2], 87

Subaru
XT Coupe 4 (2WD) [2], 86
Justy (2WD) [1], 89
Coupe, Sedan, Wagon Turbo (4WD), 86-87

Volkswagen
Golf, GTI, 88-90
Passat [1], 90
Vanagon (2WD), 87

Volvo
740 Series Turbo, 89

[1] *Avoid automatic transmission.*   [2] *Avoid manual transmission.*

ABOUT CU'S REPAIR HISTORIES

Thousands of readers tell us about their repair experiences with autos, appliances, and electronic items on the Annual Questionnaire. Using that unique information can improve your chances of getting a trouble-free car, washing machine, TV set, or other product. See the Frequency-of-Repair charts starting on page 317 and the brand repair histories starting on page 361.

FREQUENCY OF REPAIR RECORDS, 1986-1991

The following charts are the most comprehensive picture available of automotive reliability. The data for the charts come from the subscribers to CONSUMER REPORTS, who tell us each year about their automobile problems. The 1991 Annual Questionnaire on which these records are based brought in reports on more than 635,000 cars, reflecting subscribers' experiences between April 1990 and March 1991.

We combined these responses with those from past years to provide the predicted reliability judgments that you'll find in the recommendations of 1992 cars starting on page 282. New-car buyers can check the repair records of earlier models for problems that may crop up in a current model. In 35 years of publishing these repair records, we've found that a model's black or rosy past was often a prologue to a black or rosy future.

Used-car buyers can check a specific model to identify vehicles to avoid or trouble spots to investigate thoroughly. With an older car, ask about problems flagged in the charts. The necessary repair may have already been made.

How to read the repair records. On page 318, we sum up what constitutes the **trouble spots.** You'll see the average problem rate for all models in the survey year by year. In the repair records themselves, symbols show how a model compares with those averages. To earn ◐ or ◓ for a specific trouble, the model's problem rate had to differ by at least 2½ percentage points. To earn ● or ○, the model had to differ by at least 5 percentage points. An asterisk indicates insufficient data and a blank square means the car lacked that feature. For example, a 1988 model rated ● for body hardware had a problem rate of at least 14 percent (the 1988 overall average of 9 percent plus the 5-point difference).

If the average problem rate is very low, as it often is in young cars, it's difficult for any model to do substantially better than average. With our criteria, it's impossible if a trouble spot's average was less than 2½ percent. The only spots in which newer cars score better than average are those in which trouble tends to show up early—body hardware, body integrity, and the electrical system.

The **trouble index** compares the overall trouble experience, summed up overall trouble spots, of a given model with the average experience of all models of the same model year.

The Frequency-of-Repair charts also give the **cost index**, an indication of the average maintenance and repair costs faced by the owners of each model. The symbols in the cost index indicate how far a model departs from the average maintenance and repair costs for other models of that year. We give no cost index for the 1991 models; most of their costs should have been covered under warranty. The cost of accident repairs, tires, and batteries are omitted.

To be rated ◐ or ◓ for either the trouble index or cost index, a model had to differ from the average by at least 15 percent; to be rated ● or ○, it had to differ by at least 35 percent.

Cars develop problems not only because they're getting older, but also as a consequence of the miles they are driven. The more miles driven, the faster things tend to wear out or fail. We asked respondents to state the number of miles on the car, and we adjusted our tallies to minimize differences due solely to mileage.

Trouble spots explained

Trouble spot	Includes	'86	'87	'88	'89	'90	'91
Air-conditioning	Compressor, expansion valves, leakage, fans, electronics.	12%	9%	7%	5%	3%	1%
Body paint	Fading, discoloring, chalking, peeling.	10	7	6	4	3	2
Body rust	Corrosion, pitting, perforation.	7	4	3	2	1	[1]
Body hardware	Window, door, seat mechanisms; locks, seat belts, head restraints.	12	10	9	8	7	4
Body integrity	Air or water leaks, wind noise, rattles and squeaks.	10	9	9	9	9	5
Brakes	Power-boost and hydraulic systems; linings, disks, drums; antilock system.	15	13	11	8	5	2
Clutch	Lining, pressure plate, release bearing, linkage.	10	8	5	3	2	1
Driveline	Drive joints, rear axle, differential, wheel bearings, drive shaft, four-wheel-drive components.	4	3	2	2	1	1
Electrical system	Starter, alternator, battery, controls, instruments, wiring, lights, radio, horn, accessory motors, electronics.	17	16	14	11	8	5
Engine cooling	Radiator, heater core, water pump; overheating.	9	7	4	2	1	1
Engine mechanical	Rings, cylinders, pistons, bearings, valves, camshaft, turbocharger, oil leaks, engine overhaul.	9	7	5	3	2	1
Exhaust system	Exhaust manifold, muffler, catalytic converter, pipes, leaks.	15	10	5	2	1	[1]
Fuel system	Stalling or hesitation; carburetor, choke, fuel pump, fuel injection, computer, fuel leaks, emissions controls.	11	10	7	5	3	1
Ignition system	Plugs, coil, distributor, timing, electronic ignition, too-frequent tuneups, engine knock or ping.	6	5	3	2	1	[1]
Steering/suspension	Linkage, power unit, wheel alignment, springs or torsion bars, ball joints, bushings, shocks, strut assembly.	13	10	8	6	4	2
Transmission (manual)	Gear box, gear shifter, linkage; leaks, malfunction, or failure.	4	4	4	3	2	1
Transmission (automatic)	Transaxle, gear selector, linkage; leaks, malfunction, or failure.	8	5	5	4	3	2
Cost index	Average cost of repairs and maintenance.	$410	$340	$270	$200	$110	[2]

Average problem rate

[1] Less than 0.5 percent. [2] No index for this year, since most repairs covered under warranty.

REPAIR RECORDS 319

Trouble Spots	Acura Integra '86–'91	Acura Legend '86–'91	Audi 4000, 80, 90 4 '86–'91	Audi 5000, 100, 200 '86–'91
Air-conditioning				
Body exterior (paint)				
Body exterior (rust)				
Body hardware				
Body integrity				
Brakes				
Clutch				
Driveline				
Electrical system (chassis)				
Engine cooling				
Engine mechanical				
Exhaust system				
Fuel system				
Ignition system				
Steering/suspension				
Transmission (manual)				
Transmission (automatic)				
TROUBLE INDEX				
COST INDEX				

Trouble Spots	Audi 5000, 100, 200 Quattro '86–'91	BMW 318i '86–'91	BMW 325 Series (2WD) '86–'91	BMW 5 Series '86–'91
Air-conditioning				
Body exterior (paint)				
Body exterior (rust)				
Body hardware				
Body integrity				
Brakes				
Clutch				
Driveline				
Electrical system (chassis)				
Engine cooling				
Engine mechanical				
Exhaust system				
Fuel system				
Ignition system				
Steering/suspension				
Transmission (manual)				
Transmission (automatic)				
TROUBLE INDEX				
COST INDEX				

Legend:
- ✻ Insufficient data
- ● Much worse than average
- ◐ Worse than average
- ○ Average
- ◉ Better than average
- ◍ Much better than average

320 REPAIR RECORDS

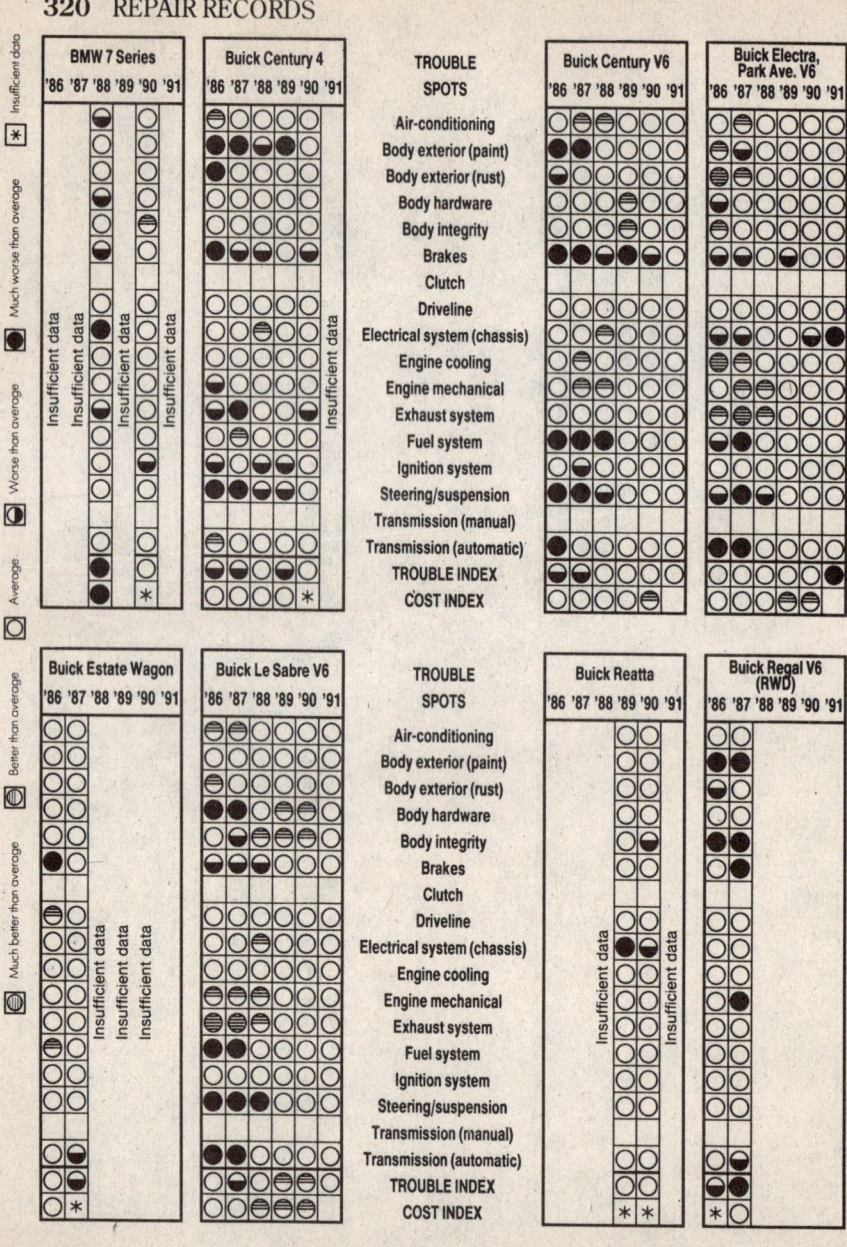

Legend:
- ○ Insufficient data
- ✱ Much worse than average
- ● Worse than average
- ◐ Average
- ○ Better than average
- ◉ Much better than average

Trouble Spots

Trouble Spots	BMW 7 Series '86–'91	Buick Century 4 '86–'91	Buick Century V6 '86–'91	Buick Electra, Park Ave. V6 '86–'91
Air-conditioning				
Body exterior (paint)				
Body exterior (rust)				
Body hardware				
Body integrity				
Brakes				
Clutch				
Driveline				
Electrical system (chassis)				
Engine cooling				
Engine mechanical				
Exhaust system				
Fuel system				
Ignition system				
Steering/suspension				
Transmission (manual)				
Transmission (automatic)				
TROUBLE INDEX				
COST INDEX				

Trouble Spots	Buick Estate Wagon '86–'91	Buick Le Sabre V6 '86–'91	Buick Reatta '86–'91	Buick Regal V6 (RWD) '86–'91
Air-conditioning				
Body exterior (paint)				
Body exterior (rust)				
Body hardware				
Body integrity				
Brakes				
Clutch				
Driveline				
Electrical system (chassis)				
Engine cooling				
Engine mechanical				
Exhaust system				
Fuel system				
Ignition system				
Steering/suspension				
Transmission (manual)				
Transmission (automatic)				
TROUBLE INDEX				
COST INDEX				

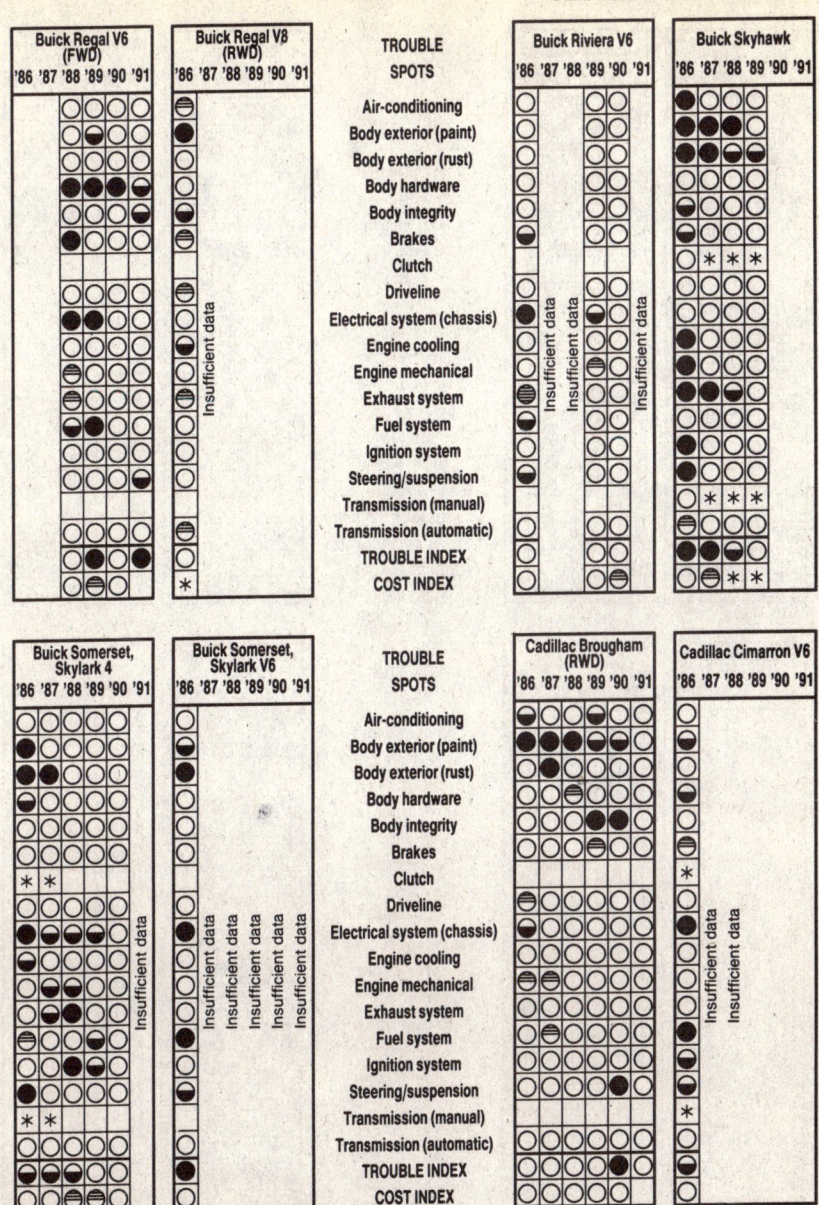

REPAIR RECORDS 321

Trouble Spots — Buick and Cadillac Models ('86–'91)

Trouble Spots	Buick Regal V6 (FWD)	Buick Regal V8 (RWD)	Buick Riviera V6	Buick Skyhawk
Air-conditioning	— ○ ○ ○ ○ ○	○ — — — — —	○ — ○ ○ ○ —	● ● ○ ○ — —
Body exterior (paint)	— ○ ◐ ○ ○ ○	○ — — — — —	○ — ○ ○ ○ —	● ● ● ◐ — —
Body exterior (rust)	— ○ ◐ ○ ○ ○	○ — — — — —	○ — ○ ○ ○ —	● ● ◐ ◐ — —
Body hardware	— ● ● ● ● ○	○ — — — — —	○ — ○ ○ ○ —	○ ○ ○ ○ — —
Body integrity	— ○ ○ ○ ○ ○	○ — — — — —	○ — ○ ○ ○ —	○ ◐ ○ ○ — —
Brakes	— ● ○ ○ ○ ○	◐ — — — — —	◐ — ○ ○ ○ —	○ ○ ○ ○ — —
Clutch	— — — — — —	— — — — — —	— — — — — —	— * * * — —
Driveline	— ○ ○ ○ ○ ○	◐ — — — — —	○ — ○ ○ ○ —	○ ○ ○ ○ — —
Electrical system (chassis)	— ● ◐ ○ ○ ○	○ — — — — —	● — ○ ○ ○ —	● ● ○ ○ — —
Engine cooling	— ○ ○ ○ ○ ○	○ — — — — —	○ — ○ ○ ○ —	○ ◐ ○ ○ — —
Engine mechanical	— ◐ ○ ○ ○ ○	○ — — — — —	○ — ○ ○ ○ —	○ ○ ○ ○ — —
Exhaust system	— ○ ○ ○ ○ ○	◐ — — — — —	◐ — ○ ○ ○ —	○ ○ ○ ○ — —
Fuel system	— ◐ ○ ○ ○ ○	◐ — — — — —	◐ — ○ ○ ○ —	○ ◐ ○ ○ — —
Ignition system	— ○ ○ ○ ○ ○	○ — — — — —	○ — ○ ○ ○ —	○ ○ ○ ○ — —
Steering/suspension	— ○ ○ ○ ○ ○	○ — — — — —	○ — ○ ○ ○ —	○ ○ ○ ○ — —
Transmission (manual)	— — — — — —	— — — — — —	— — — — — —	○ * * * — —
Transmission (automatic)	— ○ ○ ○ ○ ○	◐ — — — — —	◐ — ○ ○ ○ —	◐ ○ ○ ○ — —
TROUBLE INDEX	— ○ ○ ○ ○ ○	○ — — — — —	○ — ○ ○ ○ —	● ● ◐ ○ — —
COST INDEX	— ○ ○ ○ ○ ○	* — — — — —	○ — ○ ○ ◐ —	○ ◐ * * — —

Regal V8 (RWD): Insufficient data '87–'91. Riviera V6: Insufficient data '87, '91. Skyhawk: Insufficient data '90, '91.

Trouble Spots	Buick Somerset, Skylark 4	Buick Somerset, Skylark V6	Cadillac Brougham (RWD)	Cadillac Cimarron V6
Air-conditioning	○ ○ ○ ○ — —	◐ — — — — —	● ○ ○ ○ ○ ○	○ — — — — —
Body exterior (paint)	● ● ○ ○ — —	◐ — — — — —	● ● ● ● ● ◐	○ — — — — —
Body exterior (rust)	● ● ○ ○ — —	● — — — — —	○ ○ ○ ◐ ○ ○	○ — — — — —
Body hardware	◐ ◐ ○ ○ — —	◐ — — — — —	○ ○ ◐ ○ ○ ○	◐ — — — — —
Body integrity	○ ○ ○ ○ — —	○ — — — — —	○ ○ ○ ● ● ○	○ — — — — —
Brakes	○ ○ ○ ○ — —	○ — — — — —	○ ○ ○ ○ ○ ○	◐ — — — — —
Clutch	* * — — — —	— — — — — —	— — — — — —	* — — — — —
Driveline	○ ○ ○ ○ — —	○ — — — — —	◐ ○ ○ ○ ○ ○	○ — — — — —
Electrical system (chassis)	● ◐ ◐ ◐ — —	● — — — — —	○ ○ ○ ○ ○ ○	● — — — — —
Engine cooling	○ ○ ○ ○ — —	○ — — — — —	○ ○ ○ ○ ○ ○	○ — — — — —
Engine mechanical	○ ◐ ◐ ○ — —	◐ — — — — —	◐ ◐ ○ ○ ○ ○	○ — — — — —
Exhaust system	○ ◐ ◐ ○ — —	● — — — — —	○ ○ ○ ○ ○ ○	○ — — — — —
Fuel system	◐ ◐ ○ ○ — —	◐ — — — — —	○ ○ ○ ○ ○ ○	● — — — — —
Ignition system	○ ○ ○ ○ — —	○ — — — — —	○ ○ ○ ○ ○ ○	○ — — — — —
Steering/suspension	● ○ ○ ○ — —	○ — — — — —	○ ○ ○ ● ◐ ○	◐ — — — — —
Transmission (manual)	* * — — — —	○ — — — — —	— — — — — —	* — — — — —
Transmission (automatic)	○ ○ ○ ○ — —	○ — — — — —	○ ○ ○ ○ ○ ○	○ — — — — —
TROUBLE INDEX	◐ ◐ ○ ○ — —	● — — — — —	○ ○ ○ ◐ ○ ○	◐ — — — — —
COST INDEX	○ ○ ◐ ○ — —	○ — — — — —	○ ○ ○ ○ ○ ○	○ — — — — —

Somerset/Skylark 4: Insufficient data '90, '91. Somerset/Skylark V6: Insufficient data '87–'91. Cimarron V6: Insufficient data '89–'91.

322 REPAIR RECORDS

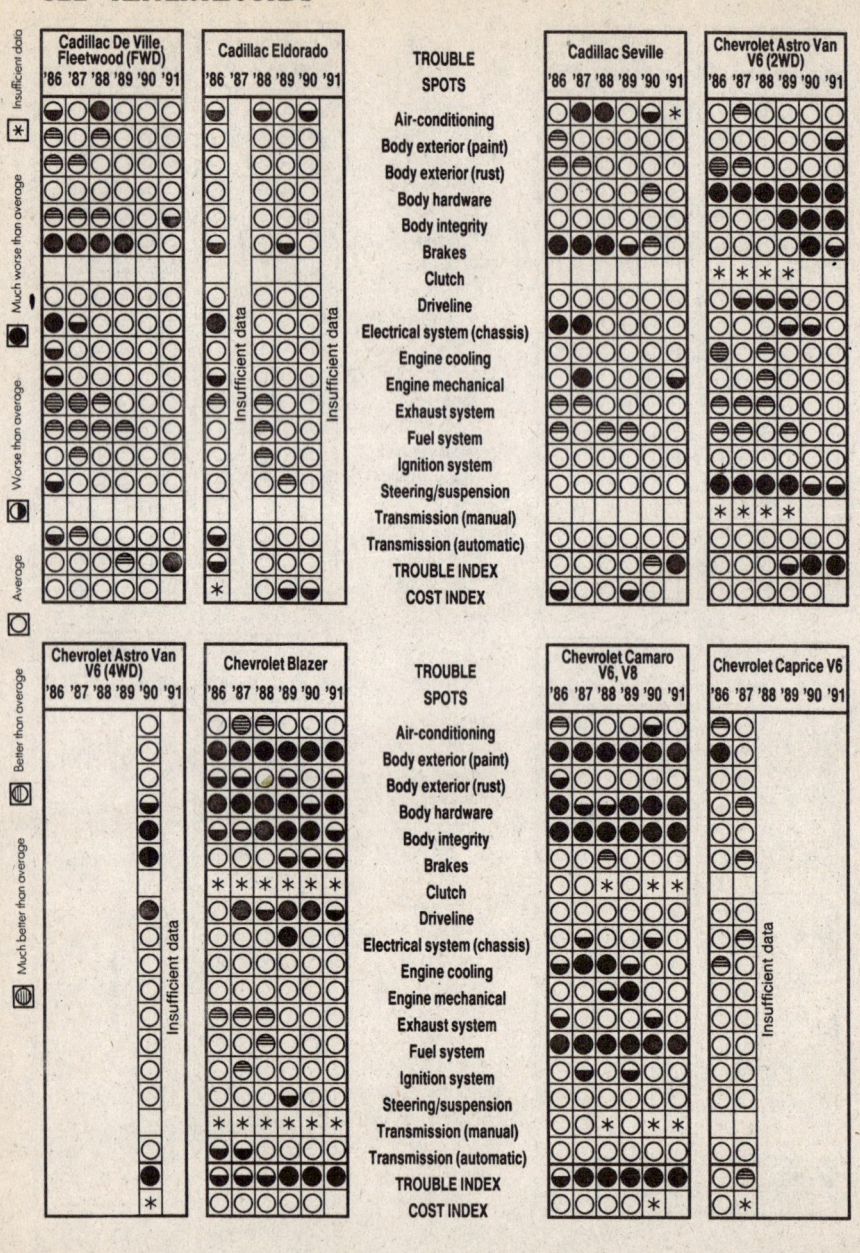

Legend
- ✶ Insufficient data
- ● Much worse than average
- ◐ Worse than average
- ○ Average
- ◑ Better than average
- ◉ Much better than average

Trouble Spots

Trouble Spot	Cadillac De Ville Fleetwood (FWD)	Cadillac Eldorado	Cadillac Seville	Chevrolet Astro Van V6 (2WD)
	'86 '87 '88 '89 '90 '91	'86 '87 '88 '89 '90 '91	'86 '87 '88 '89 '90 '91	'86 '87 '88 '89 '90 '91

'87–'90 Eldorado and '87–'90 Seville columns marked "Insufficient data".

Trouble Spot	Chevrolet Astro Van V6 (4WD)	Chevrolet Blazer	Chevrolet Camaro V6, V8	Chevrolet Caprice V6
	'86 '87 '88 '89 '90 '91	'86 '87 '88 '89 '90 '91	'86 '87 '88 '89 '90 '91	'86 '87 '88 '89 '90 '91

'86–'89 Astro Van V6 (4WD) and '88–'91 Caprice V6 columns marked "Insufficient data".

Trouble spots listed (both halves):
- Air-conditioning
- Body exterior (paint)
- Body exterior (rust)
- Body hardware
- Body integrity
- Brakes
- Clutch
- Driveline
- Electrical system (chassis)
- Engine cooling
- Engine mechanical
- Exhaust system
- Fuel system
- Ignition system
- Steering/suspension
- Transmission (manual)
- Transmission (automatic)
- TROUBLE INDEX
- COST INDEX

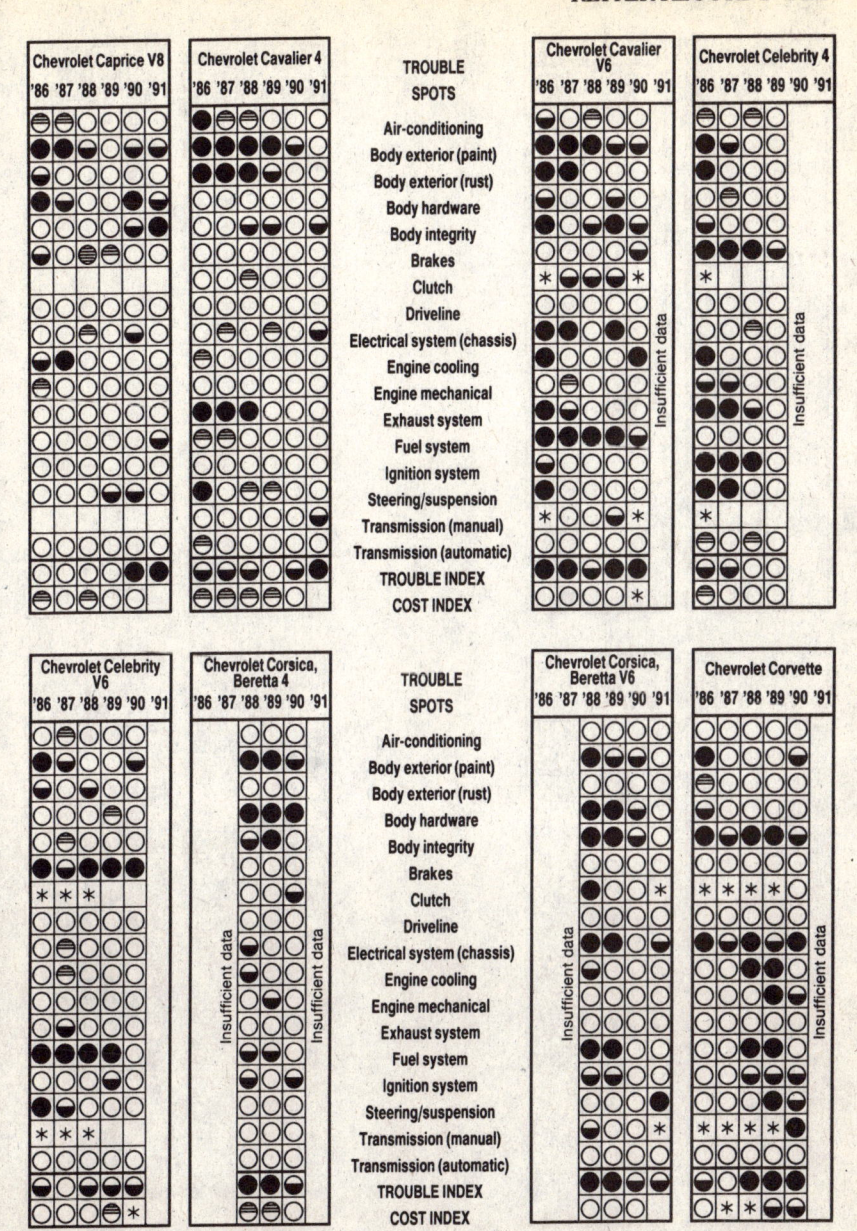

REPAIR RECORDS 323

TROUBLE SPOTS

Trouble Spot	Chevrolet Caprice V8	Chevrolet Cavalier 4	Chevrolet Cavalier V6	Chevrolet Celebrity 4
Air-conditioning				
Body exterior (paint)				
Body exterior (rust)				
Body hardware				
Body integrity				
Brakes				
Clutch				
Driveline				
Electrical system (chassis)				
Engine cooling				
Engine mechanical				
Exhaust system				
Fuel system				
Ignition system				
Steering/suspension				
Transmission (manual)				
Transmission (automatic)				
TROUBLE INDEX				
COST INDEX				

Years: '86 '87 '88 '89 '90 '91. Chevrolet Celebrity 4 '90–'91: Insufficient data. Chevrolet Cavalier V6 '91: Insufficient data.

Trouble Spot	Chevrolet Celebrity V6	Chevrolet Corsica, Beretta 4	Chevrolet Corsica, Beretta V6	Chevrolet Corvette
Air-conditioning				
Body exterior (paint)				
Body exterior (rust)				
Body hardware				
Body integrity				
Brakes				
Clutch				
Driveline				
Electrical system (chassis)				
Engine cooling				
Engine mechanical				
Exhaust system				
Fuel system				
Ignition system				
Steering/suspension				
Transmission (manual)				
Transmission (automatic)				
TROUBLE INDEX				
COST INDEX				

Years: '86 '87 '88 '89 '90 '91. Chevrolet Corsica, Beretta 4 '86–'87: Insufficient data. Chevrolet Corsica, Beretta V6 '86: Insufficient data. Chevrolet Corvette '91: Insufficient data.

324 REPAIR RECORDS

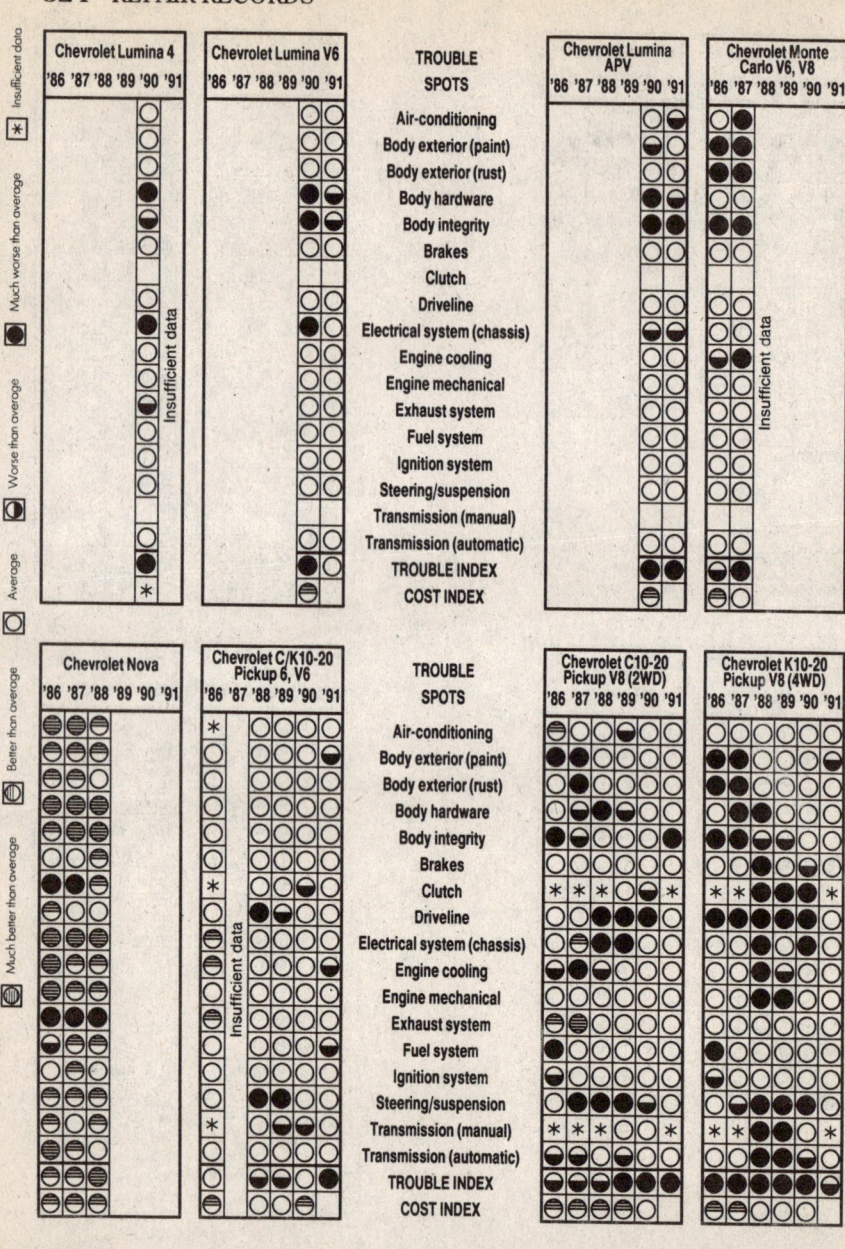

Legend:
- ✳ Insufficient data
- ● Much worse than average
- ◐ Worse than average
- ◑ Average
- ○ Better than average
- ⊖ Much better than average

Chevrolet Lumina 4 ('86–'91)
Data only for '90, '91 (most years insufficient data)

Chevrolet Lumina V6 ('86–'91)
Data only for '90, '91

Chevrolet Lumina APV ('86–'91)
Data only for '90, '91

Chevrolet Monte Carlo V6, V8 ('86–'91)
Data only for '86, '87; remainder insufficient data

Chevrolet Nova ('86–'91)
Data for '86–'88; '89–'91 blank

Chevrolet C/K10-20 Pickup 6, V6 ('86–'91)
'86 insufficient data; '87–'91 data

Chevrolet C10-20 Pickup V8 (2WD) ('86–'91)

Chevrolet K10-20 Pickup V8 (4WD) ('86–'91)

Trouble Spots
- Air-conditioning
- Body exterior (paint)
- Body exterior (rust)
- Body hardware
- Body integrity
- Brakes
- Clutch
- Driveline
- Electrical system (chassis)
- Engine cooling
- Engine mechanical
- Exhaust system
- Fuel system
- Ignition system
- Steering/suspension
- Transmission (manual)
- Transmission (automatic)
- TROUBLE INDEX
- COST INDEX

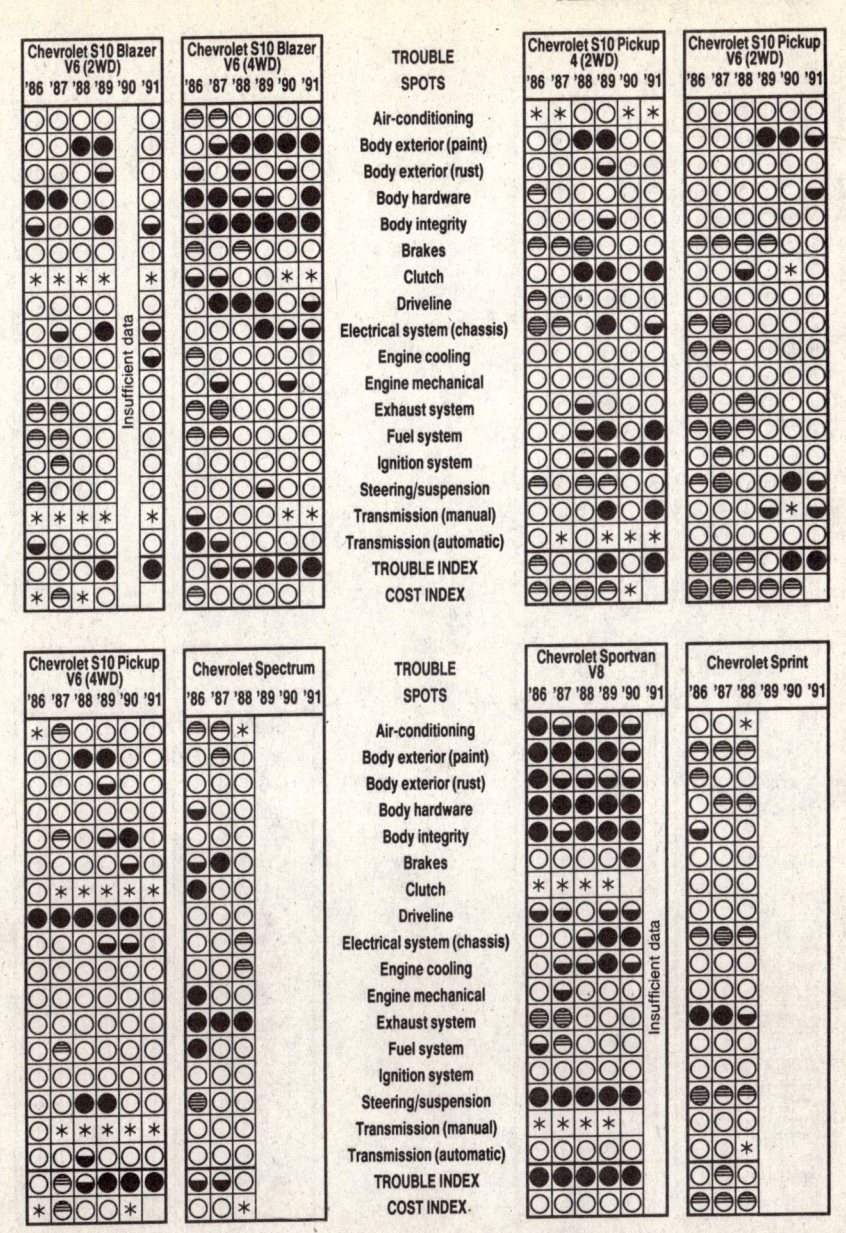

REPAIR RECORDS 325

TROUBLE SPOTS	Chevrolet S10 Blazer V6 (2WD)	Chevrolet S10 Blazer V6 (4WD)	Chevrolet S10 Pickup 4 (2WD)	Chevrolet S10 Pickup V6 (2WD)	Chevrolet S10 Pickup V6 (4WD)	Chevrolet Spectrum	Chevrolet Sportvan V8	Chevrolet Sprint
Air-conditioning								
Body exterior (paint)								
Body exterior (rust)								
Body hardware								
Body integrity								
Brakes								
Clutch								
Driveline								
Electrical system (chassis)								
Engine cooling								
Engine mechanical								
Exhaust system								
Fuel system								
Ignition system								
Steering/suspension								
Transmission (manual)								
Transmission (automatic)								
TROUBLE INDEX								
COST INDEX								

Years covered: '86 '87 '88 '89 '90 '91

326 REPAIR RECORDS

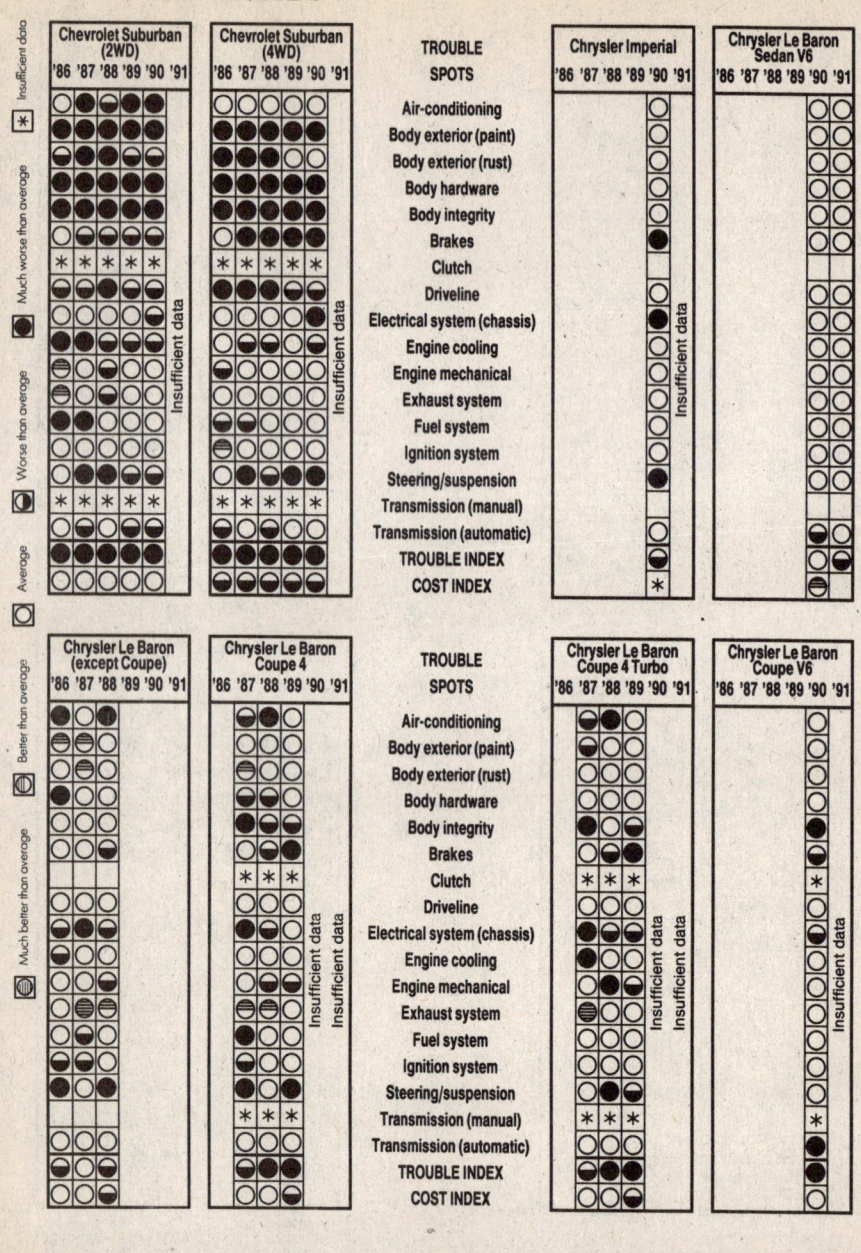

Legend
- ○ Insufficient data
- ● Much worse than average
- ◐ Worse than average
- ◓ Average
- ◑ Better than average
- ◒ Much better than average
- ✱ Insufficient data

Trouble Spots

Trouble Spot	Chevrolet Suburban (2WD)	Chevrolet Suburban (4WD)	Chrysler Imperial	Chrysler Le Baron Sedan V6
	'86 '87 '88 '89 '90 '91	'86 '87 '88 '89 '90 '91	'86 '87 '88 '89 '90 '91	'86 '87 '88 '89 '90 '91

Trouble Spots listed (rows):
- Air-conditioning
- Body exterior (paint)
- Body exterior (rust)
- Body hardware
- Body integrity
- Brakes
- Clutch
- Driveline
- Electrical system (chassis)
- Engine cooling
- Engine mechanical
- Exhaust system
- Fuel system
- Ignition system
- Steering/suspension
- Transmission (manual)
- Transmission (automatic)
- TROUBLE INDEX
- COST INDEX

Trouble Spot	Chrysler Le Baron (except Coupe)	Chrysler Le Baron Coupe 4	Chrysler Le Baron Coupe 4 Turbo	Chrysler Le Baron Coupe V6
	'86 '87 '88 '89 '90 '91	'86 '87 '88 '89 '90 '91	'86 '87 '88 '89 '90 '91	'86 '87 '88 '89 '90 '91

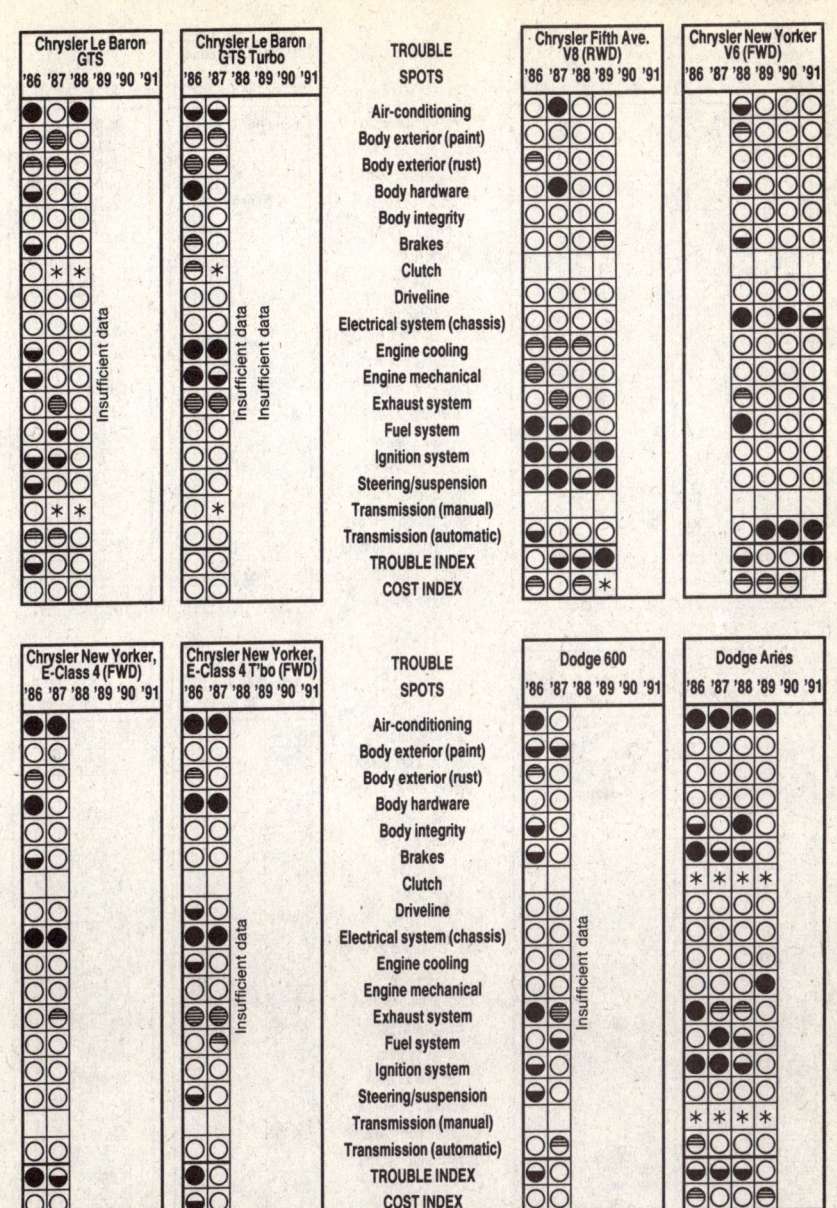

REPAIR RECORDS 327

Trouble Spots

Trouble Spots	Chrysler Le Baron GTS '86–'91	Chrysler Le Baron GTS Turbo '86–'91	Chrysler Fifth Ave. V8 (RWD) '86–'91	Chrysler New Yorker V6 (FWD) '86–'91
Air-conditioning				
Body exterior (paint)				
Body exterior (rust)				
Body hardware				
Body integrity				
Brakes				
Clutch				
Driveline				
Electrical system (chassis)				
Engine cooling				
Engine mechanical				
Exhaust system				
Fuel system				
Ignition system				
Steering/suspension				
Transmission (manual)				
Transmission (automatic)				
TROUBLE INDEX				
COST INDEX				

Insufficient data for later years of Chrysler Le Baron GTS and GTS Turbo.

Trouble Spots	Chrysler New Yorker, E-Class 4 (FWD) '86–'91	Chrysler New Yorker, E-Class 4 T'bo (FWD) '86–'91	Dodge 600 '86–'91	Dodge Aries '86–'91
Air-conditioning				
Body exterior (paint)				
Body exterior (rust)				
Body hardware				
Body integrity				
Brakes				
Clutch				
Driveline				
Electrical system (chassis)				
Engine cooling				
Engine mechanical				
Exhaust system				
Fuel system				
Ignition system				
Steering/suspension				
Transmission (manual)				
Transmission (automatic)				
TROUBLE INDEX				
COST INDEX				

Insufficient data for later years of Chrysler New Yorker E-Class 4, E-Class 4 T'bo, and Dodge 600.

328 REPAIR RECORDS

Legend
- ✳ Insufficient data
- ● Much worse than average
- ⊖ Worse than average
- ◐ Average
- ○ Better than average
- ◍ Much better than average

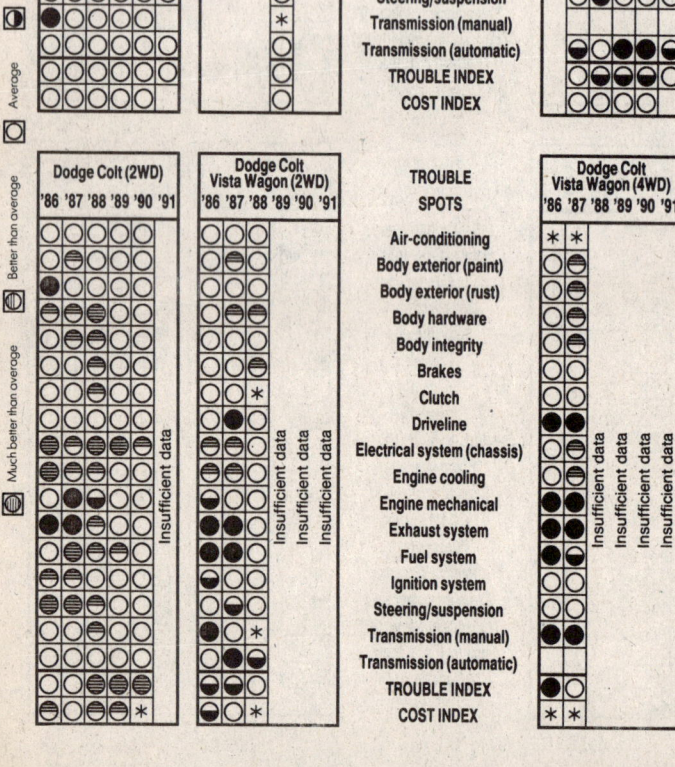

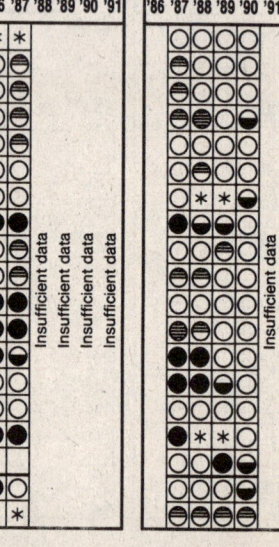

Trouble Spots

Categories (rows):
- Air-conditioning
- Body exterior (paint)
- Body exterior (rust)
- Body hardware
- Body integrity
- Brakes
- Clutch
- Driveline
- Electrical system (chassis)
- Engine cooling
- Engine mechanical
- Exhaust system
- Fuel system
- Ignition system
- Steering/suspension
- Transmission (manual)
- Transmission (automatic)
- TROUBLE INDEX
- COST INDEX

Vehicles (top row), model years '86–'91:
- Dodge Caravan 4
- Dodge Caravan 4 Turbo
- Dodge Caravan V6 (2WD)
- Dodge Grand Caravan (2WD)

Vehicles (bottom row), model years '86–'91:
- Dodge Colt (2WD)
- Dodge Colt Vista Wagon (2WD)
- Dodge Colt Vista Wagon (4WD)
- Dodge Dakota Pickup V6 (2WD)

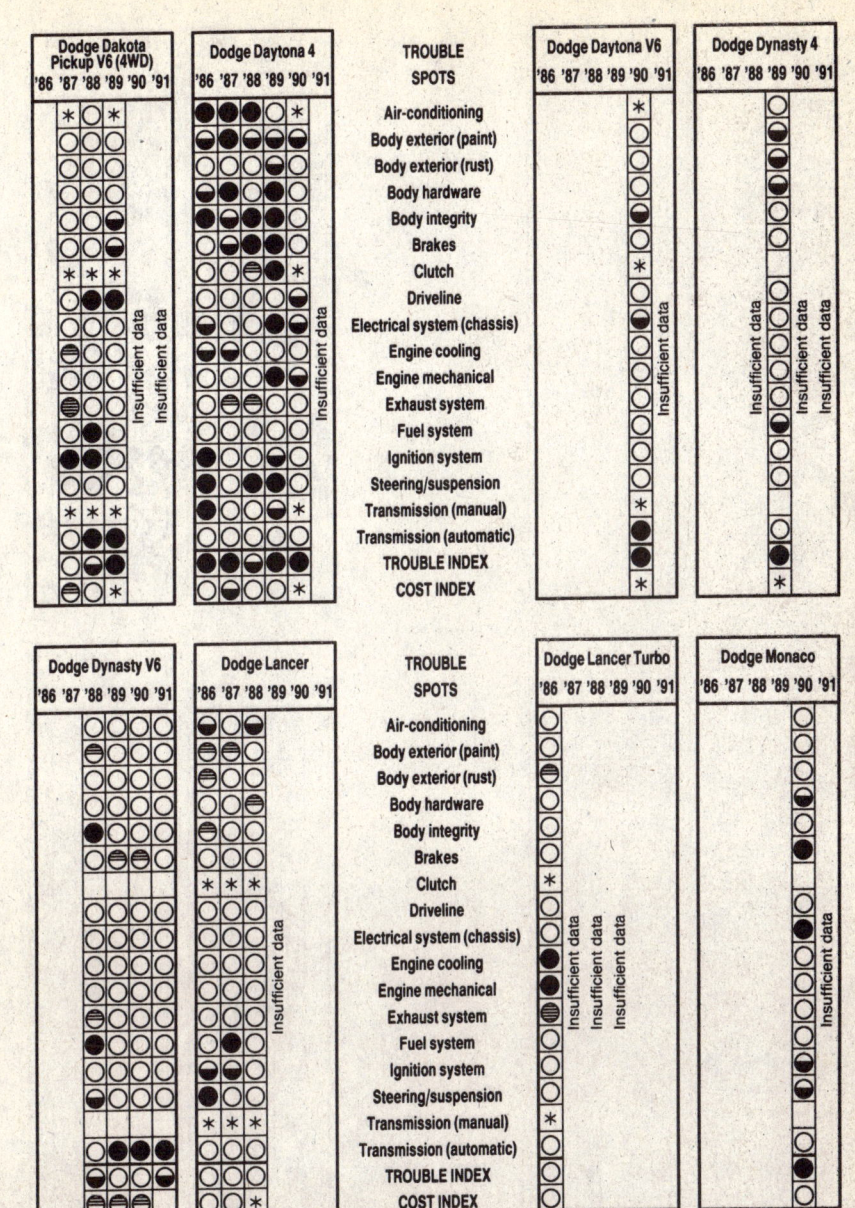

REPAIR RECORDS 329

TROUBLE SPOTS

Trouble Spot	Dodge Dakota Pickup V6 (4WD)	Dodge Daytona 4	Dodge Daytona V6	Dodge Dynasty 4
	'86 '87 '88 '89 '90 '91	'86 '87 '88 '89 '90 '91	'86 '87 '88 '89 '90 '91	'86 '87 '88 '89 '90 '91

Trouble Spot	Dodge Dynasty V6	Dodge Lancer	Dodge Lancer Turbo	Dodge Monaco
	'86 '87 '88 '89 '90 '91	'86 '87 '88 '89 '90 '91	'86 '87 '88 '89 '90 '91	'86 '87 '88 '89 '90 '91

Trouble spots listed:
- Air-conditioning
- Body exterior (paint)
- Body exterior (rust)
- Body hardware
- Body integrity
- Brakes
- Clutch
- Driveline
- Electrical system (chassis)
- Engine cooling
- Engine mechanical
- Exhaust system
- Fuel system
- Ignition system
- Steering/suspension
- Transmission (manual)
- Transmission (automatic)
- TROUBLE INDEX
- COST INDEX

330 REPAIR RECORDS

Legend:
- ✳ Insufficient data
- ◐ (filled) Much worse than average
- ◑ Worse than average
- ⊖ Average
- ◯ Better than average
- ◉ Much better than average

Dodge Omni, Charger, America — '86 '87 '88 '89 '90 '91

Dodge Raider — '86 '87 '88 '89 '90 '91
Insufficient data for '88–'91

TROUBLE SPOTS
- Air-conditioning
- Body exterior (paint)
- Body exterior (rust)
- Body hardware
- Body integrity
- Brakes
- Clutch
- Driveline
- Electrical system (chassis)
- Engine cooling
- Engine mechanical
- Exhaust system
- Fuel system
- Ignition system
- Steering/suspension
- Transmission (manual)
- Transmission (automatic)
- TROUBLE INDEX
- COST INDEX

Dodge Ram 50 Pickup 4 — '86 '87 '88 '89 '90 '91
Insufficient data for '90–'91

Dodge Ram B150-250 Van V8 — '86 '87 '88 '89 '90 '91

Dodge Ram D/W 100-250 Pickup V8 — '86 '87 '88 '89 '90 '91

Dodge Ramcharger — '86 '87 '88 '89 '90 '91
Insufficient data for '89–'91

Dodge Shadow — '86 '87 '88 '89 '90 '91

Dodge Spirit 4 — '86 '87 '88 '89 '90 '91

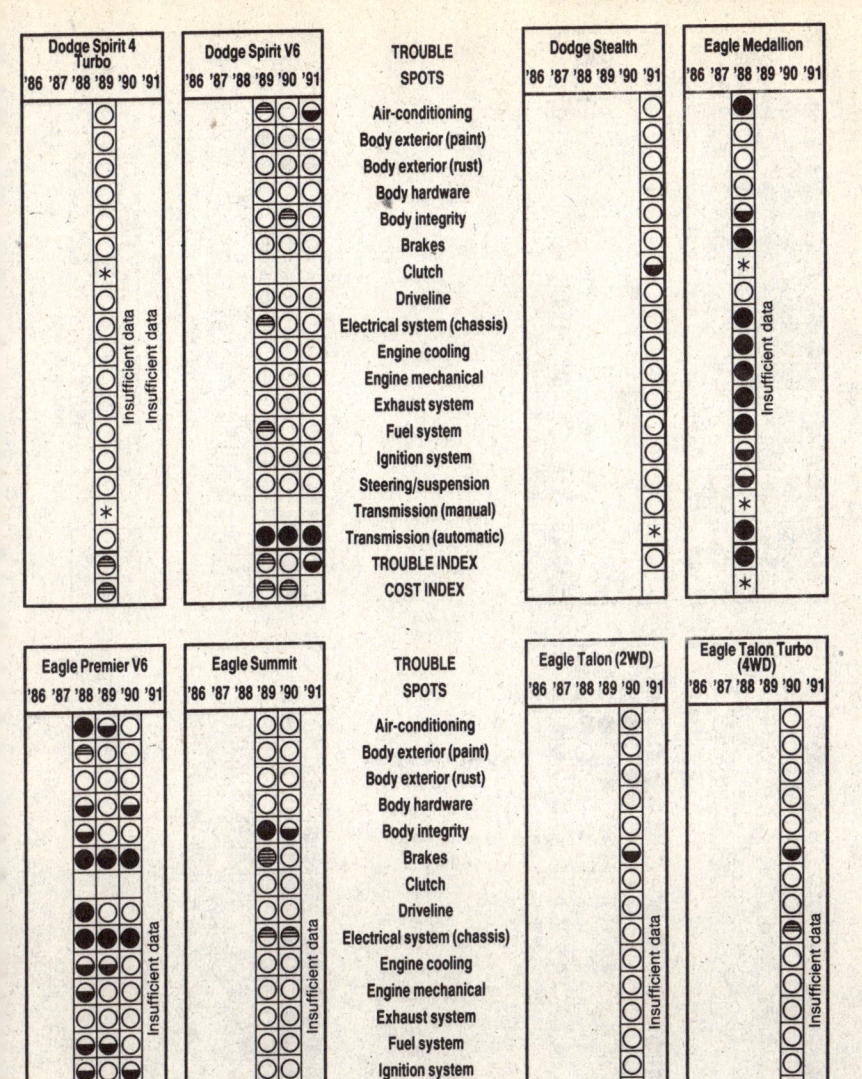

REPAIR RECORDS 331

TROUBLE SPOTS

Trouble Spot	Dodge Spirit 4 Turbo	Dodge Spirit V6	Dodge Stealth	Eagle Medallion
Air-conditioning				
Body exterior (paint)				
Body exterior (rust)				
Body hardware				
Body integrity				
Brakes				
Clutch				
Driveline				
Electrical system (chassis)				
Engine cooling				
Engine mechanical				
Exhaust system				
Fuel system				
Ignition system				
Steering/suspension				
Transmission (manual)				
Transmission (automatic)				
TROUBLE INDEX				
COST INDEX				

Years shown: '86 '87 '88 '89 '90 '91

Trouble Spot	Eagle Premier V6	Eagle Summit	Eagle Talon (2WD)	Eagle Talon Turbo (4WD)
Air-conditioning				
Body exterior (paint)				
Body exterior (rust)				
Body hardware				
Body integrity				
Brakes				
Clutch				
Driveline				
Electrical system (chassis)				
Engine cooling				
Engine mechanical				
Exhaust system				
Fuel system				
Ignition system				
Steering/suspension				
Transmission (manual)				
Transmission (automatic)				
TROUBLE INDEX				
COST INDEX				

Years shown: '86 '87 '88 '89 '90 '91

332 REPAIR RECORDS

Legend
- ⊘ Insufficient data
- ✻ (asterisk)
- ● Much worse than average
- ◐ Worse than average
- ◑ Average
- ○ Better than average (○ with variations)
- ⊖ Much better than average

TROUBLE SPOTS

- Air-conditioning
- Body exterior (paint)
- Body exterior (rust)
- Body hardware
- Body integrity
- Brakes
- Clutch
- Driveline
- Electrical system (chassis)
- Engine cooling
- Engine mechanical
- Exhaust system
- Fuel system
- Ignition system
- Steering/suspension
- Transmission (manual)
- Transmission (automatic)
- TROUBLE INDEX
- COST INDEX

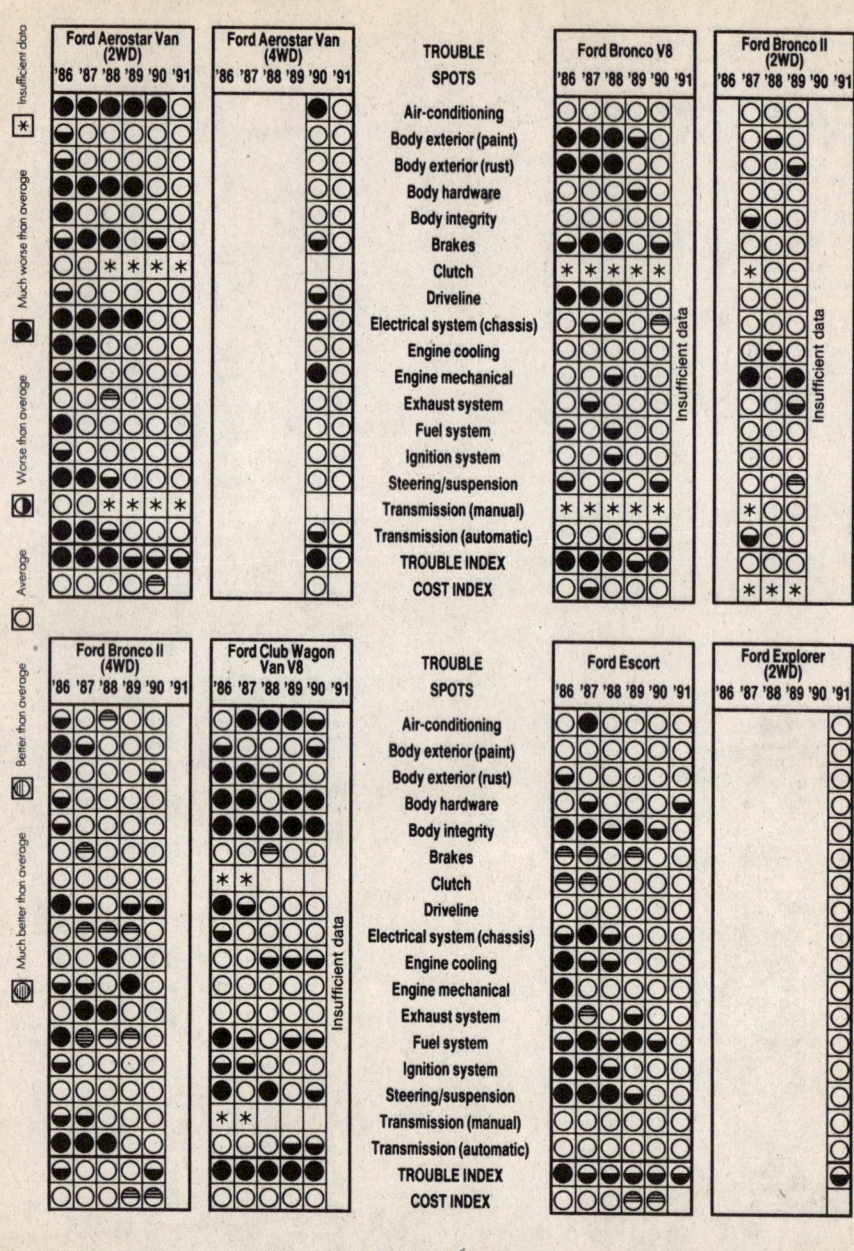

Vehicles covered ('86–'91):
- Ford Aerostar Van (2WD)
- Ford Aerostar Van (4WD)
- Ford Bronco V8 — Insufficient data ('91)
- Ford Bronco II (2WD) — Insufficient data ('90, '91)
- Ford Bronco II (4WD) — Insufficient data ('91)
- Ford Club Wagon Van V8 — Insufficient data ('91)
- Ford Escort
- Ford Explorer (2WD)

REPAIR RECORDS 333

Ford Explorer (4WD) / Ford F150-250 Pickup 6 (2WD) / Ford F150-250 Pickup 6 (4WD) / Ford F150-250 Pickup V8 (2WD)

TROUBLE SPOTS	Ford Explorer (4WD) '86–'91	Ford F150-250 Pickup 6 (2WD) '86–'91	Ford F150-250 Pickup 6 (4WD) '86–'91	Ford F150-250 Pickup V8 (2WD) '86–'91
Air-conditioning			* * * ● ○ / Insufficient data	
Body exterior (paint)				
Body exterior (rust)				
Body hardware				
Body integrity				
Brakes				
Clutch				* (last column)
Driveline				
Electrical system (chassis)				
Engine cooling				
Engine mechanical				
Exhaust system				
Fuel system				
Ignition system				
Steering/suspension				
Transmission (manual)				* (last column)
Transmission (automatic)			* * * * ● ○	
TROUBLE INDEX				
COST INDEX		○ * * ○ ● ○		

Ford F150-250 Pickup V8 (4WD) / Ford Festiva / Ford LTD Crown Victoria / Ford Mustang 4

TROUBLE SPOTS	Ford F150-250 Pickup V8 (4WD) '86–'91	Ford Festiva '86–'91	Ford LTD Crown Victoria '86–'91	Ford Mustang 4 '86–'91
Air-conditioning		Insufficient data (early & late)		Insufficient data
Body exterior (paint)				
Body exterior (rust)				
Body hardware				
Body integrity				
Brakes				
Clutch				
Driveline				
Electrical system (chassis)				
Engine cooling				
Engine mechanical				
Exhaust system				
Fuel system				
Ignition system				
Steering/suspension				
Transmission (manual)				
Transmission (automatic)				
TROUBLE INDEX				
COST INDEX				

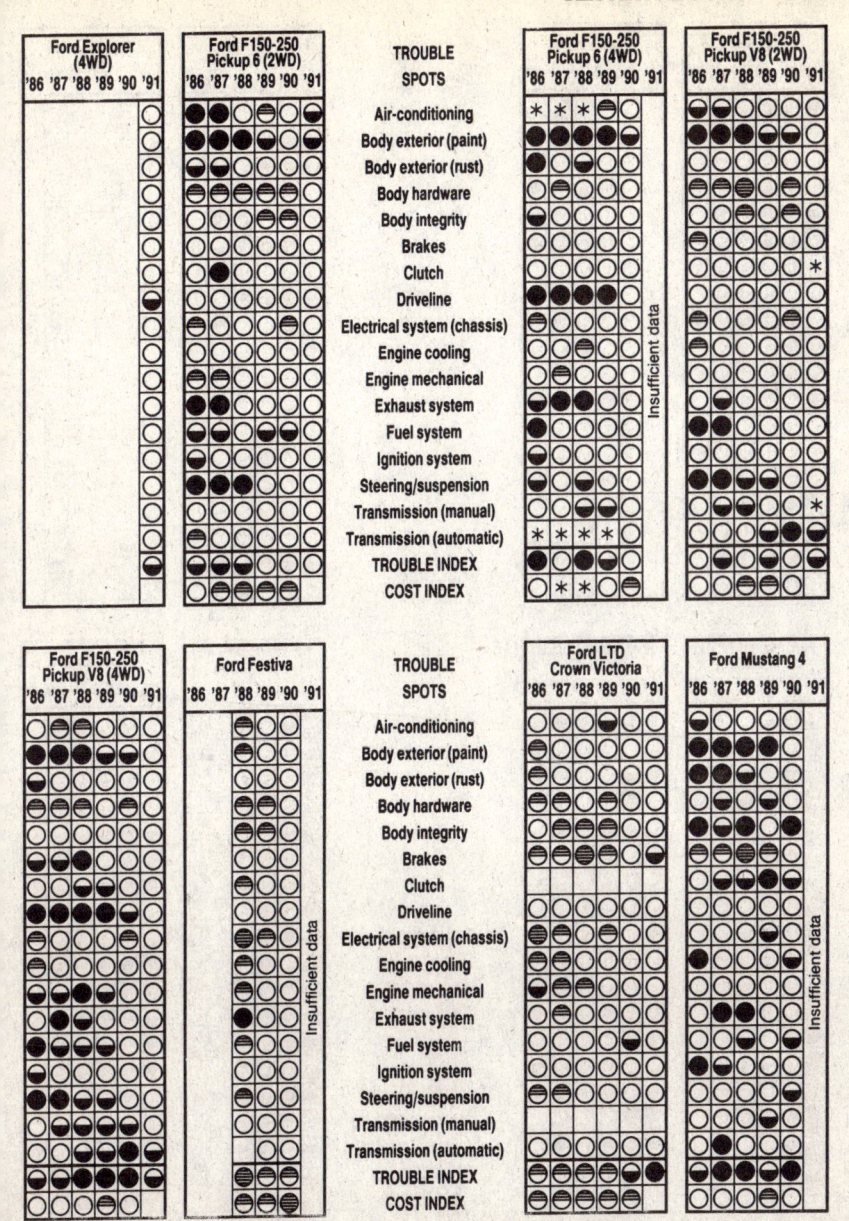

334 REPAIR RECORDS

Legend:
- ⊛ Insufficient data
- ● Much worse than average
- ◐ Worse than average
- ⊖ Average
- ○ Better than average
- ⊙ Much better than average

TROUBLE SPOTS	Ford Mustang V8 '86–'91	Ford Probe 4 '86–'91	Ford Probe 4 Turbo '86–'91	Ford Probe V6 '86–'91
Air-conditioning				
Body exterior (paint)				
Body exterior (rust)				
Body hardware				
Body integrity				
Brakes				
Clutch				
Driveline				
Electrical system (chassis)				
Engine cooling				
Engine mechanical				
Exhaust system				
Fuel system				
Ignition system				
Steering/suspension				
Transmission (manual)				
Transmission (automatic)				
TROUBLE INDEX				
COST INDEX				

Insufficient data noted for several columns.

TROUBLE SPOTS	Ford Ranger Pickup 4 (2WD) '86–'91	Ford Ranger Pickup V6 (2WD) '86–'91	Ford Ranger Pickup V6 (4WD) '86–'91	Ford Taurus 4 '86–'91
Air-conditioning				
Body exterior (paint)				
Body exterior (rust)				
Body hardware				
Body integrity				
Brakes				
Clutch				
Driveline				
Electrical system (chassis)				
Engine cooling				
Engine mechanical				
Exhaust system				
Fuel system				
Ignition system				
Steering/suspension				
Transmission (manual)				
Transmission (automatic)				
TROUBLE INDEX				
COST INDEX				

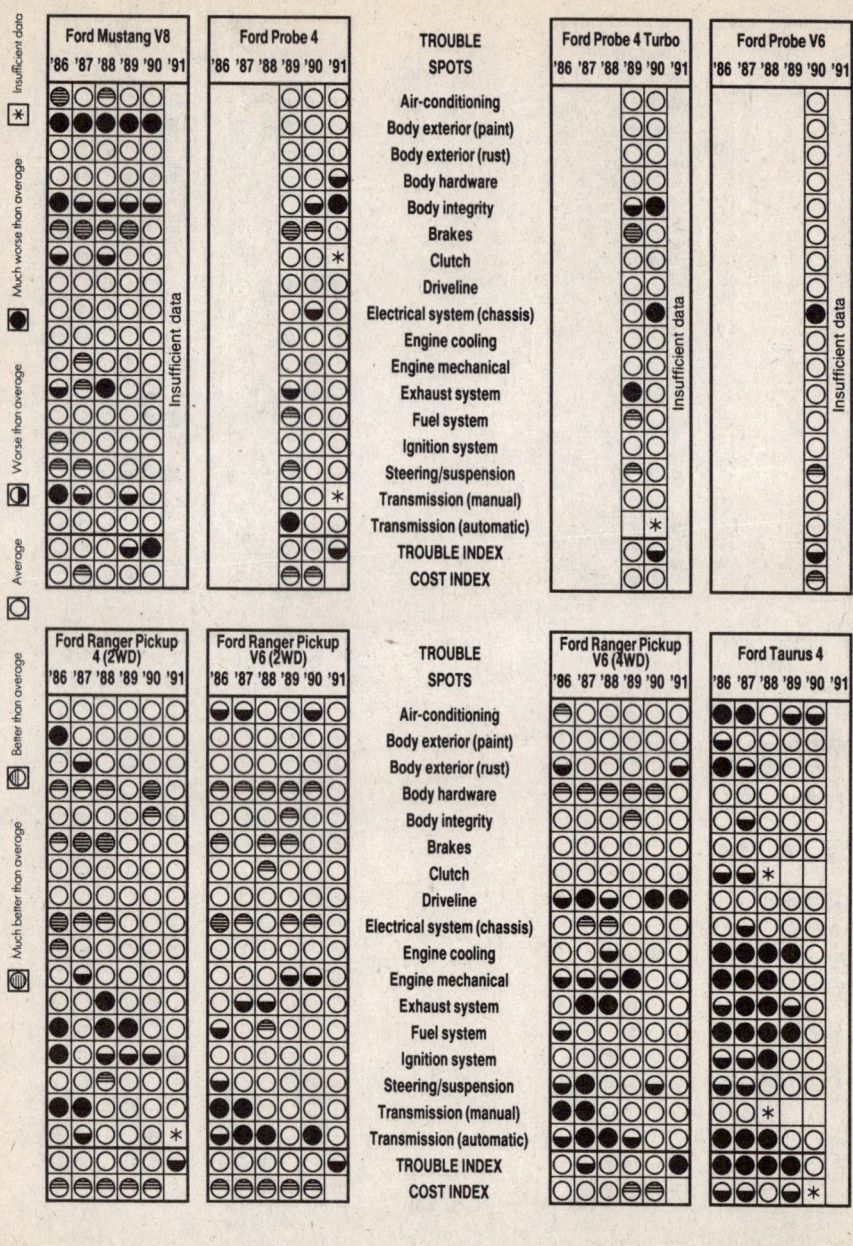

REPAIR RECORDS 335

TROUBLE SPOTS	Ford Taurus V6	Ford Tempo (2WD)	Ford Thunderbird 4 Turbo	Ford Thunderbird V6

TROUBLE SPOTS	Ford Thunderbird SC V6	Ford Thunderbird V8	Geo Metro	Geo Prizm

Table contents show repair record symbols for model years '86–'91 across the following trouble spots:

- Air-conditioning
- Body exterior (paint)
- Body exterior (rust)
- Body hardware
- Body integrity
- Brakes
- Clutch
- Driveline
- Electrical system (chassis)
- Engine cooling
- Engine mechanical
- Exhaust system
- Fuel system
- Ignition system
- Steering/suspension
- Transmission (manual)
- Transmission (automatic)
- TROUBLE INDEX
- COST INDEX

Ford Thunderbird SC V6, Ford Thunderbird V8: Insufficient data for several years.

336 REPAIR RECORDS

Legend (left margin):
- ✱ Insufficient data
- ● Much worse than average
- ◐ Worse than average
- ⊖ Average
- ○ Better than average
- ◐ (filled variant) Much better than average

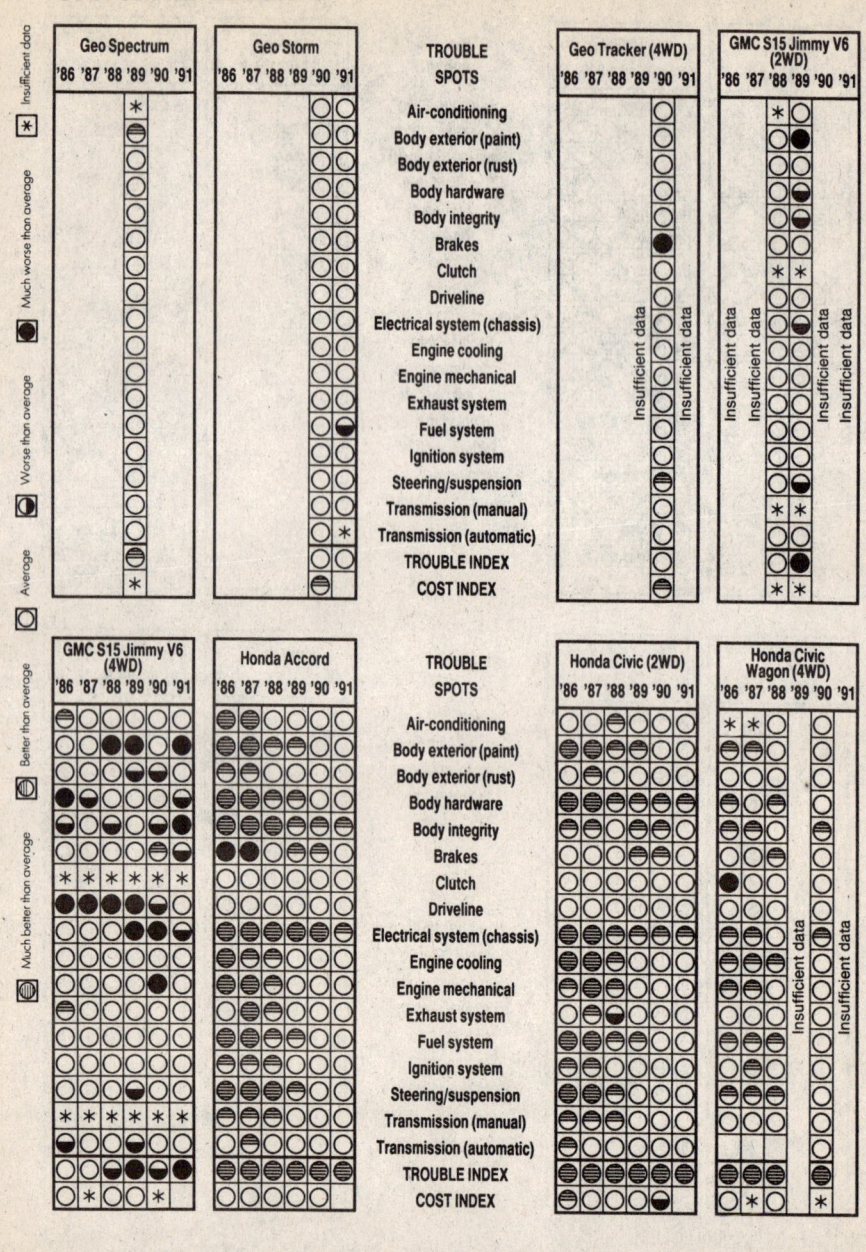

Trouble Spots

Trouble Spots	Geo Spectrum '86–'91	Geo Storm '86–'91	Geo Tracker (4WD) '86–'91	GMC S15 Jimmy V6 (2WD) '86–'91
Air-conditioning				
Body exterior (paint)				
Body exterior (rust)				
Body hardware				
Body integrity				
Brakes				
Clutch				
Driveline				
Electrical system (chassis)				
Engine cooling				
Engine mechanical				
Exhaust system				
Fuel system				
Ignition system				
Steering/suspension				
Transmission (manual)				
Transmission (automatic)				
TROUBLE INDEX				
COST INDEX				

Trouble Spots	GMC S15 Jimmy V6 (4WD) '86–'91	Honda Accord '86–'91	Honda Civic (2WD) '86–'91	Honda Civic Wagon (4WD) '86–'91
Air-conditioning				
Body exterior (paint)				
Body exterior (rust)				
Body hardware				
Body integrity				
Brakes				
Clutch				
Driveline				
Electrical system (chassis)				
Engine cooling				
Engine mechanical				
Exhaust system				
Fuel system				
Ignition system				
Steering/suspension				
Transmission (manual)				
Transmission (automatic)				
TROUBLE INDEX				
COST INDEX				

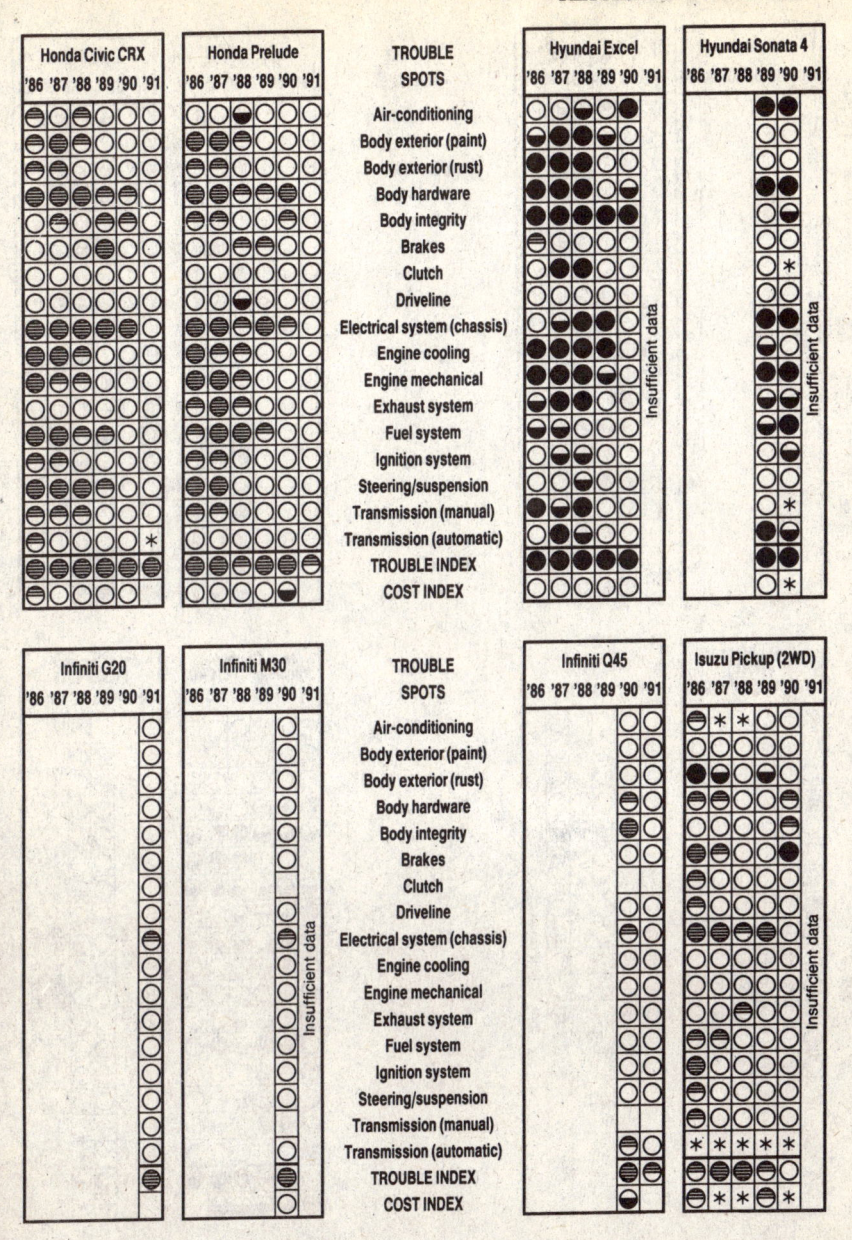

REPAIR RECORDS 337

TROUBLE SPOTS	Honda Civic CRX '86–'91	Honda Prelude '86–'91	Hyundai Excel '86–'91	Hyundai Sonata 4 '86–'91
Air-conditioning				
Body exterior (paint)				
Body exterior (rust)				
Body hardware				
Body integrity				
Brakes				
Clutch				
Driveline				
Electrical system (chassis)				
Engine cooling				
Engine mechanical				
Exhaust system				
Fuel system				
Ignition system				
Steering/suspension				
Transmission (manual)				
Transmission (automatic)				
TROUBLE INDEX				
COST INDEX				

Hyundai Excel '91 and Hyundai Sonata 4 '86–'88, '91: Insufficient data

TROUBLE SPOTS	Infiniti G20 '86–'91	Infiniti M30 '86–'91	Infiniti Q45 '86–'91	Isuzu Pickup (2WD) '86–'91
Air-conditioning				
Body exterior (paint)				
Body exterior (rust)				
Body hardware				
Body integrity				
Brakes				
Clutch				
Driveline				
Electrical system (chassis)				
Engine cooling				
Engine mechanical				
Exhaust system				
Fuel system				
Ignition system				
Steering/suspension				
Transmission (manual)				
Transmission (automatic)				
TROUBLE INDEX				
COST INDEX				

Infiniti M30 and Isuzu Pickup (2WD) '91: Insufficient data

338 REPAIR RECORDS

Legend:
- ✳ Insufficient data
- ● Much worse than average
- ◐ Worse than average
- ⊘ Average
- ◓ Better than average
- ◉ Much better than average

TROUBLE SPOTS

Trouble Spot	Isuzu Rodeo V6	Isuzu Trooper, Trooper II 4	Isuzu Trooper, Trooper II V6	Jaguar XJ6
	'86 '87 '88 '89 '90 '91	'86 '87 '88 '89 '90 '91	'86 '87 '88 '89 '90 '91	'86 '87 '88 '89 '90 '91

(Years '86–'90 insufficient data for Isuzu Rodeo V6; Jaguar XJ6 '86, '87 insufficient data; Isuzu Trooper V6 '86, '87 insufficient data)

Trouble Spot	Jeep Cherokee 4 (4WD)	Jeep Cherokee 6 (2WD)	Jeep Cherokee, Wagoneer 6, V6 (4WD)	Jeep Comanche Pickup 6, V6
	'86 '87 '88 '89 '90 '91	'86 '87 '88 '89 '90 '91	'86 '87 '88 '89 '90 '91	'86 '87 '88 '89 '90 '91

Trouble spots listed (both tables):
- Air-conditioning
- Body exterior (paint)
- Body exterior (rust)
- Body hardware
- Body integrity
- Brakes
- Clutch
- Driveline
- Electrical system (chassis)
- Engine cooling
- Engine mechanical
- Exhaust system
- Fuel system
- Ignition system
- Steering/suspension
- Transmission (manual)
- Transmission (automatic)
- TROUBLE INDEX
- COST INDEX

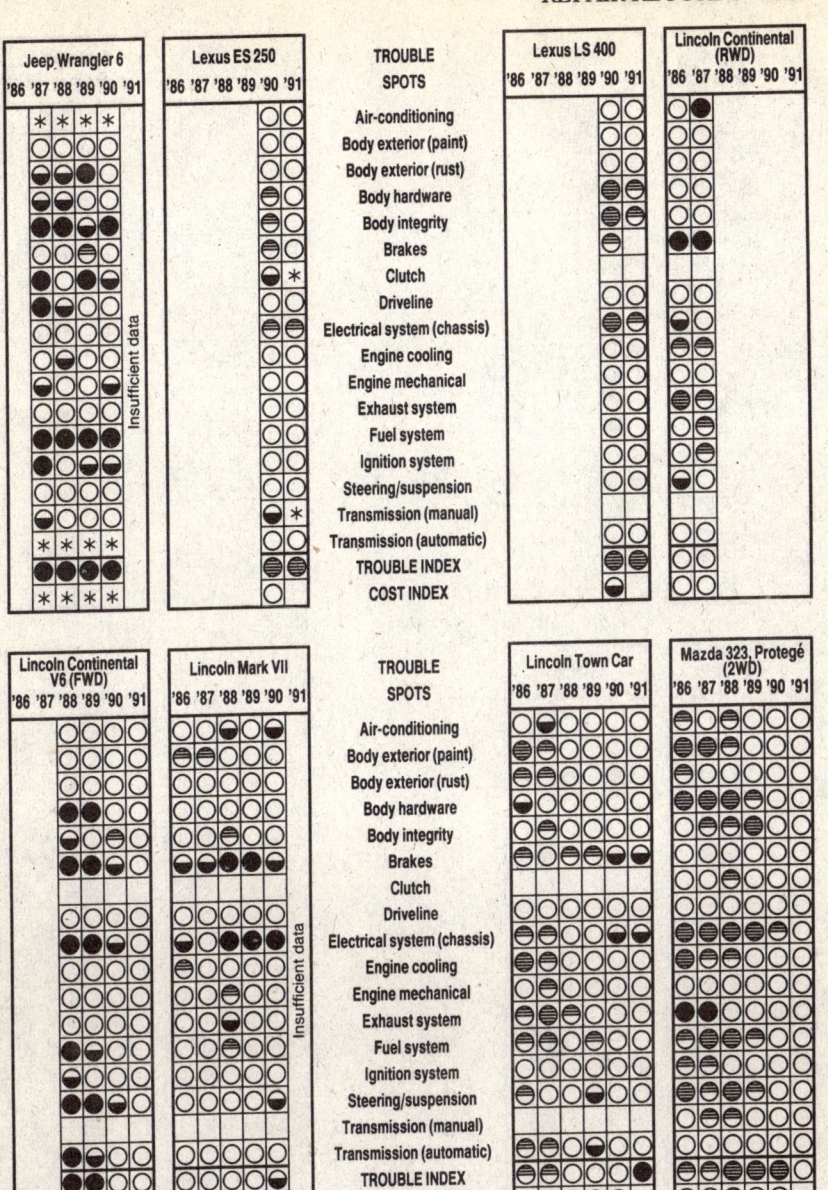

REPAIR RECORDS 339

Trouble Spots ('86–'91)

Trouble Spot	Jeep Wrangler 6	Lexus ES 250	Lexus LS 400	Lincoln Continental (RWD)	Lincoln Continental V6 (FWD)	Lincoln Mark VII	Lincoln Town Car	Mazda 323, Protegé (2WD)
Air-conditioning								
Body exterior (paint)								
Body exterior (rust)								
Body hardware								
Body integrity								
Brakes								
Clutch								
Driveline								
Electrical system (chassis)								
Engine cooling								
Engine mechanical								
Exhaust system								
Fuel system								
Ignition system								
Steering/suspension								
Transmission (manual)								
Transmission (automatic)								
TROUBLE INDEX								
COST INDEX								

Insufficient data for Lexus ES 250 ('86–'89), Lexus LS 400 ('86–'89), Lincoln Continental RWD ('89–'91), and Lincoln Mark VII ('91).

340 REPAIR RECORDS

Legend
- ✳ Insufficient data
- ● Much worse than average
- ◐ Worse than average
- ◑ (horizontal bar) — (see scale)
- ○ Average / Better than average
- ◉ Much better than average

Mazda 626 / Mazda 626 Turbo / Mazda 929 / Mazda MPV 4

Trouble Spots	Mazda 626	Mazda 626 Turbo	Mazda 929	Mazda MPV 4
	'86 '87 '88 '89 '90 '91	'86 '87 '88 '89 '90 '91	'86 '87 '88 '89 '90 '91	'86 '87 '88 '89 '90 '91
Air-conditioning				
Body exterior (paint)				
Body exterior (rust)				
Body hardware				
Body integrity				
Brakes				
Clutch				
Driveline				
Electrical system (chassis)				
Engine cooling				
Engine mechanical				
Exhaust system				
Fuel system				
Ignition system				
Steering/suspension				
Transmission (manual)				
Transmission (automatic)				
TROUBLE INDEX				
COST INDEX				

Note: Mazda 626 Turbo '89, '90, '91 — Insufficient data. Mazda MPV 4 '91 — Insufficient data.

Mazda MPV V6 (2WD) / Mazda MPV V6 (4WD) / Mazda MX-5 Miata / Mazda MX-6

Trouble Spots	Mazda MPV V6 (2WD)	Mazda MPV V6 (4WD)	Mazda MX-5 Miata	Mazda MX-6
	'86 '87 '88 '89 '90 '91	'86 '87 '88 '89 '90 '91	'86 '87 '88 '89 '90 '91	'86 '87 '88 '89 '90 '91
Air-conditioning				
Body exterior (paint)				
Body exterior (rust)				
Body hardware				
Body integrity				
Brakes				
Clutch				
Driveline				
Electrical system (chassis)				
Engine cooling				
Engine mechanical				
Exhaust system				
Fuel system				
Ignition system				
Steering/suspension				
Transmission (manual)				
Transmission (automatic)				
TROUBLE INDEX				
COST INDEX				

Note: Mazda MPV V6 (4WD) — Insufficient data for most years.

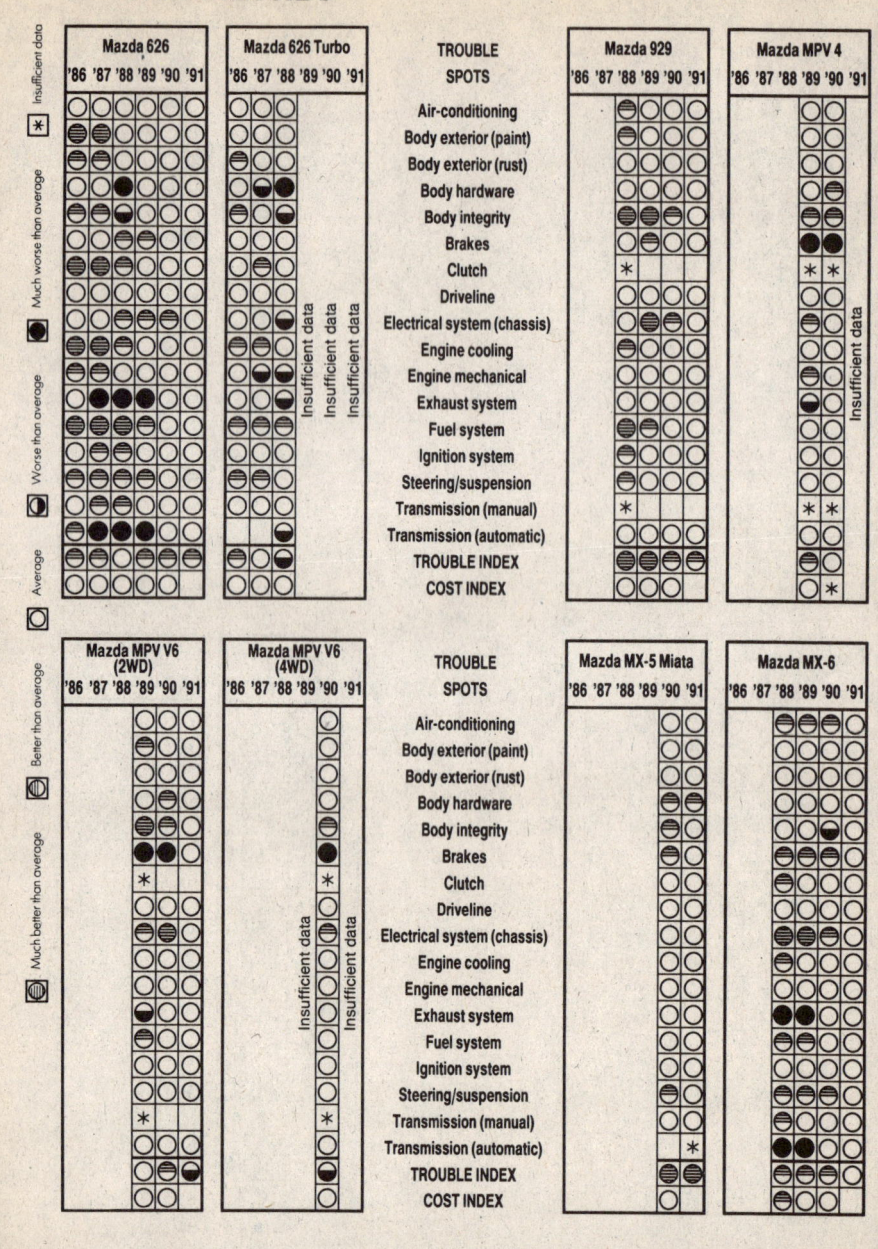

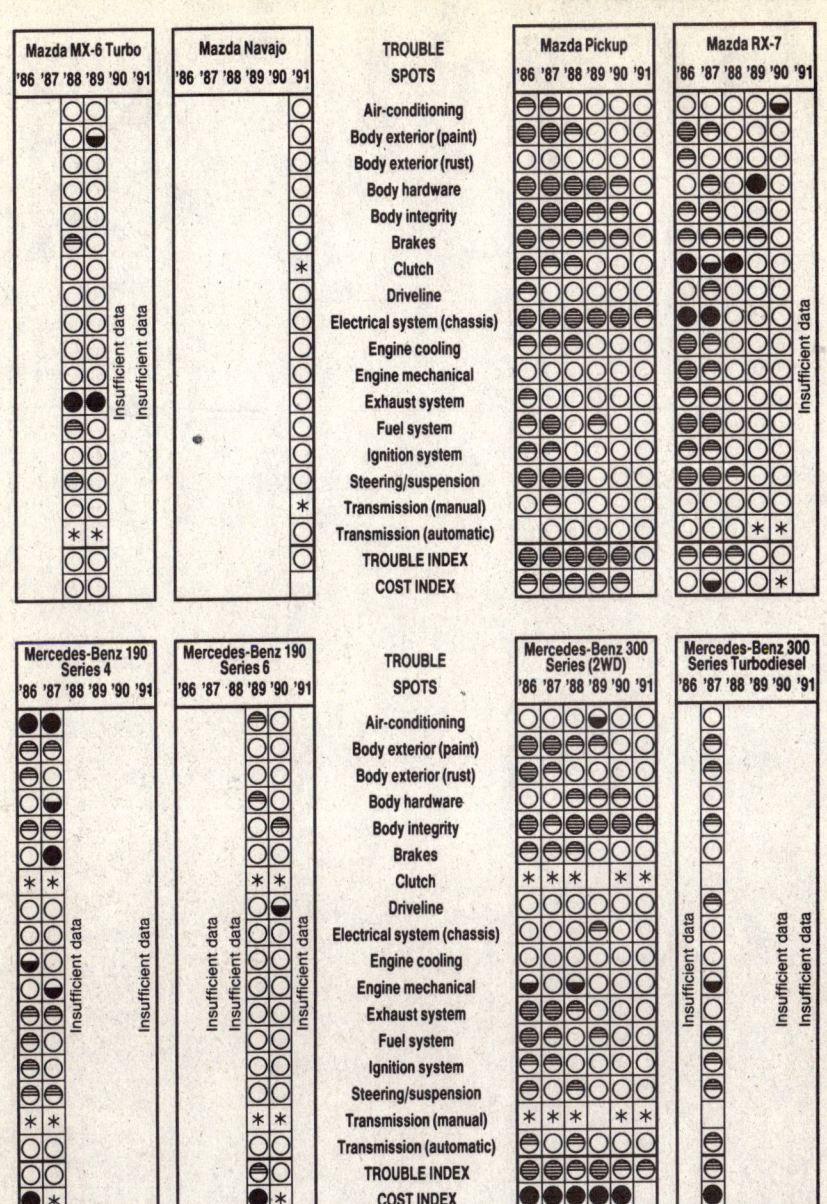

REPAIR RECORDS 341

Trouble Spots

Trouble Spot	Mazda MX-6 Turbo	Mazda Navajo	Mazda Pickup	Mazda RX-7
Air-conditioning				
Body exterior (paint)				
Body exterior (rust)				
Body hardware				
Body integrity				
Brakes				
Clutch				
Driveline				
Electrical system (chassis)				
Engine cooling				
Engine mechanical				
Exhaust system				
Fuel system				
Ignition system				
Steering/suspension				
Transmission (manual)				
Transmission (automatic)				
TROUBLE INDEX				
COST INDEX				

Years covered: '86 '87 '88 '89 '90 '91

Trouble Spot	Mercedes-Benz 190 Series 4	Mercedes-Benz 190 Series 6	Mercedes-Benz 300 Series (2WD)	Mercedes-Benz 300 Series Turbodiesel
Air-conditioning				
Body exterior (paint)				
Body exterior (rust)				
Body hardware				
Body integrity				
Brakes				
Clutch				
Driveline				
Electrical system (chassis)				
Engine cooling				
Engine mechanical				
Exhaust system				
Fuel system				
Ignition system				
Steering/suspension				
Transmission (manual)				
Transmission (automatic)				
TROUBLE INDEX				
COST INDEX				

Years covered: '86 '87 '88 '89 '90 '91

342 REPAIR RECORDS

Legend
- ☀ Insufficient data
- ● Much worse than average
- ◐ Worse than average
- ◑ Average (shown as half-filled)
- ○ Better than average
- ⊖ (horizontal bar) Better than average
- ⬤ Much better than average

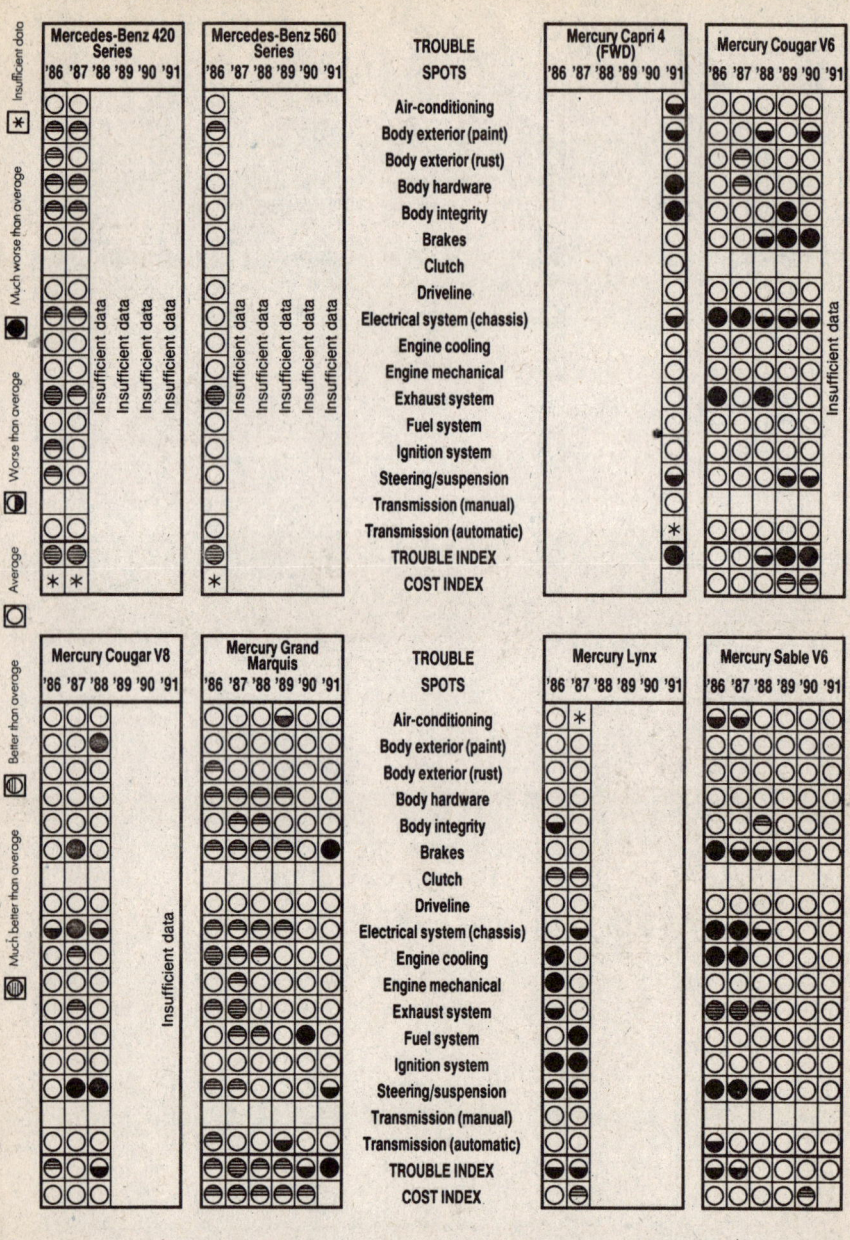

Trouble Spots

Trouble Spot	Mercedes-Benz 420 Series	Mercedes-Benz 560 Series	Mercury Capri 4 (FWD)	Mercury Cougar V6
	'86 '87 '88 '89 '90 '91	'86 '87 '88 '89 '90 '91	'86 '87 '88 '89 '90 '91	'86 '87 '88 '89 '90 '91

Years '88–'91 for Mercedes-Benz 420 and 560 Series: Insufficient data.
Mercury Cougar V6 '91: Insufficient data.

Trouble Spot	Mercury Cougar V8	Mercury Grand Marquis	Mercury Lynx	Mercury Sable V6
	'86 '87 '88 '89 '90 '91	'86 '87 '88 '89 '90 '91	'86 '87	'86 '87 '88 '89 '90 '91

Mercury Cougar V8 '91: Insufficient data.

Trouble Spots (categories listed)
- Air-conditioning
- Body exterior (paint)
- Body exterior (rust)
- Body hardware
- Body integrity
- Brakes
- Clutch
- Driveline
- Electrical system (chassis)
- Engine cooling
- Engine mechanical
- Exhaust system
- Fuel system
- Ignition system
- Steering/suspension
- Transmission (manual)
- Transmission (automatic)
- TROUBLE INDEX
- COST INDEX

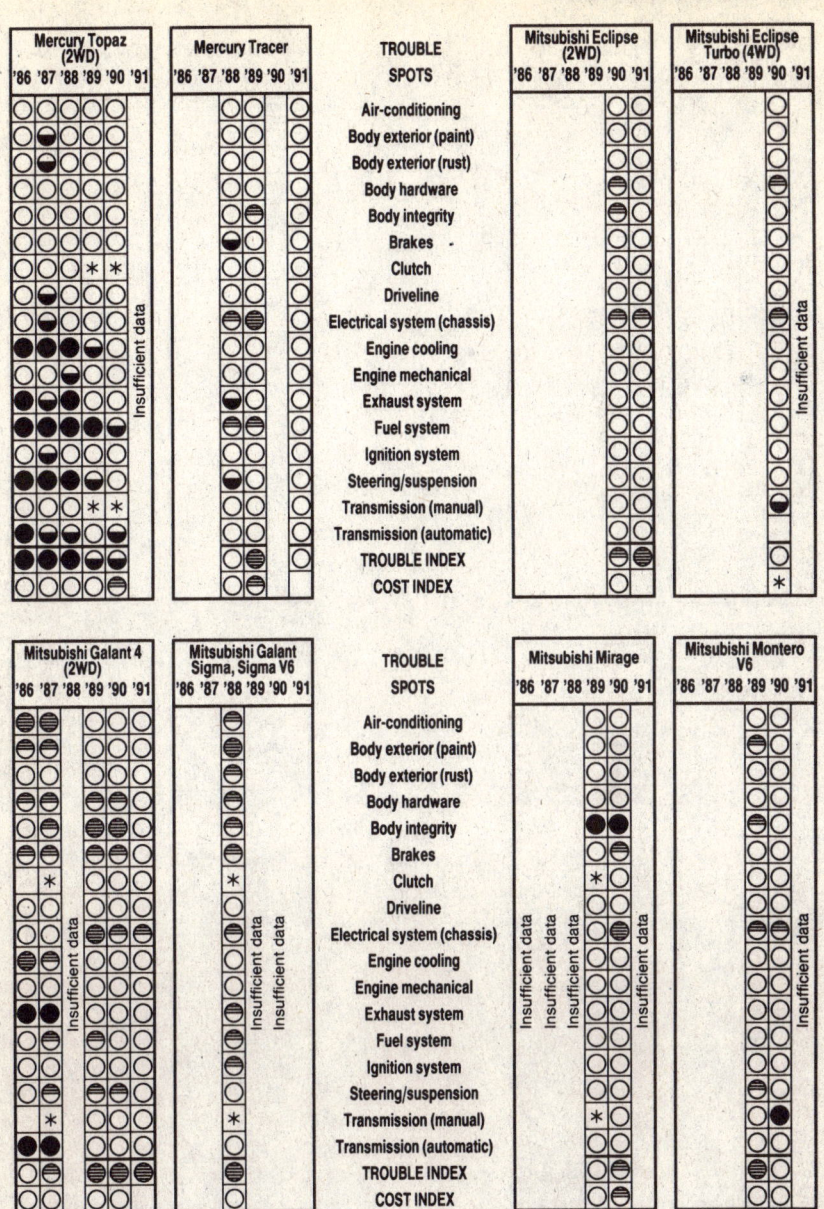

REPAIR RECORDS

Trouble Spots	Mercury Topaz (2WD) '86–'91	Mercury Tracer '86–'91	Mitsubishi Eclipse (2WD) '86–'91	Mitsubishi Eclipse Turbo (4WD) '86–'91
Air-conditioning				
Body exterior (paint)				
Body exterior (rust)				
Body hardware				
Body integrity				
Brakes				
Clutch				
Driveline				
Electrical system (chassis)				
Engine cooling				
Engine mechanical				
Exhaust system				
Fuel system				
Ignition system				
Steering/suspension				
Transmission (manual)				
Transmission (automatic)				
TROUBLE INDEX				
COST INDEX				

Trouble Spots	Mitsubishi Galant 4 (2WD) '86–'91	Mitsubishi Galant Sigma, Sigma V6 '86–'91	Mitsubishi Mirage '86–'91	Mitsubishi Montero V6 '86–'91
Air-conditioning				
Body exterior (paint)				
Body exterior (rust)				
Body hardware				
Body integrity				
Brakes				
Clutch				
Driveline				
Electrical system (chassis)				
Engine cooling				
Engine mechanical				
Exhaust system				
Fuel system				
Ignition system				
Steering/suspension				
Transmission (manual)				
Transmission (automatic)				
TROUBLE INDEX				
COST INDEX				

344 REPAIR RECORDS

Legend:
- ○ Insufficient data... (symbols key on left margin)
- ✱ Insufficient data
- ● Much worse than average
- ◐ Worse than average
- ⊖ Average
- ◑ Better than average
- ⊜ Much better than average

TROUBLE SPOTS	Mitsubishi Pickup 4 (2WD) '86–'91	Nissan 200SX 4 '86–'91	Nissan 200SX V6 '86–'91	Nissan 240SX '86–'91
Air-conditioning				
Body exterior (paint)				
Body exterior (rust)				
Body hardware				
Body integrity				
Brakes				
Clutch				
Driveline				
Electrical system (chassis)				
Engine cooling				
Engine mechanical				
Exhaust system				
Fuel system				
Ignition system				
Steering/suspension				
Transmission (manual)				
Transmission (automatic)				
TROUBLE INDEX				
COST INDEX				

TROUBLE SPOTS	Nissan 300ZX '86–'91	Nissan Maxima '86–'91	Nissan Pathfinder (4WD) '86–'91	Nissan Pickup 4, V6 (2WD) '86–'91
Air-conditioning				
Body exterior (paint)				
Body exterior (rust)				
Body hardware				
Body integrity				
Brakes				
Clutch				
Driveline				
Electrical system (chassis)				
Engine cooling				
Engine mechanical				
Exhaust system				
Fuel system				
Ignition system				
Steering/suspension				
Transmission (manual)				
Transmission (automatic)				
TROUBLE INDEX				
COST INDEX				

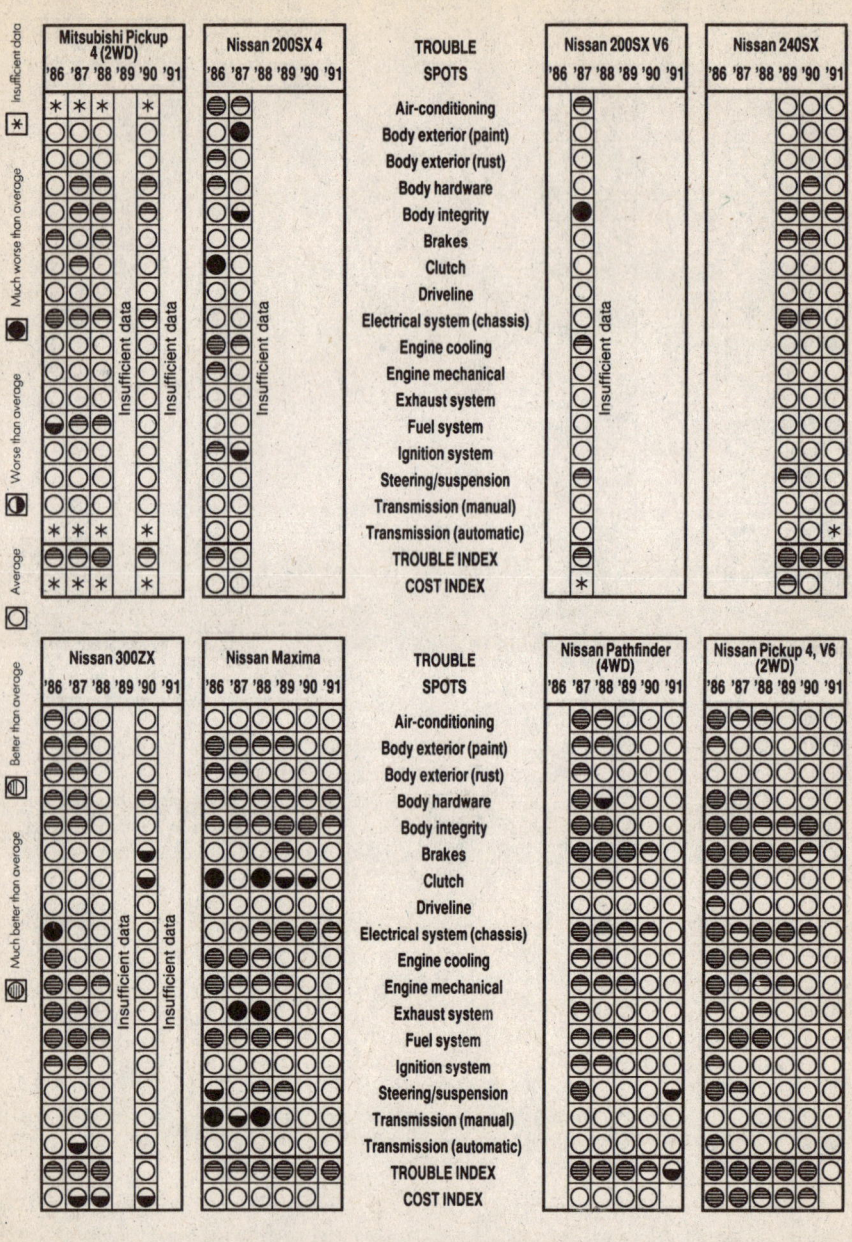

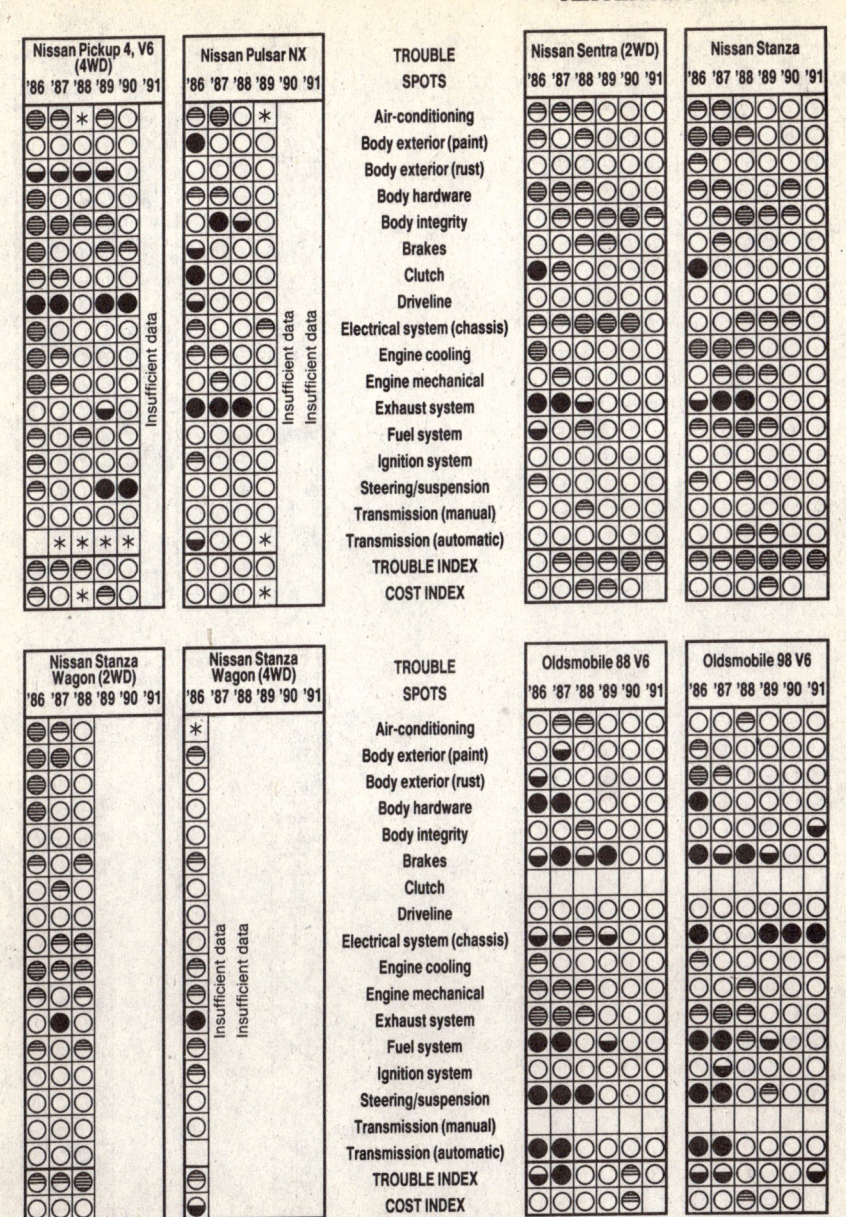

REPAIR RECORDS 345

Trouble Spots	Nissan Pickup 4, V6 (4WD) '86-'91	Nissan Pulsar NX '86-'91	Nissan Sentra (2WD) '86-'91	Nissan Stanza '86-'91

(Repair record charts with symbols indicating reliability ratings across model years '86-'91 for each trouble spot listed below.)

Trouble Spots:
- Air-conditioning
- Body exterior (paint)
- Body exterior (rust)
- Body hardware
- Body integrity
- Brakes
- Clutch
- Driveline
- Electrical system (chassis)
- Engine cooling
- Engine mechanical
- Exhaust system
- Fuel system
- Ignition system
- Steering/suspension
- Transmission (manual)
- Transmission (automatic)
- TROUBLE INDEX
- COST INDEX

Note: Nissan Pulsar NX shows "Insufficient data" for '90 and '91.

Trouble Spots	Nissan Stanza Wagon (2WD) '86-'91	Nissan Stanza Wagon (4WD) '86-'91	Oldsmobile 88 V6 '86-'91	Oldsmobile 98 V6 '86-'91

Note: Nissan Stanza Wagon (2WD) and (4WD) show "Insufficient data" for later years.

346 REPAIR RECORDS

Legend:
- ○ Average
- ◐ Worse than average
- ● Much worse than average
- ✱ Insufficient data
- ◒ Better than average
- ⊖ Much better than average

TROUBLE SPOTS	Oldsmobile Custom Cruiser Wagon '86–'91	Oldsmobile Cutlass Calais 4 '86–'91	Oldsmobile Cutlass Calais V6 '86–'91	Oldsmobile Cutlass Ciera 4 '86–'91	Oldsmobile Cutlass Ciera V6 '86–'91	Oldsmobile Cutlass Supreme 4 (FWD) '86–'91	Oldsmobile Cutlass Supreme V6 (RWD) '86–'91	Oldsmobile Cutlass Supreme V6 (FWD) '86–'91
Air-conditioning								
Body exterior (paint)								
Body exterior (rust)								
Body hardware								
Body integrity								
Brakes								
Clutch								
Driveline								
Electrical system (chassis)								
Engine cooling								
Engine mechanical								
Exhaust system								
Fuel system								
Ignition system								
Steering/suspension								
Transmission (manual)								
Transmission (automatic)								
TROUBLE INDEX								
COST INDEX								

REPAIR RECORDS 347

Oldsmobile Cutlass Supreme V8 (RWD)
Trouble Spot	'86	'87	'88	'89	'90	'91
Air-conditioning	○	⊖	○			
Body exterior (paint)	●	●	●			
Body exterior (rust)	○	○	○			
Body hardware						
Body integrity	●	●	●			
Brakes	⊖	○	○			
Clutch						
Driveline						
Electrical system (chassis)	⊖	○	○			
Engine cooling	○	○	○			
Engine mechanical	○	○	○			
Exhaust system	⊖	○	○			
Fuel system	○	○	○			
Ignition system	○	○	○			
Steering/suspension	○	○	○			
Transmission (manual)						
Transmission (automatic)	○	○	○			
TROUBLE INDEX	○	○	○			
COST INDEX	⊖	○	*			

Oldsmobile Silhouette
Trouble Spot	'86	'87	'88	'89	'90	'91
Air-conditioning					○	
Body exterior (paint)					○	
Body exterior (rust)					○	
Body hardware					●	
Body integrity					○	
Brakes					○	
Clutch						
Driveline					○	
Electrical system (chassis)					○	
Engine cooling					○	
Engine mechanical					○	
Exhaust system					○	
Fuel system					○	
Ignition system					○	
Steering/suspension					○	
Transmission (manual)						
Transmission (automatic)					○	
TROUBLE INDEX					○	
COST INDEX					⊖	

Oldsmobile Toronado
Trouble Spot	'86	'87	'88	'89	'90	'91
Air-conditioning			○	○	○	
Body exterior (paint)			○	○	⊖	
Body exterior (rust)			○	○	○	
Body hardware			○	○	○	
Body integrity			○	○	○	
Brakes			○	○	○	
Clutch	Insufficient data	Insufficient data				Insufficient data
Driveline			○	○	○	
Electrical system (chassis)			○	○	●	
Engine cooling			○	○	○	
Engine mechanical			○	○	○	
Exhaust system			○	○	○	
Fuel system			○	○	○	
Ignition system			○	○	○	
Steering/suspension			○	○	○	
Transmission (manual)						
Transmission (automatic)			○	○	○	
TROUBLE INDEX			○	○	⊖	
COST INDEX			*		*	

Plymouth Acclaim 4
Trouble Spot	'86	'87	'88	'89	'90	'91
Air-conditioning				○	○	○
Body exterior (paint)				○	○	○
Body exterior (rust)				○	○	○
Body hardware				⊖	⊖	⊖
Body integrity				○	○	○
Brakes				○	○	○
Clutch				*	*	*
Driveline				○	○	○
Electrical system (chassis)				⊖	○	○
Engine cooling				○	○	○
Engine mechanical				●	○	○
Exhaust system				○	○	⊖
Fuel system				○	○	○
Ignition system				○	○	○
Steering/suspension				○	○	○
Transmission (manual)				*	*	*
Transmission (automatic)				○	○	○
TROUBLE INDEX				⊖	○	⊖
COST INDEX				⊖	○	⊖

Plymouth Acclaim V6
Trouble Spot	'86	'87	'88	'89	'90	'91
Air-conditioning				⊖	○	○
Body exterior (paint)				○	○	○
Body exterior (rust)				○	○	○
Body hardware				○	⊖	○
Body integrity				○	○	○
Brakes				○	○	○
Clutch						
Driveline				○	○	○
Electrical system (chassis)				○	○	○
Engine cooling				○	○	○
Engine mechanical				○	○	○
Exhaust system				○	○	○
Fuel system				○	○	○
Ignition system				○	○	○
Steering/suspension				○	○	○
Transmission (manual)						
Transmission (automatic)				●	●	●
TROUBLE INDEX				⊖	○	○
COST INDEX				⊖	○	○

Plymouth Caravelle
Trouble Spot	'86	'87	'88	'89	'90	'91
Air-conditioning	⊖	○	○			
Body exterior (paint)	○	○	○			
Body exterior (rust)	⊖	○	○			
Body hardware	○	⊖	○			
Body integrity	○	○	○			
Brakes	○	○	○			
Clutch				Insufficient data		
Driveline	○	○	○			
Electrical system (chassis)	⊖	○	⊖			
Engine cooling	○	○	○			
Engine mechanical	○	⊖	○			
Exhaust system	○	●	○			
Fuel system	○	●	○			
Ignition system	○	○	○			
Steering/suspension	○	○	○			
Transmission (manual)						
Transmission (automatic)	○	○	○			
TROUBLE INDEX	⊖	⊖	○			
COST INDEX	*	⊖				

Plymouth Colt (2WD)
Trouble Spot	'86	'87	'88	'89	'90	'91
Air-conditioning	○	○	○	○	*	
Body exterior (paint)	○	⊖	⊖	○	○	
Body exterior (rust)	⊖	○	○	○	○	
Body hardware	⊖	⊖	⊖	○	○	
Body integrity	○	⊖	⊖	○	○	
Brakes	○	○	○	○	○	
Clutch	○	○	○	○	○	
Driveline	⊖	⊖	⊖	⊖	⊖	Insufficient data
Electrical system (chassis)	○	○	○	○	○	
Engine cooling	⊖	○	○	○	○	
Engine mechanical	○	⊖	○	○	○	
Exhaust system	●	●	○	○	○	
Fuel system	○	●	○	○	○	
Ignition system	○	○	○	○	○	
Steering/suspension	⊖	○	○	○	○	
Transmission (manual)	○	○	○	○	○	
Transmission (automatic)	○	○	○	○	*	
TROUBLE INDEX	○	⊖	⊖	⊖	⊖	
COST INDEX	⊖	○	⊖	○	*	

Plymouth Colt Vista Wagon
Trouble Spot	'86	'87	'88	'89	'90	'91
Air-conditioning	*	*		*		
Body exterior (paint)	○	○		○		
Body exterior (rust)	○	○		○		
Body hardware	○	⊖		○		
Body integrity	○	⊖		○		
Brakes	○	○		○		
Clutch	○	○		○		
Driveline	●	○		○	Insufficient data	Insufficient data
Electrical system (chassis)	○	○	Insufficient data	○		
Engine cooling	○	○		○		
Engine mechanical	⊖	○		○		
Exhaust system	●	⊖		○		
Fuel system	●	○		○		
Ignition system	○	○		○		
Steering/suspension	⊖	○		○		
Transmission (manual)	⊖	○		○		
Transmission (automatic)	*	⊖		*		
TROUBLE INDEX	○	○		○		
COST INDEX	*	*		*		

348 REPAIR RECORDS

Legend: Insufficient data (*) | Much worse than average | Worse than average | Average | Better than average | Much better than average

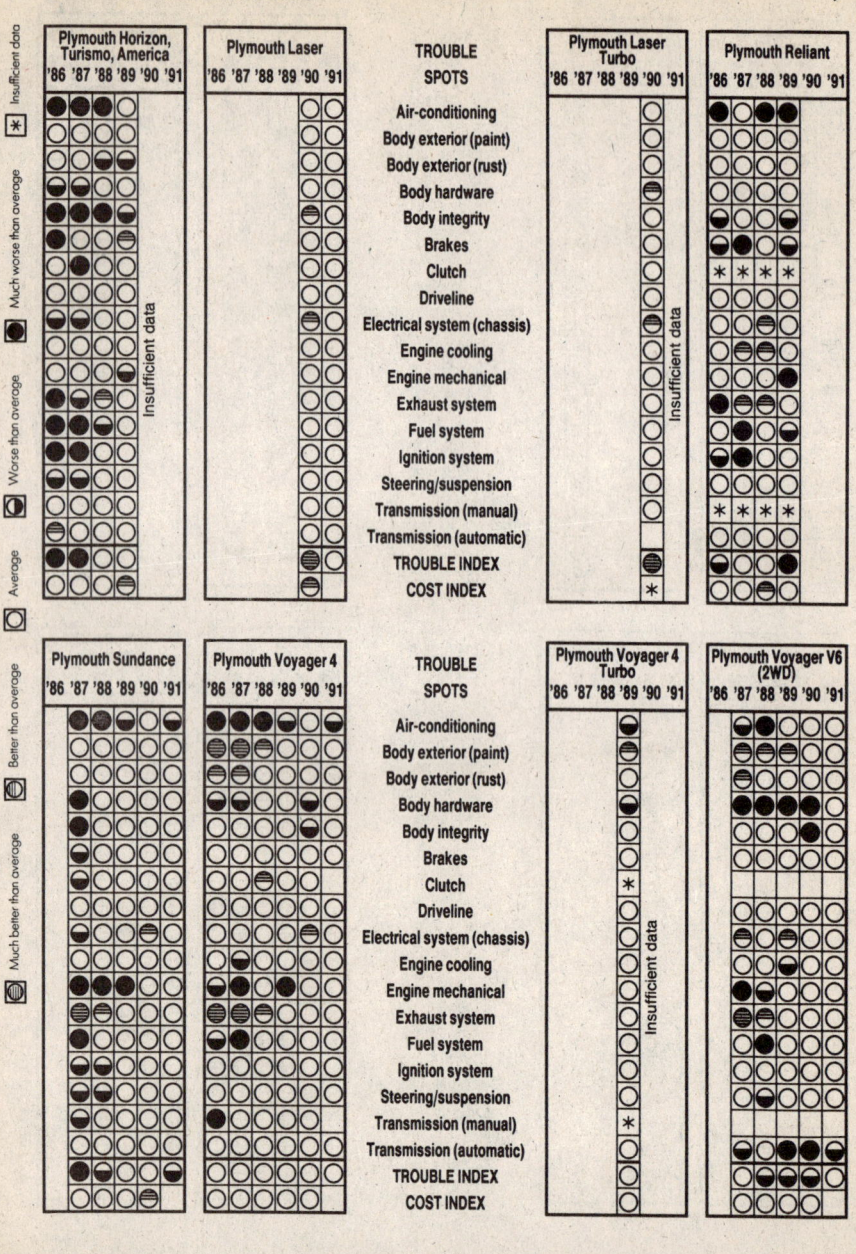

TROUBLE SPOTS

- Air-conditioning
- Body exterior (paint)
- Body exterior (rust)
- Body hardware
- Body integrity
- Brakes
- Clutch
- Driveline
- Electrical system (chassis)
- Engine cooling
- Engine mechanical
- Exhaust system
- Fuel system
- Ignition system
- Steering/suspension
- Transmission (manual)
- Transmission (automatic)
- TROUBLE INDEX
- COST INDEX

Models shown (years '86 '87 '88 '89 '90 '91):
- Plymouth Horizon, Turismo, America
- Plymouth Laser
- Plymouth Laser Turbo
- Plymouth Reliant
- Plymouth Sundance
- Plymouth Voyager 4
- Plymouth Voyager 4 Turbo
- Plymouth Voyager V6 (2WD)

REPAIR RECORDS 349

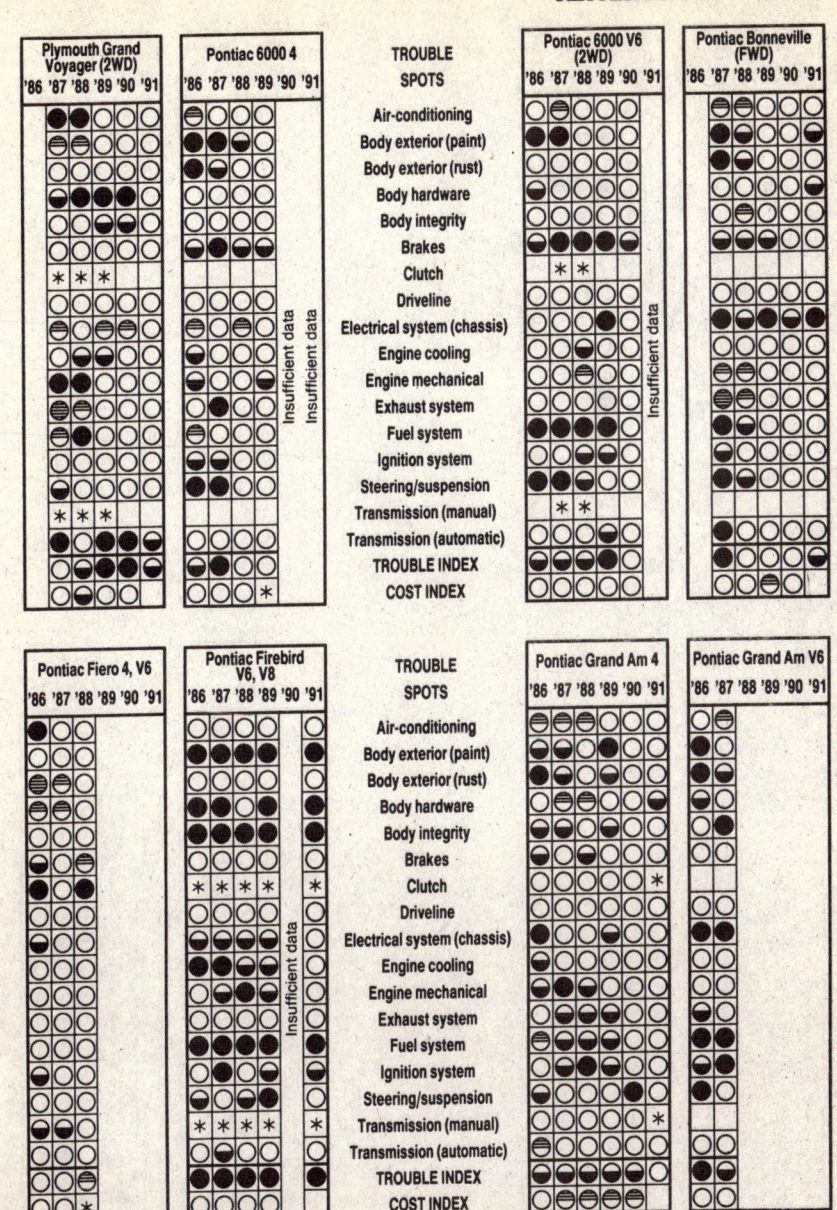

350 REPAIR RECORDS

Legend:
- ✳ Insufficient data
- ✱ Much worse than average
- ● Worse than average
- ◐ Average
- ○ Better than average
- ◑ (Better than average)
- ⊜ Much better than average

Trouble Spots

Trouble Spots	Pontiac Grand Prix V6, V8 (RWD) '86–'91	Pontiac Grand Prix V6 (FWD) '86–'91	Pontiac Le Mans '86–'91	Pontiac Sunbird 4 '86–'91
Air-conditioning	Insufficient data			
Body exterior (paint)				
Body exterior (rust)				
Body hardware				
Body integrity				
Brakes				
Clutch		✱ ✱ ✱ ✱		✱ ✱ ✱ ✱
Driveline				
Electrical system (chassis)			Insufficient data	Insufficient data
Engine cooling				
Engine mechanical				
Exhaust system				
Fuel system				
Ignition system				
Steering/suspension				
Transmission (manual)		✱ ✱ ✱ ✱		✱ ✱ ✱ ✱
Transmission (automatic)				
TROUBLE INDEX				
COST INDEX			● ✱	

Trouble Spots	Pontiac Trans Sport '86–'91	Porsche 944 '86–'91	Saab 900 Series '86–'91	Saab 9000 '86–'91
Air-conditioning				
Body exterior (paint)				
Body exterior (rust)				
Body hardware				
Body integrity				
Brakes				
Clutch				✱
Driveline		Insufficient data		
Electrical system (chassis)			Insufficient data	Insufficient data
Engine cooling				
Engine mechanical				
Exhaust system				
Fuel system				
Ignition system				
Steering/suspension				
Transmission (manual)		✱ ✱		✱
Transmission (automatic)				
TROUBLE INDEX		✱ ●		
COST INDEX				✱

REPAIR RECORDS 351

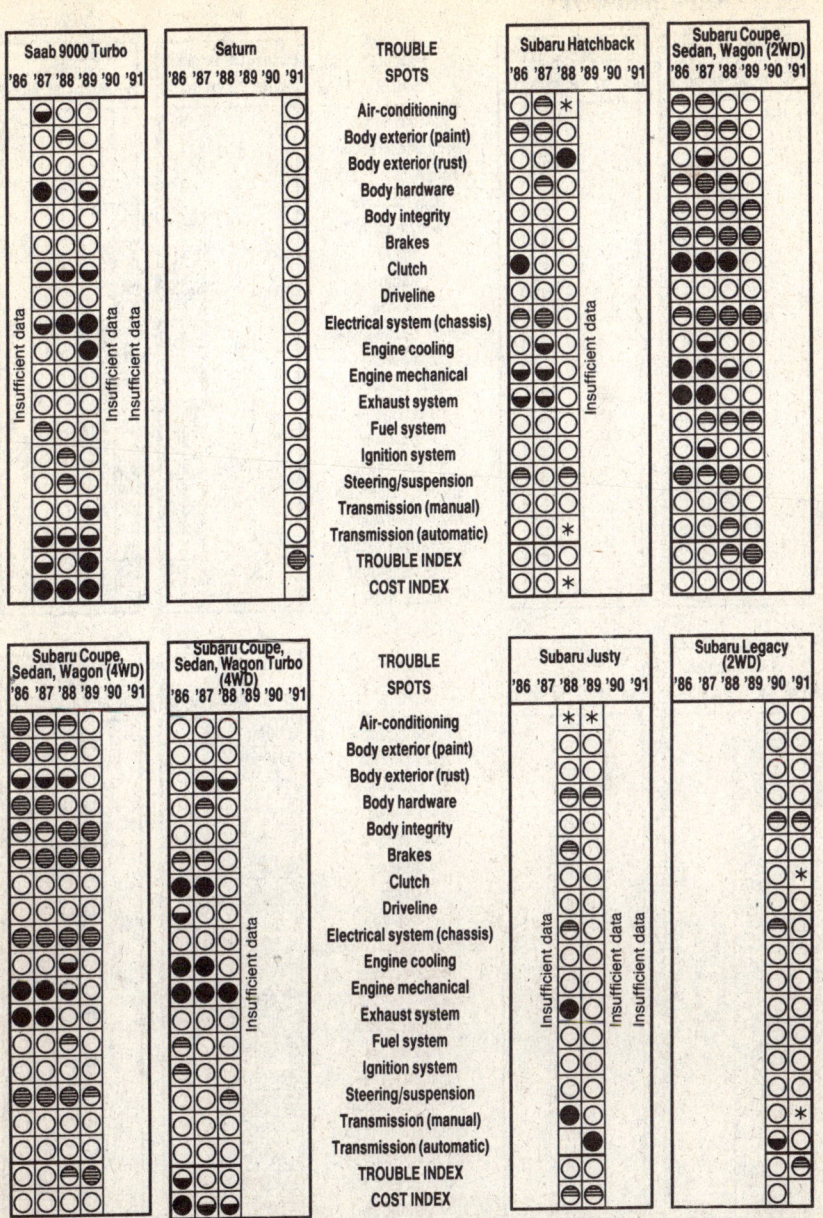

Saab 9000 Turbo
'86 '87 '88 '89 '90 '91

Insufficient data for '86, '90, '91

Saturn
'86 '87 '88 '89 '90 '91

Insufficient data for '86–'90

Subaru Hatchback
'86 '87 '88 '89 '90 '91

Insufficient data for '89, '90, '91

Subaru Coupe, Sedan, Wagon (2WD)
'86 '87 '88 '89 '90 '91

Subaru Coupe, Sedan, Wagon (4WD)
'86 '87 '88 '89 '90 '91

Subaru Coupe, Sedan, Wagon Turbo (4WD)
'86 '87 '88 '89 '90 '91

Insufficient data for '91

Subaru Justy
'86 '87 '88 '89 '90 '91

Insufficient data for '86, '90, '91

Subaru Legacy (2WD)
'86 '87 '88 '89 '90 '91

TROUBLE SPOTS

- Air-conditioning
- Body exterior (paint)
- Body exterior (rust)
- Body hardware
- Body integrity
- Brakes
- Clutch
- Driveline
- Electrical system (chassis)
- Engine cooling
- Engine mechanical
- Exhaust system
- Fuel system
- Ignition system
- Steering/suspension
- Transmission (manual)
- Transmission (automatic)
- TROUBLE INDEX
- COST INDEX

352 REPAIR RECORDS

Legend:
- ☐ Insufficient data
- ✱ Much worse than average
- ● Worse than average
- ◐ Average (half-filled)
- ○ Better than average
- ⊖ Much better than average (horizontal bar in circle)

Trouble Spots	Subaru Legacy (4WD) '86–'91	Subaru Loyale (2WD) '86–'91	Subaru Loyale (4WD) '86–'91	Subaru XT Coupe 4 (2WD) '86–'91
Air-conditioning				
Body exterior (paint)				
Body exterior (rust)				
Body hardware				
Body integrity				
Brakes				
Clutch				
Driveline				
Electrical system (chassis)				
Engine cooling				
Engine mechanical				
Exhaust system				
Fuel system				
Ignition system				
Steering/suspension				
Transmission (manual)				
Transmission (automatic)				
TROUBLE INDEX				
COST INDEX				

Trouble Spots	Suzuki Samurai '86–'91	Suzuki Sidekick (4WD) '86–'91	Toyota 4Runner 4 (4WD) '86–'91	Toyota 4Runner V6 (4WD) '86–'91
Air-conditioning				
Body exterior (paint)				
Body exterior (rust)				
Body hardware				
Body integrity				
Brakes				
Clutch				
Driveline				
Electrical system (chassis)				
Engine cooling				
Engine mechanical				
Exhaust system				
Fuel system				
Ignition system				
Steering/suspension				
Transmission (manual)				
Transmission (automatic)				
TROUBLE INDEX				
COST INDEX				

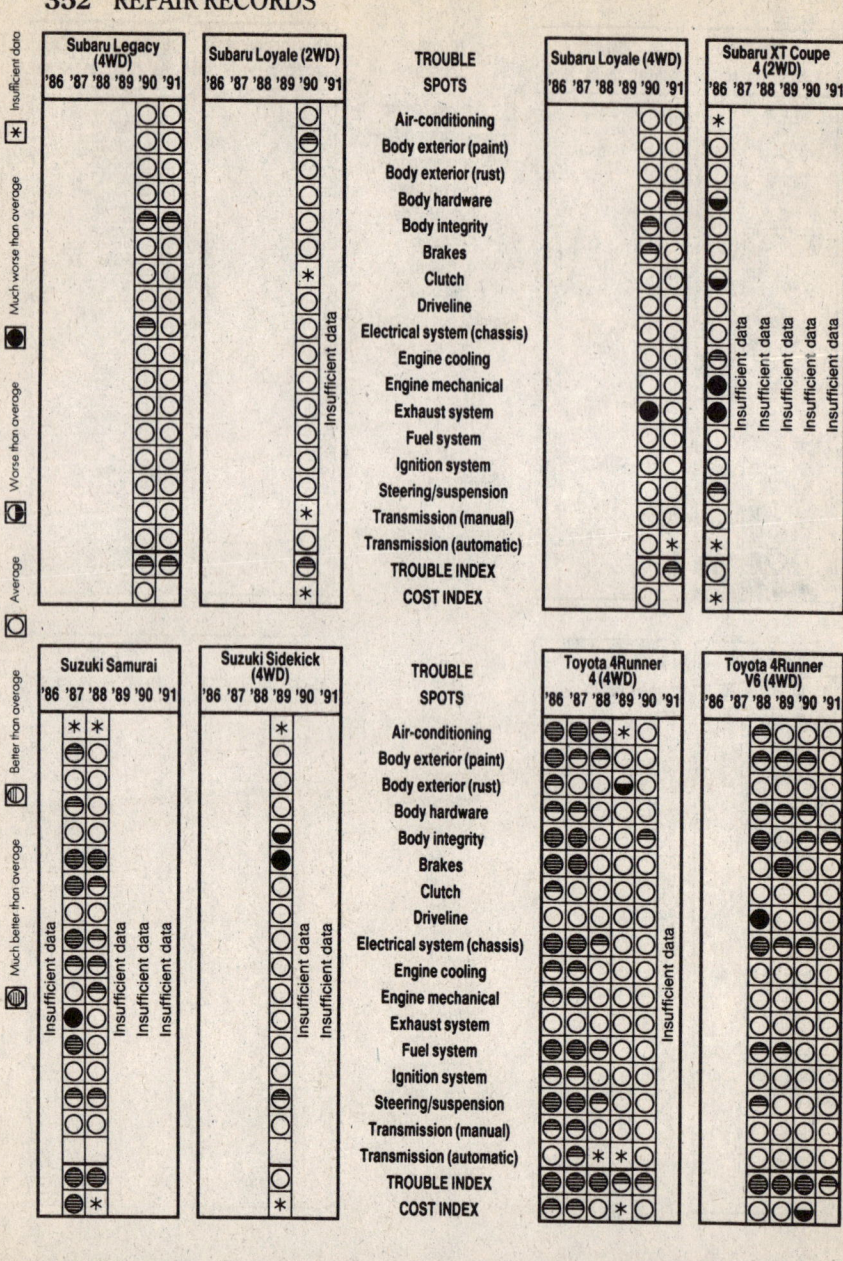

REPAIR RECORDS

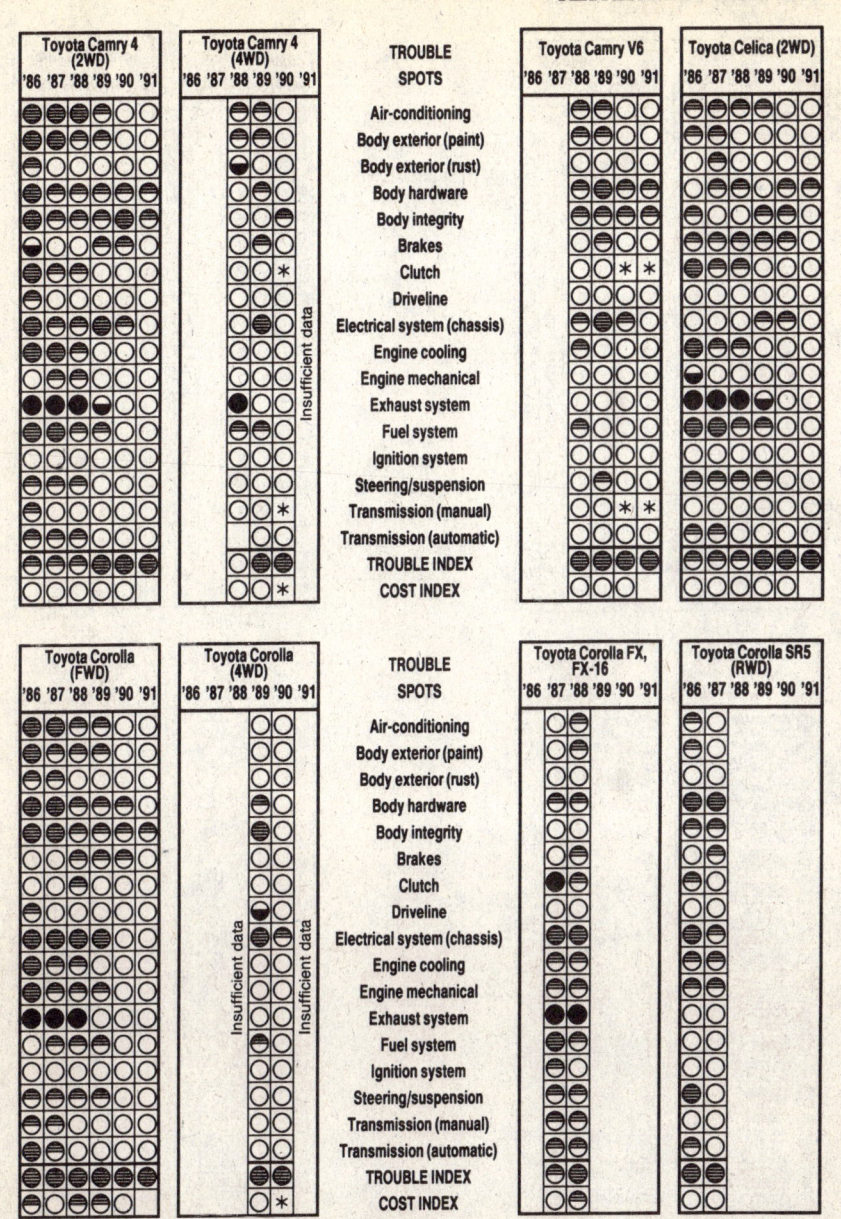

TROUBLE SPOTS

Trouble Spot	Toyota Camry 4 (2WD)	Toyota Camry 4 (4WD)	Toyota Camry V6	Toyota Celica (2WD)
Air-conditioning				
Body exterior (paint)				
Body exterior (rust)				
Body hardware				
Body integrity				
Brakes				
Clutch				
Driveline				
Electrical system (chassis)				
Engine cooling				
Engine mechanical				
Exhaust system				
Fuel system				
Ignition system				
Steering/suspension				
Transmission (manual)				
Transmission (automatic)				
TROUBLE INDEX				
COST INDEX				

Years covered: '86 '87 '88 '89 '90 '91

Toyota Camry 4 (4WD): Insufficient data for early years.

Trouble Spot	Toyota Corolla (FWD)	Toyota Corolla (4WD)	Toyota Corolla FX, FX-16	Toyota Corolla SR5 (RWD)
Air-conditioning				
Body exterior (paint)				
Body exterior (rust)				
Body hardware				
Body integrity				
Brakes				
Clutch				
Driveline				
Electrical system (chassis)				
Engine cooling				
Engine mechanical				
Exhaust system				
Fuel system				
Ignition system				
Steering/suspension				
Transmission (manual)				
Transmission (automatic)				
TROUBLE INDEX				
COST INDEX				

Years covered: '86 '87 '88 '89 '90 '91

Toyota Corolla (4WD): Insufficient data.

354 REPAIR RECORDS

Legend
- ⊖ Insufficient data
- ✻ Much worse than average
- ● Worse than average
- ◐ Average
- ○ Better than average
- ⊘ Much better than average

Toyota Cressida

Trouble Spots	'86	'87	'88	'89	'90	'91
Air-conditioning	○	⊖	○	○	○	○
Body exterior (paint)	⊖	⊖	○	○	○	○
Body exterior (rust)	⊖	⊖	○	○	○	○
Body hardware	⊖	⊖	⊖	○	○	○
Body integrity	⊖	⊖	⊖	⊖	○	○
Brakes	✻	✻				
Clutch						
Driveline	○	○	○	○	○	○
Electrical system (chassis)	⊖	⊖	⊖	⊖	⊖	○
Engine cooling	⊖	○	○	○	○	○
Engine mechanical	○	⊖	○	○	○	○
Exhaust system	⊖	⊖	⊖	⊖	○	⊖
Fuel system	⊖	⊖	○	○	○	○
Ignition system	⊖	⊖	⊖	○	○	○
Steering/suspension	⊖	○	○	⊖	○	○
Transmission (manual)	✻	✻				
Transmission (automatic)	⊖	○	○	○	○	○
TROUBLE INDEX	⊖	⊖	⊖	⊖	○	○
COST INDEX	○	○	○	○	○	○

Toyota Land Cruiser Wagon

Trouble Spots	'86	'87	'88	'89	'90	'91
Air-conditioning			○	⊖		○
Body exterior (paint)			○	○		○
Body exterior (rust)			○	⊖		○
Body hardware			○	○		○
Body integrity			⊖	⊖		○
Brakes			○	○		○
Clutch	Insufficient data	Insufficient data			Insufficient data	
Driveline			○	○		○
Electrical system (chassis)			○	○		○
Engine cooling			○	○		○
Engine mechanical			○	○		○
Exhaust system			○	○		●
Fuel system			○	○		○
Ignition system			○	○		○
Steering/suspension			⊖	○		○
Transmission (manual)			○	○		○
Transmission (automatic)			○	○		○
TROUBLE INDEX			⊖	⊖		○
COST INDEX			○	✻		

Toyota MR2

Trouble Spots	'86	'87	'88	'89	'90	'91
Air-conditioning	⊖	⊖	○	✻		○
Body exterior (paint)	⊖	⊖	○	○		○
Body exterior (rust)	○	○	○	○		○
Body hardware	⊖	⊖	○	○		○
Body integrity	⊖	⊖	⊖	○		○
Brakes	⊖	⊖	○	○		○
Clutch	○	○	○	○		○
Driveline	○	○	○	○		○
Electrical system (chassis)	⊖	⊖	○	○		○
Engine cooling	⊖	○	○	○		○
Engine mechanical	○	⊖	○	○		○
Exhaust system	⊖	⊖	⊖	⊖		○
Fuel system	⊖	○	○	○		○
Ignition system	⊖	⊖	○	○		○
Steering/suspension	○	○	○	○		○
Transmission (manual)	○	○	○	○		○
Transmission (automatic)	○	○	✻	✻		✻
TROUBLE INDEX	⊖	⊖	⊖	⊖		○
COST INDEX	⊖	⊖	✻	✻		

Toyota MR2 Turbo

Trouble Spots	'86	'87	'88	'89	'90	'91
Air-conditioning						○
Body exterior (paint)						○
Body exterior (rust)						○
Body hardware						○
Body integrity						○
Brakes						○
Clutch						○
Driveline						○
Electrical system (chassis)	Insufficient data				Insufficient data	●
Engine cooling						○
Engine mechanical						○
Exhaust system						○
Fuel system						○
Ignition system						○
Steering/suspension						○
Transmission (manual)						○
Transmission (automatic)						○
TROUBLE INDEX						○
COST INDEX						

Toyota Pickup 4 (2WD)

Trouble Spots	'86	'87	'88	'89	'90	'91
Air-conditioning	⊖	⊖	⊖	○	○	○
Body exterior (paint)	⊖	⊖	⊖	○	○	○
Body exterior (rust)	●	◐	○	○	○	○
Body hardware	⊖	⊖	⊖	○	○	○
Body integrity	⊖	⊖	⊖	⊖	○	○
Brakes	⊖	⊖	○	○	○	○
Clutch	○	○	○	○	○	○
Driveline	⊖	○	○	○	○	○
Electrical system (chassis)	⊖	⊖	⊖	○	○	○
Engine cooling	⊖	⊖	⊖	○	○	○
Engine mechanical	⊖	⊖	○	○	○	○
Exhaust system	⊖	⊖	⊖	○	○	○
Fuel system	⊖	⊖	⊖	○	○	○
Ignition system	⊖	⊖	⊖	○	○	○
Steering/suspension	⊖	⊖	⊖	○	○	○
Transmission (manual)	⊖	⊖	○	○	○	○
Transmission (automatic)	⊖	⊖	⊖	⊖	⊖	○
TROUBLE INDEX	⊖	⊖	⊖	⊖	⊖	○
COST INDEX	⊖	⊖	⊖	⊖	⊖	○

Toyota Pickup 4 (4WD)

Trouble Spots	'86	'87	'88	'89	'90	'91
Air-conditioning	⊖	⊖	○	○	○	✻
Body exterior (paint)	⊖	◐	○	○	○	○
Body exterior (rust)	●	●	○	○	○	○
Body hardware	⊖	⊖	⊖	○	○	○
Body integrity	⊖	⊖	⊖	⊖	○	○
Brakes	⊖	●	○	○	○	○
Clutch	○	○	○	○	○	○
Driveline	⊖	⊖	○	◐	○	○
Electrical system (chassis)	⊖	⊖	⊖	○	○	○
Engine cooling	⊖	⊖	○	○	○	○
Engine mechanical	⊖	⊖	○	○	○	○
Exhaust system	⊖	⊖	⊖	○	○	○
Fuel system	⊖	⊖	○	○	○	○
Ignition system	⊖	⊖	○	○	○	○
Steering/suspension	⊖	⊖	○	○	○	○
Transmission (manual)	○	○	○	○	○	○
Transmission (automatic)	○	○	✻	✻	✻	✻
TROUBLE INDEX	⊖	⊖	⊖	○	○	○
COST INDEX	⊖	⊖	○	○	○	○

Toyota Pickup V6 (2WD)

Trouble Spots	'86	'87	'88	'89	'90	'91
Air-conditioning			○	○		
Body exterior (paint)			○	○		
Body exterior (rust)			○	○		
Body hardware			○	○		
Body integrity			⊖	○		
Brakes			●	○		
Clutch			○	○		
Driveline			○	○		
Electrical system (chassis)			⊖	⊖	Insufficient data	
Engine cooling			○	○		
Engine mechanical			○	○		
Exhaust system			○	○		
Fuel system			○	○		
Ignition system			○	○		
Steering/suspension			○	○		
Transmission (manual)			○	○		
Transmission (automatic)			○	○		
TROUBLE INDEX			○	⊖		
COST INDEX			○	○		

Toyota Pickup V6 (4WD)

Trouble Spots	'86	'87	'88	'89	'90	'91
Air-conditioning		⊖	⊖	⊖	○	○
Body exterior (paint)		⊖	⊖	○	○	○
Body exterior (rust)		⊖	⊖	⊖	○	○
Body hardware		⊖	⊖	⊖	○	○
Body integrity		⊖	⊖	⊖	○	○
Brakes		⊖	⊖	○	○	○
Clutch		○	○	○	○	○
Driveline		○	○	○	○	○
Electrical system (chassis)		⊖	⊖	⊖	○	○
Engine cooling		○	○	○	○	○
Engine mechanical		○	○	○	○	○
Exhaust system		⊖	⊖	○	○	○
Fuel system		○	○	○	○	○
Ignition system		⊖	○	○	○	○
Steering/suspension		⊖	○	○	○	○
Transmission (manual)		○	○	○	○	○
Transmission (automatic)		✻	○	○	○	✻
TROUBLE INDEX		⊖	⊖	⊖	○	○
COST INDEX		✻	⊖	○		

REPAIR RECORDS 355

Trouble Spots	Toyota Previa (2WD) '86–'91	Toyota Previa (4WD) '86–'91	Toyota Supra '86–'91	Toyota Supra Turbo '86–'91

(Data charts for Toyota Previa 2WD, Toyota Previa 4WD, Toyota Supra, and Toyota Supra Turbo across trouble spots: Air-conditioning, Body exterior (paint), Body exterior (rust), Body hardware, Body integrity, Brakes, Clutch, Driveline, Electrical system (chassis), Engine cooling, Engine mechanical, Exhaust system, Fuel system, Ignition system, Steering/suspension, Transmission (manual), Transmission (automatic), Trouble Index, Cost Index.)

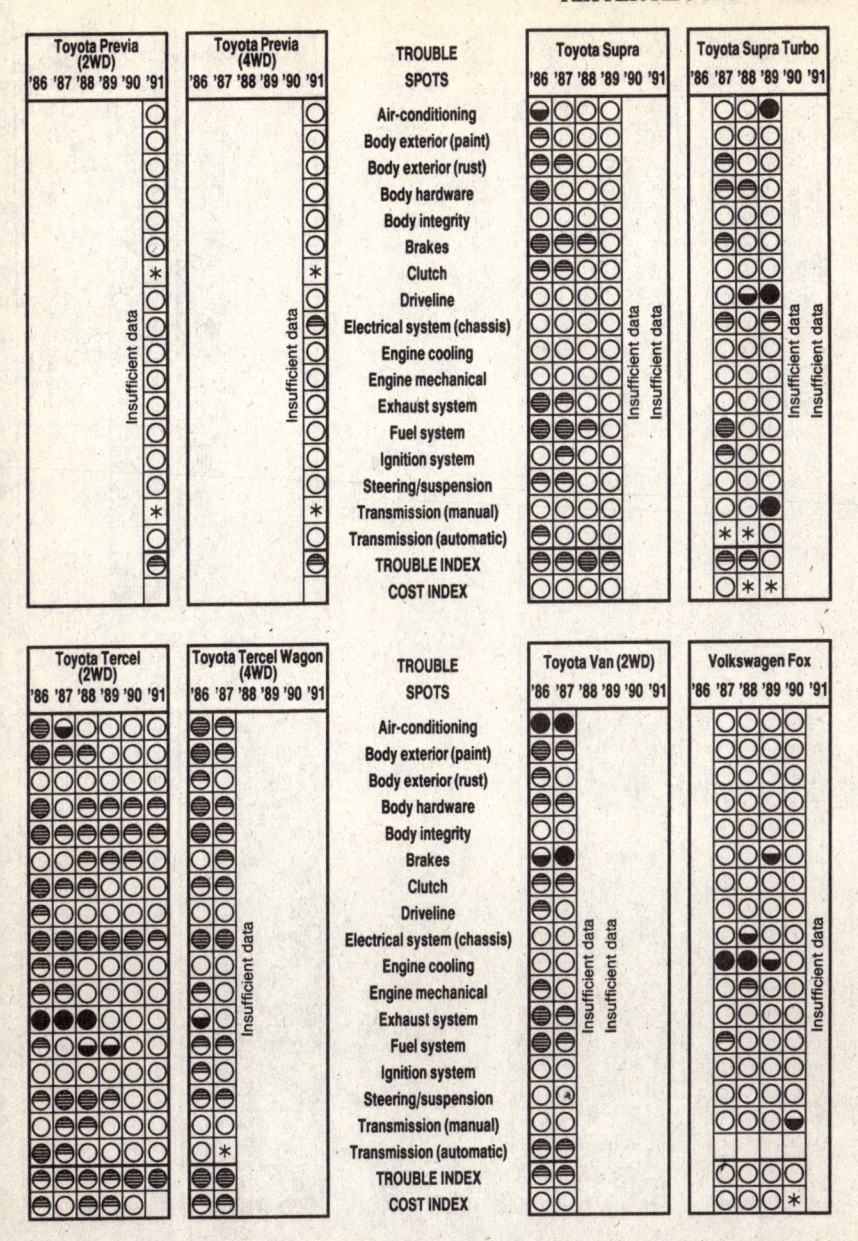

Previa (2WD): Insufficient data for '86–'90; '91 data shown.
Previa (4WD): Insufficient data for '86–'90; '91 data shown.
Supra: data '86–'89; Insufficient data '90–'91.
Supra Turbo: data '86–'89; Insufficient data '90–'91.

Trouble Spots	Toyota Tercel (2WD) '86–'91	Toyota Tercel Wagon (4WD) '86–'91	Toyota Van (2WD) '86–'91	Volkswagen Fox '86–'91

Tercel Wagon (4WD): data '86–'87; Insufficient data '88–'91.
Toyota Van (2WD): data '86–'87; Insufficient data '88–'91.
Volkswagen Fox: data '87–'90; Insufficient data '91.

356 REPAIR RECORDS

Legend:
- ✱ Insufficient data
- ● Much worse than average
- ◐ Worse than average
- ○ Average
- ◑ Better than average
- ◉ Much better than average

TROUBLE SPOTS	Volkswagen Golf, GTI '86–'91	Volkswagen Jetta '86–'91	Volkswagen Passat '86–'91	Volkswagen Vanagon (2WD) '86–'91
Air-conditioning				
Body exterior (paint)				
Body exterior (rust)				
Body hardware				
Body integrity				
Brakes				
Clutch				
Driveline				
Electrical system (chassis)				
Engine cooling				
Engine mechanical				
Exhaust system				
Fuel system				
Ignition system				
Steering/suspension				
Transmission (manual)				
Transmission (automatic)				
TROUBLE INDEX				
COST INDEX				

TROUBLE SPOTS	Volvo 240 Series '86–'91	Volvo 740 Series '86–'91	Volvo 740 Series Turbo '86–'91	Volvo 760 Series Turbo '86–'91
Air-conditioning				
Body exterior (paint)				
Body exterior (rust)				
Body hardware				
Body integrity				
Brakes				
Clutch				
Driveline				
Electrical system (chassis)				
Engine cooling				
Engine mechanical				
Exhaust system				
Fuel system				
Ignition system				
Steering/suspension				
Transmission (manual)				
Transmission (automatic)				
TROUBLE INDEX				
COST INDEX				

Owner Satisfaction

"Would you buy that car again?" is a question we ask hundreds of thousands of subscribers on each year's Annual Questionnaire. As might be expected, owner satisfaction starts to slip as a car ages. On average, the newest cars in our survey—the 1991 models—won a 93 percent vote of confidence from owners. That average drops to 91 and 87 percent for 1990 and 1989 models, respectively. Scores for the worst cars plunge even more dramatically after only a year or two.

With satisfaction so uniformly high for 1991 cars, we turned our attention to the 1989 and 1990 models. The table below translates our readers' yes and no votes into a satisfaction index for some 200 models. For a 1990 vehicle to earn an above or below average score, it had to differ from the model-year average by 5 percentage points; to earn well above or well below average, the car had to be some 10 points away from the average. Comparable spreads for 1989 models were 3 and 6 percentage points. We haven't included cars no longer available in 1992 and cars with too few votes to be judged reliably.

OWNER SATISFACTION

Better ← ⊜ ⊖ ○ ◐ ● → Worse

Make & model	1989	1990
Acura Integra	⊖	⊖
Acura Legend	⊖	⊖
Audi 5000, 100, 200	○	⊖
BMW 325i	○	○
BMW 5 Series	○	○
BMW 7 Series	[1]	○
Buick Century 4	○	◐
Buick Century V6	○	○
Buick Le Sabre V6	⊜	⊖
Buick Park Avenue	⊖	○
Buick Regal V6 (FWD)	◐	○
Buick Riviera V6	○	○
Buick Skylark 4	○	●
Cadillac Brougham (RWD)	○	○
Cadillac DeVille, Fleetwood	⊖	○
Cadillac Eldorado	○	○
Cadillac Seville	⊖	○
Chevrolet Astro Van V6	○	◐
Chevrolet Astro Van V6 (4WD)	[2]	○

Make & model	1989	1990
Chevrolet Blazer (4WD)	◐	●
Chevrolet Camaro V8	●	◐
Chevrolet Caprice V8	○	○
Chevrolet Cavalier 4	◐	◐
Chevrolet Cavalier V6	◐	◐
Chevrolet Corsica, Beretta 4	●	●
Chevrolet Corsica, Beretta V6	●	●
Chevrolet Corvette	○	○
Chevrolet Lumina 4	[2]	●
Chevrolet Lumina V6	[2]	◐
Chevrolet Lumina APV	[2]	○
Chevrolet Pickup C/K 10/1500-20/2600 6, V6	○	○
Chevrolet Pickup C/K 10/1500-20/2600 V8	○	○
Chevrolet Pickup K 10/1500-20/2600 V8 (4WD)	○	○
Chevrolet S10 Blazer V6	◐	●
Chevrolet S10 Blazer V6 (4WD)	◐	◐

[1] *Insufficient data.* [2] *Not marketed in model year.*

Listings continued

358 OWNER SATISFACTION

Make & model	1989	1990
Chevrolet S10 Pickup 4	●	●
Chevrolet S10 Pickup V6	○	●
Chevrolet S10 Pickup V6 (4WD)	◐	◐
Chevrolet Sportvan V8	○	●
Chevrolet Suburban	○	○
Chevrolet Suburban (4WD)	○	○
Chrysler Imperial	[2]	○
Chrysler Le Baron V6	[2]	○
Chrysler Le Baron Coupe 4	◐	[1]
Chrysler Le Baron Coupe 4 (turbo)	◐	[1]
Chrysler Le Baron Coupe V6	[2]	○
Chrysler New Yorker V6 (FWD)	○	○
Chrysler New Yorker Fifth Avenue V6 (FWD)	[2]	◐
Dodge Caravan 4	○	○
Dodge Caravan V6	○	○
Dodge Grand Caravan V6	○	○
Dodge Colt	⊖	○
Dodge Dakota Pickup V6	○	○
Dodge Dakota Pickup V6 (4WD)	◐	[1]
Dodge Daytona 4	●	[1]
Dodge Daytona V6	[2]	○
Dodge Dynasty 4	○	[1]
Dodge Dynasty V6	○	◐
Dodge Ram 50 Pickup 4	○	[1]
Dodge Ram Pickup D100-250 V8	○	○
Dodge Ram Van/Wagon B150-250 V8	○	○
Dodge Shadow	◐	○
Dodge Spirit 4	⊖	⊖
Dodge Spirit 4 (turbo)	○	[1]
Dodge Spirit V6	○	○
Eagle Premier V6	●	●
Eagle Summit (Hatchback & Wagon)	⊖	○
Eagle Talon	[2]	○
Eagle Talon (4WD)	[2]	⊖
Ford Aerostar Van	○	○
Ford Aerostar Van (4WD)	[2]	○

Make & model	1989	1990
Ford Bronco V8 (4WD)	○	○
Ford Club Wagon V8	○	○
Ford Escort	⊖	●
Ford Festiva	⊖	⊖
Ford LTD Crown Victoria	⊖	○
Ford Mustang 4	●	●
Ford Mustang V8	○	○
Ford Pickup F150-250 6	⊖	○
Ford Pickup F150-250 6 (4WD)	○	○
Ford Pickup F150-250 V8	○	○
Ford Pickup F150-250 V8 (4WD)	○	○
Ford Probe 4	⊖	○
Ford Probe 4 (gas, turbo)	⊖	○
Ford Probe V6	[2]	○
Ford Ranger Pickup 4	○	◐
Ford Ranger Pickup V6	○	○
Ford Ranger Pickup V6 (4WD)	⊖	○
Ford Taurus V6	⊖	⊖
Ford Tempo 4	●	●
Ford Tempo 4 (4WD)	●	[1]
Ford Thunderbird V6	○	○
Ford Thunderbird SC V6	[1]	○
Geo Metro	○	◐
Geo Prizm	[1]	○
Geo Storm	[2]	●
Geo Tracker	[1]	○
GMC S15 Jimmy V6	○	[1]
GMC S15 Jimmy V6 (4WD)	○	○
Honda Accord	⊖	⊖
Honda CRX	⊖	⊖
Honda Civic	⊖	⊖
Honda Civic Wagon (4WD)	[1]	⊖
Honda Prelude	⊖	○
Hyundai Excel	●	●
Hyundai Sonata 4	●	●
Infiniti M30	[2]	○
Infiniti Q45	[2]	⊖
Isuzu Pickup	○	○
Isuzu Trooper II, Trooper 4 (4WD)	○	○

OWNER SATISFACTION

Make & model	1989	1990
Isuzu Trooper II, Trooper V6 (4WD)	○	○
Jaguar XJ6	●	○
Jeep Cherokee 6	○	○
Jeep Cherokee 6 (4WD)	○	●
Jeep Wrangler 6 (4WD)	◐	●
Lexus LS 400	[2]	⊖
Lincoln Continental V6 (FWD)	◐	○
Lincoln Mark VII	◐	○
Lincoln Town Car	⊖	⊖
Mazda 323, Protege	⊖	⊖
Mazda 626	⊖	⊖
Mazda 929	⊖	⊖
Mazda MX-5 Miata	[2]	⊖
Mazda MX-6	○	○
Mazda MX-6 (turbo)	○	[1]
Mazda MPV 4	⊖	○
Mazda MPV V6	⊖	⊖
Mazda MPV V6 (4WD)	[1]	⊖
Mazda Pickup	⊖	⊖
Mazda RX-7	○	○
Mercedes-Benz 190 Series 6	○	○
Mercedes-Benz 300 Series	⊖	○
Mercury Cougar V6	○	◐
Mercury Grand Marquis	⊖	○
Mercury Sable V6	⊖	⊖
Mercury Topaz 4	●	●
Mercury Tracer	⊖	○
Mitsubishi Eclipse	[2]	○
Mitsubishi Eclipse (4WD) (turbo)	[2]	⊖
Mitsubishi Galant 4	⊖	⊖
Mitsubishi Mirage	○	○
Mitsubishi Montero V6 (4WD)	○	⊖
Mitsubishi Pickup 4	○	○
Nissan 240SX	○	○
Nissan 300ZX	[1]	⊖
Nissan Maxima	⊖	⊖
Nissan Pathfinder (4WD)	⊖	⊖

Make & model	1989	1990
Nissan Pickup 4	⊖	○
Nissan Pickup 4 (4WD)	[1]	○
Nissan Pickup V6	○	○
Nissan Pulsar NX	○	[1]
Nissan Sentra	○	○
Nissan Stanza	⊖	⊖
Oldsmobile 88 V6	○	○
Oldsmobile 98 V6	○	○
Oldsmobile Custom Cruiser Wagon V8	○	[1]
Oldsmobile Cutlass Calais 4	○	◐
Oldsmobile Cutlass Supreme 4 (FWD)	[2]	◐
Oldsmobile Cutlass Supreme V6 (FWD)	◐	◐
Oldsmobile Cutlass Ciera 4	○	○
Oldsmobile Cutlass Ciera V6	○	◐
Oldsmobile Toronado	[1]	○
Oldsmobile Silhouette	[2]	⊖
Plymouth Acclaim 4	⊖	○
Plymouth Acclaim V6	○	○
Plymouth Colt	⊖	⊖
Plymouth Laser	[2]	⊖
Plymouth Laser (gas, turbo)	[2]	⊖
Plymouth Sundance	◐	○
Plymouth Voyager 4	○	○
Plymouth Voyager V6	○	○
Plymouth Grand Voyager V6	○	○
Pontiac Bonneville (FWD)	⊖	⊖
Pontiac Firebird V8	●	[1]
Pontiac Grand Am 4	◐	◐
Pontiac Grand Prix V6 (FWD)	○	○
Pontiac Le Mans	●	[1]
Pontiac Sunbird 4	◐	●
Pontiac TransSport	[2]	⊖
Saab 900	◐	○
Saab 900 (turbo)	[1]	[1]
Saab 9000	○	○
Saab 9000 (turbo)	○	[1]
Subaru Justy	◐	[1]
Subaru Legacy	[2]	○

[1] *Insufficient data.*

[2] *Not marketed in model year.*

Listings continued

360 OWNER SATISFACTION

Make & model	1989	1990
Subaru Legacy (4WD)	2	⊖
Subaru Loyale	2	○
Subaru Loyale (4WD)	2	○
Suzuki Sidekick (4WD)	○	1
Toyota Camry 4	⊖	⊖
Toyota Camry 4 (4WD)	⊖	○
Toyota Camry V6	⊖	⊖
Toyota Celica	⊖	⊖
Toyota Corolla (FWD)	⊖	⊖
Toyota Corolla (4WD)	⊖	⊖
Toyota Cressida	⊖	⊖
Toyota 4Runner 4 (4WD)	⊖	○
Toyota 4Runner V6 (4WD)	⊖	○
Toyota Land Cruiser Wagon	⊖	1

Make & model	1989	1990
Toyota MR2	○	2
Toyota Pickup 4	⊖	⊖
Toyota Pickup 4 (4WD)	⊖	⊖
Toyota Pickup V6	○	⊖
Toyota Pickup V6 (4WD)	⊖	⊖
Toyota Supra	○	1
Toyota Supra (gas, turbo)	⊖	1
Toyota Tercel	○	○
VW Fox	●	●
VW Golf	●	●
VW Jetta	○	●
Volvo 240 Series	○	○
Volvo 740 Series	○	○
Volvo 740 Series (turbo)	○	○

1 *Insufficient data.*
2 *Not marketed in model year.*

How objective is CU?

Consumers Union is not beholden to any commercial interest. It accepts no advertising and buys all the products tested on the open market. CU's income is derived from the sale of CONSUMER REPORTS and other publications, and from non-restrictive, noncommercial contributions, grants, and fees. Neither the Ratings nor the reports may be used in advertising or for any other commercial purpose. Consumers Union will take all steps open to it to prevent commercial use of its materials, its name, or the name of CONSUMER REPORTS.

REPAIR HISTORIES

Washing machines 362	VCRs 366
Clothes dryers 362	13-inch TVs............................367
Side-by-side refrigerators 363	19- and 20-inch TVs 367
Top-freezer refrigerators 363	25- to 27-inch TVs 368
Microwave ovens 364	Compact-disc players 369
Dishwashers 365	Lawn mowers 370
Ranges 365	

Every year, CONSUMER REPORTS asks its subscribers to share their experiences with various products by answering questions on the Annual Questionnaire. One result is the automobile Frequency-of-Repair charts, which you'll find in the auto chapter. Another result is what you'll find in this chapter—repair histories for various brands of major appliances and electronics items.

The graphs that follow represent the percent of products in each brand that have ever been repaired, as reported to us by subscribers in the survey. It's important to keep two things in mind: Repair histories apply only to brands, not to specific models of these products. And the histories, being histories, can only suggest future trends, not predict them exactly. A company can at any time change its products' design or quality control so substantially as to affect their reliability. But our findings over the years have been consistent enough that we are confident the repair histories presented here can greatly improve your chances of getting a more trouble-free brand of clothes dryer, range, TV set, or other product.

Note, too, that the repair histories of different products are not directly comparable. Data for each graph have been adjusted differently—to compensate for differing age distributions, for instance—and the experiences summed up by different graphs may cover different years of purchase. For example, the electronics products our readers own have generally been purchased more recently than their appliances. The electronics items thus have had fewer years in service for problems to occur. The text associated with each graph explains exactly what type of product is covered and whether any special assumptions were made in the graph's preparation.

Use these graphs in conjunction with the product reports elsewhere in the Buying Guide. You'll find the most recent repair histories in the pages of the monthly CONSUMER REPORTS.

WASHING MACHINES

Based on nearly 255,000 responses to our 1991 Annual Questionnaire. Readers were asked about any repairs to a full-sized washer bought new between 1981 and 1991. Data have been standardized to eliminate differences among brands due solely to age. Differences of less than 3 points aren't meaningful.

TOP-LOADING WASHERS (Fewer ← Repairs → More)

- Hotpoint
- Maytag
- General Electric
- Whirlpool
- Speed Queen
- Sears
- Montgomery Ward
- White-Westinghouse
- Frigidaire

FRONT-LOADING WASHERS

- White-Westinghouse

Scale: 0% – 40%

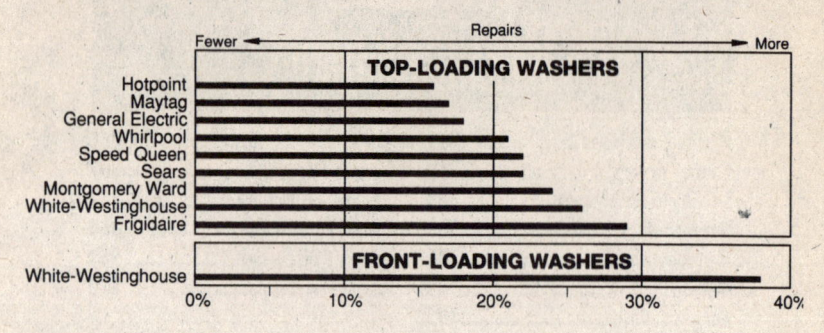

CLOTHES DRYERS

Based on more than 185,000 responses to our 1991 Annual Questionnaire. Readers were asked about any repairs to a full-sized (electric or gas) clothes dryer bought new between 1984 and 1991. Data have been standardized to eliminate differences among brands due solely to age. Differences of less than 3 points aren't meaningful.

ELECTRIC DRYERS (Fewer ← Repairs → More)

- Maytag
- Whirlpool
- Hotpoint
- Amana
- General Electric
- Sears
- Speed Queen
- White-Westinghouse
- Montgomery Ward
- Frigidaire

GAS DRYERS

- Whirlpool
- Sears
- Hotpoint
- Speed Queen
- General Electric
- Maytag
- White-Westinghouse

Scale: 0% – 40%

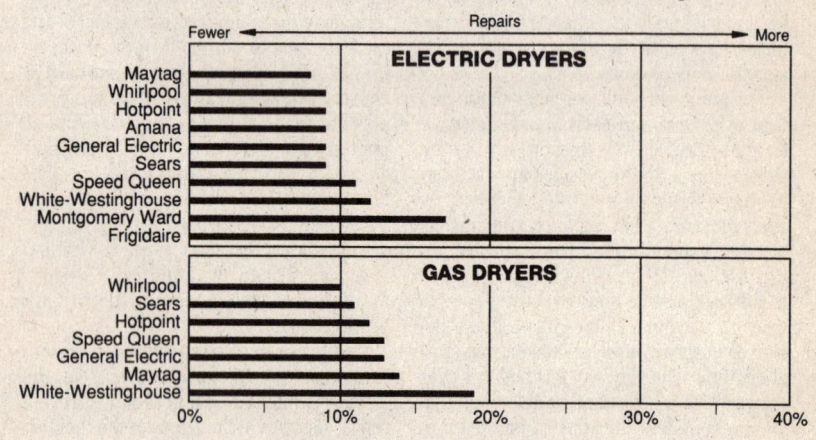

REPAIR HISTORIES 363

SIDE-BY-SIDE REFRIGERATORS

Based on almost 24,000 responses to our 1991 Annual Questionnaire. Readers were asked about any repairs to side-by-side, two-door, no-frost refrigerators bought new between 1985 and 1991. Data have been standardized to eliminate differences among brands due solely to age. Differences of less than 4 points aren't meaningful.

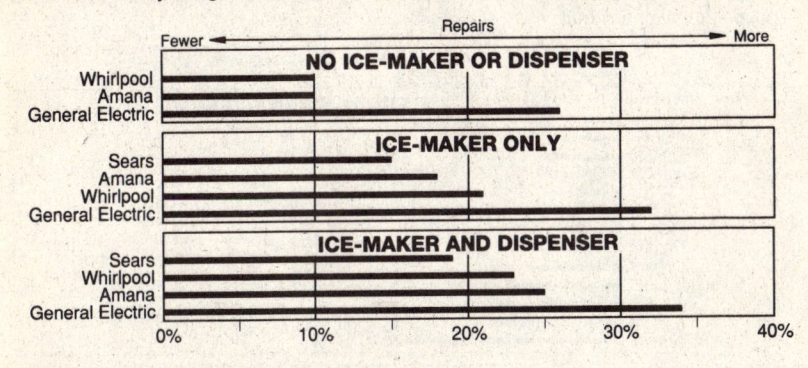

NO ICE-MAKER OR DISPENSER
- Whirlpool
- Amana
- General Electric

ICE-MAKER ONLY
- Sears
- Amana
- Whirlpool
- General Electric

ICE-MAKER AND DISPENSER
- Sears
- Whirlpool
- Amana
- General Electric

TOP-FREEZER REFRIGERATORS

Based on over 98,000 responses to our 1991 Annual Questionnaire. Readers were asked about any repairs to top-freezer, two-door, no-frost refrigerators bought new between 1984 and 1991. Data have been standardized to eliminate differences among brands due solely to age. Differences of less than 3 points aren't meaningful.

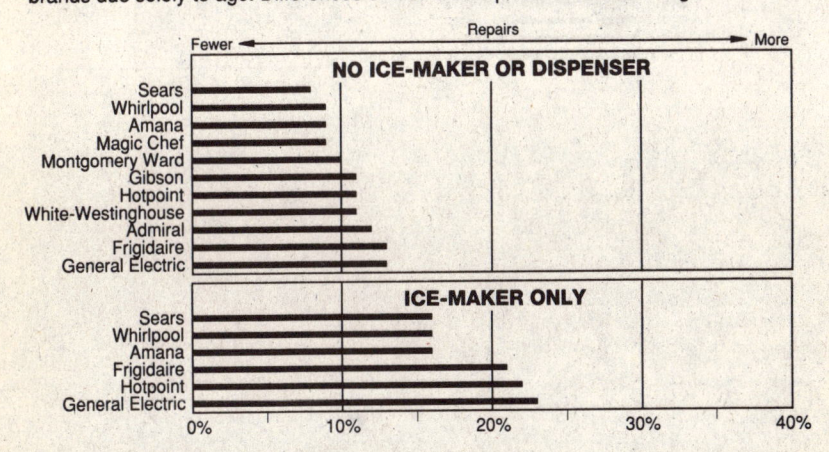

NO ICE-MAKER OR DISPENSER
- Sears
- Whirlpool
- Amana
- Magic Chef
- Montgomery Ward
- Gibson
- Hotpoint
- White-Westinghouse
- Admiral
- Frigidaire
- General Electric

ICE-MAKER ONLY
- Sears
- Whirlpool
- Amana
- Frigidaire
- Hotpoint
- General Electric

MICROWAVE OVENS

Based on over 135,000 responses to our 1991 Annual Questionnaire. Readers were asked about any repairs to intermediate- and full-sized microwave ovens with electronic touch controls bought new between 1986 and 1991. Data have been standardized to eliminate differences among brands due solely to age. Differences of less than 3 points aren't meaningful.

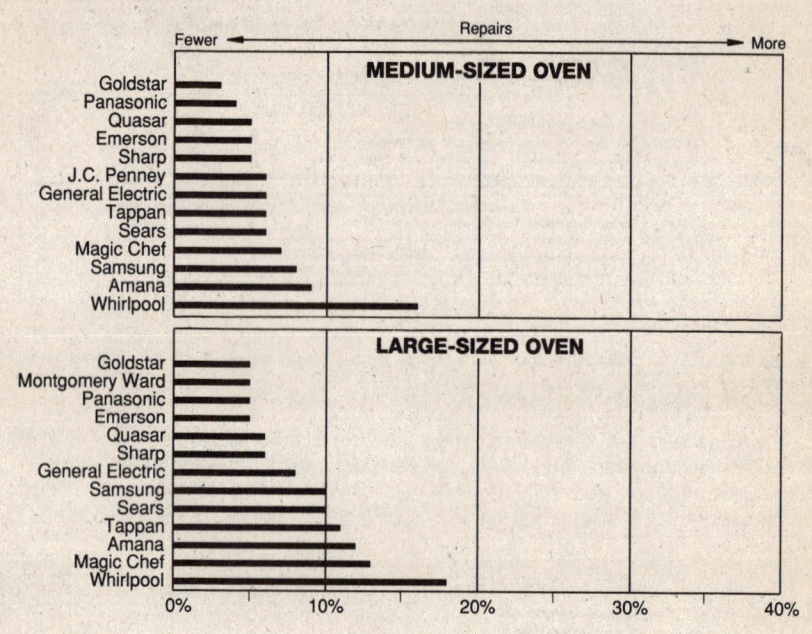

MEDIUM-SIZED OVEN

(Fewer ← Repairs → More)

- Goldstar
- Panasonic
- Quasar
- Emerson
- Sharp
- J.C. Penney
- General Electric
- Tappan
- Sears
- Magic Chef
- Samsung
- Amana
- Whirlpool

LARGE-SIZED OVEN

- Goldstar
- Montgomery Ward
- Panasonic
- Emerson
- Quasar
- Sharp
- General Electric
- Samsung
- Sears
- Tappan
- Amana
- Magic Chef
- Whirlpool

(Scale: 0% – 10% – 20% – 30% – 40%)

REPAIR HISTORIES 365

DISHWASHERS

Based on over 154,000 responses to our 1991 Annual Questionnaire. Readers were asked about any repairs to installed dishwashers bought new between 1986 and 1991. Data have been standardized to eliminate differences among brands due solely to age and how much the dishwashers were used. Differences of less than 3 points aren't meaningful.

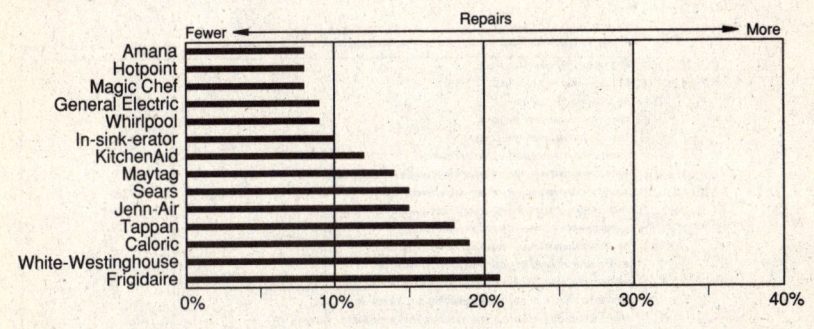

RANGES

Based on more than 39,000 responses to our 1991 Annual Questionnaire. Readers were asked about any repairs to a freestanding, single-oven, self-cleaning (electric or gas) range bought new between 1986 and 1991. Data have been standardized to eliminate differences among brands due solely to age. Differences of less than 4 points aren't meaningful. Repair rates for White-Westinghouse varied somewhat by purchase year.

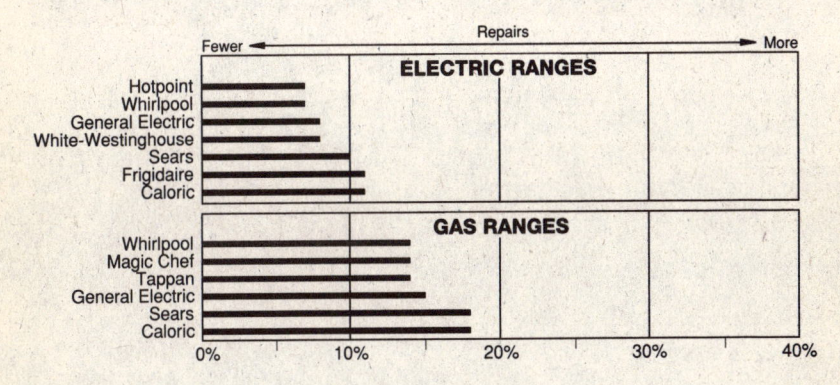

VCRs

Based on over 177,000 responses to our 1991 Annual Questionnaire. Readers were asked about any repairs to VCRs bought new between 1986 and 1991. Except for Sony, all are VHS format. Data have been standardized to eliminate differences among brands due solely to age and how much the VCRs were used. Differences of less than 3 points aren't meaningful.

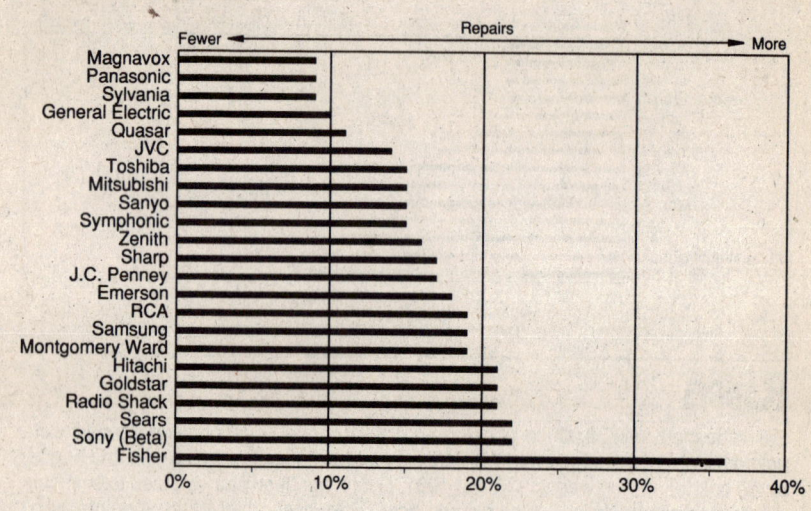

Brand	Repairs
Magnavox	~9%
Panasonic	~9%
Sylvania	~9%
General Electric	~9%
Quasar	~11%
JVC	~14%
Toshiba	~15%
Mitsubishi	~15%
Sanyo	~15%
Symphonic	~15%
Zenith	~16%
Sharp	~16%
J.C. Penney	~17%
Emerson	~18%
RCA	~18%
Samsung	~19%
Montgomery Ward	~19%
Hitachi	~21%
Goldstar	~21%
Radio Shack	~21%
Sears	~22%
Sony (Beta)	~22%
Fisher	~36%

REPAIR HISTORIES

TELEVISION SETS: 13-INCH

Based on more than 56,000 responses to our 1991 Annual Questionnaire. Readers were asked about any repairs to a 13-inch color TV bought new between 1986 and 1991. Data have been standardized to eliminate differences among brands due solely to age. Differences of less than 3 points aren't meaningful.

Repairs: Fewer ← → More

Brand	
Hitachi	
Panasonic	
JVC	
Sharp	
Mitsubishi	
Montgomery Ward	
Toshiba	
RCA	
Sears	
Quasar	
J.C. Penney	
Sony	
Zenith	
Emerson	
General Electric	
Goldstar	
Magnavox	
Sylvania	

Scale: 0% — 10% — 20% — 30% — 40%

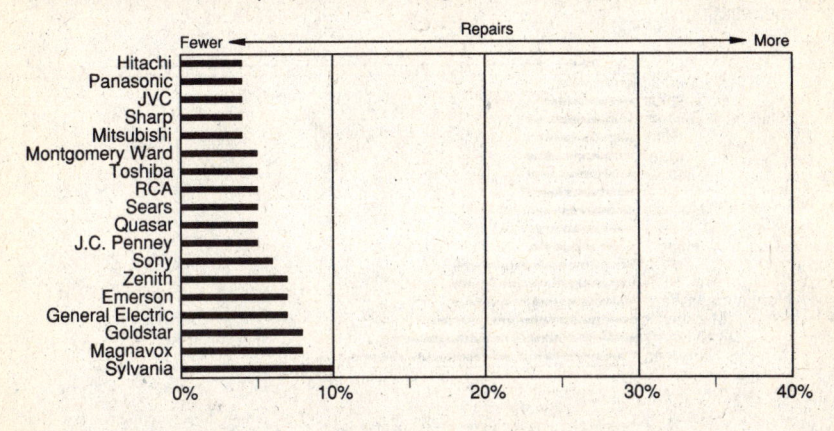

TELEVISION SETS: 19-INCH AND 20-INCH

Based on over 121,000 responses to our 1991 Annual Questionnaire. Readers were asked about any repairs to a 19-inch or 20-inch color TV with remote control bought new between 1985 and 1991. Data have been standardized to eliminate differences among brands due solely to age. Differences of less than 3 points aren't meaningful.

Repairs: Fewer ← → More

Brand	
Panasonic	
JVC	
Mitsubishi	
Toshiba	
Hitachi	
Quasar	
General Electric	
Sony	
Sears	
Sharp	
RCA	
Montgomery Ward	
Sanyo	
Magnavox	
Zenith	
Samsung	
Goldstar	
Sylvania	
Emerson	

Scale: 0% — 10% — 20% — 30% — 40%

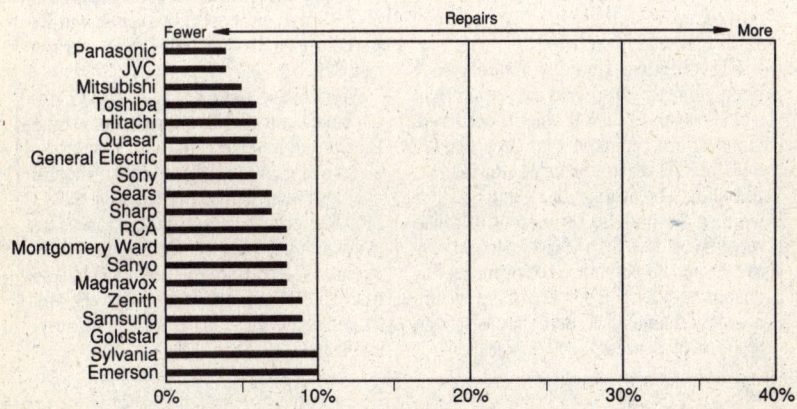

TELEVISION SETS: 25-INCH TO 27-INCH

Based on more than 97,000 responses to our 1991 Annual Questionnaire. Readers were asked about any repairs to a 25-inch to 27-inch color TV with remote control and stereo sound bought new between 1986 and 1991. Data have been standardized to eliminate differences among brands due solely to age. Differences of less than 3 points aren't meaningful.

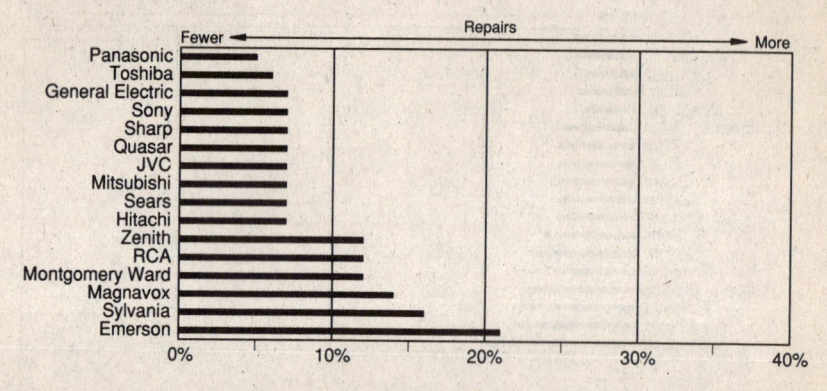

Brand	Repairs (Fewer → More)
Panasonic	~5%
Toshiba	~6%
General Electric	~7%
Sony	~7%
Sharp	~7%
Quasar	~7%
JVC	~7%
Mitsubishi	~7%
Sears	~7%
Hitachi	~7%
Zenith	~12%
RCA	~12%
Montgomery Ward	~12%
Magnavox	~14%
Sylvania	~16%
Emerson	~21%

HOW MUCH DO REPAIRS COST?

For some of the products whose repair histories are listed here, our surveys also collect information about repair costs. Here's what readers told us about the cost of repairing these products between April 1990 and March 1991.

CD players. Changer models have been slightly more repair-prone than single-players. When problems occurred, our readers reported that they usually took their player to a factory-authorized repair shop. The average bill: about $80. For single-play models, 18 percent of those repairs cost less than $50; 49 percent, $50 to $99; and 33 percent, $100 or more. For changer models, 16 percent of the repairs cost less than $50; 45 percent cost $50 to $99; and 39 percent, $100 or more.

VCRs. About one in six models purchased by our readers since 1986 has needed repairs. Of those models repaired since April 1990, 22 percent cost less than $50; 45 percent cost $50 to $99; and 33 percent cost $100 or more. The average bill: $79.

Microwave ovens. Large-sized models have been slightly more troublesome than medium-sized models. For large-sized ovens, 40 percent of those repairs cost less than $50; 29 percent cost $50 to $99; 31 percent cost $100 or more. The average repair bill: $70. For medium-sized ovens, 42 percent of the repairs cost less than $50; 31 percent cost $50 to $99; and 27 percent cost $100 or more. The average repair bill: $65.

COMPACT-DISC PLAYERS

Based on over 115,000 responses to our 1991 Annual Questionnaire. Readers were asked about any repairs to a single-play or changer tabletop model bought new between 1988 and 1991. Data have been standardized to eliminate differences among brands due solely to age and how much the CD players were used. Differences of less than 3 points aren't meaningful.

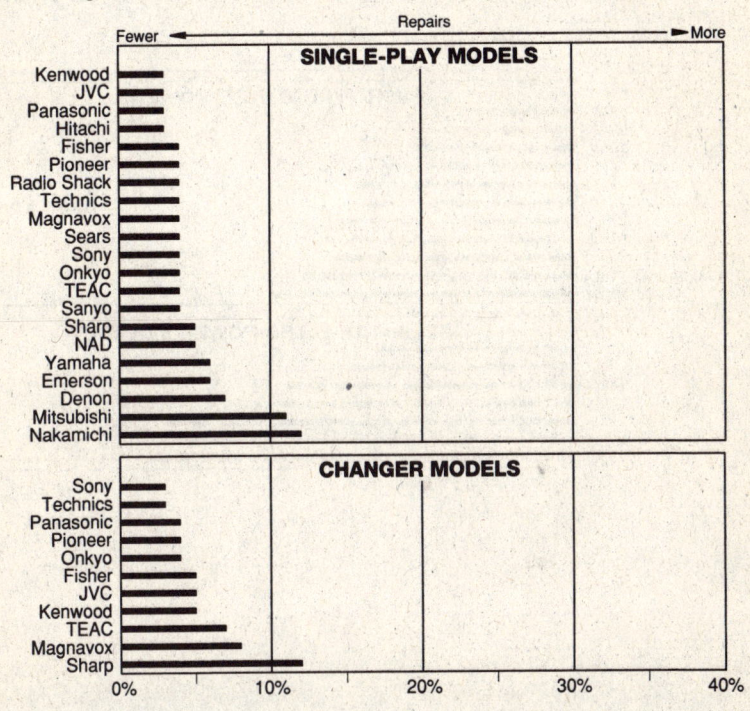

SINGLE-PLAY MODELS
(Fewer ← Repairs → More)

- Kenwood
- JVC
- Panasonic
- Hitachi
- Fisher
- Pioneer
- Radio Shack
- Technics
- Magnavox
- Sears
- Sony
- Onkyo
- TEAC
- Sanyo
- Sharp
- NAD
- Yamaha
- Emerson
- Denon
- Mitsubishi
- Nakamichi

CHANGER MODELS

- Sony
- Technics
- Panasonic
- Pioneer
- Onkyo
- Fisher
- JVC
- Kenwood
- TEAC
- Magnavox
- Sharp

(Scale: 0% – 40%)

Lawn mowers

Based on more than 52,000 responses to our 1991 Annual Questionnaire. Readers were asked about any repairs to a walk-behind (push or self-propelled) gasoline mower with between 3.5 and 5.0 horsepower and a cutting swath of 20 to 22 inches bought new between 1986 and 1991. Data have been standardized to eliminate differences among brands due solely to age. Differences of less than about 4 points aren't meaningful.

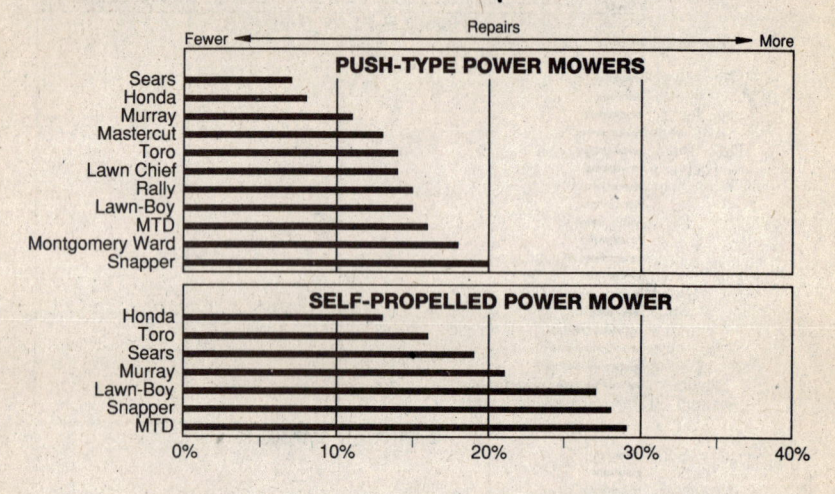

Fewer ← Repairs → More

PUSH-TYPE POWER MOWERS

Brand	Repairs
Sears	~7%
Honda	~8%
Murray	~11%
Mastercut	~13%
Toro	~14%
Lawn Chief	~14%
Rally	~15%
Lawn-Boy	~15%
MTD	~16%
Montgomery Ward	~18%
Snapper	~20%

SELF-PROPELLED POWER MOWER

Brand	Repairs
Honda	~13%
Toro	~16%
Sears	~19%
Murray	~21%
Lawn-Boy	~27%
Snapper	~28%
MTD	~29%

PRODUCT RECALLS

Children's products	371	Motorcycles	384
Household	375	Motor homes, trailers	385
Cars	377	Vehicle accessories	385
Trucks & vans	381	Miscellaneous	386
Child car seats	383		

Products ranging from cars to toys are recalled when there are safety defects. Various Federal agencies—the Consumer Product Safety Commission, the National Highway Traffic Safety Administration, the U. S. Coast Guard—monitor consumer complaints and injuries and, when there's a problem, issue a recall. A selection of those recalls are published monthly in CONSUMER REPORTS. This section covers recalls from October 1991 through October 1992. For the latest information, see the current issue of CONSUMER REPORTS.

CHILDREN'S PRODUCTS

Aprica Rockin Rollin Rider toy car.
Could tip and injure child.

Products: 400 toys, model 92090, sold in '91 for $110-$120. Ride-on car can be converted to rocking toy or push-walker. "Aprica" appears in white lettering on both sides and is molded into bottom of yellow plastic rocker base.
What to do: Return toy to store for refund.

Big Bird battery-powered toothbrush.
If batteries are installed improperly and leak, hazardous material could seep out of device and cause serious injury.

Products: 330,000 toothbrushes, marketed under the Ideal and Tyco brands, sold '86-91 for $10.
What to do: For refund, mail toothbrush to Tyco Ind. Toothbrush Recall, 540 Glen Ave., Moorestown, N.J. 08057.

Blue Box Toys Activity Water Ball.
Could break into small parts and choke child.

Products: 15,000 toys, model 33012, sold 2/91-12/91 for $10. Yellow plastic ball is 6½ in. in diameter and has large tube down middle with magnifying glass and handle on one end and flip-up screen on other. Embossed on screen: "Blue-Box Toys, Made in Singapore." Ball also contains 4 activities: red paddle wheel, pink circle with blue button, retractable pink fish attached to 11-in. cord, and "aquarium" with 5 fish and pinwheel.
What to do: Return toy to store for refund.

Buddy L. Motorized Zipper toy airplanes.
Wings may break into small parts and choke child.

Products: 267,000 toys, models 3135, 3137, 4160, 4635, and 4637, sold 1/89-2/91 individually or in packs of 2, 3, or 4, for $2-$7.50 each. Airplane is 3 in. long with 2¼-in. wingspan, has 3 black tires, and comes in various colors. Embossed on bottom of toy are words "BUDDY L CORP. 1989 PATENT PENDING MADE IN CHINA." Some toys have "BUDDY L" printed on sides. Package labeling reads in part, "Pull 'Em Back Let 'em Zip!"
What to do: Return toy to store for refund.

Butterfly bracelet.
Could break, releasing small parts that could choke child.

Products: 12,000 bracelets sold at school and church carnivals and in stores in Ariz., Colo., Ill., and Kan. 7/90-2/91 for 20¢. Bracelets consist of small yellow, orange, green, and pink plastic butterflies about 3/8 inch wide, strung together on elastic string with black beads between butterflies.
What to do: Return toy to store for refund.

Childcraft cribs.
Slats may be loose or missing, posing entrapment hazard.

Products: 1735 cribs, models 15811, 15821, 15961, and 15991, sold after 9/88. Model number appears on bottom of headboard.
What to do: Check side rails. If slats are loose or missing, return side rails to store for replacement.

Cosco Youth Options toddler beds with arched headboard and footboard.
Child's head could become trapped between arches or between mattress and arch, resulting in serious injury or death.

Products: 155,000 red or white tubular steel beds sold 12/90-3/15/92 for $50. Check label on mattress support; recalled beds contain code 10T22 or 10T23.
What to do: Call 800-468-0174 to receive modified parts. Before calling, note date code on label and measure distance between top 2 arches of headboard so Cosco can provide appropriate modification parts.

Disney Poppin' Sounds Pull Train by Mattel.
If toy breaks, small balls in smokestack dome could fall out and choke child.

Products: 400,000 toys sold '90-91.
What to do: Return toy to Nancy Nelson, Mattel Consumer Affairs, 15930 E. Valley Blvd., City of Industry, Calif. 91744. Consumers will receive refund and discount coupon toward purchase of any Mattel toy.

Esco Imports toy nursing bottle.
Nipple could come off and choke child.

Products: 600,000 toys sold 5/82-1/91 in Ia., Ill., Ind., Ky., La., Mich., Miss., N.Y., Ohio, Okla., Tex., Utah, and Wisc. for 29¢-59¢. Toy is 3 in. high with rubber nipple and pink or blue cap. Label reads "Polythene Nursing Bottle...Esco...3/211...Made in China." Some are marked "Bottle Baby."
What to do: Return toy to store for refund.

Evenflo Disney pacifiers.
Cartoon character on pacifier could come off and choke child.

Products: Pacifiers decorated with Mickey Mouse, Minnie Mouse, Donald Duck, or Daisy Duck characters, sold 12/90-7/91 for $2-$3.
What to do: Mail pacifier to Evenflo, P.O. Box 1206, Ravenna, Ohio 44266-1206 for replacement or refund.

GapKids baby booties.
Decorative button could come off and choke child.

Products: 5000 booties sold 9/9-10/2/91. Corduroy booties, available in sizes 0-3, are navy, burgundy, yellow, green, or purple, with button sewn on top of Velcro flap fastener.
What to do: Return booties to store for refund and bonus $15 gift certificate.

Good Lad Co. toddler girls' two-piece outfits.
Decorative buttons could come off and choke child. Also, decorative pin poses puncture hazard.

Products: 360 outfits consisting of solid-colored shirt and striped skirt with suspenders, sold 3/91-4/91 for $19. Tag on neck seam of shirt pictures girl and boy dolls and reads in part: "PETE's PARTNER, A Good Lad Company, Made in Philippines."
What to do: Return outfit to store for refund.

Graco Converta-Cradle swing.
Could suffocate infant.

Products: 169,000 swings with straight (not curved) legs and cradle that swings infant from head to foot, sold since 1/90 for $99. Device consists of swing stand and motor, infant seat/carrier, and cradle. Recall involves only cradle portion of swing.
What to do: Call 1-800-942-1700 to learn how to get $25 refund or other Graco product.

PRODUCT RECALLS 373

House of Lloyd Infant's Playmat and Special Skunk toys.
Small parts could come off and choke child.

Products: 21,000 Special Skunk stuffed toys and 7200 Infant's Playmat toys sold at home demonstration parties 5/89-12/89. Skunk sold for $12, Playmat for $35. Playmat, sold as cat. no. 3182, stock no. 130189, measures 36 x 32 in. It has furry tan bear face with black button eyes, plastic nose, 1 striped cloth ear and 1 dotted cloth ear, striped bow at neck, quilted stomach, and 4 stuffed tan paws. Toy also comes with rattle, teething toy, and mirror that can be attached to one of three paws with Velcro. Fourth paw contains squeeze toy and applique of house. Front of paw says "TOUCH me." Black and white skunk, sold as cat. no. 4155, stock no. 510052, is 7½ in. tall and 3½ in. wide, has plastic eyes and nose, curled tail, and suction cups attached to legs and arms. Message on stomach:"GOD MADE ME SPECIAL."

What to do: For refund, return toy to House of Lloyd Inc., Merchandise Recall, 601 S. 291 Hwy., 5555 W. GeoSpace Dr., Independence, MO 64056.

Island Wood Products wooden swing sets (various brands).
Protruding bolts pose serious laceration hazard.

Products: 8500 swing sets with glider sold 9/89 through 1991 for $247-$550 under following names: Fort Apache, Islander, Kitty Hawk, Lookout Tower, Pirates Fort, and Treetop.

What to do: Call 800-729-5033 for new bolts and nuts.

Jak Pak Inc. Rain or Shine dolls.
Small parts could come off and choke child.

Products: 6939 dolls, model JP #0137, sold 1/90-12/91 for $2-$3. Brown plastic doll stands 6¼ in., has brown-rooted hair and painted facial features. It comes with removable raincoat that fastens with Velcro, removable shoes and socks, and nonremovable underwear. Doll's head, arms, and legs move at main body joints. Package label reads in part: "Rain or Shine Doll…1988 JAK PAK Inc. Milwaukee, Wisc. 53201, Made in China."

What to do: Return toy to store for refund.

Kenner Colorblaster pressurized-air spray art toy.
Toy could come apart forcefully and injure child.

Products: 292,000 toys, model 14290, sold 5/91-11/91 for $30. Toy consists of hand pump, plastic cylinder, and airbrush attached to cylinder. Only toys with L-shaped hooks used to lock handle to cap are affected. Recall does not apply to modified model 14290-02.

What to do: Return toy to store for refund or call 800-327-8264 for modified pump assembly.

Kransco Power Wheels Porsche battery-powered child's ride-on car.
Power switch could malfunction, resulting in inability to stop.

Products: 12,000 toys, powered by 18-volt battery, sold 8/21-10/1/91 for $359-$399. Models with 12-volt battery are not involved in recall.

What to do: Call 1-800-348-0751 for new switch and replacement instructions. Consumers may return unit to service center for repair.

Little Tykes Crib Center toy.
Excess lead in paint poses health hazard if ingested by child.

Products: 16,300 toys, model 1525, sold 11/91-1/92 for $20. Toy is designed to be mounted on crib rail and measures 18½ in. long, 3¾ in. wide, and 14½ in. high. It includes 9 activities, including red and white cylindrical candy-cane roller. Label on packaging reads in part: "CRIB CENTER, LITTLE TYKES, MADE IN USA." Model no. is molded on back of toy, next to company's toll-free telephone number. Recall does not affect redesigned toy with purple- and white-striped candy-cane roller.

What to do: Return toy to store for refund or exchange for other product.

Multicolored hollow plastic play cars.
Tires could come off and choke child.

Products: 10,000 car sets sold 9/1/89-12/91 for $3 mostly at the following stores: Bargain Time, Britts, Elmore, McCrory, H.L. Green, Kress, McClellan, T.G.& Y., Silver Kittinger, Newberry, and G.C. Murphy. 4½ in. cars have solid black tires and were sold in packages of eight, with two cars each in yellow, red, green, and blue. The words "INDUSTRIA ARGENTINA" are embossed on front and rear windshield wipers and undercarriage. Packaging reads in part: "Play Cars, 8 Colorful Freewheeling Cars. No. 25, Made in Argentina by Andresito."

What to do: Return toy to store for refund.

MYKIDS Bump-and-Go Wonder Loco train engine.
Wheels and axles could break into small parts and choke child.

Products: 4000 toys, model 7801, sold at Aldi supermarkets in Ill., Ind., Mo., Ohio, and Wisc., 10/20/91-11/2/91 for $5. Battery-operated engine is yellow, red, blue, and black with decals that read "No. 30 wonder Loco." Toy is 7 in. long, 7⅛ in. high, 5¼ in. wide, and has wind-up key on top. Engine has blinking lights and "steam" whistle.

What to do: Return toy to store for refund.

Newco Swing-N-Slide swing seats.
V-shaped hooks connecting belt seat to swing chains pose laceration hazard if not fully closed.

Products: 500,000 seats sold since 1986. Seats were sold separately or as part of Scout and Pioneer model swing kits. Seats with V hooks bear words "Swing-N-Slide."

What to do: Crimp or hammer hooks until metal touches. If hooks cannot be closed adequately, call 800-888-1232 for replacement hooks.

Novelty pacifier 'necklace' sold at Claire's Boutiques accessory stores.
Necklace is not intended for children; chain poses strangulation risk if worn around child's neck.

Products: 5943 necklaces sold 1/91-4/91 for $4. Latex pacifiers are clear or amber colored and have beaded or chain necklace attached to handle. Item was sold unpackaged.

What to do: Return to store for refund.

Peg Pounder workbench toy.
Small plastic nuts could choke child.

Products: 12,800 toys, model no. 8839, sold 9/89-11/89 for less than $2. Plastic toy consists of red workbench and 8 shape-sorting slots that hold matching yellow and blue pieces. Set also comes with yellow or blue hammer and wrench. Label on box reads in part: "Peg Pounder, BACO, Made in Yugoslavia for New Brite Products Ltd., Royton, Lancs, England."

What to do: Return toy to store for refund.

Ranger International Corp. Wooden Pre-school Puzzles (no. 401) and Mini Wooden Puzzles (no. 404).
Pegs and clock hands could come off and choke child.

Products: 1400 toys sold 1/90-6/91 for $4. Puzzles depict various pictorial scenes. Package labeling reads in part: "SUMMCO, Wooden Puzzle with Easy-Lift Knobs for Little Fingers, Ranger ..."

What to do: Return toy to store for refund.

Rawlings Batting Tee game.
Metal stake that anchors tethered ball could pull loose from ground, causing severe injuries.

Products: 16,000 games, model no. TBK-2, sold since 1987. Game has Rawlings name imprinted in red on white plastic home-plate stand.

What to do: Return game to store to receive redesigned batting tee.

Sesame Street nursery set.
Small parts could come off and choke child.

Products: 12,000 toys, style 71700, sold 2/91-9/91 for $4. Set consists of Ernie finger puppet with orange and yellow rubber duck, orange and yellow swing set, and blue bath tub on feet with white faucet and white handles. Packaging reads in part: "Nursery Set Finger Puppets with Accessories, Made in China, F.W. Woolworth Co., New York, N.Y."

What to do: Return toy to store for refund.

Sesame Street Big Bird and Happy Face Animal mouse and elephant pacifiers.
Could break into small parts and choke child.

Products: 844,000 pacifiers, made by Playskool Baby Inc., sold since 1989.

What to do: For refund, return pacifier to store or mail to Playskool Baby Inc., Consumer Service Dept., 200 Narragansett Park Dr., P.O. Box 200, Pawtucket, R.I. 02862-2000.

Sportcraft and Wilson (Foremost) Batting Tee games.
Metal U-shaped stake that anchors corded ball could come out of ground suddenly and forcefully, causing severe injury.

Products: 150,000 games sold under Sportcraft label since 1980, and 70,000 sets sold under Wilson name since 1986. Game consists of 5-sided stand, or "tee," and ball tethered to elastic cord anchored to ground with stake. Games with a 1¼-in. common washer tying ball directly to base are not being recalled. Brand name appears on base of stand.

What to do: Return game to store for refund.

Stuffed rabbit plush toy.
Eyes and nose could come off and choke child.

Products: 300,000 toys sold 1/92-3/92 for $4 or more. Toy is white, 14 in. high, with pink ears, feet, and nose. Attached tag reads in part: "Style #1011-1 Reg. No. PA.-3692 (RC)." Sold in stores including Boscov's, Hallmark, Venture, and Woolworth stores.

What to do: Return toy to store for refund.

Symphony Loco toy train.
Could break into small parts and choke child.

Products: 3850 battery-operated toys, style no. 3037, sold at Toy Liquidators stores 1/89-12/91 for $8. Toy consists of see-through, red-plastic locomotive and comes with built-in castanets, cymbals, xylophone, and drum. Stickers on both sides of engine show young boy conducting orchestra. Package reads in part: "Battery Operated Symphony Loco Mysterious Action, Made in Hong Kong, Distributed by Blue Box, New York, N.Y."

What to do: Return toy to store for refund.

PRODUCT RECALLS 375

Tara Toy Corp. Sesame Street Push Power action figures.
Toys could break into small, sharp pieces that pose choking and laceration hazards.

Products: 44,000 toys, item 75110, sold 6/91-1/92 for $4. Colorful plastic set consists of Big Bird driving red fire engine, Ernie riding on airplane, and Cookie Monster sitting on scooter with chocolate chip cookies on his back. Characters cannot be removed from vehicles. Embossed on underside of each vehicle is: "CTW JHP, INC. TARA TOY CORP. MADE IN CHINA."

What to do: Return toy to store for refund.

Wind-up Row n Row Boat plastic water toy.
Could break into small, sharp parts, injuring child.

Products: 2000 toys sold since 1/91 for $3. Toy is 5½-in. long and 3½-in. wide and contains either an alligator or hippopotamus. Hippopotamus, which is green and has soft rubber head with painted facial features, comes in boat with yellow oars, red deck, white bottom, and blue wind-up key. Alligator, which has yellow body and green soft rubber head with painted facial features, comes in boat with beige oars, blue deck, white bottom, and red wind-up key. Both boats are decorated with decals that resemble blue water.

What to do: Return toy to store for refund.

Wisdom Blocks Train Set wooden pull toy.
Small parts could come off and choke child.

Products: 3400 toys, model WP262, sold 3/89-5/89 for $7-$10. Toy measures 15½ in. long and 3½ in. high and consists of natural-wood engine and 2 natural-wood cars. Engine and cars each have 4 free-moving wheels. Cars have 3 blocks that sit on pegs. Each side of block contains letter of alphabet with picture and name of object that begins with that letter. Engine has smokestack, 1 alphabet block, and 28½-in. long pull string.

What to do: Return toy to store for refund.

World Wrestling Federation Sling 'Em-Fling 'Em toy wrestling ring.
Rigid corner posts pose risk of severe injury if child falls on them.

Products: 1.4 million toys sold 1985-89 for up to $20. Toy has 18½-in. square plastic base that's 3½ in. high. Four 9½-in. blue plastic posts snap in, one at each corner. Red, white, and blue elastic bands form ropes around ring. Molded into plastic on underside of ring are words: "1985 LJN TOYS LTD. TITAN SPORTS INC. MADE IN U.S.A."

What to do: Return ring posts to MCA Inc., parent company of LJN Toys, in exchange for free children's book. For information, call 1-800-531-9336.

HOUSEHOLD

Amana room air-conditioners.
Control switch could overheat on "Off" position and cause fire.

Products: 130,000 208/230-volt air-conditioners sold 6/87-10/91 for $500-$600. Recalled models include ES1123A (mfg. no. P6968407R and serial nos. 8707011078 to 8806126842); ES2183A (mfg. no. P9938605R, serial nos. 8709034615 to 8806086274); 12C3A (mfg. no. P6968413R, serial nos. 8808061439 to 9105092687); 12C3A (mfg. no. P6968419R, serial nos. 8810098399 to 8811057379); 12C3A (mfg. no. P6968420R, serial nos. 8908098339 to 9011051971); 12C3B (mfg. no. P1118108R, serial nos. 9106053390 to 9109199032); and 18C3SA (mfg. no. P9938613R, serial nos. 8810062411 to 9105078912). Identification nos. are beneath removable front grille. First four digits of serial no. stand for year and month of manufacture; thus, 8707 represents July 1987.

What to do: Unplug air-conditioner and have switch replaced. For nearest Amana service center, call 800-262-3121.

DeLonghi, Sears, and Welbilt portable heaters.
Could cause fire.

Products: 3.6 million oil-filled electric heaters made in 1980-88. Heaters are beige or tan and look like small radiators. DeLonghi heaters have silver sticker with two-digit code noting year of manufacture ('80-88) on underside of metal box housing controls. Recalled Sears and Welbilt models carry code no. 816F next to UL label on side of control box.

What to do: Phone 800-874-0981 for new control panel or to arrange for replacement panel.

Duracraft 16-in. brass- and platinum-plated fans.
Spinning fan blades could break and cause injury. Also, retaining clips may not hold grilles together.

Products: Model DP-161, selling for $40, and models DP-1601 and DP-1602, selling for $60.

What to do: Check bottom of fan base for date code; first two digits represent month of manufacture; last two, the year. If fan was made before 2/91, call 800-882-0064 for new blades, grille clips, instructions.

Hamilton Beach electric handheld mixers.
Fan in motor could break apart and fragments could contaminate food.

Products: 600,000 mixers, models 230 and 232, sold 4/90-4/91 for $10-$20. Model number and date code are on underside of mixer housing. Included on appliance nameplate are several cautionary statements, the name "Hamilton Beach Inc.," and "Made in China." Date codes are stamped in ink on housing near nameplate. Model 230 bears date codes 1290 to 1691 (12th week of '90 through 16th week of '91); model 232 carries codes 3890 to 1791.

What to do: Call 800-341-3333 to find out how to receive replacement mixer.

Micro-Dome food preserver.
Pressurized plastic container could explode during or after removal from microwave oven or if container is hit or dropped. Also, device may allow food to become dangerously contaminated.

Products: 18,600 food preservers sold since 9/87 for $50. Appliance was sold for use in microwave ovens to preserve fruit, vegetables, and prepared dishes. It can accommodate one standard metal-lidded canning jar at a time.

What to do: Call 800-736-2330 for instructions on getting $50 refund.

Mr. Coffee QB1 nonelectric microwave coffeemaker.
Cone-shaped brewer section could separate from cup and scald user.

Products: 338,850 coffeemakers sold 5/90-6/91 for $10-$13. Recall does not involve QB1 microwave coffeemaker with basket-type filter.

What to do: Remove metal blade from bottom of brewer and mail to Mr. Coffee, 24700 Miles Rd., Bedford Heights, Ohio 44146. Company will provide basket-style brewer section and replacement filters.

Norelco wrinkle remover/ fabric steamer.
Exposed wiring in power cord poses shock hazard.

Products: 56,880 steamers, model TS-60, distributed since 9/91 and sold for $17-$22.

What to do: Check date code stamped on metal blades of electric plug. If first three digits of four-digit code are 241 through 281, examine power cord for tears. Company says steamer is safe to use if no tears are present. If cord is damaged, return steamer to store or mail to Norelco Consumer Prods. Co., TS-60 Product Return Dept., 440 N. Medinah, Roselle, Ill. 60172. State whether you want replacement steamer or refund.

Nutone ceiling fans.
Mount could crack and allow fan to fall.

Products: 310,000 36-in. and 52-in. fans, sold 5/83-12/85, including Decorator, Hacienda, Sea Island, Slimline, and Verandah models.

What to do: Call 800-352-4287 to identify recalled devices and arrange for installation of redesigned mount.

Simplicity Deluxe garment steamer.
Fill plug could pop out, allowing hot water or steam to cause severe burns.

Products: 5600 electric steamers, models Y1211 and Y1237, sold in fabric stores since 8/89.

What to do: For refund, return steamer to store or mail it to Steamer Refund, c/o Pentapco Inc., 963 Newark Ave., P.O. Box 261, Elizabeth, N.J. 07207.

Toastmaster model D126T toaster.
Switch may not shut off heating element after toasting cycle, causing fire, burn, or shock hazard.

Products: 8857 chrome-finish toasters, bearing date codes EL101 to EL158, manufactured 4/89-6/89 and sold for $30-$35. Model number and date code appear on crumb tray.

What to do: For replacement toaster, phone 1-800-527-3069 or write: Operations Manager, Toastmaster Inc., Second and Vine Sts., Boonville, Mo. 65233. Note: This recall first appeared in the September 1990 issue of Consumer Reports. We're repeating it because of a low return rate from the first recall notice.

Woods Wire Products remote-control receiver.
Could short circuit, causing fire hazard.

Products: 6000 receivers, model 1468, sold 1/91-10/91 for $10-$15. Receiver plugs into electrical outlet and is used with remote handheld transmitter to operate home-electrical devices. Label on back of receiver

PRODUCT RECALLS 377

reads in part: "III Woods No. 1468, UL Listed Appliance Control 19U4, CHK'D 91." Product carton is labeled "III Woods Transmitter and Receiver, Christmas Tree Light Control Kit, No. 1467T."

What to do: Return receiver portion of device for inspection and, if necessary, replacement. Mail to: Woods Wire Products Inc., P.O. Box 2675, Carmel, Ind. 46032-6675. Company will reimburse postage.

CARS

'91-92 Alfa Romeo Spider.
Map light in glove compartment could short-circuit and cause fire.

Models: 1800 cars made 9/90-12/91.
What to do: Have dealer replace map light and attachment bracket.

'90 Audi 100 and 200.
Vehicle's load capacity is missing from label inside fuel-filler door.

Models: 5900 cars made 7/90-12/90.
What to do: Have dealer attach new label.

'91-92 BMW 318.
Ice buildup in throttle housing could speed up engine and prevent slowing down promptly.

Models: 15,200 cars made 6/90-11/91.
What to do: Have dealer install redesigned throttle housing and reroute crankcase-ventilation-system hose.

'92 BMW 325i and 325iA.
In severe head-on crash, driver's seat could rise, increasing risk of injury from steering wheel.

Models: 22,416 cars made 3/91-4/92.
What to do: Have dealer install damper under seat cushion to prevent change in seat height.

'91-92 Buick, Oldsmobile, and Pontiac cars.
Parking brake might not prevent vehicle rolling.

Models: 20,765 cars made 4/91-5/91, including '91 Buick Park Avenue and Oldsmobile 88 and 98, and '92 Buick Le Sabre and Pontiac Bonneville.
What to do: Have dealer replace parking-brake lever.

'92 Buick, Chevrolet, Oldsmobile, and Pontiac models with automatic transmission.
Transmission might not work properly in Reverse. Also, transmission could remain in Reverse even though shifter is in Neutral, resulting in unexpected vehicle movement.

Models: 10,141 cars, made 10/91-11/91, including Buick Century and Regal, Chevrolet Lumina, Oldsmobile Cutlass, and Pontiac Grand Prix.

What to do: Have dealer check and, if necessary, replace transaxle.

'86-87 Buick, Oldsmobile, and Pontiac cars with V6 engine.
Engine could stall intermittently.

Models: 1.3 million cars including '86-87 Buick Century, Electra, Le Sabre, Park Avenue, and Riviera (all with 3.8-liter engine), '86 Buick Le Sabre (with 3.0-liter engine), '86-87 Buick Skylark and Somerset (with 3.0-liter engine), '86-87 Oldsmobile Cutlass Calais (with 3.0-liter engine), '86-87 Oldsmobile Cutlass Ciera, 88, 98, and Toronado (with 3.8-liter engine), '87 Pontiac Bonneville (3.8-liter engine), '86-87 Pontiac Grand Am (with 3.0-liter engine).
What to do: Have dealer make necessary repairs (free of charge through the end of 1992 on cars with up to 100,000 miles). If owner has already paid for repair work, contact dealer to seek reimbursement. For more information, call automakers' customer assistance lines: 800-521-7300 for Buick, 800-442-6537 for Oldsmobile, or 800-762-2737 for Pontiac.

'90 Buick Reatta and Riviera.
Brake indicator light on dash may not work.

Models: 18,904 cars made 8/89-3/90.
What to do: Have dealer make necessary repairs in computer module.

'91-92 Buick Roadmaster, Chevrolet Caprice, and Oldsmobile Custom Cruiser.
Hood could open suddenly, blocking driver's view.

Models: 224,588 cars made 10/89-8/91.
What to do: Have dealer replace secondary hood-latch assembly.

'91 Buick Skylark, Oldsmobile Calais, and Pontiac Grand Am with power windows.
Short circuit could lower window unexpectedly and overheat control module, causing fire hazard.

Models: 37,030 cars made 1/91-5/91.
What to do: Have dealer replace "express-down" control module.

378 PRODUCT RECALLS

'87-91 Cadillac limousine conversions.
Rear brakes aren't effective enough.

Models: 699 vehicles, made 10/86-2/91, including '87-91 Brougham conversions by Allen Coachworks; '87-90 Brougham conversions by Ultra Limousines; '88-91 Brougham conversions by Classic Limousines; '88-91 Brougham conversions by Dabryn Coach; '88 and '91 Brougham conversions by Royale Limousines; '88 and '91 Brougham conversions by Limousine Works; '90-91 Brougham conversions by Executive Coach Builders; '90 Brougham conversions by Federal Coach; '90 Brougham conversions by Picasso Coach Builders; and '91 Fleetwood conversions by Krystal Coach.

What to do: Have dealer replace original 1-in. brake cylinder with 1 1/16-in. cylinder.

'91 Chevrolet Beretta and Corsica.
Steering wheel could come off.

Models: 36,364 cars made 3/90-10/90.
What to do: Have dealer tighten nut securing wheel.

'88-90 Chevrolet Beretta and Corsica.
Front shoulder belts could fail.

Models: 722,884 cars made 1/88-7/90.
What to do: Have dealer replace shoulder-belt retractors and necessary hardware.

'87-88 Chevrolet Beretta and Corsica.
Hood could open suddenly, blocking driver's view.

Models: 290,408 cars made 6/86-11/87.
What to do: Have dealer replace primary and secondary hood-latch assemblies and support bracket.

'89 Chevrolet Corsica.
Wheels could crack and come off.

Models: 19,603 cars, with styled steel wheels, made 1/89-8/89.
What to do: Have dealer replace wheel assemblies.

'91 Chevrolet, Buick, Oldsmobile, and Pontiac cars.
Guide loops for front shoulder belts may crack, causing belts to give inadequate crash protection.

Models: 347,866 cars made 2/90-2/91, including Chevrolet Cavalier and Lumina, Buick Regal, Oldsmobile Cutlass, and Pontiac Grand Prix and Sunbird.
What to do: Have dealer add reinforcing plates to cracked guide loops.

'92 Chevrolet Cavalier and Pontiac Sunbird.
Hood could open suddenly, blocking driver's view.

Models: 3212 cars made 8/91.
What to do: Have dealer inspect hood-latch assemblies and, if necessary, install new secondary hood-latch spring.

'91 Chevrolet Cavalier and Pontiac Sunbird.
Front door frame, which anchors safety-belt housing, could collapse in accident, resulting in safety-belt failure.

Models: 41,718 cars made 12/90-1/91.
What to do: Have dealer replace belt interlock striker studs.

'84-91 Chevrolet Corvette.
Safety belts could jam in retractor and become unusable.

Models: 231,833 cars made 2/83-5/91.
What to do: Have dealer inspect and, if necessary, replace safety belts.

'90-91 Chrysler, Dodge, Eagle, and Plymouth cars and vans with antilock brakes.
Brake fluid could leak from high-pressure hose and reduce stopping ability.

Models: 80,000 vehicles made 3/90-7/91, including '90-91 Chrysler Imperial and New Yorker, '91 Chrysler Town and Country, '91 Dodge Caravan and Monaco, '90-91 Dodge Dynasty, '91 Eagle Premier, and '91 Plymouth Voyager.
What to do: Have dealer replace ABS hose.

'91 Chrysler Fifth Avenue, Imperial, LeBaron, and Salon; Dodge Dynasty and Spirit; and Plymouth Acclaim.
Front safety belts could fail.

Models: 130,000 cars made 7/90-11/90.
What to do: Have dealer replace belts' latch engagement.

'89 Chrysler LeBaron and Dodge Daytona.
In regions where road salt is used, disc-brake linings could separate, resulting in increased stopping distances.

Models: 41,000 cars made 8/88-12/88.
What to do: Have dealer replace front and rear linings on cars with 15-in. brakes. Replace only rear linings on cars with 14-in. brakes.

PRODUCT RECALLS

'92 Chrysler LeBaron.
Hood could open suddenly while car is moving, blocking driver's view.
Models: 17,000 cars made 8/91-2/92.
What to do: Have dealer adjust secondary hood latch so it engages properly.

'87 Dodge Charger and Omni and Plymouth Horizon and Turismo.
Fuel could leak and cause engine fire.
Models: 95,000 cars made 11/86-3/87.
What to do: Have dealer replace fuel-pressure regulator.

'88-89 Dodge Shadow and Plymouth Sundance.
Automatic shoulder belt could malfunction.
Models: 115,000 cars made 5/88-6/89.
What to do: Have dealer replace necessary parts.

'90-91 Ferrari (various models).
Steering could develop excessive play, impairing control.
Models: 645 cars, with vehicle identification numbers lower than 87898, made 7/89-1/91, including '90-91 Testarosa and 348 and '90 Mondial.
What to do: Have dealer replace locknut in upper steering column.

'89-90 Ferrari 348 and Mondial.
Aluminum fuel-line fittings could corrode and break, spilling fuel and, possibly, causing fire.
Models: 812 cars, with vehicle identification numbers below 88386, made 7/89-12/90.
What to do: Have dealer install redesigned fuel hoses.

'90-91 Ford Crown Victoria.
Rear-brake hoses could leak, causing partial brake failure.
Models: 25,000 cars with 5.8-liter V8 and police performance package.
What to do: Have dealer inspect and, if necessary, reroute and replace brake hoses.

'84-85 Ford Mustang and Mercury Capri.
Tongue could detach from webbing of front safety belt, causing belt failure.
Models: 306,000 cars made 9/83-8/85.
What to do: Have dealer make necessary repairs.

'86-92 Ford Taurus and Mercury Sable station wagons.
Child could accidentally lock self in rear storage compartment or footwell area of rear-facing third seat and be asphyxiated.
Models: 654,000 vehicles made 10/85-5/92.
What to do: Have dealer replace self-latching assembly with one that locks only with key.

'86-87 Ford Taurus and Mercury Sable.
Prolonged exposure to road salt could corrode brake discs, reducing braking effectiveness.
Models: 325,000 cars made 10/85-8/87.
What to do: Have dealer install new front brake rotors.

'92 Ford Taurus station wagon.
Liftgate could open suddenly, allowing passenger or cargo to fall out.
Models: 1300 station wagons made 3/91-8/91.
What to do: Have dealer replace liftgate latches.

'82-85 Honda Accord.
Road salt could corrode fuel filler or breather pipe, resulting in fuel leak and, possibly, fire.
Models: 903,219 cars made 8/81-9/85.
What to do: Have dealer inspect and, if necessary, replace pipes.

'91 Honda Accord.
Light in cargo area could short-circuit, causing fire hazard.
Models: 19,688 station wagons made 11/90-5/91.
What to do: Have dealer remove washers behind cargo area light and, if necessary, replace light assembly.

'86-89 Hyundai and Mitsubishi models.
Malfunction of emissions-control component could melt plastic air-filter case and cause engine-compartment fire.
Models: 895,000 cars including '86-89 Hyundai Excel and '87-89 Mitsubishi Precis.
What to do: Have dealer replace defective part.

'91 Isuzu Rodeo.
Transmission-fluid dipstick could show incorrect fluid level, possibly leading to overfilling, leakage, and fire hazard.
Models: 3023 multipurpose vehicles with automatic transmission, made 5/90-10/90.
What to do: Have dealer replace dipstick.

PRODUCT RECALLS

'92 Jaguar XJ-S.
Engine wiring could chafe against air-conditioning system, causing short circuit and vehicle stalling.

Models: 700 cars made 7/91-8/91.
What to do: Have dealer reposition protection plate for air-conditioning expansion valve to avoid contact with harness.

'89-91 Jaguar XJS.
Fuel-injector hose could leak and cause fire.

Models: 11,000 coupes and convertibles with Marelli ignition system, made 11/88-4/91.
What to do: Have dealer install shorter high-tension lead and, if necessary, replace fuel injector and injector hose.

'92 Lexus SC400.
Defective computer could cause rear antilock brakes to drag, increasing stopping distances, accelerating brake wear, and hampering control.

Models: 1415 cars made 4/91-6/91.
What to do: Have dealer replace antilock brake/traction-control computer and, if necessary, repair brake damage.

'89 Mazda MPV.
During low-speed stops, rear brakes could lock up unexpectedly, making vehicle difficult to control.

Models: 29,824 cars made 7/88-6/89.
What to do: Have dealer install redesigned rear brake-shoe assembly.

'93 Mazda MX6.
Front suspension could fail, causing loss of control.

Models: 2450 cars made 2/92-4/92 at Flat Rock, Mich., plant. (Ask dealer to check vehicle identification no. to determine where car was made.)
What to do: Have dealer inspect and, if necessary, tighten retaining bolts for lower ball joints.

'84-88 Mercedes Benz 190.
Parking brake could release, allowing vehicle to roll away.

Models: 96,541 cars made 8/83-12/87.
What to do: Have dealer replace parking-brake grip.

'91 Oldsmobile 98 and Pontiac Bonneville with automatic transmission.
Transmission shifter may not show proper gear position, resulting in unexpected vehicle movement.

Models: 6866 cars made 12/90-7/91.
What to do: Have dealer modify shift-control cable.

'91 Peugeot MI16.
Engine wiring could rub against alternator and short out, stalling the engine and possibly causing fire.

Models: 689 cars made 1/90-3/91.
What to do: Have dealer inspect and, if necessary, repair engine wiring harness.

'92 Pontiac Bonneville with automatic transmission.
Transmission shifter might indicate wrong gear, resulting in unexpected vehicle movement.

Models: 1570 cars made 5/91-7/91.
What to do: Have dealer install retaining clip on shift-control cable bracket.

'92 Pontiac Sunbird.
Defective accelerator cable could prevent engine from slowing when pedal is released.

Models: 22,452 cars made 3/91-1/92.
What to do: Have dealer replace accelerator control-cable assembly.

'89 Porsche 911 Turbo.
Fuel line could leak and cause fire.

Models: 975 cars made 6/88-4/89.
What to do: Have dealer inspect and, if necessary, replace fuel line. Also, reroute fuel line to clear brake-pad wear indicator bracket.

'83-87 Renault Alliance and Encore.
Heater could rupture and spew hot coolant into passenger compartment, posing risk of burns to driver's feet.

Models: 540,000 cars made 7/82-6/87.
What to do: If you see leakage or if windshield fogs, have dealer replace heater core.

'85-87 Subaru DL, GL, and XT.
Road salt could corrode rear suspension components, making vehicle difficult to control.

Models: 147,000 cars made 8/84-11/86.
What to do: Have dealer rustproof or replace inner control arms.

PRODUCT RECALLS 381

'92 Subaru Legacy.
Fuel tank may have been punctured during assembly; fuel could seep out and cause fire.

Models: 9500 cars and wagons made 7/91-1/92.
What to do: Have dealer inspect and, if necessary, replace fuel tank.

'90-91 Subaru Loyale.
Transmission could shift out of Park unexpectedly.

Models: 19,763 cars, including front- and 4-wheel drive vehicles with 3-speed automatic transmission, made 8/89-3/91.
What to do: Have dealer repair Park mechanism.

'88-91 Subaru XT6.
Power-steering pump could malfunction, causing intermittent increase in steering effort.

Models: 13,000 cars made 6/87-9/90.
What to do: Have dealer make necessary repairs.

'87 Toyota Camry.
Liquid spilled onto dash could seep into electronic mechanism that controls motorized safety belts, causing belt to malfunction.

Models: 175,923 cars made 8/86-7/87.
What to do: Have dealer install protective cover over electronic control unit.

'91-92 Toyota MR2.
Steering wheel might not absorb crash forces properly.

Models: 26,395 cars made 1/90-11/91.
What to do: Have dealer replace steering wheel.

'87-90 Volkswagen Cabriolet and '87-88 Scirocco.
Fuel tank could crack and leak, causing fire hazard.

Models: 51,000 cars made 8/86-8/89.
What to do: Have dealer inspect and, if necessary, replace fuel tank.

'90 Volkswagen Cabriolet.
Air bag might not deploy in crash.

Models: 8500 cars made 8/89-7/90.
What to do: Have dealer secure air-bag harness wire to dashboard crossmember to prevent chafing.

'90-91 Volkswagen Cabriolet.
Plastic panel that prevents engine from getting wet could jam accelerator linkage, causing unexpected vehicle movement.

Models: 11,300 cars made 8/89-11/90.
What to do: Have dealer install bracket to reinforce panel.

'90-92 Volkswagen Cabriolet.
Fuel could seep into engine compartment and cause fire.

Models: 18,000 cars made 8/89-3/92.
What to do: Have dealer secure fuel hose to fuel rail with self-tightening clamp.

'91 Volkswagen Fox.
Fuel line could rub against intake manifold, leak, and cause fire hazard.

Models: 2000 cars made 10/90-3/91.
What to do: Have dealer replace fuel line.

'85-90 Volkswagen Golf, GTI, and Jetta.
Heater could rupture and spew hot coolant onto driver's feet.

Models: 650,000 cars made 8/84-1/90.
What to do: If you see leakage or if windshield fogs, have dealer replace heater core.

'90-91 Yugo GV Plus.
Water could seep into electronic ignition unit through rubber seal, causing short circuit and stalling.

Models: 3676 cars made 12/89-1/91.
What to do: Have dealer replace seal.

TRUCKS AND VANS

'91 Chevrolet, GMC, and Oldsmobile light trucks and multipurpose vehicles.
Fuel could leak from tank in rollover, causing fire or explosion.

Models: 102,885 vehicles, made 1/90-2/91, including Chevrolet S10, T10, and Blazer; GMC S10, T10, and Jimmy; and Oldsmobile Bravada.
What to do: Have dealer replace fuel-tank sender seals.

'91 Chevrolet and GMC pickup trucks.
Brake line could rub against splash shield in front wheel housing and leak, causing failure of front brakes.

Models: 654 trucks, made 1/91, including Chevrolet K100 and K200, and GMC K150 and K250.
What to do: Have dealer replace splash shield.

382 PRODUCT RECALLS

'85-86 Chevrolet and GMC G30 light trucks.
Steering components could separate, resulting in loss of vehicle control.
Models: 166,624 vehicles made 8/84-8/86.
What to do: Have dealer install brace at left lower control arm.

'87-91 Chevrolet Astro van conversions.
Front and middle safety belts may not provide proper protection in crash.
Models: 185 vehicles, made 1/87-1/91, modified by ASC Colamco.
What to do: Have dealer relocate safety-belt anchor bolts.

'92 Chevrolet Truck and GMC vans with automatic transmission.
Engine can be started while transmission is in Forward or Reverse, resulting in sudden vehicle movement.
Models: 10,642 vans made 3/91-9/91, including Chevrolet G100, G200, and G300 and GMC G10, G20, and G30.
What to do: Have dealer reroute transmission cable.

'91 Chrysler Town and Country, Dodge Caravan, and Plymouth Voyager with antilock brakes.
Brake fluid could leak, reducing stopping ability and increasing possibility of brake lockup.
Models: 10,492 minivans made 6/91-7/91.
What to do: Have dealer replace ABS pump if last six digits on pump are between 052300 and 059262.

'92 Dodge Caravan and Plymouth Voyager.
Brake pedal could come off.
Models: 360 minivans made 8/91.
What to do: Have dealer replace brake pedal.

'92 Dodge D150 Ram pickup truck.
Parking brake may not be fully engaged even though it appears so, and vehicle could roll away.
Models: 800 pickup trucks made 11/91.
What to do: Have dealer install parking brake cable assembly with proper length spring.

'91 Dodge Dakota pickup with 2-wheel drive.
Right front brake hose could rub against tire and wear through, decreasing stopping ability.
Models: 38,000 pickups made 7/90-5/91.
What to do: Have dealer check routing of hose and replace it, if necessary.

'90-91 Ford Aerostar, Explorer, and Ranger.
Transmission could jump out of gear when shifter is in Park, resulting in unexpected vehicle movement.
Models: 683,000 vehicles, with 4-speed automatic transmission, made 8/89-8/91, including '90-91 Aerostar, '91 Explorer, and '90 Ranger.
What to do: Have dealer install new Park pawl.

'87-88 Ford Aerostar vans.
Liftgate could drop suddenly.
Models: 112,000 vans made 4/87-1/88.
What to do: Have dealer replace liftgate attachments.

'90-91 Ford Econoline van conversions.
Rear safety belt may not adequately restrain passenger in crash.
Models: 1010 van conversions, by Glaval Corp. of Elkhart, Ind., made 10/90-3/91.
What to do: Have dealer install new safety-belt anchorage.

'92 Ford trucks and multipurpose vehicles.
In cold weather, water could enter door-latch release and freeze, preventing door from latching securely or being opened from inside.
Models: 190,000 vehicles made 7/91-11/91, including F150, F250, F350, F450, F600, F700, F800, Ranger, and Bronco.
What to do: Have dealer replace door-latch release cables and water shields.

'90-91 Mazda MPV van.
Rear brakes may grab as linings wear, hampering stopping ability and operation of antilock brake system.

Models: 95,074 vans made 6/89-6/91.
What to do: Have dealer replace rear-brake assemblies.

'91 Mazda Navajo.
Transmission shifter might not engage when placed in Park, resulting in unexpected vehicle movement.

Models: 33,540 pickup trucks, vans, and multipurpose vehicles, with automatic transmission, made 8/6/90-7/29/91.
What to do: Have dealer install new Park pawl.

'90-91 Range Rover.
Brake lights could fail.

Models: 8151 vehicles made 2/89-5/91 with high-mounted center brake light and antilock brakes.
What to do: Have dealer replace brake-light switch at brake pedal.

'80-90 Toyota Land Cruiser.
Fuel tank could crack and leak, causing fire hazard.

Models: 38,500 vehicles made 9/80-12/89.
What to do: Have dealer replace fuel tank.

CHILD CAR SEATS

Century 580 infant safety seat.
Instructions for routing shoulder belts through seat are unclear. If belts are misthreaded, child might not be protected adequately in crash.

Products: 644,313 seats, model nos. 4580, 4581, 4583, and 4585, made 7/86-12/89.
What to do: Call 800-837-4044 for revised threading instructions.

Century child safety seats.
May not adequately protect child in crash if installed according to Spanish-language label.

Products: 727,343 seats, type 1000 STE, 2000 STE, 3000 STE, and 5000 STE, made 12/90-10/91. Model nos. include: 4153, 4163, 4180, 4253, 4261, 4263, 4265, 4266, 4365, 4366, 4367, 4368, 4369, 4380, 4381, 4460, 4470, 4475, 4476, 4480, and 4490.
What to do: Call 800-937-4766 for corrected label.

Cosco child safety seats.
May not adequately protect child in crash.

Products: 9500 Soft Shield and Soft Shield Auto Trac seats, models 02-090, 02-190, 02-290, 02-790, and 02-890, made 10/30/89-6/30/90.
What to do: Phone 800-544-1108 for harness retainer and installation instructions.

Cosco Deluxe Commuter child safety seat.
Foam-filled seat pad isn't sealed at seams. Child could tear out foam and choke on it.

Products: 5041 child seats, model 02-086, made 10/12/87-2/2/88.

What to do: Call 1-800-544-1108 for redesigned seat pad.

Evenflo booster seat (models 470 and 471) and Seven Year child safety seat (models 453 and 454).
Push pins that attach pads to seat frame could come off and choke child.

Products: 162,967 seats made 2/87-8/88.
What to do: Call 800-233-5921 for redesigned push pins and replacement instructions.

Kolcraft Dial-A-Fitt II child safety seat.
In rear-facing position, seat could fail to protect infant adequately in crash.

Products: 7787 seats, model 180-600, made 11/90-8/91.
What to do: Call 800-453-7673 for new plastic seat shell.

Kolcraft Perfect Fitt child safety seat.
Seat cushion could burn too quickly.

Products: 164,385 seats, model no. 180-200, made 1/88-7/91.
What to do: Call 800-453-7673 for redesigned cushion.

PRODUCT RECALLS

Kolcraft Perfect Fitt child safety seat.
Might not protect child adequately in crash.
Products: 40,000 seats, model nos. 180-150 and 180-200, made 3/89-10/90.
What to do: Call 1-800-453-7673 for parts to reinforce seat shell.

Kolcraft Playskool child safety seats.
Foam seat cushion could burn too quickly if exposed to fire or extreme heat.
Products: 13,500 seats, models nos. 140-155 and 180-400, made 12/89-8/90.
What to do: Contact Kolcraft at 800-453-7673 for replacement cushion.

Kolcraft Traveler 700 child safety seat.
Excessive tension between springs and armrest could cause plastic to split and injure child.
Products: 48,742 seats made 1/91-8/91.
What to do: Call 800-453-7673 for new seat shell without springs.

Renolux GT 5000 Turn-A-Tot child safety seat.
Might not protect child adequately in crash. Also, models with striped seat covers could burn too quickly.
Products: 24,463 seats made 2/90-4/91.
What to do: Call 800-476-5273 for replacement base and seat cover.

MOTORCYCLES

'87-88 BMW motorcycles.
Front brake line could wear from contact with fuel tank or speedometer cable, resulting in reduced braking effectiveness.
Models: 1122 motocycles made 4/87-9/88, including '87 R80RT, and '88 R100RS and R100RT.
What to do: Have dealer install necessary parts to protect brake line.

'88-90 Harley-Davidson FL and FX motorcycles.
Positive battery cable could cause short circuit and fire.
Models: 34,693 heavy softtail motorcycles made 6/88-7/90.
What to do: Have dealer replace cable.

'90-91 Harley-Davidson motorcycles.
Headlights and brake lights could go out suddenly.
Models: 61,386 motorcycles made 2/90-6/91.
What to do: Have dealer replace 30-amp circuit breaker.

'92 Harley-Davidson motorcycles.
Brake pads could come off their backing plate, preventing motorcycle from stopping adequately.
Models: 2658 motorcycles made 7/91-8/91.
What to do: Have dealer replace brake pads.

'93 Honda CBR900RR motorcycle.
Front brake pads may continuously rub against rotor. As rotor overheats, it may warp, reducing brake performance.
Models: 1254 motorcycles made 1/92-2/92.
What to do: Have dealer inspect and, if necessary, replace brake pads and rotor.

'91 Kawasaki ZX1100 motorcycle.
Rear brake hose could rub against brake rotor and leak, reducing stopping ability.
Models: 1760 motorcycles made 9/90-10/91.
What to do: Have dealer reroute brake hose.

MOTOR HOMES, TRAILERS

'82-86 Coachmen motor homes.
Propane gas could leak from furnace into living quarters, causing explosion hazard and respiratory distress.

Models: 46,239 motor homes, with Hydro Flame furnace with RV28SBR59 and RV28SBR68 ITT valves, made 1/82-12/86, including Cross Country, Fan, and Frolic, Midas, MRV, Pathfinder, Shasta, and Travelmaster.

What to do: Have dealer replace ITT valves with redundant gas control valves.

'92 Coleman Cedar, Roanoke, and Royale fold-down camping trailers.
Bumper could fall off and cause accident.

Models: 366 trailers made 2/92.
What to do: Have dealer replace bolts that secure bumper.

Wedgewood Designer Range, Medallion Range, and Slide-in Cooktop
Installed in various motor homes. Could leak gas.

Products: 46,000 appliances with Robertshaw control valves, made 1/1/91-9/15/91. Model numbers of recalled appliances begin with C or R.
What to do: Have dealer install control valves with properly torqued fasteners.

'91 Fleetwood Bounder motor homes.
Furnace could discharge deadly carbon monoxide into cabin.

Models: 135 motor homes made 6/91-7/91.
What to do: Have dealer align exhaust furnace vent tube.

'87-90 Fleetwood motor homes.
Steering wheel could come off steering column.

Models: 20,413 motor homes, on General Motors P30 chassis, made 6/86-10/89, including: Bounder; Eagle; Eleganza; Pace Arrow; Southwind.
What to do: Have dealer inspect steering assembly and, if necessary, install retaining clip for steering-wheel nut.

'90-92 Holiday Rambler Limited motor homes.
Hydraulic fluid could leak from cooling fan, causing fire hazard in engine compartment.

Models: 186 37 ft. and 40 ft. motorhomes on Gillig chassis made 3/89-8/91.
What to do: Have dealer check for leaks and make necessary repairs.

'90-91 Itasca and Winnebago 320RB, 321RB, 321RL, and ICN36RA motor homes.
Furnace can draw air over range top, causing downdraft that could extinguish burner flame and allow LP gas to seep into cabin. Also, downdraft could cause flame to melt burners.

Models: 352 motorhomes made 6/90-3/91.
What to do: Have dealer install partition between appliances.

'91 Itasca Windcruiser and Winnebago Elandan motor homes.
Generator assembly could drop out onto road.

Models: 383 motor homes made 9/90-9/91.
What to do: Have dealer install bolts to support generator.

VEHICLE ACCESSORIES

Cordovan Grand Prix radial G/T tires.
Could fail.

Products: 120 tires, size P205/70R14, made during week of 11/17/91; identification no. PJKECEBR461.
What to do: Return tires to store for replacement.

Kelly Springfield light-truck tires.
Could fail if inflated and loaded as per incorrect labeling.

Products: 1009 tires made 4/91-5/91, size LT225x75R16, with DOT nos. PJ1LA1LV171, PJ1LA1LV181, and PJ1LA1LV191.
What to do: Have dealer replace tires.

Sears Diehard battery.
Case could crack and leak acid, causing injury and battery failure.

Products: Batteries sold 5/20/91-9/11/91 in Del., Washington, D.C., Md., NYC boroughs of Brooklyn and Staten Island; Long Island, NY, Pa., northeastern Va., northern W. Va. To find out if battery is involved in recall, look for the model number on the sales slip rather than on the battery. Recalled batteries include model numbers 43224, 43225, 43234, 43258.

What to do: Return battery to Sears Auto Center for replacement. For more information, call 1-800-666-1112.

Western Auto Patriot Ultra Supreme 770 polysteel tubeless radial tires.
Could fail.

Products: 1157 tires made 7/91, size P175/70R13, with DOT nos. U9EVUBW261, U9EVUBW271, and U9EVUB281.

What to do: Have dealer inspect and, if necessary, replace tires.

MISCELLANEOUS

A.O. Smith liquid-propane and natural-gas water heaters.
Oversized flue baffles could release excess carbon monoxide, which can cause illness or death.

Products: 29,000 30- and 40-gallon water heaters distributed 4/16-7/9/91. Recall involves FSG and PGX models with serial nos. beginning with MD91, ME91, MF91, and MG91.

What to do: Call 1-800-538-9642 to arrange for replacement of flue baffle.

Do-It-Yourself paint-brush set.
Paint on brush handles contains excess lead, which is toxic.

Products: 6000 brush sets sold 2/90-3/91 for $3.35. Set consists of 5 camel-hair brushes: 2 half-inch flat-edge brushes, 1 quarter-inch flat-edge brush, and 1 #2 and 1 #4 round-pointing edge brush. Wooden handles are painted in assorted colors. Package reads in part, "DO-IT-YOURSELF HOBBY & CRAFT BRUSHES" and has no. "033572-10001-4" printed beneath bar code on back of package.

What to do: Return brush set to store for refund.

Geneva Generics' Prenatal Vitamins With Folic Acid in 100-tablet bottle.
Bottle lacks child-resistant closure. Iron content of tablet could cause serious illness or death if child swallows four or five tablets at one time.

Products: 70,000 bottles sold since 1990.
What to do: Return vitamins to store for refund.

Grumbacher artists' paint brushes.
Handles contain excessive lead.

Products: 332,761 paint brushes with wooden handles sold 1/90-1/92. Products include set numbers 1140C Do-It-Yourself Utility Brush set of 5, listing for $7.95 (recall involves only red-handled black-bristle brush and yellow-handled ox-hair brush). Also, 1141C Artcraft Hobby and Ceramic Brush set of 3, for $7.75. Also, No. 2 green, No. 3 blue, No. 4 yellow, and No. 5 red brushes, sold for less than $1 in Hobby/Craft Brush Assortment countertop display 114D. All are marked "CAMEL HAIR KOREA." Various brushes marked M. GRUMBACHER SABLE KOREA, M. GRUMBACHER CAMEL KOREA, and M. GRUMBACHER OX KOREA are recalled as well.

What to do: Return brushes to store for refund. For more information, call 1-800-346-3278.

K Mart plastic resin patio chairs.
Could collapse.

Products: 101,300 chairs sold 12/90 through summer of 1991. White molded plastic chairs, which have "Suncraft" stamped on underside of seat, were sold separately or as part of 9-piece "Moroccan Sand" patio set.

What to do: Return chair to K Mart for replacement.

Patriot 52-in. A-frame swimming-pool ladder.
Handrails could bend in use and trap and injure fingers or hands.

Products: 7500 ladders, models X4932-01 and X4932-06, sold 4/90-10/1/91, mostly in eastern U.S. To identify recalled units, check model number listed on instruction sheet in packaging. (Ladder itself bears no identifying marks.)

What to do: Call 1-800-235-0185 for special parts to prevent gap from forming.

PRODUCT RECALLS 387

Pull-Up Exerciser and Maxi Rower stomach exercisers.
Could break during use and cause severe injuries.

Products: 1.5 million Pull-Up Exercisers sold '81-89 and 701,365 Maxi Rowers sold '84-89. Devices were sold by Hanover House Ind., a catalog company. Recall pertains only to exercisers sold by mail-order. Pull-Up Exerciser consists of footrest bar and handlebar connected by spring that is stretched by user. Maxi Rower consists of metal frame with 2 springs, each with separate handle. User sits on rolling seat with feet in footrest attached to frame.

What to do: Call 800-338-2670 for retrofit kit to fortify Pull-Up Exerciser or for credit on Maxi Rower good toward purchase of other Hanover House product.

Quarter-in. gas hose used in various barbecue grills.
Hose could leak and cause fire or explosion.

Products: 60,000 feet of ¼-in. hose manufactured 9/3/91. Lettering on outside of hose reads: "5561 MH8749 UND. LAB. INC. R LIST L.P. GAS HOSE ISSUE No. D-1723 MAX WK. PRESS. 350 PSI (2.4 MPa) 1750 PSI BURST 09/03/91 C.G.A. Type I."

What to do: Return grill to store for replacement or credit. For information, call Parker Hannifin Corp. at 1-800-472-6844.

Toro Vision II Irrigation Controller.
Poses electrocution hazard.

Products: 7500 devices, models 189-06-01, 189-66-01, and 189-96-01, sold 9/89-12/90. Metal cabinet of system is white with red "Toro" logo and key lock on door. A "Vision II Series" paper label appears inside door. Irrigation controllers with gray or tan plastic cabinets are not being recalled.

What to do: Phone company at 1-800-367-8676 toll-free (1-800-255-8676 in California) or ask contractor who installed controller to assure that system is properly grounded.

Yazoo high-wheel gasoline-powered lawn mowers (various models).
Mowers intended for commercial use may have been sold to consumers in southern and northeastern parts of U.S. Lack of blade-stopping safety mechanism increases risk of injury. Note: This is not recall, but a warning and a notice. It applies only to mowers purchased for personal use, not those intended for industrial, commercial, or professional use.

Products: Self-propelled and push mowers made 1982-91, including models S22B, P22B, P22W, S22W, P24B, P24W, S24B, S24W, S26B, and S26W. Models retailed for $750-$900. Bright-yellow decal states: "NOTICE. THIS MOWER DOES NOT MEET CPSC SAFETY REQUIREMENTS".

What to do: Call 1-800-892-4505 to arrange for retrofit with three-second blade-stopping mechanism.

Buying Guide Index

This index is for information in the 1993 Buying Guide. For a four-year index of CONSUMER REPORTS, see opposite.

Air cleaners 192
   Ratings 205
Air-conditioners 188
   mid-sized, Ratings 200
Automobiles
   batteries 270
      Ratings 279
   buying a new car 306
   buying a used car 309
   child safety seats 273
      Ratings 276
   Frequency-of-Repair records 317
   owner satisfaction 357
   recommended 1992 cars 282
   security systems 271
   tires 268

Bathroom cleaners 209
   Ratings 222
Bicycle helmets 129
Bicycles, recreational 128
   exercise 124
Blenders 24
   Ratings 36
Blood-pressure monitors 165
   Ratings 175

Cable television 63
Calculators, printing 145
   Ratings 151
Camcorders 71
   Ratings 99
Camera lenses, zoom 109
   Ratings 118
Cameras 109
   automation 113
Cassette decks 81
   mid-priced, Ratings 102
Chippers/shredders 246
   Ratings 262
Cleansers, household 209
   Ratings 218
Clothes dryers 47
   Ratings 54

Coffee grinders 31
Coffee makers, automatic drip 29
Compact-disc players 80
   Ratings 97
Computer printers 143
   Ratings 162
Copiers, home 140
   Ratings 150

Detergents, dishwasher 210
   Ratings 220
Dishwashers 15
Dishwashing liquids 209
   Ratings 221

Espresso machines 30
   Ratings 42
Exercise equipment 123
   stair climbers 124
      Ratings 131
   treadmills 123

Fans 186
   Ratings 202
Film-processing labs 116
   Ratings 120
Food choppers 26
   Ratings 41
Food mixers 27
   Ratings 39
Food processors 26
   Ratings 34

Glass cleaners 209
   Ratings 218
Grills, gas barbecue 247
   Ratings 265

Headphones, stereo 77
Helmets, bicycle 129
Home theater 61

Irons, steam 49
   Ratings 59

CONSUMER REPORTS INDEX 389

Laser-disc players 71
Laundry products 51
Lawn mowers 241
   mulching, Ratings 249
   self-propelled, Ratings 252
Lead-testing kits 231
Loudspeakers 76
   Ratings 106

Microwave ovens 7
Mouthwash 170

Oral irrigators 172
   Ratings 184

Paint removers 230
   chemical strippers, Ratings 238
   heat guns, Ratings 239
Paints & stains 224
   interior latex paint, Ratings 232; 234
   matching surface to finish 226, 227
Paper towels 210
   Ratings 217
Printers, computer 143
   Ratings 162

Ranges, gas and electric 10
Receivers, stereo 73
   mid-priced, Ratings 89
Refrigerators 12
   side-by-side, Ratings 18
   top-freezer, Ratings 21
Remote controls 64
Running shoes 125
   Ratings 134

Stair climbers 124
   Ratings 131
Stereo systems, compact 84

String trimmers 243
   Ratings 255
Sunscreens 173

Tapes, audio 83
Tapes, video 70
Telephone-answering devices 147
   Ratings 156
Telephones, cordless 146
   Ratings 159
Television sets 65
   13- and 20-inch, Ratings 94
   27-inch, Ratings 86
Tennis racquets 127
   Ratings 136
Tillers & cultivators 245
   Ratings 259
Toaster ovens 32
Toasters 32
Toothbrushes, electric 171
   Ratings 182
Toothpaste 168
   Ratings 177
Tripods 114
   Ratings 119
Typewriters 141
   Ratings 154

Vacuum cleaners, handheld 212
   Ratings 214
Video cassette recorders 68
   hi-fi, Ratings 91

Walkabout stereos 78
Washing machines 44
   Ratings 56
Water treatment 194
Word processors 141
   Ratings 154

CONSUMER REPORTS FOUR-YEAR INDEX

This index covers issues of CONSUMER REPORTS, from January 1989 to October 1992. Entries in bold type are Ratings reports. *indicates correction or follow-up notes.

Advertising
   and children .... Aug 90, 518
   in schools .... May 89, 286

   video news releases .... Oct 91, 694
AIDS .... Mar 89, 142
Air cleaners .... **Feb 89, 88**; Oct 92, 657

in-duct type .... Oct 92, 662
ozone generation .... Oct 92, 661
Air-conditioners
   large .... **Jul 90, 474**
   medium-sized .... **Jul 89, 432; Jul 92, 420**
   small room .... **Jun 91, 384**
   windowless .... **May 91, 344**
Air pumps, electric .... **Oct 90, 676**
Airlines .... **Jul 91, 462**
   bankrupt .... May 91, 302
   fares .... Jun 89, 363; *Jul 89, 481
Alar .... May 89, 288; *Aug 89, 490; Jul 90, 446
Alarms, burglar .... **Feb 90, 104**; *Apr 90, 208
Annuities .... Sep 90, 592
Apple juice .... **May 89, 283**
Apples and *Alar* .... May 89, 288; Jul 90, 446
Aspirin, half-dosage .... Jun 92, 354
Audio components, *see* stereo components
Automobile brokers .... Sep 89, 593
Automobile dealers, influence on newspapers
                                           Apr 92, 208
Automobile-rental companies .... **Jul 89, 477**
Automobiles & automotive equipment
   air-conditioners, CFCs
                         Apr 91, 211; Apr 92, 209
   anti-theft devices .... **Feb 92, 96**
   audio equipment .... **May 91, 303**
   back-up light, beeping .... Jan 92, 6
   batteries .... Jul 90, 445; **Oct 91, 683**
   battery booster cables
                    Jan 89, 22; *Jun 89, 353
   battery disposal .... Apr 91, 211
   body dimensions .... **Apr 92, 276**
   brake-repair shops
                    Aug 89, 528; Apr 90, 210
   bumpers, strength of, window sticker
                                   Apr 92, 208
   buying a new car .... Apr 92, 241
   buying a used car .... **Apr 92, 280**
   child safety seats
             Sep 90, 573; **Jan 92, 16**; *May 92, 345
   crash tests .... Apr 92, 211
   defects .... Apr 90, 228
   emergency gear .... Apr 92, 248
   emission-control repairs .... Jan 90, 6
   fanbelts, emergency .... Aug 89, 491
   Frequency-of-Repair records ... **Apr 92, 251**
   headlights .... Apr 89, 201
   imported utility vehicles .... May 89, 330
   lawsuit, Nissan .... Feb 90, 73
   loudspeakers .... **May 91, 310**
   maintaining .... Apr 90, 211
   mechanical specifications .... **Apr 92, 271**
   minivans, alleged dumping of .... Oct 92, 635

   motor-oil labels .... Apr 90, 210
   motor-oil recycling .... Apr 91, 210
   muffler-repair shops
                    Aug 89, 528; Apr 90, 210
   new cars, 1992 models .... **Apr 92, 217**
   optional equipment .... Apr 92, 238
   owner satisfaction .... **Apr 92, 269**
   recalls summary .... Feb 89, 84
   recycling .... Apr 91, 211
   replacement parts .... Apr 89, 201
   rustproofing .... Aug 90, 506
   service contracts .... Apr 90, 226
   Suzuki Samurai .... May 92, 294
   tire sidewalls, how to read .... Apr 92, 209
   tires, all season .... **Feb 92, 75**
   Toyota Camry .... Sep 92, 558
   warranties, secret
                       Apr 89, 214; *Aug 89, 490
   windshield treatment .... Aug 91, 514

Bacon .... **Oct 89, 647**
Baking pans .... Feb 90, 75
Banking
   basic services .... Jan 91, 7
   checks, lost .... Feb 89, 74
   checks, ordering .... Feb 89, 74
   joint accounts .... Jul 89, 458
Barbecue sauces .... **Jul 91, 498**
Basements, water damage .... Feb 90, 82
Bathroom cleaners .... **Sep 91, 603**
Bathroom spas .... **Jul 89, 467**
Bathroom tissue .... **Sep 91, 606**
Batteries, dry-cell .... **Nov 91, 720**
Battery recharger .... Sep 90, 575
Battery tester .... Nov 91, 701
Beans, baked .... **Jan 89, 14**
Beech-Nut .... May 89, 294; Jun 89, 354
Beef .... Aug 90, 507
   brand-name .... Sep 90, 575
Bicycles
   automatic transmission .... Jun 91, 377
   exercise .... **Nov 90, 746**
   Fuji .... Oct 90, 641
   hybrid .... **Nov 90, 739**
   mountain .... **Oct 91, 650**
Bicycle-tire insert .... May 89, 285
Binoculars .... **Jul 89, 444**
Blankets .... **Oct 91, 696**
   electric .... **Nov 89, 711**
   safety .... Nov 89, 715
Blenders .... **Jun 92, 383**
Blood-pressure
   high .... Jan 90, 48
   how to lower it .... May 92, 300

CONSUMER REPORTS INDEX 391

monitors .... **May 92, 295**
Blue jeans .... **Jul 91, 456**; *Oct 91, 640
Bonds .... Sep 89, 579; *Oct 89, 669
   mutual funds .... **Jun 90, 428**
   savings bonds .... Jan 90, 6
Bottles, insulated .... **Aug 89, 519**
Brake and muffler shops
                 Aug 89, 528; Apr 90, 210
Bread bags, lead in .... **Mar 91, 141**
Breakfasts, fast-food .... **Sep 91, 624**
Breast cancer .... *Mar 89, 193; Aug 89, 498
Broom, cordless .... Oct 90, 641
Buckets, five gallon, infant and toddler
   drowning hazard .... Feb 92, 73
Burglar alarms .... **Feb 90, 104**; *Apr 90, 208
Butter .... **Sep 89, 551**
   shake-on substitute .... Aug 89, 489

Cable television .... Sep 91, 571; **Sep 91, 576**
Cakes
   low-fat .... May 91, 301
   microwave .... Jul 89, 429
Calculators, printing .... **Aug 91, 527**
Camcorders
       Mar 90, 162; *Apr 90, 208; **Mar 91, 184**;
       Mar 92, 161
Cameras
   disposable .... May 90, 302
   electronic .... Oct 89, 609
   35mm SLR .... **Nov 90, 758**; *Mar 91, 201
Canadian health-care system ..... Sep 92, 579
Canola oil .... Jul 89, 429
Carafes .... **Aug 89, 519**; *Oct 89, 669
Carbonated waters .... **Sep 92, 569**
Carpet cleaners .... **Jan 91, 14**
Car-rental companies .... **Jul 89, 477**
Cassette decks
       Mar 89, 160; Mar 90, 184; Mar 91, 164;
       Mar 92, 184
   digital audio .... Oct 90, 660; Mar 91, 165
Cereals
       Oct 89, 638; *Nov 89, 676; *Jan 90, 65
Certificates of deposit
                 Mar 89, 153; Jun 89, 392
Cesareans .... Feb 91, 120
Chain saws .... **May 90, 304**; *Feb 91, 133
Chair sales promotion .... Feb 91, 73
Cheese, American .... **Nov 90, 728**
Chicken, fresh .... **Feb 89, 75**
Child safety seats .... Sep 90, 573
Chili, canned .... **Oct 90, 688**
Chippers .... **Jun 91, 414**
Cholesterol .... Mar 90, 152
   and coffee .... Jan 91, 40

Cholesterol-Reducing Paks .... Mar 90, 141
Chronic fatigue syndrome .... Oct 90, 671
Cleansers, scouring .... **Jan 90, 61**
Clock radios .... **Sep 89, 558**
Clothes dryers .... **Oct 89, 616**; **Jan 92, 44**
Coffee and cholesterol .... Jan 91, 40
Coffee filters (and dioxin) .... Jan 91, 47
Coffee grinders .... **Jan 91, 48**
Coffee makers .... **Jan 91, 42**
Coffees .... **Jan 91, 30**
   gourmet .... Jan 91, 33
   instant .... **Jan 91, 36**
   microwave .... Jan 91, 41
Coins, investment .... Jul 91, 483
Colas .... **Aug 91, 518**
Cold remedies .... Jan 89, 8; Feb 91, 73
College, saving for .... Oct 91, 661
Comforters .... **Nov 89, 706**
Compact-disc players
       Jan 89, 27; Mar 89, 165; **Mar 90, 185**;
       Mar 91, 166; **Mar 92, 187**
   portable .... Sep 90, 574
Compact-disc rings .... May 89, 285
Computers
   handheld .... Jun 90, 377
   home .... **Jan 91, 23**
   laptops .... **Sep 89, 564**
Conditioner, hair .... **Jun 92, 395**
Condoms .... **Mar 89, 135**
Consolidators, airline tickets .... Jun 89, 363
Contact lenses .... Jun 89, 411
Cooler chests .... **Jun 89, 403**
Copiers
   pocket .... Feb 90, 74
   small .... **Jan 92, 51**; *May 92, 345
Creamers, nondairy .... Nov 90, 701
Credit cards
   choosing .... May 90, 315
   disclosure required ... Jan 89, 7; Sep 89, 550
   purchase protection .... Jul 92, 432
   transactions, signature only ..... Mar 90, 142
Credit ratings
       Oct 90, 648; May 91, 356; Jul 91, 453;
       Nov 91, 710; *Jan 92, 6
Credit-repair scams .... Nov 89, 677
Culinova dinners .... Feb 89, 73
Cushions, infant bean-bag .... Jun 90, 377

Debit cards .... Jun 90, 422
Dehumidifiers .... **Jul 90, 479**
Delivery dates .... Apr 90, 209
Dental floss .... **Apr 89, 504**
Detergents
   dishwasher .... **Feb 92, 81**

392 CONSUMER REPORTS INDEX

dishwashing liquids .... **Sep 91, 592**
  hand-laundry .... **May 89, 297**
  laundry .... **Feb 91, 100**
Diapers.. **Aug 91, 551**
Diet............................Oct 92, 644; Oct 92, 652
Dimmers, light-bulb .... **Oct 92, 669**
Dishwashers .... **May 90, 342**
Doorbell remote chime .... Oct 89, 610
Driwater (plant sitter)...................... Jul 92, 414
Drug companies
  influence on the news .... Mar 92, 142
  marketing to doctors
              Feb 92, 87; *May 92, 345
Drugs, generic............................May 90, 310
Dryers, clothes ....**Oct 89, 616; Jan 92, 44**

Egg substitutes........................... Jul 91, 455
Eggs...Oct 89, 650
Electronic measurer ....Jan 92, 5
Electronic organizers .... **Nov 91, 768**
Emergency-response system ....Jan 91, 5
Espresso machines.................... **Nov 91, 728**
Estrogen therapy......................... Sep 91, 587
Exercise equipment, home
  bicycles .... **Nov 90, 746**
  stair climbers............................ **May 92, 315**
  treadmills.................................. **Nov 90, 752**
Extension cord
  outdoor......................................Sep 89, 550
  retractable .... Mar 91, 141
Eyeshadows................................ **Feb 91, 96**

Fabric softeners........................ **Feb 91, 109**
Facial cleansers .... **Jun 89, 408**
Fans........................... Jul 89, 437; **Jul 92, 415**
Fast-food chains
  breakfasts .... **Sep 91, 624**
  nutrition .... Jul 91, 453
Fats in food .... Mar 90, 158; *Feb 91, 133
Film ....Nov 89, 687
Film-processing labs
        Aug 91, 558; *Nov 91, 776
Finishing sanders........................ **Sep 90, 628**
Fish, safety of.............................. Feb 92, 103
Flashlights.................................... **Sep 92, 573**
Flatware, stainless-steel............. **Mar 91, 188**
Flea killers ....Aug 91, 563
Food mixers................................**Jul 91, 486**
Food processors .... **Aug 92, 502**
Food wraps .... **Feb 89, 120**
Frozen desserts, low-fat.............**Aug 92, 483**
Frozen dinners .... **Jan 90, 44**
Furniture, upholstered...................Jan 89, 33

Garbage bags, degradable .... Feb 89, 73
Garden pests .... Jun 91, 419; *Oct 91, 640
Gasoline Jan 90, 8; *Apr 90, 211; Feb 91, 75;
    Apr 91, 212; *Jun 91, 423
  alternative fuels............................Jan 90, 11
  fuel economy..........Apr 90, 210; Apr 91, 210
Genetic screening .... Jul 90, 483
Glass cleaners ....**Oct 89, 611; Jan 92, 22**
Green marketing ....Oct 91, 687
Grills, gas ....**Jul 91, 491**
Guaranteed investment contracts . Jul 90, 447

Hair dryers ....**Aug 92, 532**
Hairbrush, melting .... Aug 90, 505
Hamburgers .... Aug 90, 507
  microwave .... May 90, 303
Hammers, claw ....**Jul 91, 470**
Hand-laundry detergents ....**May 89, 297**
Headphones, stereo................... **Sep 89, 596**
Health care, waste and abuses
          Jul 92, 435; *Oct 92, 625
Health claims (food) .... Mar 90, 153
Heaters, portable electric ....**Nov 89, 724**
Heating pads, cordless.................May 89, 287
Hedge trimmers ....**Jun 90, 403**
Helmets, bicycle..........................**May 90, 348**
High blood pressure ....Jan 90, 48
High chairs .... **Oct 90, 649**; *Feb 91, 75
HMOs ....**Aug 92, 519**
Holiday advice
      Nov 89, 678; Nov 90, 702; Nov 91, 711
Home, sale of, defect disclosure . Aug 92, 482
Home security .... Feb 90, 96
Home theater ....Mar 91, 155; Mar 92, 150
Hot Pockets ....Jan 90, 5
Hotel and motel chains.................**Sep 90, 576**
Hypertension...................................Jan 90, 48
Hysterectomy .... Sep 90, 603

Ice cream, nonfat .... Oct 91, 641
Ice-cream bars ....**Aug 89, 492**
Infant formula, pricing................... Mar 91, 142
Insurance
  automobile .... Oct 91, 641; **Aug 92, 489**
  collision damage waiver
              Jan 90, 7; Jun 91, 377
  safety devices ....Oct 91, 641
  credit life......................................Oct 90, 642
  disability .... Jul 92, 449
  health
      Aug 90, 533; Sep 90, 608; Nov 90, 703;
      Mar 92, 141; Sep 92, 579
  homeowners ....**Sep 89, 572**
  life ....Jan 89, 7

long-term care
  Oct 89, 664; **Jun 91, 425**; *Aug 91, 514;
  *Nov 91, 710
Medigap policies
  Jun 89, 375; Jan 91, 6; Sep 91, 616
student accident .... Sep 91, 573
Interactive multimedia .... Jun 92, 388
Interest rates and saving .... Aug 92, 488
Investing, asset allocation .... Jun 92, 394
Irons, steam .... **Jan 91, 8**
  travel .... **May 90, 357**; *Jun 90, 437

Jeans .... **Jul 91, 456**; *Oct 91, 640
Jet-Stream Oven .... Apr 90, 209

Labeling, food
  May 90, 326; Jan 91, 6; Jan 92, 32;
  Oct 92, 623; Oct 92, 654
Label-maker .... Aug 89, 491
Lactose-reduced products .... Mar 89, 133
Ladders
  fire-escape .... Oct 91, 642; *Nov 91, 776
  stepladders .... **Sep 90, 624**
Laser-disc players .... Mar 92, 159
Laser surgery .... Aug 91, 536
Laundry boosters .... **Feb 91, 107**
Laundry products and environment
  Feb 91, 105
Lawn darts, ban .... Jan 89, 5
Lawn mowers
  choosing .... Jun 90, 392
  low-priced .... **Jun 90, 394**; *Aug 90, 565
  mulching .... **Jun 91, 408**
  self-propelled .... **Jun 92, 368**
Lawn tractors .... **Jun 89, 368**
Lawns, chemical-free .... Jun 90, 399
Lead .... *Sep 89, 550
  in bread bags ..... Mar 91, 141; *Sep 91, 574
  ceramics test kit .... Jun 90, 378
  water testing .... Jul 89, 430; Jul 91, 454
Life preserver, wrist .... Jun 90, 378
Light bulbs .... **Jan 90, 20**; *Feb 90, 133
  compact fluorescent .... **Oct 92, 664**
  "energy-saving" .... Aug 91, 513
  halogen .... **Oct 92, 664**
  life extenders .... Aug 91, 513
Loans
  automobile .... Apr 90, 210; *Jun 90, 437
  home-equity .... Jan 89, 7; Nov 90, 714
Locks, door .... **Feb 90, 98**
Long-term care insurance
  Oct 89, 664; **Jun 91, 425**; *Aug 91, 514;
  *Nov 91, 710
Longevity products .... Jan 92, 7

Loudspeakers .... **Mar 89, 166**
  low-cost .... Mar 90, 180
  mid-priced .... **Oct 90, 655**; **Mar 91, 162**
  small .... *Feb 89, 72
  surround-sound .... **Mar 92, 189**
Luggage
  hard-sided .... **Jul 90, 448**
Luggage carts .... **Jul 90, 453**

Mail-order companies .... **Oct 91, 643**
Margarine
  Sep 89, 551; *Aug 90, 565; Mar 91, 196
Mascaras .... **Feb 91, 91**
Meals, prepackaged (combinations)
  May 92, 293
Mercury-amalgam fillings .... May 91, 316
Microwave meals for children .... Oct 90, 642
Microwave ovens ... **Mar 89, 145**; **Nov 91, 733**
  canning with .... Sep 89, 549
  compact .... **Nov 89, 692**
  cooker for chicken and fish .... Sep 91, 575
  large .... **Nov 90, 733**
  pressure cooker in .... Nov 89, 677
Microwave/convection ovens ...... **Sep 89, 580**
Milk, economics of .... May 92, 330
Money-market funds
  Mar 89, 153; May 89, 316
Mortgages .... Jan 92, 26; Feb 92, 84
  escrow accounts .... Oct 90, 668
  real-estate brokers .... Feb 91, 74
  refinancing .... Mar 92, 148
  reverse-mortgages .... Oct 92, 637
  servicing .... Jul 89, 441; Jun 91, 378
Motel chains .... **Sep 90, 576**
Mouthwashes
  Aug 89, 504; Jul 91, 454; **Sep 92, 607**
Moving companies .... **Aug 90, 527**
Mutual funds .... Oct 89, 615; Nov 89, 698
  bond funds .... **Jun 90, 428**
  money-market funds
    Mar 89, 153; May 89, 316
  stock funds .... **May 90, 330**

National Highway Traffic Safety
  Administration .... Feb 89, 84
Nursing-home insurance
  Oct 89, 664; **Jun 91, 425**; *Aug 91, 514
Nutrition .... Oct 92, 644
  fast-food chains .... Jul 91, 453
  Nutrition IQ .... May 90, 322
  Nutrition pyramid, USDA
    Oct 91, 663; Jul 92, 413

Olive oil .... **Oct 91, 667**; *Jan 92, 6

394 CONSUMER REPORTS INDEX

Opener, jar & bottle, electronic .... Sep 92, 558
Oral irrigators .... **Sep 92, 614**
   battery-powered .... Oct 92, 626
Orange juice .... **Feb 91, 128**
   labeling .... Jun 91, 377
Organizers, electronic .... **Nov 91, 768**
Ozone layer .... May 89, 322

Packaging, modified-atmosphere
                                   Mar 90, 141
Paint removers .... **May 91, 340**; Jun 92, 353
Paint roller .... Oct 92, 626
Paints
   basement .... **Feb 90, 84**
   exterior trim .... **Sep 90, 619**
   latex interior .... **May 91, 335**
   semigloss interior
                     May 89, 317; *Jun 89, 352
   waterproofing .... **Feb 90, 84**
Pancake mixes .... **Jan 92, 56**
   bottled .... Jan 91, 5
Pancake syrups .... **Jan 92, 60**
Pancakes, frozen .... **Jan 92, 56**
Paper towels .... **Jan 92, 28**; *May 92, 345
Pasta, fresh .... Mar 90, 141
Pasta-salad mixes .... May 89, 286
Paycheck stubs .... Jan 89, 18
Peanut butter .... **Sep 90, 588**
Pens, gift .... **Nov 91, 712**
Personal balance sheet .... Sep 92, 567
Pest Strip .... Jul 90, 445
Pesticides, risk assessment .... Oct 89, 655
Pet sprays .... Jan 90, 6; Aug 91, 563
Pets, pest-free .... Aug 91, 563; *Nov 91, 776
Piano teacher, electronic .... Nov 91, 718
Picnic jugs .... **Jun 89, 403**
Popcorn .... **Jun 89, 355**
Popcorn poppers .... **Jun 89, 360**
Postal scale, handheld .... Oct 92, 627
Pot pies, frozen .... **Jan 90, 44**
Potato chips .... **Jun 91, 379**
Pots and pans, nonstick .... Jan 92, 5
Price fixing .... Sep 91, 574
Printers, computer .... **Sep 91, 610**
Privacy .... May 91, 356

Radiant barriers .... Mar 90, 142
Radio/tape players, automobile ... **May 91, 303**
Radon .... Oct 89, 623
   video .... Jan 90, 5
Ranges
   electric .... **Feb 89, 80**; **Mar 90, 144**
   gas .... **Feb 89, 80**; **Aug 90, 522**
Razors
        May 89, 300; **Aug 90, 505**; Sep 91, 575

   electric .... **Nov 89, 718**
Real-estate agents ..... **Jul 90, 460**; Feb 91, 74
Real-estate auctions .... Jun 90, 388
Real-estate investment .... Sep 91, 630
Receivers, stereo
   low-priced .... **Mar 89, 156**
   mid-priced
       Mar 90, 174; **Mar 91, 160**; **Mar 92, 182**
Recession, preparing for
         Jan 91, 20; Feb 91, 90; Mar 91, 194;
         May 91, 314
Recycling
   automobile batteries .... Apr 92, 208
   automobile tires .... Apr 92, 208
   motor oil .... Apr 92, 208
Refrigerator compressor, GE ...... May 89, 287
Refrigerators
   bottom-freezer .... **Jul 92, 456**
   compact .... **Aug 91, 532**
   side-by-side .... **May 91, 346**; **Jul 92, 456**
   top-freezer .... **Nov 89, 729**; *Jan 90, 65
Remote controls
       Mar 89, 170; Mar 90, 172; Mar 91, 157;
       Mar 92, 180
   universal .... Jul 90, 446
Restaurants, chains .... **Jun 92, 356**
Retin-A .... Feb 89, 112
Retirement communities .... Feb 90, 123
Retirement plans
         Jan 90, 16; Feb 90, 122; Mar 90, 150;
         *Jun 90, 437
Rice .... **Jun 90, 424**
Rights of consumers .... Jan 89, 20
Running shoes .... **May 92, 308**

Salt and hypertension .... Jan 90, 48
Salt Sensor .... Feb 90, 73
Sanders, finishing .... **Sep 90, 628**
Savings and loan bailout .... Nov 89, 679
Savings plans .... Feb 89, 78; *Apr 89, 277
Saws, chain saws. **May 90, 304**; *Feb 91, 133
Scales, bathroom .... **Jul 89, 461**
Scissors and shears .... **Oct 92, 672**
Screwdrivers, cordless .... **Aug 89, 535**
Sears advertising .... Mar 89, 133
Shampoos .... **Feb 89, 95**; **Jun 92, 395**
   ammonia odor .... Oct 89, 610
Shavers, electric .... **Nov 89, 718**
Shoes, walking .... **Feb 90, 88**; *Mar 90, 201
Shower heads, low-flow .... **Jul 90, 470**
Shredders .... **Jun 91, 414**
Silver plate, kit to restore .... Jan 89, 6
Skates, in-line .... **Aug 91, 515**
Skillets, electric .... **May 90, 317**
Snow throwers .... **Oct 89, 659**

CONSUMER REPORTS INDEX 395

Soaps, hand	Oct 90, 644
Social Security	Jun 91, 398; Jul 91, 474
Spaghetti	**May 92, 322**
Spaghetti sauce	**May 92, 322**
Spell checkers	**Oct 91, 672**
Spiffits	Feb 90, 74
Spot removers	Sep 90, 573
Stair climbers	**May 92, 315**
Standard of living	Jun 92, 392
Steamers, clothes	**May 90, 357**
Steamers, food, electronic	Sep 92, 557
Stereo components	
*Jan 89, 65; **Nov 89, 688**; **Nov 90, 710**; **Nov 91, 748**	
Stereo systems, compact	**Nov 90, 704**
Stock funds	**May 90, 330**
Stock tables	Aug 89, 534
Stoves, *see* ranges	
String trimmers	**Jun 92, 363**
on wheels	Aug 92, 481
Suits, men's and women's	**Sep 92, 559**
Sun Spots	Jul 91, 455
Sunscreens	**Jun 91, 400**
Swimming pool alarms	Jun 89, 353
Table Sweep	Aug 89, 489
Tampon labeling	Jan 90, 5
Tape measure, digital	May 90, 302
Tapes	
audio cassette	Mar 89, 160
video	**Sep 90, 584**
Tax audits	Mar 89, 172
Taxes	Mar 91, 143
earned income credit	Feb 92, 73
reduced income-tax withholding	May 92, 333
refunds	Mar 89, 202
Tea	**Jul 92, 468**
Telephone-answering machines	
Jan 89, 46; *Feb 89, 72; **Nov 91, 750**	
autointerrupt	Jun 89, 353
Telephone service	
and hardware alternatives	Jan 89, 54
from overseas	Jul 89, 429; *Aug 89, 539
Telephones	**Jan 89, 40**; *Feb 89, 72
cordless	**Nov 89, 680; Nov 91, 756**
Television, channels	**Sep 91, 576**
Television, high definition	Oct 89, 627
Television sets	
antenna	Jan 89, 5
choosing	Mar 90, 173
closed-caption decoder	Jun 89, 354
large screen	
Feb 89, 114; Mar 89, 171; *Apr 89, 277; **Mar 91, 180**	
miniature	**Aug 89, 524**
19-, 21-inch	**Feb 90, 76**; *May 90, 369
13-inch	**Feb 90, 76**
27-inch	**Mar 92, 156**
Television/VCR combos	**Aug 90, 560**
Tennis racquets	**Aug 92, 543**
Thermometer, ear	Mar 92, 141
Thermometer, meat, electronic	Aug 92, 481
Tick Garde	Aug 89, 489
Tick killers	Aug 91, 563
Tillers	**May 91, 329**
Tire inflator, aerosol	Oct 90, 643
Tissues, facial	**May 89, 332**
Toaster ovens & toaster/oven broilers	
Jun 90, 384; *Sep 90, 633	
Toasters	**Jun 90, 380**
with microchip	May 91, 301
Toilets, low-flush	
Jul 90, 466; *Aug 90, 565; *Oct 90, 640	
Tomatoes, canned	**Jul 89, 472**
Tooth-whiteners	Jul 92, 413
Toothbrushes	Aug 89, 504
electric	**Sep 92, 611**
Toothpaste	**Sep 92, 602**
tube	Nov 91, 709
Toys, unsafe	Nov 90, 716
Trade schools, abuses by	May 92, 303
Travel tips	Jul 90, 454; *Sep 90, 633
Treadmills	**Nov 90, 752**
Treasuries	Apr 89, 260
Tripods	**Aug 90, 512**
Truth in Savings law	Jun 92, 353
Tuna, canned	**Feb 92, 116**
Turbo Wash	Nov 91, 709
Typewriters	**Nov 91, 763**
Umbrellas	**Sep 91, 619**
Upholstered furniture, cleaning	Feb 92, 128
Vacuum cleaners	**May 89, 307**
handheld	**Jul 92, 451**
Vaseline Lip Therapy	Feb 91, 75
Video cassette recorders	**Mar 91, 181**
dual-deck	May 91, 302
hi-fi	**Mar 92, 158**; *Jun 92, 355
high-priced	**Mar 89, 167**; *Apr 89, 277
how to program	Mar 92, 160
low-cost	**Mar 91, 168**
Videotapes	**Sep 90, 584**
Vinyl floor coverings	**Oct 92, 639**
Viralizer	Jan 89, 12; *Jun 92, 355
Walkabout stereos	**Oct 91, 656**
Warranties	
auto service contracts	Apr 90, 226

396 CONSUMER REPORTS INDEX

extended ....Jan 91, 21
Ford dealers ....Apr 90, 211
General Electric ....Feb 90, 73
house ....Feb 90, 74
secret (auto) ....Apr 89, 214; *Aug 89, 490
Washing machines
  Mar 89, 188; Feb 91, 112; Aug 92, 537
Water, reverse-osmosis systems .. Jan 90, 36
Water, test kits for ....May 92, 293
Water distillers ....**Jan 90, 39**
Water filters
  Jan 90, 33; *Apr 90, 211; *May 90, 369

Water pollutants
  Jul 89, 430; Jan 90, 30; Jul 91, 454
Water safety, selling ....Jan 90, 27
Water softeners............................. **Jan 90, 41**
Whirlpools, portable ....**Jul 89, 467**
Window-cleaning products .... Mar 89, 134
Woks ....**May 90, 317**
Word processors .... Oct 90, 662; Nov 91, 763
Wrenches, cordless..................... Mar 90, 142
  sockets, adjustable ....Jan 90, 7

Yogurt ....**May 91, 323**

STATEMENT OF OWNERSHIP, MANAGEMENT, AND CIRCULATION
(Required by 39 U.S.C. 3685)

1. Title of Publication: CONSUMER REPORTS. 1A .Publication No: 0010-7174. 2. Date of Filing: September 18, 1992. 3. Frequency of issue: Monthly, except semi-monthly in December. 3A. No. of Issues Published Annually: 13. 3B. Annual Subscription Price: $22.00. 4. Complete Mailing Address of Known Office of Publication: 101 Truman Avenue, Yonkers, New York 10703-1057. 5. Complete Mailing Address of the Headquarters of General Business offices of the Publisher: 101 Truman Avenue, Yonkers, New York 10703-1057. Full Names and Complete Mailing Address of Publisher, Executive Director, Editor, & Executive Editor. Publisher: Consumers Union of United States, Inc. 101 Truman Avenue, Yonkers, New York 10703-1057. Executive Director, Rhoda H. Karpatkin; Editor: Irwin Landau; Executive Editor: Eileen Denver. 7. Owner: (If owned by a corporation, the names and addresses of the individual owners must be given. If owned by a partnership or other unincorporated firm, its name and address, as well as that of each individual, must be given. If the publication is published by a nonprofit organization, its name and address must be stated.) Name: Consumers Union of United States, Inc., a nonprofit organization. Address: 101 Truman Avenue, Yonkers, New York 10703-1057. 8. Known Bondholders, Mortgagees, and Other Securities (if there are none, so state): None. 9. For Completion by Nonprofit Organizations Authorized to Mail at Special Rates (Section 432, 12 DMM only). The purpose, function, and non-profit status of this organization and the exempt status for Federal Income tax purposes has not changed during preceding 12 months. 10. Extent and Nature of Circulation.

	Average no. copies each issue during past 12 mo.	Actual no. copies of single issue published nearest to filing date
A. Total no. of copies (net press run)	5,669,000	5,686,000
B. Paid and/or requested circulation		
1. Sales through dealers and carriers, street vendors and counter sales	125,000	78,000
2. Mail subscription (Paid and/or requested)	5,232,000	5,292,000
C. Total paid and/or requested circulation (Sum of 10B1 and 10B2)	5,357,000	5,370,000
D. Free distribution by mail, carrier or other means Samples, complimentary, and other free copies	46,000	46,000
E. Total distribution (sum of C and D)	5,403,000	5,416,000
F. Copies not distributed		
1. Office use, left over, unaccounted, spoiled after printing.	74,000	77,000
2. Return from news agents	192,000	193,000
G. TOTAL (sum of E, F1 and 2—should equal net press run shown in A)	5,669,000	5,686,000

11. I certify that the statements made by me above are correct and complete. Louis J. Milani, Business Manager

More Books About Money

from Consumer Reports Books

- How to Settle an Estate. (#2501H) $18.95
- Your Bank—How to Get Better Service. (#2480P) $12.95
- The Mortgage Book. (#2511P) $15.95
- Life Insurance. (#2322P) $11.95
- Personal Computer Buying Guide. (#2434P) $12.95
- Our Money, Our Selves. (#2499P) $16.95
- Consumer Reports Money-Saving Tips. (#2512P) $14.95
- Guide to Baby Products. 3rd Ed. (#2454P) $12.95

Consumer Reports Books

MONEY-BACK GUARANTEE

Mail to: **Consumer Reports Books**, 9180 LeSaint Drive, Fairfield, OH 45014-5452

CODE	BOOK TITLE (PLEASE PRINT CLEARLY)	QTY.	PRICE EA.	TOTAL
			$	$
	1993 Desk Calendar	1	~~$9.95~~	FREE
			SUBTOTAL	$

SHIPPING AND HANDLING: Order value (excluding premium)
- Orders up to $25 (shipped book rate in U.S.) — $2.50
- $25.01-$35 (shipped book rate in U.S.) — $3.50
- **Orders $35.01 or more (shipped book rate in U.S.) — FREE**
- UPS orders (any value) in continental U.S. — $5.00
- Canadian and International orders (any value) $5.00 (U.S. funds only)

SHIPPING & HANDLING	$
CANADIAN/INTL. SURCHARGE	$
TOTAL	$

Method of payment: ❏ Check enclosed for full amount
Charge to my: ❏ MasterCard ❏ Visa Exp. Date: Mo.____ Yr.____

Card Number ☐☐☐☐☐☐☐☐☐☐☐☐☐☐☐☐

Signature _____
Name _____
Address _____ Apt. ____
City _____ State ____ Zip ____

We will ship your order within 72 hours of receipt. Please allow four weeks for delivery of Book Rate Orders. All books are paperback unless otherwise noted. CU publications may not be used for commercial purposes.

FREE with your order: $9.95 value **Consumer Reports 1993 Desk Calendar**

4P2CT

FOR FASTER ORDERING CALL 1-513-860-1178

SEE BACK COVER FOR MORE BOOKS FROM CONSUMER REPORTS BOOKS

Give $1000. Get a whole lot more.

Giving away $1000 may not seem like a way to increase your assets. But consider all you get back when you give $1000 to Consumers Union:

1. You become a Lifetime Member of Consumers Union.

2. You receive Consumer Reports every month for the rest of your life.

3. Your name is inscribed on the permanent Honor Roll to be installed in the new Consumer Reports National Testing and Research Center.

4. You get a tax deduction.

5. Your Lifetime Membership is acknowledged in a special listing published periodically in Consumer Reports—unless you'd prefer to remain anonymous.

6. Your contribution helps build a stronger Consumers Union. This means better values in the products and services you buy. Safer products for you and those you care about. More protection against fraud and deceit. A fairer world for the consumer—in so many ways.

As you may know, CU accepts no contributions from business. No outside advertising. No contributions larger than $5000 from anyone.

More than 4500 of our readers have increased their assets by contributing $1000 to Consumers Union. Join them by becoming a Lifetime Member today. Please use the coupon when you send your check.

Yes, I'd like to enjoy the benefits of Lifetime Membership in Consumers Union with a tax deductible contribution of:
- ☐ $1000 ☐ $1500 ☐ $2000
- ☐ Other $ _____ (Maximum: $5000)
- ☐ My check is enclosed.
- ☐ I wish to contribute in quarterly installments.
- ☐ My first installment is enclosed.
- ☐ I cannot be a Lifetime Member now, but here is my gift for $ _____

Name _____
Address _____
City _____ **State** _____ **Zip** _____

Name to be entered as Lifetime Member (if different): _____
- ☐ Yes, you may list my name in Consumer Reports.
- ☐ Don't list my name.

Mail this coupon to:
CONSUMERS UNION
101 Truman Ave., Yonkers, N.Y. 10703   ELGGG

CONSUMERS UNION OF U.S., INC., 101 Truman Ave., Yonkers, N.Y. 10703, is a not-for-profit, tax-exempt organization, contributions to which are tax-deductible in accordance with law. Contributions are not accepted from any commercial interest. A copy of our latest financial report filed with the New York Department of State may be obtained by writing: Office of Charities Registration, Department of State, Albany, NY 12231, or from CU at the address above.

CALL 1·900·446·1120!

($1.75 PER MINUTE. EXPECT TO SPEND 5 OR MORE MINUTES FOR A TYPICAL CALL.)

IT'S THE BEST WAY TO PRICE THAT USED CAR!

Before you buy, sell or trade-in a 1984-1992 model vehicle, call Consumer Reports. The price you'll hear reflects current market conditions in *your* region of the U.S. and takes into account the vehicle's age, mileage, major options and general condition.

The service costs $1.75 per minute (expect to spend 5 or more minutes for a typical call). You'll be charged on the long-distance portion of your phone bill. Call on a touch-tone phone 7 days a week between 7:00 am and 2:00 am ET. (Sorry, no service available in certain areas of the country and for Alaska and Hawaii.)

WHEN YOU CALL... HAVE THIS INFORMATION READY:

- Zip Code
- Model year
- Mileage
- Model name or number
- Number of cylinders
- Major options
- Condition of vehicle

1992 MODEL PRICES AVAILABLE JAN. 1993

Consumer Reports
USED CAR PRICE SERVICE

The Consumer Reports

The smart way to

Deal with your dealer. Save hundreds of dollars. Know the facts—Dealer Invoice vs. Sticker Price.

Here's what you'll get:

■ A computer printout comparing sticker price to the dealer's invoice.

You'll see the base price, plus every factory installed option (and option package) for the exact make and model you choose. You can figure out exactly what equipment you want and you'll know the dealer's cost for every single item!

■ Factory Rebate Information.

You'll receive information on both Factory-to-Customer and Factory-to-Dealer Incentive programs. Just like the printouts, these rebate programs are updated continuously to give you the most current information available. All you do is make your best deal, then subtract the rebate from the bottom line!

To order by mail:

Mail us this coupon, today!

EXAMPLE **FORD TAURUS GL 4DR SEDAN**

PLEASE PRINT	MAKE	MODEL	EXACT STYLE	UNIT COST	TOTAL COST
1ST CAR				$11	$11
2ND CAR				$9	$20
3RD CAR				$7	$27
4TH CAR				$5	$32

NAME

ADDRESS

CITY   STATE   ZIP

FREE with 3 or more printout orders: our HOW TO BUY A NEW CAR booklet! (Regular price $3.95!)

QD